THE
APPROXIMATE
PARENT

Discovering the Strategies
That Work with *Your* Teenager

© 2012 Michael Y. Simon
5665 College Avenue, Suite 340C
Oakland, CA 96618

The information in this volume is not intended as a substitute for consultation with healthcare professionals. Each individual's health concerns should be fully evaluated by a qualified professional.

Printed in the United States of America

This book is printed on acid-free paper.
Cover and book design by Jennifer Durrant (www.jenniferdurrantdesign.com)
Edited by T. Rhae Watson (www.twobirdsediting.com)
Print Production & Coordination by Joshua Pfeffer (www.pfef.com)

Last digit is print number: 9   8   7   6   5   4   3   2   1

**Publisher's Cataloging-in-Publication
(Provided by Quality Books, Inc.)**

Simon, Michael Y.
    The approximate parent : discovering the strategies
that work with your teenager / Michael Y. Simon.
    p. cm.
    Includes bibliographical references and index.
    LCCN 2012935741
    ISBN 978-0-9852276-9-2
    ISBN 978-0-9852276-8-5

    1. Child rearing. 2. Parent and teenager.
3. Adolescent psychology.   I. Title.

HQ799.15.S56 2012   649'.125
                QBI12-600085

THE APPROXIMATE PARENT

Discovering the Strategies That Work with *Your* Teenager

MICHAEL Y. SIMON

Fine  Optics Press
OAKLAND, CA

CONTENTS

FOR MY FATHER,
a deeply kind, flawed man who died far too early,
and for my son, who I hope will someday come
to see me, too,
as both flawed *and* kind.

Acknowledgments

This is either the easiest or the most difficult part of a book to write, since so many people have helped along the way to make this book possible.

It is a huge understatement to say that this book would not have been completed without the assistance of my editor, T. Rhae Watson, herself a writer and parent. I deeply appreciate her guidance and sensibility throughout. Jennifer Durrant provided the beautiful design for the cover and interior of this book, and her generosity of spirit has touched this work in many ways. Joshua Pfeffer coordinated the production of this work. His craftsmanship made it look beautiful despite the technical complexities.

I want to thank and acknowledge Joshua Coleman, Ph.D., Kathleen Dadasovich, B.S., Patt Denning, Ph.D., Thomas de Zengotita, Ph.D., Fred Hoerner, Ph.D., Laurie Kahn, M.A., Jeannie Little, L.C.S.W., Christine Mallon, Ph.D., Jul McLeod, J.D., Nancy McWilliams, Ph.D., Teresa Pantaleo, Ph.D., Lynn Ponton, M.D., and Annie Spiegelman (the "Dirt Diva"), who each read all or parts of the manuscript in various states of undress and offered wise counsel that I believe made this work stronger and more helpful for parents. Each of these outstanding people—parents, educators, authors, and clinicians among them—does something *daily* (often all day) to help make our world better for other people. I want to acknowledge, too, my colleagues in clinical practice and the school counseling worlds in Northern California who every day make the work meaningful and alive.

As you will learn in reading this work, I believe strongly in the power and necessity of *mentorship* as a key value. Without my mentors, past and present, neither this book nor my life's work would exist. I've been blessed to have some of these mentors in my life in close ways and for long periods of time. Other mentors have been primarily intellectual mentors—people whose work inspired my thinking, clinical practice, and way of being in the world. Ruth Goldman, Ph.D., Harvey Peskin, Ph.D., George Araki, Ph.D., Jerry Needleman, Ph.D., and Jean W. Burnett, MFT, are five mentors in the former category. I cannot imagine my life without these stunningly kind, wise people, all of whom think and feel in ways that build bridges and ease suffering in the world. I carry George with me in memory and heart but wish I could spend just one more five-hour afternoon lunch with him at the Chinese restaurant on Taraval Street, talking about the nexus of philosophy, psychology, religion, health science, and...*everything*, since for George, everything was in relation, always.

Dr. Needleman is Dr. Needleman. Anyone who has ever met this man had the rare opportunity to know more the importance of *attention* and receive the grace that is his attention.

The second category of mentors is much wider, but no less meaningful. I am forever indebted in the best ways to: Carl Rogers, Ph.D. (a fellow longtime Chicago resident, and a primary reason for my becoming a therapist); Nancy McWilliams, Ph.D. (whose writing about psychology, psychotherapy, and diagnosis made me want to be an engaged, *involved* clinician); Joseph Weiss, M.D., and Harold Sampson, Ph.D.—above all—along with Michael Bader, PhD., Jack Berry, Ph.D., Jessica Broitman, Ph.D., Marshall Bush, Ph.D., Janice Cumming, Ph.D., John Curtis, Ph.D., Lewis Engel, Ph.D., Steven A. Foreman, Suzanne Gassner, Ph.D., Paul Ransohoff, Ph.D., Lynn O'Connor, Ph.D., Judith Pickles, Ph.D. Alan Rappoport, Ph.D., George Silberschatz, Ph.D., Denny Zeitlin, M.D., and so many others in the San Francisco Psychotherapy Research Group, the San Francisco Psychoanalytic Institute, and the old Mt. Zion Hospital in San Francisco, who all showed me *eminently* useful theory with heart; G. Alan Marlatt, for his exemplary, lifelong work on the causes and treatment of addiction—and whose recent passing we mourn; David Shapiro, Ph.D. (whose beautifully deep, descriptive work brought theory and life together in most powerful ways); Mick Goodrick (for demonstrating a long time ago the value of approximation and practice); Bill Frisell (for the soundtrack of all my theory-making); Father Raimundo Pannikar-Alemany (who showed me that religious studies was about much more than religion); Professor Jurgen Habermas (a great thinker who tries unceasingly to employ his brain for the public good); and Professor Jacques Derrida, who died before I (and I'm sure many others) could tell him how much his relentless *Differance* meant to us. Prof. Derrida was instrumental in my decision to (sort of) leave philosophy and return to clinical psychology. I'm forever grateful.

It seems strange or perhaps just right that Dr. Peskin, a clinical psychologist with a penchant for philosophy, led me to initially leave the profession to study philosophy and religion, and Prof. Derrida, a philosopher with a penchant for psychology, led me back again to clinical work. Bless you both.

A special thank you to Laura Konigsberg, Ph.D., an inspiring educator who cares deeply about adolescents and contributed to many productive discussions over the years about teens and status.

Mike Riera, Ph.D., has been a quiet presence throughout this work and an inspiration for writing about and working with teenagers. I, along with so many others, truly appreciate his work on behalf of children and teens.

Ruth Goldman, Ph.D., deserves mention again, although there just aren't words for what Ruth has meant in this life. Ruth has been an example for me—for much of my adult life—of what fierce intelligence, elegance, kindness, compassion, and perseverance look like in human form. Because of Ruth, *I* remember *fidelity*.

This book and my work could not happen without my clients and the thousands of people with whom I've had the immense privilege of working over the last (nearly) 20 years—*especially* the teenagers, each of whom I love a lot. The same is true of those in the Village who helped my own child throughout the years, who are too many to name, lucky for me. Alison Ehara Brown deserves special mention—she knows why.

And a special attention must be paid to the Internet, wherever you are. I likely would not have written this book if I'd had to spend months and months of tedium retrieving materials and getting citations (like in the good old days of searching microfiche in library stacks). I suspect, as you'll read in this book, that the Internet doesn't care about me in the way that I care about the Internet. We probably should break up, but...

Jennifer A. Spitz is another quiet figure behind this work. It is a literal fact that this book would not exist without her being in the world. Much love, right in her direction. And for Selena, who knows how the important things work—and why things *stop* working—and what to do about it, my enduring love.

More than thank you to B., who inspired the long *work* of this book and helped me with a particular pathogenic belief: I figured, if *you* can write one of the most beautiful cycles of music I've ever heard, I can at least *try* to write a book. The pen is back in your hand: My ears and the ears of the world are listening for a long time to come.

This work was enabled by the deep support of my partner, Andreea, and her father and mother—especially Pavel. When we take leave of friends or family, we sometimes offer the throwaway line, "take good care." Andreea and Pavel are two people who stand as exemplars of what it really means to *take care* with someone. The Talmud says, "The highest wisdom is kindness." They are both *very* wise.

Finally, for Ryan. I know you're not a teenager anymore. But this book is for you and because of you. You made real the possibility of trying to figure out how to *approximate* being a good enough parent. I know I am still slouching toward that possibility. What else can I do?

Introduction

It's 2012 and today is my son's birthday. More about that in a moment.

I quickly get annoyed with books that begin with a long list of the author's pedigree. This is often, but not always, done to convince you right from the start to relax your critical stance on the material you're about to read and surrender (to some degree) to the author's expertise. My hope is that you will *not* relax, but will in fact employ your critical stance on the material you're about to read. I don't want to convince you that I'm an expert. It would be better if the more you read, the more *you* felt like an expert. But I would like you to know something about my motivation for writing *The Approximate Parent*.

My great grandfather, my grandfather, my father, myself, and my son were all born 26 years apart. Today, my son will turn 26. So, recently, I started wondering what I was going to get his dorsolateral prefrontal cortex for its birthday. I have also done a lot of wondering about what his dorsolateral prefrontal cortex was going to give me (and him) this year. This is the year that—by most neuropsychological accounts—his brain development will be largely complete. If my son had been my daughter, that brain development would have been mostly complete about 12 to 18 months ago.

These are strange things to think about, right? Not for me. For the last 16 years I've worked as a psychotherapist in private practice. For about six of those years I served as a high school counselor. And many of those same years were spent as a teacher, researcher, and public speaker on adolescent development and parenting teens and preteens. So, I think a lot about the amygdalae and just what gets adolescents' ventromedial prefrontal cortex firing. I know—weird.

But when I was trying to "parent" my teenager, I was thinking in more practical terms, about what motivated my son to do what he was doing and what it all meant.

Why would he take *those* risks and not other risks? Why was he so ready to spend time, energy, and attention on most things I found of dubious value, and so busy avoiding many the things I wished he loved doing? What were we really arguing about? I spent a lot of time thinking about how to get him up in the morning and more time than that trying not to get angry with him. I would say I spent an average amount of time (whatever the metrics are on that, I don't know) trying to remember that I loved him, especially when I felt that I didn't like him very much.

When my son was 16 years old he was caught by the California Highway Patrol "driving" 103 miles per hour (in *my* car) through the Caldecott Tunnel, a structure that separates North Oakland from its eastward neighbors. I believe that since he was traveling at 103 miles per hour at 1:30 in the morning, "careening" might be a more descriptive than "driving." Anyway, the next day, when I was finally calm enough to talk to him without yelling, I asked him the question most parents ask: *What were you thinking?* (Expletive deleted.) He didn't pause very long. He looked me clean in the eye and calmly but with a tinge of annoyance at my lack of understanding said, "Well, if I'd *known* the cop was going to be there, I wouldn't have been speeding."

One of the many stunning things about his answer (at the time) is that it made complete sense to him. And when I tell this story to teens, they just stare back at me; some nod their heads in understanding and obvious agreement, as if they're thinking, "Yeah, of course, that's right, *what's your point?*" However, when I tell this story to parents, it gets a good laugh about 98 percent of the time. Parents immediately recognize how *ridiculous* this answer is. But the truth is, from the perspective of the cognitive neuroscientist studying adolescent maturation and development, from the biological-social-psychological perspective of the adolescent pediatric specialist, the clinical psychologist, marriage and family therapist, or social worker or sociologist, the teenagers are right *not* to laugh. My son's logic was impeccable and a perfect example of healthy, normal development. When parents laugh, thinking his answer ridiculous, it's because they aren't thinking about what is normative for a 16-year-old. They are laughing, in a state of mild panic and anxiety, in the semi-conscious but firm hope that someday their child will still be alive to look back and realize that logic is (now, from an adult perspective) *ridiculous*.

Adolescents' feeling, thinking, and social lives make a lot of sense to me. That was not always the case, though.

In 1998 I founded an online support community for parents, educators, and mental health professionals called Practical Help for Parents. In 1998 my son turned 12. Those two events are related not just by correlation. We're talking about causation. The conventional wisdom at that time was that there was no manual on parenting teens. I certainly couldn't find one. And I sure needed one. My training in clinical psychology did not exactly prepare me to intelligently deal with a teenager. I remembered something about Erik Erikson and that the entrance into puberty for children was the beginning of a series of tasks oriented toward the development of a unique identity—under the pressures of multiple and sometimes contradictory demands of society, family, school, friends, and the like. He called the particular developmental dilemma most associated with adolescence "ego identity formation versus role confusion."

In other words, if your adolescent daughter does not adequately negotiate the development of a stable and pro-social identity, she will experience role diffusion—problems with who she is and how she fits into the world (and what her adult roles are to be).[1] But if she does successfully negotiate this developmental period, she "wins" a particular personal value or strength: *fidelity*. By "fidelity," Erikson meant, in my understanding, *the ability to see the world as it is—flawed and imperfect and full of setbacks and roadblocks—and to persevere, to commit, to stay engaged with the world of self and others, despite what a mess it is.* She sees the good and bad in the world but still makes commitments and they are freely pledged with integrity, a sense of authorship and agency. Excellent: That sounds good to me.

Okay, got it. My son is developing his *identity*. And that task is absolutely crucial, because if he doesn't do it well, he's going to have a hard time engaging with the world as an adult. In truth, though, all that knowledge told me was: I am in *big* trouble.

I do remember vividly that though there wasn't a manual for teens, there sure was a manual on parenting *children*. I remember as a kid sneaking into my father's "den" to look at his copy of Benjamin Spock's *Baby and Child Care*. As far as I knew (and many parents agreed) that was *the* Instruction Manual. I remember reading that book, in quick, stolen snippets, fascinated and horrified. I deeply wanted to know the source of that secret logic my parents had to be using to make decisions about what I could and couldn't do. But I think I also wanted to know just as intensely why *I* was doing what I was doing.

My own search for a manual on parenting teens, then, began in 1998. Late that year I literally stumbled into a talk on teenagers given by a high school counselor, and after that, things began to slowly make more sense. In 1995 Dr. Mike Riera published *Uncommon Sense for Parents With Teenagers*,[2] and three years later, I'd found my manual. The book has by now helped countless parents understand and translate seemingly impenetrable teenage behavior. Mike's presence, professional support, and compassionate, deep knowledge about what makes teens tick stands as an inspiration throughout this work.

By 2012 the conventional wisdom was that there were now *thousands* of manuals on parenting teens. It's your call. What kind of teen do you want in your home? Want a book on raising a "Self-Reliant Teen in a Self-Indulgent World"? You might want to just skip that and move right to the next level, "Raising Teen 2.0," which argues that there is no such thing as adolescence and no real reason that you should have conflict with your teenager. Want to parent to "Your Teen's Strengths"? You should also learn the 7 Secrets of Highly Effective Teens. I know you'll want to "Avoid the 10 Worst Things Parents Do," won't you? How about just skipping all this and going for a "Whole New Mind," since in the future, right-brainers are going to rule the world?

I am not trying to ridicule these books, which now number into the thousands. Some of them are very good. But there are problems with some of them—particularly the self-help genre books for teens[3]—and this *specialization* approach to parenting is, I believe, almost all about marketing, not parenting. This is ultimately confusing and increases the feeling that you are "doing it wrong" or will never really be able to keep up with all the information required to parent your teenager.

The last two decades have seen a flood of books, popular and empirical research articles, seminars, workshops, podcasts, e-books, TED talks, and YouTube videos about how to raise teenagers. In fact, I recently read an article by one of the most respected editors I know that warns authors that of all the books you could write, the one you *shouldn't* write is a book on parenting teens—unless you're an eminent doctor. I guess I ignored that advice.

Research on brain development has also exploded in the last 12 years in particular, promising to help us all further fine-tune the way we understand and parent kids, especially teens. The transition from "trickle" to "flood" of information about parenting teens was rapid, and in many ways paralleled the growth of the Internet itself.

Most notably, in 2001 Jacqueline Lerner, Richard Lerner, and Jordan Finkelstein introduced an edited work of 178 of the country's brightest minds engaged in understanding adolescent development. The result of that work, *Adolescence in America: An Encyclopedia*, is a 918-page tome, packed with an array of article-entries from "abortion" (the first entry) to "youth outlook" (the last entry). While there are the usual problems with multi-volume, multi-contributor work, such as inconsistency of terminology—what one writer means by "shy" or "adolescent" may be very different than one another writer means—it would be hard to imagine it leaves much out. And this was neither the first, nor will it be the last encyclopedia covering adolescents and their development.[4] I wanted a manual for parents of adolescents...I got an *encyclopedia* for parents of adolescents.

If you haven't already asked, you should be asking: What is the purpose of yet another book on adolescents? The encyclopedia (and thousands of other books) have already been written. I'm going to try to answer that here, and with the rest of this book.

While I founded Practical Help for Parents as a way of creating community between myself (as a therapist, parent, and teacher) and others (parents, other mental health professionals, and educators/school administrators) who were struggling to figure out how to best work with their teenagers, it became clear to me early on that part of the supportive function of this community would be to take the quickly growing body of research and writing about teens, comb through it, and present the "good stuff."

I wanted this information so that I could help myself and my son, and the information was also a crucial part of my developing professional knowledge. Also, I knew that parents, teachers, school officials, and other mental health professionals seldom had the kind of time to go through the materials. How could we make good use of the limited and precious time we had to make sense of all the information on parenting teens? Practical Help for Parents became one answer to that question, in the form of an online community designed to help disseminate some of this information. My work took the form of a series of workshops, trainings, keynote speeches, and parent education meetings in the Bay Area and across the country, in which complex materials were translated for busy parents and professionals, in a manner designed to be very practical and relevant. I wanted people to hear the "good stuff" and be able to go home (or into their clinical practice or their school) and immediately make use of it, in an entertaining way that would reduce their confusion and tension and help them feel more efficacious in their various role(s) in support of teens. That function (research review, assessment, and, in some cases, dissemination) is still necessary but no longer sufficient.

This book is for parents of teenagers and even for those who aren't sure whether they yet have an adolescent in the house. It's also for educators, mental health professionals, and anyone else who works with adolescents and wants to understand them better. But I've written this primarily for parents who want support in figuring out how to best understand, support, and work with *their* teenager through the many phases of adolescence. *The Approximate Parent* is meant to live somewhere near your bedside and to be picked up again and again over the course of many years; it can be, but it isn't designed to only be read all at once and put away.

On the other hand, if you do read this straight through over a few days or weeks, you might get something else from the experience, for example: a strong sense that there are many commonalities between what you and your teen are going through and what other families are dealing with; a much clearer idea of how the ideas in the book translate into specific actions with your teen; or a wider appreciation of the lifeworld of your teen and other American teenagers. So you should read it all straight through, right?

This little dilemma or seeming contradiction is really at the heart of *The Approximate Parent*. It is not a contradiction; it represents the strength of this work, because it is an illustration of the idea that *one size cannot fit all and still be effective for everyone.* Some parents will read the whole book (or try to) and feel overwhelmed. Others will find that it doesn't "click" for them unless they keep reading and looking at all the different contexts in which teens are acting, thinking, and feeling. You may be a person who can't read too much at a time and your neighbor may prefer to jump around, reading the end first and the beginning last. *I believe in parents and theory-making—and putting those two things together.* I believe that if you give people really good information and the knowledge that there are many different ways to succeed—that can all look different from the others—you have something really useful and powerful. That's how this book talks about parenting adolescents, and so it had better walk its walk and function the same way, right? That's why there isn't a right way to read this book: You have to discover the strategy for making use of this information, and that means if it's going to "work" for you, you'll end up thinking a lot, and being creative and engaged.

So when you find your family in the midst of dealing with the powerful effects of digital media, you might read Chapter 4 very intently. Or you could have thumbed through the contents and seen Chapter 8 on Family and wondered how you could possibly be teaching your teenager when you weren't intending to. If you're getting curious (or a little worried) but basically feel okay about how you and your teen are handling issues of drugs, alcohol, and parties, you might read the first part, but not all of Chapter 5. If your child is between 10 and 12 and you can just feel adolescence slowly moving into your household, you might be very interested in Chapter 1, to see what's normal for a teenager during the early stages of adolescent development. Or you might just look ahead to Chapter 9, because you want to know just what constitutes good mental health for an adolescent. As your teenager gets older, you might want to read the book again, from the start… this time taking in the first five or six chapters as you realize that certain strategies for understanding and working with your particular teenager are emerging and others are no longer working. Overall, *The Approximate Parent* is meant to be a companion to you—when you need it—in the incredibly difficult and often all-consuming job of parenting your teenager.

This book is not the "answer." It will not be the "best parenting book ever written," making all the others irrelevant and obsolete.[5] We live in an era of largely unchecked hyperbole, where what counts most is what you can sell to the American public. I can say, though, that in my experience growing up, the hearts and minds of others—in book form—have truly served me and changed the way I lived my life. I intend this work to reflect what I believe are my own values: I want to be of service. What that means to me is that I wish this book to serve you, and ultimately to *help* you translate what teens do in terms that make sense, so that you have some practical ways of responding to the challenges of safely helping, supporting, and loving your child from adolescence into early adulthood. In that way, it is very much inspired by the practicality of Mike Riera's view of teens, but you'll find it very different in important ways.

Over the last 16 years of clinical practice, and in the last 14 years since my son hit adolescence, I hope I've gained some perspective not only on the tasks of parenting and supporting American teenagers, but also on the cultural contexts—or what philosopher Jurgen Habermas called the *lifeworlds*[6]—in which we're all trying to figure out how to do this. *And those lifeworlds have changed enormously since 1998.*

Parents often want to do things the "right way," and now there are hundreds if not thousands of (often contradictory) approaches to parenting teens. And in a postmodern world, there are no Truths, only truths, or truthiness, at best.[7] Everyone has his or her own opinion; there is no "right" way. "Science" is just a choice of one explanatory narrative among many. I now have sitting in a bookcase next to my desk—yes, I still have actually books—a collection of writings done between 1997 and 2011 that claim to make the definitive case for (and against): the necessity and utility of homework; adolescence as a mere social construction; praising your child; and at least 100 other binary opposites reflecting crucial or controversial aspects of adolescence.

So—what *is* the point of yet another book on teens or adolescent development? In order for this book to have a shelf (or cloud) life longer than a few months, it has been structured differently than most books about parenting teens. It does not aim to tell you just what should do when you find marijuana in your son's backpack. It is not packed with clinical vignettes from my psychotherapy practice that illustrate what a brilliant therapist I've become.[8] That kind of approach is avoided because there are *too many* factors that go into connecting, guiding, and intervening with your teen. It just isn't practical to give you a *protocol* for each of these situations. The marijuana scenario is a "mini crisis," and since a crisis situation is usually very fluid, it makes more sense to me to use a *practice*-driven approach rather than one that is *protocol*-driven.

In *protocol-driven* decision-making, if Situation A happens, you implement Protocol 1. For example, if you find marijuana in your child's backpack, you: a) confront your child immediately, but calmly; b) call the police to "scare them straight" or teach them about the consequences of illegal use or possession of drugs, and then; c) get them drug tested, so you can be aware of what drugs they are currently using, to guide your future decisions.

Some parents will read that "protocol" and find it helpful and reasonable. Other parents will read that protocol and find it presumptuous, overreactive, and unnecessarily confrontational. If, based on my experience or background, I tell you that *that* is the way, as a good Christian, or as a caring Muslim, to approach your teenager, then my advice on parenting has even more weight behind it for you, assuming we share the same background. *Protocol-driven* decision-making is linear. It uses formulas and *advance* plans and its worth is based on whether you correctly implemented the plan or not. There are plenty of "parenting teen" books out there like this, especially around parenting difficult teens in difficult situations. Some of them are really helpful, thoughtful, and smart. But if what the author tells you to do doesn't work, the author still gets the money and can always just say you didn't implement the plan correctly. With *protocol-driven* decision-making, *it's so much easier to feel like you've irretrievably failed* and you need to wait for the next time that particular crisis comes up to "practice." But chances are, you won't want that particular crisis to *ever* come up again.

The approach in this book is *practice*-driven. The idea is to support your response to likely situations that come up in parenting your teen by: a) letting you know what is normal and expectable with American teens in 2012; and b) helping you tell the difference between the expectable and something abnormal that might require the help of a professional. *Practice-driven* decision-making *fits* parenting teenagers. This approach is not as linear, because parenting teens is not linear. It requires active, in-the-moment engagement, taking into account variables in your and your child's situation and considering those in relation to the resources/options you have available at any given time. When you combine the situational variables with your available options/resources you get strategic priorities, not "the Answer." *You get strategic priorities and ways to move ahead, which will change with each situation.* Whether or not something you do "works" is evaluated on the basis of whether you more or less carefully considered the factors involved, whether your intervention was more or less wisely chosen and coordinated. *You can always get better and you can always try again. Always…any time you want and are able.* I believe this approach helps support your *own* parenting values and expertise, and expand it by taking into account what others and I have learned about adolescent development.

Protocol-Driven Decision-Making

"If Situation A, use Protocol 1"

Linear, uses formulas

Evaluation: right or wrongly executed

Practice-Driven Decision-Making

"Situational Variables x Available Resources/Options = Strategic Priorities"

Not so linear; "approximating goals"

Evaluation: more or less carefully considered; more or less wisely chosen or coordinated

In a *practice-driven* approach to parenting teens, you will want to know as much as you can about what the situational variables are and what your available resources might be. So, knowing what is going on with adolescents' brains, bodies, and emotions is more useful if you also know about the context, or the *lifeworlds,* in which adolescents develop in the early part of the 21st century.

I hope *The Approximate Parent* will provide you with a way to cut through the glut of information on parenting and adolescent development and provide powerful ways of thinking about the most important areas of your teenager's life. Then, if you want to go into depth about these key areas, we'll make it easy to wade through the large reservoir of materials so you can continue your own research and decision-making. But I have to confess that as a former teacher and ongoing student (of philosophy), I'm more interested in the question of *how* we live our lives with one another and how and whether we incorporate what we believe and cherish into what we do with our kids. That's why I've chosen an approach that is about *developing strategic priorities*—so that you can best implement and bring to the fore *your own* priorities in raising *your particular teenager,* but with the understanding that he or she will have his or her own priorities, needs, and preferences in the development of his or her identity.

About the Structure of the Book

This book is informed by the work of many others, in a wide variety of fields from philosophy, critical theory, sociology, cognitive science, neurobiology, and neuropsychology to art, literature, poetry, religious studies, and music. That's because I like these areas of exploration and experience and they make up my personality and cognitive style. Many times, though, I eventually find that apparently solid research about teenagers (or myself) turns out to be wrong or incomplete. In fact, just about everything I read turns out to be incomplete in some way. I am going to go out on a limb and say that given enough time everything I think I really know will turn out to be incomplete. *Ouch.* On the other hand, that is an excellent mindset for parenting, and so *The Approximate Parent* is, in many ways, modeled after that idea.

Most chapters in the book will present a primary essay on the main subject area, based on my *lifeworld,* as a father (and child), psychotherapist, speaker, teacher, and student. The essay portion of the chapter will always (at least) be informed by a combination of research and clinical material, but is intended to provide a rich, new, exciting, or stimulating way of thinking about what you are going through as the parent of an adolescent. I might fail, but I'm hoping that reading these chapters will increase your overall engagement and curiosity about parenting your adolescent. I am absolutely confident that if you feel more engaged and curious about your teen, you will be a better parent and person.

Each chapter will also include a list of "Practical Parenting Tips" for that particular subject area (just like on the website), and, finally, a list of resources for further exploration of that topic. Take what you like, and leave the rest. Or come back to it later to see if there's something in it for you. The way I write and think about teens might change what you do completely (or not at all), or it might change *some* things in *subtle* ways.

Throughout the process of writing *The Approximate Parent*, I wanted to give parents particular bits of advice or insight along the way. For example: if your son is a senior in high school, you'll be fighting with him more about the difference between who he *insists* he is (an adult, ready for college or moving out) and who he *actually seems* to be (an adult-looking person who may still not be turning in homework, finishing college applications on time, looking for summer work or "getting it together" in the most basic of ways). Or, when you're daughter is a junior in high school, she will likely "go underground," and be more private than ever about what she thinks, feels and does. Or that when your son is a sophomore, he will turn into a kind of "hypocrisy-detecting machine," capable of processing, at blinding speeds, the difference between what you *say* and what you *do*, making certain to comment on your growing credibility gap. Maybe these little tidbits make you smile in recognition and you want more of them. But in truth, *that* book has already been written, many times. Mike Riera's work is such a pleasure for parents to read, in part, because Mike is so good at recognizing the developmental "flavors" of family and school life with teenagers. It's not just that the book has been written, though. It's also a matter of noting again that this book isn't really that kind of book, precisely because one size doesn't fit all, and if I tell you what "juniors are like," there's a good chance I'll miss *your* junior. And that's the point. *I don't want to give you a list of things you have to do correctly or tell you how your teen will be.* This book is about giving you practical theories—ways of thinking and feeling about your teenager—and then it's up to you. That is very purposeful, because it allows you and I, together, to work in a way that is very similar to the way that I'm suggesting you could work with your teen: theory and practice, always together, always in combination, *approximating an answer best suited to you and your particular teen.*

മ

Chapter One begins with a question that often begins the relationship with parents in my psychotherapy practice. It's not that they call me and ask, "Do I have a teenager in my house?" But that is *figuratively* what they're asking, because many parents call and want to know what is "wrong" with their child. The first part of my job is to work together with these parents to figure out whether, in fact, there is *anything* wrong with their child. I would say that about half the time the issue is that something is *right* with their child, only the parents don't know they no longer have a child in the house, they have a preteen or teen residing with them. And the "problematic" behavior that makes the parent want me to tell them what's wrong is actually age- and developmentally appropriate behavior that, although annoying and vexing, indicates that the parent has a very healthy teenager in the house.

This chapter is not a cutting-edge, scientific treatise on your teen's development or teen development in general. I'm not pretending to be a neuroscientist, but I do have an intense interest in the subject and am partial to scientific research as a source for thinking about and understanding my world. This is a good example of James Baldwin's wisdom that children often fail to listen to, but never fail to imitate their parents; my father was a research scientist for much of his life and I can't seem to get away from that.

Once adolescence begins what *was* "normal and expectable" changes—forever. Chapter One ("Do I Have a Teen in My House?") will take you through the changes that accompany the beginning and progression of adolescence. I mentioned earlier that research into adolescent development and maturation has exploded in the last two decades, fueled by brain imaging studies and the rapid dissemination of information facilitated by the Internet. We're going to make use of that body of research to provide a context for looking at the main issues that parents (and teens) face in moving into young adulthood in America. This work keeps returning to the overall lifeworlds and contexts in which you are raising your children. That's one reason why there is an entire chapter on digital media and media literacy—because you cannot possibly think about strategic priorities of any kind (let alone in parenting) in America without knowing what's at stake with digital media. *This is the water in which American teenagers swim.*

In Chapter Two, "The Big Problems," we explore the main reasons that parents come in to see me—the behaviors that they most experience as *problematic*: 1) disrespectful, disorganized, or antisocial behaviors; 2) arguing and general oppositionality; 3) separation/behaviors concerning autonomy; 4) risk-taking behaviors (drugs, alcohol, fighting, sports, driving, criminality); and 5) mood-related issues (changeability and variability of mood, intensity of mood, and difficulty regulating mood). The chapter explores the links between the *normative* trajectory of brain development and the behaviors that worry parents, providing a way to think about the challenges in less anxiety-provoking ways.

The next chapter brings us into the heart of the matter for American teens— the subject of "Identity Development, Relationships, and Status."[9] While there are many more studies and writings on adolescent identity development since and in addition to Erik Erikson[10], it's still all about *identity.* Teens are always trying to find out who they are (and who they are *not*) and who they want to be in the future. Figuring out "who you are" is largely about figuring out *what* you're feeling, *why* you're feeling that, and *what to do* about it. In my opinion *this is the most important skill for adolescents to develop*. Why? Because if your teenager does not know how to experience, articulate, and manage his emotions in healthy ways, he will do so in the *easiest* ways possible, that is to say, in the same ways that other humans manage their emotions: by the ingestion of drugs and alcohol, by having sex, by taking risks, or by self-injurious behavior. In other words, when teens cannot regulate their emotional lives, their risk of death increases.

Teens die primarily because of accidents/risk-taking behaviors (48 percent, with motor vehicle accidents accounting for almost three quarters of all deaths from unintentional injury), homicide (13 percent), and suicide (11 percent). All the main ways in which American teenagers die are related to *affect regulation*—that is, difficulty with understanding, articulating, and managing emotions. This is why it is the most important skill for a teenager to learn. And please believe me, they could really use your help to learn the complex sub-skills associated with this main developmental task.

But, *status*? What is that doing here?

Teens (and adults) care a lot about status for a simple reason: because most people tend to be nice to us according to the amount of status we have. It is no coincidence that the first question adults tend to ask new acquaintances is "What do you do?" It is also no coincidence that teens automatically have lower status, because they rarely have an answer to the question, "What do you do?" that involves the description of their job, the status of their job, and the amount of money they make.[11]

It seems important to mention here that I work with teens because they are in general, in my opinion, sensitive, caring, bright, creative, funny, deeply feeling, and, when I'm lucky enough that they will let me *really see them,* honest and insightful in breathtaking ways. But in my travels across the United States, talking with teenagers and their parents, I have learned important things about how teens suffer in 2012. Many American high school students, especially those in the private school world, almost regardless of geographic location, socioeconomic status, cultural and ethnic background, feel that they have the right to be rich, to have high-profile publicity, celebrity looks, and high-status jobs. These mindsets are partly the expression of our deep national belief that everyone has equal opportunity to acquire status in America. And we desire to be rich, look great, and have high status because we want the approval (and love) of our world. Sometimes this approval is a matter of survival, and sometimes it's an issue of how much suffering we will or won't experience. In the United States, identity development and status (or more important, *anxiety over status*) are intertwined. This is one good example of why it is crucial to understand not only that teens seek to establish their identities in and with the world of others, but also that they do so in the context of concern over their status.

Social and media critic John Culkin once remarked that, "Whomever discovered water, you can be certain it wasn't a fish." Chapter 4 ("Parenting in the Digital Age") illustrates the inexorable and mutually influencing links between adolescent development, identity, status, and digital media. This chapter represents a modification of Culkin's quote: "Whomever discovered the ongoing, mutually reinforcing effects of digital media on teens, you can be certain it wasn't a teen." These days, it's getting more difficult for the person who discovers these effects to be an adult, either. But many, many very smart people are trying to figure this out, and this chapter will tell you about their work and why I argue that *media literacy is the most important kind of education you could possibly give your child if they live in the United States in the 21st century.*

A good number of the questions and concerns I get from parents around the country have to do with the subject of Chapter 5, "Alcohol, Drugs and Parties." This gets so much attention for obvious reasons: The attraction is understandable and powerful, but the consequences can be lethal. You probably care about alcohol, drugs, and parties for one or more of the reasons that other American parents care: because you want to protect your child from danger, pain, and disappointment; because you're worried about the physical, psychological, and emotional effects of drugs and alcohol; because you equate parties with sex and are worried your child will have sex and get pregnant or get someone pregnant; because you worry that your child isn't responsible enough to make the sorts of complicated decisions necessary to stay safe (not to get hurt physically, psychologically, or emotionally); or because you partied and used drugs and/or alcohol (or a loved one did this) and you know what can happen and fear your teenager might make similar mistakes.

Many of you raise similar concerns about your adolescent's friendships and sexual relationships, in part because the lines between friendship and sexual relationship have been steadily blurring for many American teenagers. I'm only talking about those teens that live on the East or West coasts or in a major population center, though, right? Not necessarily. I wouldn't (and most researchers wouldn't) say that *your* old world of courtship, dating, and strict distinctions between friendly, romantic, and sexual relationships cannot be found anywhere in the United States. But it is important to remember that the water that teens swim in is the ocean of digital media. So while your teen may still go on a "date" or may refrain from sex until marriage or have other traditional ideas around relationships and sex, the digital world in which teens connect with one another *does not reflect this traditional reality.*

The television programs, e-books, graphic novels and cartoons, videos, games, films, radio, social media sites, chat sites, web browsers, cellphone advertisements, and e-readers also do not usually reflect the same views of sex and relationships you grew up with. So Chapter Six ("The Sexual Culture of American Teens") explores another basic premise of the book: that understanding what it means for teens to develop identity by creating and maintaining friendships, acquaintances, and partners (sexual or otherwise) requires an understanding of digital media. The entertainment industries—primarily television, film, and the music business—were all highly influential in adolescent identity development in 1993. But after 1994, the content and influence of these industries changed in dramatic ways. As we'll see, the advent of the 24/7/365 always-connected, always-plugged-into-digital-media teenager is here to stay for the foreseeable future. And *that* is changing just about everything, including relationships and sex.

Chapter 7 ("Protecting the Wish to Learn") presents some of the barriers to learning that arise for adolescents in the United States. While the chapter explores some of the problems associated with private and public schools—violence, poverty, racism, mental health disorders, learning disabilities, bullying, harassment, and aggression—it doesn't focus on what to do about these challenges. Research and recommendation about policy in these areas continues apace. The chapter also looks at the barriers caused by a failure to understand the difference between *learning* and going to school. As more educators, policymakers, parents, and students recognize the problems of "teaching to the test," and "racing to the top," we need to refocus our attention on providing the experiences of engagement, curiosity, and perseverance that are parts of *real* learning. What *are* we learning from our students—about their will and wish to learn, in a world of digital media, where status easily overwhelms the formation of identity? We'll visit that in Chapter 7.

In Chapter 8, we turn our attention to what happens in the background of family life. Fathers and mothers often have different parenting values and styles, and your child can make use of these differences in style, tone, and substance. But you know you are not raising your teen in a vacuum. Other children or adults may be present full- or part-time in your home. The normal pressures of raising children can be overwhelming and can make it easy to stop enjoying(or forget how to enjoy) your teenager—an experience they need to have with you. Living with anybody, let alone an adolescent, is challenging, and as your teenager becomes more physically, emotionally, and intellectually capable, your own capacities will feel *tested*. The feeling of being tested by your adolescent's provocative speech, strong feelings, and level of engagement (or disengagement) can be wearing and can feel very personal. Chapter 8 offers an exploration and application of a cognitive-interpersonal theory called "Control-Mastery" theory to thinking about what happens in your family, as a whole. We introduce a different concept of "testing," to help you understand the pushes and pulls of family life in a fashion that illustrates how much of the strain of family life has to do with the various ways in which our teens are trying to *approximate* what to do and how to feel in order to make you proud and happy without giving up their own (often different) wishes for their own life.

Sometimes the challenges that interfere with learning and identity formation in general come from *mental health difficulties*. Parents want to know if their child might be depressed, anxious, or dealing with a learning disability. But in close to two decades working with youth, I've never been asked: "Do you think my teen is mentally *healthy*?" Mental health cannot be solely addressed when things go wrong. So Chapter 9 ("Does My Teen Have Good Mental Health?") attempts to provide a framework for thinking about what makes your teen mentally healthy and how to support that good health. This chapter gives you the groundwork for working on your competency as a health *scientist*—a concept introduced in Chapter 1. It's difficult to know how to approximate your goals if you don't know what the goals are, beyond "surviving adolescence," "having them be happy," or "getting them into college." These are not bad goals; they are just not specific enough to give you a practical "theory for action."

It's a good bet that you are reading this book because you believe very strongly that your job as a parent of teens includes playing *a,* if not *the* major role in the ethical development of your child. Our final chapter, "The Ethical Dimension of Parenting Teenagers," is arguably the backbone of *The Approximate Parent.* This chapter is a kind of meditation on ethics, character, and the teaching of values to our children. You might remember that I said I'm more interested in the question of *how* we live our lives with one another and how and whether we incorporate what we believe and cherish into what we do with our kids. That's ethical development. But I'm not trying to get you to parent by my values. This is a book about helping you parent by *your own values,* by giving you practical ways of understanding—informed by the voluminous body of materials about adolescents from the disciplines of psychology, cognitive science, medicine, neurobiology, philosophy, sociology, and culture and media studies—what your teens are doing, thinking, and feeling. We also need to know *how* or *whether* they receive what you are doing, thinking, and feeling. I want to help make your lives easier, to help you enjoy your teen more and to feel interested, curious, and more competent in working with the teens in your life. I believe that requires the teaching of values and responsibility, including the importance and even necessity of failing, and persevering when things don't go well or the way you want them to. Remember *fidelity*?

Do I Have a Teen in My House?

Did you hate science in high school (or love it but find it difficult)? Do you have AD/HD? Then I want to talk to you for a second. I'm not joking here—I know firsthand what it's like to try to read material that is technical or scientific and stay focused on it without feeling overwhelmed. I wouldn't tell you to skip this chapter; it's got some fun, intriguing material in it. Plus, we usually know more about our cars then we do about our own brain anatomy and what it allows us to do. And I think it will help to know some of the *current* theories of brain development and how they relate to what your teenager is (or isn't) doing. This can help to provide a sense of the *practical* significance of our current neuropsychological understanding of adolescent development. If your eyes start to glaze over or this gets too technical or jargon-laden, you might come back to this chapter later, after you've read about the areas of the book that interest you more. Much of the information on brain development is spread through the other chapters, too, in a less detailed form.

Adolescent development is "complex and asynchronous." That's the kind of statement you would read in a textbook for researchers about adolescent development. In fact, you can read it on page 4 of *The Adolescent Brain: Learning, Reasoning, and Decision Making,* a recent book (and one of the best) about adolescent brain development.[1] That phrase is extremely accurate but it makes me want to take a nap. I prefer Ken Winters's description—he says adolescence is like having "a child driving a Formula One race car."[2] A very complicated, extremely powerful instrument is in the hands of someone who is excited to have access to the vehicle, but doesn't know what it means to have that much power at their disposal, much less how to use it.

There are some fantastic books available on adolescent development, written by people much smarter than me, who are doing cutting-edge research on teen development and maturation.[3] This isn't one of those books, but if you're interested in what you read here, you can find those books at the end of this chapter.

By the way, it's helpful to know the difference between those two terms. When we discuss *maturation* we mean the biological unfolding, physical growth, and primarily genetic influences on what happens in our human bodies. When talking about *development,* we mean maturation *plus* experience and learning (education), which is influenced over time (history) by family, culture, cognition, language, personality, etc. I know this is simplistic (or maybe way too complex), but I think of this way:

> *Maturation* = what your child is *likely* to become, in a particular sequence, related to being a human (the fact of genetics), and mostly because of *his/her* particular genes

> *Development* = what happens with all facets of your son or daughter in time and over time, due to the mutually influencing experiences of life

These mutually influencing experiences are both conscious and nonconscious, but I believe most involve nonconscious processes and apperceptions, which are faster, often more efficient, more accurate ways of responding to our own bodies and the world of others, than our conscious thought processes.[5]

This way of thinking about maturation, now that I think about it, doesn't make things clearer. A human ovum is fertilized and off we go. Development and maturation are happening. But even that is inaccurate. Things were in play already, because of the combination of development and maturation of the humans (your biological parents) involved in the production and fertilization of that ovum. And things were already in play because these things happened in a lifeworld with its own particularities, given the complexity of history/histories. This seems abstract, but what it means is that what happened to your paternal grandfather has a bearing, for example, on whether your grandkids do or don't get diabetes or depression—more on that later in the chapter.

In other words, who your teen is and who she will become isn't just about the *linear* unfolding of her genetics, as if there was no context for this biological unfolding. A human becomes who she or he will be in context, *always.* And that context is different for every person, making each person different. That is, in my opinion, true even (or especially) when you have two humans who together help create and raise many children in the same household.

You would think (and you would be right) that two children born to the same parents, in the same household, in roughly the same historical period, fed with roughly the same food, exposed to roughly the same environmental influences, talked to and played with relatively equally, would have a lot in common. But you would be incorrect if you thought that they *should* be very similar in their development, just because all those other things happened.

You might be surprised how many people call my psychotherapy office to make an appointment because they had one child who turned out one way (the easy, good, relatively unproblematic one) and another child who turned out another way (the difficult, challenging, problematic one). Oftentimes those parents of preteens, teens, or "emerging adults" are pained, angry, disappointed, or confused[6]—really, it is all a kind of grieving—over the huge discrepancies *between* their different children. Left "unchecked," this disappointment and grief over what children do or do not become can have long-lasting effects, according to psychologist Joshua Coleman, author of *When Parents Hurt*. A longtime and wise colleague, Dr. Coleman has recounted over the years the intense conflicts and pain occasioned by both parental and child disappointment in the ways child-rearing happened in the family. In our exceedingly mobile society, grown children often move away from or cut off their parents as a result of this anger and deeply felt disappointment. The consequence can be grandparents cut off from grandchildren, grown children who avoid or won't talk to their parents, and a whole lot of suffering.

Parents don't always say it, but they wonder, *"How could this happen?"* Another equally understandable question they have, and don't usually ask out loud, is, *"How can I get the child I'm having trouble with to become more like the one I'm enjoying a lot more?"* The answer is almost always: You cannot do that. You have two *different* (or *very* different) children, and that is what development and maturation are all about. And so, who your teen is and will become is always "about" geography and your genetics and what happened with her father in Oradea in 1965 or her grandmother in Lagos in 1942 and about where she lives now and what kind of food she has access to (and what she chooses or is induced into choosing) and whether she is bullied or has AD/HD or practices the clarinet frequently. And parents and caregivers do not "produce" children or teens, as if development flows in only one direction. I couldn't agree more with fellow Chicagoan and writer Peter De Vries, who is quoted as saying, "Who of us is mature enough for offspring before the offspring themselves arrive? The value of [parenthood] is not that adults produce children but that children produce adults."[7] Or, consider my absolute favorite definition of maturation, often attributed to Erma Bombeck: "Maturity is doing what you want, even if your parents want you to do it."

What This Work Is and Is Not

This chapter is not a cutting-edge, scientific treatise on your teen's development or teen development in general. I'm not pretending to be a neuroscientist. I just have an intense interest in the subject and am partial to scientific research as a source for thinking about and understanding my world. Why? Probably in no small part because my father was a researcher. This book is informed by research and other genres of work—the work of many others, in a wide variety of fields from philosophy, critical theory, sociology, cognitive science, neurobiology and neuropsychology to art, literature, poetry, religious studies, and music. That's because I am interested in these areas of exploration and experience and they help make up my personality and cognitive style.

Most chapters in the book will present an essay on the main subject area, informed by a combination of research and clinical material, but intended to provide a rich, new, exciting, or stimulating *way of thinking* about what you are going through as the parent of an adolescent. I'm hoping that reading these chapters will help you feel more engaged and curious about parenting your adolescent, in turn making you a better parent and person. Each chapter will also include a list of "Practical Parenting Tips" for that particular subject area (just like on the website), and, finally, a list of resources for further exploration of that topic.

The way I write and think about teens might change what you do completely or not at all or it might change some things in subtle ways. That's the point. I don't want to give you a list of things you have to do or need to do correctly. I'd like to give you a way of thinking and feeling about your teenager, and then it's up to you. That is very purposeful, because it allows you and me to work together in a way that's very similar to the way that I'm suggesting you could work with your teen.

Adolescent Development and Maturation, Or: Do I Have a Teen in My House?

Do you have a teen in your house? It is really good to know the answer to that, because it helps you know what is normal and expectable and whether to take their behaviors (and words) as personally insulting as they sometimes seem.

There are an estimated 42.6 million adolescents (children between the ages of 10–19) in the United States, and that number is expected to hit 53 million by 2050.[8] If you consider the broader definition of adolescence as stemming from just prior to puberty (since puberty and onset of adolescence are not the same)[9], then the estimate would be closer to 70 million individuals or more; we're looking at the age span of 9-25. This population is more ethnically and racially diverse than the general population, and that diversity is increasing, varying by region of the country,[10] with most adolescents living in the South, followed by the Midwest, West, and Northeast (35.7 percent, 23.5 percent, 22.7 percent, and 18.1 percent respectively)[11]. Most adolescents live in the suburbs, rather than in rural areas,[12] and over 66 percent of teens 12–17 live with both parents—representing a decreasing trend of teens living in two-parent households. Finally, race matters. Black and Hispanic youth tend to experience poverty much more frequently than their Caucasian and Asian/Pacific Islander peers—almost three times as much.

So, are you living in a suburb in the South? Good chance you have a teen in your house. But let's try to get a bit more specific than that.

It might be instructive to start with a stereotype about teenagers and then work our work toward the specific. First of all, if you have an adolescent in your house, you might have encountered what I like to call OYH Syndrome—which stands for "Oh, yeah, huh?" This phrase is encountered—although it can also be a sort of blank, sheepish look you get—when you ask your child, for the fourth time, to take out the garbage or to feed the cat or dog or to do just about anything for you. You might have heard your child say, "In a minute, Mom" or "After this show is over" or "After I get through this level" (on the video game). But being the good mom that you are, you let your child do what he said he wants to do, only after he's promised that he will then, finally do (fill in name of chore). Once you've gone through all this and you remind your child that they still didn't do (fill in name of chore), he looks up at you and says, "Oh, yeah, huh?"

Your child isn't trying to purposely work your last nerve. It is more likely that if your child is in middle school and doing this kind of thing (often) and is also often forgetful and seems to be in a cloud somewhere, they have OYH Syndrome. But it may also mean that adolescence has begun, because adolescent brains—in part due to the effects of neural pruning—can present to us like anterograde amnesia patients. That's the kind of amnesia where long-term memories remain intact but there is incomplete or impaired recall for recent events and difficulty with creating new memories. If you add in the idea that adolescent brains respond more fully to relevant and emotionally salient material (of which taking out the trash is not an example), then you get easy forgetting, distraction, and difficulty remembering "non-crucial" tasks. So, the stereotype of the forgetful, absent-minded, foggy middle-schooler (preteen or teen) has some truth to it and it is one way of seeing whether your child has entered adolescence. Now let's get to a decidedly more scientific way of understanding the onset of adolescence.

Why Puberty and the Beginning of Adolescence Aren't the Same

Puberty is a word for the neurobiological processes by which your son or daughter becomes capable of sexual reproduction, i.e., able to produce a child. Puberty usually starts when increasing amounts of leptin (a protein produced in the fat cells) are present in the body. If your teen's body produces enough leptin and body fat, it probably signals a structure in the brain to start the hormonal changes that will begin puberty.

The period of puberty usually takes about 3–5 years for boys and 5–7 years for girls, but there really isn't a length of time demarcated for puberty to last. If the process happens too soon (at the age of 6)[13], too quickly (less than two years)[14,] or too slowly (more than five years for boys and seven years for girls)[15], something might be off and you should check in with your son or daughter's doctor. Puberty largely starts with changes in the brain, as chemical messages are sent to the sex organs (ovaries/testes) that will eventually result in an increase in sexual feelings and significant changes to the musculature, skin, bones, hair, breasts, sexual organs, and the brain itself. Your children should get taller, heavier, and begin to look more like an adult and less like a kid.

In the United States, the average age for a girl to start puberty is at 10½ years of age, with the normal range being from about 7¾ to 13. The span of puberty for girls, then, is usually from about 9 to 16 years of age, but again, there is no set time period. The average age at which puberty starts has significantly dropped over the last 150 years[16]—it used to be closer to 16.

For girls, the onset of puberty is usually signaled first by the growth of breasts; their periods usually start (on average) at 12½ to 13 years of age. Other common changes include change in body odor, growth of pubic hair, presence of acne, and increasing height. African-American and Hispanic girls usually begin puberty a bit earlier than their Caucasian peers.

For boys, average onset of puberty is about 11½ to 12 years of age, with a range between about 9½ to 13½ years old. The length of puberty is usually about 3–5 years. Boys usually begin puberty with the growth and "dropping" of their testicles and increase in penis size, followed by changes in body odor, growth of pubic, facial, and axillary (armpit) hair, increase in height and weight, and deepening of the voice.

The *timing* of puberty is related to both genetic and environmental factors, such as disease, nutritional condition, amount of environmental stress, exposure to chemicals, the people you're surrounded by (or not surrounded by) in your life setting. By the end of reading this book you will be tired of hearing me say "it is always about genes and environment in interaction," because this is true of all elements of development and I'm aiming to help us get rid of that "nature versus nurture" idea.

As I discussed earlier in the chapter, the *beginning of puberty* is not the same thing as the *beginning of adolescence;* adolescent development and puberty are not different names for the same thing. Puberty is mostly about biological maturation and has to do with the changes described above. These changes are neurobiological and physiological changes influenced by the interaction of genes and environment. *Adolescent development* is an umbrella term, referring to all of the interactions between genes and environment, biology and biography. *Puberty* is a set of processes that make up *one* aspect of adolescent development—sexual maturity.

So while this book disagrees with the notion that "there is no such thing as adolescence," it's still not hard to see why someone might make that argument. If puberty and adolescence are not the same, then when does "adolescence" begin? How do I actually know if I have an adolescent in the house?

There is no one answer to that question and that's why some folks probably think "adolescent" is a meaningless term. If you think of adolescence as primarily a *biological* event, then you can argue it begins with puberty and ends when significant physical maturation, especially in the brain, slows and stops; that would be about 24-"ish" for young women and about 12 to 18 months later for young men. If you think of it as primarily a *cognitive* event, then you could argue it begins when a child develops the ability to "think more like a grown up" or develops what Swiss psychologist Jean Piaget called "abstract thinking" and other adult-like capacities for reasoning, imagining, and complex perspective-taking. If you think of the beginning of adolescence as a *neurological* event, you might say that it begins with some of the earliest brain chemical/hormonal changes spurred on by puberty. The production of important growth and sex hormones in the body significantly affects social relationships, because they affect thinking and perception. If you work in the "human sciences" like *psychology, cultural anthropology, or sociology,* you might look at the beginning of adolescence as when the child becomes able to understand and take on certain social roles such as being able to love, work, cooperate, learn, and organize activities in more adult ways.

There is a period of adolescence and it is identifiable. It is just that it is a complex period of human development and can be described in many different ways and through the optics of many different disciplines of knowing. So, that's why there is no agreement on when adolescence begins or what it is. That's not necessarily a problem, in my view. I actually think disagreement is *sometimes* a very good thing. It is good that we argue over what's important and true and real. It would be better if we could do that, though, without having to destroy others, figuratively and literally.

This is an important illustration of why this book is called *The Approximate Parent.* I research and gather data about how lots of people and lots of disciplines view adolescence, and then apply them to my thinking about and work with teens. If my approximated theory of "adolescence development" helps me *truly help teens,* then the theory is a keeper, until a better one comes along. I pretty much know when I need a new theory or an upgrade: I *hurt* physically or mentally. *Something doesn't work anymore.* It's like picking up a hammer to swing it and noticing there is no head on the hammer. The balance is off. I feel worried or anxious. People are getting angry at me or not interacting (or wanting to interact) with me. I'm unhappy or frustrated (more than just for a few days or a week). Those are my signals. When something *feels* like it isn't working and hasn't worked for a while, it's probably time for a better, improved, tweaked, or otherwise new theory.

This approach works because it fits how human beings learn. We're hard-wired to perceive anxiety and pain, to make assessments about what we need and what works and what doesn't. People in therapy ask me all the time, "How can I *miss* something I've never had?" You can miss something you've never had or want something different or have something feel "off" because the working of human biology is easily and readily described by its propensity to *detect*—often with exquisite precision—*experiences of "abnormality."* And our bodies are always giving and getting biological and psychological clues as to what we're missing and what we need. Since we have to start somewhere—wherever our mindsets/state of our biological organism are, whatever social location and cultural environment we're in and whatever we're doing—we are always *starting with theories* of what we want and need and how to get it. These processes of figuring out where we are, what we want, and what we need: 1) are ongoing as long as we're alive and healthy; 2) are set in motion by the interaction of genes and environment and themselves impacted by genes and environment; and 3) are mostly nonconscious, because, I believe, they are too fast, too complex, and too pervasive to be happening within our *conscious* awareness. In any instance, what we're aware of is only a small piece of the pie of what happens with us humans.

These processes of detecting and responding, which I call "theory making" or "approximating," describe *how we figure out who we are, what we want, and what to do about it*. We all do this: It's how you and I and our teens learn, so let's use it to our advantage. But just because we all do it doesn't mean it's "good" or "true" or "accurate" or without bias or problems. That's why it's also helpful to try to understand what could go wrong with the process of theory-making, how it could be distorted or biased or not functioning well. I call that "health science."

Being a *health scientist* encompasses the way I approach both mental and physical health (which are two sides of the same coin). One of the coolest, most useful and engaging things we can do in taking care of ourselves and our children is to be and teach our children to be a health scientist. You do this by being interested in and curious about what theories we are making about our health, what the biases and problems are with those theories, whether they are "working," and curious what to do when they're not. Being a health scientist implies *approximate parenting* because it is always about observation, data gathering and collection, correction and refinement...and starting again. It incorporates psychologist Kurt Lewin's wise saying that "there is nothing so practical as a good theory." By definition, a *good* theory is never a *final* theory.

The Characteristics of Adolescents

Okay, you've got it. Just because you see the signs of puberty in your child doesn't mean you have a "full-blown" adolescent in the house. There is not necessarily a need to panic yet. Of course, if you notice one day that your son has a few hairs on his upper lip, it could be poignant, but not necessarily panic-inducing. I usually get a call when there are "behavioral" indications of adolescence presence. That's what is confusing. Because adolescence and onset of puberty are not the same, you can see signs of adolescent development *before* puberty—and I believe this happens more often in the United States than in other countries. This phenomenon of a *child* sounding and looking like a *teenager* happens more frequently and sooner in countries where exposure to Western media and culture is high, where digital media use is high. If you're the parent of a pre-adolescent in a country with unfettered, uncensored Internet access, good luck.

It could be that your child has discovered thong panties (yes, they are marketed to kids) and she wants to wear them. It could be that she wants to dress up and look like one of her Bratz dolls. It could be that he starts swearing and talking back to you or your partner or arguing about every last thing. It could be that he wants to start lifting weights and getting 'bigger muscles" and is becoming very focused on appearance. Or you might find these behaviors—usually associated with one gender—being exhibited by another gender. Your child might seem more withdrawn or sullen or want more privacy; your son or daughter might start locking the door to the bathroom when they had previously shared with you all aspects of what they did in there.

If these types of things are happening in your household, you might be surprised or even anxious, because you could be thinking your child is *too young* to be a teenager, and you're *not ready* to parent a teen. Since development is "asynchronous," it follows that some signs of adolescent development can and will show up earlier than others, based upon the interaction between genes and environment. It's not that the Internet directly *causes* teenage-like behavior. But access to the Internet and all forms of digital media—don't forget television, which is on the Internet, anyway—can and does promote adolescent-like behavior. Why?

It's good for business, that's why. There are plenty of companies that are looking at (and doing) the exact same research that informs this book, and this research is being used to sell products to your child, by appealing to the powerful wish to grow up and to be more mature. There is plenty of research being done and utilized by thousands of companies on just how many times your child will have to bug you/ask you to buy something before you'll cave in and buy it. A lot, if not most of this advertising know-how ends up affecting digital media. It's the business of separating you from your money, via your child. That's *big,* big business because everyone involved in it—and you know this if you're involved in it—knows that parents want to do right by their children and don't generally like saying "no" to them.

Lest you think I'm blaming everything on the Internet and digital advertising, let me say that the presence of an older (adolescent) child in the family also represents a powerful motivation for your younger child to start adopting adolescent behaviors. It's easy for younger kids to simply associate age with privilege (because they do in fact usually go together). If a child wants and feels a need for more power, that seems the obvious route: *Get older faster.* I would say that the odds of you wanting help and calling someone like me are significantly higher if: 1) you've got teenagers in the house alongside younger children; and 2) everyone in the household is a digital media consumer. Someone should do *that* study (or please send it to me, if it's already done).

As you understand by now, this book is intended to provide you with some practical theories to apply to what you're seeing and feeling. It's not about giving you The Answers. So first we'll quickly look at current *principles*[17] of overall human development, then go to contemporary theories of adolescent brain development, and in summary highlight how those maturational changes (which, as you'll see, are "top down") can show up as a teenager in your house (or classroom or office).

I want to pause to note, here, that principles and theories are different. A *principle* denotes comprehensive, fundamental laws and rules—usually related to the workings of nature—that are accepted as true. Principles are the things that don't change; they carry the immutable "truths" of life. These days many Americans seem to be at war over Principles. You might not like a principle, but you can't really argue with it—it's usually thought of as being *beyond* you, or any individual. A *theory* involves an analysis of a set of facts in relationship to one another; facts can change or be rearranged, forcing new analyses. Theory-making involves belief, risk, and speculation, forcing us—if we have integrity—into the land of the hypothetical and circumstantial. Theory pushes and pulls toward the plausible, the approximate. It is a composite, community effort, for the sake of investigation. Theory and theory-making cannot be divorced from *practice* and the *practical,* because doing so would blur and eventually erase the distinction between what we merely think and imagine to be workable—given human limitations—and what we *assume, without further investigation, to be true.* In this view, parenting cannot be *principle-driven.* It can keep its eye on principles, but it must be *practice-driven.*

The Organizing Principles of Human Development

Human development seems to be organized along lines helpfully described by seven principles. Let's look at these now:

1. *Development happens from the top down* ("the cephalocaudle principle"). Children get the most control of their head first, and then control slowly comes to lower parts of the body. Each newly won developmental step affects subsequent steps; that's partly why it's hard to walk without pretty decent gross motor control of the arms first.

2. *Development happens from the center to the periphery* ("proximodistal development"). Gross motor coordination happens before fine motor coordination (arm control before finger control, for example). The spinal cord is going to develop first because the outer parts of the body (limbs) and peripheral nervous system require a well-developed spine (in all its functions).

3. *Development is always about maturation and environment, in interaction.* Certain biological changes may be "programmed" to happen in a certain order in the human, but their rate of unfolding, and whether they unfold smoothly are influenced by everything in the person's internal and external environment. That means you—if you are your child's biological parent—are in both your child's external and internal environments, in some way. Certain biological changes (maturation) must happen in order for certain other biological and developmental changes to happen. For example, in learning theory we talk about the idea of "readiness," to describe the fact that certain brain changes must take place in order for your child to speak. Other changes must take place in the brain for your child to understand language.

4. *Development moves from more simple structures to more complexity* (although to me, it's all pretty complex). This one seems pretty obvious. Skill acquisition—whether language, speech, thinking and problem-solving, or moving your body—grows in complexity as the human develops. Children understand things first in concrete ways. If you say to your 3-year-old child, "Mom is a little under the weather," it might be confusing; but it might be fine for your 7-year-old, depending upon his or her level of cognitive development. The brain and other physical structures start out with the *basics* and eventually (if healthy) grow in capacity.

4. *Development is always happening and is both additive and cumulative, although not always linear.* As suggested already, one skill usually builds upon another skill, and one stage of development lays the ground for another. There is a *usual* or normative sequence to the acquisition of skills and capacities. These sequences are not set in stone, however; they can change and sometimes must adapt, depending upon the environment. But in general, mastery in one area is followed by predictable mastery in other areas. And it doesn't stop. It might be distorted or disturbed or go awry, but it isn't going to stop until we die (and then, who knows?).

6. *Development happens from the "general" to the "specific."* Just watch a human newborn flailing, a lack of motor coordination among the limbs. They are behaving from instinct, and their behavior often looks completely un-goal-directed. It isn't actually the case, as even seemingly uncoordinated behaviors are highly purposeful, like early eye-gazing, arm and leg movement, and vocalization. But a child will, for the most part, be able to do something generally before they can *refine* the more specific aspects of any particular behavior. That is true of both physical and psychological phenomena, which are always related.

7. *Development unfolds in different time frames for each person.* While children might all go through the *same* general developmental stages and phases, no two children will go through them at exactly the same rate. This is especially important in the United States, where we can get very focused on being first and doing it "right." It's normal for a child to walk at 10 months and it's normal for a child to walk at 18 months. It's normal for your child to be toilet-learned at 3¼ years of age and it's also normal to be toilet-learned at 4¼ years of age. If the preschool you *must* send your child to requires that your child be toilet-learned prior to entry, you are much more likely to start worrying that your child is "behind" in his development. However, this requirement has nothing to do with *normal* development and everything to do with whether or not the preschool staff wants to change diapers or not.

It just doesn't help to compare your child to another child. Principle 7 has an important corollary: Different structures and functions *within* the person unfold at different rates. Your child can be more advanced emotionally than intellectually or vice versa. This is an important principle to keep in mind for your child's entire lifespan, *especially in adolescence.*

This overview is from the top down, so we're going to go deeper by starting at the top, with your adolescent's brain.

The Brain During Adolescence

Anatomical development (of the brain) is related to but not the same as *functional* development. That means that as your child's brain changes, they will have the *capability* for new behaviors, ways of thinking and feeling. But it doesn't necessarily mean they'll use them. Anatomical development means you get a fully formed arm. It doesn't mean that arm will belong to a major league baseball pitcher—that, too, is a matter of genes and environment. Having only *one* fully formed arm can be enough to have a great fastball. So, same with the brain. The brain, during adolescence, is rapidly changing.

Your brain is described by some scientists as having three main structures: the *cerebellum* (below the back of the brain, regulating balance, posture, and movement/motor coordination, and involving emotional processing and other cognitive functions)[18], the *cerebrum* (the largest area of the brain, "divided" into frontal, parietal, temporal, and occipital lobes), and the *brain stem* (which includes the midbrain, pons, and medulla), which is connected to the spinal cord, responsible for controlling many of our *automatic* and motor functions. The brain stem and related structures regulate eye and mouth movement, sensation of pain and temperature, perception of loud and soft, involuntary muscle movements, sneezing, coughing, swallowing, and the like. The brain stem is a very old (evolutionarily speaking) part of the brain. Depending upon the type of scientist you are, you might describe the brain in different ways, and see different structures as the *major* parts of the brain. Some scientists include the emotional center or limbic system as a kind of fourth major "part" of the brain. Other scientists, such as Joseph LeDoux (one of my favorites), suggest that the idea of the limbic system is outmoded and inaccurate[19]— it's much more about the junctions and spaces *between* the neurons (synapses) that count, thus the title of his book *Synaptic Self*. As a musician, I'm particularly fond of the idea that it's the space between the notes we need to pay attention to.

Your brain is (hopefully) encased in your skull, which is made of bone. It is also surrounded by a tough membrane called the *dura* that protects the brain and spinal cord. Inside the skull is a layer of cerebrospinal fluid (CSF) that protects the brain and spinal cord, circulating throughout the brain and spinal canal. All of these protective features have made it difficult until recently to use imaging to see the brain or see the brain at work. Magnetic Resonance Imaging (MRI) technology has changed all that, and the advent of that technology is a main reason why you're reading about brain development in this book. The early 1990s were a game-changer, with the advent of MRI and the invention of the modern Internet. These two technologies are rapidly changing the way we think, feel, and act in the world. Dr. Jay Giedd— one name you should definitely know—is one of the pioneers in the field of using MRI technology to understand the brain, especially the adolescent brain.

Our next discussion largely follows the work Dr. Giedd (and his colleagues) detailed in the new volume *The Adolescent Brain: Learning, Reasoning, and Decision Making*.[20]

Giedd and others most commonly describe the brain as consisting of four kinds of tissue that make up the "cerebral volume" and weight of the brain:

1) Gray matter (GM, mostly cell bodies, dendrites, axons, blood vessels, and extracellular space);

2) White matter (WM, named for the color of myelin or the fatty tissue that surrounds the axons and increases the speed and efficiency of chemical message processing in the brain);

3) Cerebrospinal fluid (CSF, which offers some protection for the brain, allows it to be buoyant inside the skull and keep a certain chemical balance while helping to facilitate blood flow to the brain); and

4) "Other" tissue (skin, bone, and blood vessels or vasculature).

The overall course of maturation for the adolescent brain includes:

1) A peak in the total volume of the four tissue types (above) at about 10½ for girls and 14½ for boys, followed by a decrease;

2) A peak in the overall volume of cortical and subcortical gray matter (GM) during adolescence, with different areas peaking at different times, followed by a

decrease. Decreases in GM (probably) related to proliferation of synaptic (neural connections) material and thinning ("pruning") of those neural components that are not strengthened through use; and

3) An *increase* in the volume of white matter (WM) during childhood and adolescence, with the pace of increase being potentially dramatic, with some regions showed a 50 percent increase in a two-year period.[21] Increases in WM are (probably) related to *myelination,* which allows for *100 times* speedier transmission of signals down the axon and up to 30-fold increases in the frequency of "firing" of a particular neuron.

There are other important changes in the cerebellum, ventricles, and within the cortical and subcortical regions, including areas of the brain that, if abnormalities develop, are particularly vulnerable to the creation of neuropsychiatric disorders. This seems, at least in part, related to problems with the temporal lobes, amygdalae, and hippocampus—all major parts of the brain connected to how we feel, use language, and remember our experiences.

In other words, there is a lot of rapid construction happening, and while the end result of that construction will likely be a much more capable, thoughtful, calm, smarter, kinder, emotionally stable child, there is also a lot that go wrong during this period of development.

ELEVEN MAJOR CHARACTERISTICS OF ADOLESCENT BRAIN DEVELOPMENT

Figure 1 provides an overview of 11 Major Characteristics of Adolescent Brain Development. In this section, we'll go through each of these changes in more detail. They'll be referred to throughout the book, because these brain changes (maturation) have a huge influence on what teens do and why they do it (their development).

Maturation from Back to Front

The first areas of the brain to develop and roughly "finish" development include the areas of the brain (like the *cerebellum*) that have to do mostly with physical coordination of movement and sensory processing. Two other very important structures— the *nucleus accumbens*, which is heavily involved in regulating motivation to seek rewards, and the *amygdalae,* two almond-shaped areas, one in each hemisphere of the brain, associated with emotional processing and evaluating pleasure and aversive stimuli—generally develop later than the sensorimotor areas. Finally, some of the areas of the brain primarily involved in higher cognition ("Executive Functions"), such as the *dorsolateral prefrontal cortex* (DLPFC), are the last to finish developing; these areas support growing competencies in organizational ability, judgment/generalizing from the specific, response inhibition (and holding back now for something good later), and multitasking. By "multitasking," I don't really mean the activity of checking your email online while you're texting on your phone. This kind of "multitasking" is more like weighing stimuli and making decisions about what to attend to, with multiple sources of information and differing priorities attached to each of those possible inputs.

As we'll discuss later, some scientists believe that the adolescent brain is characterized by a *relative imbalance* in developmentally based capacity between the emotional center of the brain (the so-called "limbic system," which includes the *nucleus accumbens, amygdala, hippocampus, olfactory bulbs, thalamus,* and other structures) and the *ventromedial* (VPF), *orbitofrontal* (OFC), and *dorsolateral prefrontal cortices* (DLPFC), which are involved in the experience of fear, risk evaluation, decision-making, and the organizational functions noted above. The *ventral tegmental* area, located in the central cortex and associated with the dopamine/pleasure-reward system, also develops *earlier* than the frontal cortices. These are by no means the only important "structures" of the brain, but they are the structures most talked about in the popular press in relation to adolescent development.

You might think, especially because the popular media describes it this way, that this state of affairs means that kids are primarily emotional and don't really think much until they're older and their frontal cortices are more developed. This is inaccurate, although there is a grain of truth to it. Why? Well, think about Principle 7, above. That would indicate that every child's brain is developing at a different rate than every other child. And different areas develop more or less faster than others, because of genetic and environmental factors in combination. One child can (and will) have more highly developed executive functioning capabilities than another. And even if that particular child has a propensity toward considering information and acting based upon its emotional salience and relative pleasure, it doesn't mean she isn't "thinking" about her actions, prioritizing them or weighing risk and reward. It just means that her ability to do so in a way that favors a more rational, long-term view might not be as strong, and given environmental influences (such as peer opinion or available resources for her to implement and back up her decisions), the balance might be tipped more easily toward an "emotionally laden" decision. It may also mean that she relies less on "gist-based" thinking—which is faster and more efficient, but not always accurate—in her decision-making and evaluation of risk and reward than she does on the more analytical (and slower) type of decision-making.[22]

It is true, though, that the capacity for *faster* and more efficient thinking is a trait of adulthood and more maturity. And this efficiency goes hand in hand with *myelination* and *synaptic pruning* of the frontal cortices.

Figure 1. Characteristics of Adolescent Brain Maturation and Development

CHARACTERISTIC	DESCRIPTION
Maturation from back to front	The areas of the brain primarily involved in higher cognition (DL-PFC or "Executive Functions") develop last, including organizational abilities, judgment/generalizing from the specific, response inhibition (and holding back now for something good later), and multitasking.
Maturation from center to periphery	There may be an imbalance in maturation that favors the limbic system over the Dorsolateral Prefrontal Cortex (DL-PFC) functions; this means that what is emotionally relevant for teens gets "processing time" priority over what might be "logically" good for them—but this is different than "lacking intelligence."
Brain development is a matter of nature x *nurture*	The idea of neuronal plasticity during adolescence is rooted in the capacity of the brain to be changed by the environment and experience; it's no longer about "nature vs. nurture"; development is always both maturation and experience in the lifeworld.
Plasticity is at its zenith during adolescence	The changeability of the adolescent brain is an absolute hallmark of and central piece of adolescent brain research.
Connectivity of neuronal structures is key to development	Brain maturation isn't just about increased speed; it is equally about "turning on" and connecting previously unconnected parts of the brain.
Brain development is linked to the centrality and rapidity of white matter (WM) changes	The "white" of white matter is owing to the color of myelin, the adipose "sheathing" that wraps around parts of the nerve cell, allowing much faster conductivity of electrical impulses in the brain.

CHART CONTINUES ON NEXT PAGE

CHARACTERISTIC	DESCRIPTION
Gray matter (GM) development peaks during adolescence and then gradually decreases	Unlike WM changes, which increase throughout adolescence, GM volume decreases over adolescence, possibly in relation to the "pruning" of cellular structures that are overproduced leading to adolescence ("Use it or lose it").
There are definite sex differences in maturation/development	Brain size and speed of maturation varies widely between boys and girls and among boys and girls.
There are wide individual variations in development (within and among teens)	The size of one boy's brain can be double the size of a same-age male brain, and still be within the norm. There is a very wide range in how different teens' brains develop, and they can all be "normal."
Risk and reward are assessed by teens in fundamentally different ways than by adults	Changes in adolescents' brain dopamine systems now appear key to how reward-motivated behaviors develop .
The adolescent brain is uniquely vulnerable to pathology	Teens are incredibly resilient, physically, but also incredibly vulnerable during synaptic proliferation and pruning.

And you'll remember something else about neurons—they are wrapped in a fatty substance called *myelin,* which helps (significantly) speed chemical signals down the neuron. Well, some of the neurons are wrapped, some are not, and some are being wrapped. That process is called *myelination,* and it is not yet complete in adolescence. *This incompleteness is a hallmark of adolescence.* It keeps going throughout adolescence. As we noted earlier, there is an *increasing* of "white matter" (WM) in the adolescent brain, as more and more nerve cells are made more efficient and faster in functioning through myelination. And the process of *making* or "activating" certain neurons and neuronal groups is not yet complete. The increase in neuronal production seems to reach a peak at around 11 for girls and about 12½ for boys, before they start getting "pruned back." This pruning back process is what may account for the significant *decrease* in gray matter (GM) in the adolescent brain, which begins fairly early in adolescence. When the pruning is done—at some point after high school—you have a very efficient, quicker functioning, more "mature" brain.

However, these processes of having the nerves wrapped in myelin—which speeds up chemical messaging in the neuron, and from neural network to neural network—occurs at a different rate than the "pruning back" of neural connections that are not highly utilized. Pruning begins in the striatum and sensory motor cortices, and is finished relatively early in adolescence, along the "back to front" principle. The frontal cortices *continue* to be pruned throughout adolescence. And this is not a linear process. Pruning and neural development and growth are happening simultaneously. Some connections are being rapidly pruned back while others are in rapid connection mode, especially between the prefrontal cortex and the subcortical regions associated with pleasure, risk, reward, and emotion.[23]

Maturation from Center to Periphery

As mentioned previously, adolescents *seem* to demonstrate an imbalance in maturation that favors the limbic system over the frontal cortices (e.g., DLPFC functioning). This would follow the basic developmental principle of maturity from center to periphery. Until recently this principle suggested theories about development highlighting the priority of emotionally *relevant* data getting "processing time" priority over what might be "logically" good. "Head versus heart" seemed to be an apt metaphor for this state of affairs. But like most theories that operate on binary opposites, it's usually only a matter of time before new evidence comes to light that reveals the limitations of an either/or model.

We generally expect our teens to do more and understand more as they get older, to get smarter with age and experience. Teens are often thought of in *both* ways: either as being at the height of their cognitive abilities or "ruled" by their emotions. Worldwide comparisons of academic achievement (based on test performance) show lower scores overall for high schoolers versus middle or elementary school kids.[24] And we are all familiar with the often-intense emotionality of adolescents and the link between these strong feelings and apparently poor choices. So, which is it? Are teens intelligent and growing in intelligence or are they primarily emotionally driven?

Well, part of the problem is that intelligence and rational decision-making are not the same thing—it turns out that's another false binary. Adolescents can be highly intelligent *and* highly irrational, as the capacities described by each term are *complementary,* different sides of the same coin of "higher cognitive functioning."

Let's explain this by going back to the little story I told in the Introduction about my son getting caught speeding. His explanation was, "If I'd known the cop was going to be there, I wouldn't have been speeding."

I believe that my son was and is highly intelligent (and at least his IQ score demonstrated something about that "fact"). So, how could an intelligent being give such a stupid answer? Because it *wasn't* stupid. If you think that his behavior was the result of irrationality (associated with emotionality)—that teens just do stupid, crazy things because they can or because they get pleasure or excitement—then his answer was dumb. But if, in analyzing his *decision* to speed as part of a *rational* process, you emphasize the strong feelings of invulnerability and tendency to discount negative outcomes (getting caught) in proportion to the rewards (fun and exhilaration), you get a calculation in which speeding at 1:00 A.M. seems like a pretty good idea. Additionally, some researchers have found—and my own professional and parental experience supports these findings—that kids take risks and agree in retrospect that the risk was a poor choice.[25]

I think it makes a big difference if you know that your teen's poor choice was not the complete *absence* of rationality but the ongoing *presence* of temptations (of all kinds, many of which are highly rational, like not losing a friend or being embarrassed), which can raise *procedural* difficulties with multitasking, i.e., thinking more analytically about the decision *at the time* the decision has to be made, in order to avoid the consequence. I actually believe my son: If he'd *known* the cop was going to be there (and he *thought about that at the time of the decision*), he would not have been speeding. But this makes many of the problems we associate with adolescence learning problems, not *character* problems. For that matter, it also makes many *character* problems, issues of *learning*. In other words, parents often think their teens are acting badly on purpose, because they have something unformed or malformed in their moral development, when in fact it's just a matter of complex behavior that your teen has yet to learn.

If you're parenting in a two-parent household, one parent might tend to say (about the speeding incident), "At least he's okay; boys will be boys." The other parent might say, "Are you kidding me? He needs consequences and punishment and you're not taking this seriously enough, because if this keeps up he's going to be living in a van down by the river!" The first response is helpful in that it lowers the emotional temperature around the incident, which *allows* for learning to happen, but "boys will be boys" is not enough. It doesn't really teach your son much that is of practical use, other than, *Oh, okay, sweet, since I am a boy, I will do that again.* But punishment and angrily/fearfully implemented consequences without discussion, modeling, and "failure analysis" also do little to foster the learning process. Perhaps a combo theory would work?

Brain Development Is a Matter of Nature x Nurture

Brain development is a product of the interaction between genes and environment. Nature vs. Nurture is a false dichotomy that no longer characterizes the way scientists (or many other professions) look at the influence of culture or environment on behavior and biology. One aspect of a more updated way of understanding the interaction is in the science of *epigenetics*.

Human epigenetics involves studying the way inherited characteristics (our genes or "genotype") can produce a variety of different outcomes or traits in an individual (what the person looks like and functions like, on an observable level, or "phenotype").

Every cell of your body has in its nucleus molecular/chemical "instructions" for maintaining existence, growing, and developing. That molecule is DNA (deoxyriboNucleic acid), and it gets to you (and makes you you) because your biological parents provide *chromosomes*—thread-like structures that carry the DNA molecules. Most human cells contain 46 chromosomes (23 pairs); 22 pairs (autosomes) look the same in males and females, and the last pair—the sex chromosome—looks different. Females usually have two copies of the X chromosome, while males have one X and one Y. The chemical information in DNA, which has the shape of a double helix, is stored in a code made up of four base pairs (nucleobases): adenine (A), guanine (G), cytosine (C), and thymine (T). Don't worry, we're almost done. *All* that information about what your teenager (and you) look like and do from the chemical information of four nucleobases? Not quite…that's what we're getting to. Human DNA has about 3 *billion* bases, and most of them are the same from person to person. The order in which these bases appear and connect to one another determines what biological materials are *available* for building your son or daughter (DNA-wise). Another important thing to know is that DNA can replicate itself.

So what you can observe (or what a scientist with a good MRI machine, a few electron microscopes, and a huge budget can observe) about your daughter, for example—the structure of her cells, other biochemical and physiological properties, her behavior and what she does with her behavior (such as whether she likes to take risks or not)—are part of her *phenotype*. Her phenotype is always the result of her genetic inheritance (genotype) and her history—what happens with her (her environment).

So, your children might have almost the same genotype, since you conceived them both. If you have one boy and one girl, you already know your kids are likely to have a different sex chromosome. But the DNA they got is always going to be *modified* in some way in relation to their inner and outer environments. So, not all people with the same genotype look and act the same, and not all people who look and act the same have the same genotype.

One way you can see this at work is with human disease or mental illness. A study done in Sweden, for example, demonstrated that if a father did not have enough food during certain critical periods in his development right around puberty, his offspring were *less* likely to die of heart disease. If food was plentiful for that father's *father*, his sons were less likely to die of diabetes.[26] Similar changes are being studied with regard to mental health issues, such as autistic spectrum disorders,[27] schizophrenia, addiction, mood disorders such as depression and anxiety-related illness, and AD/HD and other processing and attentional issues.[28] Many different types of scientists working together are studying the relationship between genetic and environmental factors in development, and luckily for us, many of them are focusing on adolescent development.

One common misconception, though, is that a certain gene can *cause* a disease (like alcohol dependence or AD/HD). It just doesn't happen that way. But if there are problems with the nucleobases or problems translating information or problems with "DNA methylization at key regulatory regions...resulting in histone modification" (just trust me on this), scientists are beginning to understand how those *cellular* changes can result in observable changes in mood, mood regulation, or attentional difficulties. Epigeneticists and psychologists together are studying how those cellular changes can be brought upon by environmental factors.

You might remember that the DNA your child has only gives an amazing *blueprint*. You can have a blueprint, but that doesn't mean the electrician shows up to wire the structure on time or even shows up at all. You can have problems with the materials, due to sunlight or water exposure or infestation. A group of workers may start the roof but fail to finish it, affecting other parts of the construction and delaying the completion of the job or changing major aspects of the build.

In humans, one single fertilized cell changes into the huge range of all the other types of cells in your body, such as nerve cells, skin cells, muscle cells, spinal fluid, blood vessels, and the list goes on. This happens because some genes get activated as the cells continue to divide and other genes get suppressed.[29] So things can "go wrong" during this process, in terms of which *genes* get activated or suppressed, and some of these things have to do with *epigenetic* influences. This is a growing and important field of science whose promises include a much better explanation for how choices like smoking, drinking, sexual activity, abuse, exercising, risk-taking, and all the other things that concern you as a parent—such as proneness to physical and mental disease—significantly affect your child and his or her future. You're born with *your* genome—the particular collection of genes that makes up your genetic inheritance. But your *connectome*—the particular way in which the entire collection of neural connections in your brain is wired—is arguably what makes you *you,* and different than everyone else, despite the fact that humans share so much, genetically speaking. The connectome is the result of experiences—your unique experiences. And the neurons get wired differently in four main ways: by the connections between neurons getting stronger or weaker (reweighting); by getting rid of or growing new synapses (reconnecting); by developing or withdrawing branches (rewiring); and by new neurons being grown and existing neurons being pruned (regeneration). Neuroscientists like Sebastian Seung believe these "four R's," representing the way that neurons end up connecting, change because of each person's individual experiences.[30]

One positive consequence of this way of thinking is that parents who are all too ready to feel omnipotently responsible for everything and get hamstrung by guilt can finally stop asking, "Is this all my fault?" and start asking, "What can I do to respond to this?" It can't really ever be *all* your fault, and whatever combination of genes *x* environmental factors are involved—histone suppression problems or parenting choices—there will always be things you can do to mitigate the effects. You might want to think of it as a "harm reduction" approach to parenting. More to the point: You *always* matter to your child. Which brings us to our next characteristic of adolescent brain development: *plasticity*.[31]

Plasticity Is at Its Zenith During Adolescence

This theory is related to the principle that biology and environment are always "in conversation" in the developing human. Changeability is an absolute hallmark of the adolescent brain and a central piece of adolescent brain research. There are plenty of arguments (of course) about the significance of this plasticity. Three of the major researchers in this area—Michael Merzenich, Edward Taub, and William Greenough—have written about and demonstrated three types of plasticity. These types of plasticity (or ability to reorganize in response to a change in the internal or external environment) are thought of as "experience-independent," "experience-expectant," and "experience-dependent."[32]

According to Donald O. Hebb, who we'll meet again in a minute, connections between neurons get strengthened (or weakened) depending on whether similar things are going on with nearby neurons. Certain kinds of synapses (now called "Hebbian" synapses) are stronger when the presynaptic and postsynaptic neurons are firing at the same time.[33] The brain "changes itself," so to speak, as it responds to differential or similar neural activation patterns.

The second type of plasticity is "experience-expectant." This suggests that the main way that the brain develops capacities throughout development is by producing the scaffolding of neural structures and then "waiting" for input from (primarily) inside or outside the body. This allows for the brain to produce and/or overproduce neurons and neural structures in a rough way and get rid of those structures (not reinforce them) on an as-needed basis. Cool. Sort of. You might imagine that this is the most frequently occurring type of plasticity and the easiest to "activate," because you're basically starting with a structure already in place that will either strengthen or diminish. If the "expected input" arrives, the structure develops along a normal path. If the cell(s) keep waiting for Godot, who never shows, there will be abnormal maturation or no maturation at all. This type of plasticity is extremely "hopeful" in the sense that it indicates that if certain kinds of accidental or deliberate deprivations occur during the course of human development, they may be able to be reversed.

The last type of plasticity—"experience-dependent plasticity"—is really what we call true *learning,* because it refers to something out in the environment influencing something in the brain. You might say that the other two types of plasticity are also learning, but "we" are not doing it. Ugh. We're going to avoid a philosophical debate here, but it's important to me to ask: *What* learns? If "my" cells learn to fire together, aren't *I* learning? If someone teaches "me" a song, *what* of me learns it? The physical changes that take place are probably related to Hebbian plasticity ("experience-expectant plasticity") anyway, so we're still dealing with cellular changes in either case. But with experience-dependent plasticity, I can more easily *feel and think,* "I'm learning." The involvement of affect, emotion, and cognition in the processes of neural plasticity are themselves part of the environment, too, and affect brain changes as well (to a point). But to *what* point, we don't know, and this is an important area for study, especially with adolescents. By the way, I actually think that there is immense power in the idea of not taking credit for the learning, necessarily, and thinking of it as, "The body learns." I think it's more accurate, and more useful, and opens more possibilities, but that's just me. It's my prejudice that it helps us be better *health scientists.*

So, scientists have learned that the brain can and does basically rewire itself when injured, or when undergoing repeated experience, especially before neural pathways are more established and are still being formed in relation to experience. They know this from animal studies, studies of human injury involving pathologies of our psychology and our neurology, which are, we should repeat again, inexorably linked, as there are always psychological and physiological correlates of experience. Plasticity is the rule, not the exception; it doesn't only happen when we're healing and the brain is forced to find new ways of doing things. It is part of the developmental capacity of the human to adapt to its environment, throughout the lifespan, although during adolescence—when there are a proliferation of neurons and neural networks waiting to be used and activated (or not used and deactivated)—it is especially critical time. This is a time where it really pays to think about what is going on in the environment and how it affects the *course* of development. Of course, infancy and toddlerhood are other critical times to consider environmental influences vis-à-vis plasticity, but adolescence is when the production of neurons and neuronal material reaches its peak. Plasticity is a concept that represents an astounding way of thinking about not only *that* nurture happens, but *how* "nurture" happens and that it cannot be separated from our genetic inheritance.[34]

I think it is worth remembering, especially in relation to teenagers, that when we think about repeated "experience" reinforcing or rewiring certain functions, that experience is not just experience *outside* the body. We are talking about the experiences of thinking and feeling, too. Any experience, really, has the possibility to transform and shape the brain. We all know now that our brains change in response to practice and new experience. That's learning (of a kind). But in a fascinating series of experiments conducted by Alvaro Pascual-Leone[35] and his colleagues at Harvard, he showed that if you took a group of people who had never played the piano, and divided them into two groups charged with the task of learning a simple melody—one group that would practice playing the piano by actually *striking* the keys and a second group that would only sit at the keyboard and *imagine* striking the keys—both groups showed *identical changes in their brains, regardless of whether they touched the keys.* Thinking repeatedly about taking an action is an experience that changes our brains. Nature *versus* nurture? Nope. Thought *versus* experience? Nope.

I think parents have seen evidence of this process for a long, long time. When Chess and Thomas described the "slow-to-warm-up" temperament in children and talked about a kind of approach to new experience that included a lot of "mental rehearsing," they were describing a similar linkage between thought and experience.[36] It is a good bet that if your slightly shy 5-year-old—who upon first going to a community pool clings tightly to your leg and only after some time reluctantly circles the pool a while before dipping a toe in the shallow end—is likely mentally *rehearsing* the task of jumping in. She might do this for the first three trips to the pool and on the fourth visit, jump right in, much to your surprise.

The scary thing, though, is that our brains are really quite blind to this process of adaptation. Your brain doesn't "happily" grow dendrites as the neural strands thicken and connections grow more powerful and efficient. It just happens. Your neurons don't really "care" if the result of repetitive experience and neurological plasticity is that "you" get good at baseball, Tweeting, checking e-mail, playing piano, using weed, or looking at Internet porn. Experiences of "reward" do not *equally* reinforce the repetition of behavior within an individual—for example, something that gets you to exercise today might not get you to do it tomorrow. And one type of experience is not equally reinforcing or pleasurable among individuals. For some (like me), learning algebra was not immediately pleasurable. I have to confess it barely provided more than two minutes of pleasure in my lifetime. This becomes extremely important when we talk about drugs, alcohol, parties, risk-taking, and sex, and learning and ethics. Okay, it's important for everything.

There is an idea that we'll discuss in Chapter 5 regarding the effects of drugs and alcohol that I want to preview here. In short, the effects of any drug (chemical) are always mediated by three main things: the *drug itself,* the *person using the drug,* and the *setting in which the drug is used.* No two experiences are the same for any two people, because these three factors always change, within and between individuals. In order to help your children understand and for you to understand the consequences of drug and alcohol use, it helps tremendously to know as much as possible about these three things.

Well, neurochemicals are *chemicals,* no? What any neurochemical or combination of neurochemicals *do* is always going to be influenced by the neurochemical itself ("drug"), the *set* (in this case, think of the genetic inheritance/DNA of the person and the current psychophysical condition of the person), and the *setting* (what is going on prior to, during, and after the introduction of these neurochemicals into the system). What this means for our purposes is that as parents we can't just look at our child and think that their experience will be the same as ours, or their siblings, or their friends, just because it contains "similar" elements. This is a simple but powerful thing to understand.

It means that knowing that your neighbor's child is playing World of Warcraft "all the time," and is getting all A's in school and is on track for Harvard, isn't enough information to know whether *your* son is going to have problems with it. It means that just because you didn't smoke weed and nobody in your family is addicted to any substance, doesn't mean your child won't be. It means that just because your daughter is fantastic at playing the violin, this doesn't mean that she will be good at remembering to feed the dog or playing the clarinet, for that matter. It means that what causes addiction for one may or may not cause addiction in another; that what strikes your son as exciting may not strike others as exciting. I think you get the idea.

What seems like a rather banal idea—that each person is different from another and we'd do well not to assume too much—is actually, in my opinion, a very powerful idea. Who we are is rooted both in our stars and in ourselves; if we really remembered this, every day and most minutes of the day, we would probably feel less confused, angry, and anxious in trying to understand what our particular child (or children) is up to. Think of the implications:

> We would probably jump less quickly to conclusions about whether something was either (or purely) good or bad for our kids, because we'd have to watch and study and wait to find out, based upon some trial and error. You'll notice I didn't say we'd "give up" deciding right from wrong or good from bad...just that we would move probably to "wait and see."

> We would probably compare our kids less with their siblings and our friend's kids, because we'd really *get* that other children's neurobiology, genetics, and experience will shape them differently than they'll shape your child, by necessity.

> We would probably be very curious as to what combination of factors were at play with this or that particular event or choice or mood or major change in our child's (or our own!) life.

Connectivity of Neuronal Structures Is Key to Development

Brain maturation isn't just about increased speed; it is equally about "turning on" and connecting previously unconnected parts of the brain. We've already met McGill University psychologist and pioneer in learning theory Donald O. Hebb, who developed and researched the idea that has come to be known as "Hebb's Law":

> When an axon of cell A is near enough to excite cell B and repeatedly or persistently takes part in firing it, some growth process or metabolic change takes place in one or both cells, such that A's efficiency, as one of the cells firing B, is increased.[37]

These days we just say, "Neurons that *fire* together *wire* together." You now know that this is a *type* of learning based upon experience-expectant plasticity. As groups of neuronal cells begin to work faster (due to myelination), they also work more *often* together, with nerve impulses firing more frequently, causing other nearby and distant groups of neuronal groups to also fire. The presence of this myelin "insulator" allows for a much more finely tuned and timed process of transmitting chemical information throughout the brain. We've seen how different parts of the brain have different primary functions. So just imagine that the process of myelination allows for more functions and capabilities of the brain to come *together* and to have this activity happening in a more *coordinated* and quicker fashion. Powerful stuff! But I've also suggested something about how delicate these processes are and that neuronal connections are just as easily diminished as enhanced.

Dr. Michael Merzenich—a pioneer in the field—showed how certain structures in the brains of primates shrunk or enlarged in response to increases in activity of certain body parts. This was a strong illustration of the "use it or lose it" idea. It's not so much that you will "lose" a part of brain, just that the brain is a highly efficient organ. If parts aren't being used, they'll often be taken over nearby structures to increase *other* functional capacities.

Dr. Edward Taub's work demonstrated that even small changes in the mapping features of the subcortical regions of the brain—like those in and near the brain stem—can cause larger changes in other areas of the brain, as it reorganizes itself in relation to these subcortical changes.[38]

Finally, Dr. William Greenough's work showed that the brains of rats changed in direct response to their early environments, such as in relation to how much they were free to wander and explore new situations, have new social contacts, and in general, in relation to the novelty in their environments beyond just having their basic food and water needs met.[39] Yes, I know, rats are not humans. And even though they have a lot in common with us, we always have to be careful about the translatability of animal studies to human development.

One thing we can say for certain at this point: The theory of plasticity in adolescent brain development is as close as you can get to a guarantee that no two teens (or people in general) can or will be identical, regardless of genes, and that development is an *approximation* on multiple levels, not a straight line. Plasticity doesn't mean that *everything* in the brain can change, based upon experience. It means that *some* things can change, and can change dramatically.

Brain Development Is Linked to the Centrality and Rapidity of White Matter (WM) Changes

White matter refers to the color of *myelin,* the adipose "sheathing" that wraps around parts of the nerve cell (axons), allowing for much faster (100 times faster) conductivity of electrical impulses within single neurons and among neurons and neuronal groups throughout the brain. Since chemical messages travel down the axon faster, it allows the neuron a kind of "quicker reset" time, meaning that the neuron can transmit its chemical messages much more quickly—up to 30 times faster. The brain therefore has a 3,000-fold increase in processing "power" as a result of the process of myelination. So, myelination is very important and that's why you've probably been hearing about it in the media in the last five to ten years or so.[40]

The largest structure of white matter is the *corpus callosum* (CC), a wide, flat collection of neurons underneath the cortex. This "structure" connects the hemispheres of the brain and functions like a kind of intra-hemisphere communications bridge. Many gender-related differences in the *corpus callosum* have been discovered with the advent of MRI technology, including handedness[41]; and abnormalities in the structure of the CC have been implicated as a possible cause of autistic spectrum disorders. Interestingly enough, Laurence Kim Peek, the man who provided the inspiration for the film *Rain Man,* was born without a *corpus callosum.*[42]

The size of the *corpus callosum* increases from the age of 4 to about 20, and dramatically increases during adolescence. While the two hemispheres have already been in communication for a long time, *increasing* myelination in other parts of the brain allows areas to "connect" and come online to the entire system, so to speak. More myelin means more information, more quickly processed, about more things going on in the internal and external environments. Increased myelination also contributes to the inhibition of axon growth and an increase in synapses (the junction between the neurons) throughout the brain.[43] And according to some, like Dr. LeDoux or Dr. Seung, and those with the most powerful neuroimaging equipment, it's all about the synapses and the particular ways the neurons connect (the *connectome*).

The growth of white matter in the brain is intimately tied to all sorts of dynamic brain activity, allowing for improvement in language, reading, memory, and response inhibition—all gains you might expect from the "learning" of the body at the neuronal level in response to environmental influences. This knowledge about the relationship between WM growth and "increased capacity" of adolescent brains—stimulating so much improvement in cognitive functioning—has called for better explanations for why teens get into so much trouble and take the risks that they do.

Gray Matter (GM) Development Peaks During Adolescence and Then Gradually Decreases

Unlike WM changes, which increase throughout adolescence, GM volume peaks and then decreases over adolescence, possibly in relation to the "pruning" of cellular structures that are overproduced leading to adolescence (i.e., "Use it or lose it"). As GM (cell bodies, dendrites, axons, blood vessels, etc.) decreases, so do synapses, in a process that scientists think reflects the increasing specialization, organization, and coordination of functions throughout the brain, and especially between the subcortical areas of the brain and the frontal cortices. Jay Giedd's groundbreaking work—upon which much of the science in this chapter is based—also showed significant gender differences in maturation in areas like the amygdala and hippocampus.[44] It's still not clear yet what it means, though, that boys have significant increases in the size of the amygdala over girls and girls have significant increases in hippocampal volumes over boys. Likewise, it's not clear exactly *when* various parts of the brain are more or less sensitive to the effects of environmental influence.

There Are Definite Sex Differences in Maturation/Development

Brain size and speed of maturation varies widely between boys and girls and among boys and girls. For our purposes, it's important to note that most neuropsychiatric disorders have different developmental trajectories in boys and girls; this makes sense given how areas develop at different rates and undergo pruning at different rates. Girls start puberty earlier, start the process of neuronal proliferation earlier, and start and finish the pruning and myelination processes earlier than boys in many structures of the brain. These are likely connected to the commonplace wisdom that girls "mature" faster than boys, taking fewer and less dangerous risks. Most scientists theorize that these different developmental paths are related to the effects of the quantity and timing of sex steroids (hormones) on brain maturation during adolescence. As you've already read, the pruning and myelination processes are certainly related to the growing capacities of teenagers around cognitive/intellectual and emotional functioning, which effect planning, judgment, empathy, understanding, organizing, and learning of all kinds. We'll visit these gender differences and their impact throughout the book.

However, while there are statistically significant differences between rates of mental health disorders, height, weight, and overall brain structure between men and women, Giedd notes that nobody can yet reliably tell the difference between a male and female brain on an MRI brain scan.[45] Much of the *meaning* of the differences discovered are yet to be understood, and we're not yet at a point where reliable gender-based interventions can be planned for the kinds of problems that teens (and parents) face.

There Are Wide Individual Variations in Development (Within and Among Teens)

The size of one boy's brain can be double the size of a same-age male brain, and still be within the norm. There is a very wide range in how different teens' brains develop, and they can all be "normal."[46] Examples are easily multiplied across each area of internal and external development, from the rate at which neural pruning occurs in particular parts of the brain to the timing, rate, and quality of development around spatial relations, hearing, physical coordination, emotional "intelligence," and risk-taking. For example, you can have an overall trajectory moving toward "balance" between functions and processes linking the "limbic system" and dorsolateral prefrontal cortex, but this "trajectory toward balance" doesn't tell you much about how *your* son is going to respond to rewards, for example. Knowing that balance is the developmental *goal* doesn't tell you about *your* son's "reward sensitivity" or how strongly his brain will respond to the presence, frequency, or type of reward. It doesn't tell you about how *your* son is going to process and evaluate risk and make decisions. It tells you about the destination, not the journey. So this principle of wide variation is inherent within and across all areas of individual and group development.

Risk and Reward Are Assessed By Teens in Fundamentally Different Ways Than By Adults

This section is worth more page-time, for reasons that I think you already understand—this is one of the main things you're worried about, in parenting your teenager.

Changes in adolescents' brain dopamine systems now appear key to how reward-motivated behaviors develop. It would be easy to just move quickly over that sentence, so I'm slowing us down to call attention to it again. The importance of dopamine in the brain (as a neurotransmitter highly implicated in learning) and body (as a chemical that can help raise heart rate and blood pressure) accounts for its focus in the media. It also means that dopamine will be discussed as being responsible for *everything* that happens in the brain. This isn't the case, so let's look at what it does seem to do.

Most of the dopamine receptors in the brain are located in the midbrain, with many of the axons from this region projecting into the nucleus accumbens and prefrontal cortex. The presence of dopamine in the frontal lobes affects how chemical signals travel to other parts of the brain, and thus impacts what information gets where in the brain. Problems with dopamine production or distribution can cause a host of neurocognitive problems having to do with attention, memory, concentration, multi-tasking, and problem-solving. As you might imagine, it is implicated as playing a major role in Attention Deficit/Hyperactivity Disorder (AD/HD), but it is also implicated in problems like Parkinson's disease and schizophrenia. Too much or too little dopamine in certain areas of the brain affects sensitivity to reward and pleasure, motivation, mood, sleep/waking cycles, and voluntary motor activity (for example, in Parkinson's disease). Most rewards, from the small pleasures of desiring and getting certain kinds of food (appetite) and figuring out how something works, to the big pleasures associated with drug addiction, are intimately tied to the workings of this particular chemical.

Dopamine affects responses to new experience—with increased levels in the brain occurring *generally* during adolescence (more than in childhood or adulthood)—and *specifically* in response to rewards, and thus in connection to learning. Dopamine can be found intravenously—where it doesn't cross the blood-brain barrier—or in the brain, inside cell bodies and outside them, "traveling" throughout the brain system. How dopamine is transmitted throughout the brain can be affected in part by how much of the chemical is *taken up* from the synapses of the cells and/or how much of the chemical is *released* from dopamine-containing cells. It can be released into the brain *independent* of other neuronal activity or somewhat systematically (but irregularly) in bursts from the cell body itself. It's fairly simple, from the "end-user" point of view: If you have increased levels of dopamine in certain parts of the brain, you feel *good*. You know—the feelings of satisfaction, pleasure, focus, and "everything's going to be alright." You know—the feelings many of us live for. Having fun (low-effort, high-reward activities associated with pleasure, relaxation, and well-being), eating, and having sex significantly trigger dopamine release. If you think of it that way, you'll get how important dopamine is: It's related to at least two activities that produce feelings associated both with *individual survival* and *survival of the species.*

Interesting enough, if actions are repeated, but rewards for those actions delivered at unpredictable intervals, dopamine levels in the brain rise. Think of playing a slot machine. The longer you play the game, and the more unpredictable the reward delivery, the more money you'll put in the slot machine. If, when you do an activity, rewards are distributed evenly, at regular intervals, brain dopamine levels remain constant. If no rewards are received, dopamine levels in the brain can drop. And just as important to consider are the effects of low or decreased levels of dopamine—or activities that deplete dopamine in the brain, like the ingestion of certain drugs and alcohol—as low levels of dopamine are shown to reduce motivation, energy levels, feelings of pleasure, concentration, mood, sex drive, lactation, weight maintenance, heart rate regulation, regular gait, having a regular period, ability of the body to regulate sugar production, and many other key functions. Basically, low or diminished dopamine levels mean you'll feel bad and your body won't function properly.

For both reasons of desire and avoidance, dopamine is key. You get why we want to repeat any experience we have that significantly increases the brain dopamine level. Dopamine, serotonin, and norepinephrine are three extremely important and powerful chemicals in the body. Most of the medications humans take related to mood problems (depression, anxiety, etc.) and pain relief of all kinds work with these three chemicals. How the world, yourself, and others *feel* to you are related to these chemicals. *Now* we can talk about risk and reward.

I mentioned earlier that dopamine levels, overall, are higher during adolescence. One reason for this might be that since adolescence is all about identity formation and sexual development, dopamine plays a key role in stimulating teenagers into new behaviors; dopamine helps spur us out into the world of new experiences with others and ourselves. We do something, *it feels good,* and we want to do it again. This reward-based system is one powerful description of how we learn new behaviors and reinforce the desire for certain feeling states.

Let's think about risk-taking from the reward side. So, first, you have to forget about risk as something *dangerous* or aversive and assume for a moment that if we really had a choice, we would all want to experience something that feels *good* over something that feels *bad*. Think of your teenager. He isn't thinking, "I want to take this risk." But he might be thinking, "Ohhh, *that* might be cool." Then he's got to figure out whether to actually do that thing, whatever it is. He'll have to try something (relatively) new. That is a "risk." There are two main theories, then, for why adolescents take risks, if you think of a "risk" as simply the decision to consider and pursue a new behavior.

It could be that adolescent brains—and their pleasure/reward systems—are kind of immature and therefore, under-responsive to rewards. That makes sense, right? Their brains are not as developed as adults in terms of "milking" the good feelings from experiences and so they need practice at it. Most adolescents might need more intense and more frequent rewards in order to feel really good, whereas adults have learned to get pleasure more regularly and easily. It's not really about getting pleasure from "the *small* things in life," as much as it is about getting pleasure from *more* things in life, big and small. As we know, teen brains generally get good at what they practice. As they practice understanding what is pleasurable and what to avoid out in the big world, they get to a point of regulation and stability around rewards, risk-taking, and pleasure in general; in other words, they "grow up" and become "more adult."

But another theory proposes that teenagers are really sensitive, *oversensitive* to dopamine production and release in the system. This theory interprets risk-taking as an increased sensitivity during adolescence to seeking out those behaviors and feeling states that heavily favor the *good* feelings. It isn't until later in early adulthood that they come to understand better the (relative) pleasures of forestalling the immediately pleasurable for the longer-term goal—a primary executive function of the brain. Teenagers live in the *now,* and if it feels good now, it must *be* good. Whoops, that wasn't so good. *What* wasn't so good? Well, sneaking out of the house to see my boyfriend felt great. Sex felt great. Driving 103 mph on the freeway felt great. Getting caught by my boyfriend's mom didn't feel great. Getting grounded didn't feel great. Worrying about my missed period—not so good. $257 ticket—not *that* fun. Now your teen has some experience of pleasure and pain and an association between the two. But learning takes time. After all, I got caught once—*maybe that won't happen the next time.* If I do the same thing over and over and the reward is there regularly, but so is a consequence I'm not thrilled about, the reward loses its really *strong* thrill. It still might be great, but it's not *all that.*

Both of these theories of risk-taking make sense and there is evidence for both—so this is still an open question. But we have to remember that not only are adolescents as a whole different from adults and children in the way they respond to and assess risk and reward. They are different from one another, too. Your teenager maybe a "high nucleus accumbens" responder...*or not.* Your teenager may be more willing to take a risk to get the large (dopamine) reward—they may have more dopamine receptors in the brain to begin with. In other words, *whether your particular teenager is a high-risk-taker is dependent upon biology and environment in interaction.*

Cocaine, nicotine, and amphetamines all provide huge increases in dopamine release in the brain. But these drugs may also significantly alter the way dopamine normally functions in the brain. One of the hallmarks of addiction is that we persist in a behavior (using a drug or participating in some activity) because it once gave us enormous pleasure and we want to return to that same level of pleasure. It may be that certain social/biochemical experiences give us the great jolt once or a few times, but after that our brains are not capable of reproducing that same experience. We keep chasing the original high, but the source of that original high actually disrupted the ability of the body to respond again at that level. That's how it seems to work. Addiction is about reaching a level of tolerance to the more pleasurable effects of the experience and about not being able to stop desiring the experience, even though it is no longer returning rewards and even though the negative consequences far outweigh the dopamine jolt.

The Adolescent Brain Is Uniquely Vulnerable to Pathology

Teens are incredibly resilient, physically, but also incredibly vulnerable during synaptic proliferation and pruning. Here's one particularly spectacular example.

Since the Golden Gate Bridge was completed in 1937, almost 1,500 people have jumped off the main deck, which is situated 220 feet above very cold water and very strong currents. Over 98 percent of those who jump will die, either from the impact from the fall itself—which at 75 mph is going to kill most people—or from drowning, immediately after the fall. Most people who do survive have serious long-term injuries; only 4 percent ever walk again. And then there is a *teenager* from a Sonoma County high school. On a clear day in early March 2011—supposedly on a dare, during a school field trip—he climbed over the railing on the bridge's east sideway and jumped. *Then he swam to shore.* He reported feeling a little sore and had some bruises.[47]

While adolescence is arguably the most resilient and healthiest period during the lifespan, the overall rates of disease and death increase between 200–300 percent during this period. Death and disease during adolescence are often related to problems with control of behavior and emotion, as indicated by increased rates of accidents, suicide, homicide, depression, substance abuse, eating disorders, reckless behaviors, violence, and risky sexual behaviors.

I use this example because it so well touches on both ends of the spectrum of adolescence. The police investigating the incident said—and the teen confirmed—that this was not a suicide attempt. I believe that is true. But it was a suicidal *gesture*. A suicidal gesture is any self-directed action that a person denies was an attempt to commit suicide, but that could easily result in injury or death. A suicidal gesture cannot easily be explained as normal adolescent risk-taking behavior—like unprotected sex or riding a dirt bike without a helmet. Many adolescents explain suicidal gestures as behavior they attempted "just to see what would happen," but their reasoning is often highly irrational. Just about any reasonable human would think that jumping off the Golden Gate Bridge would kill them. So, if you're attempting to do something you pretty much know will kill you—and you just do it, on a dare, thinking it's no big deal—you're either under the influence of a drug or you're dealing with a mental health issue like depression.

The example illustrates, on a *macro* level, the confluence of adolescent vulnerability and resilience. On a micro level, we've talked about how frequently, pervasively, and rapidly the brain is changing, with new "systems" coming online, many dependent on experiences in the world *in connection with* the healthy unfolding of more genetically determined brain changes.

The delicacy of these changes make the adolescent much more vulnerable to a variety of psychiatric problems, which are in turn related to the kinds of behaviors that end up hurting and killing our teenagers.[48]

The most common type of psychiatric vulnerability that shows up with adolescents and in adolescence has to do with *anxiety* and related disorders. One of primary reasons that we experience anxiety has to do with problems learning which cues in the environment signal safety and which signal danger (and unlearning which cues signal threat, when the threat doesn't exist anymore). We'll discuss this idea in Chapter 8 on Family, in terms of how children can easily learn to associate threats with certain conditions but are very slow to unlearn them. It's also relatively "easier" and more efficient from a brain perspective to experience a threat once and assume it *will* be there again, rather than assume it *won't be*. Although the science is in its infancy, there is some evidence from animal studies to suggest that abnormalities with some particular genes may play a role in increasing risk for anxiety and depression. This may result in "faulty" and hypersensitive detection of danger/threat in the environment—the condition of anxiety.

As we'll discuss often in this book, much risk-taking behavior can be thought of as a problem of *imbalance* between those areas of the brain most associated with emotion and threat assessment *and* those structures in the prefrontal region of the brain, most associated with fine-tuned analytic thinking. Although pruning and myelination are going on in both areas of the brain, we've already seen how myelination of the frontal cortical structures happens last, in general. Projections of neurons need to extend from the central brain structures into the frontal areas and "connections" need to be made between areas for the increased capacities we associate with adult decision-making to occur.

Most of the researchers referred to in this book agree with some version of this "imbalance model," which points to relative differences in maturity between the cortical and subcortical regions of the brain and the control functions in the prefrontal cortex as providing the main reasons why adolescents tend to take bad risks. But some recent research suggests that it is the adolescent brain's *hyper*sensitivity to rewards and signals for avoidance that make it particularly vulnerable to increased risk-taking and psychiatric problems such as anxiety.[49] The tendency to overestimate anger or to respond quickly and intensely (before calming down) to situations that are not all that threatening may have to do with less "functional connectivity" between the prefrontal cortex and the amygdala, specifically. As mentioned earlier, difficulty with extinction—that is, with unlearning a previously learned behavior—can be associated with immature connectivity between these two areas of the brain. Your experience with your teen might be that you've told him several times that he doesn't have to worry about your withdrawal or your sour face—you're just tired from a particular work stress and it's not about him. Yet he continues to react to you as if you're ready to be irritated with him, long after your work stress disappears. People who tend to have more anxiety, in general, find it harder to unlearn anxiety cues, even after repeated exposures to safe situations.

It's difficult to actually "see" the immature amygdala-ventral prefrontal cortex (vPFC) network of neural connections in humans, but studies of many other animals demonstrate that this immaturity in the "network" is characteristics of most species during adolescence. Teens who go through trauma—especially teens with heightened perception of danger signals in the environment (those with higher anxiety)—are more vulnerable to developing psychiatric disorders during this period of their life. Several studies of mood and anxiety disorders in adults show that imbalances in the amygdala-vPFC network are present[50], with those adult brains showing significantly greater activity in the amygdala relative to the prefrontal cortex.

Of course, it makes sense to consider, too, that as teens go through stressful experiences in which their more reasoned judgment does or cannot come into play, they experience more negative social consequences of this more-emotional way of responding to the world. If this relative imbalance between amygdala-vPFC processing does not improve, you can imagine that more and more people will have trouble communicating with and positively responding to these teens. The social-relational problems that go along with "not being able to handle things," or "being too emo or aggro" (too emotional or too aggressive) in turn add to the difficulties of adolescence, further complicating the picture. The point here is that because a teen's success (or lack thereof) in the social world and his self-evaluation are related to how well his brain is developing—and how well his brain is developing is related to his ability to understand and regulate his emotions—the teen is extra vulnerable to deficits, delays, and other problems with normal brain development during adolescence.

How Do All These Brain Changes Impact Adolescent Behaviors?

The "impact" is what the rest of the book is about. While a headline that reads "Gray Matter Pruning Issue Causes Male Teen, 16, to Send Naked Pictures of Girlfriend Over Internet" might get you to click on a link or buy a magazine, what the headline suggests doesn't really work that way in real life. Knowing that neural pruning happens generally *later* in boys than girls and that boys have significantly higher amygdala volume doesn't mean boys do dumb things longer, act on emotion more, or think about their decisions less, across the board, than girls. And if you know this, and tell a friend (or a few friends), you're already approximating a better intervention strategy with your picture-sending child, and you're not working from outmoded stereotypes about adolescent motivation.

Therefore, part of the purpose of this chapter is to allow you to think about some of the key internal characteristics of your changing adolescent, in order to approximate strategies for *intervention*. That sounds so formal. It's simply about figuring out when to step in and when to let your teen work things out, with a host of issues. You probably want to observe and gather data—a lot of data—on what kinds of risks your teen takes, how often, and under what conditions. This level of attention might be difficult for you given the circumstances of your life. Or it might be something that feels natural for you to do.

Funny, but many of us did this when our children were very young: We wrote down milestones like first tooth, first crawl, first walk, first words, or cute little utterances along the way. We took photographs of our children and organized them unconsciously by developmental phases and new capabilities. Many parents stop or significantly slow down this collecting and data gathering behavior as their teenagers refuse the prying eyes of their parents (and the camera) and generally start to clam up about and hide their milestones *and* difficulties. But every child is different. Sometimes openness to family experience and sharing is easier *within* genders, and sons can find it easier and more desirable to get closer to their fathers during adolescence—especially before leaving home—and daughters get closer to their mothers. Divorce, separation, and conflict in the family during early and middle adolescence can quickly and significantly impact these alliances, depending upon your circumstances (and your child's temperament, cultural factors, biological vulnerabilities... you know, "environment"). And then your child might be highly social, very engaged with others (and you) and still talk often and openly to you about her trials and tribulations. Is it a wonder that children who do this tend to fare better in school, at home, and in their mental health? Sometimes that's great parenting and sometimes it's the luck of the environmental draw, but usually if it's all going well, it's both...just like when it's all going badly, it's both.

In 2001, A. Rae Simpson, Ph.D. released a beautiful, thoughtful compilation study, "Raising Teens: A Synthesis of Research and a Foundation for Action." The study was part of the Project on the Parenting of Adolescents carried out by the Harvard School of Public Health.[51] Many of the same central, outstanding researchers, clinicians, and educators cited throughout this book participated in the Harvard review study. In the end, the study identified "The Ten Tasks of Adolescence":

1. Adjust to sexually maturing bodies and feelings

2. Develop and apply abstract thinking skills

3. Develop and apply a more complex level of perspective-taking

4. Develop and apply new coping skills such as decision-making, problem-solving, and conflict resolution

5. Identify meaningful moral standards, values, and belief systems

6. Understand and express more complex emotional experiences

7. Form friendships that are mutually close and supportive

8. Establish key aspects of identity

9. Meet the demands of increasingly mature roles and responsibilities

10. Renegotiate relationships with adults in parenting roles

I just mentioned that you might need to know the internal "characteristics" of your changing adolescent, in order to approximate strategies for intervention. The tasks above are the areas of intervention—or at least areas of decision-making about intervention.

In conclusion, Dr. Simpson wisely notes that the list above is not constituted in this particular order for any particular reason, nor are the descriptions of particular items *new* in the history of studying how adolescents develop. Teens are working on all of these tasks, all the time, and as you know, some start earlier than others, and each task is going to progress at differing rates, person by person. As almost every study of adolescent development confirms, most teens get through this list of tasks, having developed relatively unscathed. The Harvard parenting project notes that "a number of factors can put teens at risk, including:

> [...] special needs and learning disabilities; early deprivation that precluded developmental foundations; devaluation and discrimination regarding such issues as ethnicity, class, immigrant status, or sexual orientation; lack of adult support; physical or emotional trauma; mental and physical illness; family dysfunction; poverty; neighborhood and community dysfunction and violence; and shortages of opportunities for developing competencies."[52]

You'll note no emphasis on gene-environmental factors and no mention of the special challenges brought to the fore by the explosion of digital media and the Internet, specifically, in the lives of our children. The Harvard study has a total of *six* references to the "Internet" or "brain development" in the entire 98-page report. That's because it was written in 1999/2000 and published in 2001. And that's why the rest of this book takes up, in various forms, each of those 10 tasks, always in the light of what I consider to be the profound changes introduced by the Internet and the ubiquity of digital media use among American teens. The context is also set by the preliminary but nonetheless useful information coming out about adolescent brain development—thanks, as well, to digital technology and increases over the last 15 years in computing speed and power (just like the adolescent brain)! So while the *tasks* of adolescence have not changed much, the *context* sure has.

Practical Help Tips

1) Who your teenager is and who he or she will become is always a matter of nature and nurture, in interaction with each other, unfolding over time. What happens with your children *cannot* be completely your fault, nor can your influence be discounted. Let's start getting practical about this and stop arguing about whether parents matter in the lives of their teens or whether parents are the reason those teens get so messed up.

2) Find a way to keep up with one or two good sources of research on adolescent development. It's not as difficult or overwhelming as it might seem, and it puts you in a better position to make theories about how to intervene with your teenager. The Pew Charitable Trusts and the Kaiser Family Foundation are two high-quality sources for information about development. If you subscribe to their information feeds, you get summaries of research every couple of weeks—this makes it much easier and less time-consuming.

3) A corollary to item 1: Research is often wrong, inaccurate, or eventually outdated. This doesn't mean you shouldn't read or trust research. Research gives you new ways to think about old problems. Read, try some things out, and collect your own data, but be prepared to let your theories (or the theories in the research) go when they don't serve you anymore. You'll know when something isn't working—you'll hurt in some way. It doesn't mean you were duped—it means you're adapting and being an "Approximate Parent."

4) Parents have the job of teaching their teens to be good health scientists. You do this by being interested in and curious about what theories we are making about our health, what the biases and problems are with those theories, and whether they're "working"—and curious what to do when they're not. Being a health scientist implies *approximate parenting* because it is always about observation, data gathering and collection, correction, and refinement...and starting again. It incorporates psychologist Kurt Lewin's wise saying that "There is nothing so practical as a good theory." By definition, a *good* theory is never a *final* theory.

5) Media literacy (for you and your children) is *a*, if not *the* key ingredient in becoming a good *health scientist*.

6) Teens are able not only to process information analytically and logically but also to respond and "think" with their feelings and emotions. Their capacities for emotional reasoning and more analytical ways of thinking about problems are developing at the same time, but at different rates. If your teen tends to feel things deeply and can get "lost" in that, help them with analyzing. If your teen is more intellectual and analytic, help support their ability to know what they feel.

7) *Maturation and development are not the same.* Maturation is about the building materials your child has for the project—and the organizational principles behind how those building materials are formed. Development is about the back and forth between you and your child, between the influences of the environment with the building materials, and back again. When things are not going the way you'd like, try to remember to think about: What is maturation and what is development? How can I accept the materials my teen has to work with, and help with the construction and organization of those materials?

8) *No two teens (or any other two people) are the same, nor could they ever be.* This isn't some humanistic metaphor about "no two precious snowflakes being the same." If you find yourself comparing your child with a brother, sister, your child's friend, or yourself/your partner, find a way to stop that mental activity (safely). It just can't help you deal with what's going on with your child, at that moment.

9) *Puberty and adolescence are not the same.* Just because puberty hasn't begun doesn't mean you aren't parenting an adolescent. Adolescent-like behavior, feelings, thoughts, and attitudes can begin before puberty.

10) *It helps to know the principles of adolescent development in order to make theories about the practice of parenting adolescents.* If you know, for example, that all normal brain development follows from the simple to the complex—and that therefore skill acquisition for teens has to follow from the more simple to the more complex—this knowledge could very naturally change your expectations. Your teen won't "get it right" the first time, as a matter of course. Your teen will mess up and do *less* than you want in the beginning of learning anything new. Your teen will do something well once and then forget it; or they will do something well for a while and then do it less well, as they practice and figure out their own theories for what works and why. You can count on these things—it helps you *not* take this "asynchrony" (unevenness) of learning and development personally.

11) The whole brain participates in functioning—we don't just use 10 percent of our brains. But that doesn't mean this functioning is smooth, even, or balanced. Your teen needs the entire period of adolescent maturation (that is, until the mid-20s) to fully power up. Even then, changes will occur, new capacities will grow and others diminish. Their brains are highly *plastic* (changeable), but not everything is changeable and that plasticity has only recently been studied. So, while teen brains *tend* to get good at what they practice, there's no guarantee that if they practice something enough they'll be great at it, or that it's the *right* thing to be practicing.

12) It significantly helps to know not only what your teen is maturing toward but in what context they are doing it. Your daughter's goals for herself and your goals for her are dependent upon *context.* Try to learn about and understand digital media—the digital world is the "water" your teenagers are swimming in, so to speak. It forms a large part of the *context* for development.

Suggested Reading: *Do I Have a Teen in My House?*

The "Suggested Reading" lists are by no means comprehensive. I'm including what I consider to be the most informative, practical, relevant, or comprehensive readings on the topic(s) of the chapter. In other words, if you have limited time, these are the works I believe you might want to explore first. It doesn't mean all of these books are "easy reads." Sometimes a listed book will be very difficult, but worth the time.

Chess, S., & Thomas, A. *Know Your Child: An Authoritative Guide for Today's Parents.* New York: Basic Books, 1989.

Dreikurs, R., & Soltz, V. *Children: The Challenge. The Classic Work on Improving Parent-Child Relations—Intelligent, Humane & Eminently Practical.* New York: Plume, 1991.

Fonagy, P., Gergely, G., Jurist, E., & Target, M. *Affect Regulation, Mentalization, and the Development of Self.* New York: Other Press, 2005.

Hinshaw, S., & Kranz, R. *The Triple Bind: Saving Our Teenage Girls from Today's Pressures.* New York: Ballantine Books, 2009.

LeDoux, J. *Synaptic Self: How Our Brains Become Who We Are.* New York: Penguin, 2003.

Lieberman, A. F. *Emotional Life of the Toddler.* New York: Free Press, 1995.

Riera, M. *Uncommon Sense for Parents of Teenagers.* Berkeley: Celestial Arts, 1995.

Seung, S. *Connectome: How the Brain's Wiring Makes Us Who We Are.* New York: Houghton Mifflin Harcourt, 2012.

Spear, L. *The Behavioral Neuroscience of Adolescence.* New York: W. W. Norton & Company, 2009.

Stern, D. N. *The Interpersonal World of the Infant: A View from Psychoanalysis and Developmental Psychology.* New York: Basic Books, 2000.

2

The Big Problems

Spoiler alert: We're going to begin and end this chapter talking about *emotions*. Teens have problems. You have problems. You have problems with their problems. You want to help them with their problems and you want them to avoid the really big problems. Many of their behaviors that you feel are problems, though, are not "problems." They are *questions*. I'll explain that soon enough. But let's start this chapter with another prejudice of mine and an axiom of my thinking about parenting adolescents.

Whatever you choose to do, whatever strategy you adopt, no matter what book you get it from, and this applies to everything in this book, each of those strategies is no better than how you're feeling—in what emotional state you are—when you implement the strategy. And, with every intervention you make, you will be teaching your teenager something about your values. You just cannot escape this. So think of it this way: You might have the perfect strategy (that works in the lab and has been tested with rats, bunnies, monkeys, and humans and is FDA-approved), but if you implement it while you're exhausted, enraged, disengaged, or distracted by your own problems, that strategy *will not work as intended.*

Therefore, I take it as an axiom that *whatever emotional state you're in while you're parenting conveys more to your child than the content of what you're doing with them, no matter how perfect your intervention looks "on paper." In other words, to para-phrase Marshall McLuhan, "your emotional state is the message."* But the lousy (and hopeful) part here is not only that your emotional state is the "lede" of the story, in journalistic terms. It isn't just that if you're enraged, children will primarily feel the rage and respond to that, rather than the strategy. It isn't just that your strategy won't work. It is also my experience that *you will be teaching them something about your values, too.* If you scream at your child, "Don't yell at your sister!" you might get your child to be quiet for a while that afternoon, or it may "work" for a few weeks, months, or years as a means to get your child to pay attention and feel the sting of doing something wrong. But you might also be teaching them that it's okay to say one thing and do another. You may be modeling the value that "hypocrisy" is okay if it's a strategy implemented by someone more powerful than they are. Or you might be teaching them the value of acquiring power, so that then they, too, can implement that "yelling" strategy. These aren't the only values being taught in the example above, but what you cannot escape is that in these moments, your emotional state is a delivery vehicle—the medium is the message.

Yelling at your child is not always the wrong thing to do. In fact, it can be done with love and be exactly the right thing to do, but I would argue that *that* depends upon your emotional state at the time, and the state of your literal and figurative heart. Most kids *know in their bones* when you are out of control and haven't made anything close to a "choice" about your behavior. Most know when your choices, even if unpleasant, are actually something considered and rooted in your best self. And that will be true for every intervention you make, whether it's about sexual behavior, drugs and alcohol, homework—you name it, this will abide, in my opinion.

Yes, that is a bit (or extremely) depressing, right, because "exhausted, enraged, disengaged, or distracted by my own problems" practically defines what it can feel like to parent your teen. So, you might be thinking, "Thanks very much, Michael, you've just told me I can't possibly be a good parent, because I am not likely to be in a good state when I'm doing it." Nope, that isn't the case. We can use these things to our advantage as parents and you'll see that in play especially around dealing with drugs, alcohol, and parties (Chapter 5).

We're all in this both alone and together. There are certainly times when we're *really in* those difficult states. The less money we have or the more worry over money we have, the more those states might creep in or just sit down upon us. The worse our health is, the more we might be in one of those states. The more tragedy or trauma or violence or racism or lack of regard[1] we have to cope with in our lives and in the lives of people we love, the more our emotional states will imperfectly fit the ideal parenting state of "calm, firm, matter-of-fact, loving, but meaning business."

But that doesn't mean we shouldn't know what we're aiming for and what the effects of *not* being in those more ideal emotional states would be. I fail every day. I promise you that. The challenge, though, is to persevere, in the face of that imperfection, my own imperfection. Remember *fidelity*?

Changing Historical View of Adolescents and Their Problems

"Youth are inclined to contradict parents and tyrannize their teachers."
—*Socrates,* 449 B.C.E.

Evidently not much has changed since 449 B.C.E. One thing that is clear in the historical record is that Socrates seems to have contradicted many people and tyrannized his teachers. Was he biased in his assessment?

I don't think that's really the point. *How* culture understands the human adolescent—and whether Western culture even grants the fact of adolescence as a distinct period in human maturation—is what I'm most concerned about. In 1904, when G. Stanley Hall wrote that adolescence was a period of *sturm und drang* ("storm and stress"), he had plenty of historical company in his opinion, which, like Socrates', was formed based on keen, naturalistic observation, much as Piaget and Erikson and many of the so-called "modern" Western theorists of childhood development. We've come a long way since G. Stanley Hall's vision and exploration of adolescence[2], although we still use many of Dr. Hall's basic areas of inquiry.

Developmental psychologists like Richard M. Lerner and many others have advanced efforts at empirical, larger-scale longitudinal research on adolescents. Now studies and attendant programs like the National Longitudinal Study on Adolescent Health or the Youth Risk Behavior Survey are common, providing ongoing, in-depth information on a wide variety of developmental issues for adolescents.

Michael Apted's breathtaking *Up Series* films, beginning with *7-Up!,* captured for a wide audience, for the first time, a filmed record of British children's social development. Beginning in 1964, Apted followed the same group of children—to the degree that they participated—every seven years, into their fifth decade of life. This piece—while not an empirical research study—still gave a rather stunning look at *development,* in general. The organizing theory of that film was a dictum often attributed to St. Francis Xavier, "Give me the child until the age of 7, and I will show you the man." This Jesuit "challenge" was a way of weighing in more heavily on the side of *nurture* as the dominant shaping factor in human development. But the reason why I call this piece of work "stunning" is because it allows us to see the power of *both* nature and nurture: *7-Up!* and its sequels now stand as a visual testimony to the end of the nature/nurture debate.[3]

Both Raymond William's *Keywords* and Michel Foucault's provocative writings shed some light on the historically situated and contentious process of defining adolescence specifically, and on *definition* in general. Forces in a culture, according to Williams, always fight to define words, because of the political and social power that goes with being able to define what appears as "natural" or the Truth. But there are discernible patterns to this process of definition. In times of relative prosperity, adolescence is seen by Western culture as a relatively stable, short period of time, which is negotiated fairly easily by young humans who are capable of a great deal. The more prosperity in the culture, the more capable the adolescent and the less help he or she needs to successfully mature. In more difficult economic times, the period of adolescence is seen as longer, requiring more work, more strife, and more support. Adolescence extends into young adulthood more forcefully and it is rockier, with more rebellion.[4]

The *how* of understanding adolescence, though, is what has undergone the biggest historical change, thanks in large part to advances in digital technologies. By the mid-1990s, adolescence came to be understood as a series of unfolding, highly plastic neurobiological events, best understood by the rapidly burgeoning brain sciences and imagining technologies like MRIs, fMRIs, and PET and CAT scans. Much as "science" was under political attack as the final arbiter of Truth, it was asserting itself as the locus of the most accurate, up-to-date way of understanding what it means to be an adolescent human. It would be only a slight exaggeration to say that studying adolescent development became studying adolescent *brain* development. In 2012, the most cutting-edge studies of what adolescents think, feel, and do either involve some kind of brain research, or are somewhat "old-fashioned." This book, my speaking career, and my psychotherapy practice is filled with references to many of those studies. It is an incredibly exciting time to be interested in adolescent development. But it is also very confusing, overwhelming, and, in my view, somewhat troublesome.

Competing Narratives

The "modern" period in the "West"[5] can be defined in many ways, but one way to think of what is modern is to consider it as a historical period when Western culture exploded with *many* ways of thinking about and representing what is True, Right, and Good, and what is False, Wrong, and Bad. Prior to the so-called European Enlightenment, most questions of Truth were settled by religion—questions of "what is" and "how is it" were addressed by and in reference to God. Science, education, anthropology, sociology, and all the things we understand today as constituting the activities of the human sciences were the purview of religion and supported (or condemned) according to how well they represented the glory of God. To think that matters of God could be settled without reference to the Bible, Torah, or Qur'an was considered blasphemous. As this shifts to the point where humans feel and act as if Reason is as important as Revelation, we have the shift to the *modern*. What some writers in the 20th century began to call the *postmodern* is the shift from the dominance of Reason to the reason of dominance, or Plato's definition of rhetoric as "the stronger bullying the weaker." It looks like this: There is no one way of describing reality any longer. Every definition, every word, every phenomenon is up for debate. There is no Truth, only truths. All arguments are equally valid, and even the fact of "arguing" or "using reason" to convince someone is a "choice." Some people are "deciders" and they just use their gut feelings to know what to do. Some people are "intellectual elitists" who think and think and are just hamstrung by having to logically think through things and have logical coherence in their arguments. I'm not saying either one is *bad*; they are just choices and it's up to you to pick a way of thinking, feeling, and acting and not worry about how it fits with God or Science. Or worry about how it fits with God or Science. It's up to you, it's all relative and it's all a choice. That's the *postmodern* period.[6]

With the rise of new digital technologies in fields of science and publishing, for example, it is increasingly easier to advance *your* narrative of the Truth. Of course, it helps if you have access to some deep-pocketed capital investors, some powerful servers, and a good PR firm.

One thing this meant for parents is that by 1995 or so, it was getting harder and harder to figure out what to do with our sons and daughter. Many in the country went through some significant increases in personal wealth and prosperity in the 1980s (although many didn't).[7] But for those who did, many began to wonder in the 1990s whether they were giving too much, too fast to their children. Was it always such a good idea to be highly involved in your child's life? What happened to the "good old days" of the 1960s, when kids ran free, disappearing sometime in June when school ended and reappearing only sporadically for food, and then grudgingly again around August or September to go back to school? And what about those kids, anyway? Aren't we spoiling them with all our attention and time? Isn't the whole "teenager" thing an invented concept to begin with? Maybe there is no such thing as adolescence and it's about time we got rid of high school and homework and get kids prepared for the real world and stop coddling them. And how about *competition*? We should get kids prepared to compete at the highest levels academically and in the world of work, because we're falling behind. No child should be left behind. And that's why *competition* is wrong and bad. Everybody should cooperate and gain something just for trying. Our children's self-esteem is in the garbage bin and if we don't help kids feel better they'll keep using drugs and joining gangs and hurting themselves and others. No more first-place gold medals; everyone gets a gold medal! Let's give our kids a gold medal for taking emotional risks, because emotional intelligence is the most important thing. And empathy. And arguing. And conflict. Oh, yeah, and most of what you think you know about teens is wrong.

Each of those often-conflicting views is represented by multiple books on the subject, by equally situated experts, all with valid opinions. Just like this book. That is our historical situation, and it's hard to get around. It's one of the reasons why I didn't write this book earlier—because it was difficult to imagine that this book wouldn't just add to the cacophony. Each new book that comes out tells us, directly or indirectly, that we're doing it wrong. Each new book that comes out tells us what we need to know to be "good" parents of teens. In 2012, here's what we need to know about, in no particular order:

- Temperament

- Parenting Roles and Styles

- Adolescent Brain Development and Maturation

- Normative Adolescent Physical, Social, Neurobiological, and Psychological Development

- Conflict Management and Resolution

- Affect Regulation and Management

- Sleep Hygiene

- How to Access Effective, Affordable Healthcare

- Depression, Anxiety, and other Mood Disorders

- Drugs and Alcohol: Use, Effects, and Risks

- Eating Disorders and Healthy Eating

- Adolescent Sex, Sexuality, and Youth Sex Culture

- Self-Harm (Cutting and other Self-Injury)

- Learning Disabilities and Attentional Difficulties

- Peer Relations, Friendship, Bullying, Social Aggression, and Violence

- Trends in New Media (Multitasking; Social Networking Technology Development and Adoption; Risks and Hazards of New Media; Advertising Effects; Media Literacy)

- Youth Culture and Trends

- School Options, Choices, and Processes

- Teaching Ethics, Morals, and Values

- And much more...

It should be easy to understand, then, how the amount of information we are expecting to learn and incorporate, during a period of stress and insecurity (for parents and kids alike), in a culture of competing narratives about what constitutes "Truth," could make us tired and more conflict-prone. And I mean "us." I don't mean the 99 percent versus the 1 percent. I talk to plenty of parents with six- and seven-figure incomes that are struggling with the same things, even if they aren't struggling with having enough money.

This situation can and does also lead to guilt and avoidance/withdrawal—two really lousy things to be feeling or doing while you're trying to do the hard work of getting your adolescents into adulthood. I guess my response, though, is rather than go silent, I'm going to just try to state my biases as best I can and stick to responding to what parents say they want help with: *the big problems*.

What Do Parents Say Are "The Big Problems"?

In 1995 I started keeping a list of the kinds of problems about which parents were calling me and asking for help. I also started looking around online and finding "help" sites for parents raising teens. I began to closely follow one of our local treasures, the UC Berkeley Parents Network[8], to see what parents were writing to other parents about. After I began Practical Help for Parents, I started doing informal online polls, asking parents to tell me what they thought were the hardest parts of parenting teens. Pretty much, the Big Problems came down to these:

1. Disrespectful, Disorganized, or Antisocial Behaviors

2. Arguing and General Oppositionality

3. Separation/Autonomy: When, Whether, How They Communicate How Much They Hide (Privacy)

4. Risk-Taking Behavior

5. Difficulties Related to Mood

If the list above hits home, you'll want to get right into it. It's important to keep in mind, though, that the "Big 5" could be rearranged and presented in very different ways, and many of the examples of "problems" overlap with one another. For example, problems with mood could be discussed under "Arguing and General Oppositionality." This overlap is precisely the point: Many of the "problems" of adolescence are expressions of normal stages in adolescent maturity. If you know what's normal and expectable for an American teen in 2012, you will likely feel less stressed and take their behavior less personally. That's the goal.

Disrespectful, Disorganized, or Antisocial Behaviors

These are the behaviors that are difficult to understand and get parents pretty riled up: 1) Lying and Cheating; 2) Lack of Demonstrated Empathy; 3) Social Disengagement; and 4) Immaturity in Executive Functioning.

LYING AND CHEATING

Parents usually really dislike being lied to. It feels so insulting and disrespectful. When you discover a lie, it's like getting punched in the stomach. Those statements seem true enough. But here are some other true enough things: We teach our kids to lie, early and often, and kids are good at lying, particularly teenagers, because they do it almost all the time, about almost everything. One more thing—they pretty much *have* to do it.

Why? Well, for starters, teenagers really want two things…badly. The first thing they want is *privacy*. Privacy provides a "backstage" for trying out new behaviors, thoughts, and half-baked ideas, without immediate condemnation, disapproval, correction (or *approval*, for that matter). Remember: Maturity is doing what you want, even if your parents want you to do it. So, if you're immature—and teenagers are, by virtue of their level of development—then you often don't want to do what you want if your parents want you to do it. Or you may feel very ambivalent or confused about wanting the same things as your parents. But in most cases, teens need some place where they can try things out and be "themselves" as a way of developing their *own* identity. This identity will (and must) be different and unique, but still in relationship to *your* identity. If your teen lies to you, it serves to keep his or her behavioral choices, thoughts, and feelings away from your immediate consideration and response. So "lying" can function as a way of creating and preserving a space for your teen's *own* identity. Come on: Didn't you lie to *your* parents? And I'll bet you didn't do it because you were bad or evil. You probably did it at least sometimes to keep something of yourself "safe" until you were ready to expose it to your parent's scrutiny.

When I worked as a high school counselor, I conducted an annual survey on cheating and plagiarism. The results were fairly consistent: About 80 percent of our students cheated/plagiarized materials. That number stayed pretty even until 2007, when the percentage went up significantly. *Think our kids aren't watching what we're doing?*

This "cheating" behavior included things like copying homework from each other, taking materials off the Internet and passing them off as one's own, the old-fashioned but still-utilized "crib notes" on the hands, and high-tech cheating using phones, laptops, and other digital devices. I organized student-led panels on cheating and plagiarism and students spoke eloquently and openly about why they cheated. But the number one reason was not "I didn't know the material" or "I just *had* to get a good grade on that assignment." The number one reason they said they cheated was: "It saves me time." Everyone cheats, right?

The Josephsen Institute of Ethics regularly conducts research and performs national surveys looking at teens and lying, cheating, and plagiarism, as well as a host of other behaviors. The Institute is concerned with understanding the development of ethics in youth. Every two years the Institute conducts an extensive, detailed survey of American adolescents' views on honesty and integrity, especially in the schools. The 2006 survey noted that while 84 percent of high schoolers said that "half or more of the people that knew them would say they were one of the most ethical people they know," and 93 percent were "satisfied with their own ethics and character," over 70 percent of those same students admitted to having cheated one or more times in the past year. Those percentages did not change significantly in subsequent surveys. In 2002, Michael Josephson, president of the Josephson Institute, wrote:

> The evidence is that a willingness to cheat has become the norm and that parents, teachers, coaches and even religious educators have not been able to stem the tide. The scary thing is that so many kids are entering the workforce to become corporate executives, politicians, airplane mechanics, and nuclear inspectors with the dispositions and skills of cheaters and thieves.[9]

Scary, definitely. But because I tend toward being something of a smartarse, I have to ask: Given the near-collapse of the markets after 2007 and what we've found to be the causes of financial instability, isn't the willingness to cheat a sign of *readiness* for corporate America?[10]

In addition to the work of the Josephsen Institute, several other important researches have been or are being done on lying behavior. The Penn State study was one of the best recent studies on lying because it explored why teens lie, what they lie about and what supports them in telling the truth more often. That study in particular noted that 98 percent of teenagers lied to their parents regularly.[11] Here's a sample list of what teens lie about:

1. How they spend their allowance
2. Whether they have or don't have money/where they got it
3. What clothes they put on away from the house
4. What movie they went to, and with whom
5. Whether they're hanging out with people you approve of

6. Whether they're actually going to the place they say they're going

7. Whether they're going to stay at the place they say they're going to

8. How they spent the afternoon, if the parent is still at work (and sometimes even if they aren't at work)

9. Whether a chaperone or adults were at a party

10. Whether they rode in a car driven by an intoxicated or high individual

11. Whether their homework is done

12. Whether their homework is started

13. Whether they have homework

14. What music they're listening to

15. How much and what kinds of drugs and alcohol they've tried and use

16. Their relationship status

What do we mean by "lying"? There are many ways to lie, but in the main, you could represent a deliberate falsehood or you could just not tell the whole story. The latter is the method of choice for teens. They hold back the relevant details, and they do so not primarily to gain some advantage, like getting to go out when the parent would otherwise say "no" to the request. Okay, they do that, too. But according to the Penn State study, the main motivation for lying was very clear: Teens lie to protect the parent-child relationship and to avoid parental disappointment.

Darling and her colleagues' work at Penn has also demonstrated that teens tell their parents *less* when the parents are permissive and friendly with them, and they lie equally to parents who are strict and unbending in their rules. If that's true, then what kind of parent response or situation seems to call for more truth-telling? As it turns out, teens lie less when they can argue more with their parents, without getting shut down. Teens are three times more likely to lie than to attempt a protest of the rules, because most teens will tell the truth only if they have some hope that their parents will "give" on something. Teens will risk telling the truth and thus risk arguing if the argument results in a new freedom or the possibility of a new freedom. It might stress you out to argue with your teen, but they take it as a sign of respect and they also use the occasion (believe it or not) to learn about your values.[12] What the Penn State study showed is that teens feel good when they can argue over the *rules* and that they do not see this as fighting over your *authority*. So, as it might turn out, the family that argues well and has moderate conflict is consistently rated as having better parent/child adjustment (by both parent and child) than families who have no conflict or frequent conflict.[13]

The second most common motivation for lying is *to not disappoint you and ruin your relationship*. Huh? Yes, that's right. Teens hate disappointing their parents. There are important reasons for this, having to do with kin altruism, shame, guilt, and belonging.[14] But for now, let's just say: Your kids love you and they don't want you to not love them or to feel they've ruined the relationship they have with you.

And, yeah, I'm sorry to have to remind us of one very important fact: Teens *also* lie and cheat because they learn to lie and cheat very early, as children—*from us*.

NurtureShock profiles another key figure in the world of research on how and why children lie: Victoria Talwar at McGill University in Montreal. In the chapter "Why Kids Lie," author Po Bronson explains that Talwar's work on lying and cheating demonstrated that children begin to lie as early as 3 or 4, when they can tell the difference between a lie and the truth. Children also cheat, when given the chance to gain an advantage and when that advantage is considered pleasurable. Their lies and "cheats" are often cute or innocent, and parents tend to let them slide. But Talwar's work shows that kids don't stop lying when their inaccuracies are overlooked—*they do it more and get better at it*. Children disapprove of lying and people who lie—just as we teach them to do—but they still do it. And almost all teenagers, as you'll recall, think that lying and cheating is wrong, yet almost all of them do it. Sure, teens and children lie to cover "bad" behavior, but they also do so for a variety of other reasons, including to gain power when they feel disadvantaged, to vent frustration or get attention, and a host of other reasons that have to do with "smoothing out" or balancing difficulties in social relationships, including and especially with parents. But how do they develop these strategies to begin with? Talwar says they learn it by observing us do it, from a very early age. They hear you whisper to your partner "I'm not here," when you don't want to talk to your mom right now. They see us smile and laugh with the friend we just told another friend we were angry with. The list could fill many a book. "Little lies" that we excuse for reasons of social cohesion are, nonetheless, lies. They watch us do it, and by the time they are 4, they know what we're doing and they see it works for them, too. James Baldwin was right: Children aren't great at listening to us, but they're excellent at imitating us. It might be one little reason, too, that lying and cheating bothers us so much when our kids do it. It's one of many instances we're not exactly happy about them being like us.

LACK OF DEMONSTRATED EMPATHY

Teens usually feel things very deeply. It's not uncommon for your teen to have difficulty separating their own feelings and difficulties from those of close others—including you. Teenagers are like tuning forks for each other, *sympathetically* buzzing in concert when any one of them is "struck," especially struck *down*—it is a kind of "feeling with" the other person. But sympathy and empathy are very different, though related.

When I think of the difference between those two capacities, thoughts of two particular teens come to mind. The first is of a 17-year-old girl who, on the eve of graduating from high school, told me the story of how a friend of hers had gotten kicked out of high school three years before. This friend was evidently involved in drugs and alcohol use (and a few other things) early on. But what really got to her was how her friend's departure from school was done quietly and kept secret from everyone at the school; school officials refused to discuss the case and nobody really knew what happened. All that students knew was that something big had happened and this other student's "life was ruined." What struck me, though, was how she related the story to me, and then at the end said, "You know, they thought we'd just forget it. I never will forget it. That's not something you forget."

The second memory recalled a similar sentiment. I was working at a school that had recently suffered the tragic loss of one of its students. I was privileged to attend the memorial service at the school, which was held about 15 weeks after the student died. The memorial, primarily organized by the students, deeply supported by very caring, kind faculty and administration members, was beautiful, devastatingly sad, and poignant. Toward the end of the memorial, a student stood up and said about her friend, through unceasing tears, "I will never, ever in my life forget her. Not for a minute. I will think of her every minute of every day and I'll never forget."

Both of these teens are describing the enormous capacity for sympathetic connection with others, especially close peers. It's important to note, however, that part of the poignancy in both cases is in the fact that they will, of course, forget. In the second case, she will *have* to forget, in order to grieve in a healthy way and move on. I don't mean that she'll forget her friend completely. I mean that the normal course of living will take over, and hopefully she will have many thoughts and many feelings—beautiful and sad ones—that are not about her friend and the loss.

Both of those stories illustrate something about how *perspective* and a *more complete understanding of time*—two essential components of empathy—are developmental acquisitions, not givens. Teenagers for the most part focus more heavily on the now, as opposed to the past or the future. Adolescents more easily feel and think about the future as the extension of the *present* moment, into eternity. Do you remember feeling that way? If you do, you'll know more in your gut why your teen feels that *right now* is all that matters. If now hurts, what does tomorrow matter? I need and want to feel better now. If now feels great, what does tomorrow matter? I need and want this moment to last forever...who cares about tomorrow? Is tomorrow a source of hope, if now is lousy? Or is it a source of desperation, if now is lousy—since tomorrow will be the same as today?

Empathy—what Heinz Kohut called the "capacity to think and feel oneself into the inner life of another person"—requires more than being able to feel something like what another is feeling. It requires *perspective,* to know that those feelings are not yours and that the history, trajectory, and causes of another's thoughts and feelings are not and cannot be the same as yours. Carl Rogers described this best when he said that empathy in therapy was the ability "to sense the client's world as if it were your own, but without ever losing the 'as if' quality."[15] In order for adolescents to be good at empathic connection and not just sympathetic connection, they need to have many significantly developed capabilities that will be discussed in Chapter 9 on mental health. Above all, they need good capacities for *mentalization*, judgment, emotional regulation, and complex perspective-taking, all of which are related to maturation of the prefrontal cortex—the last area of the brain to develop.

What do we mean by "demonstrated" empathy? When your teenager insists on being driven, bought, cooked, or helped with something, interrupting what *you're* doing regardless of your state of consciousness or mental or physical health, it feels like your teen has no empathy. Parents often think (and sometimes say) things like, "Can't you see I'm busy?" "Do you think I have nothing to do except drive you back to school to get something you left there?" "Do you not remember I had surgery on my foot last week; think I might be a little tired?" Your teens feel your exasperation with their needs or demands. Even if they act entitled to you dropping what you're doing to serve them, they often feel guilty for putting you out. Sometimes they feel intensely guilty, often in relation to how much you show your frustration, anger, or upset about their "selfish" demands. *But they still want what they want.* They feel your upset because they buzz in sympathy with you, and have likely been doing so since they were babies. We're wired with the potential, as humans, to be exquisitely tuned to the same channel as our children, and they to us. Your children want, more than anything, for you to be happy. Yes, that's right. It's what they want most of all. I'll explain more later, but just trust me on this for a moment. So teens often feel *too much* sympathy for us, and it results in guilt and shame, which often interferes with the encoding of new information into the brain.

Here's the picture, then, for when a "lack of empathy" presents itself. Your teen comes to you and wants something, because that's what teens do. They want it now and they want your help to get it. That's how it's been for, say, 15 years.

You're busy or in pain or enjoying yourself and don't want to drop your needs and desires. You've done that for, say, 15 years, and you're tired. You feel torn between giving them what they want and meeting your own needs. You might feel angry at being put in this position. So you might snap, "Can't you see I'm busy? Could you not have asked me this three hours ago when I was out?" "SORRY," your daughter snaps back, "I can't remember everything!" And now you're both angry and irritated. You might feel she's selfish and doesn't care about your life and needs. You might even yell *that* at her. She feels you're selfish and don't care about her life and needs. She feels guilty. But she still wants it. You feel guilty or angry or disrespected or torn or all of those things.

Your daughter, in that moment, is not demonstrating much empathy, but there is plenty of sympathy happening. You are both upset, in no small part *because* the other is upset. She wants you happy. You want her happy. That isn't happening. You want her to understand your perspective, that it's a bad time to be interrupted and you're tired. She wants you to understand her perspective, that she's anxious about what she asked you for, it's connected to something she values and she wants your help in getting it. You might even *get* her perspective (and that's why you feel torn about what to do). But she isn't getting your perspective, and that hurts and makes you feel frustrated. If you "give in" and give her what she wants, she "wins" again— you're always putting her first, if she whines enough.

Your daughter needs a better-developed prefrontal cortex and higher capacity for mentalization. She's not demonstrating empathy. That's exactly what she needs to learn to do. *What are you going to do, to help her develop those things?* That's the real question at moments like this. She isn't trying to make you angry. She is asking you for instruction, about a set of behaviors and capacities that she doesn't quite have under her belt.

In fact, almost every behavior that parents find problematic is actually a *question*. The question is usually in this form:

> "Hi Mom, what's up? Here is an example of something I am not very good at yet. I have a vague inkling that I need help with this issue. I need your help, but since I'm all about figuring out my identity and not simply repeating yours, I can't really ask you this directly, but what I want to know is...*How do I get better at this thing I just demonstrated for you?*"

It might not feel like it at the moment, but you have a *choice* to make. So, go ahead and be pissed off at her. Yell at her, too. Tell her she's good-for-nothing and never thinks about you, or that she's spoiled. If you're divorced, tell her she's selfish, *just like her dad.* Just be sure that your behavior teaches the value you want to teach, because the emotional state you're in will not fail to teach her something about the question she is asking. If yelling "You only think of yourself!" is the answer you want to give to her question of "How do I do this better?" then go ahead and give that answer.

I know I'm being facetious and that most of you don't want to give that answer. But the problem is that we're tired and irritated and feeling disrespected and that's what comes out. So, have some compassion for yourself and realize you'll blow it. You can always try again, you can always learn something new and realize you did it in a way that didn't work. So go back and apologize and tell your daughter exactly that. Come to think of it, isn't that just what you want your daughter to learn about how empathy works?

SOCIAL DISENGAGEMENT

"Why is it so hard for my son or daughter to make friends?" If that question is followed by "It never used to be that way," then you're probably pretty worried. What about if your teen used to have a lot of friends and now only has one or two good friends? What if they don't have any friends and are not at all involved in school activities? Has your teen stopped talking to you and/or joining you at family or social functions?

If you're asking these questions and your teen doesn't talk much to you about what they do or don't think or care about, then you're likely experiencing their social disengagement as a big problem. I've purposely included questions, though, that could point in *at least* two directions. Each of the items listed above could be a sign of normal development or an indication of abnormal development. That's why the focus of this chapter is to help you figure the difference between the normal/expectable and the indicator of a problem that requires professional help.

Having Friends

The narrowing down of a friendship group is predictable and often normal. In middle school your child might have a group of 10–15 good friends, with an inner circle of 5–6 really good friends that shifts in relation to a host of interpersonal factors including gradual or sudden changes in interests, normal individual (or group) conflicts, geographical moves or changes in accessibility to individual members of the friend group. Gossip is rampant in middle school, and shifts in the "in group" can change rapidly, without a particular member even knowing *why* the shift happened, since it all happened quickly and "out of earshot." With so many children living their lives online and via text message, news travels significantly faster than in the days—your days—when the telephone was likely the dominant mode of teen communication outside of the school setting. Funny—it still is a dominant mode of communication, just not as a device to "talk" into. The normative processes of establishing and maintaining *status*—your standing among others or whether or not the "world" loves you—can be enormously painful. At least 40 percent of the clients who come into my therapy practice come in initially to deal with some kind of interpersonal pain or conflict but end up dealing with or uncovering deeply painful feelings of grief, sadness, fear, and humiliation related to an incident or series of incidents in *middle school* (6th–8th grade, or roughly from the ages of 10–14). It should come as no surprise that the starting point—the onset of the second decade of life—roughly corresponds to the onset of puberty and the beginning of adolescence.

Young teens can therefore experience upset around social engagement (and pull away for a while from particular friends or socializing in general) for expectable reasons. They can disengage because of moves to and from their familiar neighborhood and school, changing interests, challenges to physical health, embarrassment or worry over physical, cognitive, or cultural differences, or because of the changes related to the onset of puberty we discussed in the last chapter. This is an especially important arena of both social engagement *and* disengagement, since the hormonal changes of puberty—which foster increases in attraction to peers—can also lead to the physical or mental changes that put a child at risk for embarrassment, humiliation, and withdrawal.

It is normal for your teen to have to find balance between "putting oneself out there" and "hiding." This goes with puberty and intensifies as the changes—such as breast development, voice deepening, acne, hair growth, and physical coordination (or lack thereof)—multiply. Some of the psychological and cognitive changes of the early teenage years—more "foggy" thinking, difficulties with understanding and correctly perceiving facial expression and tone of voice, embarrassment about and fear of being evaluated—all contribute to a normal wish to be disengaged with others. It's not a silly thing to think that the presence of a sweet, loving pet can offer some salvation during this time. I've heard from so many teens (and adults, too) that their beloved pet helped assuage many a lousy day in middle school. "I don't care! At least Snowball loves me." A powerful sentiment, indeed.

But at times the disengagement, which starts off as a part of the normal pushes and pulls around friendship and intimacy, ends up moving more toward the problematic. Your 11-year-old might have had a few friends upon entering middle school but you now realize he no longer invites anyone to the house or wants to go to out. He plays video games during almost all of his free time. He's not interested in talking to your friends when they come over and not open to attempts to get him to visit with peers. He isn't exercising. Teachers might describe him as nice enough, but very quiet or a "loner" or "quirky." His teachers don't dislike him at all but feel they don't "get a good feeling for him." He seems "happy" enough, and says he's okay, but he's mostly playing a single-player game (as opposed to a multi-player game), and that's all he wants to do. His media use isn't varied—no music, television, radio, or film, just video games.

Yes, you should be concerned about this kind of disengagement from a world of others. I'm not saying he has a disorder. I'm saying he's showing some risk signs, because of the level or intensity of his lack of contact with others. It would be a different picture if he were upset about not having friends and expressing some desire, to someone, to change this situation. It might still mean a problem was present, but the prognosis would be better. Again, all these things don't mean there is a problem that needs to be *changed*. But it might mean that you need the eyes of a professional to determine whether there is a problem like a verbal or nonverbal learning disability, attentional difficulty, processing disorder, anxiety or mood disorder or other psychological disorder affecting communication and social skills (like Asperger's), or even a medical disorder that impacts the endocrine system. All of these conditions affect the desire and ability to be social. But even if one or more of these conditions are present, it doesn't mean your teen won't be okay and happy and successful. "Not being normal" and "not being successful at life" is not the same thing. I know of one particular boy who, at 11, fit the above description perfectly. He struggled in high school, too. He's now 26 and he's rich and married with a child, running a software company.

Worrying About What's Normal

"Normal" is usually thought of as referring to what happens most often or what is "natural." The second denotation of the word is where trouble often begins. Thinking of something as "unnatural" usually brings up mostly negative thoughts and feelings. What is *unnatural* is "non-human" and to be avoided and condemned, fixed, or removed.

So what do I do with my own experience that says that many of the best things in life are the things that happen the least often, or are unfamiliar, quirky, weird, unexpected, or abnormal? I want to be exceedingly clear about this, so I'm putting it in bold type: **When I say "not normal," or "abnormal," or "problematic," what I mean is:** *the signal to get more information and do more data-gathering.* That's it. I don't mean "bad" or "morally wrong" or "hopeless." And I'm not just being politically correct. This is how I think and feel about the concept of developmental *normality.*

It's important to consider your child's temperament, too. If your child is "slow to warm up" or on the shy side[16], then you might know your child has always preferred his own company or the company of one close, safe person.

The same behavior can mean different things. Children can hyper-focus on one thing and one thing only because they have a psychological disorder or because they have passion or both (or neither). Children can pull away from school and friends because they are being bullied and harassed in very subtle ways (at school or online).

Social aggression, bullying, and harassment reach their peak in middle school. It is one of the most powerful and formative experiences in adolescence and it can have lasting, pervasive, negative effects. But if a child can find the support of peers (and peers get involved when bullying or social exclusion or aggression are happening), then a bullying experience can become crucial in the development of a sense of personal efficacy and belief in the positive power of community.

Aren't I making this more difficult, then, by showing how a sign or symptom can be either an indication of a problem or a normal event, even a strength? I hope not, because it's often true of the phenomena of adolescent development. Your daughter is "hiding" in her room. She could be really stressed, depressed[17], and withdrawn, or she could be "processing" the events of her 7th grade day privately or online with others, about to emerge in a few hours and want some dinner, happy to share some of her day with you. You son has "no friends" right now, because all he wants to do is play the guitar. Your son, who seems happy, has a ton of friends—and they're all selling weed, getting high, and breaking into cars and homes.

We return to a major theme of this book. Many other books have been written about the problems of adolescence, including problems of social disengagement. I'm going to give you a list of some of these books at the end of the chapter. You *don't actually need to know* all the possible scenarios and factors for determining how to make a differential diagnosis between normal and not normal. I think that it's plenty good enough for the "Approximate Parent" to know how to tell when something *feels off* or *isn't working*. In terms of adolescent psychological development, you just need to be able to pay enough attention to your child to tell when something has changed (especially rapidly) or is having negative consequences for their mental health (see Chapter 9).

Here's how it works: Are you are arguing all the time with your child about his seeming disengagement? Has it gone on a long time, more than a few months? Is it just a matter of you having a different temperament than your child; is that what's getting you worried? If your child has always been this way (whatever "this way" is), it's often an issue related to biological and psychological temperament. If it's a new behavior and a rapid shift, that's a different story. If it's causing conflict and upset at home, at school and in social relationships, then something isn't working. That's a *signal* that it's time for a new theory and approximation. That means more data-gathering. No need to panic. It's just time for *help, and possibly a new theory*.

IMMATURITY IN EXECUTIVE FUNCTIONING

This is the easiest "problem" to talk about, because it's pretty much coexistent with adolescence. In other words, immaturity of executive functioning describes the *normal* state of things. Many of the other challenges caused by this lack of maturity are also normal problems of adolescence. That does not, of course, mean that these problems are easy to deal with, should be ignored, or do not require your approximations, interventions, and theory-making capacities—in other words, your executive functioning capacities. In fact, the demonstration of your executive functioning capacities plays an absolutely crucial role in the development of your teenager's capacities. We learn by observation and by having behaviors demonstrated and modeled for us.

As you've already learned in Chapter 2, teens do not have fully formed prefrontal cortices, and this means that the good stuff that you'd like them to demonstrate is still under construction, and often unevenly so. Two very smart folks in the fields of theoretical and applied cognitive neuroscience —Tim Shallice and Don Norman— have identified some situations where just responding the way we've always responded wouldn't really be sufficient, productive, or best:[18]

1. Situations involving planning or decision-making;

2. Situations involving failure analysis (problem-solving, error detection, and refinement);

3. Situations in which practice has not been possible or is limited or where new combinations of behaviors are required;

4. Situations that are threatening, high-risk, or difficult; and

5. Situations in which avoiding old habits or overcoming strong temptations are necessary for mastery of the new set of circumstances.

Your teenager might well ask, "Why I can't I just do what I've *already* learned to do? I'm 11 or 12 now and things have gone pretty well; what's the problem?"

First of all, many of us already tend to resist doing something *new* anyway (unless it's really fun). Despite the heavy emphasis on research in this book, both as a means of informing parents and as a description of the ways that humans figure out how to do what they do, there are biases in research and biases in the human perceptual processes. I've asked us to be good *health scientists* and to model that behavior for our children. But we have to remember that sometimes the most important thing we can do when we're trying to figure something out is to fail, and *not* ignore the failure. Americans are a positive-thinking lot. We tend to frown upon others and ourselves unless they exhibit a "can do" attitude. If we do "fail," we're supposed to shake it off, forget about it, and move on. I've come to understand, though, that this can be highly problematic.

We get some insight on the problems around bias and ignoring from Jonah Lehrer, who wrote:

> The reason we're so resistant to anomalous information—the real reason researchers automatically assume that every unexpected result is a stupid mistake—is rooted in the way the human brain works. Over the past few decades, psychologists have dismantled the myth of objectivity. The fact is, we carefully edit our reality, searching for evidence that confirms what we already believe. Although we pretend we're empiricists—our views dictated by nothing but the facts—we are actually blinkered, especially when it comes to information that contradicts our theories. The problem with science, then, isn't that most experiments fail—it's that most failures are ignored.[19]

We already tend to ignore failures and act in accordance with what we know. If you just look at the list of behaviors on the previous page that *require* novel approaches (and new theories) above, you'll see a list that describes, with frightening accuracy, the real challenges of your adolescent's life. These "tasks" or capacities describe the behaviors, thoughts, and feelings necessary not only for your teen to survive, but also for them to learn and master new skills, develop relationships, and feel satisfied and happy with themselves and what the world has to offer.

And that brings us to Baba Shiv's Chocolate Cake. No, that is not my Russian grandma's delectable after-meal treat. Baba Shiv is a Stanford Business School professor, trained in engineering, management, and marketing. He's a key figure in a growing field called "decision neuroscience" and "neuroeconomics." Lots of people (and I say people, since corporations are "people" according to the Supreme Court) want to know Baba Shiv and be his *good* friend. It's not just because he's such a nice man with a calming, uplifting presence. A Stanford student gives a hint as to why so many people, corporate and otherwise, want to know him:

> In the first session alone, after instructing everyone to call him "Baba," he took apart a model of the human brain and gave a whirlwind tour of its emotional circuitry, presented the intellectual history of emotions in decision making, and managed to tie it all in with, among other things, emotional branding in Coke and Pepsi TV ads, Best Buy's problem with product returns, and Google's $3.1 billion purchase of DoubleClick. Throughout, Shiv wove in research results that he calls "frinky"—not a dictionary word but one his son made up to mean counterintuitive and funky.[20]

In 1998, Dr. Shiv and his colleague Alexander Fedorikhin designed and carried out a really elegant experiment. Participants were first asked to complete a task—either the memorization of a one-digit number or a seven-digit number. The memorization of *seven* digits is significant in this experiment because it is a reference to Alan Baddeley and Graham Hitch's model of *working memory*.[21] Even though there are other refinements to the theory of how memory works, Baddeley and Hitch's theory, developed in the 1970s, is still highly influential. The theory suggests that our short-term memory works via two systems that store information—a "phonological loop" (PL) and "visuo-spatial sketch pad" (VSSP). The first system stores the sounds of language, refreshing them over and over again. Think of how you might remember a phone number for the first time: You usually say to yourself, "Okay, 4322882, 4322882, 4322822."[22] The second system, as the name implies, keeps visual and spatial information and functions to construct and change around pictures of information. These two systems—and they are much more complicated than I'm describing here—function rather automatically (all systems being normal). But they work in connection with and can be influenced and overridden by the executive functioning systems of the brain. As we just discussed, these systems help direct attention, suppress *automatic,* irrelevant, or non-critical responding, and coordinate other processes of the brain to establish a hierarchy of functioning, so that while many brain tasks are being done, the most important ones can dominate so that we can reach a goal. In other words, this is about multitasking and setting priorities. The memorization of seven digits (plus or minus two) is considered to be stretching our short-term cognitive capacity and relates to the idea of *cognitive load* or just how much information we can process cognitively at any one time, given the relationship between automatic processes and things we want to *choose* to do otherwise. I'd like to give a shout out to cognitive psychologist George A. Miller, who was instrumental in thinking up much of this stuff in the 1950s.[23]

Back to the chocolate cake. After participants were given a task to do, they were then interrupted and asked if they wanted a snack of either chocolate cake or fruit salad. Yum. Which participants *overwhelmingly* chose the chocolate cake? You probably knew intuitively that the ones who were asked to memorize the seven-digit number chose the *cake* much more often than they chose the fruit salad. The study was interpreted to mean that people, when carrying a higher cognitive load, are more stressed and likely to opt for the "bad" choice (the habitual, automatic, and impulse-driven choice) rather than listen to the rational mind that says, "Maybe I shouldn't really have 400-plus calories right now."[24] We have to be careful about the interpretations of this study, though. To characterize the desire for glucose under stress as "bad" misses the point. It isn't "bad." It's what the body wants, and there are some good reasons for it that aren't just about "when we're stressed, we don't think well." Our bodies need more exogenous (introduced from the outside) glucose in proportion to how large a load we're carrying (cognitive or otherwise). It's just that many of us have a hard time separating out a *real* emergency, requiring huge spikes in blood glucose (for flight or fight), and those events that just *feel* like emergencies. If we're trying to memorize a seven-digit number, we don't really require a huge slice of chocolate cake (although some of you might disagree). If you're about to fight a tiger, you might want (and need) a chocolate cake, heavily frosted—or at least an equivalent amount of calories. There are, though, *better* choices for calorie intake if we've got a cage match coming up with a tiger. We don't want to just get a huge rush of glucose; we might want a slower-burning source of energy, to fuel our fight over the long haul. But this knowledge has developed over time from a lot of trial and error. And it explains why high-level athletes don't have all their training meals at the donut place next to the stadium.

So the chocolate cake experiment shows us a lot about executive functioning, decision-making, and the "wisdom" of the body, and how sometimes that "wisdom" needs to be overridden. That's what the executive functions are for. But the more you stress a person, the harder it is to access those functions. And for teenagers, it's already hard to access those functions, because the neural *connections* they need for maximum performance of executive functioning are just not fully developed yet. Those neural connections develop over time, through experience, and sometimes that experience includes a lot of chocolate cake...or drugs...or sex. All things that, in the body's wisdom, it *wants and needs*. But we also need the capacity to decide some things about how to stimulate the needed biological changes in our system, for example: Donut vs. Orange; Great Conversation vs. Sexual Intercourse; Extreme Sports vs. Gang Activity. Both sides of those choices can offer similar biological "benefits." But each choice in the pair has significant *additional* consequences that are not immediately apparent, or sometimes not apparent in advance of the choice. By the time we reach adulthood, we've usually had some experience with sex and donuts. But the experiences with sex and donuts, on the way to adulthood, in the absence of mature executive functioning, is what makes parents feel that this immaturity of executive functioning can cause "Big Problems."

So immaturity in executive functioning might mean that it's hard for your teen to override what he wants to do or has always done in favor of what he should do in order to reach a goal (your goal or his goals), be safe, or make an ethical decision. The so-called executive functions are needed for conscious, deliberate action, especially when automatically responding in another way is pleasurable or habitual or otherwise "the order of the day." Easy, right...to see how normal immaturity in executive functioning accounts for so many of what we feel are the "Big Problems" of parenting teenagers?

Arguing and General Oppositionality

There are three main kinds of opposition in the family that usually result in arguments:

Opposition to the **Rules**: Arguing About What's Okay

Opposition to Your **Reality**: Arguing About "What Is"

Opposition to Your **Values**: Arguing About "What Matters"

If your teen isn't in big trouble, it's likely that behaviors related to this category are going to be present and responsible for at least some of your suffering in parenting him or her. My then-13-year-old son and I once spent 15 minutes arguing about whether the sky was blue or not. It's not that he was coming up with some fancy theory based on refraction, optics, and the nature of atmosphere to argue that "blue" was the incorrect way of describing the sky. He wasn't arguing over *shades* of color. He was saying: It's *not* blue; end of story, you're wrong, I'm right. This was an argument over "what is," or about what we each perceive as the nature of reality. Reality: What's *that*, you might ask? What my son was arguing about was a simple point that I was missing. He was actually offering a brief philosophical treatise on phenomenology that went something like this:

> Dude, listen. There's no *Reality*. There is *your* reality and there is *my* reality. You can say whatever you want but it doesn't make it *true*. Besides, if I agree with you and we get to a consensual version of Reality, then I might as well give up on the project—written in my very DNA, and expressed in my behaviors—to find my own identity, e.g., what *I* feel, think, want, and wish, and theories about how to go about doing that in the best way. So, go ahead and fight me. I actually kind of like seeing your face get red and your eyes bulge a bit and I'm sitting here thinking "You are so stupid and lame and insecure arguing over the color of the sky with me, as if it really matters." I can stop whenever I want, and in fact, I will stop, *now*. That, too, will also piss you off. Sweet.

I know, it's cruel, but teens often really do have to do this kind of thing, and it helps them develop their own identities as well as a host of other super important skills like affect management, logical thinking (yes, even when their arguing is illogical), cognitive multitasking, verbal self-confidence, performance skills under pressure, and a bunch of other executive functions. It can also represent a kind of "risk-taking" activity that is important for the development of a host of other executive functions.

In fact, *moderate* amounts of arguing in the household are associated with *higher* levels of family satisfaction, in contrast to families that discourage or avoid arguing or participate in it all the time.

All "normal" arguing has a similar structure and function, whether it's about rules, reality, or what matters. It is your adolescent's attempt to figure out for themselves what they feel, think, and want to do, in contradistinction to your thinking, feeling, and doing (the rules, the reality, and what matters). Arguing can represent a conflict of needs, a conflict that might be apparent or perceived. Let's look at the sleep/bedtime example.

Your daughter wants to stay up later (until 1 A.M.) and you want her to get to sleep (at 11 P.M.). Big deal. *You're not her.* If she wants to be awake and you want to be asleep, what's the problem? (That's likely what she's thinking, at first.) Well, I'll *tell you* what the problem is. (That's likely what you're thinking, at first.) She might keep you up with her loud music or stomping around the kitchen. She might have to be up at 6:15 A.M. so that *you* can get her to school on time, and that leaves only 5¼ hours of sleep. Adolescents need about 9¼ hours of sleep for maximal functioning. Yeah, how often does *that* happen? Anyway, we have a *difference* here of 4 hours; that's half of a workday—*your* workday. And the difference between you being able to function tomorrow might be the difference between whether the music is on and there's noise or you're worrying about how much sleep she's getting.

How about her needs? The music might help her calm down and actually allow her to get to sleep eventually. Being awake that late may allow her time to think about things that are bothersome or exciting for her. She might want to be online with a friend (or *potential* friend) who can't get online until his or her parent(s) get to sleep. Besides, adolescent sleep patterns almost always shift to later onset of sleep and a need for later waking times. It's not her fault that school starts about 2–4 hours too early for the adolescent brain and body and ends at the wrong time. The noise? Are you *kidding me*? It's almost turned down all the way. She can't believe you can even hear it. Are you standing next to the bedroom with your ear to the wall? You're so boring, anyway, I mean, you *read* for pleasure. Just go to bed and *read* and leave me alone.

She has some very important identity- and physical-development needs happening. It's not personal. There's a real conflict of needs here (and a lack of mature executive functioning, mentalization, and empathy skills).

I like this example because it's the kind of argument that contains opposition in all three forms—about the rules, and what is, and about what's important. In this argument, your daughter thinks the 11 P.M. bedtime rule is arbitrary or punitive or unfair or selfish or doesn't take her needs into account. In this argument, you hear "noise" and it makes you agitated and she hears "music" and it makes her happy.

And in this argument, she wants time with friends, to set her own bedtime and live by her own rules and have needs and wants respected and acknowledged—that is what matters and what is salient. You might remember that teens primarily process information in terms of its salience, especially emotional salience. So, the more salient the reason for the behavior of staying up later—for example, if the person she is waiting for is a love interest or best friend or she can't fall asleep without her trustworthy routine, whatever that is—the more she'll want and need to be able to be in opposition to you and assert her views about each aspect of the argument.

Nancy Darling and Linda Caldwell were the two researchers (from Penn State) whose work was highlighted in the book *NurtureShock*.[25] Po Bronson and Ashley Merryman's book helped publicize Darling and Caldwell's work about why teens lie, and illustrated that for teens, arguing and lying are related—often inversely. As mentioned earlier, teens will often refrain from telling the truth if they feel that they won't be able to *productively argue toward some shift* in the rules, the reality, or agreement about what matters. Arguing is therefore normative, because it is a primary method for establishing identity and negotiating the conflict of needs, normal between *any* adolescent and *any* adult in the same proximity for a long period of time. As Darling and Caldwell and other researchers[26] have demonstrated, communication between your teen and you, even (and especially) if it involves a moderate amount of argument and conflict, is associated with better outcomes.

Here we arrive at yet another irony, and what is fast becoming an accepted theory in adolescent development and a statement about why it seems to be inherently conflictual. A certain amount of argument and opposition happens because it must, for purposes of identity development. A certain amount of arguing happens because of the immaturity in executive functioning (e.g., lack of demonstrated empathy, advanced planning, and impulse inhibition) and other brain functions that take time to develop (e.g., ability to accurately gauge facial expression and understand and regulate affect). A certain amount of arguing happens because no two persons are the same and negotiation over differences in needs is always necessary and much better than abandoning the relationship instead. A certain amount of arguing actually stimulates the development of the very capacities we're hoping our teens had already developed. In other words, in order for your teenager to become the adult you'd like, arguing has to happen. The same idea, illustrated in the quote attributed to Jim Horning, Stanford computer scientist—which he attributes to Sufi sage Mulla Nasreddin—applies to adolescent risk-taking, needs for privacy, "separation," and difficulties with mood regulation: "Good judgment comes from experience [and] experience comes from bad judgment." The need for *experience* to get to the point of making better choices, faster and more often, is beautifully demonstrated by Abigail Baird's research at Vassar College, and we'll look at that in the section on risk-taking behaviors.

Separation/Autonomy: When, Whether, How They Communicate How Much They Hide (Privacy)

The issue of "related autonomy" is discussed more fully in Chapter 9 in relation to mental health. It's important to emphasize, here, though that teens don't really *separate* from their parents. I don't mean they'll never move out, just that your child doesn't need to (psychologically) leave you behind forever. By the time your child reaches adolescence, for better or worse, many of your values are already "in there," gleaned from years and years of watching your behavior and taking in, consciously and nonconsciously, how it *feels* to be around you. Your teens have already been approximating and forming theories for a long, long time. It boils down to this process: *I watch what my closest caregivers do, with me and others. I take ample notice of how it makes me feel (and I also won't fail to notice how it makes others feel). I link up those two things and make decisions about whether those behaviors are good or not and therefore, whether I want to learn and repeat them.*

This process (which is not one, but many) is happening all the time and is primarily nonconscious. But my cells register the effects and make use of that "information." It is another description of epigenetics and the interaction between genes and environment and biology and biography. Since it's been going on for your child's entire life (albeit in different ways at different states of cognitive and physical capacity), your child has had a lot of time to be taught by you about who you are and who you want them to be. Adolescence is yet another developmental time period that sets the background for a process that's already been happening. But this time period allows for more arguing about and implementing their version of what they've learned so far. It allows—because of rapidly expanding cognitive and physical capacities—the trying out of *alternatives* to what they've learned from you and close others, about whom they are, what they want to be, and what to do about it. I know this is incredibly scary. When teens "try out alternatives" to what *you* want them to do, the choices they make can result in accident or death. And their "alternative" choices can and probably will bring them into conflict with you much more often, since you presumably *already* learned much about which alternatives to parental ideas, wishes, and behaviors are effective or desired and which are not.

You love your children. You've taken care of them, arranged and managed their lives and been through terror, panic, fear, joy, and immense uncertainty, through each period of their life. *You're attached with them.* You might understand (intellectually) that one day they'll leave home or "strike out on their own" with their own ideas, and make their own decisions—just not yet, because they're nowhere near ready, right? You know they're not "ready" because you know how unready you were at their age. You know they're not ready because every day they do something that shows you, without a doubt, that they are not ready to move out or start a family and generally make it in the world at large without your daily input. You see and feel their immaturity and you want to protect them from harm. Plus, you might actually really like your child's company. Or you might really need *their* help. So "separation" can be extremely anxiety-provoking for parents, and signs and indicators of "separation" can cause conflict, worry, attempts to control, limit or manage the behaviors (like getting socially or sexually close to others, wanting privacy, not participating in family events or not sharing, purposely withholding important information or lying).

So that I can stop putting "separation" in quotation marks, let's talk about what they're actually doing. Your child is working toward a developmental milestone called *related autonomy,* and it's a major component of teen mental health. Here's what *related autonomy* might sound like, if we could listen in, not to the words, but to the meaning of the inner dialogue of a teenager trying to realize this developmental milestone:

> I am a teenager. I am almost an adult. My job is to be and become my Self. My very own Self. I want to do it myself. I *should* do it myself. But I need my parents. I need my friends a lot, but that's not really a problem to me. I guess I need teachers; I don't know, it depends upon the teacher. I love some (or all) of my extended family and care what they think, too, but not like with my parents. *I hate disappointing them.* I'd rather they punish me and get it over with than "be disappointed." I just want what I want, and want it *now,* and I wish they'd understand. What I want is increasingly different than what my parents want. I say I don't care, but I do. *It makes me feel guilty.* But instead, I usually get angry, then they get angry back and sort of punish me and strangely I feel better…kind of a distraction from the guilt, and I feel more okay to want what I want. I'm selfish. No, I'm not; they're selfish. It will be so great to leave—*I think.* I really want them to be happy. And happy with me. I want to be happy, too. *How do I have both of those?* Thank God it's the weekend.

Your adolescent is trying to find a balance between what they need, want, and should do about those needs and wants, with what they imagine or are told that *you* need, want, or think should be done. They want you to be happy and they want to be happy, and they really don't want to have to choose between the two outcomes, but they *will* do so. They want to stay *in relation* to you. They also want to feel and know and actually be competent actors *in* their own lives and capable *authors* of their *own* story. This is a normal conflict of adolescence, and however it all gets figured out is your child's degree of related autonomy. If the balance is tipped too far to the side of acting only on their own behalf (too much emphasis on the "self"), then problems can occur. Likewise, problems result if the balance skews too much to the side of acting only on *your* behalf or on the behalf of *others* (too much emphasis on the "self-in-relation").

We've now talked about how adolescents are highly motivated to establish their own identity, to avoid embarrassment, to maximize low-effort, high-reward ("fun") activities, to seek and repeat novel behaviors that increase pleasant feelings, and to avoid disappointing you or having unpleasant experiences. We've noted, as well, how these motivations register as highly salient to them. So, to sum up:

Michael's Nine Rules for Adolescent Action

1. Activity, whenever possible, should be fun and enjoyable.

2. Activity should not be repetitive, unless the repetition is fun and enjoyable.

3. Activity should not look like parental-type activity.

4. Activity should not make me feel ashamed, embarrassed, or humiliated.

5. Activity should not get me praised if the praise indicates it is the type of behavior my parent is likely to do or makes me too stressed or pressured about repeating the same level of success that garnered the praise.

6. See Item 1. If activity does not equal "fun," and I absolutely have to do it, then that un-fun activity should be quickly followed by a fun activity or at least something of my own choosing.

7. Fun, non-embarrassing activities should also, if at all possible, primarily represent me as a competent adult in the world, to the adults I know.

8. Activity should not disappoint people I love, especially my caregivers.

9. Activity should not result in disapproval, condemnation, rejection, abandonment, significant correction, or removal of support of any kind; *none* of those things are fun and *most* of those things humiliating.

Think about the things you'd like to know about your adolescent's life and how many of them conform to the list of "rules" above. Now, you understand *privacy* and *doing things without you*.

PROBLEMS WITH COMMUNICATION

Many issues surrounding communication problems have to do with the ways in which people feel and think—especially about communication. It is both absolutely amazing to me that people can communicate and also a completely banal fact of existence. We communicate. This common understanding—that subjects, you and me, communicate or don't communicate and then understanding happens or it doesn't—drives most of our thinking about misunderstanding and problems with communication. But this "basic" notion doesn't well describe how communication "works."[27]

For purposes of this book, let's emphasize a connection between the way people feel and the fact of communication. I like many theories about emotions, but for now I'm working from a perspective of something called the "appraisal theory of emotions."[28]

The very basic idea is that when we experience any emotion(s), that experience is rooted in our evaluation (appraisal and interpretation) of events and situations in the world, others and ourselves. By the way, there isn't just *one* appraisal theory, there are many—different camps of thought based upon various criticisms and elaborations of the basic theory. Some people think that since parts of the theory aren't being proved in scientific experimentation, it's wrong. Some people like the theory but don't like certain emphases or parts of the theory—for example, that it doesn't emphasize enough the role of *affect* (the automatic physiological arousal that is always happening as a result of our experience). Cognitive behavioral theorists might think about the example below as a description of the physiological responses to "activating events."[29] Here's an example from later in the book (Chapter 9):

> Imagine you're a camera operator, filming two people going to see one of those old-fashioned B horror movies. One person watches the film with a look of intense engagement, excitement, and pleasure as they engage in the experience. The other person looks terrorized, worried, and scared and eventually has to leave. "Wasn't that a blast?" asks the friend. The other answers, "Are you kidding me, that was that most awful thing I've ever seen! I never want to do that again!"

In this example, two people had the same stimuli, and similar affective responses, but had very different *emotional* experiences. This difference is accounted for, says appraisal theory, based on the different interpretations that each person was giving to the experience of seeing that film. Appraisal theory is a way of explaining why individuals vary in their emotional reactions to the same event; and it is a heavily *cognitive* model because it puts a premium on our cognitive interpretation of events as a cause for emotional response variation. Some appraisal theorists talk about "emotion…in the absence of physiological arousal" and that is why the theory is often criticized.[30] I can understand that criticism. I don't think that such a condition exists—emotion without physiological arousal. I think the state of "without physiological arousal" is more accurately referred to as "death."

There is a connection between how we describe and experience our emotions and our cognitive interpretation of physiological states. I take as a starting point Schacter and Singer's findings from their still-influential 1962 experiment[31], which is referred to as the *two-factor* theory of emotions: one factor is the physiological state of arousal and the second factor is the cognition (thought, belief, etc.) that makes the best sense of the situation. So, there is an activating event (anything that happens in the world, or in ourselves, for that matter) and there are various physiological responses (increase in heart rate, sweating, pupil dilation, muscle tension) and awareness of the response, which gives rise to an interpretation of why it is happening. I believe that the interpretation will be based upon a host of factors, including previous exposure to similar stimulation, visual and body memories of similar events, current overall physiological state of health at the moment of the event in question, amount and quality of neurochemicals released in the system, events that happened just prior to the activating event in question, and imagination about future events. But the basic premise goes like this: activating event, additional physiological responses, cognitions (interpretations), new physiological responses in relation to the interpretation, and on it goes. It's important to note that the physiological arousal cues themselves are activating events for new rounds of feeling and thinking. I would put an even finer point on it: There is no such thing as the "same" stimuli or "same" response, because a human response to neurochemicals is always a matter of mindset, setting, and the neurochemical itself—an equation that speaks to the ever-changing nature of things.

In other words, *our emotional responses are always a combination of biology and biography,* and that's why two people do not and cannot have the same responses to the same stimuli. Two people who see the same movie and both loved it are still not having the *same* response. They could have similar overall responding patterns, but they aren't and won't ever have the same response—they are not the same people. One person who sees the same movie twice will not have the "same" response. That's axiomatic for my thinking about just about everything. It's all *case-specific;* each human is simultaneously unique and similar to another. That belief explains well enough why I'm amazed that we communicate and understand one another at all *and* why the fact that we are always communicating seems banal. This fact has important implications for understanding adolescent health and mental health, especially as regards decision-making around risk.

The process of figuring out what to do, based upon experience, is always rooted in the emotional experiences of "regret," "confidence," and "stress." The experiences of those phenomena for teens (and adults) are not separated from reasoning processes. And that "reasoning" will involve appraisals of the affect involved in the experience. In other words, how you interpret the bodily sensations that go with trying healthy behaviors strongly affects motivation to repeat them. One study puts it like this: "Although dual process models tend to separate affect and cognition into two different systems, our results make salient how meaningful behavior requires an ongoing interdependence between the two systems."[32]

But people do respond in somewhat overall consistent ways, emotionally, and some of that responding is highly predictable. Explain that, genius. Okay, I'll give it a shot, thank you. Imagine how life would be if you really lived and experienced it with the absolute certainty that nothing was certain or going to be repeated. For purposes of illustration, let's say you're lucky enough to have both feet intact. Every time you opened your eyes and swung your feet over the side of the bed, it was a real question as to whether the floor would be there. Let's say you're lucky enough to have teeth. And you might or might not find teeth when you stuck the toothbrush in your mouth when doing your morning brushing. Let's say you're lucky enough to be aware of your emotions and your physiological responses and "you" (in this case, I mean, your conscious thinking process) could determine precisely how much norepinephrine had been secreted in your brain and gut and were highly aware of and could differentiate each type of physiological arousal cue and had exquisite memories of the very subtle differences in meaning associated with each state and could rapidly (in milliseconds) process all the memories and thoughts and fantasies associated with this particular state, etc. First of all, you'd have to have a very different level of consciousness available to you than most of us have now. In other words, we might need a different or very differently wired brain, because as it stands now, there is the "cognitive load" problem. Can you imagine, in your current state of being, attending to *all* of that stimulation, in a conscious way, and processing it all effectively and still acting in the world? I can't. And that is why, I think, we have so much activity going on in the background (like the "assessment" processes being done at the cellular level, in response to neurophysiological changes in the organism) and nonconscious thoughts and feelings in relation to those cellular events. *Almost all of it,* in fact, has to go on in *background.* It provides us with too high a cognitive load, otherwise. And what we get as a byproduct of all that is a *theory*—an approximation (or appraisal) of what's going on and why. Usually that theory (and in this case, the *theory takes the form of an emotion*) is good enough for determining action. And that's mostly what we need.

You swing your feet over the side of the bed and assume the floor is there: Good enough for me. You don't want to have to imagine it's an open question every time. You imagine seeing this person and based on your biology and biography, you imagine it will "feel" a certain way. Good enough for me. You don't want to have to imagine it's a question every time. But what if you *did* have to imagine it every time and had to keep scanning the environment for cues and clues to how it would be *this* time. Unless your capacities radically changed, you can guess how it would be; that state is called *anxious*. It's not pleasant. People who have disorders of anxiety oftentimes are people who kind of "know too much," are scanning too much and know all too well that things are contingent. These folks worry about how things are going to be, all the time. You might say that, from a Buddhist perspective, that an anxious person's perception that everything is arising anew at each moment is *essentially correct*. But you'd better be a Zen monk if you're going to *really know* that or you're going to be too anxious to function. That's why, I think, we come up with "theories" about what's happening with others, the world and ourselves. We "theorize" in all different ways; *emotions are an approximation. Emotions are a kind of theory about others, the world, and ourselves.*

I didn't make this up. I just think it's practical and it works and I agree with it for now. Many people have thought similar thoughts and written about it them, for instance Sigmund Freud, Joseph Weiss, and Harold Sampson (and many of their colleagues). I never met Freud, and I've heard a lot of crazy things about that guy. But I did meet Joe and Hal—and was able to train with them—and they were able to think about, talk about, and help people by taking a lot of what Freud wrote and re-translating it into their own theory that is highly practical, doesn't actually contradict very many other theories of psychology, psychotherapy, and psychopathology, and allows people to change. They also developed the theory, with so many other good people at the old Mt. Zion Hospital in San Francisco and with members of the San Francisco Psychoanalytic Institute and a group of researchers and clinicians who eventually founded the San Francisco Psychotherapy Research Group.

These folks found, through decades of empirical research on the psychotherapy process, that the conditions and interventions that help people change and reduce their suffering are highly individualized, always case-specific, and largely carried out by the people themselves. They called this theory "Control-Mastery" because they found that people exert and exhibit a great deal more *control* over their nonconscious mental functioning than was previously thought[33] and that people organize their unconscious processes toward the *mastery* of trauma and the kinds of problems that keep people from pursuing their healthy, normal developmental goals in life. The theory is more democratic than most, and while it recognizes that we have strong influence over and with others, it posits mutuality as the cornerstone of all interaction, alongside the need and wish for individual self-efficacy, a feeling of authorship, and a fundamental desire for health in functioning.[34] *It is a theory of related autonomy.* It is not a Pollyannaish theory, but it is essentially respectful of the Other, recognizes the power of each individual, and is, in the end, hopeful. I like that. And I hope it's helpful to you because it's a really fine and effective optics for thinking about teenagers. We'll talk much more about this very useful theory in Chapter 8 on Family.

Miscommunication is always happening between people. We think we are communicating, meaning that we think others understand us and get what we say and do. But we are always making little and big errors of judgment and are always biased in our perceptions. There are plenty of good studies on what these biases are.[35] We oftentimes don't "get" or understand others. Not even therapists always get or understand others—we just get paid to *try.* We get paid to try to understand, with the pledge that we'll work during our careers to keep understanding and making theories about and testing out what gets in the way of understanding.

One big error we can all easily make is the one referred to above—the error of thinking that similar experiences cause similar feelings (in ourselves or others). We do *that* approximating for a reason—it's faster, more efficient, and less anxiety-provoking than being open to everything as if it were a brand-new experience. That's where being an *Approximate Parent* can be helpful. If you know your emotions are an *approximation* of what's happening, you won't necessarily use emotional reasoning. Trying not to use emotional reasoning is one of the skills you want your teenagers to learn and to use. Emotional reasoning is figuring from your feelings: I feel bad so things must *be* bad. It is a cognitive distortion. That statement will sometimes, but never *always* be true. Since I've lived this long I know that "bad" feeling states often accompany long-term good changes. I've seen this in every area of my life. I have finally learned to more often judge my particular feeling state from this long-term perspective and with the knowledge of that perceptual reasoning error. Teens live in the now, so emotional reasoning is the order of the day. Please just know this and it might help you not get angry when they employ this cognitive error.

Our cognitions and our emotions are almost always approximations, for the reasons I described above—it's more efficient that way, and good enough for getting things done in the world. But when things go wrong—like in the instances of conflict, argument miscommunication, and lack of understanding, which make up much of existence—it might help you to remember that everyone involved has probably been operating on approximations and not certainties. Your teen has been operating on *more* approximations than you because they feel things more deeply and reason from their feelings more often, especially since they lack experience. Your teen might insist or think or feel that you've gotten it wrong because they feel so strongly about their position. That's not because they're bad or you raised them wrong. That's how it works. Here's some things they don't know but you can know:

1. They don't necessarily know that their amygdalae are immature and can interpret neutral faces as registering anger.[36]

2. They don't know that they favor sensory and motor activities over more complex, high-cognitive-load tasks (in other words, sports over homework, partying over rational discussions of philosophy).

3. They don't know that their immature *nucleus accumbens* leads to a heightened interest in novelty and excitement—self-reflection on past experiences...not so much.

4. They don't know that their lack of development around executive functioning skill-building and lack of prefrontal cortex development (which is a primary but not the *only* area of executive functioning activity) results in poor planning and poor judgment.

5. They don't know that their underdeveloped *amygdalae* make it: a) hard to regulate their emotions; and b) easier to feel "hot," high-intensity emotions more than cold, sober ones that mitigate emotional reasoning errors.

6. They don't know that their lack of a fully developed theory of mind makes it easier to think that what they feel and think is what others feel and think, and that it prevents them from accurately and consistently knowing that others are always different and always have their own unique thoughts, feelings, and reasons for acting the way they do.

7. They don't know that the balance between judgment, emotionality, and decision-making/reasoning doesn't really kick in fully until brain development is complete in the mid-20s (and that brain development is usually complete for girls first).

8. They don't know that the current state of underdevelopment in their brain means they aren't good at complex perspective-taking and they are prone to care more about their own needs than the needs of others.

Normal problems with communication happen because stuff doesn't get communicated—because of the lying, holding back relevant details, or lack of awareness discussed above. Communicating information also "doesn't happen" because of the normal need for privacy. And normal problems with communication are always happening, simply because your teenager doesn't know about the list of things above. For all these reasons, misunderstandings and problems with communication are going to happen more often and more intensely with adolescents. As they mature these problems will decrease. (See Chapter 9 for what constitutes adolescent mental health.)

If you've taken all this into account and the arguing, withdrawal, aggression, and lack of productive communication is still happening or worrying you, then it's time for a new theory and probably time to get help. Lack of consistent, semi-effective communication can also be the result of a learning disability, attentional difficulty, or mental health disorder like depression, anxiety, or a developmental disorder like Asperger's. It can be the result of a medical condition that is temporary or permanent. If the information above doesn't help you get oriented to the problems of communication, then it might mean one of these other reasons is in play and it's time for professional help to sort it out.

Risk-Taking Behavior

I don't think I really need to tell you why you and other parents feel that this list constitutes the Biggest of the Big Problems. These are the problems that can lead to accident, injury, and death. This section is therefore going to be about risk and how teenagers understand and respond to risk.[37]

There is a list of readings for follow-up at the end of each section. One of the readings on that list for this chapter is Dr. Lynn Ponton's 1998 book *The Romance of Risk: Why Teenagers Do the Things They Do.* That book should probably be on the shelf of every American parent. There are a few other books that I feel that way about, and they're all recommended someplace in this book.

Dr. Ponton is an adolescent psychiatrist at University of California, San Francisco. She's spent her career serving at-risk youth and families. Her book approaches the subject of risk in a similar way to *The Approximate Parent,* insofar as she is clear to make the distinction between normal and problematic risk-taking. Normal risk-taking behavior is about your child implementing Mulla Nasreddin's dictum that "good judgment comes from experience [and] experience comes from bad judgment." Ponton writes:

> Current thinking is beginning to acknowledge that adolescence is a time of risk-taking that is not solely harmful, and, in fact, that *frequent risk-taking is a normative, healthy, developmental behavior for adolescents.*

It is during adolescence that young people experiment with many aspects of life, taking on new challenges, testing out how things fit together, and using this process to define and shape both their identities and their knowledge of the world.[38]

Let's look again at Norman and Shallice's list of situations that require executive functioning and therefore require *practice*:

1. Situations involving planning or decision-making;

2. Situations involving failure analysis (problem-solving, error detection and refinement);

3. Situations in which practice has not been possible or is limited or where new combinations of behaviors are required;

4. Situations in which are threatening, high-risk, or difficult; and

5. Situations in which avoiding old habits or overcoming strong temptations are necessary for mastery of the new set of circumstances.

These "tasks" or capacities describe the behaviors, thoughts, and feelings necessary for your teen to learn and master new skills that are crucial for healthy development into adulthood. Most of these situations involve risk-taking to a greater or lesser degree, because they are all mostly new situations and situations in which the lack of experience/practice can only be mitigated by more experience and practice, so that risky behavior (over time) becomes less risky or dangerous.

Fine, let them experiment with a new hairstyle or wearing boots instead of tennis shoes. But that's not enough. What's enough, then? Unfortunately for you (and I hope not for them) they will have to have some practice and experience in all areas, including sex, drugs, alcohol, driving, managing emotions, maintaining and creating new friendships, learning at school, and almost all areas of living. Does my child need experience in *fighting*? Come on! Well, your particular child might not need experience in fighting, but another child might. Your child might need experience, though, in avoiding fighting or avoiding gang activity or avoiding unprotected sex or avoiding drinking or avoiding self-injury. Your child might also need (and want) experience in *helping their friends* deal with any or all of these things. This desire to help a friend can get your child into the thick of things that are dangerous and highly risky, too, even if they aren't directly participating in specific high-risk behaviors.

Some of your teen's risk-taking is going to be a behavioral way of arguing about the rules. Remember from earlier in the chapter that all teen behavior (especially risk-taking) that parents find problematic is actually a *question*. The question usually looks something like this:

> "Hi Mom. Here is an example of something I am not very good at yet. I have a vague inkling that I need help with this issue. I need your help, but since I'm all about figuring out my identity and not simply repeating yours, I can't really ask you this directly, but what I want to know is...*How do I get better at this thing I just did?*"

It helps to be physically accessible to your child, then, during adolescence, so they can get *quick* answers to their "behavioral questions" about risk. Ponton is keen to note that adolescents want and need your presence and will use it to help correct and refine their choices around risk—they just won't necessarily tell you that's what they are doing, for all the reasons we discussed about identity and privacy. If you respond to your teen's risk-taking by throwing up your hands and just "trusting" they'll be okay, they will, for the most part, interpret that as a sign you don't care about them. When you are willing to argue about the rules, they interpret that as a sign of care. When you can give in a little about the rules, they interpret that as a sign of respect. But it doesn't mean that you're going to be getting their appreciation, acknowledgment, and understanding of your care in a way that you recognize or want—not just yet. They need you to monitor and guide them, but the thanks don't usually come until later. In my experience teens start giving some of the love back around 17 or so...and it can seem to disappear again during senior year and then reappear later. The more secure they feel in their identity, the more they can show their appreciation. In the main, mitigation of problematic risk-taking occurs with your presence, limitations on how much money you give, and the presence of structure and alternatives to dangerous risk-taking. *Unlimited access to money, unstructured, unsupervised time, low parental involvement, and lack of parental guidance and monitoring significantly increases risk-taking behavior and is associated with higher incidences of all kinds of problems with healthy adolescent adjustment.*[39]

The bottom line is that one size doesn't fit all. Every child has a different propensity toward risk-taking, evaluates risks and rewards differently, has different needs for privacy, and differently assesses what constitutes risk, reward, pleasure, aversion, and danger. We explored that idea in Chapter 1, in looking at differential rates of development of the central and frontal cortices. Every child feels similar things in a different way than their peers. Each child responds slightly differently (behaviorally) to the presence of a group, and so each child responds differently to "peer pressure." Minimizing the problems associated with risk-taking is about: 1) knowing how teenagers function, in general; 2) knowing *your* child; and 3) putting those two things together. What area of development might my child be working on? (See Chapter

9, for example, on components of mental health development.) Are there any safeguards I can introduce them to, knowing full well that what I think of as "safety," they'll think of as "hassle"? Thinking about risk-taking in this way will help lower your worry and anxiety about some of the risks your child is taking and help you to see some of that behavior as healthy (albeit nerve-wracking).

It's worth noting here that parents (and I) worry about some of these risks because the dividing line between healthy risk/experimentation and something more dangerous is a thin line. A case in point is the issue of pornography and related sexual materials. While certainly not confined only to males, I've heard more and more in my practice about how the easy and constant access to pornography has created a number of difficulties for my clients, young and older. We know that it used to be that if you were coming up in the Baby Boomer generation and were a teenager naturally curious about sex and the human body, you had three main options, at least until you met someone: *National Geographic* magazine, the Sears catalog underwear section, or a copy of *Playboy* magazine, found in an alley somewhere or stolen from your older brother's bedroom. That all changed in 1994, with the beginning of the Internet as we know it today. It became possible—for free—to see just about any image (moving or still, and in real time) of just about any type of sexual activity imaginable (and unimaginable). Boys especially seem to be more prone to being overstimulated by the constant availability of sexual images and videos, and "healthy curiosity" can pretty quickly turn into something that looks more like an addiction, significantly changing the way one feels about sex and sexuality, men and women and oneself. *When* that line gets crossed is hard to determine, and so parents worry about the risky aspects of so much easy exposure to all kinds of sexual material. More about this in Chapter 6.

In order to complete this section, let's look at the powerful work of two neuroscientists and developmental psychologists, Professor Abigail Baird at Vassar College and Adriana Galvan at UCLA—two more of my favorite researchers on adolescent development. They are both exceedingly smart, but I like their work largely because they "get" teenagers and both know how to design cool experiments that tell us about how teens really feel, think, and make decisions.

My grandmother lived with our family, when I was a teen. She was a mix of tough and sweet, and being from Russia she liked some of the Americanisms she collected over the years. When I said something ridiculous she'd reply, "Get out of town." Sometimes it was "Go play on the freeway" or "Go jump off a roof." You might think this was cruel, but when she said it was always sweet and silly and I knew for certain she didn't mean it. However, it was probably not the right thing to say, given the state of maturity of two important neural systems: my prefrontal cortex and my striatal system. These are the areas of the brain that undergo the kinds of developmental changes that seem to contribute to adolescent risk-taking behavior.[40] And we'll soon see, thanks to Dr. Baird, why suggesting that a teen jump off a roof might not be a good idea. Here's a preview: If you tell a teen to "Go jump off a roof," he'll actually *think* about it, whereas most healthy adults will dismiss it out of hand immediately.

Adriana Galvan and her colleagues derived—from mice and men—the *imbalance model* of emotional development in adolescents. Based on neuroimaging studies of adolescents and studies based on rodent models, they describe two systems working simultaneously, but not yet in coordination and balance, that will hopefully characterize late adolescence and early adulthood. One component system is the more rational, analytical side of brain promoted by activity (mostly) of the prefrontal cortex. The other component system runs more automatically and intuitively, largely thanks to the subcortical, affect-related systems (sometimes called the limbic system).

When research on the prefrontal cortex and executive functioning exploded in the 1990s, the story that got to the popular press and has stayed in the foreground is that all the problems we've been talking about in this chapter are related to prefrontal cortex immaturity. But the imbalance model suggests that the more mature limbic system of the adolescent is what dominates information processing. You'll remember that the brain develops from back to front and from the center to the periphery. So it's not just that a teen's prefrontal cortex isn't yet developed, it's that the limbic system, which has developed earlier, holds sway. Some of the consequences that follow from the imbalance between these two systems include the tendency for low-effort, reward-seeking behaviors ("fun") and a related tendency for a kind of overexaggerated production of dopamine associated with getting a reward. Translation: Fun stuff feels *really* good.

The *imbalance model* isn't the only model out there to explain risk, but like all good theories it doesn't contradict other current theories, and the various theories complement one another. Other models include the idea that teens have varying and variable decision-making competence; they do in fact consider risk versus reward, but sometimes, for example, they tend to overemphasize the rewards and downplay the risks. That is not inconsistent with the imbalance model. Yet another model describes how adults use a kind of "gut" or hunch-based way of avoiding risks and that teens are in the process of developing this *quicker* "gist-based" way of assessing risk versus reward.[41] Development is complex and asynchronous. That was the scientific way of saying that adolescence is like having a child driving a Formula One racecar. All the models of risk-taking in adolescence, though, recognize that teens are feeling and thinking about risks and rewards—they aren't just acting purely on impulse or seeking only pleasure, and they aren't stupid.

In fact, one recent study by Gregory Berns and his colleagues at Emory University suggests that increased risk-taking and engagement in dangerous behavior is associated with *higher levels of prefrontal cortex development* (in that the brain is more highly myelinated) and not *lower* levels of prefrontal cortex maturity.[42] His study really begs the question of how you and I (and your teen) define "risk." It's hard to get agreement among adults on what constitutes risk, and "dangerous" or "risky" behavior may just be—at least in some cases—"behavior that is more adult than the chronological age would suggest." This certainly fits what Berns found in his study about the relationship between increased risk-taking and more, not less, *highly* developed cognitive capacities in those adolescents who took more risks.

Let's get back to my grandma, though, and jumping off a roof. Grandma, meet Abigail Baird. In a study aptly named "What Were You Thinking?"[43] both adults and teens were asked to decide whether an activity was a good idea or bad idea. Dr. Baird and her colleagues studied the brain activity of both the teens and the adults to see what *areas* of the brain were active during the process of responding to scenarios like jumping off a roof or biting down on a lightbulb. The adults seemed to be using the parts of the brain that create mental imagery, along with parts of the brain that signal distress (and avoidance behavior). Both areas of adult brain activity happen quickly and automatically—it's a gut instinct; you just *know* it's bad. Teens, however, use different parts of the brain to decide whether the scenario is good or bad. They still pick the same items as *good* or *bad* as the adults do, but they take longer to do it for a fascinating reason—they are thinking and reasoning more about the choice. The teens' decisions are more *thoughtful* than the adult, but seriously—how much time do you want your teenager to thoughtfully consider whether or not to jump off a roof? Not much. You want your teenager to quickly get the gist of something that is dangerous and avoid it, just as quickly as you can know that biting down on a lightbulb is a bad idea: No *thought* necessary. But you have *experience* and can combine immediate visceral clues and visual imagery to form a rapid "gist" about "bad" and "good."

Dr. Baird's study points to the unmistakable importance of the role played by *experience* in a teen's developing thinking and feeling life. Teens use different strategies for theory-making, and the theories—remember, emotions are theories—are different than adult theories for decision-making. So, this points to one way in which teens assess risk and reward differently than adults. Well, if teenagers don't find jumping off a roof automatically too risky and something to be avoided, what do they find immediately aversive?

In a 2010 *Scientific American* article, Dr. Baird discussed a study by fellow researcher Gregory Berns that answers the above question succinctly.[44] The Emery University study took adolescents between 12 and 17 and asked them to listen to a short clip of music and make two ratings—one about how familiar they were with the music and another indicating their like or dislike of the selection. The clip was played twice. The second time around, they were asked again to rate their response to the song. When teens weren't told how popular the song was, they changed their minds about how much they liked the song the second time around by about 12 percent. When told, though, that the song was popular (based on numbers of online downloads), they switched their ratings 22 percent of the time, on average. But did they rate the song higher or lower once they found out how popular it was among their peers? I tend to be a bit of a contrarian and if I know a lot of people like a movie, I'll more often avoid seeing it. Well, not the kids. When they changed their own ratings, based upon others', *they changed toward the popular view 80 percent of the time.* Big deal, right? It's just peer pressure, we all know that; teens care what their peers think. But it's more important than that. Berns went on to investigate what was going on in their brains as they were making their decisions about likeability.

Berns and his colleagues found significant increases in brain activity in those areas of the brain *not* associated with pleasure-seeking—not what you might expect if a teen was having the experience of "liking" the songs *more* the second time around. Instead, they found that brain regions that were firing—the anterior cingulate cortex and motor cortex and frontal poles—were highly associated with *danger, pain, and anxiety.* The more an individual teen changed his or her rating toward the popular view, the higher his or her level of pain and anxiety. Baird wrote that the authors of the study viewed the results as being explained by the *aversion and dissonance caused by seeing yourself out of step with your peers.* Her summary of the authors' conclusion: "[C]onforming seems to be motivated not by the positive utility of behaving like your peers, but instead out of anxiety and pain at the prospect of being a 'contrarian.' "

Dr. Adriana Galvan at UCLA, another of the most important researchers on adolescent risk-taking and assessment, has not only conducted a number of studies on risk and reward, but is also one of the people who most strongly suggest how important context (environment) is in influencing risk-taking and reward-seeking behavior in adolescents. Her work points to the importance of *emotional salience,* or the idea that, among other things, teens process information according to whether or not they feel it matters to them (is "salient").

One particularly clever study involved children and adults in game play, as brain activity was being observed using Functional Magnetic Resonance Imaging (fMRI). Rewards were given as part of the game play that involved risk-taking and rewards for that risk. Young children showed brain activity related to pleasure and reward when they received *any* reward at all and adults responded *in proportion* to the reward, meaning that the bigger the reward, the bigger the brain response.

But adolescents responded *only* when the reward became emotionally salient, that is to say, when the reward was *huge* for them. Basically their brains say "ehhh, whatever" to small and medium-size rewards and only "light up" when the reward is large. Teens develop a kind of "tolerance"—just as drug addicts do—in response to small and medium rewards. Even prefrontal cortex activity *slows* in relation to decreases in nucleus accumbens responding. In other words, the more salient the reward, the less they're thinking and analyzing.

But not all teens respond the same. Teens whose nucleus accumbens was highly involved rated risky behaviors as more exciting and more worth the reward than those who were lower nucleus accumbens (NA) responders. In the "high NA responding" teens, small risks and excitements don't figure as emotionally salient, and these teens show greater receptivity to the feelings and opinions of others. Although the findings are complicated, it appears that only some adolescents will be high risk-takers and experience the dopamine-related feelings of euphoria associated with risky or dangerous behaviors. Once again, we have more confirmation for the idea that not all teens are the same, and their responses are a result of complex interaction between biology and biography.

Many teens fear and would rather avoid being evaluated, condemned, or rejected by others. Some teens find it absolutely *dangerous,* as if their very *survival* was at stake.

> "If you're not on MySpace, you don't exist."—Skyler, 18, to her mom[45]

A teen uses her thinking and feeling in order to make decisions—even mature-level thinking—but she may nonetheless make bad decisions or take big risks, especially when the risk registers for her as emotionally salient and the subcortical structures of the brain "win out" over "thinking it through." Galvan's recent work has shown that under the pressure of peer rejection, social discomfort, or other additional environmental factors, the balance can be "tipped" to the side of a bad decision or overestimation of reward versus risk.

So teens can act and feel differently and change their behavior if they *fear* being rejected or judged. Context and emotion are intertwined, context and risk-taking are intertwined—this is Galvan's point in thinking about adolescent risk-taking, and it's worth remembering.[46]

Difficulties Related to Mood

When we think about teenagers, I think we most often imagine some picture involving changes in the *intensity, frequency,* and *regulation* of emotional/affective states. Scientists use phrases like "adolescent-typical alterations in arousal, motivation, and emotion."[47] Parents use phrases like "What the hell is wrong with him?" or "She's like that Tasmanian devil on Bugs Bunny—one moment up, the next down, but always all over the place!"

Most parents just think, "It's just being a teenager" or it's "raging hormones." Yes, the continual release of sex steroids, especially during the onset of puberty, does play some role (but not a major role) in influencing mood and behavior during adolescence. The gonads also produce non-steroid hormones like lutenizing hormone (LH), follicle-stimulating hormone (FSH), and gonadotropin-releasing hormone (GnRH). These play a role in sexual development but are not sex steroids, *per se.*

But there are other hormones at work, too, like those released by the adrenal glands, located right above each kidney. The adrenal glands produce epinephrine, norepinephrine (adrenaline), cortisol, aldosterone, testosterone, DHEA, DHEAS, androstenedione, and estrogens. Cortisol is a stress hormone but that doesn't mean it causes stress. It is involved in things like weight management, heart function, maintenance and repair of skin and bones, fighting infections, memory functioning, and consolidation of episodic memory during sleep.[48]

What a cocktail, right? Temple University Professor of Psychology Laurence Steinberg is one of the foremost researchers on adolescents and has spent most of his adult life helping adolescents and their families in one way or another. Some of Dr. Steinberg's work in the last decade notes how difficult it is to demonstrate that hormones (at any particular time period in adolescence) are the primary factor in the variability or intensity of mood.[49] It's likely that hormonal factors do influence mood, but the effect is not necessarily *direct* and immediate, i.e., the release of a particular hormone does not trigger an immediate increase or decrease of negative or positive feeling. Hormonal effect, too, is one of those context-dependent events.[50]

At this point, you can probably guess where we're going. We've already seen that different "systems" in the brain develop at different rates, as a result of normal maturation and environmental factors that affect the unfolding of brain maturation. We've seen how a propensity to read and respond to "hot" emotions means that events are more often experienced and thought of as more intense. We've talked about the different sense of "time" for teens and how the pressure is on to feel *now,* figure it out *now,* and do it *now.* Most of the entire chapter on "the big problems" has touched on the various ways in which affect, emotion, and external environment (as well as the internal brain) influence adolescent ability to process and respond to their own and other's emotions.

And by now you know my prejudice that brain chemicals are like drugs, and the effect of a drug is always dependent upon the drug itself, the mindset, and the setting.

So my theory, for now, is that emotions, too, are the result of the environment interacting with your particular teenager, and *vice-versa*. We've seen how interpretation and thinking plays a role in just what emotion your teen (or you) will have in response to any given activating event. We've seen how teens are especially prone to misunderstanding and miscommunication and how that influences our own ability to communicate. Increased levels of cortisol are often present under stress. But as mentioned earlier, the "stress hormone" cortisol does not cause stress.

Studies of patients with post-traumatic stress disorder (PTSD), a condition that can follow prolonged exposure to trauma or single incidences of particularly intense trauma and loss, show that cortisol levels are actually lower in PTSD patients. Bessel van der Kolk and others showed that, contrary to what we thought (based on *animal* studies), people with PTSD release *lower* levels of cortisol under stress. He hypothesized that without enough cortisol in the system, the body's capacity to reduce stress responses is diminished, making it harder for the body to recover after a stressor.[51] The body's release of cortisol is a mechanism designed to *decrease and reverse* the stress response, not increase it. But if you are under stress a lot, and a lot of cortisol is continually being released, your body is going to learn to start *expecting* stress, even if it's not forthcoming. The body also strongly associates the *amount* of cortisol with the severity of the stress. And we get "good" at (or at least make adaptations for) responding to those events we *expect* to experience. Teens are under an enormous amount of stress, much of the time. Increased levels of cortisol and other stress hormones also change our thinking and can result in cognitive distortions under those conditions of stress. We are more likely to think in "all or nothing" terms or experience any one of a number of distortions in cognition that can increase interpersonal misunderstanding and raise blood pressure quickly.[52]

What stress is my teen under? *Doing homework, being with friends, and living for free?* you might think. Our final section shines a light on what teens think about and experience as the problems of adolescence, and you'll see they are under a lot of stress. Once you read the last section, you might want to ponder: *Do these things influence the quality, intensity, and ability to regulate their mood, in addition to the normal factors having to do brain development?*

What Do Teens Say Are Their Problems?

If time (and book space) had permitted, I would have loved to do a large survey on just what teens feel are their problems *with* parents. I think it would be helpful for you to know how teenagers, in general, see this question, since we've been primarily focusing on what parents see as the "big problems." So in the place of a survey study, I'm drawing on years of an informal study, done simply by keeping a list of what teens have told me in my clinical practice about the kinds of things they are dealing with that feel like "big problems." Here's the list, below. You might want to really study this list, because I believe it describes a lot of what normally goes in your son or daughter's head, when they get to thinking about what is happening in life.[53]

What Teens Normally Think Are the "Big Problems"

What do I do when I get angry? Upset? Anxious? What level of feeling is normal? What do I do when I feel out of control?

What do I do if I'm hurting/depressed/suicidal? Do I tell anyone?

What do I do about making/keeping friends, bullying, harassment, rumors, and gossip? Am I "in" or "out"? How do I get "in," or do I give up on that or pretend it doesn't matter? What do I do when friends are in trouble?

What do I do when what I feel and want is different from what my parents feel and want? How do I balance what I want/need with what others want?

How much and what kind of alcohol and/or drugs should I have? How do I get it? How do I not get in trouble? How do I say "no"?

What behaviors on the sexual spectrum are okay to do, what do they mean, what do they obligate me to? What is my sexual identity? Am I gay, straight, bisexual, transgender? What do I do about that? Do I tell my parents? What do I do about how I feel? Will this knowledge make me rejectable?

What do I look like—am I cute/hot, etc.? Do others notice? Do I want the attention? For girls: If I'm developing breasts, having my period, etc., what does it mean and how can I manage using those changes to create relationships versus getting unwanted attention, demands, wishes as a result of bodily changes? What do I need to do about my body (lose weight, gain weight, hide it)? For guys: Am I good looking? How do I deal with my sexual feelings (having them or not having them)?

Why can't I control my brain and what do I do about it?

How do I stop or control/direct my thinking, especially if it is focused on something negative?

Am I crazy, sick, lazy, depressed, or abnormal? What is my "definition" as regards the things I don't understand? How much of a problem is it?

If you (my parent) is depressed, angry, abusive, withdrawn, etc., how do I not abandon you, but get as much time away from you as possible? Do I have to feel what my parents feel? What my friends feel?

How can I make my parents happy and not feel like a total baby...or like I'm betraying myself? How much like my parents do I have to be to be loved?

How can I have fun and enjoy myself without feeling too guilty, embarrassed, ashamed, or humiliated?

How much do I try to measure up to what I see on television, movies, etc.?

How can I get the stuff I want? How much is too much to have and still be a good person?

How can I not be embarrassed?

How is what went wrong my fault? How is what went wrong not my fault?

Why don't you "get it"? Who does...and how can I be with *them* more without making you feel too bad?

And last but not least, the thing every teenager asks themselves, struggles with, and is constantly trying to figure out, if someone they love is hurting, angry, or in pain of any kind:

What is the cause of the pain? How long will it last? How much of my life will be affected?

Teenagers (and adults) have a very, very hard time moving on and turning their conscious and nonconscious energies toward healthy development, until they get an answer to that last question, in relation to their own or another close person's suffering. *How* they answer that question will determine how well they grieve, so they need your close help with that question. As I'm fond of saying, "Living *is* grieving." Your teen needs help thinking about his identity as a person who has strengths *and* weaknesses, problems *and* solutions. Your teen needs help understanding that some of her "big problems" are normal, but that is a fine line to walk. You can't help her realize that some of her problems are normal, developmentally, by telling her not to worry about them or by any other form of minimization. That will, in fact, *increase* the strength and intensity of how she brings her questions (her "problem" behaviors) to your doorstep. *Identity formation* is a complex set of processes, and we'll turn our attention to that next.

Practical Help Tips

1) Whatever intervention or strategy you choose with your son or daughter will only be as good as the emotional state you are in when you implement the strategy.

2) Your behavior and feelings are always teaching something to your teen. Just *what* your behavior and feelings teach is something you can be more aware of and have more control over.

3) Adolescents lie because we model the behavior for them early on, but also because they're trying to preserve their relationships with us. If your teen knows it makes you happy to hear the truth, and you're willing to listen to their explanations—even to the point of arguing and debating some about the reasons for their choices—they'll lie less often and provide you with more of the information you need to help keep them safe.

4) Teen behaviors—especially the more problematic behaviors—are questions. Their behaviors are ways of figuring out how to get better, safer, more effective means of accomplishing the goals they were aiming for in their "troublesome" behavior.

5) Brain development research is in its infancy and is often done with animal studies. Beware of mass-media dissemination of study results.

6) Helping your teen understand, articulate, and regulate his or her emotions are arguably the most important tasks during middle and high school. Emotionality and reasoning are neither separate nor opposed brain processes. Arguments and negotiation help develop needed brain/life skills for teens.

7) Digital media are changing the way teens think, feel, and behave. If we only focus on the *content* of those media, we lose the message—that the influences of digital media are bi-directional, powerful, and pervasive.

8) Forget about nature versus nurture. (The "versus" is the problem. It's not either/or, it's both/and.)

9) Imaging studies help begin to explain why teens take risks, lie, make so many misjudgments (and need to)...but they do not prove that adolescents *must* rebel or get into trouble.

10) Effects of myelination, over-proliferation of neurons, and neural pruning during adolescence mean that the prefrontal cortex and other parts of the brain are unfinished: The amygdalae and central cortical systems may at times, for some teens, hold sway over more analytically based information processing; the result can be an increase in misunderstanding and conflict.

11) Teens absolutely need safe places/privacy to practice and fail at many things, and many opportunities to do so. Good judgment comes from experience, which comes from bad judgment.

12) But teens also need to hear from us: Harm and risk-taking is reduced around sexual behaviors and drugs/alcohol use when ongoing conversations take place at home.

13) Alcohol, marijuana, and nicotine are drugs of choice, in that order. The span of 10–18 is a crucial time for brain development and drugs/alcohol may have permanent effects.

14) Teens say that the parent-teen relationship is still the most crucial one, despite their reliance on friends.

15) Teens in general develop more perseverance, work harder, use less drugs/alcohol, have less contact with the law, and report more satisfactory relationships when they talk more often with their parents, have family meals together, and have clear, consistent limits (and can argue the limits).

16) Try to understand the difference between arguing and disrespect and help teens maintain important relationships and repair strains in those relationships.

17) Do less. Deal with your guilt/worry separately. Do very little for your teens if they don't interact with you with respect *and* take the lead. It's all about intrinsic motivation.

18) Global praise is counterproductive in a variety of different ways: It induces task avoidance, dependence (less autonomy), anxiety, risk aversion, and withdrawal.

19) Let others support you in gathering all this information; don't do it all alone.

20) See A. Rae Simpson's smart and thorough 2001 report (The Harvard Parenting Study) for highlights on specific recommendations for parenting teens, based on an overview of researches, studies, and practice. Check out her new website, too, at http://hrweb. mit.edu/worklife/raising-teens/

Practical Help Tips, Part II: Weighing Interventions with "The Big Problems"

1) ***Before you intervene,*** try to ask yourself:

a) Am I interfering with my child's learning something important if I rescue them or get involved?

b) Am I intervening too soon or with too much information (am I overindulging them)?

c.) Who is this about? Am I doing something to meet my own needs or my child's needs?

d) What will be the likely results of violating their boundaries/privacy/trust?

e) Is there another way to get the information I need to help them be safe, without directly violating their privacy?

f) Have I taken into account, in crafting a response:

   i) My own developmental stage

   ii) My own temperament

   iii) My recent past behavior and individual history

   iv) My family history

   v) My current mood and ability to have a calm conversation

   vi) My level of education about the issues involved in the problem

g) Have I taken into account, in crafting a response:

   i) My teen's developmental level and mental health capacities

   ii) My teen's temperament

   iii) My teen's past behavior and individual history

   iv) My teen's family history

   v) My teen's current mood and ability to have a calm conversation

   vi) My teen's level of education about the issues involved in the problem

Suggested Reading: *The Big Problems*

The lists in the "Suggested Reading" sections are by no means comprehensive. I'm including what I consider to be the most informative, practical, relevant, or comprehensive readings on the topic(s) of the chapter. In other words, if you have limited time, these are the works I believe you might want to explore first. It doesn't mean all of these books are "easy reads." Sometimes a listed book will be very difficult, but worth the time.

Coontz, S. *The Way We Never Were: American Families and The Nostalgia Trap.* New York: Basic Books, 1993.

Cooperman, S. A., & Gilbert, S. D. *Living with Eating Disorders (Teen's Guides).* New York: Checkmark Books, 2009.

Costin, C. *The Eating Disorder Sourcebook: A Comprehensive Guide to the Causes, Treatments, and Prevention of Eating Disorders.* New York: McGraw-Hill, 1999.

Dellasega, C. *The Starving Family: Caregiving Mothers and Fathers Share Their Eating Disorder Wisdom.* Wisconsin: Champion Press, 2005.

Kurcinka, M. S. *Kids, Parents, and Power Struggles: Winning for a Lifetime.* New York: Harper Paperbacks, 2001.

MacKenzie, R. J. *Setting Limits with Your Strong-Willed Child: Eliminating Conflict by Establishing Clear, Firm, and Respectful Boundaries.* New York: Three Rivers Press, 2001.

Nelsen, J. N, & Erwin, C. *Parents Who Love Too Much: How Good Parents Can Learn to Love More Wisely and Develop Children of Character.* New York: Three Rivers Press, 2000.

Nelsen, J. N., & Glenn, H. S. *Raising Self-Reliant Children in a Self-Indulgent World: Seven Building Blocks for Developing Capable Young People.* New York: Prima Lifestyles, 1988.

Nelsen, J. N., Lott, L., & Glenn, H. S. *Positive Discipline A-Z, Revised and Expanded 2nd Edition: From Toddlers to Teens, 1001 Solutions to Everyday Parenting Problems.* New York: Three Rivers Press, 1999.

Neumark-Sztainer, D. *"I'm, Like, SO Fat": Helping Your Teen Make Healthy Choices about Eating and Exercise in a Weight-Obsessed World.* New York: The Guilford Press, 2005.

Ponton, L. *The Romance of Risk: Why Teenagers Do the Things They Do.* New York: Basic Books, 1998.

Riera, M. *Uncommon Sense for Parents of Teenagers.* Berkeley: Celestial Arts, 1995.

Seligman, M. E. *The Optimistic Child: Proven Program to Safeguard Children from Depression & Build Lifelong Resilience.* New York: Harper Paperbacks, 2005.

Simmons, R. *Odd Girl Out: The Hidden Culture of Aggression in Girls.* New York: Mariner Books, 2003.

Wallerstein, J. S. *What About the Kids? Raising Your Children Before, During, and After Divorce.* New York: Hyperion, 2003.

3

Identity Development, Relationships, and Status

Not long ago, a trend started on YouTube, the most popular site worldwide for teens who are interacting with online video content.[1] Young girls—as young as 9 or 10—began posting homemade videos posing the same question, "Am I Pretty?" This trend was followed by an increase in related video postings with preteen and teen girls asking, "Am I *Ugly*?"

Aided by a computer (usually located in the bedroom), a webcam, and minimal digital media skills (with video uploading), the girls tell their stories: "I'm called ugly at school; leave me comments and let me know whether or not I'm pretty." Some young girls try to cajole their imagined audiences, providing "nice" pictures of themselves, taking down their hair and smiling the best smile they can muster. And boy, do they get comments. Most of them are horrific: "Not even a paper bag would work!" writes one of the less vitriolic commentators. "You're a fat, ugly pig, you make me throw up!" writes another who chose not to hold anything back. Not all of the comments are mean or negative; some provide the self-esteem and confidence-boosting feedback these girls long for, telling them they're "truly beautiful" or "gorgeous just the way they are." Some comments—possibly from worried parents—warn the girls to stop the activity altogether, fearing the activity will lead to depression and even suicide.

Early in 2012, one of the rather pretty, shy middle-school girls who posted a video online was invited to appear on *Good Morning America* to talk about her Am I Pretty/Am I Ugly video. As it turns she wasn't quite in middle school. Sophia Roessler was 21 years old and apparently an artist doing an experiment. She posted this explanation online:

> PLEASE READ: I am a 21 year old artist, and I made this video
> four months ago as a piece about the struggles a girl transitioning into

womanhood must go through. It is a difficult and confusing experience, and my video aims to express some of the feelings associated with this uncertain period of life. The video acted as a social experiment as well as commentary on this disturbing trend, and has recently gained a lot of media attention, from jezebel.com to Good Morning America. Part of the reason I made this video is because I understand where these girls are coming from on a personal level. I'm sure many commenters on other videos, as they have with my video, say that beauty comes from within. I completely agree with this, but you hear it a lot and it can lose its meaning. What I want to say is this: no one in middle school thinks they are pretty. Even the girls that you think are perfect are also insecure. Love yourself for who you are, or a lot of time will be wasted standing in front of a mirror nit picking about something other people don't even notice. Don't hate yourself for no reason. The sooner you start loving yourself the sooner life gets easier. Adolescence is something that every one experiences, and most people say middle school was the worst time of their life. It was for me, but it's gone uphill from there, high school was better, and college was great. Some features that I like all of the time, and some features I like only some of the time. You are beautiful and unique and if anyone says otherwise, it is because they are insecure, and making other people feel bad makes them feel better. Now get off the internet and go eat ice cream!!!! here is a interview I did with the Kansas City Star: www.kansascity.com2012/02/24/3450112/kc-students-am-i-pretty-video.html.

Date: 3/3/12
Views: 191276

There is so much about this phenomenon that repeats, recapitulates, and reinvents other adolescent and adult experiences. First of all, this young woman was engaging in a kind of *identity play* online, which involved the deliberate misrepresentation of her age and the purpose of her activity. For Sophia, she's in the process of formulating and implementing her own online values and ethics—and these evidently include lying and misrepresentation in an *experiment* that does not include *consent* of her subjects. I'm pretty sure the human subjects review committees at most colleges and universities would pause before they approved Sophia's project.

The "Am I Pretty" videos echo the proliferation of "Hot or Not" websites, photos, and videos of the 1990s which showed (mostly women) in all states of dress and undress, asking to be "rated" on a 1 to 10 scale. Little "quizzes" and "tests" still abound on sites like Facebook, providing some kind of rating of the overall degree of "hotness," "sexiness," or "interestingness." And like much of online behavior, people say and do things they would never do "in real life," as strangers leave horribly severe feedback for the young people using the medium to get an always-needed boost of confidence and self-esteem.

However shocking, this phenomenon should not be surprising, if you consider the characteristics of teens, the characteristics of digital media, and what happens when you combine the two. That's what the next chapter is all about. The "Am I Pretty?" videos are just one of many examples that demonstrate that any investigation of adolescent identity formation in America cannot ignore the bidirectional, mutually influencing effects of digital media on youth. Online and connected: That's now the primary cultural context for adolescent identity formation. And we'll soon see the implications of the primary tasks of adolescence being carried out in the digital world: *For American teens, identity formation, relationships, and status—and anxiety over status—are all of one piece, mediated by digital media.*

The Rise of Research on Adolescents

The last 25 years could have been called "the quarter-century of the adolescent." The 1990s and the past decade have seen a tremendous rise in the sheer number of pages devoted to understanding the teenager. Professor Laurence Steinberg, from my *alma mater* Temple University—and one of the preeminent researchers on adolescent development—notes that the empirical study of adolescents barely existed just 25 years ago. As mentioned in the Introduction, most of the 20th century produced three major figures writing about adolescent identity and development: Sigmund Freud, Jean Piaget, Erik Erikson, and that's about it. That doesn't mean that intelligent others were not interested in adolescents or did not write about them, but the work of Freud and Erikson dominated the landscape. Erikson taught at a private school in Vienna, trained at the Vienna Psychoanalytic Institute, went through psychoanalysis himself, and was an acquaintance with Freud's daughter Anna. Erikson continued Freud's work, even as came to disagree with significant aspects. It's interesting to note that he also studied with Maria Montessori—herself a pioneer in understanding childhood and identity development.[2]

After the development of Erikson's theory of *identity formation* in adolescence, most of the new research centered on just what you might expect—the question of why adolescents were doing the kinds of problematic things that drove parents nuts. Most research attempted to do what this book is attempting to do, which is to deemphasize the ironclad link between "adolescents" and "problems." Most of that research was unsuccessful in decoupling the focus on problems with adolescence itself. The process of adolescents developing a cohesive, continuous sense of their own identity—a process identified by Erikson as the *normative* developmental course—has been primarily studied from the perspective of what goes *wrong*, rather than what goes *right*.

Today, many of Piaget's theories about cognitive development have been demonstrated as outmoded, and the shift has gone to "information-processing" models dominated by the computer-calculation metaphor of processing. Laurence Steinberg's and Amanda Morris's 2001 review of adolescent development frameworks notes that Erikson's work is basically still taught in schools, although rarely studied empirically.[3] But the studies in the last 25 years have shown a high degree of agreement about some things related to adolescence.

For example, most research has shown that just because teens have problems *during* adolescence doesn't mean those are "problems *of* adolescence." Many teens get drunk and abuse alcohol during adolescence. That *could* be *problematic*. However, most teens do not develop alcohol-use disorders—that would be a problem *of* adolescence, if the developmental period were highly associated with certain negative outcomes. In addition, problems like depression or anxiety often have roots that predate adolescence; the meeting up of adolescence with earlier difficulties in mood regulation can *deepen* a problem—or trigger a new version of it—but not necessarily be the "cause" of the problem. Most of the research has also agreed that arguing and dissension in the ranks increases with the onset of puberty and that Mom gets most of the brunt of that arguing—sorry, moms.

Despite the lack of interest in the ongoing empirical validation of Erikson's theories—and shifts in the foci of current research driven by imaging studies and brain development concerns—his theories persist and are still elegant and useful. Steinberg and Morris's review highlights many of the researches over the last 25 years of looking at adolescent identity formation—this in combination with Erikson's earlier work will give you a starting point for thinking about what identity development means. But the real changes in the last 20 years have much less to do with the sorts of components that make up a sense of stable identity and much more to do with *the means by which and contexts in which* teenagers now attempt to form a more adult sense of self. You got a taste of that in the opening of this chapter.

The Major Components of Identity Formation

In Erikson's books *Childhood and Society* and *Identity: Youth and Crisis* (as well as other works), he described a view of lifespan development (the "Eight Ages of Man") and specifically adolescent development. Each of the eight "ages" referred to a psychosocial *stage* that each person passes through, from birth until death. Erikson divided the stages of adulthood into three "ages" including young adulthood, middle age, and older adulthood. This is a stage theory, not an age theory, meaning that there are no rigidly set chronological ages that begin or end any particular stage. Erikson, too, thought in terms of *epigenetics*, and understood the formation of identity as being the result of biology and environment.

Erikson formed his theory, in part, through naturalistic observation—through the study of the Oglala Lakotaone—one of the seven tribes of the Lakota people, part of the Great Sioux Nation. At the time of Erikson's study, the Lakota peoples' way of life was in tremendous upheaval, having been subject to a series of wars, forced relocation onto reservations, and treaties broken by the American government. They had taken from them their interdependent relationship with the buffalo—their main source of sustenance—and day-to-day life was an echo of its former powerful rhythm, thanks to one of the more shameful historical policies of the American government. But this was a valuable time to consider how the most vulnerable in a social group—the children—negotiate the entry into an adult life and adult roles that are no longer clear, well demarcated, and solid.

No doubt through observation of a struggling people, Erikson strongly believed that our biology and biography in combination provided each person with a set of eight major stages to be traversed over the course of a lifetime. He wrote, too, of "sensitive" periods during which a crisis—corresponding to the eight ages (or stages)—needed to be avoided or resolved, before moving into the next stage. It's not exactly accurate to put it that way since the individual *moves into each subsequent stage with whatever level of crisis resolution they've achieved*; life doesn't wait for us to "get it right." If the sensitive period is passed and the crisis of that stage resolved, the individual takes with them a psychosocial *virtue* or *strength*. If the individual does not resolve the crisis of that particular period, he or she acquires a certain *danger* and *vulnerability* that carries forward.

For example, if the fourth stage ("Industry vs. Inferiority")—the one associated with middle childhood/elementary school—is successfully negotiated with others, then your daughter learns the pleasures and rewards of task mastery; she learns to do things correctly, well, and to an internal as well as an external *standard*. She gains the strength of *competence*. But if things are not well-negotiated during this period, she will not feel competent and industrious; instead she will begin to associate feelings of frustration, hindrance, and *inferiority* with her growing sense of self. This is the stage of *tools, technology, and task mastery*. In Chapter 9 we'll discuss the connection between task mastery and self-esteem. It's important to say, now, though, that the "degree" or quality of your preteen's self-esteem as he or she *prepares to enter adolescence* is crucial.

When writers talk about the "eight stages" and adolescence in general, they often skip over consideration of this fourth stage—but the beginning of adolescent identity cannot be adequately considered without looking at it. The fourth stage has so much bearing on thinking about identity formation in the digital world:

> [S]ince industry involves doing things beside and with others, a first
> sense of division of labor and of differential opportunity, that is, a sense of

the *technological ethos* of a culture, develops at this time. We have pointed in the last section to the danger threatening individual and society, where the schoolchild begins to feel that the color of his skin, the background of his parents, or the fashion of his clothes rather than his wish and his will to learn will decide his worth as an apprentice, and thus his sense of *identity*...[4]

It's important to pause for a second and consider what Erikson is saying about the "technological ethos" of a culture. First of all, the word *ethos* comes from the Greek, denoting character or the morals or ideals of a community. *Ethos* is the "accustomed place," or habitat. It's a word with some fascinating meanings and uses, all of which are worthwhile in thinking about adolescents. The word has connections to Orpheus and the Orphic mythology of music having the power to transform the hearer—whether a rock or a human! *Ethos* can refer to the power of music to change the very behavior, emotions, morals, and spirit of the listener. *Ethos* is related to *ethikos,* the Greek origin of the English *ethics*. I think that Erikson was evoking all of these meanings in suggesting that the school-age child was learning about what was expected of him or her with regard to the world of inner effort and outer work. This orientation to work alongside and with others is related to character formation and leading an ethical life. In order to enter the adult world of others and be able to "make a living," the child needs to be able to learn and have an *active wish to learn* that is not overshadowed by an undue focus on a lack of technological skill and mastery, inability to work alongside others (difficulty forming friendships and mutual relationships), or the pervasive dangers of racism or anxiety over status.

I'm continually *amazed* that Erikson first wrote this in *1950,* and that's partly why I'm utilizing his work to talk about the contemporary aspects of identity formation. This one paragraph still speaks to the current challenges (and dangers) surrounding identity formation, because it points to the links between status, relationship formation, and the *technological ethos* of the culture, racism, learning, character, and ethical development. In 2012 America, the *technological ethos* of the culture appears to point to a kind of Internet-based Orphic machine, with the power to change (or at least shape) the behavior, emotions, and ethics of the listeners. Teens are listening intently to this "music" in a world of skills and tools constituted increasingly by computers and acumen with digital media.

Identity formation doesn't just spring forth in adolescence. As with other human capacities and developmental achievements, identity formation is an *additive* process. Earlier developments help make subsequent developments possible. So, preteens (elementary-age children), according to Erikson, are (hopefully) moving into adolescence having forged a successful relationship with the "world of skills and tools," from the contexts of school and play.

Children pass through four stages *on the way* to the main stage of early adolescence, "Identity vs. Role Confusion,"[5] and one stage *afterward,* as early adulthood begins.

1. *Trust vs. Mistrust* (Infancy)
   Child develops a belief that the environment can be counted on to meet his or her basic physiological and social needs.

2. *Autonomy vs. Shame and Doubt* (Toddlerhood)
   Child learns what he/she can control and develops a sense of free will and corresponding sense of regret and sorrow for inappropriate use of self-control.

3. *Initiative vs. Guilt* (Early Childhood)
   Child learns to begin action, to explore, to imagine as well as feeling remorse for actions.

4. *Industry vs. Inferiority* (Middle Childhood/Elementary School)
   Child learns to do things well or correctly in comparison to a standard or to others.

5. *Identity vs. Role Confusion* (Adolescence)
   Develops a sense of self in relationship to others and to own internal thoughts and desires. (Later work has shown two substages: a *social identity* focusing on which group a person will identify with; and a *personal identity* focusing on abilities, goals, possibilities, and the like.)

6. *Intimacy vs. Isolation* (Young Adult)
   Develops ability to give and receive love; begins to make long-term commitment to relationships.

Steinberg and his colleague pointed out that the description of developmental tasks at each stage has held up well over time, but the *timing* of the stages—particularly the intense identity formation behaviors of adolescence—have been shown to occur much *later, and not with the onset of puberty.* This probably matches most of our experiences as parents, as does the delay or lengthening of the fifth stage, which Erikson calls "this most decisive stage," well into our teenagers' early 20s. As expected, the timing of the stages of adolescent development would be related to socioeconomic and other environmental factors.[6] Erikson wrote that "childhood proper comes to an end, Youth begins." And with the beginning and

121

progressive development of Youth, goes a series of identity formation tasks to be negotiated:

1. Deal with new ways of thinking and feeling about *sameness* and *continuity*

2. Deal with a rapidly changing body, including significant changes in reproductive organs

3. Deal with a constantly palpable concern and anxiety over how you look (physically, socially, and psychologically) in the eyes of others

4. Linking up the skills you learned in childhood with adult-like and adult-sanctioned activities, without appearing to be a child

5. Find models and mentors for your "final identity" and, related, find new "adversaries" in the fight for your own sense of self

6. Develop a solid sense of who "I am," but in the context of pressures to fit certain *prescribed* social roles demarcated by friends, family, class, ethnicity, and the like; this sense of who you are must fill certain social obligations and roles around industriousness, e.g., "finding a career"

7. Figure out your sexual identity—what you desire, like, love, and how that takes shape in behavior and self-identification

It's a wonder any of us get through this partial list of tasks. They sound like full-time jobs to me. And on top of this, we ask our teens to go to school and actually learn something useful—and keep their wish and will to learn! When these main tasks of identity formation do not go well, the danger faced is "role confusion." Erikson noted the extra pressures that LGBTQQ (Lesbian, Gay, Bisexual, Transgender, Queer, and Questioning) kids face—although he didn't use the acronym in 1950 (or 1963, when his second edition of *Child and Society* was published). But he did note that kids whose sexual identity was in question or doubt had a special vulnerability to disorders of mood. Likewise, if teens cannot find an occupation or "sense" of career, they too face this vulnerability, feeling that they do not know where they belong. A teen, Erikson notes, can *over-identify* with the "heroes of cliques and crowds," to compensate for the lack of a coherent feeling of self-identity. This makes access—24/7/365 access—to media celebrities (actors and actresses), sports figures, popular musicians potentially more problematic as teens either fail to maintain or measure up to the idols and their lifestyles.

In this stage, the identification (and over-identification) with heroes is a kind of practice for falling in love—which Erikson notes has only peripheral connections to sexuality. This kind of "falling in love" is more about seeking and discovering one's own desired-identity-in-process "reflected and gradually clarified" in another person. We fall in love with the qualities of others we wish ourselves to have. The process of seeing your own identity reflected back to you requires the beginnings of a more mutual way of relating. Erikson notes, poignantly, "This is the reason why so much of young love is *conversation* [italics mine]." If Erikson were living today he might say, "This is the reason why so much of young love *should* be conversation—preferably offline."

Role confusion can also result when your teen struggles to find *any* place to belong, at school, with friends, or in the neighborhood. Erikson spoke about the pain of exclusion during this period, pointing to the cruelty of being "out" when you so much want to be "in"—whatever the grouping. Exclusion on the basis of skin color, fashion, aesthetics, cultural background, and all types of preferences, including sexual, are equally painful, particularly as "difference" is celebrated (intellectually) while it is often punished in practice. These kinds of exclusion and intolerance—and the establishment of who and what is "in" and who and what is "out"—suggest another danger that I'm quite certain Erikson would be writing about today, if he were alive: *adolescent anxiety over status.*

Erikson sounds like a kind, well-meaning (research psychologist) parent when he cautions that "such intolerance [is] a defense against identity confusion." I think he's probably very correct, but I'm not sure how many teens would be assuaged by hearing, "She's just being mean because *she* doesn't know who *she* wants to be, yet!" If you know *your* teen, you'll know if this will work or not.

Identity formation also involves teens acting in ways that even *they* don't really believe in, but need to try on in an effort to find a cohesive sense of self amidst many roles and peer pressures. Many teens are busy (nonconsciously) testing you, other adults, and especially their peers to find out about their own and others' capacities to do what they say they'll do and be loyal and committed. Commitments and promises made and broken provide the testing grounds of a developing teen's identity. Speaking of promises made and broken, Erikson speaks of the teen mind as "an ideological mind," one that is keenly and continually searching for the kind of personal and social values that would organize identity and serve as a guide in the adult world. In this way, the teen mind is essentially *political*, wondering consciously and nonconsciously whether they would make a good leader and whether those that do become the "leaders" in the adult world will serve the world well. Teens must therefore constantly measure the distance between what people say and what they do, and in a related way, keep a tender eye on who they are versus who they wish to be, without becoming cynical, apathetic, or harshly critical of self or other in the process. This points to the virtue or psychosocial strength that Erikson believed that an adolescent would gain by successfully achieving "ego identity" and avoiding the "identity crisis" of adolescence: *fidelity.*

The concepts of fidelity and *agency* are complexly related and are not explored in depth here.[7] I touched on the idea of fidelity in the Introduction as the *ability to see the world as it is—flawed and imperfect and full of setbacks and roadblocks—and to persevere, to commit, to stay engaged with the world of self and others, despite what a mess it is.* A teen that emerges from this stage successfully will see the good and bad in the world, others, and himself, but can and does makes *commitments* that are *freely pledged,* by someone with integrity, a sense of authorship and agency. Erikson stressed the importance of this experience of "freely choosing" to commit, and knew that it had lifelong implications. He was referring to the possibility of finding a partner, forming a mutual, long-lasting relationship, a community to belong to and help build, a career in which to thrive, and the ability to form long-lasting friendships in an ever-changing world, with ever-changing role requirements. In gaining the guiding value of *fidelity* we also see the crucial need to *persevere* in the face of difficulties, since "success" with any of those life goals—career, family, friends, community—is never a once-and-done proposition. We must often try again and again, adjusting along the way.

As noted earlier, the identity formation tasks of adolescence require the strengths hard won in earlier stages. Those strengths, he writes, must be *tested* in each subsequent stage; the strength gained in one stage allows the developing child to *take chances* in the next stage. After the *Identity vs. Role Confusion* stage, what comes next?

> He is ready for intimacy, that is, the capacity to commit himself to concrete affiliations and partnerships and to develop the ethical strength to abide by such commitments, even though they may call for significant sacrifices and compromises.[8]

Erikson's still-vital work points in the direction of some of the most interesting and potentially difficult challenges for teens in 2012—the creation of an identity capable of perseverance, commitment, and "the ethical strength to abide by such commitments."

Adolescents and Status Anxiety in America

We have already explored the idea, and will return to it repeatedly in this book, that American adolescent identity development is bound up in the notion of a self that comes to blossom with others, because of others, and under the anxiously imagined gaze of peers. In other words, identity is about *self in context* and *related autonomy*. It is not about "separation," *per se*. This is an outdated notion, that adolescents "separate" from their parents and caregivers during this developmental period. American popular consumer culture, specifically, is set up to help kids feel they are entering adulthood through the acquisition of status and its rewards. Teens learn to want more, feel entitled to more, and ride the conveyer belt of a never-ending cycle of material desires, albeit without much education about or a felt sense of what it might feel like to really belong or feel "satisfied."

While plenty of books are marketed to teens (and parents of teens) aimed at helping them navigate the teenage years, none address directly the issue of *status anxiety* as a critical reason for teens' unhappiness. Many books address some symptoms of adolescent unhappiness, such as body image problems and "low self-esteem," but I have yet to read anything that puts anxiety over status squarely in the center of the despair I see so often in teens at school and in my psychotherapy office.

Madeline Levine's *The Price of Privilege* and Denise Clark Pope's *Doing School* are two stellar recent examples of literature rooted in research showing that many teenagers—especially the more affluent ones—are depressed, unhappy with their bodies, under a great deal of stress, and emotionally unprepared for college.[9] It is no coincidence that Madeline, Denise, and myself are all located in and writing from the Northern California Bay Area, all within shouting distance of Silicon Valley—the leading wealth and innovation generator of California and arguably of the United States. Those two books outline how, despite stereotypes of privilege, more affluent teens are in the kind of crisis of identity of which Erikson wrote. It seems clear that the acquisition of wealth is not a buffer against this crisis, and may actually engender some adolescents' stress. In our culture, many teens believe they have the right to be rich, to acquire high-profile publicity, celebrity good looks, and high-status jobs, and these beliefs are causing great distress among young people, especially to the degree that it is getting harder to attain those goals.

This section aims to provide you with some tools to understand how the phenomenon of *status anxiety* is at the heart of many teens' problems and threads its way into what many have come to feel is the "natural" angst of teenage years. I don't believe this anxiety is at all "natural," but the ubiquity of digital media and their pervasive orientation toward self-representation make it very easy to conflate status with true peer acceptance and belonging. It quickly becomes too easy, therefore, for American young people to feel it is somehow natural and normal to hate yourself for not having what your peers have.[10]

With the national housing and global financial markets in tenuous condition, having barely survived collapse, families scrambling to salvage their 401(k), and fiscal insecurity the rule for a growing majority, what do we now know *for certain* will be the rewards of hard work? I'm not being entirely facetious when I say that even cheating to get ahead isn't paying off as reliably it used to. What happens to a teen's worldview—and developing sense of self—when all the things they saw their parents reach for to secure their status and broadcast their success may no longer be available? As a psychotherapist, educator, and speaker on adolescent trends and issues since 1995, I've come across tens of thousands of teens that cannot separate their own true and authentic passions from the uncanny experience that they are constantly performing for an audience. They believe their rewards for "great performances" as son, daughter, athlete, or student are fame, celebrity good looks, money, a great job, and everything America promises as high-status success. But these same teens—the so-called "good" kids with skyrocketing rates of depression, suicide, alcohol and drug use, self-injury, and crippling anxiety—wonder why all their stellar academic achievement, acceptance at prestigious universities, fancy cars, expensive vacations, connected friends, and hot partners leave them feeling empty, lost, and fraudulent rather than happy and satisfied. It sickens me that this past fall saw a record number of suicides in some of the most "successful" Bay Area public and private schools.

I don't think we need another self-help book for teens, though. In some ways these books are part of the problem, because the genre can focus almost exclusively on the *individual,* and the very individualized sense of self that is cultivated by forces of state and market. This form of self-help often (deliberately) forgets to situate the self in the contexts of history, culture, media, or society. These kinds of books make it easy to hate yourself for not being happy—which, given the technologies and sciences of how to be happy, means that there is something wrong with your very self.

I hope this chapter, and the entire book (on final analysis) brings together the critical insights of author Alain de Botton, who pleads for a need to find "more than one way to be a success at life," and the cautionary wisdom of cultural critic John Culkin, who believed so strongly that in a dynamic democracy and market economy, "intelligent and critical consumers are likely to end up as the best kinds of humans."

> That the manufacture of consent is capable of great refinements no one, I think, denies. The process by which public opinions arise is certainly no less intricate than it has appeared in these pages and the opportunities for manipulation open to anyone who understands the process are plain enough.

> The creation of consent is not a new art. It is a very old one that was supposed to have died out with the appearance of democracy. But it has not died out. It has, in fact, improved enormously in technic, because it is

now based on analysis rather than on rule of thumb. And so, as a result of psychological research, coupled with the modern means of communication, the practice of democracy has turned a corner. A revolution is taking place, infinitely more significant than any shifting of economic power.

Within the life of the generation now in control of affairs, persuasion has become a self-conscious art and a regular organ of popular government. None of us begins to understand the consequences, but it is no daring prophecy to say that the knowledge of how to create consent will alter every political calculation and modify every political premise... It has been demonstrated that we cannot rely upon intuition, conscience, or the accidents of casual opinion if we are to deal with the world beyond our reach.[11]

American writer, reporter, and political commentator Walter Lippmann wrote these rather prescient words almost 100 years ago. The *lifeworld* of the teenager, almost completely defined by the influences of the state and the market, feels/appears natural to the teenager, even as the source for rebellion against the awesome forces of the consumer markets. Teens might rebel against consumer culture, but they still go on Facebook, YouTube, and MySpace, wear the same jeans, want the same cache due to how they dress, how they speak, what music they listen to, how they have sex and with whom. Whatever you think of the Occupy movement, it's worth noting that it wasn't a couple weeks after the protests began and people were getting pepper-sprayed in the streets that popular culture icon Jay-Z was busy selling (and making a profit) on "We are the 99%" T-shirts and apparel.

The market sees things differently than you do.[12] For example, in their online advertisement for services, U.K. market research firm Intersperience note how the purpose of their business is to "bring us closer to the thoughts and actions of customers, in the moment, as it happens." They and thousands of other similar companies are watching your online activity like a hawk for clues to how, what, when, where you make purchases and how you go about making these decisions.

Facebook, Google, and MySpace are powerful market research instruments, as are most of the instruments of "democratic youth culture"—the wider cultural context in which teen identities are forged. When your teen (or you) go on Facebook and talk about what you *want* and what you *like,* and you click that little thumbs-up sign, it enables corporations and market researchers to discover, reinforce, and persuade you to buy what they're selling. This same company, Intersperience, released some of the results of an extensive survey in 2012 demonstrating that a significant number of U.K. consumers would feel "sad" or "lonely" if deprived of online connection:

The project, which surveyed a nationally representative sample of more than 1,000 individuals aged from 18 to over 65, included a challenge to participants to get through one full day without using technology and to record their reactions to the experience. While the idea of no Internet had prompted widespread anxiety, people reacted just as, if not even more strongly, to the prospect of foregoing technology altogether, even for 24 hours. Giving up technology was considered by some to be as hard as quitting smoking or drinking, while one survey participant described it as "like having my hand chopped off."[13]

"Hand chopped off," indeed. Whether or not this information makes Intersperience CEO Paul Hudson happy, I don't know. But I do know that *knowing* this information—and the much more extensive and expensive information you can buy from Intersperience or Axciom or hundreds of other companies like this—makes advertisers very happy indeed. This is not a secret (anymore), and this propensity and strength of connecting via digital media is what feels "natural" in the lifeworld of the teenager.

WORRY ABOUT STATUS: HOW TO FAIL WITHOUT FAILING

Status and status anxiety are descriptions of phenomena that deeply impact everyone living in the United States. In 2004 Alain de Botton published one of *those* books. I mean, the kind of book that changed how I think about and organize my life, like Mike Riera's *Uncommon Sense for Parents with Teenagers* did for me, six years prior. De Botton, a philosopher and social critic, wrote *Status Anxiety,* and while that book is mainly about adults and anxiety over status, it quickly got me thinking about how easy it is for teenagers to secretly hate themselves and have confusion about their roles in America.

I am primarily concerned about status and the American *teenager* because worry over status can lead to depression and suicide at worst and at best, increased anxiety and feelings of failure. This is in part because teens—for reasons we discussed in Chapter Two—do not yet have fully developed capacities to put things into perspective, to understand accurately their own or others motivations, emotions, and behaviors. They each have a mind, but not a fully developed *theory of mind.*[14] Everything hits them harder, and in each moment feels final and often unchangeable. It is much more difficult for your teen to think of the "big picture" or the "long haul," and the speed and attendant impatience supported by communication using digital media mean that misunderstanding and the "gravity" of that (mis)understanding happen quickly. How many times have you had or heard of a conversation that goes something like this?

Mom: What's wrong? Come on, it's dinner.

Daughter: Nothing's wrong. I'm not eating.

Mom: What do you mean, nothing? You've been moping around for the last three hours and are obviously bothered by something.

Daughter: Well, fine. It's Shannon.

Mom: What about her?

Daughter: I kind of said something to her in math today that pissed her off and now she isn't talking to me. We're not friends anymore.

Mom: Honey, listen, are you crazy? You and Shannon have been best friends since second grade. You are still friends.

Daughter: You don't understanding anything! It's done. I've texted her like 12 times since school and she's not on Facebook. She hasn't responded to any of my offlines and I can't see her page anymore. I don't want to talk about it. I'm not eating.

(2 hours later)

Mom: What are you doing?

Daughter: I'm hungry, I'm eating.

Mom: Oh, your appetite is back. You seem better.

Daughter: Yeah…everything is fine. Shannon's Facebook page went down and I guess she had practice right after school today and because she was up too late last night her Dad took her iPhone away, so she wasn't getting texts.

Daughter: So, what, everything is okay now?

Mom: Uh-huh. She wasn't mad at me at all. She actually thought what I said was kind of funny.

For teens, feeling bad about themselves or their situation happens quickly. According to psychologist Don Nathanson, when we're ashamed, we have four basic ways to respond and defend ourselves against the painful feelings associated with shame.[15] The experience of shame is one of the most ubiquitous experiences of adolescence. If you remember your own adolescence, you'll know what I mean. So, picture the four points of a compass. North on the compass is *avoidance*. South on the compass is *withdrawal*. On the eastern point of the compass you'll see *attack self*; to the west lies *attack other*. Nathanson called this the "compass of shame," and these constitute the four basic defenses against this painful experience. If your daughter is using language indicating she "sucks" or is "bad" or "awful" (attack self) or she is busy blaming everyone but herself for everything that's going wrong (attack other), you can safely assume she feels ashamed about something. Tread lightly.

That's fine if I tell *you* to tread lightly. You can do that (if you're not too tired or upset at the moment). But you can't really tell the content of digital media to "tread lightly." It's not actually that practical to monitor your teenager's Facebook account and make sure that nothing is going on there that could make your teen feel ashamed. Nonetheless, while Facebook and other social media sites offer amazing ways to connect with other people, they also offer very quick, powerful ways to become ashamed, because these are the locations *par excellence* for identity development. This is a prime social location for your teen to see who is up, and who is down, who is hot or not, who has been "friended" or "unfriended," what clothes people are wearing, what cars they drive, what vacations they took (or will take), how *many* Facebook (and "real life") friends they have, what bands, movies, TV shows, and YouTube videos they like. The list is pretty endless. This is the list of things that Erikson considered the great danger of society—that these kinds of status concerns would overshadow "the wish and will to learn."

Most teens can negotiate this roller coaster of status assessment, but some cannot. And those teens are, according to a recent study, prone to depression, possibly as a result of the constant temperature-taking of their status online.[16] We need to be very careful about these studies, though, and it's hard to draw conclusions from any particular clinical report.

Nonetheless, one of the most straightforward paths to hating yourself is to fail at what mainstream American culture says matters most: accumulating wealth; being successful financially and in your chosen career; being well known; having celebrity good looks; being happy and pursuing endeavors that make you personally happy, which can overlap with accruing wealth and spending it, and having a great job, falling in romantic love or having the world love you (fame, celebrity, approval, etc.). In short, many of these areas of life that matter most concern status, and much of the suffering that follows from their pursuit involves status anxiety, a subject that gets pretty quickly to the heart of what matters and what doesn't.

THE NEGATIVE IMPACT OF STATUS ANXIETY ON TEENS

Status—from the Latin *statum* or standing—refers to the amount and type of goodies given to us by others: material goods and services, control over our own time, comfort and/or a lightening of physical, geographical, and psychological burdens or barriers, and perhaps most important, responses from other people who help you feel cared about and just plain great to be you. You've likely been hearing for decades how important "self-esteem" is in identity development. Well, if there is indeed a strong connection between positive identity development and how strong and hopeful we feel about ourselves—the capability and capacity of our minds, bodies, and spirits—then it makes sense to be concerned about phenomena that interfere with that accurate, positive assessment of those things for teens, right? At the very least, it would seem reasonable to be aware of those things that positively and negatively affect self-esteem and to try to mitigate and/or transform the negative influences while highlighting and multiplying the positive ones. That is why media literacy is so important. If you (and your teen) do not know what and how their esteem is being shaped—and understand ways to respond to those influences—then your teen's identity is being controlled, not developed. It cuts pretty quickly to what it means to live as a free citizen in a democracy, doesn't it?

High status accords what author Alain de Botton describes as the sense of personal value, "conveyed through invitations, flattery, laughter (even when the joke lacked bite), deference and attention."[17]

Status anxiety, something so universal that it rarely gets mentioned directly, is a kind of deep anxiety and suffering about what others think of us: about whether we're judged a success or a failure, a winner or a loser. *Status anxiety* is the intensive and pervasive worry about whether the world—*your world*—loves you. De Botton notes that "we see ourselves as fortunate only when we have as much as, or more than, those we have grown up with, work alongside, have as friends or identify with in the public realm."[18] Think there aren't a lot of sources of suffering in caring about whether your world loves you? Well, thanks to the Internet, television, film, radio, and mass market books, teens (and adults, too) *now have the entire world as a reference group* about whether they're in or out, hot or not, a winner or a loser. As de Botton writes,

> People who hold important positions in society are commonly labeled "somebodies," and their inverse "nobodies".... Those without status are all but invisible: they are treated brusquely by others, their complexities trampled upon and their singularities ignored.[19]

We care about our status for a simple reason: because most people tend to be nice to us according to the amount of status we have. Teens care tremendously about their status because they are busy consciously and unconsciously figuring out who they are and who they want to be, i.e., developing their identities. *Teenagers derive feelings and thoughts about their identity primarily in relation to others and how others see them and feel about them.* You can try to tell your teens something we've probably all heard at least once in our lives: "It's how you feel about yourself, not what others think of you that is most important." It is a very solid piece of advice and might reflect some very important values of yours. Try to hold off on saying it, though. More about that bit of advice later.

It is no coincidence that the first question adults tend to ask new acquaintances is "What do you do?" It is also no coincidence that teens automatically have *lower* status because they rarely have an answer to the question, "What do you do?" that involves the description of their job, the status of their job, and the amount of money they make.[20]

It seems important to note here that I work with teens because they are, in general, in my opinion, sensitive, caring, bright, funny, deeply feeling, and, when I'm lucky enough that they will let me truly see them, honest and insightful in breathtaking ways. But in my travels across the United States, talking with teenagers and their parents, I have learned important things about how teens suffer.

Many American high school students, especially those in the independent school world, almost regardless of geographic location, socioeconomic status, cultural and ethnic background, feel that they have the right to be rich, and to have high-profile publicity, celebrity looks, and high-status jobs. These mindsets are partly the expression of our national belief that everyone has equal opportunity to acquire status in America. Teens desire to be rich, look great, and have high status because they want the approval (and love) of their world. Who can blame them? Sometimes this approval is a matter of survival, and sometimes it is an issue of how much suffering they will or won't experience.

> The approval of others may be said to matter to us in two very different ways: materially, because the neglect of the community can bring with it physical discomfort and danger; and psychologically, because it can prove impossible to retain confidence in ourselves once others have ceased to accord us signs of respect.[21]

The desire to be successful, to be accorded respect, to be noticed and affirmed is hard to escape. Think teens don't care? It may not seem obvious, but I think that the first question they usually want answered when they meet someone new is, "Do you love me?" It is also the second, third, and fourth question, and until this question is answered, they may not be able to comfortably move forward with their life—at least not for a few moments.

Yes, I know that isn't literally true. If a 15-year-old male walks into a neighborhood convenience store, he doesn't really want to know if the clerk behind the counter loves him. The 15-year-old wants his Mountain Dew, hot dog, Slim Jim, or donut and wants to leave. But here's the thing: If the clerk looks at your son as if he's there to rip off the store—just because he's a teenager—or if the clerk doesn't smile at your son (even though your son might ignore him anyway because, after all, he's "only" a clerk), your son might just feel a little worse.

Or consider this: Your daughter, a high school junior, is asked by the teacher to help her deliver some important papers to the high school office. If your daughter is taking a moment-by-moment temperature of her degrees of status (and in most cases, she is), she might feel a slight increase in status at being asked to run this errand. As she jumps up to help out the teacher, the girl sitting next to her notices her Doc Martens and whispers, "Dude, the '90s called; they want their boots back." Of course, your daughter is wearing *her* Docs *ironically,* and thinks the girl who commented is an idiot, because your daughter knows that Doc Martens were big in the 1990s among so-called "Goths" and your daughter is anything but a Goth or trapped in the '90s, style-wise. Your daughter wears Docs because she's cool, and can consciously cross between fashion boundaries and meanings. Besides, the "idiot" who commented—your daughter believes—is wearing Baby Phat and *she means it.* Your daughter leaves the classroom and shrugs off the stupid comment, but it kind of bothers her that someone—*even an idiot*—might think she was out of style or not conscious about her style choice. *Slight dip in the status temperature.* Depending upon how resilient your daughter is, this little comment can be forgotten by the time she gets to the high school office, or it can ruin her entire day.

I think that it's safe to say that especially for American teenagers, these little, seemingly banal moments of rising or falling status happen hundreds of times a day. These moments—where in an instant your teen is deciding whether another values, approves of, or ultimately loves them—powerfully influence whether your teen: a) ends up feeling pretty good about him or herself at the end of the day, or b) wishes they could get all new clothes, another car, a bigger home, a replacement set of parents, or a whole new life (or want to end the life they have). I am not kidding.

In short, much of a day in the life of every teenager is filled with opportunities to enjoy slight rises or endure significant drops in status. And because the lives of teenagers are packed with these moments—delivered at lightning speed via glance, text, or email—they have lots of opportunities to feel miserable about where they stand as a human being. So, it becomes easy, in a sense, to be a teenager and to hate oneself, depending upon how vulnerable your teen is to those drops in status, and depending upon how far your teen thinks or feels they fell. Remember, teenagers' brains are set up to misinterpret and misunderstand. And those conversations about how far they fell are not likely to reach you, so that you can help correct their perceptions. Those "quiet" conversations happen in your son or daughter's own mind, and are likely to be about how they look (and how they feel about it), whether they're being noticed by the right person(s) and ignored or left alone by the wrong ones, or whether they're bored, tired, scared, or hungry, and what to do about these states of being. Right about now you should be thinking that there must be an incredibly strong connection between your teen's ability to understand, articulate, and manage their emotions—what I called the most important developmental task for adolescents—and status and identity development. You would be absolutely right.

Two Great Love Stories

If, as author de Botton suggests, every adult life could be said to be defined by two great love stories—the story of looking for someone to love and that of seeking love from the world—then teenagers are living in between these two grand narratives. These paths promise to give your son or daughter what they most want: a) someone nearby to confirm their desirability at this very moment, and b) the wider world to confirm and reward their very existence beyond this moment. These two wants and needs are part of the "falling in love" process that Erikson sees as a normal part of identity development. This confirmation can take so many different forms: money and the power to purchase what you wish; social and political power to influence those close and far; and attention and fame. If your teen is watching reruns from the now-passé HBO series *Entourage* or MTV's *The Hills,* they're watching representations of young people who—at that moment in time, anyway—had a pretty easy time getting a "yes" to the question of whether the world loves them. In short, the main characters (Vinny and Lauren, respectively) are depictions of high-status individuals.

For most American teens, the issue of whether they're loved and whether the world is a sufficiently rewarding place is not yet settled. Status is elusive and ever changing. One day you're in, the next you're out. You're a millionaire? Big deal. In 2010 there were estimated to be between 3.1 and 9.8 million millionaires[22] in the United States. By 2020, that number is expected to double. What about the almost 4 million families knocked off the millionaire map during the Great Recession? If you are among that group of folks—or if you know someone in that group—ask yourself whether the drop in status affected them. As the income inequity in the United States continues to widen, there will continue to be higher status accorded to millionaires, but it will begin to be about being a billionaire, in terms of whether you are considered to have "real" wealth.[23] Of course, if the dollar is devalued during some kind of international monetary crisis, then we'll see some pretty major changes in what constitutes status in America.

But I digress. Remember back in middle school when the biggest deal was finding a place to sit at lunch? It really matters whether or not you find a place for yourself. For teenagers, it's arguably impossible to ignore whether they're in or out, hot or not. Finding just one person who loves you, unalterably, is fantastic, but it's hard to take in if you don't feel that the world loves you, too. And we envy those who seem to have more goodies than we do. That seems to matter. De Botton wrote:

> It is the feeling that we might, under different circumstances, be something other than what we are—a feeling inspired by exposure to the superior achievements of those whom we take to be our equals—that generates anxiety and resentment.[24]

Let's go back to that question of the good parental advice, that they would do well to care more about what they think of themselves over what others think…and to remember that Mom/Dad/Grandma always love you. If things went pretty well for your child during the years between birth and about 14, then your child pretty much knows that you love them. *But the teen years are not so focused on whether your parents or grandparents love you.* When I ask teenagers whether hearing Mom or Dad say, "Well, *I* love you honey," actually takes the sting out of getting shot down by the person whose attention you want, or whether it helps them feel better about their body, about 95 percent of teens say no. Knowing your parents love you doesn't really get you into your college of choice, either. If your parent's love were all it took to make everything better, most American teenagers would be doing just fine. Your parents might pretty much annoy you, but you know they love you. That's not really the issue. De Botton writes:

> In an ideal world, we would be more impermeable. We would be un-shaken whether we were ignored or noticed, admired or ridiculed. If some-one praised us insincerely, we would not be unduly seduced. And if we had carried out a fair assessment of our strengths and decided upon our value, another's suggestion that we were inconsequential would not wound us. Instead…we typically turn to the wider world to settle the question of our significance.[25]

The roads to real misery are legion: violence, poverty, racism, homophobia, sex-ism, depression and other mental illnesses, the loss of loved ones, and so on. These are sometimes unalterable tragedies, through which we become aware of power and powerlessness. It is not hard to suffer or feel miserable if you experience these in your lifetime. But the misery caused by suffering over status is not obligatory, even though it is a ready option for just about every teenager. You and I don't want it to be so easy to suffer in those ways.

In 2012, the dominant messages in our culture—the lifeworld of the teenager—is populated by a strong belief that there is only one path that counts to being Successful. Even teens that don't consciously believe this to be true will often feel guilty, or somehow "wrong," for not being Successful in certain prescribed ways. For example, I talk to teens every day that secretly or not-so-secretly feel pretty bad:

For not being rich.

For not being famous.

For not having a rich, famous, or beautiful mom or dad.

For not having a traditional family.

For being "different."

For not being "different."

For being different than the mainstream and celebrating that, but secretly wishing they weren't all that different.

For feeling like a phony because they are not all that interested, really, in Darfur or diversity or helping the homeless when they know they are supposed to be, and actually want to be, interested in people who are suffering.

This basic idea that there is only one path for being successful at life is, I believe, a dangerous idea, and I think it's responsible for making millions of teenagers miserable. I'm not some radical arguing that it's *bad* to be rich or famous. I'm just making the reasonable proposition that no teenager should suffer from clinical depression or want to kill themselves if they aren't Successful in these traditional ways, especially as it becomes more and more difficult to reach those levels and types of success in American life.

As an aside, the striving and anxiety over status is currently making quite a few adults pretty miserable, too, as gaining the same level of wealth and commercial success seems more and more out of reach in the lingering aftermath of one of the most difficult economic recessions and crises of confidence our nation has ever seen. So, here's my assertion: The easiest way to be at risk for hating yourself (as an American teenager) is to live in America without questioning issues of status and anxiety over status. Why? To answer this, we have to look at Erikson's understanding of *fidelity*:

> Fidelity is the ability to sustain loyalties *freely pledged* [italics mine] in spite of the inevitable contradictions [and confusion] of value systems. It is the cornerstone of identity and receives inspiration from confirming ideologies and affirming companions.[26]

The teenager's ability to make commitments must be done "freely." This is an absolutely key point. For Erikson, if the choices, commitments, and loyalties of the teenager are the result of a healthy process of identity development, then their choices must conform to two standards: The adolescent must "(a) perceive alternatives, including the option of not choosing (or delay choosing), and (b) understand themselves as 'being in charge' when selecting among these possible options."[27]

James Cote's understanding of the "freely pledged" commitment also includes a teenager's trust or "believing in" his or her own agency ("being in charge"), requiring a "sensed 'psychological distance' between self and possible commitments." In other words, the cohesive feeling of "identity" that your teenager develops should result in commitments to work, love, play, friends, and community that are freely pledged with the feeling of "being in charge." There must be more than one way to succeed at life, because each person—who is in every case unique—must choose his or her own commitments. What does it mean for adolescent development into young adulthood, if the choices for commitment are already prefigured? What if the choices and roles are no longer clear and guaranteed, as they once were?

Many parents of teens are struggling with what makes them happy and discovering that what they thought a good life was about doesn't make as much sense as it used to. But I think Culkin got it right when he wrote that "intelligent and critical consumers are likely to end up as the best kinds of humans." And that starts with being an intelligent and critical assessor of consumer culture in a democracy.

Status anxiety is about the feeling that you're losing choices. But, in truth, it is about losing what brilliant writer Thomas de Zengotita describes as "Optionality." *Optionality,* in a world mediated by mass media, is Freedom. *Optionality* is the promise of Democracy and Capitalism and provides all the Reasons for why you want to be "in the game." *Optionality* is:

1. Postmodern freedom in the overdeveloped world.

2. Perpetual mobility in an environment of options.

3. The fact that what has been chosen can (almost always) be unchosen.

The problem, however, is that you don't really have "real" choices or options in the game. *You have the appearance and multiplication of* representations of real choice—and that is what teenagers feel they might be losing. Status anxiety is really about the feeling that you're losing *Optionality.* It is the hijacking of more authentic, broader choices about identity into the narrower realm of consumer culture. Teens can pick their "mood" indicators online, which social networks they visit, choose and re-choose and un-choose their screen names and online friends, their chat icon and the background for their blogs, create new identities in multiple places, find a "second life" and live it out online, choose which products they "like"—they can click here, there, and everywhere, all of their own agency and choosing. *These* "choices" can help to create a sense of identity—*of being who you truly are.* After all, you're *way different* from your friend if dance is your mode of competition, you drive a Audi, you roll in Nike Air Jordans, wear Apple Bottoms, and have Bumble &

Bumble in your hair, than if you're a soccer playing, Prius-driving, Hollister-, Roxy-, or Juicy Couture-track-suit-wearing teen who only uses hair products from Eden Body Works. *Aren't you?*

I am quite confident that Erikson was not thinking of *brand* loyalty, when he thought about fidelity being the virtue and strength of adolescent development. I am equally confident that any executive working in digital advertising or neural marketing knows *a lot more than you do* about child development and what motivates your teenager—as well as how to exploit your teen's normal developmental strivings toward identity formation and corral them into a *way of feeling, thinking, and behaving and, eventually, a* purchase. And if you happen to get a chance to talk to someone in the field, he or she is mostly going to tell you the same thing: *We're just providing you and your family with the kinds of choices and options you want.*

Developing media literacy and being a critical assessor of consumer culture is the activity, I believe, that best provides the "psychological distance" between the adolescent "self" and the objects to which he or she chooses to commit. Without this critical distance, the choices and commitments cannot be "freely pledged." That's why understanding the impact of digital media is so important and why we'll explore that in depth in the next chapter.

Practical Help Tips

1) The development of identity is a task central to adolescence—and takes place in a digital world. The processes of identity formation and the characteristics of the digital world form unique challenges and opportunities that need to be understood by parents. Gaining media literacy and education is one very important form of supporting your teen "away from the ball" as one says in basketball. Just because you aren't directly "in on the play" at the moment with your teenager doesn't mean there isn't a lot you can do; media education is one of those things you can do.

2) Status concerns are paramount for American teenagers—whether they overtly agree or not. A teen wants to feel not only that certain individuals (and their families) love him or her, but that his or her identity is acceptable and cherished by the world at large. Worry about whether the world "loves" you or not is called status anxiety, and in the U.S., anxiety over status is intimately bound up in self-esteem and identity formation. Try to notice when your teen's worry might be about status. It won't help to tell them "status doesn't matter; you should love yourself for who you are." It might be true, but it won't really help them in the moment. You can help them notice the things you value in them that don't have to do with the kinds of rewards our society gives those with high status, e.g., cars, homes, cash, automatic deference, etc. When you do offer praise, try to praise for *specific* qualities of your teen without emphasizing how this quality can be "used" for some other material purpose.

3) Problems during adolescence are not necessarily problems of adolescence. There are normal challenges and difficulties related to identity formation that don't mean "something is wrong." It helps to know a bit about how teens develop their sense of identity and not to belittle or minimize (or over-praise) their efforts at identity formation. Teens can act in ways even they don't believe in or endorse; part of adolescence is about trying *a lot* of things just to see what fits. If your daughter goes upstairs with one hairstyle and comes downstairs with a different one, or if she starts reading a particular writer or genre that she's never read before, it's not "cute." That is about your daughter being very vulnerable around figuring out who she wants to be. It's very good for you to notice these things, but better to keep quiet about them until she brings them up in some way. And even then, it's almost always better to listen than to talk.

4) You can use Erik Erikson's work to see if your child is on track with the healthy development of his identity. If things are going well, your son will be engaged in a variety of different roles and social situations (except, perhaps, if he's temperamentally on the "shy" side). If things aren't going so well, he might be feeling inferior, expressing those feelings in behavior (and attitude), and shrinking from social contact. Can you answer these questions: "What does my teen *love*?" or "What gets my teen excited and interested?" Even if you disapprove of those things, being able to begin to commit to things is a good sign of identity development. On the other hand, if your teen hasn't figured it all out by junior year, it doesn't mean she has no identity or is unhealthy. The more intensive forms of identity development don't really occur until later in adolescence, including during the post-high-school years. All isn't lost if your child leaves high school and heads off for work, other exploration, or school without a solid sense of what he or she wants to do.

5) Identity development involves two of the biggest motivators for teen behavior: having fun and avoiding embarrassment (shame). The places that hold the promise of the most "fun" (usually low-effort, high-reward activities) often hold the possibility for the most shame. A teen having fun is a teen with his or her guard down, to a greater or lesser degree. This means that shame and fun are close cousins in the daily experiences of teenagers. Teens can be hurt the most when they are relaxed, laughing, smiling, or having any kind of fun—because at that moment, a teen might be feeling "most like myself." It's good to know this so that you don't end up unwittingly being a source of shame for them. If you need to ask them to do something or need to criticize a choice or a behavior, try to wait until later. *When* is later? *Later* is the time when they aren't right in the middle of expressing some deep commitment or connection to themselves or another.

6) One of the most important things you can do with your teenager is to help them feel there is more than one way to be successful at...anything. It's a powerful habit of mind to develop: that if you fail, there are multiple causes; that if you succeed, there are multiple causes; that there are multiple ways to think about what a "success" would be. Your teen might get annoyed with you if you model this behavior, but if you keep it low-key, you'll be teaching them something valuable. I'm talking about "reframing." For example, I remember talking to a dad once about his daughter going to play for a particular soccer team. He was convinced that there was only one team for her and if she didn't make that team, it was a disaster. She didn't feel that way; in fact, she was concerned (rightly so) that if she actually made the team, she'd be subject to a coach with a particularly nasty disposition, who'd already scared off several of the team members over the years. She loved the game and wanted to put her love of the game over the possibility of dominating during league play. So, she came up with "another way of being a success," and once Dad understood that, he could support it, despite his wish that she play for the "best" team. Discovering varying ways to understand "best"...that's the point.

7) *And one last, related point. Erikson spoke of the need for commitments that help determine a teen's identity being "freely" engaged.* I hope this doesn't sound too harsh, but adolescence is about the development of your *teenager's* identity, not your identity. If you do their work for them, don't give them the chance to try and fail (at a wide variety of behaviors), or are focused on continually letting them know how you feel and think, as opposed to supporting sharing about how they feel and think, you'll be making it difficult for them to feel they are "freely choosing" anything. Teens want to "do it themselves." That doesn't mean you shouldn't stay close enough to lend a hand. Even if your teen has a learning disability, attentional difficulty, or mental health difficulty like depression or anxiety, your teen still needs to try and fail, and gather data about what worked and what didn't. These are the experiences of identity formation that allow for the development of the quality of *perseverance.*

Suggested Reading: *Identity Development, Relationships, and Status*

The lists in the "Suggested Reading" sections are by no means comprehensive. I'm including what I consider to be the most informative, practical, relevant, or comprehensive readings on the topic(s) of the chapter. In other words, if you have limited time, these are the works I believe you might want to explore first. It doesn't mean all of these books are "easy reads." Sometimes a listed book will be very difficult, but worth the time.

Bellah, R. N. *Habits of the Heart: Individualism and Commitment in American Life.* New York: HarperCollins, 1986

Carr, N. *The Shallows: What the Internet Is Doing to Our Brains.* New York: W. W. Norton & Company, 2011.

Chin, E. *Purchasing Power: Black Kids and American Consumer Culture.* Minneapolis: University Of Minnesota Press, 2001.

Committee on Integrating the Science of Early Childhood Development & Youth, and Families Board on Children, and National Research Council. *From Neurons to Neighborhoods: The Science of Early Childhood Development.* Madison: National Academies Press, 2000.

de Botton, A. *Status Anxiety.* New York: Pantheon, 2004.

de Zengotita, T. *Mediated: How the Media Shapes Our World and the Way We Live in It.* New York: Bloomsbury USA, 2006.

Ehrenreich, B. *Bait and Switch: The Futile Pursuit of the Corporate Dream.* London: Granta Books, 2006.

Erikson, E. H. *Childhood and Society.* New York: W.W. Norton & Company, Inc., 1963.

_____. *Identity: Youth and Crisis.* New York: W. W. Norton & Company, 1994.

Fonagy, P., Gergely, G., Jurist, E., & Target, M. *Affect Regulation, Mentalization, and the Development of Self.* New York: Other Press, 2005.

Hinshaw, S., & Kranz, R. *The Triple Bind: Saving Our Teenage Girls from Today's Pressures.* New York: Ballantine Books, 2009.

Hochschild, A. R. *The Managed Heart: Commercialization of Human Feeling.* Berkeley: University of California Press, 1983.

Kindlon, D. & Thompson, M. *Raising Cain: Protecting the Emotional Life of Boys.* New York: Ballantine, 2000.

Lakoff, G., & Johnson, M. *Metaphors We Live By.* Chicago: University Of Chicago Press, 1980.

Lareau, A. *Unequal Childhoods: Class, Race, and Family Life.* Berkeley: University of California Press, 2003.

Levine, M. *The Price of Privilege: How Parental Pressure and Material Advantage Are Creating a Generation of Disconnected and Unhappy Kids.* New York: HarperCollins, 2006.

Pearce, J.C. *From Magical Child to Magical Teen: A Guide to Adolescent Development.* South Paris: Park Street Press, 2003.

Pope, D. Clark. *Doing School: How We Are Creating a Generation of Stressed Out, Materialistic, and Miseducated Students.* New Haven: Yale University Press, 2001.

Porges, S.W. *The Polyvagal Theory: Neurophysiological Foundations of Emotions, Attachment, Communication, and Self-regulation.* New York: W. W. Norton & Company, 2011.

Postman, N. *The Disappearance of Childhood.* New York: Vintage/Random House, 1994.

_____. *Technopoly: The Surrender of Culture to Technology.* New York & London: Vintage, 1993.

Riera, M. *Surviving High School: Making the Most of the High School Years.* Berkeley: Celestial Arts, 1997.

Tatum, B.D. *Why Are All the Black Kids Sitting Together in the Cafeteria? (And Other Conversations About Race).* New York: Basic Books, 1997.

Thompson, M., & Barker, T. *Speaking of Boys: Answers to the Most-Asked Questions About Raising Sons.* New York: Ballantine Books, 2000.

Twenge, J. M. *Generation Me: Why Today's Young Americans Are More Confident, Assertive, Entitled—and More Miserable Than Ever Before.* New York: Free Press, 2007.

Twenge, J. M., & Campbell, W. K. *The Narcissism Epidemic: Living in the Age of Entitlement.* New York: Free Press, 2009.

4

Parenting in the Digital Age:
Please Slow Down

Two snapshots. Snapshot one: I want you to imagine a 10-month-old child. The child has come into my psychotherapy office, carried by his mother, who is my client. But before we can all get settled in, the child turns his gaze to his mom and makes the following gesture: He raises his right hand up to chest level, extends his right pointer finger slowly, and then, crossing his midline from left to right, traces a straight line, across his midline, with both arm and finger. But he isn't finished. He quickly begins a new gesture: This time, with right pointer finger extended, he places his arm just about at midline and makes repeated upward movements, from his belly button to the top of his head.

His mother looks at him quizzically and he repeats the exact same multi-part gesture. Twice. Her brow furrows and then, after about eight seconds, a look of relaxation crosses this mother's face as she realizes what her baby wants. This gesture, Mom understands, signifies that her son wants her to unlock one of the most alluring advances in digital media—an iPad— so that he can play an old-school software game involving moving a cartoon amphibian deliberately, in upward fashion, through a serious of obstacles—Frogger.

Snapshot two: There is a video circulating on YouTube that depicts a toddler furiously poking at a magazine with her pointer finger; she alternately grasps at the magazine, then at her leg, where she ends up making the same poking gesture on her leg. It's pretty clear this toddler is responding to the magazine and her own body as if it is a haptic device.[1] The final slide superimposes these words over the video of the child: "For my 1-year-old daughter, a magazine is an iPad that does not work. Steve Jobs has coded part of her OS."

According to a 2010 study done by Internet security company AVG, "[S]mall children…are more likely to navigate with a mouse, play a computer game and increasingly—operate a smartphone—than swim, tie their shoelaces or make their own breakfast." The same company also reports that babies and toddlers "have an online footprint by the time they are six months old." The *Wall Street Journal* covered the story with the title, "Learning to Play 'Angry Birds' Before You Can Tie Your Shoes."[2]

All healthy brains are mediated by and mediate experience. Nature versus nurture is a very outmoded way of thinking. We influence the environment as it influences us, and back again, and so on. And regardless of the magnitude of each vector's influence, it seems certain that we can and do influence and are influenced by the world, others, and our own psychophysical selves. This is arguably one of the biggest philosophical and psychological "insights" of the 20th and 21st centuries.

From connection with this insight and attendant research come keywords like "intersubjectivity" and "mutuality" and "responsibility." From connection with this insight flows the psychological justification for participatory democracy, voting and civil rights, private and governmental efforts to protect the public, and an understanding of what community means.

So, these two charming little stories about babies and digital media—cute, but no big deal, right? The mainstream press, following Marc Prensky's writing, calls these children "digital natives" because they'll never know a world undefined by digital media.[3] This chapter began with the description of a gesture. It is the gesture of a 10-month old human to pursue his own happiness. What does it mean that a 10-month-old has developed the neural pathways, the learning and motivation necessary to signify that he wants to play a game on the iPad?[4] Again, big deal. Kids can and do learn sign language and easily sign to indicate their desire for food, drink, or a number of other, more complex pleasurable (and necessary) experiences. Well, maybe it means more than that, but at the very least it means if you're looking down the road for the digital future, you're looking too far. It's *now.*

Right now: Parents in my office often arrive with the same dilemmas involving digital media access and use. This week I was struck by the number of families in the very same position, worrying about the level of arguments over how, when, and whether the iPad or the laptop gets used. Parents see the possible benefits and creative potential available on digital media platforms and applications and encourage those activities. It's hard to argue against; young teens can produce professional-quality music, art, photography, and video-based projects with these tools, and learning and real connection take place in the production and sharing of those endeavors. Adolescents are *passionate* about what they can do with their digital know-how, and it's one of the few areas in life that they can be absolutely certain they know much more than the average adult. Children in middle- and high-school often have creative and multimedia-based learning projects for school and need access to online sources, resources, and software applications. And we'll soon see how persistent and frequent the usage of digital media can be.

But as normal problems with prioritizing media usage, texting, chatting, social networking activities, and homework and other school and family responsibilities conflict, a parent must look for ways of refocusing their child's attention to other important thoughts and tasks. The intervention of choice is usually to *limit* access to digital media of all kinds, since parents know that this gets their child's attention and will often motivate behavior (to get back media access). And that's when the big and constant arguments really get going. You can use your iPhone for your calculator and texting about your homework, but not for texting friends…and not all night! You can use the iPad for recording in ProTools, but you can't play Minecraft until your math is done. And you have to be asleep by 11 or you're not going to use the iPad this weekend or spend the night at your friend's house. *Yeah—right.* Teens being teens means that they'll sneak and lie and find ways to get access to the digital platform, application, or communications devices of their choice. They'll beg for access, pleading to do some *legitimate* activity—I need it for homework!—and then just happen to send a few texts or play a few games; I mean, what's the big deal? Then you catch them, feel betrayed and used, and take away more, to even greater protest. You vow to really crack down on the media use—which feels at times compulsive and out of control—and then feel guilty about depriving them of the pleasurable "good" things they do with digital media. Then, of course, you realize that the level of monitoring, parental-control setting, digital media–ectomies you have to perform hourly, daily, or weekly is way too much for you to handle, so you just give in and it all starts again. Or your own digital media use comes into sharper focus and you start to feel more ambivalent about all the limit-setting you've been up to lately. You might vow to stop the craziness, but you know that you need to have consequences and set limits of *some* kind—and that means having *some* consequences for bad choice—and you're right back to the cycle of giving or limiting access to digital media as a way to impact your child. Perhaps your child uses digital media in the classroom, too, as part of their accommodations for learning disabilities or attentional difficulties, and he or she is allowed to use a tablet or notebook computer in class to take notes, for example. This means that something that is kind of a "toy" at home becomes an "assistive device" at school. Then, your life is really going to get complicated as fighting over access to digital media takes center stage in the family. If any of the above sounds familiar to you, then welcome to parenting in the digital age. If none of the above sounds familiar…you're either very lucky or your village is *way* out of a Wi-Fi or 4G reception area.

So, let's start by saying that I have a good deal of trust in most parents. I trust our communities to figure out what is going on. But most parents—and I'm one of them—are anxious about what our teens (and ourselves) are doing with personal computers, laptops, netbooks, cellphones, iPads, iPods, instant messaging, texting, sexting, social networking, tweeting, and the content these technological devices and processes carry. There are good reasons for some anxiety, including the fact that most parents are significantly behind their children (and teens) in using and understanding how digital media work. The premise of this chapter, though, is that we ought not be, in our anxiety and wonder, too distracted by the content to forget about the digital technology delivering the content. The content is really important. And what we do and don't do with the content is important. Very important. But I have to say that I'm inclined to agree with what Marshall McLuhan wrote 46 years ago: "For the 'content' of a medium is just the juicy piece of meat carried by the burglar to distract the watchdog of the mind."[5] I'm also inclined—in the spirit of mutuality and bi-directionality—to be asking not just what our teens are doing with digital media, but what digital media is doing with our teens. I believe it is *changing* the way our brains think and how we feel.

You'll notice I didn't say that it is "ruining" the way we think and feel. But in fact critics, skeptics, and champions of digital media agree that the Internet and digital media are changing us, as we are shaping them. The disagreement—and it is a big one—is whether those changes are essentially "good" or "bad."[6]

I want to make clear that the title of this chapter isn't quite referring to the challenges and opportunities afforded our teens by being lucky enough to have been born in the digital age. It's not about the superpowers of information-gathering and processing speed and unheard-of levels of fun and engagement and connection with others, community-building and local and global problem-solving that they're in for...even though those things are part of the digital age. No, I wanted to address you about the challenges and opportunities in parenting. I am, after all, a therapist, former (but never quite former) philosopher, and educator. And always, a parent.

Parenting in the digital age is not about deciding whether you're a skeptic or an enthusiast about digital media. Some believe the technology isn't all that important; it's only how we use it that matters, and there is a lot to be happy about. Others are wondering just how to stop the shadowy and ineluctable force of technology that is out to destroy our children and ourselves, turning us all into mindless drones and slaves to a digital world. Both skeptic and enthusiast have their place. But the Internet and new digital media are changing us—our habits, ways of thinking and feeling, and probably (according to the latest research) our neurology for the short- and long-term. And because we love our children, we can be anxious and overwhelmed about these changes, which in my experience often results in a dance between overconfidence and underinvolvement and anxiety and over-involvement in our parenting choices.

As parents, we want to lessen our anxieties and figure out what's going on and what to do. But in order to do that, we'll need information and a method of understanding that doesn't overwhelm us. As in other chapters, I'm going to attempt to do that by suggesting a framework/perspective for understanding. That framework will turn out to be too simplistic in the long run—after all, we never have "complete" knowledge of something or full command of its effects. But we can start somewhere. So please join me in a thought experiment by considering three "things" (in quotes) and how they might interact: "fire," "paper" and "an unsupervised 12-year-old adolescent male." When I asked my 26-year old son what he would expect to get if he combined these three things, he replied, "Some kind of risk-filled, fun, quasi-scientific experiment." My wife, concise as she's known to be, just said: "Arson."

The three things under consideration are: 1) *adolescents and their level of development,* primarily from a neuropsychological point of view, with a focus on how and what teens learn (and how they adapt and change); 2) the *type of technology* of which we are speaking—its characteristics and how it operates; and 3) how these two types of phenomena *interact* and what their likely future effects might be. To put it simply, we want to explore teenagers, digital media, and how these two things do and are likely to interact.

Part I: The Characteristics of Teens

Figuring out the characteristics of Piece 1 of our puzzle is, arguably, the easiest step in the process. We have more tools than ever before—many of them products of the digital revolution—at our disposal to help us understand how adolescents learn and adapt. Broad advances in motivation and learning, cognitive neuropsychology, brain imagining technology, cross-disciplinary cooperative research on adolescent development that benefits from sociological, psychological, neurobiological, affect regulation, brain development, and even political perspectives have shed tremendous light on what goes on during adolescence and why. Much of this was highlighted in Chapter 2[7], but is repeated here in a slightly different format, so that it can stand on its own if you want to skip Chapter 2 and go right to reading about teens and digital media.

At some point in the last 15 years I realized that I spent most of my time thinking, reading, and talking about adolescents. Here's some of what I've found in my role as a parent, researcher, clinician, student, educator, and observer of teens:

Teens—biopsychosocial (and spiritual) beings—are humans sandwiched between the developmental milestones of puberty onset and completion of brain development: roughly from 9 to 25. This incredibly long 16-year span of modern adolescence raises some important considerations in terms of development. While many of the (especially brain) changes that teens undergo are related to biology, many are related to environment and experience. Many, if not most teens navigate adolescence with minimal difficulty, although there is evidence that there is more conflict between adolescents and their parents in American households than in other cultures.[8] The "average" young teen/preteen (from about 9½ to 12 years old) in the United States is:

1. Undergoing major changes in brain biochemistry;

2. In a bit of a cognitive fog on the way to developing what Swiss developmental psychologist Jean Piaget called "abstract thinking";

3. Relatively challenging of family and social authority;

4. Wanting more time alone and with friends;

5. Beginning to reject things and associations of childhood;

6. Intensely focused and anxious about appearance and what others think of them;

7. Having intense same-gender relationships;

8. Daydreaming a lot about who to be and how to be "me," always imagining an audience (usually a critical one);

9. Worrying about whether they're crazy or weird, and hyperfocused on what is and is not normal.

Teens, like you and I, have brains and minds. They may not, however, have a fully developed *theory* of mind. *Theory of mind* is the ability to attribute mental states—beliefs, intentions, desires, pretending, knowledge, and the like—to oneself and others, and to understand that others have beliefs, desires, and intentions that are different from one's own.[9] Having a healthy and developed theory of mind really requires the fully functioning executive functions of the prefrontal cortex. Structurally, teens have a prefrontal cortex (and other cortices). But their brain structures are not yet like yours and mine. They have neural bodies, axons, dendrites, synapses, myelin sheathing (white matter) covering the nerve bodies. But their brains are not developed until their mid-twenties, and while they are "unfinished," they are also plastic (changeable) to an extraordinary and unique degree. This neurological *plasticity* is, as we discussed in Chapter 2, a hallmark of the adolescent brain.

The billions of nerve cells in their brains,[10] with signals traveling at times almost 400 miles per hour, involving over 90 neurochemicals for neurotransmission, are not all "connected" or even "turned on." They are *ready* to be activated but they are not necessarily going to be. And the synaptic connections that are not activated are going to be pruned back during adolescence. This is a little bit like "use it or lose it," in a neurological sense—but not quite. It's more important to know that the synaptic connections that are activated and reinforced are going to grow in strength and efficiency, while others are weakened. Repeated experiences in the world fuel this process, and thanks to the pioneering work of thousands of researchers and clinicians such as Michael Merzenich, Eric Kandel, Edward Taub, and Donald O. Hebb—oh, and William James and a guy named Freud, over 100 years ago—we now know that "cells that fire together wire together."[11] I understand this in the following terms: *What teen brains practice, teen brains get better at.* This process of practice enforcing neurological structure, thus strengthening not only behavior but also propensity toward particular behaviors, *is arguably more intense during adolescence than at any other time in the human life cycle.*[12]

In a rather cruel twist of fate, it seems that risk-taking behavior seems to help create synaptic connections between the parts of the brain in the limbic system (the "emotional," "reward" and motivational centers of the brain) and the prefrontal cortex—the structure of the brain identified most with executive functioning, or the behaviors we most associate with maturity. The brain develops from the back to the front, from the cerebellum (the locus of physical coordination and sensory processing), to the nucleus accumbi (associated with motivation and reward- and pleasure-seeking), forward to the amygdala and other structures within the limbic system, and finally to the prefrontal cortex (executive functioning). Thus, executive functioning—reasoned judgment, weighing consequences, planning, generalizing from the specific, true multitasking, prioritizing, gratification delay, and impulse control—is the last to develop. In other words, teens need to take risks in order to learn which risks to take. Or as former Stanford computer scientist Jim Horning is quoted as saying—and he attributes to the Sufi sage Mulla Nasreddin: "Good judgment comes from experience. Experience comes from bad judgment."

Physically, adolescents are, by most measures, at their lifetime's peak of health and resilience. They are usually undergoing unprecedented improvements in strength, speed, reaction time, and mental reasoning ability, with levels of resistance to cold, heat, hunger, dehydration, and most types of injury absolutely guaranteed to annoy even the most sanguine 50-year-old. Yet their overall morbidity and mortality rates increase nearly 300 percent from childhood to late adolescence. The primary causes of adolescent death and disability are related to problems with the control of behavior and emotion. As we will discuss in many contexts throughout this book, when teens die, they do so because of accident, suicide, and homicide. The reasons teens die (even in the case of accidental death) are frequently related to mood disorders like depression, alcohol and drug use, and abuse, violence, poverty, eating disorders, and health problems related to risky sexual behavior. Often the reckless or risky behaviors that result in death or disability occur together; in other words, there are statistically significant correlations between all of these problematic conditions. Teens who are depressed use more drugs and alcohol. Teens who live in poverty and violence are at risk to encounter problems with the law and legal system, and to use and abuse drugs.[13] And so, helping teens understand, articulate, and regulate their emotions is arguably the single most important task during middle and high school. Why? Because if your teen cannot understand and get help with what they are feeling, when they feel bad, they have access to many ways of quickly changing their emotional state, most of which increase their risk for death and disability. Teens need the close proximity of friends, teachers, family members, and parents in order for them to develop healthy, strong affect regulation skills.

Emotionally, adolescence is a period of risk-taking, sensation-seeking, and emotionally influenced and directed behavior. Adolescents primarily process information emotionally; that is to say, information entering adolescent brains (as opposed to adult brains) seems to get firing what we now call the "limbic system"—the area involving the septum, amygdala, hypothalamus, hippocampal complex, and cingulate cortex. This is the area of the brain most involved in determining "saliency"—*does this matter to me or not?*

Saliency detection is considered to be a key attentional mechanism in humans, because it facilitates survival by allowing us to focus our limited perceptual and cognitive resources on the most pertinent subset of available data. While saliency detection involves all of the visual, auditory, and other sensory and motor cortices, we've learned that teens process information differently than we do. They seem to first want to know: Is this information emotionally relevant to me? If it is, I want to remember it; if not, I want to avoid it. It will come as no surprise, then, that teenagers gravitate toward high-excitement, high-reward, low-effort activities, as a matter of their biology. Immature and underdeveloped amygdalae mean poor modulation of emotions, with "hot" emotions more common than "cold" ones. This could be one reason teens are not particularly great, yet, at correctly interpreting the emotions and motives of others, and why teens interpret neutral and fearful facial expressions as being "angry."[14] It is worth pointing out that in the absence of facial expression, tone of voice, explanation, and conversation, misunderstanding increases even further.

Several recent important studies on adolescent motivation conducted at Vassar and UCLA[15] demonstrate that teens are, in fact, unique in their motivations. In these experiments using brain imagining, young children's brains "light up" with any reward at all. Adults respond by order of magnitude: the bigger the reward, the greater the response in the brain. But teen brains responded only when the reward became emotionally salient, that is to say, when the reward was huge (to them): Their brains say "ehhh" to small and medium-size rewards and only light up when the reward is large. The *nucleus accumbens*—a collection of neurons in the striatum of the brain, near the amygdala—is thought to play a key role in the reward and pleasure center of the brain, affecting things like addictive, aggressive, and fear-based behavior. Each half of the brain has one nucleus accumbens. And in teens, nucleus accumbens activity decreases in the face of low and medium rewards, and prefrontal cortex activity slows and even diminishes in proportion to high-reward stimulation.

Translation, please? What this suggests is that in general teen brains respond the way drug addicts' brains do: They not only seek and require greater and greater stimulation for the same perception of pleasure, but when faced with what they consider to be emotionally salient and pleasurable, parts of the brain—the prefrontal cortex—associated with judgment start shutting down. Use it or lose it meets "use it and abuse it." For teens, what is pleasurable and practiced is a moveable feast.

And so, what do they care about enough to want to do over and over again? Well, now we're really into the realm of motivation. Teens care about relationships. They care a lot about not disappointing their parents...often more so than about not disappointing their friends and partners. They also care about avoiding embarrassment. And having fun. What counts as fun? Activities that are generally low-effort and high excitement/reward and get the "limbic system" structures screaming, "This is salient to me!" But teens are also about avoidance. They want desperately to avoid what their brain signals as danger. So, what do they find dangerous? Not what we'd hope they'd find dangerous. In an amazing series of experiments at Vassar, teens and adults were shown a list of items and asked to respond as quickly as they could as to whether these ideas were "good" or "bad." Items included things like, "bite down on a lightbulb" or "eat a salad." The good news is that both teens and adults picked the same items as good and bad. The bad news is that teens took *significantly longer* to identify whether an activity was "bad." Why? Adults have experience and a kind of shorthand "gist-based" thinking to make this judgment, and teens have primarily their emotional reactions to go on, and the much slower processes of analysis—without the benefit of this more efficient "gist-based" decision making. As you might imagine, it's easier to know and respond to what's good and bad when you have a lot of experience, and the resulting rapid decision-making capacity.

But wait a moment. What is arguably more important about the work at Vassar is what was learned later. The first experiment told researchers that teens take longer to judge something as risky or dangerous because the area near the brain stem and ventromedial prefrontal cortex was not really firing when teens were making these assessments. Apparently just "contemplating" jumping off a roof didn't register as "risky" or "dangerous" enough to warrant the kind of fast response usually associated with high risk and trauma. But researchers figured out how to get this area firing for teens. How? Easy. They conducted an experiment—a kind of online poll study—during which teens were asked to simply answer some questions on a computer screen, while researchers studied their brain activity using fMRI technology. No problem. These were question about popular culture. Cool. The only minor thing was, there were going to be teens, just like them, sitting at an offsite computer screen, looking at their answers. Okay, go: "What kind of music do you like?" "What do you think of Paris Hilton?" "What websites do you like to visit?" So it turns out that if you want to get a teenager's ventromedial prefrontal cortex firing, warning them of imminent danger, just put them in a position where *other teenagers are judging their choices.* So, whether to bite down on a lightbulb, that takes some real thought…but if your desires and preferences are going to be judged by a peer—that gets a strong stress response going, higher executive functioning begins to shut down, and survival becomes the issue. The nervous system starts withdrawing blood flow and glucose to areas associated with judgment, planning, critical reasoning, and understanding emotional reaction, and starts emphasizing functioning associated with our three main choices when in danger: fight, flee, or freeze.

Teens are trying to figure out who they are and want to be, engage primarily with others their age to create, maintain, and modify their emergent identities, and they want to know what it is going to take to be loved—by themselves, others, and the world around them. It is safe to say that at no other time in human history has electronic media been involved in those processes of identity formation, socializing, and status assessment and maintenance.

STATUS, IDENTITY DEVELOPMENT, AND DIGITAL MEDIA

If, as author Alain de Botton suggested, every adult life could be said to be defined by two great love stories—the story of looking for someone to love and that of seeking love from the world—then adolescence is life between these two grand narratives. These two paths promise to give teens what they want most: a) someone nearby to confirm their desirability at this very moment, and b) the wider world to confirm and reflect back and reward their very existence beyond this moment. Erik Erikson referred to this period in teen development as a crisis of "identity development versus role confusion." This confirmation of emergent identity can take so many different forms: money and the power to purchase what you wish; social and political power to influence those close and far; and romantic love, attention, and fame.

It is worth jumping ahead to quote from a 17-year-old teenager that you'll meet in the next chapter, because she beautifully captures the link between adolescent identity development and status—the search for approval from the "world" of peers and others at large:

No matter how secure teens seem in themselves, there does exist some twinge of self-doubt, and in order to validate a healthy "self-image," teens must search externally and find validation in the world. We do not, at that point in our development, trust our own impulses, our own value-systems and beliefs.[16]

We already know that we love our teens. And most of them know we love them. But what they're not sure of—because this question can only be answered as their identity is formed—is whether the world loves them. And one of the most straight-forward paths to hating yourself is to fail at what American culture frequently says matters most: accumulating wealth; being successful financially and in your chosen career; being happy; and pursuing endeavors that make you and your family person-ally happy, which can overlap with accruing wealth and spending it, and having a great job, falling in romantic love, or having the world "show you the love" by be-stowing fame, celebrity, and other forms of public approval. In short, many of these areas of life that matter most concern status, and much of the suffering that follows from their pursuit involves status anxiety, a subject we explored in Chapter 3 that gets pretty quickly to the heart of what teens perceive as salient.

As I argued in that chapter, the desire to be successful, to be accorded respect, to be noticed and affirmed is hard to escape for adults. It is almost impossible for teens to escape, precisely because their brains can and do perceive the world through the lens of how others see, receive, and approve or do not approve of them, as a matter of normal adolescent development in America.

Part II: Characteristics of the Internet and Digital Media

Let's start by focusing primarily on the Internet, since that is arguably the most pervasive digital medium. There is another reason for focusing primarily on the In-ternet, which I'll expand upon soon.

Digital data on the Internet is:

- Easily reproducible;

- Easily shared;

- Flexibly represented;

- Flexibly modified;

- Difficult to intercept, stop, or remove;

- Moving very quickly, usually across large distances;

- Always already filtered before and in order to get to you, usual-ly based upon an algorithm favoring popularity and consensus;

- Designed to be presented and "used" in ways that relieve the end user of as many tasks as possible regarding usage and manipulation of the data (in other words, it's all about speed).

The Internet supports:

- Many to many connectivity;

- A high degree of interactivity;

- High decentralization;

- High anonymity between users, but not necessarily between end user and those who develop applications;

- Easy publishing of materials (low capital outlay);

- Fast, pervasive distribution of material, the accuracy and source of which is hard to ascertain;

- Convenience, via multiple access channels, 24/7. Say it again: 24/7. That is all the time.

If something can be digitized, it can and will be available on the Internet. And if something is available on the Internet, it is available to be shared with others. Thus, anything that can be digitized, can be shared with others: From real-time, explicit sexual activity to the entire collection of Bach compositions and performances by Glenn Gould to the current view of Tahrir Square, looking north.

So, let us think together about these characteristics of data on the Internet and about what is happening online in 2012: Teens can listen to, share, edit, create, sell, buy, and market music online; they can initiate what we used to term "phone calls" and see and hear the person with whom they are communicating, and along with that capacity goes the opportunity to see and hear anything another human being—or multiple human beings, or other animals or machines—are doing, in real time; they can create, edit, share sell, buy, and market two-dimensional static and moving images of every kind (what we used to call photography and video); they can create, run, modify, sell, distribute, and purchase software applications of every type; they can send messages "instantly," within and without all of these various software applications; and they can search and find any piece of information which can be digitized—that is to say, pretty much anything. And all of these activities can be (and often are) *monetized*.

I could spend the rest of this book detailing what humans can do with the Internet. I could spend the rest of the book detailing what humans can do themselves and with others while connected to the Internet. Multitasking between Internet-based activity and non-Internet-based activity will be, in a very short amount of time, the way that most American teens live their lives; we call it having "wired teens" or "living digital." To me, the technological device is interesting, but ultimately not as salient. Plenty of others can tell you about PCs, netbooks, public networked computers, digital music and video players, recorders and editors, digital television systems, cameras, digital video games—I mean, let's just drop the adjectival "digital," because it's all already digitized. Is there anything that isn't or won't be digitized? Is there any experience or realm of human experience that cannot or should not be digitized?

As Nicholas Carr wrote of his own experience in the brilliant and provocative work *The Shallows: What the Internet Is Doing to Our Brains*, the Internet is fast becoming, for everyone, an all-purpose medium—the conduit for most information that flows through your eyes and ears, into your mind.[17] The development of the Internet, Carr wrote, has replayed in less than 20 years—at time-lapse speed— the history of modern communications media, from Gutenberg's printing press for the distribution of books, pamphlets, and leaflets, to newspapers, magazines, radio, television, film, and the like. The printing press, book, pamphlet, typewriter, map, calculator, clock, telephone, office, radio, television, record and record player, CD player, film, and video—it's all online. It is Alan Turing's "universal computing machine," mostly limited only by the speed at which it can run.

And those speeds are dizzying; so is the amount of information and opportunity and choice available. It's got its advantages and opportunities. *Wired* magazine's tech writer, Clive Thompson, reminds us that the "perfect recall" of silicon memory can be an unfathomable boon to thinking.[18] No longer do teens need to hurt their brain trying to remember everything. Spending less time on sustained, singular tasks allows for greater multitasking and more information input. And certainly their brains are already adapting to a fast-moving, input-rich environment. Teens will take in more information, faster than we ever did. And not really need to remember as much. Every new piece of software, each new device, each new platform will offer new opportunities to extend the reach of their brains, limbs, and imaginations, and push them past limitations of time and space. These advantages accompanied the invention of writing, writing with spaces between words, paper, the printing press, the clock, and the computer. This extension of our capacities is the essence of technology.

Part III: Putting It Together: Interaction Between Teens and Digital Media

I want to suggest two orienting themes—from media and social critics Marshall McLuhan and John Culkin—to think about what is happening with our teens and digital media:

We can be certain that whoever discovered water, it was not a fish. (Variously attributed to John Culkin or Marshall McLuhan)

A new medium is never an addition to an old one, nor does it leave the old one in peace. It never ceases to oppress the older media until it finds new shapes and positions for them. (Marshall McLuhan, *Understanding Media*)

In the Kaiser Family Foundation's 2010 Report on "Media in the Lives of 8- to 18-Year Olds," we see a reason for why many adults and most teen "fish" aren't in a position to discover the "water" effects of the digital lifeworld:

As anyone who knows a teen or a tween can attest, media are among the most powerful forces in young people's lives today. Eight- to eighteen-year-olds spend more time with media than in any other activity besides (maybe) sleeping—an average of more than 7½ hours a day, seven days a week. The TV shows they watch, video games they play, songs they listen to, books they read and websites they visit are an enormous part of their lives, offering a constant stream of messages about families, peers, relationships, gender roles, sex, violence, food, values, clothes, and an abundance of other topics too long to list. [19]

American teems live with and become themselves in the two-way feedback loop provided by digital media. The technology is everywhere and will become more and more seamless in the lives of our children. That little 10-month old you imagined at the beginning of the chapter is growing up with iPads, iPods, computers, Skype, the Internet, and will never know a world without digital media. When what you use and attend to, and play with and think with every day, with others—and as a way of connecting to others—is always there and always on, it's hard, if not impossible, to notice anything but the content of those media. For anyone but the initial adopters of new technology, it is difficult to notice the effects of that technology on the self. Perhaps it is even hardest for the early adopters, because the content delivered and the fact of it being delivered is so compelling.

Three things we know for certain that adolescents do when they are in contact with the Internet and digital media: *They connect with other adolescents, they watch videos, and they buy things.* American consumers and users of digital media say they most trust advertisements that come to them online, through "branded" websites like Google, MSN, Facebook, or Yahoo![20] It's good that folks trust the advertising they encounter on these sites, because it's where they are spending most of their time. I'm just not sure *who* it's good for. Some, like media critic Robert McChesney, see this activity as the "commercial logic" of the Internet, and it is directly aimed at your teen:

The commercial logic is the idea that everything is dedicated to the idea of selling something. The whole point of the relationship with the teen is to turn them upside-down and shake all the money out of their pockets. That's the sole purpose of it—the artistic, the creative. There's traditionally been a distinction between the editorial or creative side and the commercial side. It was a common theme in our media for much of the twentieth century.[21]

McChesney argues that when it comes to the "merchants of cool," what is wanted *from* your teen in connection with digital media, the distinction between creative and commercial is now mostly gone. Most in the digital advertising industry, and especially those who pioneered neural advertising—that's right, *neural* advertising—would find the simplicity and naiveté of this book quaint and somewhat laughable. Martin Lindstrom, one of those pioneers in neuromarketing research, knows a lot about what happens when consumers are exposed to advertisements while their brain activity, pupil dilation, galvanic skin response, and minute facial muscle movements are recorded. More importantly, neuromarketing researchers are acutely interested in this data, because it helps large and small corporations turn your teenager (and you) upside-down and shake the money out of your pockets. All of those biological indicators, above, are aspects of affective responding—and knowing your affective responses helps them understand the emotional triggers that make you want to buy things.[22] The neuromarketing industry would find this book laughable because I'm explaining these phenomena to you as if they're shocking and "new." This neurological research and close collaboration with the business world has been going on for more than 30 years. It's partly responsible for why your teenagers already "love" ESPN and Victoria's Secret. It has helped to quietly define and exploit the enormous commercial potential of your teenager's highly valued, constant presence online.

Once again, Nicholas Carr writes:

It's in our home, our office, our car, our classroom, our purse, our pocket. Even people who are wary of the Net's expanding influence rarely allow their concerns to get in the way of their use and enjoyment of the technology. The movie critic David Thomson once observed that, "doubts can be rendered feeble in the face of the certainty of the medium." He was talking about the cinema and how it projects its sensations and sensibilities not only onto the movie screen but onto us, the engrossed and compliant audience. His comment applies with even greater force to the Net. The computer screen bulldozes our doubts with its bounties and conveniences. It is so much our servant that it would seem churlish to notice that it is also our master.[23]

So, we've already arrived at part three: What happens when you take a being that has the characteristics of a teen and put it together with technologies that have the characteristics of digital media and the Internet?

I'm not going to pretend to go into depth as to how our teens are using digital media. One entire book provides barely enough space to properly get at even the highlights—so much for information overload. There are a number of useful and important research-based studies on the topic, notably S. Craig Watkins' *The Young and the Digital;* danah boyd's[24] prolific work—from her UC Berkeley dissertation on the meaning of social networking for teens, to her upcoming work on the usage of Twitter and the problematic practices of solicitation, harassment, and cyber-bullying; and the cutting-edge work going on under the auspices of the Pew Charitable Trust's "Internet and American Life" Project; USC's Annenberg Center for the Digital Future; the Kaiser Family Foundation's partnership with Stanford exploring all aspects of "Youth and Media"; and the work supported by the John D. and Catherine T. MacArthur Foundation's "Digital Media and Learning" various projects, including the important 2009 work on "Young People, Ethics and the New Digital Media." You'll find these materials and links to these resources at the end of the chapter.

One author stands out among the researchers on how adolescents utilize digital media.[25] danah boyd—a senior researcher at Microsoft, assistant professor at New York University, and fellow at the highly esteemed Berkman Center for Internet and Society at Harvard—is a rock star, when it comes to influence and acclaim in the world of social media research. Her path from adolescent pain through the "saving grace" of the Internet (as she refers to it), through Brown University, University of California at Berkeley, M.I.T., Google, Yahoo!, and Tribe, and on to working at Harvard and Microsoft, is not a path that most digital natives follow.

As colleague, researcher, and fellow technology champion Clay Shirky writes of her, "The single most important thing about danah is that she's the first anthropologist we've got who comes from the tribe she's studying."[26] Now, I think danah's work is incredibly important, but when she says that "teenagers are the same as they always were," I think she's wrong. And although she argues that teens are still mostly doing everything they've always done, and that they're *sharing* it online—and this doesn't make them aliens—it just isn't the case, in my opinion, that this means that parents should all breathe a sigh of relief.[27] When danah was asked to join Microsoft, I sent her a tweet and congratulated her, and then asked her if I could "chat" with her by email. She agreed, and I proceeded to ask her pointedly whether one of my favorite researchers was about to be co-opted by working at Microsoft. I think I might have even included the John Culkin quote and essentially asked her whether she was a fish or not. She was amazingly kind in her reply (as she is, in fact), and basically said she didn't feel that her work was going to be co-opted, and that she "believed in doing public work and helping shape the world for the better." I believe her 100 percent. I'm not worried about whether someone who is arguably one of the most prolific researchers in the area of teens and digital media is going to somehow be "corrupted" by being connected to a company with a net worth of about one-quarter of a trillion dollars. I'm worried because danah is, in fact, *exceptional*. I worry *that most teens* will not be able to come to understand and make personal use of information about teens and digital media use the way danah has.

I make a point of drawing attention to danah's work because it exemplifies the essence of *one* side in an ostensible "debate" over the effects of digital media on youth and youth culture. When I say that the Internet and digital media in general are changing what counts as ethical and redefining it, just as we are changing and redefining the technology and how we use it, I will always note that this isn't necessarily good or bad, *but the fact of it happening is undeniable.* What danah does is to exquisitely document "the fact of it happening" as she tries to make sense and translate for the rest of us what it means. But to me, she's a (brilliant) fish—from the tribe she's studying—and on the "anti-Luddite" side of a debate over whether the Internet and digital media are changing the way our brains work. Therefore, she's much more likely to argue that it's "just a tool" and it's how you use the technology that counts.

WHAT ARE TEENS DOING ONLINE?[28]

As of the time of this writing, the United States Census estimates that there are 312.8 million people in the U.S., with teens (10–19) accounting for about 13.7 percent of the population.[29] Young people less than 20 years of age (78 million) makes up about 25 percent of the total U.S. population. Almost 90 percent (87.6 percent) of Americans have Internet access, twice the amount who did in 2000. In terms of online priority, most Americans go online to access social network sites and blogs (81 billion minutes total in 2011)—now far exceeding the time we use accessing email.

All categories of digital media use are dominated by *women*—with the exception of tablet use, where males now have a slight majority (53–47 percent of tablet users are male). You might be surprised to know that the largest numbers of Americans visiting social networking sites are *not* teenagers—they are white women between the ages of 18–49. White Americans currently far outnumber all other users/owners of digital media, indicating just *one* type of digital divide. As digital platforms like laptop, smartphone, home computer, HD television/digital cable television, and DVR become more integrated, the issue of accessing different content by different platforms fades into the distance; it's all about "cross-platform" engagement. One prime example of this regards "television" watching: Americans watch more television than ever but they are watching it more places and on more devices than ever, too.

Let's start with something that is now trending among those teens. As of 2012, one thing teens are starting to do much more often is access video—on their *mobile phones,* which teens still primarily use for texting, not making phone calls. YouTube is the favorite destination of teens and adults alike for video streaming. A teen in one of the Pacific Rim countries is almost 50 percent more likely to watch video on his mobile phone than the average global consumer of video by phone. Among all age groups, teens 12–17 watch the *least* amount of traditional television and, by far, do most of their television and video watching on a *mobile phone.*

When teens go online, they do so mostly to access Google. It's the site most accessed by teens in every country covered by the latest 2012 Nielsen reports on global digital media use—except for Japan, where kids like Yahoo! better. If you want to be knowledgeable about what is happening around online privacy, security, email, innovations in purchasing, and all forms of digital media usage, Google is the company to be keeping your eyes on. If you have a problem with what Google is doing, you're going to have a problem with what most other competitive companies are doing online.

Facebook is one of the top three sites accessed in every country, with the exception of Japan, where teens mostly visit FC2 and Ameba, two other social networking sites. If you're at all concerned about where your teens (and you) are getting their news and search information from, you'll need to be learning about Google, Yahoo!, MSN/Windows Live/Bing network, Wikipedia, AOL Media Network, and the *Ask* Search Network. (I hesitate to even list these sites, because it will be different—maybe radically different—in a year.) Overall, the order of amount of time spent by teens, by device:

> *Via laptop or other personal computer:* teens use Facebook mostly, then play games online, check email, and watch video/movies.

> *On mobile phones:* teens send text messages, search the Internet, go to social networking sites, make and receive calls, check email, use music or video applications, and use their camera.

And it should be noted that now almost half of all Americans are multitasking when using one or another form of media—meaning we're checking email while watching television or downloading an application while visiting a social networking site. *"Cross-platform" media use and multitasking are more the rule than the exception.*

In 2006, there were about 36 million blogs. At the time of this writing, there are now over 181 million blogs being tracked by NM Incite, a division of the Nielsen/McKinsey Company that closely watches digital media use. Sites like Tumblr,

WordPress, and Blogger are still increasing in popularity and usage among teens, although they are primarily used now by Americans in their 20s and 30s. And of course, Twitter use has skyrocketed over the last five years, with over 26 million unique visitors by the end of 2011. It seems that Americans—especially Americans from 20–35—have a lot to say about who they are and what they think.

If these activities suggest to you that teens are primarily using digital media as expressions of and ways to sculpt their identities, you're right. But if they also raised questions about the *methods* they are using to craft their identities—social networking and blogging, looking up information of all kinds, watching streaming videos, and purchasing goods and services—doing all this together with peers, uniquely exposed to what these same peers are doing, you would be *wise*. It's all *really* fun. That should remind you of "Michael's 9 Rules for Adolescent Activity" from Chapter 2 on "The Big Problems." I hope it also reminds you of Abigail Baird's research on what generates fear and anxiety for teenagers—*being evaluated and judged by their peers*. Advertisers and the advertising industry know what generates fear, avoidance, and anxiety. You need to know this, too, otherwise you and your teens are in an unfair battle for authorship of your thinking, feeling, behaving (especially purchasing) decisions. *That's what media literacy is about.*

HOW TEENS INTERACT WITH DIGITAL MEDIA

Each "highlight" below is a characteristic of teens, and the text following describes examples of how that characteristic takes shape in digital realms.

Highlight 1: Teens are capable of intense persistence in behavior.

And they are persistent in their use of digital media. In 1999 teens spent an average of 6¼ hours a day using digital media (including TV, music, audio, computer, video games, online newspapers/magazines/blogs, and movies). At that time, they still spent less time connected to digital media than they did in school. By late 2010 that number was shattered. Now teens spend an average of 10¾ hours daily exposed to digital media, and that amount is increasing as more digital media become mobile, accessible 24 hours a day, and bundled on fewer devices. While TV watching in front of a stand-alone TV set has declined for teens, TV watching has actually increased by almost 45 minutes a day because of content delivery on new media platforms. Teens are multitasking more media and cramming more content into more hours, but spending less time within an individual medium. In other words, they move more and more quickly from one content type to another, and from one media delivery platform to another.

When MySpace was sold to Rupert Murdoch's NewsCorp. for almost $600 million, some people thought he was crazy, but when participation, in less than two years, moved from 2 to 24 million kids between 12 and 20, they knew he wasn't crazy. He'd delivered 22 million eyeballs to a $20 billion dollar advertising market, because MySpace was doing digitally what kids have been doing offline for the last 60 years—hanging out with peers, expressing and defining themselves through music, style, language, and pop culture.

Since teens often possess extremely high levels of physical resilience, they are usually capable of taking on doing, feeling, and thinking more than an adult, but can also be unaware of their limits. A good example: Teens can drink more alcohol than an adult can without feeling intoxicated, but by the time they feel intoxicated, they are much more dangerously close to levels of toxicity than an adult would be. Teens are capable of great physical feats, often pushing themselves past limits, but not necessarily recognizing the limit until it has a negative consequence. This is, as we all understand, a "feature" of adolescence. But that means that we cannot ignore the effects of decreased sleep or difficulty falling asleep, increased eye strain, back/muscle aches and repetitive strain injury, increased risk of depression, and a host of other physical stress responses demonstrated with extended exposure to computers and other digital media. Research on ophthalmic issues around CRT use demonstrate that just 40 minutes of uninterrupted daily "screen" exposure increases the risk of significant eye strain and back, neck, and other muscle aches.[30] And teens are putting in almost 11 hours daily, remember? Marc Berman's research at University of Michigan showed that even brief, simple interactions with nature "produced marked increases in cognitive control...increasing effective cognitive functioning." As Nicholas Carr asked, where is the "Sleepy Hollow" on the Internet...the source for the restorative, peaceful reconfiguration our brains need to work continually, with efficiency and acumen?

Highlight 2: Teens think a lot about who to be and how to be "me."

And they are increasingly doing this online, connected with digital media. On the Internet, on their phones, while gaming, while instant messaging or text messaging, while watching television programs, while watching movies and music videos, while watching YouTube, while changing their MySpace pages or updating their status on Facebook or posting to their wall, they are participating in what new media scholar and researcher danah boyd calls "networked publics." Teens are engaged in peer-based socialization and identity formation—as they have always been—but they are radically and rapidly reconfiguring public (and private) life in the process. When they make a friend (which they may still do the old-school way, in the real world), there is a public place to post that friend's names and pictures, or to "unfriend" them after an argument. It complicates things, to be sure.

Since teens can and do use the Internet and digital media to see what goodies are being accorded to the successful, the status-worthy, their reference group for how they should be doing is now basically the entire world. You can know exactly what high-status rewards are in every country, among all peoples. Feeling bad about not being "in" or "successful" is easier than ever before, because teens' reference group for their status is larger than at any previous time in human history.

In deciding who they are and how to be themselves, teens have endless ways to present, re-present, modify, and falsify the broadest possible range of information about themselves, and unlike in face-to-face interaction, they can easily utilize digital data to support these falsified identities. Identity experimentation is a normative and normalizing facet of teen life, but online cues as to credibility, honesty, competence, and authenticity can be nearly impossible to verify. A person can readily steal or claim someone's work as their own, pay for or exchange goods or services for another to take a test, write a paper, play/advance the person in any endeavor (from game play to certification in some activity requiring specialized knowledge). Teens and adults alike can easily fake professional status, join a voluntary community with the intention of disruption, shock, or to gather data for commercial purposes or sexual exploitation. Healthy teens are inherently (and intensely) wanting connection, belonging, and community, and these impulses are easily subverted, abused, or manipulated when there is no consensus around the rules of identity "play" online. You might feel curious about your daughter exploring what it's like to pose as an NCAA-level athlete in a fake Facebook profile, but not too happy about your son posing as a cardiologist on WebMD.

Highlight 3: Teens are hyperfocused on what is and is not normal, and while they want to be "individuals," their brains signal intense danger at peer and other disapproval for straying too far from the norm.

Think of the Vassar and UCLA studies. If what registers as "dangerous" for teens are the various phenomena of being evaluated, rated, and responded to by their peers in relation to their identity choices, then one might expect anxiety and depression levels to rise as teens feel ever-more judged and publicly exposed. And this is exactly what has happened since 1994: a steady rise in levels of depression and anxiety, especially among the affluent and those with more access to the Internet and digital media. Teens who are heavy users of digital media get lower grades and report higher levels of dissatisfaction with themselves and personal relationships.

And think back to the previous chapter on identity formation. Teens must be hyperfocused on what is and is not "normal" and normative, because their job is to find a way of establishing their identities under the pressures of various roles. Teens want and need desperately to belong, and as Erikson noted over 60 years ago, healthy development often comes down to finding out if you're "in" or "out"—*for real*. But in the digital age, it is not at all easy to figure out what "is" real and what is representation. Marshall McLuhan might say that for American teens *media* really is the message and what mass (digital) media is all about is representation *as* reality. Yes, I know, I'm getting too philosophical and abstract again. Let's allow Thomas de Zengotita, author of *Mediated: How the Media Shapes Our World and the Way We Live in It*, to explain what teens (and you) are dealing with in terms of what is *real*:

> **Real real:** You fall down the stairs. Stuff in your life that's so familiar you've forgotten the statement it makes.
>
> **Observed real:** You drive by a car wreck. Stuff in your life where the image-statement is as salient as the function.
>
> **In-between real real and observed real:** Stuff that oscillates between the first two categories depending on the situation. Like, you're wearing something you usually take for granted but then you are introduced to someone attractive.
>
> **Edited real real:** Shtick you have down so pat you don't know it's shtick anymore, but you definitely only use it in certain situations. Documentaries and videos of all kinds where people are unaware of the camera, although that's not easy to detect, actually. Candid photographs.[31]

And the list goes on to include the "staged real," "edited staged real" (some reality television), "overtly unreal realistic" (an SUV blithely making its way up the side of a skyscraper), and finally, the "Unreal real: Strawberries that won't freeze because they have fish genes in them."

What de Zengotita means by "mediated" or the process of mediation "refers to arts and artifacts that represent, that communicate—but also, and especially, to their effects on the way we experience the world, and ourselves in it."[32] His book is about how mass media in general and specific ways shape our views of ourselves and the choices we make—and shape and sculpt what counts as a "Self" and as a "Choice." That's why his work is so important for understanding adolescent identity development.

In the *mediated* world that de Zengotita describes, it's difficult if not impossible at times to experience or locate the "freely pledged" commitment. He smartly points to the teen use of the expression "whatever" as the essential verbal word for the times as they "negotiate the field of options that so incessantly solicit our attention and allegiance" (p. 15). "Whatever" means whatever you want, whatever you can get, whatever you can think of or do, without limit. *It's all good,* because all options are on the table. Endless, limitless options and opportunities—*optionality.* There is barely a gadget or advertisement that doesn't allude to this. It's all about *customization,* and giving you what you want so you can be whomever you choose to be. You *choose,* you create your unique Self. You can go with a custom iPhone cover, as long as you have an iPhone. Or choose a Droid phone, if you want to be a "rebel" or don't want to stand in line for six hours waiting for your ultra-cool phone (a recent commercial directly played on this very notion). It is the representation in consumer culture of the American dream: Everyone is born equal, everyone can choose, everyone can be a Success.

I'm sorry, but *no they can't.* Teenagers especially—despite what advertising and mass media try to get them to think—know at a very basic level that they cannot do anything that want, without limit. They know this deep down, and their failure to achieve impossible levels of "success" form direct and indirect daily attacks on their self-esteem. Your son or daughter might *like* to have no limits, economically or geographically or in terms of work or whom they love (or have sex with), but as Erikson notes, the entry into adulthood is about the *narrowing* of *real* choices, and the adaptation to limitations about who you are likely to become, given the resources available to you. The entry into young adulthood is about making commitments *anyway,* and learning to grieve the losses in healthy ways. *One* teenager might be able to have "whatever" he wants, but *all* teenagers cannot.

What would it even mean for "everyone to be successful," given the accoutrements of success currently available in American culture? *A chicken in every pot?* No way: It means a *Hummer* in every driveway, two summer houses (one in Aspen and one in St. Moritz), a winter house on Maui, an apartment in Manhattan (or a cute brownstone near Prospect Park), a seven-figure income, unfettered access to quick, comfortable travel, healthy, delicious, un-genetically-modified, plentiful food, clean, plentiful drinking water, and an endless (at least for your lifetime) supply of oil (or source of renewable energy). That "lifestyle" is not something everyone can have, for reasons that seem obvious to me. And besides, even if "a lot" of teenagers could have that—say, 20 to 30 million of them—that lifestyle would quickly become passé and lose some of its status luster, because "everybody" would be at the same level. It would probably create a migration to a yurt-centered lifestyle in the desert or an increase in the construction of huge, gloating private islands populating the oceanic areas of the planet.

So "whatever" *also* means "I don't care, because I have no power to choose." Huh? How can it mean both "I have all the power and all the choices are great" *and* "I have no power to choose"? It's nothing fancy, since a word can denote a meaning and its opposite: It's called an *auto-antonym*. That's why adolescence in America right now is "literally" a "puzzle." Both of those words are auto-antonyms, as "literally" can denote something "real" or something virtual or figurative and "puzzle" can be about "posing a problem" or "solving a problem."

As teens "stray too far from the norms" of success in America, their brains signal "danger." The danger isn't real, but it is real. Or rather, it's "real real." There is no tiger at the door, waiting to maul your teenager if she doesn't wear the *right* fashion or have the *right* house in the *right* neighborhood. But the *risk* for her identity development is real, if her perception of what constitutes a real, authentic choice is narrowed down to "one way of being a success," and all teens are after the same piece of the pie.

Highlight 4: Many teens do not yet have fully developed "executive functioning" capacities (long-term planning, exercise of empathy, impulse control, priority-setting, gratification delay, organizational acumen).

These executive functions form a significant baseline of cognitive skills necessary for the full development of an ethical framework for living. Research demonstrates rather pronounced ethical "fault lines" among those growing up with the new digital media. Consensus on norms of self-representation and self-expression has not yet developed among youth online around five crucial areas: identity, privacy, ownership, authorship, credibility, and participation. And these areas are rich for the kind of unethical behaviors the 2009 MacArthur Foundation report called "bad play." The report suggests new, more troublesome norms are emerging among online youth, in which unethical, dangerous, and otherwise hurtful behaviors are not only tolerated but encouraged because of the difficulty of controlling the behavior or identifying the "sources" of "bad play." While the report does not suggest that "bad play" is becoming the norm online, it does beg the question of how and whether teens themselves are thinking about their ethical responsibilities, given the characteristics of new digital media and its high participation factor AND how and to whom teens are looking for mentoring, guidance, and support around questions of ethicality online. Are we, as parents or as educators, thinking deeply about forms of media literacies and offering the possibility of developing these literacies at home, at school, or in wider community institutions?

While most teenagers may be able to negotiate the development of these new norms just fine, there is even more recent evidence that teens are not as good at this as we might think, and can often be incredibly cruel "digital citizens."[33] Amanda Lenhart—one of the country's most important researchers on teens and social media—works for the Pew Internet & American Life Project, and recently conducted a study on how youth behave on social networking sites. Many teens report having good experiences online, but harassment, cyberbullying, and misuse of personal material (including sexual photographs) is clearly also occurring. The anonymity and rapid dissemination of information via digital media often leads to risk-taking that might be mitigated in person. As with most risk-taking phenomena in teen lives, risky or cruel teen behaviors are significantly mitigated by parent involvement—including conversations about what can go wrong when we don't treat one another well online. Teenagers, who tend to be impulsive or have difficulty focusing on one thing at a time, can also just make *mistakes* that they later regret but are hard to "take back." For example, there's a new Facebook application that efficiently and quickly lets a group of people in your Facebook circle know that you have a sexually transmitted infection (STI). What if your daughter and her boyfriend are fighting, and her boyfriend (who knows her Facebook password) impulsively decides to tell 150 of her closest friends that she's contracted chlamydia? If they patch things up later, that's a mistake that's hard to take back.

It's not just a question of "bad play" or the lack of normative consensus online. Teens (and adults) now regularly text or access digital media during meals, during religious services, during psychotherapy sessions, and at weddings and funerals. The electronic devices that we have play to our deepest emotional, psychological, and physiological needs to belong and connect. From an evolutionary standpoint, we are wired to respond to things that psychologically "tap us on the shoulder"—things like message-waiting beeps, email-received notices, and all kinds of "pop-up" reminders—because we need to know if the thing that popped up is a danger or an opportunity for pleasure. Neither teens nor adults have developed norms about when the time is right to respond to these digital cues.

Bill Drayton, prime developer of the social entrepreneur movement—a man considered by many to be on the shortlist of most influential Americans—founded the Ashoka Institute with the overarching purpose of creating citizen changemakers who can and will solve the major problems facing every world inhabitant. His belief is that the underlying bedrock of this movement centers around a singular focus on the development of the strongest possible sense of empathy in every single child. His belief, shared by many political leaders, is that this is necessary for America's economic and social survival in a global marketplace. The MacArthur report and annual publications and research of the Josephsen Institute suggest a growing "empathy" gap among digital youth and point to ways in which the very structures of digital media help to undermine the cognitive processes involved in developing empathy and what I referred to earlier as "theory of mind," an understanding not only of the Other as different but as holding an inviolable integrity.

Highlight 5: Teens' abilities around short-, medium-, and long-term memory is still "under construction" and is often dependent upon the ideas of "salience detection" and "use it or lose it."

We are beginning to see a small flood of stories in the popular press about just what is registering as "salient" for teens and what kinds of experiences they want to repeat. At a talk on "Ethics and Digital Media" in San Francisco, young and hip Rabbi Joshua Strulowitz—himself a father of three—related the story of a friend's daughter who wraps her cellphone in a plastic bag so that she can take it into the shower with her, just to make sure she won't miss a text. The rabbi wondered aloud whether this wasn't too much being in touch. Another participant at that talk, Matt Richtel, Pulitzer Prize–winning *New York Times* correspondent, makes the kind of analogy I like parents to know about: "If you are building a hut, and a lion comes into the hut, it sends a message to the prefrontal cortex to *run*. So, there is a constant dialogue going on between the prefrontal cortex and central cortex." Richtel is talking about that "tapping you on the shoulder" that happens where you need to find out if that interruption is a threat or not. For teens, he argues, there is no developed gatekeeper (this would be a well-developed prefrontal cortex) that jumps in to say, "Um, not the right time."[34] Richtel is right. But there is, however, a message that says there is "danger" afoot, if you don't or can't connect to your peers, and if the lack of connection or lack of certainty would result in a loss of status or problem with the representation of your identity. This is what those Vassar and UCLA studies are, in part, telling us: Teens feel that being evaluated negatively by their peers is the kind of danger on par with having a tiger "tap you" on the shoulder. A new American study recently confirmed the power of that "tap" on the shoulder—and told us something about salience and repetition—when it was reported that people experienced cravings around using Twitter and email more often and more intensely than they experienced cravings to use alcohol or nicotine (one of the most addictive substances studied). One of the author's lead researchers said, "Desires for media may be comparatively harder to resist because of their high availability and also because it feels like it does not 'cost much' to engage in these activities, even though one wants to resist."[35]

So, we worry about them not enhancing their abilities around memory, or their salience detection being otherwise hijacked by processes that are designed to highly stimulate the adolescent brain and draw attention. But it's not just a question of what skills and what behaviors are being practiced and developed. It is also a question of what might be lost or atrophied. We know from thousands of years of history that the ushering in of any new, transformative technologies is accompanied by the loss or diminishment of certain human capacities. Marshall McLuhan described this when he wrote that "our tools end up numbing the part of the body that they amplify"—we could alienate and distance ourselves from the amplified part and its natural function. McLuhan might not have known the science behind this phenomenon, but it is now increasingly clear that neurological plasticity means that, in actual fact, parts of us become more alienated, distant, and unused as we learn and repeat our use of new technology.[36] This isn't just more of McLuhan's "doom and gloom" scenario. One study out of the dozens of researches into these phenomenon concerns an investigation of London cabbies, who have been shown to have significant larger hippocampal volumes, testifying to their world-renowned knowledge of the impossibly difficult London street system. But GPS is changing all that. But GPS is changing all of that. As cabbies relied more on the shiny new GPS technology, certain parts of their brains began shrinking that had previously been tapped to negotiate the impossibly difficult streets of London. This same loss of capacity accompanies every major technological shift. Nicholas Carr is worth quoting at length, here:

> When the power loom was invented, weavers could manufacture far more cloth...but they sacrificed some of their manual dexterity, not to mention some of their "feel" for fabric. Their fingers, in McLuhan's terms, became numb. Farmers, similarly, lost some of their feel for the soil when they began using mechanical harrows and plows. Today's industrial farm worker, sitting in his air-conditioned cage atop a gargantuan tractor, rarely touches the soil at all—though in a single day he can till a field that his hoe-wielding forebear could not have turned in a month. When we're behind the wheel of our car, we can go a far greater distance than we could cover on foot, but we lose the walker's intimate connection to the land...the mechanical clock, for all the blessings it bestowed, removed us from the natural flow of time...the tools of the mind amplify and in turn numb the most intimate, the most human, of our natural capacities—those for reason, perception, memory, emotion.[37]

One Dutch study illustrated Carr and McLuhan's point quite distinctly. Subjects were asked to perform a complicated task while a particularly friendly computer software program gave the subjects hints, tips, and directions to solve the task more easily. Other subjects were provided with only a "bare bones" program with minimal help. Subjects in the first group dove into the task and took an early lead over the "bare bones" group, but in the end, they were significantly slower in task completion than the group with much less computer assistance. Other studies have replicated the Dutch study, finding that the more user-friendly the software interface, the less efficacious end users become as they quickly learn to externalize the problem-solving, shutting down key areas of the prefrontal and ventral and occipital cortices usually involved in complex problem-solving. This intellectual "outsourcing" apparently leaves parts of the brain under- and unemployed, affecting current and future task performance.

And while Carr is not without his detractors, who put him firmly in the McLuhan camp, out to spoil the technology party, he brings to the table what McLuhan could not—a long list of research studies, rooted in the very digital technology advances he's writing about, that show demonstrable brain effects about which he's concerned. Various technology and Internet champions like Clay Shirky or even brain development researchers who think Carr is too much of a naysayer, who's already decided that technology is "evil," don't engage him on his points—they just think he's wrong that we have something to worry much about. But Carr's remarkable work on how the Internet is changing our brains is not a lengthy tome on how we should do away with the Internet. It is a plea for media literacy and choice—telling us that technology, by its very nature, changes us, and that that can always be and has always been both a blessing and a curse.

Highlight 6: Neurological plasticity is a defining hallmark of the adolescent brain: While the basic structure and number of neurons is relatively fixed, functionality, capacity, efficacy, emphases, and preferences in cognition and behavior and a host of other qualities are highly changeable based upon environmental influences.

Nicholas Carr is keen to emphasize an important part about adolescence and learning: Teen brains get good at what they practice, and they are practicing a lot of Internet use.

> If, knowing what we know today about the brain's plasticity, you were to set out to invent a medium that would rewire our mental circuits as quickly and thoroughly as possible, you would probably end up designing something that looks a lot like the Internet. It's not that we tend to use the Net regularly, even obsessively. It's that the Net delivers precisely the kind of cognitive and sensory stimuli—repetitive, interactive, intensive, addictive—that have been shown to result in strong and rapid alterations in brain circuits and functions.[38]

Advances in digital video technology are, within a few short years, going to allow real-time access to any place on Earth, at any time. Entire generations of teens are going to grow up not knowing what it is like to *not* see people when they talk to them, or to not see what's happening in a particular area of the globe. This is going to occasion fundamental changes in the way teens experience time and space.

Teens are reading differently, when they're reading online. It is much easier now to click on hyperlinks and to shift content focus. It's not uncommon to begin reading a selection and find yourself reading something entirely different and unrelated within a few minutes. Sustained concentration on a singular task is becoming increasingly difficult and rare. "Scanning" is replacing old-style reading, and strikes teens as easier and more relevant, especially when content is mixed—words with photographs, videos, music, hyperlinks to other platforms and content—and in smaller snippets, rather than long, sustained, linear narrative format. Teens and adults alike say they often feel "smarter" the more they spend time online, but they also feel much more impatient and less able to focus. Duke and other universities have begun to study changing eye-movement and cortical function as teens increasingly no longer read left to right, but now up and down, skipping from side to side. Teens have embraced the Net's "uniquely rapid-fire mode of collecting and dispensing information."[39] And I'm not happy to report that the data so far shows that teens not only do not remember more in a hypermedia-rich environment like the Internet, they remember less, short- and long-term, and report more difficulty with memory, in general, in relation to exposure to digital media. Despite hopes and some beliefs that the Internet and multimedia-based methods would increase student engagement, attention, and performance, a 2010 paper published by USF Professor Stephen Morris showed no significant differences in learning outcomes when material was presented to college business school students using "blended" methods (conventional text reading/didactic instructional methods plus use of on-line and other new media platforms).[40] Many studies in the last few years have demonstrated that when students have access to digital media like cellphones and laptop computers with Internet access while attending class, they remember significantly less material, short- and long-term, than their counterparts who had to "suffer" through listening to the teacher talk during class, without benefit of a digital distraction. It seems that there are fairly set limits (at least right now in human history) around what we can pay attention to successfully without parts of the brain beginning to shut down or otherwise screen out input. That will most certainly change over generations, but it isn't going to change in a few years. Every major study of human multitasking shows decreased measures of performance on all levels, as we begin to pay attention to more than one thing at a time—despite the claims that teens can multitask well. I'm not saying they don't enjoy it. I'm just saying that the research doesn't support the idea that it makes them "better" or otherwise more effective at any of the activities they are multitasking.

Naysayers (and there are plenty of them) say that concerns about how the Internet is changing the way we think and feel are overblown—headline-grabbing fear-mongering akin to the madding crowds that protested the advent of books and the teaching of reading to women. In *Is the Internet Changing the Way You Think?* John Brockman asked 150 influential, extremely smart people around the world this very question.[41] It's stunning to see so many people (who aren't politicians), in one place, *not* answering a question. Many dodged the question, some answered another question of their own choosing, some said, "yes," many said "no," and a fair number said they just didn't know or it was too early to tell, but we need to be studying the effects. That seems reasonable to me. *What do you think?*

So is the Internet and access to digital media really all that important to teens? I think the answer is "yes," for many teens it is. But you might want to ask the 17-year-old Chinese teenager who sold his kidney for about $35,000 and received only 10 percent of the sale—enough to purchase both an iPad and an iPhone, which was his intended purpose in having the organ removed. It didn't turn out so well: As of April 12, 2012, his condition was deteriorating rapidly and five people were arrested and charged with illegal organ trading. Including the surgeon, and the broker who spent his time searching through online chat rooms looking for kids interested in selling any organs they might not need. It should be noted that this case was first reported by a Chinese news agency in a country not particularly known for its open and transparent media, so one can only guess that the Chinese government wasn't trying too hard to discourage this sort of behavior—which would indicate this is the sort of thing that could or would happen among many Chinese youth, and is not the act of just one particular crazy, now kidney-deficient teenager.[42]

If most adolescents are deeply desiring to engage with digital media and the Internet and they are learning new technologies and organizing their lives differently based upon those technologies—as they undeniably are—then the Internet (and digital media) are changing the way your teens think, feel, and behave. It's ridiculous to deny that. What people are arguing about, I think, is the *significance* of those changes. Political scientist Langdon Winner argues that "if the experience of modern society shows us anything...it is that technologies are not merely aids to human activity, but also powerful forces acting to reshape that activity and its meaning."[43]

Highlight 7: Teens assess most incoming information in reference to how much they like or dislike it—its packaging, the cognitive load it places upon their brains, etc. They prefer pleasurable, high-reward, high-stimulation, low-effort activities, in general.

Teens use social networking—and like it immensely. It is not a tool; it is a way of life, precisely because it registers as so highly salient, because of its structure and purpose. Social networking (which now includes instant messaging, texting, sharing photos/music, blogging, and emailing) is the activity par excellence for the developmental task of identity formation. Over 87 percent of American teens visit a social networking site at least daily, and a significant percentage of teens are always connected via digital device to one or more social networking sites. Even kids who are philosophically opposed to the "shallowness" of social networking often or eventually give in and get accounts, because while they might not feel the need to define themselves through living online, they know many of their friends are doing so and they want to stay connected to them. Social networking sites and Internet sites in general that attract teen users are designed with interfaces geared toward high-reward, high-stimulation, low-effort activities. It's interesting, however, to note that among a small group of my clients, some are consciously deciding to "unplug" from a variety of, though not all digital media platforms. These young men and women tell me they feel that being online is a waste of time and makes *them* feel like a waste of time. They still connect with digital media devices, computer, and software—but tend to do so to make art or music of some type, and highly value the face-to-face interaction with their peers and potential audiences for their works.

Highlight 8: Teens need to be able to experience, articulate, and express their feelings, and need close others to do that with. This "affect management" is one of, if not the most important skill for an adolescent, because the leading causes of adolescent morbidity are all related to difficulties with affect management.

One of my favorite writers and researchers, Antonio Damasio (at USC), explains to us that not only certain types of *thinking* require a calm state of mind. The more complex emotional experiences involving empathy, compassion, and understanding of others require neural processes that Damasio calls "inherently slow." The faster things happen in the world around us, the harder it becomes to experience emotions about the mental and emotional states of others. This seems intuitively true for most of us, and probably contributes to understanding the "bystander" syndrome that occurs when fast-moving, traumatic events occur and most of us "freeze" as a stress response, less capable of understanding our own emotional state, let alone the state of another.

I could be accused here of "burying the lede." Highlight 8 is probably the most important highlight, and it alludes to the subheading of this chapter: Please slow down. The Internet and digital media are all about *speed*. Rapidity allows for so much, especially in terms of brain function. You might remember that as neuronal connections are made during adolescence, the brain's "processing capabilities" can rise 3000 percent in terms of speed and efficiency. More connections mean more and faster learning. But parents have to ask: *What* are we learning and what are we teaching? Living life online and in the digital world means that there are rapid and often long-lasting (or permanent) consequences as a result of very quick clicks, key presses, and taps on a screen. We see this with grown adults all the time—just ask Spike Lee (or see a bit later in this chapter about the entire trajectory of media coverage of Trayvon Martin's killing). And adolescents are even more impulsive, fast to act, and more deeply and quickly feeling and acting on their choices—all the result of normal developmental forces. So it's even more important that we teach our children (and ourselves) how to *slow down* in our adoption, use, and understanding of digital media.

Teens need their peers close, and while they can tend to push parents away, they overwhelmingly report needing their parents close and "on standby." But the digital divide is not only evident by race, ethnicity, and socioeconomic status; it is also defined by age. Teens use the Internet and adopt and master new media much more quickly and more often than adults. Nearly 100 percent of teens go online, but a surprisingly high percentage of Americans between 36 and 55 (close to 20 percent) are not Internet users; overall large percentages of Internet users never go online to do instant messaging (50 percent), work on a blog (79 percent), participate in chat rooms (80 percent), or make or receive phone calls (85 percent). These are all routinely practiced by teens 8 to 18.

Social networking—one of the primary means by which teens now socialize—is not your mom's (or even your) social networking, where you met at the mall or the local park and hung out together. As researcher danah boyd reminds us, there are elements in social networking that are unique to living online. Remember those characteristics of digital data and information? In the "networked public" lives of teens, danah boyd points out, there are qualities of "persistence, searchability, exact copyability, and invisible audiences. These properties fundamentally alter social dynamics, complicating the ways in which people interact."[44] I would add, too, that since data is always available 24/7, flexibly represented, easy to manipulate and falsify, fast and easy to distribute, hard to get rid of and often created and consumed with many, many others at the same time, the chances for hurt feelings, misunderstandings, embarrassment, pain, and heartache increase, making the Internet a good place for a teen to feel bad.

Teens are not using social media, gaming, blogging, and the like to disconnect from others, becoming more isolated in front of a computer screen—they do these things to connect to others, and that's why researcher danah boyd calls them "networked publics." But teens still feel isolated and even numb—their connections online are pervasive but don't seem to get in "deeply." This seems understandable when we consider that recent research has demonstrated that the full understanding, feeling, and articulation of strong emotion, empathy, and compassion require time—longer times than those usually afforded by interactions in digital media platforms, which are usually geared toward speed in ways that face-to-face interaction is not and cannot be. Teens crave and require privacy to develop a sense of agency. But as they withdraw into the privacy of their rooms and the ear-bud-filled world of the iPod, it can become hard to distinguish the dividing line between alienation, loneliness, and the healthy privacy needed for their autonomy. Teens don't "separate" from us during adolescence, as psychologists used to say. Their autonomy is related autonomy—it is about figuring out who you are, alongside others, in relation to them.

Teens are tweeting about what's happening in their lives. Sometimes they tweet in ways that allow for "hiding in plain sight," through the use of code, "in jokes," and a variety of other techniques. They comment on things that are happening out there. Can they also write a meaningful tweet about things happening "inside," in a way that is compelling and worth paying attention to? This could be key time—even using digital media—spent in touch with their emotional, inner world...trying to articulate it.

Teens are forming and advertising their identities on Facebook and on other social networking sites. Is your teen creating different personas online and really studying their own and others' responses to these "parts" of themselves? Where are they getting the skills to analyze peer reactions to their media selves? Where are they learning *deep* media literacy? Can they create a website and web presence in a way that isn't cookie-cutter...that represents hard work, a real journey into what matters to them...or is it all going to be about Mafia Wars, Farmville, pre-packaged Facebook quizzes about "How Hot Are You" or "How Evil Are You," "What Kind of Lover Are You?" or "Who Will You Be in 10 Years?" Can your son or daughter think about, write about, draw about, play music about, dance about, argue about, hope about who they will be in 10 years, without a Facebook quiz?

Highlight 9: Teens care deeply about what others (parents, teachers, friends) think of them and use this information as primary material in identity formation. They get their main (but certainly not their only) cues about who to be, how to be, what to have, and what to do from their peer group. Therefore, status concerns are of central importance, influencing and/or informing just about every choice a teen makes...and these can be played out endlessly on the Internet.

In 1985, 8 percent of American households had a computer, and the Internet as we know it didn't exist. By 2006, over 80 percent of American homes with children had one or more computers and 92 percent had access to the Internet.

Teens get their news online, but over the last few years trustworthiness of information found online has been steadily dropping. Digital media aren't just neutral channels of information: They not only su pply content (they filter what is "worth" paying attention to) but also shape the process of thought. How do we know this? Because we know about neural plasticity and the way brains work in general—this is not unique to how "brains work under the influence of digital media." In other words, we learn and adapt, and learning and adaptation is a cellular process, as well as a social one. A study by James Evans at the University of Chicago noted that automated search engine technology tended strongly to serve as amplifiers of popular information, rapidly establishing and then maintaining a consensus about what is and isn't "important." We know from the recent heated battles over "Net neutrality" that there is an ongoing fight to determine what information gets to whom, how quickly or slowly it arrives or whether it arrives at all to you, whether that be via search engine or fragmentation processes where certain content is excluded from reaching you based on criteria decided by the Internet service provider or instrument of State power. And as we'll recall, what teen brains practice at is often what gets put squarely in front of them. It takes sustained effort, critical thinking, and solid literacy in digital media usage to ignore or temporarily set aside what is handed to you, in favor of what else might be out there. Forbearance isn't exactly the strong suit of cognitive skills for teens. Low efforts, high reward, remember?

Internet Commerce and Behavioral Targeting

The "commercial" Internet—a self-serving term for those who want you to focus on the idea that the Internet is not *all about* commerce and monetization—is one unbelievably mega-large *shopping innovation*. You know, shopping innovations…like the mall, the shopping cart, the smart Carte, automatic doors, bar codes, credit cards, coupons, mail order catalogs, and large-inventory department stores. It's really fun to go to if you're a child or preteen. There are always a bunch of people handing out free samples, coupons, ride tickets, and other enticements to try out new things. There is always the hope that you'll buy something, and then buy something else. If you're having a lot of fun all the better, because the process of separating you from your money will be less conscious, therefore less painful for you. The Internet is not *all* commercial, you might say. And besides, what's wrong with window-shopping? And what's the problem if I never even go near a store and never even get my cash or credit card out of my wallet? I'm just here to meet my friends, browse around, and that's it.

That seems fine to me. Except that that's not the way the Internet works. While you "browse around," thousands of companies have their figurative eyes and hands on you, watching every place you visit (or even look at), every purchase you do happen to make, how long you're online, and the pattern of the innocuous visits you make. It's what the Internet is—it's a place for you to go and have fun, browsing information or talking to your friends—but all for a price. The price is that your every move is going to be watched by someone whose interest is to sell you something and potentially restrict your access to certain parts of American society. That restriction might be a "good" thing, in the case of tracking potential terrorist activity online, but a "bad" thing if the information on Google search you entered five minutes ago for your 87-year old mom—"dementia care and aging"—is provided in real time to the healthcare site you're now visiting to get a quote on insurance for you and your two kids. Yes, that happens.[45] The current "basic privacy" standards on the Internet might not allow the health insurance site to know that the customer *now* entering data into the online application is *you,* but they do allow the insurance company to know that whoever you are, you were just searching about "dementia" online. There are no laws right now that prevent them for turning you down for insurance or adjusting your potential premium costs with the idea you might be a customer with a very high *utilization rate*. That is to say, you're going to be very expensive, and so they are going to charge you more.

It's not just the Internet—it's about being tracked on *all digital media.*

If you have seven minutes until your doctor's appointment, say, in Vestavia, Alabama, and your GPS location through Google analytics shows you're in Mt. Brook, the doctor's office can send you a message and let you know you're probably going to be late if you don't get going. Cool, right? I'm wondering if you can think of any situations, though, in which you might not want to be tracked or reminded. Or if that isn't the case, I wonder if you might not want someone other than Google to track you, if they happen to get their hands on that information in real time.

What are companies like BlueKai tracking? That's not hard to find out. The quote, below is from the TARGUSinfo brochure about "On Demand Insight"—that means, information that you can purchase from Targus about consumer behavior. Their brochure details just why they're *better* than BlueKai, for example, since they collect so much offline data and online data about consumers that they get a better, more intimate picture of *you and me:*

> The verified *offline* [italics mine] data accounts for not only demographics but family status, number of children, hobbies, home ownership, lifestyle patterns, hobbies and avocations, discretionary purchasing priorities, brand and product affinities, education, income and occupational status. AdAdvisor provides hundreds of persistent likely behaviors—providing a holistic view of the consumer and predictive data to corroborate online behaviors. For each AdAdvisor segment, ad servers have an extensive list of user demographics, interests, lifestyles, browsing behaviors and purchase behaviors—enabling them to resourcefully match their available inventory with their current set of advertisers.[46]

If you want a real treat, just visit their website at www.targusinfo.com and watch their little animation showing how easy it is to find a list of personally identifiable information on you the length of your arm.

That's not all. There's hardly a day that goes by that you can't read some story about "hacking," "back doors," and urban legends (and realities) about what is possible regarding digital media use and privacy (or the lack thereof). Most of you have by now heard of the British tabloid scandal involving Rupert Murdoch's newspapers. The scandal involved the illegal hacking of cellphones and cellphone voicemail, along with bribery of police officers to leak confidential information about politicians, celebrities, and other public and private figures. Dozens of reporters, editors, executives, and law enforcement personnel have been arrested.[47] It's been known for a while that the camera on your laptop can be remote-activated, without your knowledge.[48] Many in the industry are aware of illegal "back doors" and perfectly legal government-sanctioned means of access to your computer (and all the data on the computer) through the software installed on the computer. Teens (and more and more parents) are well aware of spyware which can be downloaded onto a computer, allowing people (like your parents) to track every single keystroke you make on your computer, get your entire browsing history (even if you delete it), and see screenshots of what is being done and seen online.

Behavioral targeting—the practice referred to above—has been going on (online) since the early days of the Internet.[49] This practice is made possible through a number of different technologies all geared toward connecting digital media user behavior with the characteristics of the user: ethnic background, age, gender, socioeconomic data, whether you rent or own, your annual salary, occupation, geographic information like zip codes of work and home, where you browse the Internet from when you purchase, and a host of other "data points." Behavioral targeting companies hook up with advertising companies and partner websites to allow large and small corporations alike (for a hefty price) access to this information, in order to individually target the consumer with advertisements. Some of the companies doing behavior targeting and data mining include Akami Technologies, BlueKai, Rapleaf, Invidi, eXelate, TACODA, 24/7 Real Media, Adveritising.com, DoubleClick, Atlas, and Axciom.

Some of your information mined by these companies is personally identifiable (PII), like your name, email, and social security number, and some is not ("non-PII"). Put these three pieces together—a) where you go online, how long you stay there, what you click on, in what order you do your clicking; b) all the personally identifiable information a company can get; and c) all your non–personally identifiable information—and add in the same information from hundreds of thousands of other people, and you get some pretty solid information about what consumers are doing and why.

Your information is being culled by three main methods—via browser "cookies" (a file placed on your computer), Flash cookies, and Web bugs (or "beacons"). Basically, anything you do with digital media leaves a trace that can be tracked. Politicians have known this for decades and the "smart" ones never do anything incriminating via digital media. If they want to talk to someone "privately," they go for a walk (somewhere out of the line of sight of a listening device) and chat the old-fashioned way; either that or they send old-fashioned letters. I believe it is still illegal to open someone's mail without a federal warrant.

It's important to note that this information gathering and digital "profiling" isn't just about being able to place a convenient but innocuous little ad about "the Nikon D40 digital camera" next to your Gmail window (hours after, minutes after, or as you browse online for a Nikon D40). And if you look for a D40, rather than a Canon EOS 5D Mark II, the good folks at Axciom or Rapleaf, for example, know that you're a lower-status target—and what advertisers will put in your path will be different than the high-status consumer who can afford to drop $4,500 on a digital camera. It's not just about sending you a coupon for ice cream or a well-placed ad for a new Jeep. It's also about advising media buyers about where to place "news stories" and ads that are barely disguised as "news" or entertainment features on websites that you happen to frequent, so that you just happen to read an article that is related to the thing for which you may (or may not) be shopping.

Behavioral targeting and digital "profiling" has its doublespeak and jargon, too. You are either a *target* or you're *waste*. A target is an online consumer really worth following—the patterns of their digital activities are meaningful and they're worth going after because they've got money. If not, well, you're *waste*. That doesn't mean the marketers are going to ignore you; it just means you're going to get different kinds of "options" presented to you and embedded in your digital experience. Companies are still happy to have your money; they just don't care as much about you. It's a bit like the difference between an institutional investor at a brokerage firm and being an account holder at a major bank. If you're in the latter category, you're cute but you ultimately don't matter too much, money-wise.

But what kind of target are you (or your teen)? Are you a "socially liberal organic eater" or the "single city struggler"? You might just be the "diabetic individual in the household." Even though you may *not even have diabetes*. In the brave new world of digital marketing, if you visited Diabeticlifestyle.com for your aging aunt, and you're a female, there's a good chance you'll become the "diabetic individual in the household," and will soon start seeing ads, receiving emails and coupons from Nutrisystem, or magically seeing "news" stories about Glucerna. com. You okay with that? That might all be just a little disconcerting and just mildly annoying. Things might really get interesting, though, when you visit a health insurance website in a few weeks and try to get a quote on a policy, only to find your rates are unusually high. This insurance company may very well have figured out that the person with your IP ("Internet protocol") address attached to your laptop computer belongs to "diabetic individual in the household." Now do I have your attention? Joseph Turow, author of *The Daily You: How the New Advertising Industry Is Defining Your Identity and Your Worth,* got my attention—he's the one who outlined for me how the new marketing and advertising industries work in the digital age. Who's got your *teenager's* attention? What is he or she doing right now, as you read this book?

So, you didn't agree to all this? Your teen didn't agree to this? Oh, well. It's going on and it's a multi-billion dollar business. Advertisers and corporations know that if you can afford it (and often, even if you can't) you want to buy what your teens and children want. For millions of teenagers in America, given our relative affluence in this country—it's mostly *all* disposable income. Turow provides more details for the anthropological and philosophical vision provided by Thomas de Zengotita: Mass media and corporations want your teenager's money, and they're going to try to get it by becoming the primary sources of identity development for your kids. This isn't some crazy conspiracy theory. As argued earlier, the idea is to link up, as soon as possible in the life of your child, brand loyalty with *identity*, such that your child comes to feel that choosing to buy this or that is a *natural* choice, reflective of who they *really* are and *what they really care about*. I chose Levi's jeans. Nobody *made me do that. Yes, they did*. Some of the smartest people in the world—and some not so brilliant people right out of college—are paid anywhere from a modest wage to an obscene amount of money to work very, very hard to *make you buy things*. And the work these folks do is what your teens see daily on their iPads, iPods, laptop and desktop computers, smartphones, on Facebook, Yahoo!, through Google searches, on library computers and kiosks, radio, billboards, Internet cafés, on gaming devices, on buses, at schools, in airports. Who's got your teenager's attention?

You might be thinking that your daughter isn't online all the time; she watches MTV or VH1—it's just a bunch of stupid television shows (it used to be a music video channel, but that was a different decade). In fact, you've seen one or two of them, like *Real Life* and *If You Really Knew Me*. Those are pretty good shows, in fact. They show real teens doing real things and they treat teenagers very respectfully. True. But the "we care about teenagers" division is a small division in a mega-corporation like Viacom. As media critic Mark Crispin Miller puts it, "The MTV machine doesn't listen to the young so that it can make the young happier. It doesn't listen to the young so it can come up with startling new kinds of music…[it tunes in] so it can figure out how to pitch what Viacom has to sell to those kids." The relationship between media and teenager is a symbiotic one—one that was explored beautifully in the Frontline special *The Merchants of Cool*.[50] The program detailed the collapsing distinction between culture and marketing, and showed how the creation and usurping of "cool" is the stock in trade for media giants and advertisers who want to get close to your teenagers, to help create, foster, and maintain identities that buy what they're selling.

What's the problem, you say? Am I sounding too much like a Communist who's against free market capitalism? What's wrong with consumer choice and customization? But if you're already in the camp of folks who think it is or might be problematic, then you want some answers to at least a few hundred questions. Perhaps the most important questions, though, include: What, if any, are the limits on the power of the marketplace to invade or even define privacy in the name of "just doing business"? What are the relative influences between corporate control of media and authentic individual autonomy and choice, "free" of the influences of state and market? What is the role of a public realm or vital sector between state and market that has and enforces protections *against* abuses or largely unchecked power of states and markets?[51] How and where does my child really get to decide who they are and who they want to be, without being primarily controlled or prefigured or assaulted by concerns about *buying (a product or service)* and/or *status (how and whether the "world" loves you)?*

To be fair, the problems of how much power the media and the marketplace have to define identity and shape behavior have been argued for 100 years. That argument is not exclusive to digital media. The "new" part of all this is the incredible pervasiveness and accessibility to "targets" and "waste" afforded by digital media, and the consolidation of technology, messaging, and access to consumers of all ages, all the time. I'm not a Communist. I just believe in a fair fight, and this isn't a fair fight. Trillions of dollars in technology and know-how stacked up against a 15-year-old boy or girl is not a fair fight in the battle of who gets the power to define Identity, Self, Worth/Self-Esteem.

I'm going to close this section with a somewhat tongue-in-cheek plea for parental commitment to media literacy—and for a movement to learn about the power of media (specifically digital media) to define identity for American children. It seems reasonable to me, at least in a democratic society, that if one segment of the population is going to have enormous power and influence, those subject to those influences should be *informed.* The phenomena of the digital world are never happening in one direction only, and that's true in terms of identity formation. Teenagers are participating in the creation of content and process with digital media. Researchers call these activities the creation of *participatory cultures.*

I'm not arguing for corporations to stop making money or for the digital advertising industry to just go away. I just happen to believe in *mutuality* and *consent* in a free society. I'm not against consenting adults doing what they chose to do. But we're talking here about adults versus children. Children whose brains are "massively plastic," and whose task is to figure out who they are, what they feel, what they think and want, and how they're going to live their lives. Our job is to protect our children and teens as best we can and to help give them the information they need to make consenting and informed decisions. A teenager cannot, by any stretch of the imagination, do this, without *media literacy,* including: specialized information about mass media, digital advertising, neural marketing, the role of the stand-alone media buyer, privacy and constitutional law, issues of unequal access to skills and know-how of the digital world, ethics of "play" and "work" with and "on" digital media, informed consent, identity development, and the politics of autonomy. Those are a *few* items on a very long list. *Why these things are not a major part of the high school and middle school curriculum is completely beyond me.*

Digital Media Literacy

As you know by now, I believe that every high school student in America should be required to take and pass a certain curriculum before graduating. That curricula—consisting of four yearlong courses—would be entitled "Digital Media Literacy."

Michael's Declaration of Media Literacy

Whereas I believe that relationships should be mutual, whenever possible, and

Whereas that does not mean that all parties in the relationship should be equal or that each person should be the same or do the same amount of work, and

Whereas mutuality requires an exchange of value between the people in the relationship, with each getting, giving, or otherwise providing something of mutual benefit, and

Whereas that isn't always practical or even necessary, and

Whereas some relationships are imbalanced in terms of power to give, receive, control, or otherwise limit those processes of mutual exchange and benefit, and

Whereas if there is imbalance, there should be ongoing real informed consent (not "fine print"), real disclosure, and real sharing of information, and

Whereas if an imbalance of power is so significant, e.g., between Internet service provider, digital advertising executive, digital media mogul, television or film executive, Google, Twitter, Facebook, or other search engine and social media service provider, corporation owner, oh, hell, let's just say between any mass media and the consumer, and

Whereas kids, especially teenagers, love digital media (the content and the fact of it), and use digital media to understand themselves and others and form their identities, and

Whereas there is "unequal access to experiences, skills and knowledge to prepare youths for full participation,"[52] and the ways in which media shapes perceptions and opportunities for learning about the influence of media is not transparent, and new ethical and legal standards have yet to be established with digital media, and,

Whereas the benefit to the above-named types of entities is represented by mountain-range-size piles of cash and enormous influence over the values, choices, and options of aforementioned children,

Therefore, there must be justice. And justice cannot be defined, at any time, solely by the one in whose hands predominantly rests the power to create, collect, store, disseminate, and manipulate the flow of information,

Therefore, in the interests of justice, freedom, and preservation of at least some significant areas of self-definition and identity formation not completely controlled by the forces of the marketplace, be it resolved that each parent and educator in America vow to teach children—and themselves—literacy and competency in understanding how mass media function, especially digital media in America and their relationship to privacy, choice, identity, fair play (among users in a participatory culture and between the owners of the technology and technological know-how), informed consent, and freedom.

When I give talks around the country, and parents find out that the talk that night is about "digital media," they usually come armed with lots of questions, such as:

"How many hours is it okay to allow my teenager to be online, and how can we stop arguing about it?"

"I just got the phone bill; is it normal for a teen to actually send 3,500 texts a month? When are they doing it?"

"What do I do about how much time my daughter is spending texting and on Facebook?"

"I'm worried that my son doesn't have enough face-to-face time with his friends and he's too isolated."

"What is the best online software for finding out what they're doing online and for how long?"

"When is it appropriate for my son/daughter to get a smartphone?"

"Forget about my kids. How can I stop my husband from playing (insert name of favorite game, e.g., Call of Duty, Minecraft, World of Warcraft, Sims, etc.)?"

"When does playing violent or even non-violent digital video games become an addiction?"

I can appreciate these concerns, and I do my best in these talks to give my thoughts on those questions. I know we, as parents, range from completely overwhelmed, scared, and anxious to calm and excited about living and parenting in a digital age. But this chapter is not about those specifics. I think it's important that you be thinking about something in addition to the digital content or technological device in question.

In 2009, the National Association for Media Literacy Education (NAMLE) published a policy document entitled *Core Principles of Media Literacy Education in the United States*. It defines the purpose of media literacy education as "[helping] individuals of all ages develop the habits of inquiry and skills of expression that they need to be critical thinkers, effective communicators and active citizens in today's world."[53]

Media literacy education makes real the cautionary wisdom of critic John Culkin, who believed strongly that in a dynamic democracy and market economy, "intelligent and critical consumers are likely to end up as the best kinds of humans."[54] That sentiment and the activities implied by it are foundational in this chapter and in my thinking about teens, parents, and digital media.

I will give you a very practical reason, too, for media literacy and becoming a good "educationist" about media. But I'll use Neil Postman's words to get straight to the point, which is a plea that we teach and/or support our children in developing excellent skills that help them lay bare "those ways of [people of the media] talking that lead to unnecessary mischief, failure, misunderstanding, and pain"[55]:

> Stupidity is mostly done with the larynx, tongue, lips, and teeth; which is to say, stupidity is chiefly embodied in talk. It is true enough that our ways of talking are controlled by the ways we manage our minds, and no one is quite sure what "mind" is. But we are sure that the main expression of mind is sentences. When we are thinking, we are mostly arranging sentences in

our heads. When we are thinking stupidly, we are arranging stupid sentences. Even when we do a nonverbal stupid thing, we have preceded the action by talking to ourselves in such a way as to make us think the act is reasonable. The word, in a word, brings forth the act. This provides educationists with a specific subject matter: the study of those ways of talking that lead to unnecessary mischief, failure, misunderstanding, and pain.[56]

1n 1991, Tom Lewis wrote *Empire of the Air: The Men Who Made Radio,* a history of radio in the United States.[57] Ken Burns adapted this book into a documentary the following year. One of the really interesting points from the documentary was that before radio, if you wanted live music in your house, *you had to make it.* After the advent of radio, people learned to play and make music much less on their own.

When in 1445 Johannes Gutenberg and Johann Fust set about developing and popularizing the printing press, Gutenberg was excited to put it use on a pet project he'd been thinking for a decade: printing a two-volume edition of the Bible.[58] But Fust, who had the money in this partnership, had other ideas. Large editions of perfect copies of thousands of books could be mass-produced by a few people, at a relatively inexpensive cost. What would have cost one scribe one Italian florin to produce one book, now cost three florins for 1,100 books. Equally important to remember is that this miracle was greeted all over "civilized" society by bans on reading (especially for women) and organized protests of books and reading as the tools of the devil.

But the arrival of letterpress, moveable type printing changed Western culture and the development of the Western mind, as people moved from living in primarily orally based cultures to those based on writing and reading. Scholars are still studying the sociological, historical, and psychoneurological effects of so much reading, even as we enter what some decry the age of the "death of reading." The worldwide publishing industry—an effect of Gutenberg's letterpress—was estimated, in 2006, to produce $150 billion in sales. This is $150 billion in just book sales, in a declining industry. This is a fraction of all revenues, jobs, manufacturing, communities, and the like created by the book publishing industry. But it took over 400 years for Gutenberg's revolution in reading to really catch on. That's a pretty long time to get used to a change in technology. The Internet as we know it was born in 1994. And in the 18 years since the inception of this form of digital media, most of the world's other great technological advances have now been incorporated into this one technological advance. That's not a long time to get used to a major, worldwide change in technology.

Nicholas Carr wrote—in agreement with Erik Erikson—"every technology is an expression of human will." Both men were interested in *tools* because they express and expand our powers into realms unreachable by our individual bodies and capacities alone. Our use of tools and technology—and what that experience tells us about the ethos of technology in our culture—is a fundamental part of human identity development. Carr considered this technological "reach" of new tools in terms of whether they amplified our *strength or resilience* (like with the plow), the *reach of our senses* (like with the microscope or amplifier), our ability to *reshape nature* to serve our needs and desires (as with the damn/reservoir or genetically modified crop). The fourth category referred to technology that extends our intellectual reach and mental power, and included tools like the map and the clock. Carr considered these tools "our most intimate, the ones we use for self-expression, for shaping personal and public identity, and for cultivating relations with others":

> Every intellectual technology, to put it another way, embodies an intellectual ethic, a set of assumptions about how the human mind works or should work. The intellectual ethic of a technology is rarely recognized by its inventors. They are usually so intent on solving a particular problem or untangling some thorny scientific or engineering dilemma that they don't see the broader implications of their work. The users of the technology are also usually oblivious to its ethic. They, too, are concerned with the practical benefits they gain from employing the tool.[59]

If we are concerned about the identity development of our children, it is our charge, as parents, educators, and humans, to concern ourselves with the intellectual ethic of digital media. That means asking questions and having discussions with each other about, for example, the music *we no longer make ourselves*? The benefits of hearing music through the radio seem obvious and were probably magical at the time. Taming animals extended the reach of our feet, permitting movement over long distances. Internal combustion engines supplanted transportation via animal. Car supplants horse. Jet overtakes car. Paper supplants papyrus. Writing supplants oral tradition and speech. Printing press and the mass market supplants scribe and the single copy. Digital supplants paper (books and magazines). Digital supplants radio. Digital supplants records. Digital supplants video. Digital supplants film. Digital swallows television. Are you noticing a trend here?

In each transition from an old to new transformative technology, something is lost and something is gained. New, transformative technologies become Rorschach inkblots. We project all our fears and hopes onto the "technology" itself or, in an attempt to manage those fears, we say, "it's not the technology that's bad, it's how we use it." Technology is merely a tool. We are in control of the tool. I'm asking us to imagine, for a while, that this just isn't the case. Digital media and the Internet are not evil or the work of the devil. But neither are they, in my opinion, our salvation. Remember the truths of bidirectionality and mutual influence? It's tempting to think the Internet and digital media are all good or all bad. Here's one small example from recent history.

For the last few years, the popular press in America has been beside itself with the idea that new media and social networking technologies and platforms are the best friends of democracy.[60] We can save the world by getting everyone online. Who could argue with the idea that teaching children about the online world and having the open communication that goes with social networking and peer-to-peer communication systems like text, IM, and Twitter help create an open, democratic society?

But as we witnessed in Egypt during 2011, despite the seemingly miraculous power afforded by Facebook and Twitter to organize a popular uprising, most, if not all communications tools that existed in the Egyptian social networking world were connected to corporations with deep financial, regulatory, and electronic/administrative ties to State power. What can be operated by an end-user can be manipulated, as a tool for collecting, exploiting, or misrepresenting information—or it can be shut down altogether when activities on the Internet run counter to the interests of the State. This is no less true in any other country, state, or principality where people are "living online." Influence, identity formation, learning, adaptation, changeability work in two directions, always.

Digital media are not "just tools." That, I'm afraid, is too naive a view. New, transformative technologies usher in new ways of behaving, organizing ourselves, thinking, feeling, and being. They change the way our brains work. They change what counts as salient, and how our minds and hearts figure out what matters to us. They are changing what counts as ethical and redefining it, just as we are changing and redefining the technology and how we use it. This may not be "inherently" good or bad, but it is, in my view, undeniable.

But I think the good news is that parenting in the digital age is really quite similar to parenting prior to 1994. Or rather, it is still similar to what we have figured out is needed in the last 50 or so years since I was born. Teens need their parents, friends, and teachers close, physically. They need to be listened to and talked with, in person. They need to feel and be respected and be provided opportunities to work really hard and to fail without everything being at stake. They need to see our eyes and hear our voices and feel our touch. They need to know we want to hold them when they hurt or are confused, so that they can find their own strengths. When you're with someone, near his or her body, you can feel this. Teens need limits set for them, even if they protest, but they also need to argue the limits and make cases for and negotiate new limits as they get older and get more experience. Teens need to be monitored and guided or they feel abandoned and neglected, even if they argue that you're too involved. Part of this guidance involves being close enough to direct them to or allow the subtle shuttling toward mentorship in various forms, knowing that as parents of teens, we often stand as prophets in our own land. We might need to enlist others in the teaching of media literacies, but it's still up to us as parents to think deeply about the content of that literacy.

If you've traveled on the New York City subway or London Underground, you'll know about minding the gap. Your teens are minding another kind of gap: They are paying attention to the difference between what you say and what you do. They are, as I've said, hypocrisy-detecting machines. Having battles about screen time at home? Getting upset that they never seem to stop texting long enough to give you a glance? Worried about their difficulty with transitioning off of digital media? How hard is it for them to get your attention when you're on your computer? How hard is it for you to put down the BlackBerry or the iPhone? How's your work-life balance? What do you do, that your kids can see, that cannot be rushed? What do you do, that your kids can see, that demonstrates non-technological means of understanding, articulating, and managing your emotions? One of the main points of this chapter is how powerful modeling and shaping is in forming human behavior. James Baldwin once said that "Children have never been very good at listening to their elders, but they never failed to imitate them."

As of 2012, parents are still the most important humans in the life of their teens. They are watching you and want frequent examples from you of how, when, and whether to unplug.

The Internet isn't evil. But let's be practical and use some common sense. Some of your children will become addicted to some form of digital technology. Some will rise up with the technology and what it affords. Some will fall. So, knowing that, what does that obligate you to do? What does it oblige you to do vis-à-vis your family? I think the young Rabbi Strulowitz was right when he challenged his audience at the "Ethics and Digital Media" talk, asking: "Are we asking the questions? Are we seeking to understand the ramifications? Are we trying to find the balance? We can't get anywhere if we just accept the machine or marketing mindset and just think it's cool and great." My own view is that it obligates us to become literate about the technology and its effects on us and our effects on the technology. It obligates us to teach our children at least some of what we learn, and to value and support their valuing media literacy and competency.

Media literacy is about more than understanding how digital marketers and advertising corporations go after your teen's brand loyalty and disposable cash. Understanding digital media and its effects is crucial because of what it teaches teens not only about who they are, but what kind of world they are entering—and what to do about it. The case of Trayvon Martin is a horrific example of the need for media literacy and its inexorable connection with identity development for teens.

On February 26, 2012, Trayvon Martin, a 17-year-old, unarmed high school student in Sanford, Florida was fatally shot by George Zimmerman, a 28-year-old neighborhood watch volunteer. Details of the case slowly (or quickly, depending upon your perspective) were released in the media, and by March 26, the case was creating a national firestorm of criticism over police response and media coverage. President Obama weighed in to express his grief over the killing, saying that if he had a son, he'd look like Trayvon. It's disturbing enough for all caring people that more than 8,000 black teens died from firearm-related deaths between 2000 and 2007. Almost double that amount of black young men between 20 and 24 died of firearm-related deaths during the same period. By 2007, a black teenager was almost five times more likely to die by gunshot than a white teen.[61] But that's not what came to dominate the national conversation about the tragic killing of Trayvon Martin.

Fox News reported on the story early, and regional and state newspapers picked up the story over the next couple of weeks, thanks to the efforts of Trayvon's family and attorney, who persuaded journalists to check into the story. Many of the reporters who *stuck* with the story were black and responded in very personal ways to the story—like Jonathan Capehart of the *Washington Post,* who framed his response to the story by recounting how he had been trained in the "rules" of being a black teenager in America. "Don't run in public," he was taught, defining the burden of being black in America as "carrying the heavy weight of other people's suspicions."[62] But when Spike Lee—who has over 260,000 followers on Twitter—send out a tweet that supposedly contained the address of the man who shot Trayvon, the story exploded. As it turns out, Lee sent people to the *wrong* address, forcing the family at the address to flee their own home, in fear of violence from a mob of people angry that George Zimmerman had not yet been charged in Trayvon's death. In castigating Lee, comedian Jon Stewart wryly remarked that, "Yes, sending a lynch mob to the wrong address is a bad mistake…[but] even if it was the right address, that's still a bad mistake. Sending a lynch mob to *anybody's* address is a bad mistake."[63] Stewart thought it better that Lee—a 55-year-old grown man—"leave the cyber-bullying to teenagers."

Many reporters and news anchors, urged on by Facebook and Twitter followers, began following the story more closely in late March. Tapes of the 911 calls made by George Zimmerman—who had claimed self-defense in the shooting—were released by media outlets. Civil rights activist Al Sharpton got involved and used his radio and television shows to highlight the case, calling for "ground forces" (his radio listeners) and "airstrikes" (from MSNBC watchers) to keep up the pressure in the "war" to have Zimmerman charged. Geraldo Rivera made an impassioned plea for black teenagers to stop wearing hoodies, saying that "Trayvon's hoodie killed him as surely as George Zimmerman did." Rivera's racist and nonsensical argument—

a twisted version of "the clothes make the man"—was quickly retracted, but not before members of the U.S. Senate, Congress, former Governor Jennifer Granholm, Marion Wright Edelman, and a host of athletes and celebrities started wearing hoodies in response to Rivera's comments.

On March 28, ABC News released surveillance footage of George Zimmerman going to the police station, complete with Photoshopped arrows pointing toward apparent "injuries" to Zimmerman, suggesting that his self-defense claim might be valid. NBC's *Today Show* released an *edited* version of the 911 call from Zimmerman that sounded as if Zimmerman said, "This guy looks like he's up to no good. He looks black." In fact, he didn't say that at all. The phrase, "He looks black," was Zimmerman's response to the 911 dispatcher's question, "Okay, and this guy—is he black, white, or Hispanic?" Evidently NBC thought their edited version was better.[64] Media rushed to get out Trayvon's Facebook posts, and politicians and media pundits traded barbs about whatever photographs of Martin and Zimmerman were being shown next to each version of the latest "facts" in the case. The easy manipulation and quick dissemination of digital data rapidly allowed American culture wars to multiply as pictures of Trayvon were downloaded from his Twitter feed, MySpace, and Facebook accounts and manipulated to make him appear as a "menace" and "thug," by associates at *The Daily Caller,* a conservative blog founded by Tucker Carlson (a conservative talk show host) and Neil Patel, a former Dick Cheney adviser. Even people on the other side of the culture wars seemed to need to manipulate Trayvon's image: Posters emerged that not only included protest slogans but also clearly changed features of the original photographs to "soften" Trayvon's features, making him appear more young and innocent-looking.[65]

By the beginning of April 2012, Trayvon Martin was becoming a *brand*. Sales of T-shirts, key rings, clothes, posters, bumper stickers, and buttons were available for sale in Martin's hometown of Sanford, on eBay, and on other online sales sites. It's not surprising that people wanted to share their feelings and pain about all the issues raised by Martin's killing—but it is concerning what quickly became the *primary* way of doing this sharing in a digital world, oriented toward the marketing and performative aspects of culture. One cannot help but wonder what will happen if the experience of Trayvon Martin and his family's pain are rapidly "flattened out"—in only the ways that mass media can do—so that people become "bored" of his brand, like we get bored of last year's *American Idol* winner. Will Trayvon Martin become a "hot brand" or a political movement in support of justice and peace in a nation still plagued by racism? Is there a *difference* in America? Must those two choices always rise up together and what are the effects?

What happened to Trayvon Martin was horrible; details both related and unrelated to the shooting are still coming to light as of the time of this writing.

But the coverage around this incident is one of the strongest arguments for the need for media literacy. The issues raised in just the first month after this teenager was killed are enormous, including ethical and legal issues around rapid dissemination of digital information (and misinformation), media pressures to feed a 24-hour digital media news cycle hungry for content, problems with rushes to judgment and action occasioned and supported by social media like Facebook and Twitter, and intense competition for attention by mass media outlets and public media figures who live and die by publicity, forcing a kind of "shoot, ready, aim," mentality. Most people in America now know about Trayvon Martin; that's arguably a good thing. But as you read this book, think about what you remember about the case and what has stuck in your mind. Think about what your teenager and millions of teenagers thought and felt as they saw this case unfold, especially in relation to what it means to be a *teenager,* what it means to be *black,* and what it means to be exposed to the media-hungry culture that is America. What *messages* do you think teenagers got from this series of events?

Teens need your supervision and guidance around use of digital media. Teens need to hear what you care about and love and what you think they should love, even as they reject it in favor of forming their own identities. Because as we all suspect—since it happened to us, and our parents, and their parents—just who your child is going to become is: *you,* or a hopefully somewhat improved version.

Practical Help Tips

In order to get you started thinking about media literacy for yourself and your teenager, this list of tips is from material reproduced with permission by the National Association for Media Literacy Education. The first six items form a description of media literacy education. The following questions form the core questions for beginning to understand media. These questions can also give you good ideas for talking with your teenager about the media messages they receive daily.

WHAT IS MEDIA LITERACY?

1) Media Literacy Education requires active inquiry and critical thinking about the messages we receive and create.

2) Media Literacy Education expands the concept of literacy (i.e., reading and writing) to include all forms of media.

3) Media Literacy Education builds and reinforces skills for learners of all ages. Like print literacy, those skills necessitate integrated, interactive, and repeated practice.

4) Media Literacy Education develops informed, reflective, and engaged participants essential for a democratic society.

5) Media Literacy Education recognizes that media are a part of culture and function as agents of socialization.

6) Media Literacy Education affirms that people use their individual skills, beliefs, and experiences to construct their own meanings from media messages.

QUESTIONS TO ASK YOURSELF AND YOUR TEENS ABOUT THE MESSAGES YOU RECEIVE VIA ALL MEDIA

About AUTHORSHIP
Who made this message?

About PURPOSE
Why was this made?
Who is the target audience (and how do you know)?

About ECONOMICS
Who paid for this?

About IMPACT
Who might benefit from this message?
Who might be harmed by it?
Why might this message matter to me?

About AUDIENCE & AUTHORSHIP RESPONSE

What kinds of actions might I take in response to this message?

[And I would add...What kinds of actions might I be avoiding in response to this message?]

About CONTENT

What is this about (and what makes you think that)?

What ideas, values, information, and/or points of view are overt? Implied?

What is left out of this message that might be important to know?

About TECHNIQUES

What techniques are used?

Why were those techniques used?

How do they communicate the message?

About MESSAGES & MEANINGS/INTERPRETATIONS

How might different people understand this message differently?

What is my interpretation of this and what do I learn about myself from my reaction or interpretation?

About CONTEXT

When was this made?

Where or how was it shared with the public?

[And I would add...What might have been kept from the public related to this message?]

About REPRESENTATIONS & REALITY/CREDIBILITY

Is this fact, opinion, or something else?

How credible is this (and what makes you think that)?

What are the sources of the information, ideas, or assertions?

Suggested Reading: *Parenting in the Digital Age*

The lists in the "Suggested Reading" sections are by no means comprehensive. I'm including what I consider to be the most informative, practical, relevant, or comprehensive readings on the topic(s) of the chapter. In other words, if you have limited time, these are the works I believe you might want to explore first. It doesn't mean all of these books are "easy reads." Sometimes a listed book will be very difficult, but worth the time.

Carr, N. *The Shallows: What the Internet Is Doing to Our Brains.* New York: W. W. Norton & Company, 2011.

Chin, E. *Purchasing Power: Black Kids and American Consumer Culture.* Minneapolis: University of Minnesota Press, 2001.

De Tocqueville, A. *Democracy in America,* edited by E.D. Heffer. New York: The New American Library, 1956.

de Zengotita, T. *Mediated: How the Media Shapes Our World and the Way We Live in It.* New York: Bloomsbury USA, 2006.

Hallowell, E. M. *CrazyBusy: Overstretched, Overbooked, and About to Snap! Strategies for Handling Your Fast-Paced Life.* New York: Ballantine Books, 2007.

Ito, M., et al. *Hanging Out, Messing Around, and Geeking Out: Kids Living and Learning with New Media.* In John D. and Catherine T. MacArthur Foundation Series on Digital Media and Learning. Cambridge: The MIT Press, 2009.

Jackson, M. *Distracted: The Erosion of Attention and the Coming Dark Age.* Amherst: Prometheus Books, 2008.

James, C. *Young People, Ethics, and the New Digital Media: A Synthesis from the GoodPlay Project.* Cambridge: The MIT Press, 2009.

Jenkins, H. *Convergence Culture: Where New and Old Media Collide.* New York: NYU Press, 2006.

_____. *Confronting the Challenges of Participatory Culture: Media Education for the 21st Century.* In John D. and Catherine T. MacArthur Foundation Series on Digital Media and Learning. Cambridge: The MIT Press, 2009.

Kilbourne, J. *Can't Buy My Love: How Advertising Changes the Way We Think and Feel.* New York: Free Press, 2000.

Lanier, J. *You Are Not a Gadget: A Manifesto.* New York & London: Vintage, 2011.

Lessig, L. *The Future of Ideas: The Fate of the Commons in a Connected World.* New York: Random House, 2001.

Lindstrom, M. *Buyology: Truth and Lies About Why We Buy.* New York: Crown Business, 2010.

_____. *Brandwashed: Tricks Companies Use to Manipulate Our Minds and Persuade Us to Buy.* New York: Crown Business, 2011.

McChesney, R. *Rich Media, Poor Democracy: Communication Politics in Dubious Times.* Urbana: University of Illinois Press, 1999.

Morozov, E. *The Net Delusion: The Dark Side of Internet Freedom.* New York: PublicAffairs, 2011.

Postman, N. *Technopoly: The Surrender of Culture to Technology.* New York: Vintage, 1993.

Pugh, A. J. *Longing and Belonging: Parents, Children, and Consumer Culture.* Berkeley: University of California Press, 2009.

Schulz, K. *Being Wrong: Adventures in the Margin of Error.* New York: Ecco, 2011.

Tancer, B. *Click: What Millions of People Are Doing Online and Why It Matters.* New York: Hyperion, 2008.

Turkle, S. *Alone Together: Why We Expect More from Technology and Less from Each Other.* New York: Basic Books, 2011.

Turow, J. *The Daily You: How the New Advertising Industry Is Defining Your Identity and Your Worth.* New Haven: Yale University Press, 2012.

Verklin, D., & Kanner, B. *Watch This, Listen Up, Click Here: Inside the 300 Billion Dollar Business Behind the Media You Constantly Consume.* New York: Wiley, 2007.

Watkins, S. C. *The Young and the Digital: What the Migration to Social Network Sites, Games, and Anytime, Anywhere Media Means for Our Future.* Boston: Beacon Press, 2010.

Yarrow, K. & O'Donnell, J. (2009). *GenbuY: How Tweens, Teens and Twenty-Somethings Are Revolutionizing Retail.* San Francisco: Jossey-Bass, 2009.

Youth, Pornography and the Internet. Committee to Study Tools and Strategies for Protecting Kids From Pornography and Their Applicability to Other Internet Content. Edited by National Research Council, D. Thornburgh & H.S. Lin, Washington, D.C.: National Academies Press, 2002.

Zittrain, J. *The Future of the Internet—and How to Stop It.* New Haven: Yale University Press, 2008.

5

Alcohol, Drugs, and Parties

L et's start with five basic assumptions and premises, so you know my prejudices in advance, in dealing with this subject:

Premise 1: Anything we do, or learn to do, that reduces the harm associated with drug and alcohol use is a good thing to do.

This chapter is not about telling you exactly what to do if your child is using or abusing drugs or alcohol. If your teen or preteen is already abusing drugs and alcohol, you'll need professional help for your teen and the whole family. It's crucial to understand the difference between *use* and *abuse* of drugs and alcohol. You can utilize the common-sense definition of drug or alcohol *use*: It means your teen has tried a drug or alcohol. If your teen has *tried* a drug or alcohol, your eyes and ears need to be open and you should be talking with your teen and doing reading and research for yourself. But you don't necessarily need to run to a therapist or put your teenager in rehab; as we'll see, drug "use" is very common and within the normal range of risk-taking behaviors in which American adolescents engage. It could mean your 13-year-old tried a sip of cooking wine or took a half-open beer from the refrigerator and finished it. Any consumption of drugs or alcohol is considered drug or alcohol use. Drug use should be understood in reference to the *substance*, *frequency*, *amount*, and *quality* of what is consumed. Your teen's drug/alcohol use could be one-time and light, very sporadic but heavy, ongoing and moderate, or heavy, ongoing, and related to other high-risk behaviors. At some point, we are talking about drug/alcohol *abuse,* but there are different ways of defining and different degrees of drug and alcohol *abuse*.[1] The key idea here is that from a harm-reduction perspective, the main focus is always on finding strategies to limit the harm associated with *any* kind, frequency, and amount of drug and alcohol use, including abuse. That makes *harm reduction* one of the powerful strategy-making approaches you'll want in your toolbox.

By the time we're talking about substance use in one of its most problematic forms—*addiction*—we're certainly in the realm of *abuse*. Addiction is a biopsychosocial phenomenon that takes roots in a family system, and the most effective integrated solutions for addressing addiction involve everyone in the family. That does not mean that if your family is facing a crisis that involves addiction you should run immediately into family therapy or family-based treatment. It does mean that if treatment is functioning at its best, everyone in the family will have, in the end, done something to change him or herself and confronted important aspects of drug dependence and use. Whether done separately or together, these efforts by all family members will have helped the person who was dependent upon drugs or alcohol (or suffering from any other addiction). Every effort made by the person dependent on drugs or alcohol or by a family member will aid in the reduction of harm associated with drug and alcohol use. Accumulated efforts by the individual and their family increase the effects and lasting impact of that harm reduction. So we begin with the basic premise that *anything we do or learn to do that reduces the harm associated with drug and alcohol use is a good thing.*[2] This approach is called *harm reduction* and it underpins my approach to alcohol, drugs, and parties.

Premise 2: Drug and alcohol use makes sense.

Your teenagers and preteens are not experimenting with, using, or abusing drugs and alcohol because they are irrational and crazy.[3] Drug and alcohol use makes sense. It's been a part of human history since human history has been recorded.[4] And teenagers use drugs and alcohol for many of the same reasons you or the people you know around the world use drugs and alcohol. We'll talk about those reasons, soon. But the explanation for this use and abuse does not involve being crazy. And if you know why teens (and you) use drugs and alcohol, you have more (even if it's only a little bit more) control over your choices. That's part of harm reduction theory, or what I like to think of as common sense.

Premise 3: When parents respond to drug and alcohol use with one of two primary responses—either fear/worry or overconfidence—it often leads to the same negative outcomes, namely withdrawal or overinvolvement.

If you're primarily scared about the possibility or reality of drug and alcohol use, you're likely to want to avoid dealing with them—or you might want to try to control everything in your teen's life. If you feel like you've got it covered and nothing bad will happen with your child, or you think you know what there is to know already, you're likely to withdraw. You might just as readily get overinvolved, if something difficult happens. Neither of these strategies supports the two main sources of *learning* for your teenager, who someday will not be living with you or as accessible to your control: data gathering and practice.

Premise 4: The main reason why you should learn about working with your teen around drugs and alcohol is to further the goal of safe affect regulation. This is what we talked about in the Introduction as the most important developmental task for your teenager—understanding, articulating, and managing emotions. When kids can't do that in healthy ways, they do it in ways that are quick and available—by using and abusing drugs.

You are reading this book because, in part, you want to continue to be a strong, positive influence in your teen's life. You want keep teaching them (and have them take in this teaching). If you're helping your teenager understand, articulate, and manage their affect and work with their emotions around drug and alcohol use, you are doing some incredibly important work with them and helping to keep them alive. Basic education about drug use (knowing about the drug, set, and setting, which we'll talk about below) teaches your teen:

> That there are actual rewards, for them, associated with the process of understanding, articulating, and managing their affect;

> That planning in advance is helpful (to them—not just their parents!) and increases the avoidance of pain;

> That generalizing from the specific saves time and effort;[5]

> That "getting it right" makes them feel competent and strong;

> That adjusting when things go astray and figuring out what went wrong is actually a pleasurable experience; and

> That those bad feelings pass and even contain helpful data, if they give some time and attention to them.

Sounds great, huh? Of course it sounds great. This is practically a list of executive functioning skills. And every parent wants their child to have these skills and knows that these skills won't be fully developed until the adolescents' brains are developed (sometime in their mid-20s). But you don't (and shouldn't) have to sit around and wait until your daughter reaches 25. Because if you recall that teen brains get good at what they practice doing, then teen brains need practice and teaching and learning around parties and drugs and alcohol, right? So, the goal is safe affect regulation, and the *methods* parents use to teach the skills and knowledge necessary for safe affect regulation are: a) data-gathering; b) experimenting and practice; and c) "failure analysis," or correction and refinement. This is a basic premise of this book, and of raising teens in general.

Premise 5: You would never have picked up this or any other book about teenagers unless you cared about and deeply loved your child, wanted to protect them and launch them in a healthy way out into the world.

I take as an assumption that parents care to know about drugs and alcohol because they want to protect their children from danger, pain, and disappointment; because they're worried about the physical, psychological, and emotional effects of drugs and alcohol; because they equate sex with parties and are worried their child will have sex and get pregnant or get someone pregnant; because they worry that their child isn't responsible enough to make the sorts of complicated decisions necessary to stay safe (not to get hurt physically, psychologically, or emotionally); and/or because they partied and used drugs and/or alcohol (or a loved one did this) and they know what's out there, and are afraid their teenager might repeat those mistakes. Because I take these things as basic assumptions, it means that any approach to dealing with teens, drugs, alcohol, and parties needs to take these reasons into account and consider them against whatever strategies are suggested. That is primarily why harm reduction is an underpinning to thinking through the issues of teen drug and alcohol use.

Harm Reduction

What is *harm reduction*? This approach to drug and alcohol use is consistent with the aims of the book, in its belief in the power of parents and teens (and parents and teens together) to have the greatest impact on problem-solving. Harm reduction, in the words of Columbia University professor Don McVinney, is a "perspective and a set of practical strategies to reduce the negative consequences of drug use, incorporating a spectrum of strategies from safer use to abstinence."[6] This is not my invention. And there is no need to reinvent the wheel in approaching the subjects of drugs, alcohol, and parties in our teens' worlds. As with most every approach in this book, there are numerous and repeated researches that have confirmed the efficacy and strength of this approach. In the early 2000s, I had the privilege of working with the Harm Reduction Therapy Center in San Francisco, California, and I learned from two of the best minds—Patt Denning and Jeannie Little—about this approach,[7] which they did not invent but which they have advanced significantly in the U.S. and abroad over the last three decades. Much of their incredibly useful work was based on the groundbreaking work of some of the world's preeminent research scientists, like G. Alan Marlatt and his colleagues, William R. Miller, Stephen Rollnick, James Prochaska, and Carlo DiClemente. Patt and Jeannie's own words best describe what harm reduction is all about:

- Harm reduction says that not all drug use is abuse—but all drug use does need to be safe and based on accurate information about drugs.

- Harm reduction says it is not necessary to stop all drug use to stop harm—although, for some people, that is the most efficient way, whereas for others, quitting is an unrealistic and insurmountable task.

- Harm reduction says Just Say Know (know what and how much you are using).

- Harm reduction means taking care of yourself, regardless of the status of your drug use.

- Harm reduction means getting nondiscriminatory care from others, especially health care professionals, regardless of the status of your drug use.

- Harm reduction means getting your mental health needs attended to, formally or informally, when you are suffering emotional pain or mental illness, regardless of your status of your drug use.

- Harm reduction means getting adequate prenatal care without fear of criminal sanctions, regardless of the status of your drug use.

- Harm reduction says you can still put business before pleasure, especially if your business is taking care of others, even if you continue to use drugs.

- Harm reduction means being free of punitive sanctions for what you choose to put in your body.

- Harm reduction means being free of the fear, the stigma, and the shame that accompany your choices.[8]

These last three features of harm reduction values are what often get it into trouble and invite a critical response to the approach. Think of these values in relation to your own child and you'll quickly see why. Here are some responses I've heard from parents over the years:

> "Are you kidding me? I don't want my daughter to be free of the fear and shame that goes with her choices! How in the world is she going to stop using if she feels great about her use and free of shame? That's insane."

"Being free of punitive sanctions for drug use? That's some libertarian nonsense. If there are no punishments for using drugs, drug use will sky-rocket, addicts fill feel perfectly free to increase their use and encourage the same in others. Be nice to drug users. Lovely philosophy."

"It's a black and white issue. Drug use that is safe and based on accu-rate information? That means there are 'safe and responsible' uses of drugs. That's just nuts. I don't want my son using drugs, period. Zero tolerance. This approach is going to undermine my values, apart from the fact that it's crazy. I want a world without drugs, not a world where my kid thinks it's okay to use drugs."

"You are wrong. If I talk to and educate my kids about drug and alcohol use, I might as well hand them a joint and a bottle of Jack and tell them to light it up and have a drink. What an idiot."

"Harm reduction is about half-measures. Come on! Even the Pope says harm reduction approaches to AIDS/HIV prevention are wrong.[9] Giving condoms to kids and talking about sex? That's harm reduction for sexual behavior, right? This makes no sense to me."

"I think this approach is dangerous and dead wrong. My son was abusing everything under the sun. I tried *everything*, including being his friend and talking about his drug use. If I hadn't taken so long to get him into a locked program, maybe he'd still be alive today. There is only one thing an addict needs to do: Stop using drugs, by any means. I wish I'd had him kidnapped and forced into treatment. Don't talk to me about 'harm reduction.' "

I understand these criticisms completely. I have thought and felt each one of these things. But I'm very partial to idea of giving *practical* help. That requires that I take into profound consideration not only how I would like things to be, but also how they actually are. It means looking at and working from the lifeworlds/ cultural backgrounds of teenagers and moving toward something healthful. The problem with the parent attitudes illustrated above is not their lack of heart and caring for their children. It is that these responses are not rooted in the science of drug and alcohol use and abuse; they deny the reality of continuous and wide-spread socially sanctioned use of nicotine, alcohol, and prescription drugs and other controlled substances (that by the Food and Drug Administration's guide-lines, anyway, are deemed safe, responsible, and effective); and they often result in *increased* drug and alcohol use and abuse. If teenagers are anything at all, they are well-oiled, hypocrisy-detecting machines. And teenagers know that while you want them not to drink, you drink. They know that nobody in the family really talks much to Uncle Oscar since he went to rehab for Oxycontin. They know that your mother died of emphysema or that their best friend's dad has lung cancer from smoking. They've seen the television programming and commercials, movies and videos and Internet-based media—and will continue to see them daily, 365 days a year—that depict legal (and illegal) drug and alcohol use as fun, transformative, and as playing a large role in the creation and maintenance of peer status. But in my experience, parenting stances based on punishment that have absolutely zero tolerance for drug and alcohol use—in the absence of understanding the intense cultural pressures and internal pulls teens face to use and abuse drugs and party with their friends—are often highly effective ways of: *increasing risk-taking* around drugs, alcohol, and parties; *isolating* the teenager from sources of help and support; and *negatively impacting the overall quality of relationship* between parent and child. These things happen because of the ways teens think and feel. It's not what you intend, but it's how it usually gets understood and that is what we need to work from: how *teens* understand things.

Teens are not miniature adults. You'll remember this from Chapter Two. It's practical to remember that because it means we can have our own values and approaches, but we'd do well to know how (or whether) these could be understood and adopted by your particular teen, at that particular point in their life. I want to support you in implementing your own values, but in doing so in a way that increases the possibility your teen will "get it." I'm not done explaining harm reduction as it pertains to drugs, alcohol, and parties. I'm going to do that, though, in context, where hopefully it will address some of the criticisms, make more sense to you, and not seem so "all or nothing" or "permissive" about activities that could result in the death of your child.

Before we move on and you decide whether or not this approach is crazy, take a look again at the definition of harm reduction at the beginning of this section. *Harm reduction is a "perspective and a set of practical strategies to reduce the negative consequences of drug use, incorporating a spectrum of strategies from safer use to abstinence."* Harm reduction describes a perspective and a set of practical strategies. In other words, it's about what works. It doesn't say it's okay for teenagers to use drugs. It doesn't say there shouldn't be consequences in your household, or out in the world, for drug use and abuse. Implied in the approach (and in McVinney's definition) is the idea that to reduce the negative consequences of drug use, it might be helpful to think about "safer use."

For example, if you know your 17-year-old drinks alcohol at parties, and you have the kind of relationship where you talk regularly to her, one of the things you could say to her is, "You know I trust you to be responsible about your drinking;

but you also know I'm always thinking about drug and alcohol use, that's my job. I wonder if you know that if you were to have an 8-ounce glass of water for every 8 ounces of alcohol you drank, it would help your body metabolize the alcohol, and help you not to get dehydrated." Now, this is a harm reduction intervention. It's not particularly fancy, but its 100 percent accurate, and the intervention reduces the harm associated with alcohol use. Why?

Well, it's more fancy than it looks. First, when you talk to your teenager as if they can understand things, and don't preach, but just say what you think about a subject, they feel respected. Saying you trust them (if it's even a little bit true) helps them feel respected and valued. This is arguably the opposite of being in a state of shame. Being in a state of shame interferes with the encoding of new information.[10] Most teenagers, when preached and lectured to (with that certain parental "edge" in the tone of voice), are going to be shutting down or contemplating how to never again have to listen to Lecture No. 37b about drugs and alcohol. Feeling ashamed is stressful. Having an angry, disapproving parent screaming at you is stressful. When the stress response kicks in with most human beings, one of three things happens in our bodies/nervous systems: fight, flight, or freeze (see Chapter 9). Simply, we want to get away (physically and mentally), we want to fight back (physically and mentally), or we prepare for the inevitable demise we fear awaits us due to the stressful "attack," and parts of the brain and nervous system shut down and stop thinking or listening.

Next, the information is accurate, so if they try it out, you're okay on the hypocrisy meter. This is important—being okay on the hypocrisy-detecting meter. If you tell your child that smoking marijuana will make them quickly and irretrievably psychotic and that it's easy to become addicted, they can easily Google this and find out there is no good science behind these claims. Of course, the veracity of the information they get online may be questionable, but that's not the point. They can quickly and easily see that your hard and fast knowledge is shaky. That's about the end of your credibility on the subject of marijuana and its effects for a long while.

Also, the information about drinking water interspersed with each alcohol drink actually can work to help reduce some harm. When you give your teen information that is actually useful, that is one of the most powerful forms of intervention you can make because it sets you up as a "trusted consultant." By the way, if your teenager drinks eight ounces of water after drinking eight ounces of beer, it also gives your teenager *time* to think about what he or she is doing...and that's another type of harm reduction intervention.

As we saw earlier, teens learn by doing: Good judgment comes from experience and experience comes from bad judgment. They learn by taking risks and evaluating what happened, and then reconfiguring their priorities of what to repeat and what to avoid, based on what actually happens to them. Recall the Vassar and

UCLA studies from Chapter 2? Or my son's beautiful response to getting caught speeding: "Well, if I'd *known* the cop was going to be there, I wouldn't have been speeding." Exactly right. And if your daughter knows, based upon her own experience (after not drinking water, and then drinking it at a party in between her drinks—something that is not terribly noticeable by other teens and doesn't make you look like a wimp), that this intervention works: Bingo! She might remember she heard it from you, or she might just think she thought of it herself. The latter is better, in my opinion—this is one instance where I think plagiarism is fine. As we therapist-types like to say, "It's better when you make it your own." Or as a 5-year-old likes to say, "I want to do it myself!" In the back of her mind, way deep down, in a way that might not become conscious until she hits 23, though, your daughter is probably smiling a little and thinking, "My dad is pretty smart and loves me and is pretty cool." No, I am not kidding.

That's such a sweet example, isn't it? It all goes so perfectly when it happens in a book. So, fine, harm reduction strategies work really well in books and with near-perfect 17-year-olds. But, you might say: "I know my child. He's been oppositional since birth. Talking to my son like this (if it would ever happen) would go in one ear and out the other." You might have a situation like the father from the final parent response noted earlier. In that case, the family was dealing with a long history of drug dependence, with a broad family history of drug dependence (and therefore a much higher risk of substance use disorder). In that case, abstinence is probably going to be high on the list of goals, with strategies aimed toward cessation of drug use.

I'm not equivocating. Harm reduction, by definition, is about "incorporating a spectrum of strategies from safer use to abstinence." The main point is that anything we do or learn to do that reduces the harm associated with drug and alcohol use is a good thing, from drinking water in between beers to never touching alcohol again. It's about choices and feeling empowered to act, now or at any time in the future. It is not about giving up control and admitting you have no power—at least not as the only way to get healthy. That's an absolutely fundamental premise of this book: *There is more than one way to be successful.*

As we move to the next section and look at why teenagers use and abuse drugs and why parties are so important to them, we want to know how to have *influence* with our teenagers, so that they make good decisions when they are not in our presence (which is, to say, *most of the time*). Mike Riera, the one inspiration behind this book, told us in *Uncommon Sense for Parents With Teenagers* that during adolescence, parents get fired as the managers of their child's life.[11] We spent the first 9 to 12 years or so managing everything, from doctor appointments, to what and when they eat, to just about every aspect of their free and structured time. When they hit adolescence, the push of their biology and pull (and pushes) of culture hearkens back to the days when *you,* as a 5-year-old learning to tie your shoes,[12] might have looked up at your parents and howled, "I'll do it *myself*!"

Adolescence is very much about this—about developing your own sense of identity, independent from but in relation to your parents. And that's why Mike Riera says adolescence is when you get fired as the manager of your child's life. The goal, though, to staying connected to your teenager and remaining positively influential, is to get *rehired* as a consultant. It's a brilliant metaphor and points to an approach that allows you to pass on your values to your teen, *in a way that they can take in.*

Substance Use and Adolescent Development

I don't know how you felt about science when you were a kid, but I had some very mixed feelings about it. My dad was a scientist and I wanted to understand science, but it seemed beyond me. It still often feels beyond me, but I found something as an adult I didn't have as a kid—interest and enthusiasm about science. I hope you'll stick with me through this, because this science has some pretty big implications for reducing the harm associated with drug and alcohol use for your teen.

The teen brain is under construction. We have explored some of the qualities of that maturing adolescent brain, with a special emphasis on its plasticity—a malleability of functional capacities for the component parts of the brain. In order to understand what's going on with drug and alcohol use, let's revisit some of the normal functioning of the teen brain and body.

As we saw, humans have a nervous system made up of a central nervous system (CNS, whose two main parts are the brain and spinal cord) and a peripheral nervous system (PNS).[13] The central nervous system is populated with nerve cells or neurons, each made up of three main structures:

- A cell body, which contains the nucleus that carries the main genetic information;

- A dendrite, which receives chemical "messages" from other neurons; and

- An axon, which sends chemical "messages" to other neurons.

These neurons are grouped together to form strands (some up to several feet long) that extend from the brain to the spinal cord and perform specific functions. Neurons, which generally have many dendrites but only one axon, connect to one another, forming neural networks. These neurons and neural networks are the basic parts of the nervous system, which includes the brain, spinal cord, and peripheral ganglia. The peripheral nervous system overall is what connects the central nervous system to the various other parts of the body, e.g., to the organs and limbs. One nerve in particular is very important in your, mine, and our children's lives: the tenth cranial nerve (CN 10), or the vagus nerve. It is very important in terms of how kids perceive and respond to danger, risk, and trauma—and what they do about it afterward.[14]

These neural strands don't run continuously; they reach small junctions called *synapses*. The synaptic junctions have small gaps between the neurons, which are incredibly important; there are millions of billions of these spaces. At most (but not all) synapses, a chemical signal is sent from the soma of one neuron, down its axon, to the dendrite of another. In order for the chemical "messages" to get from the axon of one neuron to the dendrite of another there must be a way of translating the chemical message across the synaptic gap. This is done with more chemicals, which are produced into the synapse to continue the message to its intended receiver. Those chemicals are called *neurotransmitters,* and there are over 90 of them involved in the transmission of impulses across neurons, over the "network." The chemical can get taken up by the dendrite of another neuron and "tell" the neuron to fire or not to fire. Some of these neurochemicals can also remain in the gaps between the neurons.[15]

And you'll remember something else about neurons—they are wrapped in a fatty substance called *myelin,* which helps (significantly) speed chemical signals down the neuron. Well, some of the neurons are wrapped, some are not, and some are being wrapped. That process is called *myelination* and it is not yet complete in adolescence. This incompleteness is a hallmark of adolescence. As we noted in Chapter 2, there is an increasing of "white matter" (WM) in the adolescent brain, as more and more nerve cells are made more efficient and faster in functioning through myelination. And the process of making or "activating" certain neurons and neuronal groups is not yet complete. The increase in neuronal production seems to reach a peak at around 11 for girls and about 12½ for boys, before they start getting "pruned back." This pruning back process is what may account for the significant decrease in gray matter (GM) in the adolescent brain, which begins fairly early in adolescence. When the pruning is done—at some point after high school—you have a very efficient, quicker functioning, more "mature" brain.

As you might remember, the pruning process happens from back of the brain to the front, and from the central structures to the peripheral. First, we get the boost to the cerebellum, and that's partly why teens are so strong and resilient, physically and with regard to their senses (except their common sense). Next we get myelination with the nucleus accumbens (NAcc), one of the neural structures highly related to pleasure, motivation (especially around seeking rewards), addiction, and perception of fear and danger (among other functions).[16] We now keep moving to the amygdalae and other parts of the so-called "limbic system,"[17] the emotional processing center of the brain that helps tell your teen not only whether something is salient, but also whether it is pleasurable or something to be avoided. And on the way to maturity you finally get to the prefrontal cortex (PFC), which is thought of as the seat of executive functioning—judgment; deriving general operating theories from specific incidents; multitasking; impulse inhibition; organization and coordination of thought and action; forbearance (thinking of consequences in advance and waiting); priority-setting, and the like. How unfair is that? The good stuff, the stuff that would help keep your kids safe, and the stuff that (because it is not yet developed) makes you angry and tired and frustrated with your teens—yeah, that area gets fully myelinated last.

What should this tell you? It tells you that teenagers, through no fault of their own, are going to favor sensory and physical activities over tasks that involve high cognitive loads. Teens (in general) are going to gravitate toward impulsive-organized risky behavior that increases in strength and frequency when you get a lot of teen-type-beings together.[18] Since teens don't have fully developed amygdalae, they are not as good at reading and understanding their own and other's emotions. Teens (in general) think that people are angry with them more often than they are, and misinterpret non-angry facial expressions as "anger." They have a hard time articulating and expressing and managing their feelings. Teens (in general) will have certain areas of their brains shut down (like the prefrontal cortex, with its propensity toward judgment and thinking) when faced with highly novel, salient, rewarding, and exciting stimuli. That's really the definition of excitement for a teen, or maybe a better word is called for: fun. Fun is often any high-excitement, low-effort activity. That teen brains gravitate toward these activities should suggest another word: party.

The overproduction, pruning, and myelination of neurons are hallmarks of adolescent maturation. These are the processes that define adolescence, from a brain development perspective[19]—and drugs affect all of these processes.

While this work is going on, the construction site has some pretty good protection—the bone of the skull and spine and the blood-brain barrier. But the peripheral nervous system doesn't have these same protections, and it is particularly vulnerable to toxins and physical injury. Toxins and risk of physical injury—that sounds to me like a Friday night for a majority of American teenagers.

The construction site can get redesigned, too. Plasticity of neuronal development means that experience (practice) can impact the trajectories of brain maturation. Recent studies have shown that IQ—a measure of intelligence once thought to be relatively stable over one's lifetime—can change by up to 20 points during adolescence.[20] New neural strand connections are made; new pathways are opened up and/or reinforced very quickly in response to repetitive behaviors. And conversely, stress and trauma can slow down development in certain areas of the brain, like the prefrontal cortex.

The Part That Worries Us Most: Addiction[21]

How does addiction work? Is it due to a lack a mental will or toughness? Is it a moral failing or failure of parenting? Is it really a "disease," or is that just an excuse for a behavior that people choose to do and think they can't control?

As a society, we are still debating these questions, amid tremendous parental guilt and anger about a complicated biopsychosocial process. Dr. Ken Winters, at the University of Minnesota, offers a very clear window into the science behind addiction. Drugs alter neurochemistry and affect the way chemical signals work in the brain. Drugs also act on those parts of the brain associated with reward and pleasure—what scientists refer to as "the reward system," "reward pathway," or "pleasure centers" of the brain. Let's call it the "reward pathway." That structure is responsible for behavior essential for our very survival, as it "instructs us" to seek food, water, sex, and care.

Drugs change the way our brains work, in part because many drugs mimic the mechanism of action of the "drugs" (chemicals) that are naturally in our systems—the neurotransmitters. *All* drugs of abuse, including the legal ones (alcohol and tobacco), activate these same natural mechanisms that are active when we, for example, eat food because we're hungry. Our nerve cells have receptor sites for these naturally occurring neurochemicals, like dopamine, for instance.

But let's back up for a second, with Dr. Winters' help, and see what happens[22] when a drug enters our brain. He explains this process using the phrase, "*Veni, Vidi, Vici*": I came, I saw, I conquered. It seems fitting that Dr. Winters had Julius Caesar in mind when he explained this process to his audience. The Roman emperor apparently wrote this in 47 B.C.E. to describe his rather *quick* war against Pharnaces II in what is present-day Turkey.

The first step: Veni. The drug *came* into the user's brain. The ventral tegmental area (VTA) responds by signaling the nucleus accumbens (NAcc), our *motivation* region, to increase the euphoria-inducing neurotransmitter *dopamine*. The VTA contains neurons that project to numerous areas of the brain, from the prefrontal cortex (PFC) to the brainstem and areas in between. The VTA is an extremely important area in the brain as it is highly involved in linking our emotions to *motivation*, especially the kinds of emotions we feel when we fall in love.

The second step: Vidi. The brain *sees* the impact of this experience. The nucleus accumbens signals the amygdalae, which are responsible for weighing whether the experience is worth repeating or whether it should be avoided. If the amygdalae say, "Yes, go for it," then the hippocampus (one of the limbic system structures associated with memory) records the experience—including the mindset and setting, you might say—and we have a lesson learned by the brain: That was awesome; I'm going to remember that! But since the prefrontal cortex (PFC) is involved, there are also

211

neural experiences being recorded that will shape future thoughts, attitudes, beliefs (cognitions), and behaviors in relation to the drug experience. Part of your teen's brain will also be involved in determining risk versus reward and deciding, "Should I do this again or was there too much of a downside?"

The third step: Vici. The drug has **conquered** the brain by giving the brain a highly pleasurable experience it wants to repeat. In a highly complicated process, two proteins— CREB[23] (a protein that helps regular gene transcription and is highly associated with long-term memory formation and neuronal plasticity) and delta FosB—are activated. CREB production is related to reduction in dopamine levels and changes in the reward pathway and can result in the feeling of *craving* or the desire to repeat the experience, which your brain has remembered is related to the ingestion of that particular drug you took. Delta FosB creates a kind of sensitivity to drugs and cues associated with prior use of the use that makes us prone to take it again.

Drugs that are highly *addictive,* then, are drugs that immediately get this process going—Veni, Vidi, Vici. You take a drug and it feels fantastic to you/your brain, through the production of the chemical dopamine. Your brain "falls in love" with the drug experience. If you continue to use and you repeat the experience, the brain begins to change and adapt. Remember, the brain is highly plastic during adolescence, and teen brains get good at what they practice. Continued drug use helps the brain get good at using, because it begins to adapt to this experience by promoting the neurochemicals and related factors that promote tolerance to the drug (needing more and more of it to get the same level of "high"), craving (the intense feeling of desire and even feeling that your very survival is at stake if you don't get the experience), and relapse (the repetition of the process again and again)—i.e, *addiction.*

It's a kind of perversion or "highjacking" of the normal processes and predilections of the adolescent brain. If you think about what we've discussed so far, you'll understand that teen brains are just the right kind of brains for developing addiction. Now that is not a scientific fact; it's a surmise. We can't exactly get a bunch of teens together and a bunch of adults together and give them cocaine and see if teens are more susceptible to addiction than adults. However, I think it is a pretty good inference, based upon our current understanding of the characteristics of adolescent brain maturation and development we've covered in this book so far.[24] But it is a scientific certainty that teens are more vulnerable to all the possible harm/negative effects associated with drug and alcohol use, including: that they are not as quick to get intoxicated as adults are when they use, but by the time they "feel" intoxicated, they are closer to toxic levels of that substance in their system; that teens are more sensitive than adults are in general to the lowering of inhibitions that go with drug and alcohol use; and that, owing to the "in construction" status of teen brains, their brains change more rapidly in response to continued drug use than a brain that is already fully developed.

Most teenagers who use drugs and alcohol do not develop substance use disorders (SUD)—they do not become addicted. (There are two kinds of substance use disorders as defined by the Diagnostic and Statistical Manual, 4th revision: either "substance abuse" or "substance dependence.")[25] However, for every year that the use of a substance is delayed, the risk of developing a use disorder goes down. If your teen gets to 21 without ever drinking or using drugs, there is very little chance they will develop a substance use disorder (about 3 percent). That's excellent, but it pertains to less than 20 percent of our teens, and that means we need to be aware of the other over 80 percent who won't get to 21 without drinking or using drugs.

Many parents worry that the use and physiological effects of "softer" drugs like marijuana or alcohol will lead to the use of harder drugs, like cocaine or heroin. This is referred to as the "gateway" theory of escalating drug use. To date, there is no credible evidence that use of marijuana leads to harder drugs, according to representative studies like the 2006 study published in the American Journal of Psychiatry.[26] But there is plenty of evidence that beginning tobacco use by the age of 12 is highly correlated with the use of harder drugs, later in life.[27] It's generally the case that the earlier the drug use, the more negative the impact on subsequent development.[28]

Parents sharing what they think, feel, and want, in a calm way, add a much-needed layer of protection to teens' peripheral nervous systems while all this construction is going on. I cannot overemphasize this fact—and one of the exciting things to me, because I am kind of a science geek, is that there is excellent cognitive and neurological science that backs up that statement. That statement is absolutely packed with goodies, so I hope you'll look at it again: Parents; Sharing; Thinking; Feeling; What they want; Calm; Protection; Nervous System; During Construction. Good stuff.

My intention is not to get you "scared" into controlling your adolescent's drug use—this is about education, so that you can make informed decisions. I hope, though, that you can find healthy ways to bring this information into your teenager's life.

What Are Teens Doing With Drugs and Alcohol?

Alcohol and drug use among American teenagers spans the range from zero use to continual use to the point of alcohol or drug dependence. The *Monitoring the Future* (MTF)[29] project is a 36-year ongoing study of how American youth think, behave, and develop values around a variety of issues in their lives. The project now focuses heavily on attitudes and behaviors around drug and alcohol use, based on surveys of about 50,000 8th, 10th, and 12th graders.

The latest (2011) survey is worth exploring as a jumping-off point for considering adolescent development and substance use. First of all, usage rates (and sometimes, attitudes and perceptions) of different drugs or alcohol change by grade level. That might seem obvious, but it was not statistically obvious until about 1995. Only cigarette smoking seemed to show these "peaks and valleys" of usage and attitudes. These days, in order of preference, teens use cigarettes, alcohol, and marijuana.

Cigarette smoking among teenagers had been in pretty rapid decline since the mid-1990s, but the rapid decline stopped in 2010, when there were slight increases in teens and preteens beginning to smoke. The perception of risk and disapproval around smoking also has leveled off. This seems important, since of all the substances, there is probably less confusion and more public information about the unqualified and expectable negative risks and results of cigarette smoking. This past year, teens and preteens seemed to go back to disapproving of cigarette smoking and usage dropped again among 8th and 10th graders, but a majority of them said it would be "fairly easy" or "very easy" to get cigarettes.

Alcohol use has been in long term (relative) decline with teens. Surprising, huh? Teens appear to be drinking and even binge drinking—having five or more drinks in a row, on at least one occasion in the two weeks prior to the survey—less every year, since the 1980s. In 1981, almost half of all seniors reported binge drinking. In 2001, there were 7 million teens binge drinking at least once a month, but the percentages were much lower than twenty years prior. And by 2011, only about 22 percent of teens report binge drinking. That's a huge reduction in the last 30 years, but from a harm reduction perspective, there is still plenty to be concerned about and plenty we can do.

Marijuana use, in contrast to cigarette and alcohol use, is *increasing* across all age groups and has been increasing since 2007, in contrast to a long period of decrease in use from 1998 to 2007. The perceived risk of using marijuana has decreased since 2006 and daily use of marijuana has increased significantly among all three age groups. One in eleven teens is a daily marijuana smoker.[30]

The prevalence of other illicit drug use varies drug by drug. This past year there were some indications of *decreases* in teen use of inhalants, cocaine (powder and crack form), Vicodin, prescription stimulants such as Adderall, tranquilizers, and over-the-counter cough and cold medicines. Use of LSD, salvia, heroin, Oxycontin, amphetamines such as Ritalin and "club drugs" (Rohypnol or "roofies," GHB, and Ketamine),[31] methamphetamine and crystal-methamphetamine, Provigil, and anabolic steroids *have not declined* over the last few years.

The 2011 MTF study notes, "One group of drugs that is not down much from peak levels is narcotics other than heroin."[32] As of the writing of this book, the use and misuse of prescription drugs among teenagers remains a problem. That makes sense, doesn't it? There has been a substantial increase since the mid-1990s in the use of medication for licit purposes; and with prescription psychotherapeutic drugs being marketed everywhere, constantly, directly to the consumer, there is a perceived legitimacy to the use of these drugs. With that goes a pervasive misuse of these same drugs—amphetamines, sedatives, tranquilizers, and narcotics other than heroin.[33]

If you want to learn more about what grade-level peers are doing and thinking about drug and alcohol use (with the information broken down in very interesting ways), the MTF study is a really good place to start. It might give you some good clues as to the characteristics and attitudes of those using, and the perceptions of risk and availability of those substances (the "mindset"), and the context for usage, including what drugs are available (the "setting").

And it might also help to be able to compare what your 8th, 10th, or 12th grader might be doing, as of 2011, with other teens. About 52 percent of all 8th, 10th, and 12th graders combined say they've drunk alcohol at least once, 31 percent say they've used marijuana/hashish at least once, and 28.7 percent say they've used cigarettes (including smokeless tobacco) at least once. By the time a teenager has reached the end of high school, about 52 percent of them have used some kind of illicit drug, including inhalants. The Centers for Disease Control data is different, though,[34] since it's looking at all youth, up to age 18. As of the last survey compilation in 2009, it showed that about 73 percent had taken at least one drink of alcohol, about 37 percent had used marijuana at least once, and 46 percent had smoked at least one full cigarette. Almost 23 percent of high school kids in the CDC-run survey said they'd given, sold, or been offered illicit drugs on school property.

What I notice immediately about these statistics is the differences between what teens tell me, what teens tell one another, and what teens think about drug and alcohol use. One articulate senior, who you'll hear more from in a moment, says:

> Just to give you a picture of the amount of people who imbibe, if you will: I'd say that out of all my many different friends at [our school], from many different social groups, different races, both sexes, etc., I would be hard-pressed to find ten people who don't drink. And I really do mean hard-pressed. Virtually everyone at [our school] drinks—it's a known fact (among the student body), and one that I gather is not expressed to parents all that frequently. There are the notable exceptions, but those are far and few between.

My experience tells me that she is close to correct. Almost all teenagers, by the time they've reached senior year, have drunk alcohol. If someone pressed me to guess at the percentage, I would say 80 percent. She would probably guess closer to 95 percent. But what the research says is that it's about 75–80 percent, given the margin of error. So, what gives? Are teens lying in the survey? Are they downplaying their alcohol use, for example? They might be underreporting their use and abuse, but it's interesting to note that teens do tend to overestimate the percentage of their peers that are drinking,[35] as well as the amount of sexual activity their peers are having.[36]

Putting Teen Drug and Alcohol Use in Context

Understanding the Complexity of Drug Use

I don't think there's a better way of introducing the subject of why teens use and abuse drugs and alcohol than to ask a teenager and listen to what they say. I've edited out the name of the school involved or other identifying information about the student, but you heard from her in the last section. Now we're going to hear from her more fully.

A STUDENT'S PERSPECTIVE ON...TEENAGERS: DRINKING AND PARTIES[37]

I am a senior at [a local public high school], and feel like I've experienced most of what there is to experience in the "party scene." To begin with, I applaud your diligence in caring about what's going on with your kids. Way too many of my friends' parents seemingly couldn't care less where their kids are on the weekends. First of all, let me lend credence to the idea that most parties have alcohol as a major part of the activities: It is not an exaggeration to say that ninety-five percent (or more) of the parties I've attended since ninth grade have included alcohol-related activities.

While the average teen may seem outgoing, my observation is that this average persona is (if you will allow a generalization) more of a mask, a facade, than anything else. Especially in the younger grades, (and I'm talking from recent experience as well as from observation,) no matter how secure teens seem in themselves, there does exist some twinge of self-doubt, and in order to validate a healthy "self-image," teens must search externally and find validation in the world. We do not, at that point in our development, trust our own impulses, our own value-systems and beliefs, enough to securely combat social pressures and norms. That, combined with the fact that [this school] is a huge, relatively impersonal institution, leads to parties that have no real core of similar-interest; as someone already mentioned, parties are generally open-invitation—in other words, anyone who hears about them is welcome to show up. So here you've got this group of kids who don't really know each other very well, who are insecure about who they are, what they think and believe, and everyone wants to be cool and say the right things and act the right way. That's a lot of pressure. So it's easy to turn to drugs and alcohol. They act as "social catalysts," making pleasant interaction possible where it previously would have been prohibitively uncomfortable. This has been my observation.

Just to give you a picture of the amount of people who imbibe, if you will: I'd say that out of all my many different friends at [our school], from many different social groups, different races, both sexes, etc., I would be hard-pressed to find ten people who don't drink. And I really do mean hard-pressed. Virtually everyone at [our school] drinks—it's a known fact (among the student body), and one that I gather is not expressed to parents all that frequently. There are the notable exceptions, but those are far and few between.

Parties generally evolve from a relatively small group of somewhat sober kids, to a mob of many drunk and high people, held together namely by the token bond of false social comfort. There's no easy solution. If your child is an upperclassman, chances are they do drink. The "cool" kids on the steps drink. So do the jocks, and the chess players. So do the "nerds" staying in at lunch to do math. (Please excuse all the gross categorizations and generalizations, but I'm trying to paint a picture.) There's virtually no group "immune"

I'm not going to try to tell you what to do, how to parent, because you are surely better equipped than I am to hypothesize on parental methods. I just want to give you the picture, to validate the rumors, to say that yes, there is a major problem that could benefit from intervention. Being a senior (yes, I know, still a baby to all of you,) I oftentimes look back at my high school career, and for the first time I can see things with a clear perspective. I certainly don't drink now, nor do I feel the need to. But back then, there was this incredibly strong urge to do so, I felt compelled not quite by "peer pressure," but by the need to find some common means of communication, and these catalysts make that communication possible.

As for parents being present during parties: I've been to some parties where parents are present, but generally the parents just don't care about drinking/drugs. (If they did, their kids most likely wouldn't have had the party in the first place, for risk of being thought of as "uncool," etc.) I've been to plenty of parties where parents just go upstairs or downstairs, and just "ignore" what's going on. And then I've been to parties where the parents actually "participate," come outside and talk to all of the drunk kids, take pictures, etc. I've been to parties where the parents actually provide the illicit substances; just a month or so ago I went to a party where the parents were home, and the host (kid) went down into the basement where her parents grow all their pot, and just used all of that for the party. This is [the West Coast], folks. You've got to expect a lot of parents, post-hippies or the like, to smoke pot. And how in the world can you expect a kid to stay away from something that's not only considered cool and trendy, and feels good, but also is validated by the action of his/her parents? So as for checking whether parents will be home or not—I'm not sure that's such an effective method for making sure your kid's going to be all right. I'm sure you already know this, but parents can be just as irresponsible as kids sometimes, and oftentimes the irresponsibility of "authority figures" is much more damaging, much more influential, than that of peers.

This letter's already pretty long, but I'd like to cover a few more things, so I'll try to cover them briefly.

Driving: While I realize that the news I'm bringing isn't all that cheerful, I can say that drinking and driving following [school] parties (in my experience) has been much less than one might expect. While the actual parties themselves are hugely irresponsible and relatively dangerous endeavors, we teens seem to have caught on to the fact that "drinking + driving = death." Generally speaking, designated drivers are appointed, and on the chance that the night ends with no sober drivers, people generally find other ways of getting home. ([Our school's] students seem much more responsible in this regard than do many of the prep-school students around [these parts]; once again, this is only my experience talking, and I'm sure exclusions abound.)

Hard drugs: While they are sometimes present, they are much less of an issue, in my experience, than are alcohol and marijuana. I've seen some psychedelics around (psychedelic mushrooms, LSD, etc.), but have only heard of (and never seen) people using cocaine/crack/heroine/amphetamines/etc.

Sex: In a word, Yes. Sex does happen at parties, although the actual deed (spelled out: intercourse) is less frequent than random pairings who make out quite passionately (which is notably juxtaposed with the lack of any kind of emotional passion between the average given pair). Take alcohol and other drugs, and mix in raging hormones, and you're bound to get some sexual situations that occur in the moment, and are regretted later on.

Enough said. I wrote this all really quickly as a response to what I've heard from you all, I hope it's helpful in some manner or fashion. Life is so much better without drugs and alcohol. It's brighter and clearer and more alive. I just wish that so many people didn't have to find that out for themselves through harsh and harmful experiences. If you have the ability to help your kid out, to help them skip these foreseen pitfalls—I would recommend that with all my heart. While a few years ago I might have said, "Let kids alone, what we're doing is not so bad, let us make our own decisions and form our own beliefs from OUR OWN EXPERIENCES," now I have taken on quite a different perspective. Although teens may project an image of mature self-sufficiency, I know from experience, and from observation of my peers, that this is somewhat of a fallacy. Don't be fooled. Keep up the good work in trying to protect your kids. If more parents took a stance, fought for the well-being of their kids, than perhaps this situation, coined the "party scene" (but actually is more accurately described as the predominant and pervasive social scene,) could be made into a much more beneficial scene, one that actually contributes to the healthy development of the person through this formative stage of our lives, not to the detriment thereof.

I have a very hard time reading that, after 12 years, without tearing up. Yes, that is one very smart and articulate teenager. But that's kind of the point here. It was written over 12 years ago, but in the meantime I have not come across anything that is quite as intelligent, relevant, and poignant. This perspective is from one who has the capacity to think about and write cogently and convincingly about her experiences. That is not a bad place to start if you want to know what teens might be thinking. It also lets you know that drug and alcohol use and partying is not relegated to the "bad," "lazy," or "stupid" kids who have no other options. And it's quite stunning that, without knowing it, she is talking about the inexorable links between normal adolescent development, identity development, status, drugs, alcohol, parties, sex, relationships, family, school, and ethical development. No, I promise I did not write this! But given that this letter touches on every aspect of adolescent development, you can see why I still haven't found a better way to start off an exploration of teens, drugs and alcohol, and parties.

This teen's letter is powerful and helpful in part because, without doing so directly, it centers the phenomena associated with teen drug and alcohol use in a broader context—one that includes the drug itself, the mindset of the person using the drug, and the setting in which those drugs/alcohol are consumed.

Drug and alcohol use among teens and adults must, in my opinion, be considered from a more complex perspective or we risk blaming the individual, increasing barriers to help, support, and treatment, and, more to the point, missing the boat on understanding why people use drugs and what to do about it. But even that is not, really, the point. If your teen is using or abusing drugs or alcohol, I want to help you figure out why *your teen* is doing that. When it comes to drugs and alcohol, one size does not fit all. If you don't know your child and the context of their substance use, you can't effectively intervene.

What Is Drug Use About? Drugs, Set (Mindset), and Setting

Figure 2. Understanding the Context of Drug Use

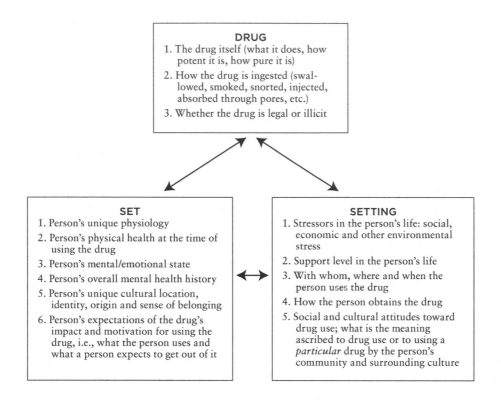

DRUG
1. The drug itself (what it does, how potent it is, how pure it is)
2. How the drug is ingested (swallowed, smoked, snorted, injected, absorbed through pores, etc.)
3. Whether the drug is legal or illicit

SET
1. Person's unique physiology
2. Person's physical health at the time of using the drug
3. Person's mental/emotional state
4. Person's overall mental health history
5. Person's unique cultural location, identity, origin and sense of belonging
6. Person's expectations of the drug's impact and motivation for using the drug, i.e., what the person uses and what a person expects to get out of it

SETTING
1. Stressors in the person's life: social, economic and other environmental stress
2. Support level in the person's life
3. With whom, where and when the person uses the drug
4. How the person obtains the drug
5. Social and cultural attitudes toward drug use; what is the meaning ascribed to drug use or to using a *particular* drug by the person's community and surrounding culture

When or if you have a crisis with your teen's drug and alcohol use, or if you just want to understand what you're seeing around you, it will help to consider it from this three-part perspective, in which the *Drugs* one uses, the *Set* (short for "mindset") of the person using the drug, and the *Setting* in which the person uses the drug all influence one another, and make up the drug use experience.

As you can see in Figure 2, the **Drug** refers to qualities of the drug itself—for example, its mechanism of action, its potency, what if anything it is "cut" or mixed or diluted with, how it's ingested, and whether that drug is legal or not. The **Set** or Mindset refers to factors like: the individual user's unique physiology (in general and at the time of any particular drug usage); whether the person is healthy or ill; their specific state of mind and overall mental health; their cultural identity, origins, sense of belonging, level of education in general and more specifically about drug and alcohol use, along with their general level of psychological maturity; expectations for what the drug will do, and conscious and nonconscious motivations for using the drug; basically, all factors having to do with that particular drug/alcohol user at that particular time in history. Finally, ***Setting*** refers to the contextual factors for the drug use, such as: physical, social, economic, and other environmental stressors and stress levels in the person's life; resiliency factors, such as social and individual supports; where you use the drug (physically and geographically) and with whom; method and source of obtaining the drugs/alcohol; and social and cultural attitudes toward drug use—in other words, how close others and members of the wider community feel and think about these drugs and what meanings are ascribed to a particular drug or drug use in general by the person's community and surrounding culture.

Several basic ideas emerge from this perspective and they are key to understanding your teen's relationship to alcohol, drugs, and parties:

1. *No two* users *of a drug are the same.* Understanding of the meaning of any particular usage is therefore dependent upon the user, their mindset, and the setting, and so by definition, even if you understand why one teenager uses a drug, you don't understand why and how every teenager (or adult, for that matter) uses that drug. If your teenage son is using substances, you'd be mistaken to assume that your daughter is using substances, or if they both are, that they're using them for similar reasons, in similar ways, and in similar contexts.

2. *No two* uses *of the drug are necessarily the same.* Every drug use incident is different, because the drug itself, the mindset, and the setting will always be different. For example, your 15½-year-old son might drink a lot of beer (the drug) at a friend's "birthday" party (the setting). Because teens generally know that birthday parties are often about getting the birthday boy or girl drunk, they often drink more, too (the mindset). But given a different context, your son might not drink that much at all. If a few of his friends get together on a Saturday night (the setting) just to hang out (the mindset), he might have two beers (the drug). Beer might not be his drug of choice. He might try mushrooms, though, while hanging out in the local park with a few friends on a Friday night. Descriptions of the multiplicity of experiences with drugs and alcohol could fill a book (and it has filled many good books),[38] and I cannot go into that much detail here. The important point is that if you understand that drug use is always different based upon the drug, set, and setting, you are in a position to make better choices about just how to intervene with your teenager. Many arguments ensue in households

because parents get nervous, seeing a "trend" of drug and alcohol use; but their teens are seeing their drug and alcohol use in fundamentally different ways, in part because the teens intuitively know that each drug experience is *not* like the other. As a parent, your first job is to educate yourself about drugs, set, and setting. Then and only then are you in a good position to help educate your teen. The word *education,* I try to remember, has Latin roots in the word *educere,* the present infinitive form of *educo,* "to lead forth." That's why lecturing is not educating. We're not trying to stuff our values into our kids; we're trying to lead them (as consultants) toward that which we value, to draw their own wisdom and growing good judgment out of them.

3. *This is the exciting part: Since drug use always involves the drug itself, the mindset, and the setting, there are always at least three sources or entry points for intervention around drug use!* If you're concerned about your teen's drug use, you can help educate them (or make sure they are getting education about drugs and alcohol, in general), you can do some good by helping them change their mindset around drug use, or you can influence the setting in which drug/alcohol use takes place. It's not all or nothing, and there is so much you (and your teen) can actually do to decrease the harm associated with drugs and alcohol. Later in the chapter I'll provide examples for interventions that target either the drug, set, or setting.

WHY DO TEENS USE DRUGS AND ALCOHOL?

I don't mean to be flippant here, but that's an easy question to answer: They use drugs and alcohol for the same reasons you use them. If you don't use them, then ask someone who does and they'll tell you (maybe not exactly in these words) that they use because:

1. They are trying to manage/change their affective states (this is often why kids are using while at school).

   a. To move from distress to relaxation (to change agitated states)

   b. To move from obsessing about an imagined or real failure to not worrying about it (to change anxious states)

   c. To move from sadness to apathy or pleasure (to medicate depressive states)

    d. To move from social awkwardness to social comfort (to "fit in," to lose inhibitions)

2. Lack of stimulation or perceived stimulation: Boredom.

    a. To stimulate parts of the brain that seem to require stimulation during adolescence (the "romance of risk" factors; propensity toward high excitement, low effort)

3. To induce pleasure; in short, because it feels good.

4. To comply with their parents or caregivers' views of them.

    a. Teens will often live "down" to expectations by acting in compliance with your view of them. If *you* think they're a screw-up, or a lazy good-for-nothing drug user, they'll act like one, so that at least your parenting perceptions can be judged accurate. Teens can also choose to act out and abuse drugs or alcohol if they feel the expectations set for them are too high and unreachable. This logic goes something like, "Well, I can't ever be that perfect, so why not just give up trying to manage my drug use at all?"

5. To be loyal to friends/family members who are using, or who are hurting or in trouble or suffering in some way.

    a. Both items 4 and 5 are complicated. But it is important to note that kids can feel very, very guilty and ashamed if someone they love or care about is doing worse than they are, or is suffering, or doesn't have some strong advantage that they have. Teens would rather sometimes be in worse shape than they're capable of if it means not "outdoing" someone they love. It is not a coincidence that of the many heroin users I've met and worked with over the years had a sibling or parent with a severe illness, disability, or significant struggle/deficit prior to their own serious drug use and abuse.

6. Because of biological factors.

    a. It appears that, at least for alcohol dependence, heredity plays a role,[39] accounting for 50–60 percent of the variance in risk for becoming dependent upon alcohol. Identical twins have a significantly higher chance of both becoming dependent on alcohol than do fraternal twins; adoptive children of those dependent on alcohol have a greater chance of developing an addiction (and that's true even when they're raised by non-alcoholic parents). There is much research to do, and many of the studies on alcoholism and genetics are done on non-humans, limiting the applicability of the studies.

b. Some of the biological and environmental factors that raise the risk for developing alcohol dependence can be present for all kinds of drugs as well. People who are addicted to one type of drug often also admit to having used or being addicted to other types before or at the same time. It seems that our biology can leave us vulnerable to a general tendency for developing addiction to substances of abuse. The overlap with other forms of addictive-type behaviors (e.g., gambling, gaming, eating disorders, sexual addictions) is present but not as large.[40]

7. Because of psychological factors and psychiatric conditions (the confluence of biological and social factors).

a. Two psychological factors that seem to set teens (and adults) at higher risk for different types of addiction are high *impulsivity* and *sensation-seeking*. For example, teens with AD/HD consistently show higher levels of drug use and substance use dependence than their peers.[41] And high levels of impulsivity in general (not just among those with attentional difficulties) are related to higher levels of various drug uses.[42] Higher levels of sensation-seeking and risk-taking are also related to increased risk of drug use and abuse.[43] Teens with anxiety (panic, social anxiety, or post-traumatic stress) as well as other mood disorders like bi- and unipolar depression are also, as you would imagine, at higher risk for substance use and abuse.[44]

b. The perception of risk also matters and affects risk for use and addiction. If your teen focuses on the "up" side and benefits of drug use *over* the adverse consequences (which teens tend to do, in any case), it increases the risk. Teens who have low risk perception, and who don't register "danger" as quickly, can easily overlook the side effects, and are at increased risk for addiction. If your teen focuses on the potential benefits over the potential adverse consequences of a drug use situation, that puts him or her at a higher for addiction. This should remind you of Chapter 2, where we discussed Adriana Galvan's pioneering work in risk detection and decision-making in adolescents.[45]

You can fill in your own blanks from here. There are certainly many reasons why people use drugs and alcohol, but we just covered most of the major reasons. Please do keep in mind that I'm consciously putting much of the science/research into the background here, to focus on what I think is practical and useful. So, for instance, I'm not going to go into all the biological mechanisms for how addiction seems to work, but I am going to talk about the elements of "risk" and decision-making, because those are so important in terms of understanding the challenges for your teen.

Before we move on to the next section, though, I want to give you some feedback I've gotten over the years from looking at the ways in which parents respond to the scary stuff around drugs and alcohol. If you're a parent and you're really scared and worried about drug and alcohol use with your child, you are likely to either withdraw or get very controlling with your child's behavior in an effort to keep them safe. If, on the other hand, you think you've got it all covered around these issues, you are likely to think that since your child is "a great kid" she won't get involved in a problematic way with drugs; you'll be "hands-off," overconfident, or might get very involved to the point of overinvolvement, since you want to make sure your child learns everything you want to teach them. I've seen that both of these responses (fear/worry or overconfidence) usually ultimately lead to withdrawal or overinvolvement. Both of those primary approaches—backing off or getting too involved—lead to very little data-gathering and very little opportunity for practice and correction. And since teen brains, as you'll remember, are busy developing (and require time and experience to develop) the "executive functions"—like advance planning, deriving general operating theories from specific instances, organization, holding off on short-term rewards for long-term benefits—if you remove data-gathering and practice from the equation, you remove two of the most important things your teen needs to develop safely into adulthood.

The two equations look like this:

Fear/Worry or Overconfidence > Withdrawal or Overinvolvement > No Data Gathering and No Practice

or

Appropriate Concern + Education/Interest = Data Gathering and Practice (At Technique and At Failure Analysis)

It's your choice. Which one do you want to work from?

Drugs, Drinking, and *Party*

That is not a typo. I'll explain, below.

This topic has been covered a lot and covered well. You know by now that I have a fondness for the breadth and accuracy of Mike Riera's work. But here I want to reply to and expand on the great job that Mike Riera has already done in framing the *setting* for adolescent drug and alcohol use. In all of his books, but specifically in *Field Guide to the American Teenager*,[46] he describes the fundamental idea that for teenagers, parties are "supercharged" and *metaphysical* events. At a party, he writes, teens are looking for relationships, fun, friendship, risk, adventure, camaraderie, sex, music, forgetting, reminiscing, time without parents (or adults), and that feeling that I remember so well from being a teenager: that *anything* can happen. Okay, so most of us know from experience, now, that in fact, nothing much usually happens at a party. But every once in a while, the most important things happen, and they happen to us. And then we're different, new and reborn, moved up in status, have a new friendship or sexual experience or just as important, a story to tell.

So what *Field Guide* helped make clear was that if you want to understand why parties are so important to your child—to the point that they'll lie, argue, bribe, sneak, and cajole their way to them, at almost any cost—you need to know that they represent an essential, paradigmatic activity of *identity development.* If you interfere with their parties, you interfere with *them,* their very being-in-process. As we discussed in Chapter 2, during adolescence *privacy* is an absolute necessity for the development of identity. They need privacy (and distance) from your gaze, your judgment, your beliefs, and your general proximity. That's why parents of teens often feel "pushed away" and unwelcome. Of course, the irony is that they actually need the opposite of those things, too, and in some ways they need you *more* during adolescence. They just find it easier to take your gaze, judgment, beliefs, and general proximity when it comes at them kind of "sideways" rather than head-on. If your presence (your identity, really) is too much in the foreground for them, they must push it away in order to have a sense that they're faithfully sticking with the project of developing their *own* identity. They must do this, and it's normal.

Parties are not all the same. If you read the student letter at the beginning of this section, you'll recall that some parties begin small, usually by invitation (not printed, but by text or Facebook posting), and then mushroom into large parties. They can get quickly out of control, through no fault of your teenager. They can get out of control without the knowledge or assent of the people who originated the party. Our student wrote, "[This] leads to parties that have no real core of similar-interest... anyone who hears about them is welcome to show up."

So, a party can be completely open to anyone who hears about it, or it can start out with eight good, close friends from the same school getting together and then morph into a party of 120, with the people who hear about it thinking they are welcome, though that might not be the case. Thus, what your teen says they're doing could be exactly what they *intend* to do, but it might not turn out that way. The party could be a chance for your son or daughter to just "chill" with a few friends. It will often, but not always, involve alcohol or weed. The party could be a "rave" or other large party happening at a location only known right before the party. That party could be massive (thousands of people), and that party will, without a doubt, include all kinds of drugs and alcohol, often drugs like MDMA ("Ecstasy" or "E")— and it could go on all night or for several days. There will be music and lots of it... maybe some gloving.

The party could be a birthday party, and the goal may be to get the birthday girl as wasted as possible. Or the party could be the kind of party typical of the school at which I worked, which was the "parents-go-out-of-town" party. There was a pretty solid unwritten rule at this private school that when your parents left, you hosted the party, and it had better be good.

Whatever the form and type of party, the majority of adolescents do use and experiment with drugs, alcohol, and sexual behavior. I know you know that. Sometimes the drugs, alcohol, and/or sex happens outside of many partygoers' or the chaperones' purview, in other rooms, in the back or front yard of a house, in cars. I'll return to this point in a bit.

Whatever the type of party, every school has its own "culture" around parties, and those cultures can clash when students of one high school (or middle school) show up at a party that is primarily for your teen's school. But sometimes this is *exactly* what the partygoers want, particularly if they go to a small school.

And finally, whatever the type of party, its attendees have two incredibly important motivations that are rooted in adolescent identity development: 1) Have fun; and 2) Avoid embarrassment. So while you might be a very permissive but knowledgeable parent and trust your son or daughter to attend parties, your teen can turn on you quickly if your goals (maximizing safety) interfere with their goals (having fun and avoiding embarrassment). You think "safety," they think "hassle." It's just that simple. Don't take it personally.

But back to the idea of parties and drinking, drugs and sex happening outside the "party." What *is* a party? The "Urban Dictionary" online has a variety of different suggestions for definitions of all kinds of words. Users vote on their favorite definitions. Let's look at the three most popular definitions of "party," because they are very instructive:[47]

227

    1. **Party**   5,522 up, 607 down

Something I never get invited to.

There was a party last night, but I wasn't invited.

    2. **Party**   1,641 up, 350 down

When everyone gets together at someone's house, get drunk, consume illegal substances like weed and coke, and trash the place completely.

(1) Sarah: Hey I'm having a few people over tonight. But keep it quiet, k?

John: HEY EVERYONE ! PARTY AT SARAHS PLACE.

(2) Wow, we had this massive party at Dana's place last night. The house got wrecked, her parents went crazy.

    3. **Party**   883 up, 220 down

    v. to consume alcohol or other substances

    n. a gathering of people to have a good time, often with alcohol involved

"Do you party?" or "Hey, let's go to a party."

The first definition is pretty cute and relatable for many of us. The second definition is relatable for many teenagers. But the third definition is really the important one, because it denotes "party" as a verb. And that is the definition that rules in 2012 for adolescents. "Do you wanna party?" can mean a lot of different things, from using methamphetamine and having sex ("party and go-fast") or getting together with a few friends to smoke a little weed and watch movies ("party and just chill") to playing music to hanging out together at a local club. So, "party" as a *verb* refers to the action(s), not the place. If you're thinking of the old meanings, "going to a party," then you might miss that "party" could be happening anywhere, at any time, with 1, 10, or 1,000 people involved. Not all parties are the same. But for teens, the purpose of partying is the same: identity development, motivated by having fun and avoiding embarrassment.

Strategies for Addressing Alcohol and Drug Use

I mentioned earlier that fear, terror, and anger are pretty normal things to feel in relation to drugs, alcohol, and partying. So, what are you going to do with your fear, terror or anger? Chances are you're going to do one of the three things human beings typically do under stress: flight, fight, or freeze. In the next section you'll see how these stress responses translate into "strategies" for dealing with drugs, alcohol, and parties.

Since Mike Riera and Joe Di Prisco published the fantastic *Field Guide To the American Teenager* in 2000—and talked about how parents respond to parties—I've yet to meet a parent who did not respond to drug and alcohol issues in the ways they described. That is, parents predominantly utilize one of four methods: 1) They anxiously do nothing and hope it goes away or works out okay; 2) They attempt to do "everything," trying to control and limit every aspect of their teenager's life to address even *potential* drug and alcohol use; 3) They become like or pretend to act like their teen's friend, so that they can influence and/or manage the effects of drug and alcohol use; or 4) They have small, ongoing interventions of many kinds, starting in pre-adolescence, about drug use, abuse, parties, peer influence, effects of drug use, genetic factors, and the like.

While parental strategies usually fall into one of these four main categories, I've also seen parents combine strategies or switch from strategy to strategy, in much the way they will try and switch overall parenting strategies (from authoritarian to authoritative to permissive and back again). Parents might start out with more fear about the subject of drugs, alcohol, and parties, and as they gain experience and feel more confident, and see some positive responses, they move toward a more collaborative strategy. But if parents start out trusting and more withdrawn (Strategy 1) and their kids get into trouble, they might quickly move into a more controlling strategy (Strategy 2). This often (but not always) backfires.

So before we explore each strategy in more detail, let's get really clear again on one key point that was introduced in Chapter 3: Whatever you choose to do, whatever strategy you adopt, no matter what book you get it from, and this applies to everything in this book, each of those strategies is no better than *how you implement,* i.e., in what emotional state you are in when you implement the strategy. And, every intervention you make, you are going to be teaching your teenager something about your values. You just cannot escape this. I'm bringing this up again not only because it's so important but also because you can use it to your advantage when you decide what strategy you want to use—you'll profit by thinking of *what values you are teaching* your teen (directly or indirectly) through the use of each strategy, and by the *emotional state* you're in when you implement it. You'll recall that even the "best" strategy, implemented in the "wrong" emotional state, won't work as intended, but it will not fail to teach them something. What that should tell you is that *timing is* almost *everything*. You might know what you want to do, but you should also know whether you're too exhausted or angry to implement it in a controlled emotional state.[48]

Now if you think back to the section on "Drug, Set, and Setting" in this chapter, you'll recall that I mentioned that drug use and abuse always occurs in a context, and that understanding why *your* teen is using drugs or alcohol is key in knowing how to intervene effectively. This primary way of approaching your teenager hearkens back to that little formula at the beginning of this chapter:

Appropriate Concern + Education/Interest = Data Gathering and Practice (At Technique and At Failure Analysis)

We're trying to avoid the other equation that looks like this:

Fear/Worry or Overconfidence > Withdrawal or Overinvolvement > No Data Gathering and No Practice

We're also trying to model something important for our teens, and that is, when problems come up, we get engaged, interested, educated, and concerned, we gather data, we practice, we fail, we adjust, and we try again. If it's true (and I believe it is) that *how* we do what we do with our teens (and children) actually teaches them more deeply and effectively than the *content* of what we do, then this practice-driven approach should work pretty well around drugs, alcohol, and parties or many of the challenges we'll encounter in the adolescent world. If you try a new one (or more) of the strategies below and you realize, upon reflection, that you still like your strategy or believe in it, I hope you'll understand that I'm not trying to take away your coping strategy. It's just that I'd like you to consider making decisions about your strategy, based in part on how teen brains respond, how they understand what you do, which is often very different than what you *intend*. In the end, you might end up choosing a new strategy not because you believe in that overall approach, but because it might more closely impart the values you believe in. That's a *practical/practice-driven* approach, as opposed to a protocol-driven approach.

The Four Main Strategies and What They Teach

Field Guide to the American Teenager outlines the all-or-nothing stances that parents can fall into regarding parties. But these stances, which are referred to as "The Ostrich" (doing nothing/avoiding), "Over My Dead Body" (absolute control), and "The CoConspirator" (trying to be your kid's best friend), apply not only to the way that parents respond to the issue of parties and party attendance, but also to all difficult issues, *including* drug/alcohol use and sex/relationships.[49] Earlier we talked about how our stress responses translate into strategies. Trying to gain absolute control over your teen ("Over My Dead Body") is a "fight" response. Adrenaline and cortisol and other stress hormones fuel it, and it is rooted in fear. Avoiding the topic ("Ostrich") is a "flight" response, and makes use of the same stress hormones, to escape the situation; that response is still rooted in fear and worry. Likewise, knowing that something bad or difficult is happening and staying still, doing nothing at all, is a "freeze" response, and is a different, more "ancient" response of the vagus nerve and autonomic and peripheral nervous systems.[50] That response signals to you that, as far as your brain can tell, there is a lion with its mouth open, fangs bared, about three seconds away from biting down on your neck. In other words, at that point, all sorts of systems shut down in your body in preparation for your demise; there is nothing you can do. The response of trying to be your child's best friend is, therefore, understandable, because it is not as stressful, even though it utilizes a good deal of *denial* about some potential big risks. However, if the choices are to feel terrified, numb, or enraged, it's easy to understand why you might choose none of those and opt for "It's all good!" The fourth strategy of using "subtle and frequent interventions" requires that you be in an optimal state (or actively work to get yourself into that state).

This theme keeps coming up, so let's name it: *You taking care of yourself is one of the first and best parenting strategies you can choose.* "Taking care of myself," what does that mean? It means that you will need to be very good at noticing, understanding, articulating, and managing your emotions; that process is key to getting what you need, in a safe, healthy way. You will probably need to do the exact thing that you are trying to teach your teenager to do. It's ironic, of course, that we are supposed (or even required!) to do with our teens the very thing they are making it extremely difficult for us to do, because of the way they behave. How is *that* fair? It's fair because we're adults and they're children, still. The onus is on us.

So, let's look at what leads to the adoption of the strategy and, more important, what it teaches your teenager.

STRATEGY 1: DOING NOTHING; I.E., "THE OSTRICH"

When parents are using this strategy, it is often because they have decided that there is nothing they can do about the powerful effects of drugs and alcohol or peer pressure, status, and parties. Since they feel overwhelmed and have decided they can't control their child, what would be the point in intervening? Or, a parent may not feel overwhelmed. He might just feel that since his teen is on the way to adulthood anyway, his job is pretty much done and he's standing back to hope for the best. The likely consequence, though, is that your child is apt to feel ignored and abandoned in some way and will feel that the unspoken bond of trust has been betrayed. Why? Because unless your child was abused or is being abused, or he or she is dealing with a mental illness, your child will usually hope and expect you to watch out for them and their safety, even if they rail against it or argue with you frequently about the details.

Sample Long-term Values/Lessons Being Taught[51]

1. When you have to confront someone you care about, the best strategy is to just ignore things and hope for the best. You probably can't do the right thing, even if you know what it is.

2. It's pointless trusting or consulting my parents because they won't get involved or will feel burdened anyway.

3. It's better not to do anything at all, than to risk doing something wrong.

4. It's better or likely that you will have to solve problems on your own, so best to be quiet and keep it to yourself when something big comes up. Confrontation, argument, and negotiation are to be avoided.

STRATEGY 2: DOING EVERYTHING; I.E., "OVER MY DEAD BODY"

In this strategy parents have decided (usually due to overwhelm/fear or over-confidence) that there is no way they can trust their teen to do the right thing. They forbid partygoing of any kind, under any circumstance, and constantly check their teen for drug and alcohol use. The teen must answer to every inquiry and the parents verify every answer. There is no aspect of a teen's privacy that cannot be scrutinized or controlled, and reductions in privacy are common.

Sample Long-term Values/Lessons Being Taught

1. I can't be trusted to do anything on my own; I'm untrustworthy and can't make mistakes on my own/can't mess up in order to learn; whatever I do, it has to be with someone who can watch me and intervene.

2. I am not capable of taking responsibility in a difficult situation. People think I shouldn't have choices, just limitations.

3. I'm still a child and need to be micromanaged or I'll be out of control.

4. I need to act like a kid, to prove my parents are right and smart about me OR I need to be "hyper-adult" to prove I'm not a child (and this, may in fact get me in over my head as I attempt to take on too much adult responsibility, too soon).

STRATEGY 3: ACTING LIKE A FRIEND, RATHER THAN A PARENT; I.E. "THE CO-CONSPIRATOR"

This strategy can also be a version of "keep your friends close and your enemies closer," and it's a strategy I see a lot of in the liberal bastion that is the Bay Area of

Northern California. We get made fun of a lot in the media, which likes to put out the idea that Berkeley or Marin or San Francisco parents are sitting around in their hot tubs, smoking weed with their kids, listening to the Grateful Dead. And that stereotype is circulated because in fact that behavior does happen. Maybe the music is different, but the basic premise applies. Now, I'm not saying this is mainly what goes on here, of course! But parents might smoke or drink or use drugs in the house or might bond with their child by telling them about their "good old days" in the '60s and '70s when they, too, got busted by the cops or pulled over for drunk driving or snuck out of the house and fooled their parents or had a party when Grandma and Grandpa went away. Or even if parents are not using drugs or alcohol with their teenagers, they might believe that staying close and connected to their teens (and their friends) while they use drugs and alcohol is a good idea. The goal and hope is that this bonding and permissiveness will encourage the child to share information about sex, drug use, and parties and will keep it all from becoming a big deal.[52] Plus, if it goes on in the house, they can keep an eye on it, right? I have heard from many parents who would never use drugs or alcohol with their kids and who are, in fact, extremely opposed to any drug and alcohol use. But even they sometimes consider whether "giving in" and being more permissive and friendly and keeping the use "close by" isn't a better idea than either controlling their teen or withdrawing completely.

Sample Long-term Values/Lessons Being Taught

1. My parents may be more concerned with what I want than with what I need.

2. I can be trusted no matter what I do and my parents are really my friends; if I mess up, it's not such a big deal (and, consequently, I can't or shouldn't really go to them, or they'll think I'm not worthy of the trust I've been given).

3. Authority is always "wrong" and to be avoided; same with hierarchy. It's wrong if someone close to me has more power than I do; it's better if we're all equal and nobody close to you has the ability to influence you too much.

4. The line between freedom and responsibility is blurry and difficult to figure out, because there are never really clear limits or boundaries around potentially dangerous activities.

STRATEGY 4: SUBTLE AND FREQUENT INTERVENTIONS OVER TIME; I.E., "NO BIG TALKS"

In this strategy (which Riera proposes as an antidote to the first three all-or-nothing approaches), the parents have decided that they will not do one "big" intervention, but will try many, ongoing, "little" interventions. These might include asking what the child thinks about the party/certain aspects of drug use; catching their child being "responsible" and subtly pointing it out or expressing their appreciation for a hard decision, well made; offering advice when it's asked for; providing conditional offers of help from time to time, or providing "cover stories" to save face, e.g., "Well, I'm still not totally okay about this party thing, but if you find that things are getting out of control tomorrow, let's arrange a phone signal and I'll come pick you up someplace where no one will see me." These kinds of interventions can be difficult if you don't have a teenager that talks with you (at least a little bit), and if you haven't been doing them before your child enters adolescence. But in this strategy, conversations and comments go along with television watching or driving in the car or putting away dishes or making dinner. Conversations or thoughts (or more important, question-asking—but not "grilling") about drugs, alcohol, and parties are just part and parcel of what you talk to your teen about. Your teen might hate it or appear not to listen when you talk about drugs and alcohol, but they take in the information and, in fact, use less drugs, less often when you do this.[53]

Sample Long-term Values/Lessons Being Taught

1. My parents still care and are available in a pinch, but they have some faith in me.

2. I'm trusted to come up with solutions on my own, because they often ask me what I think, rather than tell me what to do.

3. My intuition and "inner voice" is valued and valuable as a source of decision-making.

4. Things are not out of my control—I have choices and can get over the fear I have that I won't be able to do the right thing.

Now, it is important to note that these values are not the *only* lessons that your teen might derive from each particular style or strategy of intervention. And as mentioned earlier, strategies can backfire or communicate the wrong information if you're in an emotional state that isn't consistent with the values you're trying to impart. But I think it's safe to say that these lessons help form, at a minimum, the content of what our teens learn when we intervene.

Putting It Together

If you put together the idea of the centrality of knowing "drug, set and setting," with the idea that you teach values to your teen every time you intervene, and that those values are largely (but not solely) based on your emotional state at that time, you get a very basic approach to dealing with drugs, alcohol, and parties. For that matter, you get a very basic (and I believe, effective) approach to dealing with just about anything in the life of your teenager.

Michael's Reminder Crib Sheet

1) Consider your emotional state (and possibly wait until you're in a better place to intervene);

2) Think about what, in the end, you want your teenager to be taught about what you value, remembering that they'll read your emotional state first and only after that (if at all) take in the content; and

3) Remember that your main goal is to stay close and connected to your teen, by trying to understand them and their behavior *in context*. In this case, context = "drug, set, and setting." It takes into account developmental stage (e.g., alcohol use at 12 can be wildly different than alcohol use at 17, even though both are examples of "teen alcohol use") and a host of other contextual factors.

This approach requires getting educated about drug, set, and setting. If you only had the time to read two books on the subject, I would suggest Cohen and Inaba's *Uppers, Downers and Allarounders* and Denning, Little, and Glickman's *Over the Influence*. There are a ton of other books out there. I just think these two are extremely practical, timesaving, and rooted in some pretty effective approaches.

For a moment, go back to that adolescent boy (your adolescent boy) in whose backpack you found weed. I am *not* going to tell you what to do. Based upon the four main strategies that parents usually adopt, the following kinds of responses are possible. I've heard all of these, in fact:

"Whatever. Everybody smokes weed in this neighborhood and at his school. I smoke weed. I think it's fine and way overblown as a problem. We're all way too uptight about weed—it's a natural herb."

"Well, I guess it was going to happen at some point. If I think back to my childhood, I guess I tried things that my parents didn't know about, and I turned out fine."

"I don't understand this at all. Why is he smoking marijuana? What is this glass thing that we found in his backpack? Is he using heroin or crack? I've heard you need to heat it up to use it. Is that what the glass vial is for? Does he need to be hospitalized?"

"I want to know about military academies and boot-camp-style programs. No kid of mine is going to be smoking marijuana and turning into a delinquent; he's on lock-down until I figure out where to ship him to."

"I'm not happy about this and honestly, I'm pretty confused. I used weed and alcohol (and plenty of other things) as a kid. Things got kind of dicey for a while during my senior year and in college. I don't want to punish him, but I don't want there to be no consequences. That seems wrong, too. Should I tell him I used drugs? Then it seems like I'm a hypocrite. What am I supposed to do? It seems like every option here isn't quite the right one."

You'll notice that the example referred to was that you found weed in your son's backpack. All of these responses, however, go straight from "finding weed" to an assumption that their son is smoking it. That's a leap that may not be true. Parents do make that leap frequently and they sometimes make the leap because they don't really understand the distinctions between substance *use* and *abuse*. The chances are pretty good that if you find weed and a glass pipe in your son's backpack, he's smoking weed. But there is also a chance he's holding it for someone else. And there is also a chance that he'll tell you he's holding it for someone, when in fact he's smoking it. Or it could be someone else's weed *and* he could be smoking it. Yeah, it's complicated. But whether or not your son lies to you when confronted—or lies at first and then tells you more (the more likely scenario)—depends a lot upon your emotional state at the point of confrontation, as well as what you do and say in that confrontation. If you're primarily scared and worried or really angry, you might completely fail to consider that the weed and pipe might not be you son's stuff. You might therefore rush at your son, *certain* of what's going on.[54] That fact alone is likely to get your son to clam up or fight you, rather than talk to you—as teens often feel that they are wrongly accused of, well, *everything*.

Whether or not your own response would (or did) fall in the range of these responses, you can still think about ways to reduce the harm associated with the use of that drug (in this case, marijuana). Each of the "Practical Help Tips" in this chapter are examples of intervening around the "drug, set, or setting," in order to reduce or limit the risk of harm associated with drugs and alcohol, regardless of whether that weed in his backpack was his or not.

Practical Help Tips

1) Educate yourself about the drug, set, and setting. Read about drug and alcohol use (especially *Over the Influence, Uppers, Downers and All-Arounders,* or *Buzzed*) and be prepared to help your child help him/herself reduce the risk associated with drug and alcohol use. Don't do this because you condone drug or alcohol use. Do it because you're practical and understand that you cannot stop them from taking drugs or going to a party unless they voluntarily agree to it or they are involuntarily confined and under 24-hour guard. Know the effects of your teen's drug of choice and other frequently used drugs. Know how to mitigate some of the more harmful effects and help your teen know how to reduce the risk associated with the drugs they or their friends use. This information is very accessible.

2) Understand the legal consequences of your decisions about drugs, alcohol, and parties. You and your child should know that arrests and/or citations can be made for some of the offenses listed below. Every state and municipality is different; you can check your local municipal codes by going to www.municode.com.

    a) For example, in the state of California:

        i) There is a zero-tolerance for driving while intoxicated or distracted (if you're under 21 and have a blood alcohol level above .01 percent it's illegal).

        ii) Per the state's vehicle code, a driver can receive a $145–1,000 fine for the "wanton disregard" of a person's safety. Cell phone violations can result in a $20 fine for the first offense and $50 for the next one. Court expenses and other fees, however, usually result in a ticket totaling over $100.

        iii) Providing alcohol to a minor ("social host" ordinances) can result in a $1,000 fine, misdemeanor charge, and community service; parents and teens can also be cited for "failure to obey a lawful order to disperse," which is related to "disturbing the peace."

        iv) Loud and disorderly party ordinances exist, which when enforced, can result in fines, court appearances, or additional consequences.

v) Parents can (and have been) criminally charged for "sale of alcohol without a license" (if money was charged at a party).

vi) Teens can (and have been) charged with "possession of alcohol by a minor" (or other drugs); "drunken disorderly conduct" (CPC 415/local ordinances); "driving under the influence" (and related offenses); "vandalization of property"; and here's a new one—"irresponsible upkeep and improper garbage disposal," if garbage becomes a health hazard or eyesore.

3) *Understand that parties present opportunities to help your child develop their intuition and conscience and learn to act on their own behalf*, i.e., make decisions that are truly their own decisions.

4) *There are always good moments to ask your teen (directly or indirectly) the following important questions:*

a) "What are your values? What do you care about?"

b) "How can you make this situation not about us (the parents), but about you listening to your own, quiet voice inside that tells you the right thing to do?"

d) "As you get older, it's not so much about listening to us, but about listening to what you know in your heart and mind is right at the moment—and not having that shouted down by louder voices. What are those louder voices that make it hard to do what you know is right?"

d) "How can you not lose your own values, in the midst of different kinds of pressures in your life?"

5) *You can decide that if there is a party, you will always communicate with the parental host of the party, if possible.*

6) *You can decide, if you're going to host a party, to send out a notice/announcement via parent blog or email list* (compiled outside of school) notifying of time, date, knowledge of party, what they know about drugs/alcohol and your feelings about it, whether you'll be there, etc.

7) *"Align with Teachers (But Don't Expect them to Parent)."* As teen parenting expert and educator Mike Riera points out, in grade

school, when younger kids have problems, they go to their parents, teachers, and then friends, in that order. Teens reverse the order and go first to friends, then teachers, and finally parents.[55] It makes good sense to align with teachers because they often hear of struggles before you do. It's not about interrogating the teachers, though; it's about *knowing* the adults in your child's life and utilizing them as allies, while still respecting their autonomous work with your child.

8) *Set consistent limits*, and involve your kids in the process—let them have input, but not veto power or "final say" (the older and more mature the student, the more the input; the more successful demonstration of responsibility, the more leeway you'll give, e.g., you don't freak out when an otherwise responsible teen is home 20 minutes late every once and a while).

9) *Have a parent education night at school.* Ask teens to be involved and participate in the planning and the presentation. Have a panel of "teen experts" to talk about the issues around drugs, alcohol, and parties. You would be amazed at what teens will share with you if you just ask them and they know they won't get into trouble or ruin your relationships if they tell the truth.

10) *You can have a NQA or "Get out of jail free" card* where parents agree to pick up teens and take them home, any time, No Questions Asked (that night, anyway; it is unreasonable to expect that parents won't pursue the issue when all participants are sober and awake and things have calmed down).

11) *You can be willing to be put on an "Involved and Caring Families List" or "NQA list"* ("No Questions Asked"); these parents agree to be called on a party night to pick up any child who needs a ride and not ask questions—at least not at the moment.

12) *Adopt a "Silence = Death" policy.* This is a dramatic way of putting it, but the point is to send the message that, "In our home, we talk about drugs, alcohol use, and parties...it's on the table for discussion because we love you and will help protect you and help you protect yourself." This doesn't mean you interrogate your child or get into every aspect of their business; it does mean that you will ask questions respectfully and demonstrate your care, regardless of whether they want it or it makes them uncomfortable.

13) *You can adopt a "risk management" and "risk reduction" strategy around drug/alcohol use.* Talk to your teen about specific ways they can reduce the potential for harm.

14) Remember that good judgment requires experience, which often involves bad judgment.

15) Privileges and freedom can be linked to opportunities and demonstrations of learning and progression toward better and better choices.

16) Teens need the opportunity to fail and to try again, but as their parent you should be aware of your teen's propensity toward risk and reward-seeking.

17) Failing or making a poor choice is not necessarily a reason to yank the plug on their freedoms; "screw-ups" are always occasions for teaching planning in advance, stress management techniques, "threat" assessment, failure analysis, and a host of other important skills that can only be developed through hindsight and provide new chances to incorporate information about what does and doesn't work.

18) Remember that, as Mike Riera wrote in Uncommon Sense for Parents of Teenagers, you just might have to give up some of your short-term freedom to teach your teens long-term responsibility. Sometimes there is no greater punishment (and reward) than sentencing your teenager to spend more pleasant, engaged time with you, one-on-one.

Suggested Reading: *Alcohol, Drugs, and Parties*

The lists in the "Suggested Reading" sections are by no means comprehensive. I'm including what I consider to be the most informative, practical, relevant, or comprehensive readings on the topic(s) of the chapter. In other words, if you have limited time, these are the works I believe you might want to explore first. It doesn't mean all of these books are "easy reads." Sometimes a listed book will be very difficult, but worth the time.

Denning, P., Little, J., & Glickman, A. *Over the Influence: The Harm Reduction Guide for Managing Drugs and Alcohol.* New York: The Guilford Press, 2003.

DiClemente, C. C. *Addiction and Change: How Addictions Develop and Addicted People Recover.* New York: The Guilford Press, 2003.

Inaba, D., & Cohen, W. E. *Uppers, Downers, All Arounders: Physical and Mental Effects of Psychoactive Drugs.* Medford: CNS Productions, 2007.

Kuhn, C., Swartzwelder, S., & Wilson, W. *Buzzed: The Straight Facts About the Most Used and Abused Drugs from Alcohol to Ecstasy.* New York: W. W. Norton & Company, 2008.

LeDoux, J. *The Emotional Brain: The Mysterious Underpinnings of Emotional Life.* New York: Simon & Schuster, 1998.

_____. *Synaptic Self: How Our Brains Become Who We Are.* New York: Penguin, 2003.

Riera, M. *Surviving High School: Making the Most of the High School Years.* Berkeley: Celestial Arts, 1997.

_____. *Staying Connected to Your Teenager: How to Keep Them Talking to You and How to Hear What They're Really Saying.* Cambridge: Da Capo Press, 2003.

Riera, M. & Di Prisco, J. *Field Guide to the American Teenager: A Parent's Companion.* Cambridge: Da Capo Press, 2001.

Sheff, D. *Beautiful Boy: A Father's Journey Through His Son's Crystal Meth Addiction.* New York: Simon & Schuster Ltd., 2008.

Sheff, N. *Tweak: Growing Up on Methamphetamines.* New York: Atheneum, 2009.

6

The Sexual Culture of American Teens

Yes, we really do have to talk about sex and culture. I'm not going to give you information on how to have the "big sex talk" with your adolescent. It's not that I don't care—I certainly do—but I just hope you don't have the "big sex talk" or any other "big (fill in blank) talk" with your teenager. The brain accounts for about 2 percent of our total body weight but uses about 25 percent of the total glucose in the body.[1] Want to watch all that glucose drain from their brain? Just have a *big talk* with them.

The idea is to have lots of small talks, spread out over a long period of time, so that while the talk may still be somewhat "painful" for your teenager, it is something that they can *practice* responding to.

I'm putting this activity of talking to your teens about difficult subjects in pretty stark terms, but it doesn't mean (by any stretch of the imagination) that you shouldn't do it. It just means that if your teen is "used" to talking with you in all kinds of ways and settings—for three minutes after the lights are out and before you say good night; for six minutes after they get home from being out (if they're willing to talk); for two minutes during a 20-minute car or bus ride (if you can get the ear buds out of their ears); for 30 seconds while you're putting away the dishes; or during a long walk together (after you've talked about plenty of other things)—you can just keep talking to them in this same way, briefly, in quick conversations over time.

Many (but not all) teens like *warnings* for what is to come—it helps them think in advance about how they feel, and supports them to feel less embarrassed and ashamed, as they're allowed to muster some defenses against the impending assault on their identities: Here comes Mom to tell me again how *she* thinks *I* should be. Some of your teens don't mind if you launch right in: "So, what's up with Trevor—are you still sweet on him?" Other teens will *die* if you do that. Some teens really need a long warm-up, say 30 minutes or more of time together completely unrelated to talking about relationships and sex. This time can allow your "slow to warm up" teenager to mentally rehearse what they might tell you. So, 30 minutes of packing boxes or pulling weeds or peeling and cutting some vegetables might result in, "I'm so over Trevor" and then off you go. It's important at this point not to have too big a reaction; a simple "uh-huh," "okay," "What's going on?" or silence is usually fine. *Just keep listening.*

But as we've talked about in every chapter, one size can't and won't fit all. Some teens will complain that they don't tell you anything because you *never* ask. Some will complain that you are *constantly* asking and so they don't feel like telling you anything. Some will feel intruded upon no matter what you say (yet still want to talk); others will feel intruded upon only if you "hold court" on the subject and they don't feel you're listening to what they have to say. Many teens know that "tired adults listen more and talk less," so they'll hit you up for a talk when you're exhausted. Some don't want to look in your face—like they used to do all the time during infancy and childhood—because it's too easy to see what *you* want for them, which makes it hard or impossible to speak about what *they* want or need. They don't want your reaction (which is tantamount to the figurative *pouring* of your values and identity into their brains); yet they do want it and need it. And you want them to know how you feel and think about relationships and sex. That is your job—to *help* educate your child about sex, sexuality, and relationships.

For all of those reasons, this isn't a chapter focused on *how* to talk to your child about sex and relationships. As with all the other major "problem" areas discussed on the book—drugs, alcohol, parties, digital media, school, and learning—this topic is not approached by telling you what you *should* do, because I don't know your teen. *Do you?* If you answer, "Yes, I know my teen really well," then you're about one-third of the way to a good theory about how to talk to your teenager about sex and relationships. The next question, however, is, "Do you know *yourself* well (in relation to sex and relationships)?" If you answer, "None of your business...but yes," then you're about 66 percent of the way there. The last of the three important questions is, "Do you know the current context in America in which sex and relationships are happening?" If you begin your answer in one of these ways, you're probably in the 90 percent readiness stage, I would say:

> "Well, as a matter of fact, my name is Diane E. Levin and I am a professor at Wheelock College in Boston..."

> "Yes, I'm Stephen Hinshaw, chair of the Department of Psychology at UC Berkeley..."

"Yes, I happen to be developmental psychologist Deborah Tolman…"

"Well, yes, my name is Ariel Levy; I'm an author and I work at *The New Yorker*…"

Perhaps you work for the John D. and Catherine T. MacArthur Foundation or the Kaiser Family Foundation or have visited their websites and downloaded some of the free research publications by some of America's top researchers on friendship, sex, and relationships, or you met Deborah Roffman for coffee (hey, it could happen if you live in Baltimore) or read her *Sex and Sensibility: The Thinking Parent's Guide to Talking Sense About Sex*. You could be really up on danah boyd's work over the years and be tracking her latest research on how teens use social media and relate to one another in the digital world.

Any of these roads will get you that additional one-third of the picture in terms of supporting your sons and daughters around sex and relationships. Deborah Tolman wrote *Dilemmas of Desire: Teenager Girls Talk about Sexuality*; Diane Levin, along with Jean Kilbourne, penned *So Sexy, So Soon: The New Sexualized Childhood and What Parents Can Do to Protect Their Kids*; Stephen Hinshaw is the author of *The Triple Bind*, a really important and relevant book by a smart, caring researcher about the pressures that girls face in American culture.

There are a number of ways to get to the three parts of working with your teenager about sex, sexuality, and relationships. Referring you to these books, research institutions, and authors is a way of approaching the question of supporting your teen from the same perspective we've used before. As parents, it helps to know something about the factors *for your teen* that relate to genes and environment in interaction. It is also necessary to know about the same, *for you*. Third, it helps to understand the current American *cultural contexts* for behaviors, feelings, and thinking about sex and relationships—because they are so influential and offer the primary sources of information about those subjects.

In simple terms, if you want to understand sex and relationships for your teenagers you *have to* understand *digital media* (especially the Internet) and its impact on adolescent development around friendships, sex, and sexuality. Since 1994, the impact of digital media on sex and sexuality has created an unforeseen (to many) *revolution* in how our youth feel, think, and behave sexually. All of those changes have been driven by the engine of the adult entertainment industry finding a distribution platform based on a binary code of 1's and 0's.

That meeting of digital technology and the entertainment industry is the reason for introducing you to Ariel Levy, author of *Female Chauvinist Pigs: Women and the Rise of Raunch Culture*. If you've read her book, you're well prepared for where we're going to start our discussion about sex and relationships, and that is

245

with what Levy and others, including myself, refer to as "The Pornification of Sex." If you haven't already met Ariel Levy and her work, you might want a blankie and some hot cocoa before you continue reading.

What's New with Sex?

I'm fond of talking about my basic assumptions and premises for thinking and theory-making, and it's important to do so here. Humans demonstrate wide ranges of sexual thoughts, feelings, and behaviors, and it can be difficult for many to talk about or listen to that range of phenomena. Of course, some love to talk about sex and sexuality; that's part of our large range of individual differences in attitudes about all things sexual. So let's start with some of my ideas about sex and sexuality, so you can tell if you agree or disagree. Even if you disagree, I hope you'll read anyway, because it's not that important that you agree with my assumptions. It is, however, important what your teenager thinks, feels, and does, and that you be a good position to reflect your own values to them, in light of their choices and beliefs. So here are nine of my assumptions:

1. Knowledge about sex and sexuality, sensitive and geared to *your* child's developmental stage, is a good thing.

2. Having too little sexual knowledge too late and having too much too soon can both be problematic.

3. I don't agree with the cultural viewpoint that equates "sex" with "sexual intercourse." Sex is more than intercourse.

4. *Sexuality* is about more than sex.

5. Providing your child/teen with knowledge about sex and sexuality is always about teaching them what you value and what your values are.

6. I tend to agree with what Roland Barthes wrote of the United States, 40 years ago: "[S]ex is everywhere; except in sexuality."[1] This is the increasing trend in America.

7. Despite the apparent "ease" with which sex is discussed (and had) among youth, American boys and girls, in general, are more lost than ever about sex and relationships.

8. This one is controversial: There is no such thing as "non-relationship" sex. I'm not just playing with words. You can't engage

in sexual behavior with someone and not have a relationship
to and *with* him or her. It might be a *quick* relationship, but it's
still a relationship. It might be a bad or traumatic relationship.
It might be fantastic, but happen only once. It's still a human
relationship, and I believe that means the involved parties have
ethical obligations to each other.

9.   I tend to agree with philosopher Jacob Needleman when he
     says, "We don't *have* sex; sex has *us*."

So, first of all, your teens are in a new land, with a new language and new behaviors involved in sex and relationships—and most of the newness is accounted for
by the compound marriage between something that's been around for a *short* time
18 years (the Internet), something that's been around a *medium* amount of time (the
"adult entertainment industry"), and something that's been around *forever* (sex). It
appears from recent studies that it *isn't exactly clear what sex means to your teens,*
either.

Since we're talking about sex, sexuality, and relationships, let's talk about one
term that could potentially cover all of types of social connections: *hooking up*[3].
Most students know the term, but there is no agreement about what it means. That
is being figured out as we speak. This is equally true of *most* things that have a connection to digital media. In Chapter 4 I argued that one way of thinking about this
fact—that the process of developing norms and ethical "guidelines" for "plugged-
in" or online behavior is ongoing—is that consensus on norms must be and is being
established anew. Consensus on norms of self-representation and self-expression has
not yet developed among youth online around five crucial areas: identity, privacy,
ownership, authorship, credibility, and participation.[4] In deciding "who" and how
to be themselves, teens have endless ways to present, re-present, modify, and falsify
the broadest possible range of information about themselves, and unlike in face-to-
face interaction, they can easily utilize digital data to support these falsified identities. Identity experimentation is a normative and normalizing facet of teen life, but
online cues to credibility, honesty, competence, and authenticity can be nearly impossible to verify. Healthy teens are inherently (and intensely) wanting connection,
belonging, and community, and these impulses are subverted, abused, or manipulated when there is no consensus around the rules of identity "play" online or with
digital media. These *categories of behaviors* between adolescents—trying on new
identities, connecting in purely friendly and/or sexual ways, lying, keeping secrets,
doing the widest possible variety of activities alone, with one another, with a few or
many others all as methods to find out who you are and who you want to be—*are
not at all new*. But what is new is the *context* in which it is now primarily done, in a
world of digital mass media, fueled by social networking online. The *characteristics*

of digital data, as I noted in Chapter 4, helps to shape and influence how those other developmentally normative activities are changing.

Let's go back to "hooking up." I have personally witnessed teens using this term, and the examples below are from verbatim quotes. If you hear your teen use the term, it could mean *any* (or *many*) of these things, so try to keep an open mind about how your teen is using it. They might not be referring to the one(s) that you're most anxious about. The denotations of *hooking up* are many and variable:

A Taxonomy of "Hooking Up"

1. A one-night stand (sexual activity during one meeting, e.g., "I met this random guy at the dance and we hooked up.")

2. A "booty call" (sexual activity, usually initiated late at night, e.g., "I was so horny last night; I drunk-dialed her and we hooked up.")

3. "Random" making-out (finding someone at a party or social function you like or are attracted to or just want to kiss, e.g., "The party sucked; I hooked up with Jason, though. I guess that was okay."

4. Cheating on your current partner ("Yeah, I hooked up with her friend. Damn, I feel miserable.")

5. Sexual activity with "no strings attached" (This can also be referred to as "friends with benefits," e.g., I don't know, man, she's just some hook-up. She's chill, though.")

6. What you used to call "dating" ("Laura and I finally hooked up; I'm really happy about it—she's great. Her parents are pretty cool about it, too.")

7. Getting together (meaning just that, meeting someone, e.g., "Let's hook up on Telegraph later.")

8. The person you get your drugs from (your dealer or your friend, e.g., "I'm meeting my hook-up at 7.")

9. The act of connecting you with *anything* good at all ("Dude, he hooked me up with a Big Mac. Sweet." "Can you hook me up with some money till Tuesday?")

10. Any sexual activity *other than* sexual intercourse (this could mean kissing, sleeping together and cuddling, sexual touching, oral sex, mutual masturbation, etc. "Stephen and I hooked up this weekend at the river. I wonder if he'll call me or get all weird on me now.")

11. Any form of intimacy with someone who isn't your "boyfriend" or "girlfriend" ("Sure, we hook up every now and then, but it's not serious—we're friends.")

These variations in meanings hold for all adolescents, including college-age adolescents. Unless you're in your mid-30s and have teenage children (which is certainly possible), I can safely assume that this isn't *your* version of "relationships" and "dating." You might, though, be familiar with this term and all its many denotations, because it describes your (sexual) relationships, too. You can see the problem already, in trying to understand the terminology.

Old fogey alert: As few as 20 years ago, it was much more clear how American adolescents (and adults, too) defined the "nature" of their relationship. In addition, all of these types of social connections were understood to be "relationships." You were either in a "work" relationship, "family" relationship, a friendship or acquaintance relationship, or a sexual relationship. Sometimes those categories would cross, but then you might say, "It's complicated." But the overall understanding among most people, I would argue, was that the category had changed. A work relationship might become a sexual one. An acquaintance might become a friend. A friendship could become a sexual relationship. But there was a general sense that these categories were separate and usually clear. But when any relationship became a "sexual relationship," it changed everything. The "R" started getting capitalized.

For those of you who dated as an adolescent, you might have dated someone for a while and if you liked or loved the person, you might have been sexual with that person. The emphasis, though, was on one-to-one pairing off as the norm. Sexual activity (from holding hands to intercourse or anything else) was "supposed to be" part of a "getting to know you" process, with sexual intercourse as a possible culmination of this process. If you got to that point, it meant something about the status of your relationship—yourself and the other person, as well as something about your status in the wider community.[5]

In the new model of "dating," dating doesn't really happen as easily, unless you're in the South or Midwest, where some of the older traditions have remained. But for millions of teenagers, *they don't date.* A teen might have some kind of sexual activity on several occasions. If he or she likes the other, they might start to hang out regularly. One or both of those two people might also say, "We're NOT dating" or "We're NOT together." In your teenager's world, *group* activity is the norm; not one-to-one pairing in the way you might have done it. In the Paleolithic era, when I "dated," the worst possible thing that could happen would be to *run into somebody* else, let alone a group of people, while I was on a date. For many teenagers now, *being alone* with the person they're with sexually or otherwise is the thing they want to avoid at all costs. In the current culture of sex and relationships, sex may or may not be a way of getting to know someone. "It" doesn't have to *mean* anything: "What do you mean, *mean* something? He/she's my *friend.*"

Many parents I talk with in my clinical worlds (locally) and speaking worlds (nationally) are having trouble getting their minds around all this. They sense or know about or have read the research on problems with this way of seeing relationships, especially sexual ones. First, there are definite gender differences in terms of heterosexual "hooking up" behaviors, which usually favor males, who often don't mind having sexual contact without it "leading to anything." Even when girls in heterosexual relationships initiate sexual activity—and then often do, for complicated reasons—it's the boys that usually benefit, sexually speaking. In other words, it's not always the guys who suggested a "hook up." Girls know that guys like sex (or are supposed to like sex). They know (or think) they can gain status by pleasing the guy. So a girl may initiate oral sex ("hook up" with the guy) because it makes her cool. It has the added advantage of being a sexual activity during which she doesn't have to get undressed (or fully undressed) and possibly confront her own sensitive body image issues or worry about having her body judged by her sexual partner. A girl might initiate a hook-up (in this case, having oral sex), but it doesn't mean she's going to feel good, physically, have an orgasm or have her partner "return the favor." Thus, boys often get the better part of this relationship, even when they don't pursue or initiate it.

Gender stereotypes abound: Guys who actively "hook up" with multiple partners are considered "players" and "pimps" and receive the commensurate status rewards associated with these titles; girls are considered "sluts" or "ho's" and are also given the commensurate status rewards. If you don't "hook up" at all, you're lame, but you're less lame if you're a girl and not hooking up, than if you're a guy among guys. Many teens will tell you they don't care who's hooking up and who isn't— they're cool with whatever kids are doing; that doesn't mean they aren't thinking about it, a lot, and using it as a measure of status and normativity.

It's important to note that there's some racism mixed in here, too, since many of these terms come from parts of the black experience in America, and when the terms are adopted by whites they take on the veneer of "cool" that leaves out the more traumatic, problematic, or ambivalent experiences associated with those terms. If you're black in America and a "pimp," in the traditional sense, you're an agent for prostitution. The denotations are complicated, and many American teens—black and white—use "pimp" in a laudatory fashion these days. But it still, for the mainstream, denotes *low status*. When white American teens, use it, though, it's automatically *high status*. This is about *racism*—and it doesn't just happen with "words."

Next, teens almost always overestimate the frequency of sexual activity/hookups of their peers, and this leads to making choices that are not actually reflective of their peers. The ubiquity of "hooking up," in its wide variety of meanings, has a kind of pro-social flattening effect. It means everything and nothing much and that's great; in a sense, *every teenager is hooking up,* because hooking up refers to every social activity. If I'm 17—which is around the national average for when adolescents have their first experience of sexual intercourse—and I'm thinking that all my friends have found someone to "hook up" with (in this case, meaning "having intercourse") I can keep my status in the smaller and wider community by running into a friend at a party and dancing with her, hanging out and getting a little kiss before she leaves, and I can say, "Yeah, me and Cheryl hooked up last night, no big deal." I'm not lying. I'm just not saying *which denotation* I'm using. If someone presses me, I can always use some version of the still-viable "I don't kiss and tell" response. In the past, you could try to get out of telling, but the fact was, either you were *together* or you weren't, or you did something or you didn't, and it was going to be a big deal, usually. So, in this way, "hooking up" allows most adolescents to get in on some aspect of adolescent sexuality, as far as self-image and peer status is concerned. That isn't a problem, it's an advantage. But the pervasive use of a term that has so many meanings also, as parents would imagine (and have told me), can be problematic because it so easily leads to misunderstandings between people. You would need a lot more "relationship status" choices on Facebook than the 10 they currently list.[6]

And speaking of Facebook, which we will do a lot of in this chapter, texting and instant messaging of all kinds makes it much faster to hook up—in all ways—with less time to plan (for sex, birth control, etc.) and have second thoughts. The lack of "practice" and skill-building around meeting, talking with, and learning about someone *offline* is one of the consequences of so much of social life moving *online* into the digital realm. The distinctions are much less clear, in any case. Teens (and adults) meeting offline will nonetheless "talk" and "connect" via digital media, even in close proximity with others. Teens will and do send texts at all times (including in the shower, as you've already read in Chapter 4), and this means that "meeting" offline and "in person" can still involve a range of digital media use. It blurs the lines and language of *social connection*. Most of the teens I know don't bother to say whether they had an interaction with someone online or offline; they just "talked to," or "met," or "hooked up" with someone. That doesn't mean teenagers don't use the word "online," as I do hear them say, "I talked to Belinda *online* tonight," but that qualifier will soon drop out of the picture almost entirely, I believe.

So, at this juncture (in 2012 and in the chapter) we have a loosening of what it means to be in a relationship, a loosening of what "sex" means, and a loosening of what it means to connect with someone else. So "We had sex" doesn't necessarily mean "We had sexual intercourse," but it *can* mean that. It can also mean, "We fooled around but didn't have penile-vaginal intercourse" or "We did have sexual intercourse but it just wasn't all that big of a deal" or "We didn't have sexual intercourse but did everything else." *I know*...it's confusing.

A Wickedly Brief History of Sexual Culture

1950s: The Beginning of the End of Traditional Sex Roles and Marriage as the Norm

1960s: The Era of Civil Rights, Overthrowing Oppression, and Cultural Polarization

1970s: The Rise of Free Love, Loving the One You're With, Sexual Experimentation, Intense Cultural Polarization Between Young and Old, Hip and Square

1980s: The Excesses of Everything "Good" (and Bad). Drug distribution channels multiply like never before. Immense wealth creation and transfer out of the middle class; immense parties, drugs, and spending; immense poverty, violence, and drug use and abuse.

1990s: Whoops. Maybe We Went Too Far. Trying to figure it out and push back against the excess. **Most of your teens are born.** The Internet is born. Adult entertainment and Internet get married. Pornography distribution channels multiply like never before.

2000s: The Pornification of Sex. The decade of "Do as I say, not as I did." Lots of getting lost. Lots of pain. More transfer of wealth out of the middle class than ever before.[7]

Okay, that was a quick history, right? Not too painful. I've included some good resources at the end of the chapter if you want an *actual* history. But my lightning-quick history is to set up a few points on the way to Ariel Levy's work. I'm going to use "drug use" as an example for a moment.

The 1960s and 1970s saw large increases in drug and alcohol use, in large part due to challenges to then-dominant features of American mainstream culture. Increased frequency and amount of drug use was often felt to be (especially among adolescents) a way of challenging certain oppressive social and political norms. But illicit drug production, distribution, sales, and use had roots in a long history of criminal behavior. During and immediately after the time of the Vietnam War, drugs became big business, with the wholesale distribution of pot and cocaine, fueled by organized crime and "independent" contractors, and widely supported by the entertainment industry. I'm not a sociologist, so I'm just speaking as a parent here, but I think of this unsophisticated addition equation (even though I know it's not "additive"):

Drugs

+ Need for sociocultural change

+ Market capitalism (cash/distribution/production advances)

+ State involvement

+ Time

Lots of drug addicts, advertising and media involvement, new Victorianism, huge sectors of the economy dependent upon drug supply, use, and treatment

With a remainder: not a whole lot of political change.

The 1960s and 1970s saw large increases in public and private questioning (in the form of speech, research, writing, and sexual behavior) of cultural norms around sex and sexuality. Increased frequency and variety of sexual behavior—including challenging notions of public and private as regards sexual norms—was often felt to be a way of challenging certain oppressive social and political norms. Sexual behaviors and challenges to sexual norms increased, as did pornography and the depiction and consideration of all forms of sexuality. But illicit production, distribution, sales, and "uses" of sex had roots in a long history of criminal and criminalized behavior. In the mid- to late 1980s, and in part fueled by the increased capitalization made available by the drug trade, sex became big business. It's all about distribution channels. And in the mid-1990s, the rise of the Internet did for pornography what new distribution channels and production platforms offered to the drug trade in the late 1970s and 1980s. Pornography and access to sexual activity of all kinds, and the rise of supportive or related ancillary businesses, reached incalculable heights with the wholesale and retail distribution of sex online.

Pornography is big, big business.[8] It's almost impossible to estimate the wealth generated by and concentrated in the adult entertainment (sex) industry. Since the phrase encompasses all the commercial enterprises related to the monetization of sex and sex-related services (from the global sex trade and local prostitution—both found online everywhere from a Craigslist ad to online websites dedicated to sex tourism—to the "adult industry" comprised of films, videos, live-streaming pay-for-purchase services), it's hard to figure out how much money is related to all of those industries. The total is conservatively estimated at $150 billion annually for pornography *alone*.

So, let's look at our equation again, with a few terms changed:

Sex

+ Need for sociocultural change

+ Market capitalism (cash/distribution/production advances)

+ State involvement

+ Time

Lots of sex addicts, pornography, legitimization in the entertainment industry, advertising and media involvement, new Victorianism, huge sectors of the economy dependent upon and/or highly focused upon sex and related businesses, including those related to supply, use, and treatment of related disorders, crimes, and problems

With a remainder: not a whole lot of political change

What did change, however, among the immense culture changes of the late 1950s, '60s, and '70s, was the decrease of traditional roles and role models around relationship and marriage. Many of these shifts in marriage and relationship were the result of intensely changing gender roles in American society. *Father Knows Best*—which began on radio in the late 1940s and continued onto TV into the 1960s—said it all. *Father* knows best and he's in charge, although he's a benign and sage head of household who would sometimes defer to his wife, Margaret, as the voice of reason. Billie Gray, the man who portrayed All-American teenager "Bud" on the show, later said:

> I wish there was some way I could tell the kids not to believe it. The dialogue, the situations, the characters—they were all totally false. The show did everyone a disservice. The girls were always trained to use their feminine wiles, to pretend to be helpless to attract men. The show contributed to a lot of the problems between men and women that we see today.... I think we were all well motivated, but what we did was run a hoax. *Father Knows Best* purported to be a reasonable facsimile of life. And the bad thing is, the model is so deceitful. It usually revolved around not wanting to tell the truth, either out of embarrassment, or not wanting to hurt someone. If I could say anything to make up for all the years I lent myself to (that), it would be, 'You Know Best.'[9]

Father Knows Best ended its television run in the mid-1960s, but the effect lingered on with reruns of *The Adventures of Ozzie & Harriet, The Donna Reed Show, Dennis the Menace,* and *Leave It to Beaver,* throughout the 1960s. One notable exception to the shows that depicted traditional marital arrangements was *My Three Sons,* a show about a widowed man raising three sons. The show had no female lead or rather no *female* in the female lead role. Tough Uncle Charley fills in for the missing woman in the show, coming to the rescue to help parent the orphaned child of a family friend. No doubt each of these television shows, watched by tens of millions of Americans glued to their TV sets every night, made it clear that the keys to a happy life were traditional marriage (unless your wife dies), family, work, and a male-led hierarchy.

Educator and one of the first real parenting experts Rudolf Dreikurs explains in *Children the Challenge* how necessary social movements toward equality (of race, gender, and class) changed things for parents around *age,* too. The change and loss of traditional social and gender roles, led in no small part by the women's movement that occurred throughout the 1960s and '70s, meant that parenting, too, was losing its models: "Children should be seen and not heard" was not going to cut it anymore. Or, as Dreikurs is quoted as saying, "When Dad lost control of Mom, they both lost control of the children." Dreikurs wrote extensively about how parents were at a tremendous loss about *what to do* as parents, especially as the children pushed back more and more and wanted in on the equalization they were feeling and seeing all around them. Throw in drugs, sexual experimentation (by parents and kids), and enormous shifts in wealth,[10] and some might describe the '70s and '80s as the decades of "kids gone wild."

The Pornification of Sex: The New, Public Face of American Sexuality

Sometime in 2004, while Ariel Levy was probably very busy writing *Female Chauvinist Pigs: Women and the Rise of Raunch Culture,* and Mark Zukerberg was busy launching Facebook, I started noticing something happening particularly with my adolescent female clients; not just one, but several of them. It went something like this: I meet a 15- or 16-year-old teen and she starts talking about her friends. "So I was talking to Courtney the other day...so Ayesha was going on about how her mom is on her about homework...so I can't wait to see if Brent is around this weekend..." and on it went. I would listen, sometimes for months and months, until something would go "wrong" in a relationship or one of these teens would start talking about feeling really lonely. In each instance, I had already tallied up in my head that the number of friendships each of these girls had was close to 100, though they talked mainly about 10 or 15 really good friends. I would naively make a mental note that these kids were doing well in terms of social connection—an incredibly important measure of overall mental health and a protective factor against many of the problems that adolescents can get into. I would try to be helpful but I didn't quite understand why these girls were having trouble make use of their wide circle of friends when things were difficult. One day I said to one of my teen clients, "Well, the next time you see Tina, do you think you could ask her whether she really was feeling jealous and pushed out of your relationship with Sarah? Sometimes we make assumptions that people are mad about things that they aren't really that angry about." And my client says, without missing a beat, "Oh, I've never *met* Tina—she's an online friend." After a somewhat long pause she added, "I think that could be what's bothering me—I've *never met* any of my friends." The close to 100 "friends" of my client were online relationships, and it never occurred to her to make the distinction between "online" and "offline" or "IRL" ("in real life"). After that I finally got that I'd need to start asking about whether a friend was an "online" friend or not.

At about the same time, about a decade after the launch of the World Wide Web as we know it—ahh, I can still hear the sound of my modem connecting to America Online (AOL)—many of my adolescent female clients starting talking about exchanging some type of sexual behavior for "gifts." It's not like they talked about this with ease and without embarrassment, but they did talk: a dress for showing your breasts; new boots for masturbating on camera; a few bucks here or there or maybe just the gratitude and admiration of the person in the ether for quickly lifting her top, or pulling down her underwear, à la *Girls Gone Wild.* Sometimes this sexual behavior was with a "friend," but just as often it was with a stranger or someone my client had never met in person. Usually the male (and they were mostly males) was older, sometimes much older than the female.

If you ever had insomnia and a television set in the mid-1990s, you know about *Girls Gone Wild (GGW)*. Joe Francis is the founder of Mantra Films, which produces the video and film projects—when he isn't busy being sued and appearing in court. *Girls Gone Wild* projects are pretty much all the same, although they got more and more sexually explicit after the release of the first film in 1997. You have the same basic formula: young, attractive college-age students on spring break or at some nightclub or vacation destination being trolled by a *GGW* camera crew, and being "induced" to expose themselves or make out with one another in exchange for a *GGW* T-shirt or other branded apparel. Oh, yeah, Francis is (or was) very, very rich, at least until the IRS came calling. In the mid-1990s, most of what you would have seen on the television ads involved a girl lifting her top, exposing her breasts, and screaming. But if you purchased the subscription for monthly videos or saw the films for purchase after 1997, they showed the girls being followed to their hotel rooms or some other location and being filmed having sex or masturbating, to the delight of the young, all-male camera crew there to entice the young ladies to "get wild" for a *GGW* hat.

The *GGW* "trend," launched by Joe Francis, was rooted in a shrewd calculation that more and more of the American adolescent (and young adult) mainstream was ready for pornography. People in the adult entertainment industry already knew that Americans were ready for pornography and had already begun using the new distribution and production channels made available by the connectivity of the Internet.

In regard to the current culture of sex, it is absolutely crucial to consider two characteristics of adolescent development—brain plasticity and changes due to normal sexual maturation—along with the ubiquity of digital media. Most teens are intensely interested, curious, and actively seeking information about and experiences around sex and sexuality. Most teens are also intensely interested, curious, and actively seeking information about and experiences around digital media. In *The Shallows*, author Nicholas Carr describes the intensity with which the Internet's promise of connection calls out to teens:

> If, knowing what we know today about the brain's plasticity, you were to set out to invent a medium that would rewire our mental circuits as quickly and thoroughly as possible, you would probably end up designing something that looks a lot like the Internet. It's not that we tend to use the Net regularly even obsessively. It's that the Net delivers precisely the kind of cognitive and sensory stimuli—repetitive, interactive, intensive, addictive—that have been shown to result in strong and rapid alterations in brain circuits and functions.[11]

Because pornography is accessible all the time, and stimulates the pleasure center of the brain to produce neurotransmitters like dopamine—a substance that increases feelings of pleasure and well-being—it just isn't difficult to want to watch more and more pornography and be drawn in by the endless variation in types of sexual activity being shown. I see men, women, boys, and girls addicted to Internet pornography. Even among those who don't feel "addicted" to pornography, many still feel that pornography has radically changed the way they think, feel, and behave with regard to sex, alone and with their partners (if they have partners). This happens much more often with males than females.[12]

The bottom line is that porn is big business and very mainstream—it's a multinational, multi- billion-dollar industry that for years provided the engine of growth for the Internet. For the first ten years of the Internet, it was not only the growth engine, but also provided much of the "innovation" in advertising, sales, outreach, and marketing in the world of business.[13]

The culture around sex and sexuality, which had already undergone major changes, was changing in the United States, and more teenagers were watching pornography. It's easy to say definitively that there is an increased number of teenagers, worldwide, watching pornography on a regular basis, and that is almost entirely due to the advent of the Internet. Pornography is now accessible 24 hours a day, 7 days a week, *free,* for anyone who has access to most digital media, like an iPad, iPod, any smart phone, laptop computer, gaming device, or almost *any* device that connects to the Internet. In addition to the very wide accessibility of pornographic content, you also have in many Western advanced industrial countries the *mainstreaming* of pornography. The way that "porn stars" dress, talk, think, and respond about sex, as well as how sexual acts are depicted, has become the way many, if not most modern Americans think about what is normative in sexuality. Of course, they're wrong; most people are not having "porn sex," *but they often think they should be.* The stars are now mainstream and have crossed over to so-called "legitimate" television and movies. Ariel Levy writes about this brilliantly—especially with regard to teens—in her book *Female Chauvinist Pigs: Women and the Rise of Raunch Culture,* and that's why I keep mentioning that book. It's one of the most important works on sexual identity development in America written in the last 20 years. It is also one of the most disturbing books for parents to read and not respond, "That's not about *my* child or anyone I know," to which I have to reluctantly reply, "Yes, it is."

Part of the changes Levy describes have to do with the increasing *public* and *performative* aspects surrounding sexual behaviors that we see in the *Girls Gone Wild* ethos—the ethos of *raunch culture.* In this view, sex is public, sex is good, and it's a pleasure for everyone. If you don't have sex and/or if have a lot of it, you're on the outside. That is the clear message about sex that you get from pornography. The problematic thing, though, is not that it is *one* message about sex. After all, sexuality and sexual behavior is so varied within and across species. The problematic thing is that, as Levy writes, "What we once regarded as a kind of sexual expression, we now view *as* sexuality."[14]

Even though teens (and adults now) are getting some of their messages about sex from pornography, it doesn't mean that the "promise" of pleasure for everyone is being fulfilled. The misogyny and inequality characteristic of most pornography has also gotten transferred to adolescent sexual culture. It's not really about the girl/woman having pleasure and orgasm—it's about how *hot* she is, and the status she can derive from the currency of hotness, which is so much more about being *popular* than it is about being *beautiful*. There is really not much that's egalitarian about it.

> There is a disconnect between sexiness or hotness and sex itself. As Paris Hilton, the breathing embodiment of our current, prurient, collective fixations—blondeness, hotness, richness, anti-intellectualism—told *Rolling Stone* reporter Vanessa Grigoriadis, "My boyfriends always tell me I'm not sexual. Sexy, but not sexual." Any fourteen-year-old who has downloaded her sex tapes can tell you that Hilton looks excited when she is posing for the camera, bored when she is engaged in actual sex.[15]

Levy puts the point succinctly: *Hotness* is a currency, and sexual connecting is not a way to be *intimate (with related ethical obligations)*—it is a commodity. Thus, the salient question becomes *how to monetize* the activity, e.g., how to turn it into something that can be spent on something else. Sounds like the adult entertainment industry to me.

Female Chauvinist Pigs can be confusing for parents. Learning about it in this context—and if you tend to be liberal—you might think some of Levy's arguments must be coming from a prudish, emotionally laden, conservative critique of some of the hard-fought cultural changes of the 1960s and 1970s, which made it more possible for women to have their own voice, and their own choices about their *own* experiences as sexual beings. You might think she just interviewed the *wrong* people—and wrote a book based on the more *daring* and disturbed of kids; surely the country is in a more conservative mood, which is reflected in what the voters (and Congress) have been doing lately.

But Levy's book is based on interviews with all kinds of adolescent males and females, and kids being more sexualized in a conservative political climate isn't a contradiction—it's the triumph of commercialization. Levy describes raunch culture not as the triumph of open sexuality, more fluid gender roles, and the rise of women, but as "essentially commercial."

> Raunch culture isn't about opening our minds to the possibilities and mysteries of sexuality. It's about endlessly reiterating one particular—and particularly controversial—shorthand for sexiness.[16]

I speak pretty openly about sex and sexuality—so I hope you aren't offended by what's coming next. But it needs to be said, so you really understand the current culture of sex for our teens and arguably for many adults. All the things that go (in general) with pornography and the adult entertainment industry—publicness and performance as key ingredients in sex, a focus on male pleasure, *simulated* intense female pleasure, vibrators and dildos, masturbation, anal sex, the use of cameras (and close-ups), breast implants, butt implants, bondage and discipline, multiple sex partners, the "kinkier" the better, "sex as pure fun" (against having to "*mean* anything")—are descriptors of the current culture of sex for adolescents.

Levy interviewed many teens that were acutely aware of the pressure to represent "openness" to sexual experience with others. Levy writes:

> Anne asked me if things were different when I was in high school. I told her that it was the same in the sense that you always wished you could be the prettiest and most popular, the one who guys wanted to be with and girls wanted to be. But the obligation to present yourself as the skankiest—which means the smuttiest, the loosest, the most wanton—even before you've become libidinous (before you are "particularly sexual," to borrow Anne's phrase), is something new. When I went to high school, you wanted to look good and you wanted to look cool, but you would have been embarrassed to look slutty. Ann looked at me, baffled. "So how did you get the guy?" she asked. *"Charm?"*

Girls in particular don't necessarily want to have intercourse or be sexual at all. But they do want the attention that goes along with having a more "open" and relaxed attitude about sexuality. As Levy points out in her book and Stephen Hinshaw illustrates in *The Triple Bind*, girls are constantly trying to walk the line between being someone who dresses, acts, and *looks* they *could* and would have sex, without actually having to commit to that in terms of behavior.[17] They want to be sexy, but don't necessarily want to have sex. And that is starting earlier and earlier—and on YouTube, for example—as we saw from the example of the "Am I Pretty" trend online. That's just the way an 8-year-old prepares for the coming question: *Am I hot?*

"Why are you telling us all this? I will teach my kids something very different than this," you might say. Okay, good. But the key point here is that you do need to know what your children are facing and what messages are easy for them to derive from this shift in culture. So, here's what the digitally based mass media are feeding your teens:

Sex and sexual expression don't have to do with you, in your real life or real feelings. *It is something to achieve.*

Sex is everything and it's nothing, no big deal. There is no "sex": only "hooking up," "friends with benefits," "playing," "messing around," or "hanging out." And even though it's no big deal, it's something you must know about, and do and do "well" (like a porn star) or *you* are no big deal.

Sex is about *performance*. It isn't something you "discover" with your partner, it's a skill you learn in advance (from pornography) and then implement with someone. It's about being instrumental, not about mutuality.

Sexual activity, overall, is a reflection of or referendum on your *worth*. If you're "good at it," you have high status, if you're "bad at it," you have low status. In other words, sex is not about development (about normal human functioning, thinking, and feeling), it's a commodity or purely a matter of *style* that can be judged "good or bad."

Men are in charge of sex and the evaluation of whether this commodity is "good or bad" (saleable or not). This is not a new attitude, of course, but it is reinforced by the ways in which the mass media represent sexuality in the American cultural mainstream.

In this context, to ask yourself (or your partner, for that matter), "What does being sexual with you obligate me to, ethically, emotionally?" seems beyond "quaint." It is *irrelevant* in this context, because if this level of disconnected hypersexuality is your thing, it is, by definition, not that big of a deal. "Come on...that is the *great* thing about it—that it is not a big deal like our parent's generation made of it," say the teens I work with in therapy and talk to out in the world. *It's ironic,* I think to myself. *Many of your parents (and their generation) tried out this "no big deal" thing and made it possible for you to take it for granted. And these are the ones now thinking it might have gone a bit, or a lot, too far.*

I was once interviewed by a high school journalist on the risk of "raunch" or porn culture in America. He asked me what I felt motivated young people to watch porn. I answered, "Being human." It's not an aberration that young people are drawn to pornography and the cultural artifacts of the adult "entertainment" industry. We're all sexual beings, on a continuum of sexual desire and behavior. I'm not saying that watching pornography is "good." I'm just saying that the attraction to seeing people naked and/or doing sexual things is pretty normal for human beings.

But as few as twenty years ago, if a young boy (a minor) wanted to see pornographic images, to look at sexually titillating material of people in various states of undress, he would have to find a pornographic magazine. This wasn't easy to find. Most boys didn't have access to *moving* images of sexual behavior until after 18 years of age. Many males I know, and males I've worked with in therapy, describe something like an "A-ha!" moment for them when they discovered that it was possible to see naked people doing all kinds of things; and they could watch this whenever they wanted to. And it turns out, they *wanted* to watch it—a lot—but ended up with the feeling that they were chasing a kind of high that was only getting reached by *more* frequent and more *varied* types of sexual "input." Most men recognized that their partners couldn't possibly keep up with the frequency and kinds of sexual activity that their minds (and bodies) desired, although some of their partners tried to…usually unsuccessfully, and with growing resentment.

Now, it's possible to see anything sexual—from live, real-time sexual acts between humans (or other animals!) to images, sounds, and the like—and to participate sexually in ways that were largely unheard of or nearly impossible twenty years ago. In my view, kids are just in over their heads, sexually, and it's easy to become addicted to this kind of sexual activity, at an early age. For some complicated reasons, boys seem to more easily get addicted to pornography and online sexual behavior, but that doesn't mean it won't or doesn't happen with girls, especially as girls are more and more expected to have "enlightened" and open attitudes about sex, meaning to be more like the porn stars they hear about and see online. And sometimes the girls are taking the lead, sort of.

Ariel Levy brilliantly summarized the confusing landscape of American sexual culture for girls and boys when she wrote:

> What teens have to work with, then, are two wildly divergent messages. They live in a candyland of sex…every magazine stand is a gumdrop castle of breasts, every reality show is a bootylicious Tootsieroll tree. And these are hormonal teenagers: this culture speaks to them. But at school, the line given to the majority of them about sex is just say no. They are taught that sex is wrong until you have a wedding (they have seen those in the magazines and on the reality shows too, huge affairs that require boatloads of Casablanca lilies and mountains of crystal), and then suddenly it becomes natural and nice. *If you process this information through the average adolescent mental computer, you end up with a printout that reads something like this: Girls have to be hot. Girls who aren't hot probably need breast implants. Once a girl is hot, she should be as close to naked as possible all the time. Guys should like it. Don't have sex.*[18] [italics mine]

Identity development and sexual identity *go together* for adolescents. It is largely—from a biological point of view—what the period of adolescence is all about.

Sexual feelings, fantasies, thoughts, and behaviors, to a greater or lesser degree (and as long as the teen is developing normally) *are going to happen*. These things must happen for our species to survive—at least at *this* point in history.

Sexual identity development and digital media are a marriage made in heaven—or hell, depending on how you see it. If there is anything that fits together intently and intensely, it is the combination of sex, sexuality, identity development, and digital media. The mix is a highly powerful and volatile one.

As we saw in Chapter 3, many young girls have utilized YouTube for this purpose—or is it the other way around? The more-innocent question, "Am I *pretty?*" asked by a 9-year-old becomes "Am I *hot?*" soon enough. Levy makes the point succinctly:

> Rather than telling teens why they shouldn't have sex, perhaps we also ought to be teaching them why they should. We are doing little to help them differentiate their sexual desires from their desire for attention. Many of the girls I spoke to said sex for them was "an ego thing" rather than a lust thing...about a quarter of girls between ages fifteen and nineteen describe their first time as "voluntary but unwanted"...[19]

Voluntary, but unwanted. *That hurts*. When psychologists and researchers look at phenomena like sexting or the use of webcams and chat for sexual activity between teens, the "Am I Pretty?" videos on YouTube, the proliferation of the teen-like, raunch-culture, mini-skirt-wearing Bratz Dolls marketed to preschoolers, Christina Aguilera's "Naughty and Nice" ad for Sketchers footwear, thong underwear, short shorts and tank tops being marketed to 7-year-olds by Abercrombie and Fitch (the outfitter to the American teen), they are concerned about early and/or problematic sexualization. "Voluntary but unwanted" might just be the perfect way of describing *sexualization*.

Sexualization is the process by which a person's value is derived primarily from his or her sexual appeal or behavior, to the exclusion of other characteristics.[20] It is what Levy's book is about: the process of (especially girls) being held to a standard that equates a narrowly defined kind of physical attractiveness with sexiness. In this process, girls, for example, are sexually *objectified*, that is, made into a "thing" for others to use sexually, rather than seen as a person with the capacity for independent action and decision-making. Sexualization also describes the *imposition* of sexuality on a person, rather than a careful process of *choosing* to develop the feelings, thoughts, beliefs, attitudes, and behaviors that will make up "my sexuality." Sexualization can be contrasted with a healthy view of human sexuality as an important component of identity and mental and physical health. Satcher (2001) describes healthy sexuality as including the "fostering of intimacy...bonding and shared pleasure...and involving mutual respect between consenting partners."[21]

A 2008 report released by the American Psychological Association Task Force on the Sexualization of Girls noted some alarming evidence that the process of sexualization was indeed significant in the life of our teens.[22] In the report, researchers like Deborah Tolman, who we met earlier, provided overwhelming evidence that all forms of mass media were fully participating in the processes of sexualization. Most often this involved the sexualization of women and girls. The objectification of girls was linked to diminished cognitive capability and performance in domains such as mathematical computation and logical reasoning. Girls are already challenged, beginning in their middle school experience, to hang on to their interest and love of science, technology, engineering, and mathematics, as it becomes necessary to "defend" being excited about intellectual pursuits, especially those linked to science. Sexualization of girls is linked to the development of eating disorders (already a risk in middle school, when around 40 percent of young girls begin to "diet") and low self-esteem, and concomitantly, increased rates of depressed mood and clinical depression.[23] And as you would expect, early sexualization is linked to increased risks for diminished sexual health; girls who are more highly sexualized use birth control less often and less regularly, feel less pleasure, and have more difficulty understanding and articulating their own desires and needs, sexually. More highly sexualized girls are also less assertive about their needs overall and are more often subject to verbal harassment and sexual violence in intimate partner relationships, which the Centers for Disease Control *Youth Risk Behavior Survey* (CDC YRBS) says is about 35 percent.

All of these cognitive-behavioral changes related to sexualization have an impact on formation of identity, putting acquisition of status and pursuing healthy behavior at odds. Sexualization increases both female and male stereotyping about sex, and fosters a narrowing of views about what types of bodies and what kinds of behaviors are "normal" or "acceptable." While there appears to be an epidemic of childhood obesity in the United States that does need to be addressed, efforts to do so are complicated by problems of early sexualization. Boys know all too well how they are supposed to look: They should be "buff" or "cut"—muscular, angular, with gym-enhanced, model good-looks. Girls need to be "hot"—that is, thin, small-waisted, large-breasted (but not too large), the perfect derriere, and porcelain-smooth, unblemished skin. Girls need to be nice, extra nice, and not get angry with anyone. Boys need to be excellent at sports and smart, but not be too *intellectual*. Unrealistic expectations based on the airbrushed, Photoshop-sculpted perfect bodies of both pornography and retail advertising campaigns give teens thousands of moving and static images to compare themselves to—and worry about falling short of—on a daily basis. Teen girls, especially, are looking at the average model's body—5'11", 117 pounds—and wanting a body that belongs to less than 1 percent of the American woman. It's not much easier for boys and we see that in increasing diagnoses of eating disorders and disordered eating patterns for boys.

Sexualization is also linked strongly to the difficulty that young adult women and men say they are having with finding a partner—feeling ever more so that they want and need a *perfect* physical partner who is successful financially, exactly the right degree of masculinity (or femininity), and an impossible list of attributes, fueled by the kinds of "product" produced in Hollywood. Everyone deserves (and can now see and evaluate for themselves) what constitutes celebrity good looks, money, notoriety, and hotness—for themselves and their partners.

America is a highly sexualized culture. About one third of teens have sexual intercourse before 15, but all the research says that adolescents delay becoming sexually involved when sex is openly discussed at home. More on this in a moment, because it's a central point that addresses what you might want to do about this information.

This information may be old or new to you, but it's not here to shock or worry you. It is in this book to give you a fuller context for your decision-making, and to help you fill in the "environment" part of the equation for thinking about your teenager. I know some people will use this information to put me on "their side"—against pornography, against sex, for sex education, whatever your "side" is—or "not on their side," and that's their choice. I'm not trying to tell you what to do, I'm trying to help you teach your child your values, and you cannot do that as well without information about the *context* for decision-making. In *Female Chauvinist Pigs,* Ariel Levy helped frame part of the *political* context for your decision-making:

> But if conservatives are averse to any discussion of sex outside of marriage, liberals often seem allergic to the idea of imposing sexual boundaries or limits…and simply telling kids sex is fine isn't necessarily any more helpful than telling them sex is bad. Both of these approaches can ultimately have the same result: a silence about the complexities of desire, feminine desire in particular.

So very often, in our lives and with our teens, *silence* proves the real danger, not the hard conversation, argument, disagreement, or pain of understanding each other.

Against Silence (Unless It's There Because You're Listening)

There is an intriguing thing that happens when *a lot of money pours in, anywhere,* and experts and money substitute for real, local conversation about difficult subjects. First, there is a tendency not to talk about "it," not to talk about *the effects of the money* and *monetization* on whatever domain that money is flooding into. And there is a related tendency to stop talking about the *direct content* in a direct way. Conversations tend to move toward issues of *style,* rather than substance. As billions of dollars flow into the worlds of digital media technology, conversations are going to increasingly shut down about the technology and what it does for and against us, and become more about just *how* we use the technology. Digital media and the Internet represent technologies that are "too big to fail." The adult entertainment industry is "too big to fail." It's not about how pornography might affect adolescent identity development, it's about developing a .xxx domain so that we can have a firewall to protect kids from too frequent or early exposure to the inevitable, *too big to fail* fact of pornography, sexualization, and digital media. And sex, well, sex is going to keep happening. And communication, yes, that should probably keep happening, too. So, what's my point? Am I against sex or social connecting? No: I'm against silence with our teens (and children) on both (and all) matters, in general.

The Guttmacher Institute—one of the most respected sources of information on sexual and reproductive health—reported that 93 percent of parents said their child has benefited from sex education in high school or middle school. Almost 95 percent of parents surveyed said that sex education should cover contraception; about 15 percent of American parents wanted abstinence-only education in the classroom.

But under the George Bush administration, federally funded programs were required to discourage all unmarried people from engaging in any "sexually stimulating" behavior/activity, including kissing. State-funded programs were required to promote abstinence among people as old as 29, and total federal funding for these programs was upped to close to $180 million in 2008, an increase from $136 million just 10 years prior. Federally funded abstinence programs were studied and showed egregious errors in delivering accurate information about everything from contraceptive effectiveness, risks of abortion, sexually transmitted infection incidence rates, to basic errors about scientific facts about sex.

Let me say it clearly: Just saying "no" and trying to avoid things by not talking about them does not work. That approach hurts people. Sometimes it kills people.

I want to give two examples of this, one from the world of epidemiology and treatment of HIV/AIDS, the second from the world of race, identity, and politics.

There has been a steadily growing global campaign to fight the HIV epidemic for some time now, since the first cases appeared in the United States in the 1980s. The virus is spread very slowly and that makes it difficult to understand and combat—it doesn't move through populations in the ways the other viruses do. Part of the response to AIDS has been an effort to understand how the disease was transmitted from chimps to humans; researchers finally found a strain of the virus, HIV-1, Group M, which came from very remote regions in Cameroon and eventually migrated to the Belgian Congo in the 1960s (from Kinshasa, now the capital). From Kinshasa, the viruses spread to Haiti, and to the United States, to Europe, and back again.

In the United States, early cases of what came to be understood as HIV infection were called the "gay cancer," because for a long time it primarily infected young, healthy gay males. Many African countries basically paid no attention to the growing epidemic in their own country because HIV infection was associated with homosexuality, not heterosexual contact. And, slowly, scientists discovered that HIV rates are *much* higher where circumcision rates are lower. In addition, scientists were beginning to understand that the risk of HIV transmission was higher if a person had multiple partners. This is not uncommon in Africa, where is it more acceptable for men and women to have multiple partners outside a primary relationship.[24]

The history of the fight against HIV infection was chronicled in *Tinderbox: How the West Sparked the AIDS Epidemic and How the World Can Finally Overcome It*. Written by former Johannesburg bureau chief of *The Washington Post* Craig Timberg, and his colleague Daniel Halperin, Ph.D., the book is a counterintuitive detective's tale about how the fight against HIV and AIDS was exacerbated over and over again by the influx of large amounts of Western money, influence, and prevention "expertise." How?

All of the facts noted above took nearly 20 years to figure out, which meant that prevention efforts needed to address issues requiring frank discussions about sex and sexuality. In places like Uganda, where hundreds of thousands of lives were saved by actually reducing the spread of HIV, the rates of HIV infection went down as the Ugandans handled the frank public and private conversations about HIV infection. In Zimbabwe, infection rates also significantly declined. In both instances, people in these countries got the information and largely conducted their own successful campaigns. But, as the authors detail in the book, all this began to change as AIDS money poured in to countries formerly left to deal with the problem on their own. Rates of HIV infection rose to levels higher than a decade earlier, as more Western money and "expert help" poured in. And this trend was repeated over and over again as money and expertise poured in from European and American governments. Timberg and Halperin trace this unfortunate turn of events to the legacy of colonialism, including the paternalism that results from being a big, rich country giving advice to a smaller, poorer country. The frank conversations and spot-on efforts to target *specific* behavior (like circumcision) in many African countries—or specific *sexual* behavior, like having multiple sex partners, who themselves have multiple partners—started going away.

Tinderbox is, at the very least, a cautionary tale about how well-funded efforts that require the *curtailing* of frank discussions in favor of polite, politically correct techniques that avoid specificity or those that are *imposed* from the outside without a full understand of "local" sexual culture don't work well. In fact, they can undo the ongoing efforts of those inside the culture to do the work, based upon solid scientific information.

⌇

In 2008 Barack Obama was the first biracial person elected president of the United States. Conversations about American society being post-racial abounded. Many were tripping over their own feet in self-congratulation for the triumph of democracy and the notion of equality. Finally, the Reverend Dr. Martin Luther King's dream for us all—to judge one another by the content of our character, not the color of our skin—was being realized. But many knew better than this. Stephen Colbert poked a sharp stick at this idea when he said on his show, "Now, I don't see color. People tell me I'm white and I believe them because police officers call me 'sir.'"

Stephen Colbert might not see color, but *babies, toddlers, children, and adolescents* do. Issues of *skin color, race,* and *prejudice* are complicated—some of the most complicated issues in American society. Skin color is about melatonin, weather, and human genetics. Race is *another* matter. "Race" is about culture and control, a misguided and inaccurate way to explain something about phenotype (biological variation). The definition of "race" changes over time, because it is what Raymond Williams called a *keyword*—the locus of struggle/fight over what a word means, because of the political and social power that goes along with being able to define what appears as "natural" and "true." *Keywords* are words whose definition is fought over; how the meaning of keywords change reflects the politics and values of the times.[25]

How we *define* race is part of that fight, but there is no "race," as a valid *scientific* way to describe variations in human phenotype. So, are we beyond race and color? Well, we'd better not be. American children (and teens) need to talk about race and color, because they are part of the fabric of American society. Children see skin *color,* and they are making theories about what it *means* for them. How do I know this? Well, studies of infant development demonstrate that babies see variations in color/tone as early as one month, and are born seeing black, white, and shades of gray.[26] Other researches demonstrate that by the age of six months (but usually between three and six months), infants are noticing *phenotype*—the visually apparent aspects of faces that we normally ascribe to "racial" differences.[27]

But I prefer the more naive (or complex) explanation, depending upon how you see it. I believe that since we are theory-making animals, in terms of how we come to understand ourselves, others, and the world, that we *need* to see *color* and *difference* and need to make sense of those phenomena. You can be literally color-blind (in all its variations), but you will still see shades and differences. Humans need to come up with biological and cognitive "theories" about these differences.

So, while children can and do see skin color, their interpretations of the meanings of those colors are, in part, socially and culturally determined; that means that parents have a role in helping to shape the way their children come to understand race (which is a combination of apperception and learning from others and experience with others). To deny that you or your child (or any other person with sight) is seeing race or color is inaccurate and dangerous, in my view. Po Bronson and Ashley Merryman—the authors of *NurtureShock*—who discuss the implications of not talking about race and color in their chapter "Why White Parents Don't Talk About Race" share that view.[28]

The authors point to a 2007 study in the *Journal of Marriage and Family* showing that nonwhite parents talk about race three times more often than their white counterparts, who, 75 percent of the time, never or almost never bring it up. Kids are noticing differences, but when those experiences of "noticing" are left alone in silence for the child to understand, then misunderstanding, prejudice, and bias have no *counterweight*.

Multiculturalism and "dealing" with race and color is not about showing children books with lots of differently colored kids dancing under a rainbow. It's about real and often difficult conversation about the problematic aspects of racism, prejudice, pride, differences, and similarities.

Well-organized, well-funded college-level programs designed to increase productive, progressive understandings of race and culture show somewhat mixed results.[29] But research aimed at measuring the impact of these programs continues to show that many students—many students of color—still find unresponsive campus climates, and profound feelings of marginalization and lack of support. These conversations need to happen *much earlier*. How much earlier? Professor April Harris-Britt—one of the researchers profiled in *NurtureShock*, suggests that parents start talking to their children about race, color, and bias as soon as children can pay attention to images in a book. If your child can point out that a ball is "red" or ask what color that doggie's sweater is, it's possible to have brief but specific interactions with them around skin color—which will lead to other conversations about perception and bias.

What children learn about race from their parents and family members (and, of course, from their day-to-day experiences in the world) has a profound impact on their self-attitudes as children and adults. Talking to your child about race and color allows your child to understand difference and sameness—two enormously influential and important human concepts—and gives them the beginning of optics for understanding how to treat themselves and others. The lens through which you and your children see others shapes, to a great extent, not only their attitudes and beliefs, but what behaviors are desirable, possible, or disallowed. In other words, choosing (or teaching your child about) your lens for understanding others is an ethical matter. More important, as Bronson and Merryman and many other authors on identity development point out, not talking about race reinforces the rather natural prejudices of immature perception and thinking in children, and ideas of race at home and from family members often affect their attitudes and ideas about race as adults.[30]

Political correctness and the fear of hurting feelings can and does function to shut down real conversation that could lead to understanding and real change. This same basic lesson applies to conversations about drug and alcohol use[31] and sexual behaviors,[32] including high-risk behaviors in both domains. I've already mentioned how talking about sex (and drugs and alcohol use) in the family means a decrease or delay in the behavior in question for most adolescents. In other words, when you talk openly (and without blame, attack, or cross-examination) about drugs and alcohol, and sexuality and sexual behavior, in the home, teens wait longer to use drugs and alcohol and have sex, and when they do engage in those behaviors, they do it less frequently and with more consciousness about risks and benefits.[33] As sex educator Deborah Roffman likes to say, "talking about sex is not permission to have sex: It is permission to *talk* about sex." She and others call this being an "askable" parent. Talking about drugs and alcohol is not permission to drink and use drugs; it is permission to directly and indirectly teach your teens what you value, and in the process add to their sense of being cared for. You should know if you've gotten this far in the book that it's *not all up to you*. It's about genes and environment. What you say and do with your teen—at any given moment—won't make an irreconcilable difference in terms of his or her choices around sexual behavior. There are too many other factors involved. If your teen matures, physically, sooner than usual, this plays a role in earlier onset of sexual intercourse, for example.[34] That is one of hundreds of influential biological and social factors. It's all so overwhelming sometimes. But if sex, alcohol, drugs, digital media, and the adult entertainment industry are all *too big to fail,* then what does that leave you, in terms of influencing and shaping your adolescent's future? You and your teenager, together, having an *informed conversation*. Your engaged presence in *ongoing conversation* with your teenager helps strengthen one of the key *environmental* factors that help keep your teenager safe and happy. And knowing about some research, getting educated makes your *presence* and the choices you make when you intervene a much *closer* approximation to "getting it right" for *your* teen.

Practical Help Tips

1) These tips are found by really thinking about and answering the first four questions for yourself. You'll be able to write your own tips!

> a) Does this material make you question the prevalence of "hooking up" or "friends with benefits" or shed new light on those ideas?

> b) When kids do say "no" to having intercourse, they cite fears of pregnancy, STIs, being too young, and their parents' counsel as the primary influencing factors. If you believe in delaying intercourse or waiting until marriage, what does this suggest you should do to enhance your kids' decision to not have intercourse?

> c) When kids say "yes" to having intercourse, they cite being curious, wanting to please their partner, feeling it was the right time or the right person, or feeling ready to lose their virginity as reasons they said "yes." If you believe in delaying intercourse or waiting until marriage, what does this suggest you should do to enhance the decision to not have intercourse?

> d) If you believe that intercourse and other sexual activity is okay, given certain circumstances, what does the information in b) and c) suggest you should do to enhance your child's psychological, spiritual, and medical safety?

2) Things you can do to support your child's healthy development around sex and relationships:

> a) Work to feel more comfortable as the primary educator of your children about sexuality by starting early. For example, you can teach very young children the appropriate words for parts of the body. Try to get as comfortable saying "penis" and "vulva" as you do "elbow." As they grow older, answer their questions honestly and be willing to answer their questions about relationships, puberty, and intimacy. Forget about having one big talk; think about lots of little conversations. Are *you* confused about all this? How do you think your teens are feeling? Really? Think they have it all figured out?

b) Model mutually respectful relationships. Talk with your child about sexuality and character. Help them understand your values and stress the importance values play in your life.

c) Remember that developing a self-identity is the task of adolescence, and youth may at times feel uncomfortable talking to their parents about their thoughts and feelings, especially about sexuality. Work with them to identify other adults with whom they can talk comfortably.

d) Don't worry about: a) being "with it" or "cool"; b) knowing all the right answers; c) being embarrassed; d) figuring out the "perfect" thing to say. Be a parent who can listen to your child.

e) Work to acquire a broad foundation of factual information from reliable sources. Remember that sexuality is a much larger topic than sexual intercourse. It includes biology, gender, love, emotions, intimacy, caring, sharing, attitudes and beliefs, flirtation, and sexual orientation—as well as reproduction and sexual intercourse.

f) Connect with your son and/or daughter. Young people who feel connected to family are more likely to avoid risky behaviors in adolescence, and, in general, delay the age at which they have intercourse.

g) Think through your own feelings and values about love and sex. Include your childhood memories, your first loves and infatuations, your values, and how you feel about current sex-related issues, such as contraceptives, reproductive rights, and equality with regard to sex, gender, and sexual orientation. You must be aware of how you feel (not SURE, just aware) before you can effectively talk with your child.

h) Listen more than you speak. Enough said.

i) Remember that teens want and crave mutually respectful conversations. Try to avoid lecturing or they will shut down, even if they appear to be listening to you.

j) Don't assume your teen or any other teen is sexually experienced or inexperienced, knowledgeable or naive. Teens may portray the opposite of their real situation, in order to feel safe. Try to respond to your teen's actual question, not your own fears or worries.

k) Your friends, lots of conversations, and *lots of education* form your biggest supports. Helping teens understand the importance and implications of sexuality is as much about *media literacy* as it is about anything else.

l) Last, but not least, if the various negative phenomena of sexualization are to be successfully addressed, parents—*especially dads*—should be talking to their boys about what it means to be a good man. Parents—*especially dads*—need to be talking to boys about what they're doing, thinking, and feeling about women. It is not enough—and it's the *wrong* message too—to just identify girls as the locus of these challenges. Girls are often locked into behaviors that are "voluntary, but not wanted," and boys can lead the way out by refusing or reinventing the behaviors that define sexuality, sexiness, and "normal" in such narrow ways as our culture currently defines them. Fathers can help their sons become *leaders* of new, more mutual and more satisfying ways of being sexual beings together.

Suggested Reading: *The Sexual Culture of American Teens*

The lists in the "Suggested Reading" sections are by no means comprehensive. I'm including what I consider to be the most informative, practical, relevant, or comprehensive readings on the topic(s) of the chapter. In other words, if you have limited time, these are the works I believe you might want to explore first. It doesn't mean all of these books are "easy reads." Sometimes a listed book will be very difficult, but worth the time.

American Psychological Association Task Force on the Sexualization of Girls. 2010. Report of the APA Task Force on the Sexualization of Girls. www.apa.org/pi/women/programs/girls/report-full.pdf (accessed April 1, 2012).

Bronson, P., & Merryman, A. *NurtureShock: New Thinking About Children.* New York: Twelve, 2009.

Brown, M. L., & Rounsley, C. A. *True Selves: Understanding Transsexualism—For Families, Friends, Coworkers, and Helping Professionals.* San Francisco: Jossey-Bass, 2003.

Foley, S. F., Kope, S. A. K., & Sugrue, D. P. *Sex Matters for Women: A Complete Guide to Taking Care of Your Sexual Self.* New York: The Guilford Press, 2011.

Kilbourne, J. *Can't Buy My Love: How Advertising Changes the Way We Think and Feel.* New York: Free Press, 2000.

Kindlon, D. & Thompson, M. *Raising Cain: Protecting the Emotional Life of Boys.* New York: Ballantine, 2000.

Levin, D. E., & Kilbourne, J. *So Sexy So Soon: The New Sexualized Childhood and What Parents Can Do to Protect Their Kids.* New York: Ballantine Books, 2008.

Levy, A. *Female Chauvinist Pigs: Women and the Rise of Raunch Culture.* New York: Free Press, 2005.

Mysko, C. *Girls Inc. Presents: You're Amazing! A No-Pressure Guide to Being Your Best Self.* Avon: Adams Media, 2008.

Roffman, D. M. *Sex and Sensibility.* New York: Perseus Books Group, 2002.

Timberg, C., & Halperin, D. *Tinderbox: How the West Sparked the AIDS Epidemic and How the World Can Finally Overcome It.* New York: Penguin Press, 2012.

Tolman, D. L. *Dilemmas of Desire: Teenage Girls Talk about Sexuality.* Cambridge: Harvard University Press, 2005.

Westheimer, R. K. *Sex for Dummies.* New York: Hungry Minds, Inc., 1995.

Zilbergeld, B. *The New Male Sexuality.* New York: Bantam Books, 1999.

7

Protecting the Wish to Learn

> We have pointed in the last section to the danger threatening individual and society, where the schoolchild begins to feel that the color of his skin, the background of his parents, or the fashion of his clothes rather than his wish and his will to learn will decide his worth as an apprentice, and thus his sense of *identity*....[1]
>
> —Erik Erikson, *Childhood and Society*

> Education is a social process; education is growth; education is not a preparation for life but is life itself.
>
> —John Dewey, from Article Two, "What School Is," in *My Pedagogic Creed* (1897)[2]

Renowned musician Branford Marsalis was interviewed in 2005 for the documentary *Before the Music Dies*—a film sharply critical of the shift in the last three decades toward the unqualified commercialization of the music industry. *Holding back* was not Marsalis's strong suit in the film. "The reality is that superficiality is in...and depth and quality is kind of out," he sighs. A good portion of the film focuses on how digital technologies are revolutionizing (and threatening to destroy) most of the musical *quality* Marsalis spoke of. The film lays much of the blame on three phenomena closely associated with digital technology: MTV, the rise of the Internet, and the invention of Auto-Tune. Yes, you read that right.

We've already explored generally how the rise of music television (MTV) influenced adolescent perceptions and ideas of "cool." In the process, with the advent of the music video as the primary advertising/marketing medium and digital satellite technology opening the broadcast bandwidth, the relative *power* of conventional radio broadcasting sharply declined. The very first video played on MTV—The Buggles' "Video Killed the Radio Star"—was a self-conscious, unapologetic nose-thumbing at the futures of the traditional radio and music businesses. There is no arguing that when the video became the primary means of selling an artist, the way the artist *looked* took on an exaggerated and *primary* importance.

We've also looked more in depth (in Chapter 4) at how the characteristics of digital media—combined with the concerns of adolescents around status and belonging—can permanently inflate the power of the Internet to play a *central role* in identity formation. That leaves us with Auto-Tune—the biggest selling digital audio plug-in of all time and the invention of former Exxon seismic engineer Andy Hildebrand.

If you heard Cher's 1998 hit "Believe," you've heard Auto-Tune. It can make a singer's voice sound like a robot (as in Cher's song), or it can be used to change the pitch of a note in subtle or not-so-subtle ways (as a vocal "effect"). It has been used on countless recordings since 1998, and is often used to correct a singer's poor pitch—something that used to result in tens of thousands of dollars spent on expensive professional recording studio time (re-recording poor vocals) *or* a singer getting fired, or never getting a decent job again, at least until their vocal ability was improved. With Auto-Tune, you don't really need to sing on pitch—outstanding! But isn't that what separates someone like, say...*me*...from someone like Nat King Cole, Etta James, or Ella Fitzgerald?

Now, put together Auto-Tune on your digital audio workstation with the predominant emphasis on *looks* ushered in by the video generation, and you have the reason for why *Before the Music Dies* was made: No real reason for *quality,* when (hot, young, and Auto-Tuned) superficiality will do *just fine.* Ella Fitzgerald, the "Queen of Jazz," with perfect pitch and a vocal range of *three octaves,* was the most popular female vocalist in America for *nearly 50 years.* She sold almost 40 million records worldwide, and won 13 Grammys and countless awards in a career that spanned 60 years, until her death in 1996.[3]

Three years after Ella's death, 17-year-old Britney Spears appeared on the April 1999 cover of *Rolling Stone,* lying on her bed, her top completely open, exposing a sexy black bra and bright pink hot pants. Again, she was still 17, and *not* a porn actress; the stylists put a phone in one hand and a *Teletubby* in the other. All the fashion effects don't quite work to let you know she *isn't* in porn. Before Britney Spears turned 20, she'd sold more records than Ella Fitzgerald did in her entire lifetime, as America's most popular vocalist for half of the 20th century.[4] Britney has won one Grammy Award (2005), in the category of Best Dance Recording—for her 2003 smash hit "Toxic," a heavily sampled, heavily Auto-Tuned song, the video for which has received nearly 55 million hits on YouTube and prominently features her "assets" in a sparkling nude bodysuit for much of the $1 million music video.[5] Spears's record company spent modestly on the video: "Toxic" was only the 35th most expensive music video ever produced, way behind Michael and Janet Jackson's

$7 million "Scream" video. In an online blog earnestly entitled "Is Britney Spears a Music Genius?" the author is keen to point out Britney's winning musical sensibilities: "Six years later, if you played Toxic in a club it will still be a huge hit with the crowd because when you listen to it carefully it *sounds exactly like every other pop song on the radio today* [italics mine]."[6]

The facts speak (or scream) for themselves. How did a 17-year-old white teenager from Mississippi sell more records, make more money, and have more, um, public exposure in the first few years of her career than the "First Lady of Song" did in nearly her entire career?

Do you recall the definition of status from Chapter 3? "Status"—from the Latin *statum* or "standing"—refers to the amount and type of goodies given to us by others: material goods and services, control over our own time, comfort and/or a lightening of physical, geographical, and psychological burdens or barriers, and perhaps most important, responses from other people, who help you feel cared about and just plain happy to be you. *High* status accords what author Alain de Botton described as a sense of personal value, "conveyed through invitations, flattery, laughter (even when the joke lacked bite), deference and attention."[7]

Flattery, even when the joke lacked bite. Or, in this case: *praise, even when the music lacks quality.* Britney makes more money in a few months than I will ever make in my lifetime. I have to give her "props" for that. It's not that she has no talent. She understands the business world and she knows how to dance. But she didn't achieve this *because she's a good singer.* It happened because a male-dominated, commercially driven music business—operating via mass digital media in a highly sexualized culture that fetishizes young girls—made her rich, in the process of generating hundreds and hundreds of millions of dollars in profit for others. Britney's "take" is small potatoes compared with the wealth generated by the "Britney Industry." I know someone who has anxiety over status: Britney Spears. *Status anxiety* is the deep anxiety and suffering about what others think of us: about whether we're judged a success or a failure, a winner or a loser. *Status anxiety* is the intensive and pervasive worry about whether the world—your world—loves you. It isn't hard to imagine that this anxiety is something that a young woman whose career and identity were created and maintained by the status-generating machine would carry with her most of her days, because with status, your worth, whether the world loves you or not, is tied to whether you're *in* or *out.* Britney Spears and others like her *always* have to worry about—unless they've had a revelation or a lot of therapy and rehab—just when some sexier, *more* naked 17-year-old is going to be the "next" (younger, *hotter*) version of you.

Okay, so other than the Internet and MTV, it's all Andy Hildebrand's fault for taking the technological know-how used to map underground oil deposits and transforming it into correcting the pitch of thousands of off-key but very good-looking entertainers.[8] Dr. Hildebrand cries, "I'm innocent!" In a 2009 interview Hildebrand says he originally intended Auto-Tune as offering a powerful but very subtle aid to engineers around pitch correction. He never imagined that the effect would be set to "zero" (giving the pronounced "robotic" sound) or that it would be used so pervasively. When he invented the technology, he says, he couldn't foresee how it would be used or what impact it would have. He doesn't want to weigh in on how his invention is currently used: "I don't know if it's good or bad. I'm not a judge of that. *It's very popular, so in that sense it's good.* I don't place value judgments on things like that [italics mine]." More important was Hildebrand's summary of the whole situation: "I just give people a tool. I don't tell them how to use it."[9]

The example of Auto-Tune is just one more in a long list of supporting examples of Nicholas Carr's point from *The Shallows*—that the content of a technology (the ability to shift pitch on incoming sounds) eventually matters less than how the technology eventually influences how we think, feel, and behave (the intensely enhanced ability to push forward style over substance in music). Carr notes that we can be "too busy being dazzled or disturbed by the programming to notice what's going on inside our heads. In the end, we come to pretend that the technology itself doesn't matter. It's how we use it that matters, we tell ourselves." Of course, the implication is that we can manage the effects of technological innovation. The inventors say, "It's just a tool—how you use it isn't in my control." The powerful adopters and distributors of the technology, like media mogul David Sarnoff said of the power of mass media, say the same thing: "We are too prone to make technological instruments the scapegoats for the sins of those who wield them. The products of modern science are not in themselves good or bad; it is the way they are used that determines their value." Marshall McLuhan called this response "the numb stance of the technological idiot."[10]

By now you can understand—whether you agree or not with—Branford Marsalis's worries about the triumph of style over substance rooted in the rise of MTV and the explosion of digital media technologies and platforms. In *Before the Music Dies'* extended interview with Marsalis, he offers a surprising answer to a relatively typical question asked of successful teachers in *any* field: What have *you* learned from your students?

> What have I learned from my students? What I've learned from *my* students? Students today are completely full of shit. That is what I've learned from my students is that—much like the generation before them—the only thing they are interested in is you telling them how right they are and how good they are. That is the same mentality that basically forces Harvard to give out B's to people that don't deserve them, out of the fear that they will

go to other schools that will give them B's and those schools will make the money. We live in a country that seems to be just in a massive state of delusion where the *idea* of what you are is more important than you actually being that, and it actually works as long as everybody is winking at the same time. And if one person stops winking, you just beat the crap out of them until they start winking or go someplace else. But it's like, my students—all they want to hear is how good or how talented they are, and most of them aren't really willing to work to the degree, to live up to that.[11]

I know that Marsalis is reacting strongly here. There are plenty of people—sorry, Branford—who think he's full of hot air, and maybe that's why he plays the saxophone so well. You might disagree with him based on your experiences with your own child or your experiences as a teacher in a public or private school. You might argue that this "crisis" of style over substance—"doing" school, rather than learning in school—must be about the independent (private) school world of privileged spoiled white children in America. But Branford is responding to the same phenomena that Madeline Levine, Thomas de Zengotita, Stephen Hinshaw, Denise Clark Pope, Nicholas Carr, Ariel Levy, Alain de Botton, and many of the writers and researchers chronicled in this book have seen and written about. I am personally acquainted with many of these writers. They don't write about their concerns about adolescents in order to get rich. They are writing because they feel, in some way, *protective* of the will and wish of young people *to learn*—and they are worried about what *and how* they are learning, about themselves, others, and the world.

What *are* we learning from our students—about their will and wish to learn, in a world of digital media, where status easily overwhelms the formation of identity? That's the subject of the rest of the chapter.

Public and Private Concerns

I'm writing from a privileged position and assembling data and opinions from people mainly worried about privileged adolescents from wealthy households in private schools. These are "rich people's problems," right? I mean, after all, if you can afford to take a lesson or study with Branford Marsalis, you've got some serious money. So, maybe there's a point here. Maybe it's the "rich kids" in private schools that are having more intense identity problems—feeling empty or not knowing quite what they love (and not having the time to find out), or having a hard time really committing to something outside themselves that isn't for the purpose of a *résumé*. Maybe it's the more privileged kids from affluent families that Levine profiles in *The Price of Privilege* that truly are having higher (skyrocketing) rates of depression and anxiety disorders and "crashing" during their first year away at college, unable

281

to negotiate pressures and tasks that require the kind of autonomy they are often prevented (or stifled) from developing by being overindulged—getting so much, so easily, so soon.

Teens from affluent households have different stresses and different impediments to learning than their counterparts from less affluent families. I assume most parents want to protect a child's wish and will to learn, whether the family has enough money to live on or more money than they know what to do with. The issue at stake, though, is to figure out what *your* teenager's barriers to learning are, so that you're in a better position to choose the strategies that positively foster his or her development.

So let's do some data-gathering, with the help of your author, the Council for American Private Education (CAPE), and the National Center for Education Statistics (NCES).[12]

Why not start by looking at one private school—the school I worked at for many years. Every year we held *parent* night assemblies for each class level and I held class-level meetings with students. I always began these meetings in the same way for both parents and students, by reading them a list entitled "Who Is At Our School?" While the data varied somewhat each year, it basically looked something like this:

Who Is At Our School?

Kids whose parents have almost no money

Kids whose parents or family members became very ill or died during school

Kids whose parents divorced in the middle of school

Kids whose parents were arrested

Kids who were high and in car accidents

Kids who regularly cheat on exams and assignments

Kids who think about suicide pretty regularly

Kids whose parents or family members were reported to Child and Family Services for physical or emotional abuse

Kids who wanted to figure out whether or how to say something to a friend who they thought had an eating disorder

Kids who have eating disorders severe enough to consider hospitalization

Kids who left the school because they felt the issue of feeling accepted due to the color of their skin was not adequately addressed

Kids who have been sexually abused

Kids whose parents are extremely wealthy and/or famous in the worlds of business, medicine, or academia

Kids who at least three times during the year couldn't find their backpacks, books, phones, or sports equipment and showed up in my office in tears

Kids who were physically bullied and harassed

Kids who were afraid to tell their parents they:
- Didn't want to go to this school
- Did want to go this school
- Were gay or bisexual
- Were sexually active
- Were depressed
- Were throwing up after every meal
- Were cutting themselves
- Had been naked or exposing themselves on camera on the Internet
- Couldn't stop playing video games or chatting and were getting behind in homework

Kids who were harassed online in chat, on Facebook, on MySpace, or on a blog

Kids who sexually or emotionally harassed other kids and initially didn't think it was a problem

Kids who came in to talk to me about their relationship difficulties

Kids who have bipolar disorder, major depressive disorder, generalized anxiety disorder, post-traumatic stress disorder, anorexia, bulimia, trichotillomania, specific learning disabilities, and ADHD (primary hyperactive, primary inattentive, and mixed)

35 percent of which are not Caucasian

100 percent of which got into college, if they applied

99 percent of which, if they made it to senior year, graduated

Surprised? I know that *our* school was not unique, since I often participated in a consulting and support consortium of independent school counselors and spoke at or consulted with many of the high schools in our area. So, welcome to the "problem-free" independent school world (of Northern California). How about the *wider* world?

One in four schools in America is a private school, and most private school students go to small, religious private schools. According to late 2009 U.S. Census data, most children (85 percent) of the wealthiest American families (families with annual incomes over $75,000) go to *public* schools; about 10 percent of the nation's wealthiest families have their children *only* in private schools. As of 2009–10, out of about 55 million students in pre-kindergarten to 12th grade (PK-12), about 49.5 million are in public schools and 5.5 million in private schools. On average, about 25–30 percent of all private school students are racial and ethnic minorities:

74 percent non-Hispanic White, 10 percent non-Hispanic Black, 9 percent Hispanic (all "races"), 6 percent Asian/Pacific Islander, 1 percent American Indian/Alaska Native. On average, about 40–45 percent of all public school students are racial and ethnic minorities: 58 percent non-Hispanic White, 20 percent Hispanic (all "races"), 16 percent non-Hispanic Black, 4 percent Asian/Pacific Islander, and 1 percent American Indian/Alaska Native.

Eighty-nine percent of private school 4th graders work at or above a "basic" achievement level in mathematics, alongside 81 percent of their public school peers; 47 percent of private school students work at a "proficient" math level compared to 38 percent of their public school counterparts; and about the *same* percentage of students (7 percent in private and 6 percent in public) work at an "advanced" level of achievement.[13]

By 8th grade, the gap begins to widen between private and public school student achievement levels in math (85 versus 71 percent at "basic" level; 47 versus 33 percent at "proficient" level; and 13 versus 7 percent at "advanced" level). Very similar gaps exist in subjects such as history, civics, reading, writing, and science, with differences of up to 20 points separating those at private schools who are achieving at basic level. Those gaps usually get larger the older the child gets. Private school students, overall, take more challenging, rigorous courses in math and the sciences.

In recent, broad parent surveys, parents of children in private schools consistently rated *high* satisfaction with their schools compared with their public school parent peers (79 percent versus 52 percent say they are "very satisfied"). Private school parents consistently find the instructional quality, academic standards, disciplinary issues, and personnel interactions higher than public school parents.[14] When surveyed, over 55 percent of parents say they would like to send their child(ren) to private schools. Private school parents are more highly involved in school activities and programs and are eligible for more tax credits.

Among teachers, private school teachers say they feel more supported, experience more collaboration with peers and administration, and feel much more supported by the parent body than public school teachers do. Public school teachers outdo private school teachers on measures they would prefer not to: Almost *double* the percentage of public school teachers say they feel student misbehavior gets in the way of teaching and that tardiness and absences significantly interfere with teaching. Interestingly enough, public and private school teachers alike rated their overall job satisfaction equally high (in the 90th percentile), and about 50 percent of teachers in each setting felt their pay was adequate—with public school teachers making an average annual base salary about 30 percent *higher* than private school teachers.

When the poorest of students ends up getting to attend a private school, he or she is about *four times more likely* to eventually get a bachelor's degree than if attending a public school. A 2007 study by Dr. William H. Jeynes showed that students of color do better in private schools, *regardless* of socioeconomic status. The achievement gap, including differences in standardized test scores, is significantly smaller between majority and minority students in private schools than in public schools. The gap basically disappears between white students and African-American or Latino students, if the student is from a religiously oriented, intact family. In fact, black and Latino students at religiously oriented private schools score consistently higher than their white peers in public school. If you graduated from an independent school, though, your SAT, ACT, or AP score is most likely going to be higher than if you graduate from a religious or public school—and it will be higher than the national average. Remember—we are only talking averages. There are public high schools in Alabama or Southern California or South Carolina, for example, that consistently outperform some of the best private schools in the nation.

It seems that the private school world, serving only 10 percent of the nation's students, clearly has privilege and advantage over the public school world that most American students attend. But it's important to note that when considering achievement levels, *there were no subjects reviewed in which even private school students rated much higher than 50 percent proficiency.* Only *half* of American private school students rate near the "proficient" (or above) level of achievement and only 30 percent of public school students rate "proficient" (or above).

Here's what you are *more likely* to get, though, if you're in the 90 percent of American children who attend a public school:

> 1) Double the risk of being victimized at or on the way to or from school;

> 2) Five times the risk of being threatened with harm at or on the way to or from school;

> 3) Double the risk of being a target of hate speech at or on the way to or from school;

> 4) Six times the risk of encountering a gang at or on the way to or from school;

> 5) Four times the risk of having to avoid certain places at school, for safety reasons[15]

According to the latest U.S. Census figures, compiled in 2010, of the roughly 16.6 million high school students, two public school students drop out of school every minute. If your child drops out of school, he or she is eight times more likely to end up in prison, half as likely to vote, and is unqualified for *most* jobs. Almost 70 percent of 8th graders can't read at grade level, and 1 in 6 students is coming from a school district in a "high poverty" area. If your child is coming from this kind of school, he or she is almost 25 percent *less* likely to go to college, which means only earning 40 cents for each dollar earned by a college graduate.[16] Most of the data suggest that there are, in fact, jobs available in America, despite the Great Recession. However, there are millions of jobs available for which recent college graduates *are not qualified*. Current unemployment rates are almost four times higher for high school dropouts and two times higher for those who didn't graduate from college. In terms of academic achievement, eight years after the ink dried on the No Child Left Behind Act, the United States ranked as the 25th country in math, 21st in science, and 17th in the world in reading.[17]

☙

Dr. Victor Frankl was a successful Austrian neurologist and psychiatrist. Early in his career he began to focus on depression and, more specifically, on the factors that led people to want to commit suicide. At the age of 19, he became the head of a program to counsel suicidal students; the program was 100 percent successful in preventing suicide among its participants. From the ages of 28 to 32, he and his staff counseled close to 30,000 women prone to suicide. In his late 30s, he eventually headed up a hospital neurology department and also performed brain surgery, until the age of 37, when he—along with his wife and family—were taken to a Nazi concentration camp. In 1945, he *alone* among his family was liberated by the Americans from the concentration camp. It is safe to say that Frankl knew something about the suffering of self and others.[18]

Speaking of Americans—we have a deeply ingrained cultural ethos described by phrases like "pick yourself up by your own bootstraps." We use the *bootstrap ethos* as a substitute for "rugged American individualism." It is the "motto" of a country whose population is primarily derived through immigration—self-reliance, responsibility, and survival in the face of adversity. It is the *fine print* to Emma Lazurus's sonnet inscribed in the Statue of Liberty, "Give me your tired, your poor/ Your huddled masses yearning to breathe free."[19] In other words: Come to us, but you'd better be prepared to make it mostly on your own. We will provide a country based on the twin ideas of equality of (most) individuals and belief in the ability to pursue happiness in a "free" market. You can freely practice your religion. So, come here and take your chances—you get a shot, but not a guarantee; when all is said and done, it's up to you. The *bootstrap ethos* is used to argue *against* government entitlement programs like public assistance, social security, government pensions, Medicare, and a host of other intervention programs—on the bases of democracy and free-market capitalism. It echoes the Protestant (or Puritan) work ethic that sees hard work in the world as a sign that one has *already* been saved by God, based on the religious concept of *justification.*[20] Simply put, in Christianity, the powerful idea came to take hold (in the Reformation period) that it was Christ's sacrifice in the Crucifixion that saved humans from a state of sinfulness. Jesus has already done the hardest work; if you just have *faith* in God, you will be saved. Prior to this idea, in the Catholic world, one was supposed to do good works in the world, in addition to having faith in God, in order to be saved. But Martin Luther believed that humans could be justified, *by faith alone.* Eventually, works in the world—working hard and pulling yourself up by your own bootstraps—became important again in organizing society, but this time as *evidence* of salvation, not the *cause* of it.

So, back to Victor Frankl, because this helps orient us to the question of just what is to be done to help protect the will and wish to learn in children—and what gets in the way of that (for example, a higher dropout rate among students of color, and a figurative "dropout factory" in 25 school districts across the country).[21]

In a TV interview with Dr. Frankl, the host asked him, "What is the difference between people who are able to pick themselves up and get over life's problems and those who are not?" He answered, from a lifetime of experience:

> The decisive factor is *decision*—the freedom of choice. The freedom of choice, the freedom to come up with a decision. It *should* be; I would *like to become* this way or another, in *spite* of conditions, that should…or seem to free-determine my behavior. I *wish* to act freely, as a responsible being, which is a *human* being. I wish to act in accord with heredity and environment using—owing—what I become to them. But also, if need be, *in spite of the worst conditions.* This is exactly what you could watch and witness under severe extreme conditions of stress or of tragic conditions.[22]

When people cannot find meaning in their circumstances, when they cannot find the purpose for their suffering, despair takes hold. "Despair," Frankl said, "can be explained in terms of a mathematical equation: $D=S-M$; despair is suffering *without* meaning." This is a bit of a preview of Chapter 10, "The Ethical Dimension in Parenting Teenagers."

Making meaning is a good *strategy* for living in an imperfect world—and teens are particular good at this activity. But we have to watch just *what* meanings they are making of their suffering and their joy, because these meanings will inform their theories about who they are, and how to be with others in the world—and *that* is a preview of the next chapter.

As long as I've thrown a few controversial statements into this book, I might as well admit that I'm not all that interested in standardized test scores, AP scores, or how American students rank on achievement tests. Time for more full disclosure: I was one of those kids that *hated* school.

On Louis CK's television show *Louie*, the main character is seen attending his first PTA meeting.[23] The teacher opens the meeting by discussing how the class might consider adding more physical activities to the curriculum to deal with the "the fatigue problem." Louie raises his hand and asks for clarification about "the fatigue problem." The teacher says the problem was identified as being "a marked decline in the spirit and interest and energy of the kids here, say, usually around noon." The parents begin to weigh in, one after another, about possible causes: "They aren't given enough time to eat!" "They are being demoralized!" "You fill them with academics and don't tell them *who they are*." "It's because of the *competitive* nature of the school, of the children." "I've been reading about this Reggio teaching method from Italy; it's like Montessori except more creative." "When are they supposed to *dance*!?" "It's the academics! This school is stuck in the '70s—who still even teaches *math* anymore? The kids just need to be able to play more creatively!"

Finally, Louie chimes in, a bit shyly, the voice of reasonableness: "It's school, right, so I mean, *school sucks,* right? I mean, you do what you can to improve it...but in the end, um, there's a limit. Because it's...*school*. And... school *sucks—remember*?"

That got me laughing pretty hard—in part because it made so much sense. School isn't *supposed* to be fun or pleasant or intriguing or stimulating or actually teach you anything you care about. It's just something you get through, something you *do*—isn't it?

You know the rest of *my* story—it all must have turned out okay, since you're reading a book I've written and you know I've had a long career as a psychotherapist. I must have eventually even *read* a book. But I just *hated* high school. I went to a large public school and spent most of my time avoiding the "schooling" part of school, avoiding P.E. class and avoiding getting beaten up and bullied—which happened often. As it turns out, I had a learning disability that made learning very difficult and school overall a very difficult, shameful place to be. Teachers yelled at me; I was often called *lazy* or *stupid*. I was loath to pick up a book, let alone read it. When I went to high school, though, there was no such thing as a "learning disability" or AD/HD, and not much of any kind of special attention was paid to me (or other kids), unless there was misbehavior. The principal and all those in the vice-principal's office knew me well (and liked me, in fact, as I was there often and liked to entertain them with jokes). Teachers and administrators in the educational system of which I was a part evaluated students in one of three ways: smart, stupid, or "trainable mentally retarded." There was one other category of note: stoner. A stoner could go either way—you were smart (but stupid for being a stoner), or stupid *and* a stoner. But stoner didn't mean "substance abuse disorder." It meant "happy idiot." There were no real "interventions" or "student support services" that I knew of. There was a school counselor—and the only thing I knew about "school counselor" was that it was the punch line for many a joke. It was a synonym for "creepy guy." I finished all my requirements, graduated early, and got the hell out. I applied to several universities and got into several. They were all too expensive, so I didn't go. Nobody—and I mean, *not one person*—told me that there was such a thing as a "scholarship," where people gave you money to go to college based on having good grades (which I did). I never met our college counselor.

What saved me? Well, genetic and environmental factors, of course. First of all, I was born white (well, pink and messy, but you know what I mean). That helped... and it has to be said. If you're born white in America, you have more advantages and more status than a person of color. It doesn't matter if you're poor and white or rich and white. Whiteness means *privilege* in our society. It's no *guarantee* that *everything* will be okay. Nobody has that guarantee. But for example—and I could give many—the fact that I was white meant that the cop who picked me up *called my parents* and didn't put me in jail. The fact that I was white meant (for me, at that time, in that geographic location) that I would be in a school with mostly white children, many of whom had parents of relative affluence. It meant that my teachers—many of whom thought I was lazy or belligerent or "not living up to my potential"—didn't think that I was that way *because* I was white. And I knew that many of them thought that way about the children of color *because* of the color of their skin. This was one of the things Erikson worried about—and he had good reason to worry. The color of my skin was a *protective* factor for me in a racist society, and one of the reasons I didn't fare *worse* than I could have. Next, in addition to being a smartarse, I was also smart and that helped (even though I *felt* stupid and was told I was).

There were three other reasons—three other factors—that saved me. Here they are, in order of impact: 1) music; 2) my girlfriend; and 3) my 10th grade biology teacher. The first reason, well, that's too big and too beautiful to go into here. But it's important to say that I had a *passion* for something. I fell in love with music, playing and listening to it. If I had not become a psychotherapist, I would have pursued making music, regardless of whether I got paid to do it. I was interested in the mystery and power of music and *hungry* for it. It was so big, I could never touch it all and I knew that, and that thrilled me. It was something I could fall in love with and never stop loving. That has proven *even truer* than I knew at 12 years old when I picked up my first guitar.

The second reason—my girlfriend. I did fall in love with her, too. She was the smartest girl in school and she liked me. I still don't really know why. She helped me study sometimes and she didn't think I was stupid. She laughed at my jokes and treated me like a *person*—a whole person. As I write that, I realize how true that is, and was. I've never really thought of it that way, the crucial importance of being treated like you're *more than you feel yourself to be*. This might be one of the deepest wishes of every teenager, and I'll return to that idea in the last chapter—but through my son's eyes.

Finally, my 10th grade biology teacher, Mr. Patterson. Mr. Patterson was a legend. My sister had taken "10th grade bio" the year prior, and I'd been hearing stories about "10th grade bio" for *years,* since middle school. The apocryphal stories were terrifying—this was the year you would perform an autopsy and *dissect a live animal.* I didn't really even know what that meant...and it certainly wasn't true. But even more than "doing an autopsy," there were two things that really scared me that *did* turn out to be true. The first true thing was: *"This will be the hardest class you'll ever take."* I spent the summer before 10th grade trying to figure out how to get out of the class or get transferred to another teacher. It didn't work and there I was, in Mr. Patterson's class. The second true thing was: Everyone in Mr. Patterson's class had to do a project for the California State Science Fair.

I'll make a long story short: Mr. Patterson expected more from everyone in that classroom than I'd ever seen, and he expected more from me than *anyone* ever had. He pushed and pushed and pushed. But he did it with humor and he didn't let us slide—not for anything. And not a moment of it felt *punitive,* even though we groaned and moaned for almost the entire semester. And while this is hard to explain, I know it to be true that he never expected anything I couldn't actually do or at least make a damned good shot at. The "happy ending": I ended up winning the California State Science Fair in microbiology and in the process provided an *actual* pharmaceutical research company with new information about nitrosamine-induced mutagenesis in *E. Coli* bacterium. It doesn't sound very exciting. Bacteria are not that exciting, really. Winning the science fair was pretty fun, though—but nerve-wracking and difficult. But what Mr. Patterson gave me—what I shared with him, because of what he did—was the experience of being treated like *I was more than I felt myself to be*. It's as if he was imagining some *future* Michael, and believing in *that* Michael—knowing he could and would emerge. In the process of being challenged and respected, he helped connect up some neuron with another and I had an experience that I hadn't recognized fully up until that point: *I felt the will and wish to learn* as something palpable, as real as a hammer on a nail.

Not too far back I said that I'm not all that interested in standardized test scores, AP scores, or how American students rank on achievement tests. It's not because I'm being cavalier or "cute." It's mainly because these are measures that skip over the more important question of what is being taught and what is being learned. You might feel the same. But you also might look at the hundreds of magazine and newspaper articles that say that American students are falling behind their international counterparts and feel a twinge of worry and shame.

You might have decided to actually look up some *scientific* studies—not just popular press articles or political rhetoric—about how American kids are faring. You might have come across the results of the Fourth International Mathematics and Science study (TIMMS)—which looks at the academic performance of hundreds of thousands of students in 48 countries—and seen that only "15 percent of U.S. fourth-graders and 10 percent of eighth-graders scored at or above the advanced international benchmark in science."[24] You might have seen that Singapore and Chinese Taipei have more students performing above the international benchmark than does the United States, and that students in Singapore, Chinese Taipei, Japan, England, Korea, and Hungary all outperform U.S. students by grade 8. If you add South Korea and Finland, and about 20 additional countries to the list, you have the list of countries whose middle school students outperform U.S. students in math, reading, and science. Now you're *really* ready to get worried...or angry...or confused.

I think this misses the point, though. As parents and consumers, we need to take care not to be so mesmerized by the content of a message that we miss the importance of its form. For example, every year, millions of parents anxiously sift through something like the *U.S. News and World Report* annual college ranking issue. But do any of those college ranking stories ever tell us anything about how students do (or what they do) once they reach "the best" college? How prominent are the dropout rates for each college? How many students go on to get jobs? How many students are happy with their college choice? How many students are happy going to college and how many go because it is expected—because they are on the conveyer belt about which my student speaks in the next section?

How are those students doing in terms of physical health? How is their *mental* health? Reviews of adolescent mental health issues worldwide suggests that the magnitude, prevalence, and impact of mental health problems among adolescents has not been adequately studied.[25] We know exactly where we stand in standardized math scores, but we don't know a lot about international adolescent mental health. Should we look at the teen pregnancy rates in some of these high-performing countries? Why does the United States have the highest rate of teenage pregnancy rates among comparable countries worldwide—nearly double that of the United Kingdom, and nearly 10 times higher than Switzerland, South Korea, Japan, Denmark, Sweden, and the Netherlands?[26] Or perhaps we should look at international rates of Internet addiction and wonder why a 2006 large-scale study showed that almost

40 percent of South Korean high school students met criteria for Internet addiction, and high school students in Japan, the U.K., and Taiwan are following a similar trend?[27] There isn't space in this book for do a worldwide review of adolescent physical, mental, and spiritual health. But the point is that it seems amazingly myopic to me to look at international test scores in math or science and pronounce any country's children "better" than another's by virtue of these incredibly narrow measures of what it means to be "learning" or "developing well."

This last point is a plea for a different way of understanding your child's education and barriers to learning. I do not want to minimize, nor would I ever deny the fact that gang and family violence, drug addiction and abuse, neglect, bullying, mental health disorders like anxiety and depression (that may lead to suicide), *lack* of mental health services, and presence of learning disabilities are major barriers to learning. I would also like to suggest—plead—that one of the largest barriers to learning for American adolescents is our narrow definition of *learning*. Alongside our narrow definition of what it means to *learn* is an even narrower definition of what it means to be a "success" in America, largely defined by digital mass media and the marketplace (See Chapter 3).

So forget about how the U.S. fares internationally, then; I'll stick with my own backyard. A recent *EdSource* study of California's largest 30 public school districts showed that the Great Recession has decimated public education for 2 million students in California. Lack of mental health services? Check. California ranks dead last in the country in providing counseling for students in need, and our students are in a stunning state of need. A combination of teacher layoffs, significantly fewer instructional days, increasing childhood poverty—at the rate of 1 in 5 children statewide—and the attendant higher need for meals, medical services, counseling, and every form of student support—means the schools are under almost untenable stress. California's budget crisis—caused by the largely unregulated and speculative manipulations of the subprime mortgage mess—has brought California's (and many other state's) school system to the brink.[28] Protecting the wish and will to learn, first and foremost, must include protecting the very basic health and wellness needs of the students who still wake up every morning—many of them hungry—and want to learn. As business leaders daily bemoan the lack of qualified, dedicated young workers to fill the jobs they say they're creating or ready to create, it makes one wonder just what the private sector's responsibility is to protecting the wish to learn.

SCHOOL AND *LEARNING* ARE NOT THE SAME

In the preface to *Doing School,* Denise Clark Pope explains some of her own reasons for writing her book. She had already worked as a high school English teacher and was interested in research, but was finding very few, if any, studies that addressed the actual experience of school from the point of view of the adolescent.

She found inspiration—as many have—in John Dewey's admonition to educators that they have a "sympathetic understanding of individuals as individuals [in order to have an] idea of what is actually going on in the minds of those who are learning."[29] In the book *Doing School,* she chronicled her close shadowing of five "successful" high school students at a large, "successful" public high school. These students were seen at the school as among the "best and brightest"—students for whom the barriers to learning seemed minimal. They all got good grades, participated in community service, won awards, made commitments to others, and were well-liked by faculty and administrators.

They also cheated, lied, broke school rules, formed strategic alliances to *use* people for their own benefit, pandered to teachers, "sucked up" to the right teachers and administrators—often by learning the behavioral codes to *feign* participation, caring, and interest—"grubbed" for grades, and generally acted in ways that explicitly ran counter to their own, their parents', and the school's stated values. One of the student's studied said, "If you learn how to manipulate the system, then you learn how you can survive in high school without going nuts." What Pope found was bright students—representatives of many other "successful" students—willing to play the system, cheat to get ahead, and win at any cost, within a school system set up to reward exactly the kinds of behaviors and attitudes it was simultaneously decrying in its honor codes and mission statements. The students succeeded and went to great colleges, but also felt lousy about how they got there, often feeling significant levels of anxiety, regret, worry, and guilt over the way they'd operated.

Pope found rampant cheating among all students, not just the best and brightest, a fact confirmed by most studies of high school student behavior regarding cheating and lying (See Chapter 3). Students routinely considered cheating and plagiarism "labor- and time-saving devices" that allowed them to do the minimum and still get decent grades. Most "successful" students regularly and aggressively contested teacher grading decisions to maintain their status at the school, and regularly felt the anxiety, frustration, and regret that went along with their aggressive, sometimes manipulative approaches. Many of these same students spoke of being "robots," singularly focused on getting into the best schools.

Pope's research reminded me of one particular student-led panel on cheating that I arranged for parents. A funny thing often happens when you give students a safe chance to speak their minds: *They do it.* After listening (mouth agape) to their teens speak freely about the frequency and variety of cheating methods in school, one particular dad stood up and said, "How can you all sit up there and just talk about your lack of ethics like it's no big deal?" I sucked in my breath—certain that this was going to be a *disaster.* One of the teens slid the microphone slowly along the table toward himself, bent down slightly toward the mic, and said, without guile:

This is our life: We know you were trying to get us into the "best" pre-school before we were even born; and then it's about going to the best or the right elementary school. If we don't do well enough in the elementary school it means we don't get to the best middle school. If we don't do great in middle school we lose the opportunity to go to the best high school. And then it's all about being great in high school, getting good grades, taking APs, doing extracurriculars, the right community service, getting together the best school résumé so we can go to the best colleges…and then the best job, and on and on. We know you want this. *You put us on this conveyor belt*. You get us tutors when we're 8. You do our homework for us. You stress about where *we're* going to go to college. *You're getting what you asked for.*

That student, in that moment, became my hero. Students hear the rhetoric about "no child being left behind," but they know that it is largely up to them to make sure it doesn't happen. They watch what we do and they imitate us. They know what we value and what we want and they try to give it to us. But that is not a freely *pledged,* freely chosen commitment. Most students in Pope's study had trouble remembering anything they learned or even relating to what they were doing as "learning." Of course, they were learning a lot. The question is, though: *What* are adolescents in middle and high school learning? What sense of *purpose* are they getting from the experience, other than the self-referential purpose of "succeeding" at school (vis-à-vis getting good grades, high achievement test scores, or learning how to "work the system")? I don't quite know if this is an extremely cynical or a deeply caring response: "Well, that's how the world works, so they are learning something *very* valuable."

In the final analysis, Denise Clark Pope's important work concluded that the American school system is set up to cater to and support the students who know how to manipulate the system, and provide the adult school audience (parents, teachers, and administrators) with a simulacrum of *engagement and learning.* Her work is thoughtful, and she doesn't aggressively lay blame anywhere in particular. She describes a complicated dance between students, teachers, administrators, district policy, state and federal education policy, and the often-conflicting needs, demands, and values of the current culture. Some argue with the *interpretations* of her conclusions, believing that learning to play the system is just a *cynical*—translated, meaning "liberal"—way of talking about a positive, necessary, and somewhat "natural" process of *role socialization* for the transition to adulthood and greater responsibility for the larger, more impersonal worlds of higher education and work. Most of the students Pope spoke with wished it could be different. The parents and school officials were not at all unaware of the contradictions in the system. They realized that their students were suffering and that large, important parts of their identity formation were not being reached by the present way of "doing school." They also are not stuck in a protective bubble. The people studied in Pope's work know that they are operating in a very privileged setting and that tens of millions of other children don't have near the resources that they do. Many of them wished it could be different. Most everyone felt that it was a question of *adaptation* and survival—for everyone—and that this was the best system we have at the present time. In 2012, we're no longer making sure that no child is left behind. Now, we're *racing to the top.* Don't get me started.

The Barriers to Learning

I've alluded already—with stories and other examples—to many of the barriers to real learning that our teenagers face, in public and private schools, including: racism; anxiety and pressure over status (and the narrow, singular definitions of "success" that go with status in America); lack of adequate and consistent mental health support services in the school; a singular focus on test scores and grades as "learning"; lack of conflict resolution skills and training; bullying, harassment, aggression, and violence in the classroom and on the way to and from school—and in some cases at home; inability to correctly assess and diagnose mental health issues and learning disabilities and their effects on learning and experience with school; deficits in social skills (which are exacerbated by poverty, racism, and violence); lack of support for the calling and mission of teaching (in some cases); and an uneven distribution of resources, materials, funds, know-how, implementation, and follow-up about what works and what doesn't.

In my own case, I had a mentor who understood the importance of not only *protecting* but *diving in directly* after the wish and will to learn to help pull it out of me. He was a true *educator* and he must have known about *educere,* the present infinitive form of *educo,* "to lead forth." An educator is not necessarily a teacher in your teenager's high school. If that happens, it's a good bit of luck.

If you can, please stop doing your child's homework, focusing on the "best" (without considering the costs to your child), and rescuing them time and again so they don't have to feel the deeply wished-for *sting* of real learning. I know you won't sit back and do nothing, either. You can help by seeking out adults in your teenager's life that will help plunge them into the stream of hands-on learning, where the stakes *really* matter for reasons other than how the activity is going to help set them up for the next "best" activity. *That will take care of itself,* if learning is really happening. *The wish to learn?* What kind of nice philosophical phrase is that? Do young people really want to learn, if not motivated by grades, diplomas, and status? I have an unequivocal answer to that: Yes. Or you could ask Salman Khan, graduate of MIT and Harvard and founder of the Khan Academy, or Sebastian Thrun, former Stanford Computer Science professor, or one of the hundreds of thousands of students who signed up to take one of their free or low-cost online classes at the Khan Academy or Udacity, respectively—now, well over 160,000 of them, and that number is rising rapidly. Students log on from all over the world to take their classes, do homework, and receive a certificate of accomplishment. They do not get college credit or a degree or status bragging rights. What they do get is the same cutting-edge information that Stanford University students get, at about 2 percent of the cost of a Stanford University class, *and* a glimpse of what Bill Gates calls "the future of education."[30] It makes sense to me that Bill Gates would think that the future of education included Internet access and online course selection.

But Professor Thrun also believes he's seen the democratizing, revolutionary future of education for the masses, and all it requires is curiosity, a little bit of money, time, and a working Internet connection. This man is someone you should know about; when he's not doing television interviews or giving lectures, he's working full-time at Google on top-secret projects like Google X and the more well-known project Project Glass. Google X is basically a laboratory made up of the smartest engineering and development minds in the world, funded by a fairly endless supply of money. So far the lab has come up with inventions as stunning as the driverless car—a car that can drive thousands of miles, in almost every imaginable traffic/driving situation—and as seemingly mundane as new smart refrigerators and powerful, incredibly long-lasting lightbulbs.[31] It seems important to note, though, that MIT recently put a hold on development of their self-driving car because of problems related to the automated system's lack of ability to determine "human intent" in human drivers. As it turns out, there are "unintended consequences" to this incredible technological advance.[32] This is yet another example of Nicholas Carr's argument in *The Shallows* that the introduction of any powerful, new technology *always* brings with it both unforeseen and unintended consequences.

Project Glass puts many of your smart devices into one device—a pair of glasses—allowing you to answer phone calls, make appointments, check the weather forecast by looking at the sky, or find alternative transportation routes if your train is delayed (by just looking at the subway station). This new generation of artificial intelligence devices and inventors like Sebastian Thrun are on the rise, and they are busy learning how to make things work better. But as you'll remember from Chapter 4, this kind of learning always goes in a two-way direction. As you learn about your subway train delay, Google will be learning about where you're going throughout your day, what you what you want to do, and what you're looking at. One media observer wrote, "To be honest, when I first saw the Google Glasses video I thought that was really cool...but a moment later, I thought, 'Oh, God, there are some very serious implications in terms of privacy and data mining.'"[33] Ya think?

Why the little digression into what Google is working on, away from the subject of protecting the wish to learn? Shouldn't we be excited about all this innovation—especially with so much of it coming from young people? Shouldn't the real takeaway from teaching and learning experiments like Udacity and Khan Academy be that teens and young adults want to learn *for the sake of learning,* and they'll partner with online providers offering inexpensive, exciting ways of doing just that?

After all, *learning* is a word for how we form our identities; it is an inherent pleasure rooted in the way our brains/bodies make sense of the world. People are signing up in the hundreds of thousands to become students and learn about things like artificial intelligence and mathematics. It is terribly exciting, but it is also, always, a two-way street. Learning doesn't just flow in one direction. "I'm learning!" sounds great—so great we don't question things like: What is being learned? Who is doing the learning, and to what end? What are the benefits and real costs of that learning?

Google Glasses is an invention so stunning (and potentially scary) it calls to mind Marshall McCluhan's quote about the "juicy piece of meat meant to distract the watchdog of the mind."[34] Kids are attracted to the kinds of things Google engineers and scientists are thinking up and building right now. Google and other companies are making amazingly *cool* things. Teens will want to use these products and want to *learn,* in order to build and use these products and others like them in the future. But these digital innovations are also marketing devices, and they will help Google learn about you and your teenagers—what you see, what you do, what you think, what you buy, and where you go. The trade-off for what you and your teens get may be one you are willing to make in our digital future, but I think as parents we cannot afford to be ignorant of the future that is coming, if we want to know how to protect our children's innate wish to learn—for its own sake, rather than for the sake of Google.

ଔ

The school system as it is currently constituted in America is broken. It works well in isolated areas—to really protect the wish to learn, the most important aim of education. So, we're in a difficult situation. I honestly don't know if Sebastian Thrun or Sal Kahn (or their students) are going to lead us to the promised land of transformative education that brings high-quality, life-changing knowledge to everyone (with an Internet connection).

Dr. Frankl told us something about how any of us can survive in a difficult situation. He implored us to understand that the difference between those that may pick themselves up and get over life's problems and those who may not is the element of *decision*—the freedom of choice to come up with a decision about the way it should be, in spite of the conditions. I believe this means that there is no viable solution here without listening to adolescents and without them, in some way, leading the way toward education reform. I believe this means that more students must have more choices about what their education looks like—on a day-to-day basis. None of these "suggestions" are new. They aren't even suggestions—they are *thoughts* about the current system of learning in America. John Dewey once said something like "we only [really] think when we are confronted with a problem." Well, we have a problem. The voices we could listen to, to change things for the better—from John Dewey to Neil Postman and beyond—are still there for the listening. The voices we *must* listen to are there every day. One or more of those voices is in your house right now (or on the way home soon).

But these voices—which belong to our teens—are enamored of technology in unprecedented ways that may make seeing the enormous effects of the technologization of learning difficult, if not impossible to detect. If your son can put on a pair of Google Glasses and look at a rock formation, and instantly get information from Wikipedia or the Smithsonian on that particular geological structure, well, how *unbelievably cool* is that, and how much more engaging is that than listening to some stupid lecturer in a big hall? Does it really matter if that information comes with an advertisement or the ability of the sponsoring company to track your teen's every move? Should that be a matter of choice? Who's going to make that choice? If we're going to protect the wish and will to learn, we have to know just what we're trying to protect, don't you think? I think so, and that's why I think that one of the best things you can do with and for your teens is to know about these developments, to talk about them everywhere, with your teens, partners, friends, and colleagues.

Practical Help Tips

1) Know and practice in your daily life the idea that school is only one place for learning. Protecting the wish to learn means making it possible for your child to be wherever learning can happen. It does not have to happen at "school." *School is everywhere and it's always in session.*

2) Think about what you want your teen to learn and why.

3) Listen to your teen about their actual experiences of school. Write your own version of Denise Clark Pope's research. Please, please, please ask about more than just homework, grades, scores, tests, colleges, internships, awards, and so-called "successes." You might think if you do this, your teen will think you don't *care* about those other important things. Believe me: The chances of your teen thinking and actually *feeling* that you do not care about those things is very near zero—unless you absolutely and completely don't care about those things. And even then, they won't think you don't care—because the rest of the world does care.

4) Your teenager needs to be in the presence of as many people as possible who can give him or her the experience of being treated like he or she is more than they feel themselves to be. Almost all teenagers believe that the level of success that *you* have reached is the absolute floor—the minimum level of success—that they have to reach in order to have your approval. It doesn't really matter that you say to them, "Honey, I just want you to be *happy,* no matter what you do." They won't believe you. If you've earned a B.A., they believe they need a B.A.—just to start with—in order to measure up and please you. If you've earned a Ph.D., same thing. If you're "self-made" and you own your own business—same thing. If you're a CEO of a highly capitalized technology company and your daughter knows it...good luck. I have more higher education than I care to admit, several degrees, and I spend just about all of my disposable income on books. My son once told me point blank: *It would be so much easier if you were an alcoholic.* I'm not going to oblige him, but you get the point.

5) Our last tip is a long one. If you want to help protect your child's will and wish to learn, do whatever you can to make real the following qualities at their school. Work to make your child's school:

a) A Place Where Up-to-Date Information About Adolescent

Development Is:

- researched, regularly reported, and critically appropriated
- utilized thoughtfully by school counselors, faculty, and staff to address barriers to learning
- applied critically by faculty in the classroom to facilitate and enhance learning
- evaluated for efficacy, if/when applied in the classroom

b) A Place That Fosters Self-Reliance within Community, not Self-Indulgence in conflict with Community, and:

- personal power is recognized and enhanced, but for the purpose of building bridges into and from the wider community
- the challenges of parenting and educating amidst affluence are recognized and addressed in the school culture as well as in the classroom

c) A Place Where Student Support for Mental Health:

- is progressive, proactive, and personal
- is seen as the purview of the entire community, involving the students themselves, their parents, faculty, and administration
- is out in the open, where the culture of the school is that "We can talk about everything safely here," and confidentiality is respected and supported at all levels
- is also cognizant of its limits, and can direct students/families to appropriate community resources

d) A Place That Actively Addresses External Stressors:

- such as crises/deficits at home, school, and in the neighborhood; inadequate basic resources such as food, clothing, and a sense of security; inadequate support systems; hostile and violent conditions and personal challenges to safety
- but doesn't try to "rescue" or interfere with normal stress and its positive role in helping adolescents develop a sense of mastery; the school is not trying to unduly protect students from failure;

e) A Place Where Cross-Disciplinary, Multi-Modal Learning Is Paramount, and:

- student understanding and regulation of emotion is

not seen as "other than" learning and is understood to be tied to critical thinking

- teaching rooted in the myriad ways that students learn is not seen as a "distraction" or "problem"

f) A Place Where Teachers, Administrators, Staff, Parents, and Students Practice That:

- if you can't see it from *another* perspective, you haven't yet seen it
- listening to opposing points of view is central

g) A Place Built on Mentoring and Intra-generational Support:

- "Each one teach one"
- mentors in the wider community "adopt" mentees in the school; all ages, all ethnic backgrounds, all socioeconomic backgrounds, all sexual preferences, all types of bodies, all people of all kinds can be considered valuable teachers
- older students help/teach/support younger students
- student learn in order to teach, and teach in order to learn

h) A Place Where Parents:

- sign up for the entire ride and understand they are valued and needed from beginning to end; parent participation is active and supported by the school and other parents; parents who can't get to school or help or stay informed because they are struggling *get help* from other parents who are not struggling as much
- are provided with, welcomed to, and participate in parent education/support throughout their son/daughter's career
- are consultants in the college preparatory and application process but allow the process to be "owned" and highly directed by the student as much as possible

i) A Place Where Faculty:

- have high expectations of excellence, but do not divorce performance from character; an "A" at any cost can never be the goal
- strive for integrity and consider role models and educators one and the same
- foster diversity *and* belonging as fundamental, with a

commitment to looking beyond political correctness and "tolerance" in theory and practice

- create a college-preparatory environment by employing, when appropriate, a college-like atmosphere, e.g., seminars, round-table discussions, close reading

j) A Place Where Students:

- actively fight against the idea that "failure" is negative: success without setback, failure, frustration, perseverance, and overcoming is empty and ultimately without meaning
- actively fight against the idea that asking for help is to be avoided at all costs...that "success" usually means "doing it all on your own"
- actively fight for literacy in all media and develop deep understanding of the ways in which movies, television, the Internet, radio, and the popular press—in digital and analog forms—shapes their lifeworlds, but does not have all the power to define it
- learn by doing, on their own and in cooperation with others...where they have a strong voice but are not given the expectation that they have to run the whole show; running *parts* of the endeavor is just fine and highly desirable
- are taught with relevancy as a high priority, where their teachers and administrators can explain why what they are asking students to do is personally and socially relevant
- expect teachers to answer the question of how what they are learning connects to the wider world—and parts of that wider world that are not about status-driven concerns
- feel and act knowing that their contribution in the school and wider community *matters*!

Suggested Reading: *Protecting the Wish to Learn*

The lists in the "Suggested Reading" sections are by no means comprehensive. I'm including what I consider to be the most informative, practical, relevant, or comprehensive readings on the topic(s) of the chapter. In other words, if you have limited time, these are the works I believe you might want to explore first. It doesn't mean all of these books are "easy reads." Sometimes a listed book will be very difficult, but worth the time.

Bruner, J. S. *Relevance of Education.* New York: W.W. Norton & Company, 1971.

Darling-Hammond, L. *The Flat World and Education: How America's Commitment to Equity Will Determine Our Future.* New York: Teachers College Press, 2010.

Dewey, J. *Experience and Education.* New York: Free Press, 1997.

_____. *Democracy and Education.* New York: Simon & Brown, 2011.

Kohn, A. *What Does It Mean to Be Well Educated? And More Essays on Standards, Grading and Other Follies.* Boston: Beacon Press, 2004.

Postman, N. *Technopoly: The Surrender of Culture to Technology.* New York & London: Vintage, 1993.

_____. *The Disappearance of Childhood.* New York: Vintage/Random House, 1994.

Ravitch, D. *The Death and Life of the Great American School System: How Testing and Choice Are Undermining Education.* New York: Basic Books, 2011.

Sahlberg, P. *Finnish Lessons: What Can the World Learn from Educational Change in Finland? (Series on School Reform)* New York: Teachers College Press, 2011.

Ritchart, R., Church, M., and Morrison, K. *Making Thinking Visible: How to Promote Engagement, Understanding, and Independence for All Learners.* San Francisco: Jossey-Bass, 2011.

Thomas, D. and Brown J. S. *A New Culture of Learning: Cultivating the Imagination for a World of Constant Change.* New York: CreateSpace, 2011.

8

Family: How Parents Teach
When They *Aren't* Teaching

"I believe that what we become depends on what our fathers teach us at odd moments, when they aren't trying to teach us. We are formed by little scraps of wisdom."

—Umberto Eco, author

"Children have never been very good at listening to their elders, but they have never failed to imitate them."

—James Baldwin, author and social critic

"Where did we ever get the crazy idea that in order to make children do better, first we have to make them feel worse? Think of the last time you felt humiliated or treated unfairly. Did you feel like cooperating or doing better?"

—Jane Nelsen, author, parenting expert, and mother of 7

"Who is mature enough for offspring before the offspring arrive? The value of marriage is not that adults produce children, but that children produce adults."

—Peter De Vries, author

The content of this chapter could be derived by carefully unpacking those four quotes—as long as you slightly edit Eco's quote to include "mothers and fathers" and broaden De Vries' quote to include "the value of parenting." A kind warning: This chapter is a difficult one. It's got a lot of theory in it, but it's the chapter I hope you read slowly and come back to over and over again. The more you can take from it, the stronger you'll feel as a parent.

Much has been made in the last several decades about the concept of parenting *style*. Developmental psychologist Diana Baumrind began much of the interest in "styles" of parenting by proposing three major types of approaches to parenting: authoritarian, authoritative, and neglectful. In the 1980s Eleanor Maccoby and

J.A. Martin proposed a fourth major style, dividing neglectful parenting into either "permissive" (indulgent) or "uninvolved." Two more important researchers we've already met in other contexts—Nancy Darling and Laurence Steinberg—continued this work in the 1990s, adding new insights of their own, specifically that parenting *style* should really be understood as the *context* in which specific parenting practices occur. Additional researchers have continued the work of Maccoby and Martin, making helpful distinctions between parenting practices and parenting styles.[1]

Parenting Styles and Family Life

The concept of parenting style has been linked to a very long list of both positive and negative outcomes for adolescents, including academic performance, overall adjustment, social maturity/competencies in communication, empathy, "psychological flexibility,"[2] adjustment to new situations, sense of self-efficacy, cooperativeness and problem-solving, perseverance in task performance and completion, and even financial success.[3] All of these factors taken together could be defined as "identity formation"—the primary developmental task of adolescence. In other words, the consideration of parenting styles came to be a way of saying, *If you want your child to turn out for the best, here is the style of parenting that will do that.*

According to this idea, your parenting style is the way you go about being a parent, including: how warm or reserved you with your child; what kind of disciplinary strategies you use; how, when, and whether you communicate with your child; and what your expectations of your child's maturity are (and therefore, what behaviors, feelings, thoughts, and ideas you are expecting from your child).

An *authoritarian* parenting style[4] for teens is one in which you have strict rules and you expect them followed; if the rules aren't followed, punishment ensues. While you might spend time explaining the rules in detail, you won't be spending a lot of time offering the philosophical justification for the rules. The family is a hierarchy and the children are not at the top of that pyramid, so "Because I said so" or "Because I'm your father" are good enough reasons for the rules to be followed. You are here to make sure your children do the right thing—which is what you tell them to do, sometimes backed by a strong religious or moral code—and not to coddle them. Parents with this style sometimes think of it as "tough love," and don't worry too much about displaying affection or nurturance, because there are more important things at stake than your child's "self-esteem." Robert Duvall's portrayal of the "warrior without a war" in the film *The Great Santini* is a poignant example of an authoritarian parent.

An *authoritative* parenting style—the one generally judged "best" or "most effective" in terms of positive outcomes—is characterized by rules and high expectations, but it is more democratic, not dictatorial. Teens negotiate with their parents and vice-versa, with a premium put on listening to each other. Decision-making is multi-modal. Sometimes decisions are made completely by a parent, sometimes completely by the teenager, depending upon the nature of the decision and its consequences. Sometimes it's a joint decision. The teenager always has a voice, but doesn't always get a vote. Sometimes the decision isn't made by voting, but by decree, but that doesn't mean the parent stops caring about the impact of the decision. In this style of parenting, it's not about punishment, but about *learning,* supporting, and providing teachable moments. Parents monitor and guide their children, but respect their child's privacy, and while there is still a hierarchy in the family, with the parents having more power, power is more and more shared, the more the teen demonstrates capacity and responsible decision-making. A major goal for the parent is to help create a healthy, balanced, empathic, cooperative young adult, who can stand up for themselves but also realize that they are social beings and have an obligation to others and society.

A *permissive* parenting style is also characterized by warmth and friendliness, but the standards for the teen are unclear, since few demands are placed on them. Discipline is rarely introduced or enforced in the family characterized by this parenting style because it's so "hands off." If you discipline your child it will likely be in response to some frustration or crisis; it's usually reactive, not proactive. Permissive parents don't follow tradition and expect (and/or hope) children to basically figure things out and take care of themselves. One "benefit" of this style is that it is very conflict-avoidant, or at least, it tries to be. A parent using this style would likely use the strategy discussed in Chapter 5 regarding parties as "being my kid's friend," preferring to try to influence and communicate indirectly, if at all.

Finally, the *uninvolved* or *neglectful* parenting style borrows from the motto of many a disaffected teenager: What*EVER*. With this type of parenting style there are few if any demands, rules, or expectations. Communication is frequently negative when it happens, pointing out what's wrong, rather than what's right. Uninvolved or neglectful parents usually (but not always) provide their teens the bare minimum—food, clothes, and shelter—but there is little connection between the provision of these necessities and a close relationship. There can be many reasons for this level of disengagement and neglect, short of a parent being "evil." Parents in this situation have often themselves suffered (or are suffering) a lack of care and resources and may have overwhelming medical, mental health, family, or larger social problems involving multiple agencies, courts, and police. Taking care of a teen—especially one who is now "almost grown up, anyway"— is just not on the priority list.

As mentioned earlier, Diana Baumrind and many others who built upon her work have studied the impact of each parenting style on a variety of different outcomes, from happiness, ability to learn, and self-esteem to social intelligence and competence.

In general (and as you might expect) authoritarian parenting is usually correlated with "producing" dutiful, proficient, obedient, unhappy young adults. An authoritative parenting style seems to work best; Eleanor Maccoby's work suggests that authoritative parents turn out happy, capable kids.[5] Even when things don't turn out as planned and divorce is part of the picture, kids seem to fare much better when the parents remain cooperative (rather than "conflicted" or "disengaged") and parenting remains authoritative.[6] When parents are permissive and indulgent, children often end up feeling neglected and less happy and have trouble regulating their feelings and actions. Young adults from permissive parenting situations also tend to have trouble with authority, following directions, and following through on academic endeavors. It's not that they don't love their parents—relationships are warm, but children with permissive, indulgent parents often feel "lost" and have trouble figuring out who they are. Teens from these kinds of families are often overindulged and can have the dual experience of having everything done for them *and* still feeling somehow empty and/or neglected—or they can't quite figure out what they feel. Madeleine Levine's *The Price of Privilege* is about many of these adolescents and young adults.

Likewise, uninvolved parenting styles produce similar levels of maladjustment among adolescents. As you might imagine, if your child is coming from this situation, they are more at risk for poor outcomes with all aspects around the Ten Tasks of Adolescence described in Chapter 1. Teens who are neglected and have under- and uninvolved parents or caretakers show significantly lower self-esteem, have more trouble in social relationships of all types, and generally function at levels lower than their peers.

Okay, got it. If you happen to have read this chapter first, you don't really need to read the rest of the book now, right? Come to think of it, if you could have "peeked inside this book" in advance you could have skipped buying it altogether.

But imagine this: You're about to have a teenager in the house (in a year or so, by your calculations). It's a bit anxiety-provoking, but you're basically fine. What do you do? Well, just get some rest, buy a book on authoritative parenting styles, get yourself *Adolescence in America: An Encyclopedia,* and you're good to go.

To be honest with you, that isn't a bad plan. I would guess that hundreds of thousands, if not millions of parents would be just fine with that as a basic strategy for dealing with impending adolescence in the family life cycle. But for the rest of us, that strategy won't be enough.

Why? First of all, parenting styles can and do differ from parent to parent. Parenting styles can and do differ *within* one parent. Parents (in my experience) switch from style to style. You might be authoritative when things are going well and authoritarian in a crisis (such as one involving drugs or pregnancy or violence) or after any significant *trauma* (like job loss, forced relocation, abuse, death in the family, or divorce). Remember, trauma (in my definition) is anything that threatens ongoing engagement with close others. You might (and parents often do) have one particular style of parenting because it is largely a reaction to your own parents' parenting style (or mixture of styles or variability in style in one parent). I see that pattern most often in my clinical practice. So many times I see problems in a family based on the fact that one or both parents have *vowed* never to repeat certain mistakes of their parents, and it is *exactly* this vow—and the consequences that the parent thinks flow from this promise to themselves—mixed with the child's biology, that form the primary problems they are now experiencing with their own child.

Your dad might have been incredibly authoritarian, and you vowed never to repeat that experience for your child. You might end up having a very permissive parenting style (like your mom, perhaps) and end up feeling frustrated and really confused when you have so many "problems" with your child. You're giving him all the love and warmth and affection your dad never provided to you. What is *wrong* with your son or daughter? Don't they know how hard you had it and how hard you're trying to be a *good, warm* parent?

Perhaps the mixture of parenting styles you experienced was also confusing—with one parent doing one thing, then another, until you felt the only way of handling it was just to disengage from your parents.

Perhaps you have several children of varying ages in your house, and it's difficult to stick with one style or you feel you need a different style for each child, based on temperament, for example. This can cause trouble, as your children might (and probably do anyway) argue over "unequal" treatment—even though *unequal* treatment of each child is actually what I often think of as the "gold standard" in parenting. But there are exceptions to that, too.

How does a parenting style develop? I would bet that by now you already know how I'm going to answer that question: *It's a combination of biology and biography, genes and environment.* An overall approach or attitude toward a task as large and pervasive as parenting develops from trial and error, temperament of your child (in interaction with your own temperament), varying and variable interpretation of the "results" of our data-gathering (based upon our moods and feelings when we're evaluating), cultural/traditional factors, family size, socioeconomic status, level of education, religion, current medical and marital status, and on and on and on.

So all of these factors complicate the picture, and most families don't just work in this simple, linear fashion: Take one parenting style and apply it to one child; bingo. And even if you could do that, *life happens.* You keep developing. You're a biopsychosocial being (at very least)! That means things will change. Your child is also a biopsychosocial being. When you start multiplying the possible outcomes of complex individuals in ongoing interaction, given that things change and that everything is going to be influenced by genes and environment, that makes even parenting one teen with one style (consistently applied across a two-parent household) like changing the wheels on a moving car. That's when it's going *well*.

Genes influencing parenting styles? *Huh?* Sure. Behavioral geneticists call these "evocative effects," meaning that certain children call forth ("evoke") certain responses by the parent. Got an easy, sweet temperament child, who never has problems with transition? You're likely to have a positive parenting style, all other things being equal (which they never are). Got a difficult or slow-to-warm-up child? A child who is sensitive or oppositional or hard to soothe? You just might fall into a permissive or neglectful (more disengaged) style of parenting, because being close is *hard*. You love your child, but you might find it hard if not impossible to pick the "best" parenting style—the authoritative one. Having "evocative effects" means that the child's *genes* are influencing the parental behavior, which in turn influences the child, which in turn can influence their genes through physiochemical changes that might determine which genes turn "on" or "off" (See Chapter 1).

Now, let's add in the fact that, as we discussed in Chapter 1, researchers are usually arguing[7] over research results, validity, meaning, and significance, and even the best-intentioned, impeccably conducted research results will be overturned or revamped as new information comes to light—that's science. It's how we work: We make a theory and hold it (hopefully) until it no longer works. That phenomenon happened with the research on parenting styles, too. People argue over what a "style" means. People argue over correlation versus causation. In other words, just because two things happen "together" (are correlated) doesn't mean those two things caused each other (causation). There could be a third cause...or multiple other causes...or different kinds of causes. So, authoritative parenting is not necessarily the cause for a well-adjusted child, a happy child. Since parenting happens in a context (of genes *x* environment), it's pretty hard to pin the cause down to the style of a parent. Even Eleanor Maccoby, after all her research, ended up saying that the impact that parents have in their children's lives has been overstated by media and research. But she was not saying that parents don't matter, either. She did support, however, the underlying approach of *The Approximate Parent,* when she noted, "In any long-standing relationship, each partner must influence the other. To suggest that the parent-child relationship is a one-way street with influence flowing only from the child to the parent is, I think, absurd. Reciprocity is the name of the game between parents and children."[8]

Reciprocity and mutual influence. You've heard these themes over and over in the book. We can't and shouldn't think just about what we do with digital media; we have to think about what digital media are doing with us. We can't just think about the drug, we have to think about drug, set, and setting—and who *we* are at the time we're dealing with our teenager's drugs, sets, and settings. Following the Peter De Vries quote at the opening of the chapter, we can't just think about our parenting style, we have to think about the ways our children create that parenting style. And the ways our parents created our parenting style…and so it goes, with *everything, back and forth across the generations, from parent to child, child to parent, culture to genes, genes to culture.*

So, that's my long answer for why one parenting style or styles—or even the idea of parenting styles—or one parenting book that has all the answers for parenting your teen, won't necessarily have all the answers for *your* child. That brings us to a major if not the major point of the chapter and book (and the next section). It's all *case-specific.* One size doesn't fit all. *One size* can't *fit all. That's why parenting is so hard. That's why parenting can engender so much sadness and loss, as well as joy. That's why parenting is an ethical matter. That's why parenting is a spiritual endeavor.*

I hope you find that "argument" convincing or at least intriguing. I hope it doesn't suggest to you that it's all on you or none of it is on you. But you probably know what I'm going to say next. I'll put it in the form of a question my son would have asked me: Okay, dude, so if that's how it works, what am I supposed to do? What's a *theory* for that? How do I *approximate* that? As my grandmother would say, "Have I got a theory for you…"

A Theory for Family Living?

This section is grounded in my experience and ongoing training as a psychotherapist, but it is tested in my experience as a parent. Part of the challenges and blessings of this work came from the way in which my life was structured for so long. I would spend a portion of the day studying the theory; a portion of the day trying to apply it in a therapeutic setting with children, adolescents, individuals, couples, and families; and then most of the rest of the time directly confronting how the theory worked in relation to my own child. In other words, I was confronted daily with whether what I was preaching, so to speak, was what I was practicing. I became acutely aware of the *approximation* process that usually goes on in the background, namely:

1. Start where you are, at whatever point you find yourself in your life;

2. Keep doing what you're doing: Try to work, love, and play (and take care of yourself and others);

3. Make nonconscious and conscious decisions, minute by minute, about how to best do Item 2—this involves feeling,

thinking, believing, wishing, imagining, planning, organizing (all of which go on nonconsciously and consciously). This is what I refer to as "theory-making";

4. Apply your theory about how something in particular will (or "should") work: "What I do" and "what I feel" both represent applications of your personal theory about yourself, others, and the world;

5. Watch and note what happens (observation and data collection); this is arguably the hardest part: It involves attention and awareness and can't be "phoned in";

6. Revamp your theory (correction and revision) or don't revamp your theory; revamping or not revamping and the degree to which it all happens will be based on your experiences and interpretation(s) of the data, which will be based on who you are at that moment, which will be based on a combination of genes x environmental factors, with strong contributions of biology, biography, "mindset," and "setting";

7. Go back to number 1 and do it all again.

The process described above is very fluid. It doesn't necessarily happen in this order, but it might. It happens again and again, in concentric circles, at different speeds, with slight changes in direction. My own situation—given the work I was doing—highlighted Item 5, and thus involved a good amount of pain and sadness. When I got home or when I was dealing with the issues of being a dad, did I actually *do* what my theory suggested would work? Did I remember to observe, rather than *just* react emotionally? Was I even thinking or feeling in ways reflected by the theory? How accurate was the theory? Was it all good on paper, or in the confines or a 50-minute therapy hour—with all those built-in boundaries and limits—but not so good "in the field" with a live teenager?

I'm going to be as honest as I can be with you: I think the theory was, most of the time, better than "me." Or maybe another way of thinking of it that is less personal and less personally critically and more "scientific": As a parent, I'm as effective as my theories/theory-making at the moment, in combination with my son's theories/theory-making, given the context (and available resources and options at that time), plus or minus *grace*.

Let's put that into more familiar terms we've already seen in the Introduction to *The Approximate Parent*. We're talking about practice-driven decision-making or trying to be the "approximate" parent.

Practice-Driven Decision-Making

"Situational Variables *x* Available Resources/Options = Strategic Priorities"

Not so linear; "approximating goals"

Evaluation: more or less carefully considered; more or less wisely chosen or coordinated

Remember, this is supposed to be *practical*. You evaluate what happens and look at what you're doing—whether or not something you do "works"—on the basis of whether you more or less carefully considered the factors involved. This approach is about whether your intervention was more or less wisely chosen and coordinated. You can always get better and you can always try again. Always…any time you want and are able.

In a practice-driven approach to parenting teens, you will want to know as much as you can about what the situational variables are and what your available resources might be. This book offers you some concise information about what's going on with adolescents' brains, bodies, and emotions, because that's what the model calls for. I think it is really useful for parents to know more about the context in which adolescents develop, or the lifeworlds in which American adolescents become who they will be as young adults, in the early part of the 21st century.

So I learned a lot about how and why we *make* theories about others and ourselves, and how so many times that theory-making process can produce a "wrong" or distorted theory. I've learned that while genetic (and epigenetic) factors are very strong in developing our doing and feeling lives, they just can't be separated from the contexts in which these take root. That's where the rest of this chapter focuses. Much of the *distortion* in theory can be observed, discovered, and corrected over time. That's what I try to do each day, in my clinical practice. I also need help to do it, for myself. I need help with getting better approximations of how things *actually* work, in ways that are healthier or kinder or more accurate. I believe this very strongly, and it's one of the top three reasons why I wrote this book: *There is absolutely no reason why a therapist should have this information—about what can go wrong in the theory-making process—and you shouldn't.* What we'll discuss next, if it "falls" into the hands of parents, is not going to rob psychologists or marriage and family therapists or social workers of their abilities to make a living. I'm not giving away trade secrets, and I don't see why this information shouldn't be common knowledge. In fact, the more of this information parents have, the easier and more effective all of our work will be. I don't help every single person I meet, but I do *try to* and it often works out pretty well. If you want to do it, too, go ahead. I don't mean you should practice "therapy" without a license. I just mean, you can have the information that I use to do my work. Most of my clients have heard me say: It's not magic and it's not religion. You don't have to *believe in it.* You just have to try it and see if it works.

Control-Mastery Theory and Its Application to Parenting

Some, but not enough books have been written about Control-Mastery Theory. The people who developed the theory and did the initial and/or subsequent empirical research have largely written these books. Only one book, Dr. Steven Foreman's *Breaking the Spell: Understanding Why Kids Do the Very Things That Drive You Crazy,* specifically and in a sustained way applies the theory to issues of parenting practice and style. Steve and I worked together at the San Francisco Psychotherapy Research Group for many years, and while I left my work with this group many years ago, his work and the work of our colleagues have never left me. Joe Weiss, M.D., one of the founders of this work, died Sunday, November 7, 2004, at home, close to his wife, Dr. Estelle Rogers, herself a brilliant thinker, clinician, and artist. Hal Sampson, Ph.D.—a brilliant and uncommonly kind man—was Joe's longtime co-collaborator and is co-founder of the theory. He retired at the end of 2004. Dr. Foreman continues the legacy of their work today, as President of the Board of Directors of the San Francisco Psychotherapy Research Group.

HISTORY OF THE THEORY AND PAST VIEWS OF "PROBLEMS" AND PSYCHOPATHOLOGY

In the late 1950s Joseph Weiss, M.D., a physician who completed his psychoanalytic training at the San Francisco Psychoanalytic Institute, began to investigate just how patients made progress in treatment. He believed that psychoanalysis and psychotherapy were helpful, but it wasn't clear to him why or *how* they helped. He spent hundreds and hundreds of hours studying transcripts of audio-recorded analyses and slowly developed a series of new hypotheses about the therapeutic process. He observed, through careful study of the transcripts, that patients changed their worldviews, acquired new insights, and remembered long-forgotten events without the therapist actually making *interpretations* to the patient—the time-honored way that patients got "helped" to feel better. This flew in the face of the more classical psychoanalytic stance that explicit interpretation of *resistances* formed the central part of growth and change in therapy. I'll talk more about resistance soon, because this theory saw resistance in a *fundamentally different* and much more useful way than before, and parents often relate to their children using a version of the *old* formulation of resistance.

Throughout the 1970s and '80s at Mt. Zion Hospital in San Francisco, Dr. Weiss and Harold Sampson, Ph.D. began a formal program of investigations into *how* psychotherapy works. The interpersonal-cognitive theory they developed as an out-growth of this research has come to be known as Control-Mastery Theory. (The Mt. Zion Group is now known as the San Francisco Psychotherapy Research Group.) When I joined the group at the beginning of the 1990s, we still kept records in shoe-boxes. One of the biggest and most exciting projects for me was the idea of keeping better records and supporting the research, writing, teaching, and educational func-tions of the group using a fantastic new tool: an Apple Macintosh SE.

The theory was named Control-Mastery to emphasize the client's ability to ex-ercise a significant degree of *control* over his/her mental life and nonconscious pro-cesses, and to acknowledge the powerful wish and drive to *master* any traumatic experiences that inhibit normal development. Thus, clients are seen as constantly working in therapy to overcome their dysfunctional patterns and beliefs and *adapt* in better ways to their interpersonal realities. A frequent activity throughout my tenure as executive director of the group was to have meetings and debates about changing the name of the theory, since it reminded most of us of either some kind of kinky sadistic or masochistic reference or of some innate wish to dominate other people. These things have nothing to do with the thinking behind the theory, so the name seemed unfortunate. You can see how far those discussions got, as the name remains to this day.

Hundreds of researchers and clinicians worldwide now participate in the ongo-ing work of the San Francisco Psychotherapy Research Group. Several hundred papers and many books have been published that present research or explore new directions for study of Weiss and Sampson's theory. In 1986 much of this research was collected and presented in a groundbreaking volume entitled *The Psychoana-lytic Process: Theory, Clinical Observation and Empirical Research,* authored by Weiss, Sampson, and the Mt. Zion Research Group. In 1993, Weiss published *How Psychotherapy Works: Process and Technique,* a volume that focuses on the clinical application of the theory. It should be noted that one criticism of this theory (and its applications) is that it is too simple and simplistic. In my experience, now over 21 years, I would say that it is a theory that has profitably picked up more nuance over the years in conversation with others, but that at its base, it's as complex as it needs to be. It is first and foremost elegant, because from very solid core ideas emerges an incredibly complicated, fluid, and useful way of thinking about what happens between people.

Psychopathology According to Control-Mastery Theory

When developmental psychologists think about "normal" and "abnormal" it is usually understood as being on a *continuum* from adaptive to maladaptive. When I taught abnormal psychology, I would remind my students of Ronald Comer's "four main components of abnormality": *deviance, distress, dysfunction, and danger.*[9] We talked about how one's behavior can be deviant, distressful, dysfunctional, and dangerous but still not be *pathological,* that is, definitive of an ongoing maladaptive pattern. However, if the behavior continues over time and across situations, worsens, affects others and self more, and/or causes harm to self or others, it may very well be diagnostic for pathology. That's not a bad definition for psychological pathology, although it can be hard to pin down what "worsens" or "affects others" means or when enough is enough. It does, however, point to the important thing, in my mind, which is that psychopathology is the result of *adaptation*—an attempt and *approximation* to respond to the current environment, given the current internal and external realities at that time (yes, given genes *x* environmental factors). Pathology in this view, and in a Control-Mastery view, is not the result of evil or ill will. It is the result of our being's best available theory-making and approximation at the time.

Thinking about what psychopathology "consists of" has changed over time.[10] In the past, most people have thought of psychopathology as related to evil or badness or a war between good and evil. Psychopathology and its treatment have shifted back and forth from being a matter of evil and madness to being a medical matter of illness and treatment. For most of Western history as we know it, psychopathology was primarily a *religious* business, to be attended to by priests, shamans, rabbis, and other spiritual leaders in the community. Most views of prehistoric society are based on inference using archaeological discoveries. For example, the idea of "trephination" (or drilling holes in your head with a trephine, to release evil spirits) is based upon finding holes in the skull that date back almost 500,000 years ago. There is no definitive proof, though, that that's what the holes were drilled for. Early writings of Egyptians, Chinese, and Hebrews all have reference to demonic possession linked with abnormal behavior (like King Saul and David feigning possession to convince enemies he was inhabited by divine forces). Exorcism (coaxing the evil spirit out of the body) or use of shamanic practices (prayers, pleading with the evil, magic, loud noises, use of potions) was widely used to treat abnormalities.

The early Greeks and Roman philosophers began to describe and prescribe treatment for mental disorders: melancholia (sadness), mania (frenzied activity), dementia (intellectual confusion and decline), delusions (false beliefs), and hallucinations (imagined sights or sounds that appear real). But not all philosophers agreed that mental disorders were pathological; some believed they inspired creativity.

Hippocrates (460–477 BCE), "the father of modern medicine," believed that imbalances in the four humors (four internal fluids: bile, black bile, blood, and phlegm) caused personality and mental disorders. Want to know why a husband is beating his wife? Easy: too much yellow bile. Are you sad and can't get out of bed? Too much black bile. Treatment involved gaining balance: excess of black bile was treated with rest and a quiet life, vegetarian diet, temperance, exercise, celibacy, and sometimes bleeding. His views were apparently shared by Plato (427–347) and Aristotle (384–322), and later by the physicians Aretaeus (50–130 ACE), who suggested that emotional problems caused abnormal behavior, and Galen (130–200 ACE), who systematically outlined emotional causes (e.g., worries about money, loss of love, etc.) and distinguished them from purely physical causes (alcohol abuse, head injury) as causes of abnormality. Treatment in early Greek and Roman physicians' circles usually involved a combination of physical and psychological techniques like providing supportive environments, calming music, massage, exercise, and baths. When those failed, patients were bled or restrained with mechanical devices. Roman physicians emphasized soothing and comforting as first-line treatments.

I won't go through an entire history of thinking about psychopathology and its treatment, but it's important to note that while this thinking started changing pretty radically during the so-called European Enlightenment—and there were other, earlier periods of "enlightenment" that didn't involve the Europeans—it all changed radically after Sigmund Freud, at the end of the 19th and beginning of the 20th century. Thinking and practice in Europe and the United States began shifting away from an emphasis on "madness" and "evil"—and seeing psychopathology as primarily a religious issue—to an issue of medicine and neurology, of illness and treatment. Psychiatrists, physicians, neurologists, and eventually psychologists and other related professions—like social work and marriage and family therapy—became the new priests, rabbis, and shamans.

From the 1960s onward, in parallel with other cultural and historical changes, it began to be about *you* (and me)—the parents. It was up to us to create and change our children and deal with "what goes wrong" and make sure of "what goes right." That process might involve understanding psychology or finding a therapist, but the primary responsibility was *ours*. Since then, we've tried to shift that responsibility to teachers and the educational systems—or at the very least we've asked them to *share* the burden, as expectations and standards for being a parent rise and get more complex. After the 1950s, as ideas about families (and the world) were rapidly changing, it started getting harder for "being a parent" to just mean "having a child" and giving him or her some food, clothing, shelter, and education.[11] By the 1980s, I think that "being a parent" started, for many American parents, to be synonymous with "feeling guilty." That's in no small part because of this increase in and shift of knowledge practices to *parents* from professionals of all sorts.

In 2012, the Internet and technologies like it that can connect people and information—if used justly, openly, with checks and balances—promise to create and solidify a new (and very old) model for responding to the "what goes on" and "what to do about it" as parents: *collaboration*. This promise is by no means *guaranteed*, and that's why media literacy is so important (See Chapter 4). But the promise of collaboration and sharing of knowledge between people, between academic disciplines and specialties, between technologies, is where we're at now. It is reflected in the explosion of research, thinking, and practice in psychology on "intersubjectivity," "interrelatedness," "mutuality," "mutually reinforcing effects," and the focus on *layers of influence* as opposed to finding The Cause.

THE BASIC TENETS OF CONTROL-MASTERY THEORY: OVERVIEW AND KEY CONCEPTS

Control-Mastery Theory is an integrated theory of psychopathology and psychotherapy, so it offers explanations for how what *isn't* working in a patient's life can be transformed by the therapeutic relationship. The theory assumes that a person's *problems* are rooted in grim, constricting beliefs (called "pathogenic beliefs"[12]) that are acquired in the traumatic experiences of childhood. I'm going to add my own piece to the theory by clarifying my definition of "trauma" as: *experiences on a continuum of threat to ongoing engagement, especially with close others*. Pathogenic beliefs are attempts at *adaptation* to the current environment that warn a person (consciously and nonconsciously) against the pursuit of their normal developmental goals. Which goals? *All or any of the goals* listed in A. Rae Simpson's list of "Ten Tasks of Adolescence" (Chapter 1) or around the full, ongoing development of capacities listed as the "15 Core Components of Mental Health" (Chapter 9).

An example of a pathogenic belief would be "If I do not meet expectations now, I do not deserve to be given the chance to do so in the future; my poor performance is fate and not correctable." Many very successful adults have this kind of belief and it can contribute to perfectionism—a kind of belief or feeling that if you don't get it right at first, you're bad; a learning curve isn't allowed.

According to Control-Mastery Theory, a person comes to therapy *because* they have both a conscious and nonconscious desire to overcome their pathogenic beliefs and to pursue normal developmental goals—like being able to be easier on oneself, take time to learn, and not always have to be "perfect." You weren't *born* being a perfectionist. You were made into one, by environmental and genetic factors. Just *who* you became—for example, being a perfectionist—was based on you trying your best to figure out what to do, given the balancing act of pleasing yourself and others, and given the available genetic and social resources in your family.

So, Control-Mastery Theory emphasizes your child's urgent and continuing *need* to adapt to reality. Her best strategy for doing this—the "theory" that she will usually use and that makes the best sense from the perspective of genes and environment—is to *get along with her parents/caregivers*. Therefore she is motivated to maintain ties to her parents. She needs her parents for survival, safety, love, and security. In order to maintain these ties, a child works to learn as much as possible about her parents. She infers the moral and ethical "theories" that govern her parents' lives, which they practice in relation to her, and which they expect her to practice in relation to them. A child must know her parents' whims, needs, and desires. She examines her parents closely in order to sort out what they want, expect, and will allow. Because for her—for any child—it is a matter of life and death that she gets along with her caregivers, she will often condemn inside herself any impulses, attitudes, goals, or affective states (and related feelings or interpretations of those states) that might threaten her ties to them. But the condemnation of these impulses, attitudes, goals, or emotional states at the expense of her own normal development can result in maladaptive life patterns, held in place by these pathogenic adaptations that Joe and Hal called "pathogenic beliefs." Pathogenic beliefs are maladaptive because they warn the person against pursuing normal goals. (I personally don't like the term pathogenic *belief* because it tends to make us all think it's purely a cognitive theory, and about what "we believe."[13])

But when we adapt to our reality, we don't just change our beliefs. We change our feelings, hopes and wishes, and basic ideas about how the world works. We make up new theories, new "working models" for others and the world. If we have to change these working models[14] in ways that are maladaptive—we have made a pathogenic adaptation, and that's what Control-Mastery Theory can teach us a lot about.

I gave you an example of a common adult pathogenic belief within "perfectionism." So, let's look at how a child's pathogenic adaptation might occur. Let's imagine that you feel drained, burdened, or overwhelmed, following the your child's attempts to be close, or get help. Now, this is a normal thing for a parent to feel. But if it happens again and again, your child may develop the belief that there was something wrong with him that *caused* you to be drained, burdened, or overwhelmed by him. He might develop the symptom of a *reluctance to complain* or express his needs *for fear of draining his parent*. In other words, your son has a dilemma that I want to try to describe for him:

> Let's see. I'm not getting the help I need. I usually get that help and *should* get that help from my parents. But Mom seems unhappy about helping me. I can tell. She used to help and now she doesn't help as much or in the same way. I have a theory. I know she must love me, so that's not the problem. I know she is great and generally perfect, so *she* isn't the problem. I'm going to bet that it is *me* that is the problem. I must have too many needs or have them too often, or have specific needs that are troublesome. I wonder which ones. I know—*I'll just stop having some of these needs,* and that should perk her up. But *which* needs? I can't get rid of all my needs (or

can I?). Well, maybe if I *increase* my demands in a particular area, and she gets *really* upset, that's probably a problematic need. Then I'll curtail the need in some way—by getting rid of it, by becoming unaware when I have it, by condemning it in myself—there are bunch of ways to do that!

If a child is old enough, he might actually think this way. But usually he just has a lot of feelings and fleeting thoughts that amount to what you just read. Your child is *working out a theory of interpersonal interaction as an adaptation to reality.* This process goes on for all of us, continuously during childhood, in relation to new developmental challenges. Children observe close adults and take in data in exquisite detail. Until your child does it consciously, using *thought,* they'll do it unconsciously, using sensory data and affective responding, meaning they'll use every means that they're aware of at that time—using smell, skin temperature, heart rate, amount of eye contact, and hundreds of other signs from themselves and their caretaker—to determine what effect they have on you. And I promise you, their bodies will take in this information and adjust, and your body will do the same, in a dance we call *survival.* This overall view is now shared by thousands of different researchers and clinicians, across disciplines, and supported by empirical research over the last 80 years.

By now you might have already thought, "Well, if this is true, I'm in huge trouble, because young children don't really *think* logically very well." That's exactly right. Children are mostly egocentric and narcissistic (which is normal) in their thinking, needing, and preferring to consider how things affect *them.* So, it makes complete sense that our children will think that when things go wrong, it's about *them.* Even teenagers still think this way, much of the time. Some of that is because they have developed pathogenic beliefs/adaptations to their realities in the past, but some of it is because they're *children* and just not mature enough yet to consider how complex it all is—and that there is no *single* cause for anything. That's an adult view and it's taking me hundreds of pages to explicate just that. So, yes, it can be and often is highly problematic that children have immature cognitive capacity and they often take what we do, say, feel, and think in the "wrong" ways. That's exactly why I'm writing this chapter. *I want to help you deal with the difference between what we, as parents, mean and hope to do, and the ways our children often interpret what we do—that can lead to problems.*

Another unfortunate fact of parenting: Your children, in their immature state, can take the way they are treated and make it into a moral/ethical imperative, believing that the way they *are* treated is the way they *ought* to be treated. This fact points to the seemingly confusing problem of why children who are mistreated as children often end up choosing to be in relationships with people who mistreat them over and over again. If you're one of those people, you're not *weak* or *stupid.* You do this because you're attempting (in the way you learned how) to keep close relationships. You might have developed the pathogenic belief that being close to others and being mistreated go together and *should* go together. Being treated with consistent love and care is going to feel, to you, *unfamiliar*—literally, it will not feel like *family.*

This hardly seems fair, to put it mildly. It seems that we are destined, therefore, to do some things that mess our kids up. I believe that is 100 percent true, 100 percent of the time. *Living is grieving.* I think we should get used to that fact and move on or at least fold it into our current theory about theory-making.

So what would Control-Mastery Theory have us do to deal with problems caused by maladaptions? Since pathogenic beliefs are usually (but not exclusively) derived from interpersonal experience, help in "disconfirming" these pathogenic beliefs must also proceed interpersonally[15]: *Treatment is and always must be case-specific.* One size cannot and will not ever "fit all." You can see why I like the theory for our purposes. And you'll soon see other reasons for why the theory is useful for parenting *your* teenager and why it cannot just be in the purview of the scientist, researcher, or clinician. It has to be in the hands of parents (and even kids)! Then we can collaborate together on all of it—of course, based upon each of our resources, options, current level of development, etc., etc., etc.

Okay, we skipped ahead to 2012 from Freud, so back to Sigmund for a moment. He mostly—at least in the early part of his career—wrote about psychopathology as related to problems involving *resistance.* People get mentally ill but *resist* becoming healthy. He suggested that a patient might unconsciously repeat traumatic experiences (and lock them in as patterns of responding) in order to get *immediate gratification* or some kind of pleasurable gain. In simplistic terms, people have problems or mental illnesses because the illness was a way of them getting infantile needs met for caretaking. Mental illness allows people to stay stuck in earlier stages of development, even though they are capable of more. Since it was "easier" somehow being a kid, without the demands and responsibilities of adult, mature living, it drives the person not toward health and mastery, but toward stuckness and pathology. For example, you might get stuck in melancholia (depression) because you just can't face the realities of adult life and you can't handle certain internal (and external conflicts). Pathology is the result of a *failure to adapt.*

In *Analysis Terminable and Interminable* Freud suggested that the patient works unconsciously with the analyst to solve his problems, and the analyst helps the patient by interpreting the patient's *resistances* to getting better.[16] He called this work "defense analysis." According to Freud, much of what we think and do is driven by attempts to *avoid* certain feelings, thoughts, and actions—and we know little or nothing about any of these "shadowy" forces that control and determine our actions. Much of our functioning as human beings is, according to Freud, *unconscious and automatic,* regulated by forces beyond our control, like the drive for pleasure or the desire to harm others who interfere with our pleasure. He wrote about these forces as being beyond the influence of "reality," and just things that every human must contend with. When a human cannot deal well with Reality (and they often couldn't, according to Freud), these principles or drives will do it for you...as they often already are doing. The human being generally lives in a world of fantasies, desires, and infantile wishes (and therefore is more prone to psychopathology) unless helped by "the talking cure" (psychoanalysis).[17]

Of course, these are all huge simplifications of Freud's work, most of which was deeply complex and nuanced, and changed over the course of his lifetime of writings.

Control-Mastery Theory assumes, to the contrary, that people aren't *avoiding* reality, they are *dealing with it* the best they can. As I alluded to before, dealing with the reality of having parents and having your own needs means getting along with your parents, which implies observing them like a hawk, to figure out what your effect is on them.

This process of deep, intent watching requires "identification" with and "compliance" with our caretakers/parents,[18] and with *their* views and adaptations to reality. You could say that this deep watching takes the form of our children becoming like us, in behavior and feeling. Above all, this is about how *real experience* with others makes us who we are; it is not about how we become who we are because we really want to be infantile and get taken care of our whole lives.[19]

In one of Freud's models—called the "structural model"—he posited the idea of an *ego,* an *id,* and a *superego.*[20] The *id* (the "It") was the reservoir for all those unconscious impulses, wishes, fantasies, and desires that were too painful or terrifying to be aware of—all unbridled desire for gratification, pleasure, and destruction. The *superego* is the "conscience" or the policeman on the beat, giving us rules and injunctions to live by, keeping the peace, so to speak, by setting a high bar for our behavior, thinking, and feeling, so that we don't just act on our impulses. The superego is usually pretty harsh and punishing, though, and needs to be to keep a lid on how out of control we would be if the id ran the show. The *ego,* well, that's sort of a compromise between the two, and contains thoughts, wishes, beliefs, and feelings, some of which we're aware of right now ("conscious of") and some of which we're not aware of ("unconscious of"). Some of the information (thoughts, wishes, beliefs, affects) *could* be available to us, but we consciously vow to forget them—that's called "suppression" and it's a defense against reality we judge too harsh to accept right now. Some of the information (thoughts, wishes, beliefs, affects) is way too painful to even consciously forget, so we forget it and forget we forgot it. That's called "repression."

For Freud, *repression* is the problem, insofar as it speaks to: 1) our lack of ability to incorporate reality; and 2) the shadowy, awful contents we're repressing, proving after all that *homini homo lupus* (man is to his fellow-man a wolf). According to Freud, and for much of the history of psychoanalysis and psychotherapy in the 20th century, helping patients stop repressing these warded-off mental contents was the curative work of psychoanalysis. It was the dual processes of *repression* and *resistance* to removing the repression that caused psychopathology. That makes *remembering* the most important thing for a person to do, if they want to get better.

Freud's work provided intriguing, complex (and in many ways utterly new) ways of understanding why humans do what they do. But I think there is a lot about it that is either inaccurate or doesn't *work* for us in terms of being parents and figuring out what to do. More about that later.

TRAUMA AND THE DEVELOPMENT OF PATHOGENIC BELIEFS

The work of Joseph Weiss, Hal Sampson, Lynn O'Connor, and other members of the San Francisco Psychotherapy Research Group (SFPRG) occupies a unique place in our understanding of psychopathology in its emphasis on what they call the development of pathogenic beliefs, and the importance of *guilt* and *shame* in how pathogenic beliefs get formed in the first place.

So, we've learned that children are powerfully motivated to *adapt* to their environments (including their parents' needs). These efforts at adaptation include the acquisition of beliefs about oneself and one's relational world. A belief is termed *pathogenic* if it warns a person (accurately or not) that pursuing highly adaptive and desirable goals (which are in each instance person-specific) would be dangerous to oneself or destructive to others.[21] Pathogenic beliefs are hard to change once they develop.

An infant or child may develop such beliefs in order to maintain his ties to his parents. This can be an especially powerful motivator for teenagers. For example, your teen may become maladaptively "bad" if he infers that by being so he pleases you, by giving you the opportunity to feel morally superior. Huh? All that means is that sometimes a teen will act up and act out just to prove that *you* are right about him or her. Teens sometimes live *down* to your expectations. If you continually tell (or feel or think) that your teen is lazy, mean-spirited, stupid, or will never amount to anything, your teen—in an effort to at least keep you happy by confirming that you *know* your child well and thus are a *good* parent—will do whatever behavior confirms your view of him.

Moreover, he may *generalize* this belief, and so may continue for years to behave provocatively with anyone in authority, in an unconscious attempt to maintain his ties to that person.[22] In other words, your child can come to believe that you must be right about them, and in order to maintain a connection with someone close to you, you have to behave the way you're expected to behave. In this case, that creates a mess for your teenager and the people who he'll later meet. But why would he *generalize* this belief?

Well, it's a kind of developmental "shorthand," and it's why theory-making happens at all. It's efficient; *efficiency* is often valued in our organism over *accuracy.* If you get treated one way and learn to treat others one way, it's difficult to have to *relearn* these ways of being over and over again, with each new person. It's so much work. We develop all kinds of shorthand for figuring out what to do. Our feelings, too, are a kind of shorthand *theory* that guides us in what to do in any given moment. I discussed more at length in Chapter 2 why it makes so much sense for humans to use this shorthand, theory-making capacity.

Okay, so let's follow this example. You might have—for all kinds of reasons (say it with me: genetic *x* current/past environmental factors)—treated your son or daughter as if he or she was lazy, and was simply *refusing* to work hard. This is, unfortunately, something that might happen until you discover that your child has AD/HD (particularly the inattentive subtype). You might have battle after battle over why your smart, middle-school adolescent is refusing to just pay attention, get off the frickin' computer, stop playing Minecraft, and do his homework. You might have had similar difficulties with sustained attention in the past, especially around school. If you *believe* that his behavior is *personal* (that he could work harder but he isn't), that his behavior is *pervasive* (that it is a part of his personality or his *very being,* not just a particular behavior), and that it is permanent (that it will persist in time and is not changeable), you are likely to deem your child lazy, yourself a bad parent, and either withdraw or get overinvolved.[23] Neither of these two solutions is very useful, as we've explored throughout this book.

While pathogenic beliefs, as attempts at adaptation to one's relational world, are understood as largely developing in childhood, they are by no means only developed in childhood.[24] A person may develop new pathogenic beliefs at any time in the developmental life cycle, and in the same manner as children do, by direct treatment by close others or by inference from relational events, especially traumatic ones. In addition, a person may have an old pathogenic belief structure that is restimulated or crystallized in response to a new traumatic event or maintained by current realities and interactions.

It turns out, you should have gathered by now, that we are *always* teaching something to our children, about our children, ourselves, and the world, *especially* when we are not teaching them directly. If you stand in front of your teenager and say, "It's *good* to be on time," then they know that you have a certain opinion about "being on time." That's a powerful enough experience for your child. He wants you to be happy. He doesn't like disappointing you. So when you say, "It's *good* to do x, y, or z," he might reject that advice, but he's taking it in and considering it.

But if you are *angry or enraged* with him when you say it, he knows you *feel* a certain way about time and about *him*. If you are extremely anxious when you are rushing around, trying incredibly hard not to be late, to the detriment of all else (including everyone else's feelings), then they know you are *afraid* of something about time. If you're always late and you still say, "It's good to be on time," he is being taught that you are either hypocritical or confused or weak or struggling or all of those things.

He might react by trying to keep you (and himself) on time or he might react by being late *all the time* and ridiculing your attempts to be on time when he knows you never will be. It all depends. On what? Genes, environment, you know, the usual stuff. But we are always "teaching" something. It's just that you can have more input and control over what it is you are teaching and be conscious of how to actually teach what you *intend* to teach. That's a long process, a sacred one, and one that I think is incredibly worthwhile.

A Reformulation of Trauma

My own wish to look at definitions of trauma began, in part, out of a growing sense that standard definitions of trauma were not sufficiently relational, that is, they did not take into account enough the fact that we suffer, to a great degree, because of the real and imagined suffering *of others*. Even self-trauma, for a child, is often complicated in the ways the child begins to consider how the experience of their own trauma was or might in the future be detrimental to a close other (especially if the perpetrator of the trauma is a loved one).[25]

In a Control-Mastery approach to trauma, while childhood experiences play a central role in trauma development, there is a strong recognition that pathology often develops in the normal process of identification with close others, like parents.[26] And that means, *trauma can occur by witnessing the suffering of our parents, and identifying with them*. And when we persist, and are still okay, even when those we're close to are not (or we think they are not), we very often feel *guilty*. Again, this is a normal part of family life, and probably normative of all human life. Guilt in the face of the suffering of others is called *survivor guilt*. Survivor guilt can be conscious or nonconscious, and can be understood as a pervasive feeling of worry about being better off than others; as the belief that being alive is at the expense of a loved one or; or as the belief that there is a limited amount of the good things in life to go around, and that experiencing the good things in life will harm someone else.[27] Through the lens of survivor guilt, the pursuit of happiness is a zero-sum game: If I am happy, you can't be...or you have to be *less* happy, since I got more than you. Marshall Bush, Ph.D. wrote about the links between survival guilt, identifying with parents, and development of problems:

Traumas that befall other family members tend to produce intense un-conscious survivor guilt. Traumas that befall oneself, especially those stem-ming from parental mistreatment and rejection, often produce a deep-seated unconscious belief that one is unworthy and deserves punishment. Massive trauma can exert a pathogenic influence and create masochistic symptom-atology at any point in the life cycle. Weiss has suggested that most inhibi-tions and symptoms represent either compliances to or identifications with other family members toward whom one unconsciously feels guilty. Symp-toms may also represent mixtures of compliance and identification. The unconscious purpose of these compliances and identifications is to reduce guilt through a self-sacrificial restoration of or a display of loyalty to the injured party.[28]

In other words, Dr. Bush is saying that when we feel guilty because those we love are suffering, we usually seek some form of punishment or reduction of our own happiness, in order to be loyal to the suffering person. If I love you and you suffer, I want to equalize the situation. Control-Mastery sees these things as highly related: caring about others who suffer, feeling guilty, and the development of problems. The Control-Mastery approach to trauma,[29] guilt, and psychopathology is thus highly *interpersonal.* It takes account of the interpersonal nature of trauma and psychopa-thology as the result of the conflict between one's own needs and the perceived needs of others. This hypothesis assumes that we are born with an *altruistic* motive system and a set of biologically based prosocial instincts, like those proposed by Bowlby[30] and Hoffman.[31] It is in stark opposition with Freud's idea that we are simply wolves to one another.

But this doesn't mean that if your child is in pain over your pain, they will de-velop pathology or their mental health will be adversely affected. *Having pathogenic beliefs is not the same thing as being "mentally ill."* It just happens, and for good reasons. Children can and will develop pathogenic beliefs in relation to their parents for reasons noted above: because children don't think well (lack of cognitive ma-turity), because they think they're often the cause of everything (egocentrism), and because they love you and need you (and so will naturally identify with and comply with you in the process of developing a self and identity). The problem is that patho-genic beliefs can stop children (and teens) from pursuing normal goals.

Pathogenic beliefs, often held in place and created by intense shame and guilt, affect one's ability to maintain safe psychological distance or intimacy, the ability to maintain self-esteem, and the ability to know one's desires and aspirations.[32] Un-fortunately, those are key developmental tasks of adolescents. Some of the factors affecting the severity and intransigence of pathogenic beliefs include: age at devel-opment of the belief structures, individual temperament, current life circumstances (including interpersonal resiliency factors), and psycho-physiological status of the organism (How is affect processed? What level of cognition is the individual capable of?). Thus, pathogenic beliefs acquired earlier in life may be more dominated by issues with how our bodies respond, whereas in other pathogenic beliefs one may be more or less conscious of the bodily feelings that were connected with the belief formation process.

Anxiety, shame, guilt, envy, and sadness (and thus, depression) may all accompany pathogenic beliefs. Control-Mastery Theory places a special focus on the role of *unconscious guilt* in the formation of psychopathology. While Freud emphasized guilt in the development of psychopathology, his understanding of the nature of guilt was quite different from that of Weiss and his colleagues.

In his early theorizing, Freud saw guilt pathology as caused by the fact that we were repressing (unconsciously forgetting) all of the seedy little impulses (*id* impulses) that wanted gratification, without regard to reality. Weiss took up Freud's later work and argued that Freud had indeed opened the door for a view of guilt rooted in ego-based, altruistic concerns for the welfare of the Other. Following from this belief, Control-Mastery Theory holds that guilt can arise at any time in the developmental life cycle and develops based on the fundamental orientation of the individual to the other, and our tendency to blame ourselves for the traumatic (or traumatically perceived) experiences of close others.

Survivor guilt is not the only type of guilt we experience, and that's related to the lives of family members, in the normal course of living. Let's look at some other forms of guilt and their relationship to pathogenic beliefs and psychopathology.

On Guilt and Shame in the Family

Along these lines, then, Weiss and his colleagues identified certain types of unconscious guilt as fundamental in the development of pathogenic processes including depression,[33] the inappropriate sexualization of relationships,[34] eating disorders,[35] self-punitive, self-injuring patterns of interaction,[36] and interpersonal interactions rooted in irrational beliefs about how one already has or may in the future harm significant others.[37] The idea that *guilt* is associated with pathology (mental and physical) is not a new one and it has persisted over thousands of years of history and across cultures. The reasons for and functional workings of guilt (and shame), however, have changed.

While Weiss did not originate the concepts related below, he developed a program of empirical research with his colleagues that would eventually come to emphasize the importance of certain forms of unconscious, interpersonally driven guilt. Some of these subtypes of guilt were often already identified in the literature as *survivor guilt* (discussed above); *separation/disloyalty guilt* (worry that being separate/different from loved ones will harm them and constitute an act of disloy-alty)[38]; *omnipotent responsibility guilt* (the exaggerated sense that one is responsible for the happiness and well-being of others)[39]; *role guilt* (the guilt that people expe-rience consciously and unconsciously when they believe they have violated or are going to violate the socially sanctioned rules and regulations accepted for their sex/gender, class or ethnic group)[40]; and *self-hate guilt* (which refers to a general sense of badness indirectly related to interpersonal guilt).[41]

The first four forms of guilt are all deemed *interpersonal* because they are deeply connected to the fear of harming others. The last form, *self-hate guilt,* may occur in relation to extremely punitive parents or caregivers, and is theoretically akin to the other forms of guilt insofar as people are trying to preserve a connection to sig-nificant others by maintaining themselves as bad (in order to see the other as good). Lynn O'Connor and her colleagues noted that people might experience self-hate in an effort to ward off survivor guilt. For example, if one feels always at fault when something goes wrong (one "hates oneself"), then being hate-worthy and undeserv-ing is a way of not *outdoing* one's loved one.

Guilt has often been the emotion most associated with pathological processes.[42] Research has been less focused on the experience of *shame,* for a variety of reasons.[43] But advances in evolutionary biology, psychology, and psychoanalysis support a more inclusive view of *both* shame and guilt as playing dual roles.[44] In this more recent view, shame and guilt are emotions in service of what may be a strong, nor-mal human motivation, that is, *to belong and to maintain attachment to significant others not as a consequence of aggressive, antisocial impulses and ensuing guilty feelings, but as the result of a human organism with the biopsychosocial capacity for empathy and altruism.*[45]

In this more updated view, guilt and shame are now understood to be related to socially valued traits and behaviors,[46] and to psychological maladjustment and psy-chopathology.[47] What, then, makes a particular form of guilt or shame maladaptive?[48]

I know this is pretty technical, but if you stick with me there's a big payoff. So, here's a preview of where we're going and why I'm talking so much about shame, guilt, and psychopathology: Many of the problems you're going to encounter in your family during the adolescent years have to do with problems your teens (and you) will have around understanding and managing difficult emotions. If you un-derstand the critical role of both guilt and shame in creating and maintaining family problems, you will be in an incredibly powerful position to reduce those problems. In order to give you the power to change things, we have to look at the link between affect regulation (managing emotion) and how problems begin (the development of pathogenic beliefs).

Affect Regulation and the Development of Pathogenic Beliefs

What do I mean by *affect,* and why is it important for understanding what you do with your children? In 2012, the fields of study that deal with "affect regulation" and its relationship to self- and identity-development are hotbeds of research activity. I've mentioned in this book and usually mention at every talk I give that the awareness of, understanding, articulation, and management of affect is the most important series of tasks that your adolescent needs to learn.

So first I need to give you a few definitions, based on the earlier work of Donald Nathanson and Sylvan Tomkins.

In Nathanson and Tomkins's views, affect is the *biological* portion of emotion. Affect is what happens in the body (the biological patterns) in response to unfolding events in the world. Affective responses are very, very quick, typically not lasting more than a few seconds. According to Tomkins, there are nine innate affects,[49] but this seems to be plenty to call forth an infinite number of emotions—in the same way that there are only 26 letters in the English language and four nucleobases in DNA, but there is no shortage of possible words and sentences and no shortage of genetic configurations ("phenotypes").

Some people seem particularly sensitive to the presence of the "shame chemical" in their system, and this is important to remember.

Each *affect*, as a pattern of expression, is a specific package of information triggered in response to a particular type of stimulus. Much of the information involves the skin and muscles of the face. Affect, says Tomkins, makes good things better and bad things worse. A stimulus involving an increase in brain activity will trigger an affect that increases brain activity; a stimulus that involves a decrease in brain activity will trigger an affect that further decreases brain activity. In this sense, at least, affect motivates our behavior. For example, your school-age child is working on a puzzle. Each new stimulus (picking up and trying a new piece, looking at the puzzle from different directions) provides increasing brain activity, and both the tension and excitement mount as she nears completion of the puzzle—the stimulation of each part in this process urges her on. But if she gets frustrated as she begins the puzzle or if a disapproving adult watches her and comments, "Good luck with that; what makes you think you can finish such a hard puzzle?" she will likely feel shame. The experience of shame is associated with chemical changes in the brain that result in withdrawal and decreases in motor activity. As the brain "becomes aware" of these changes other neurological events will be triggered that will continue this decrease in overall brain activity and engagement with the task. So, in this way, our *affects* act as motivators (or de-motivators) for goal-directed behaviors. Now let's look at some other definitions regarding our emotional life.

Feeling is the *experience* of affect; this is the organism's awareness of affective response. Feeling allows for knowledge and understanding. It only lasts for a flash of recognition, as Nathanson says, and this is one reason why it is difficult to discern, especially if one has been warned against paying attention to one's bodily states.

Emotion is the complex combination of affect with memories of those affect-triggered situations, and the response to the affect triggered by new occurrences of the feelings. In other words, most everyone has the same biological response when the affect "anger" is triggered. However, we differ in how we understand, remember, and experience this affect. To understand my emotions, you must know my history. Emotions, as you know, can last quite a while.

Mood is a persistent state of emotion that can last hours, days, or weeks. Mood is triggered by a combination of thoughts, feelings, and emotions, which trigger other thoughts, feelings, emotions, and so on. A mood is like an ongoing cascade of emotions, which can be persistent because of the triggering of behavioral ways of responding to complex emotions, which in turn stimulates other emotions. These behavioral ways of responding are called "affect scripts." These affect scripts can also be understood as always "carrying with them" pathogenic beliefs that explain to the person the persistence of their feelings/emotions. In other words, affect scripts are *theories*. They are theories that explain, like a good journalist, the 5 W's and 1 H: Who is it about? What happened? Where did it take place? When did it take place? Why did it happen? How did it happen? Or as kids think about it: Who is at fault, how long will it last and how much of my life will be affected?

Don Nathanson and Sylvan Tomkins before him understood the *shame* response not as a primary affect, but as ancillary, as the impediment (or modulator) to the primary affect pair termed "excitement-joy." This seems so theoretical, but it's important. These researchers were saying that shame is basically a chemical that *reduces* a range of responses, from excitement to joy. If you are interested and excited about something and you become ashamed, your interest *reduces* in the subject at hand. If you're feeling joyful about something and shame enters the picture, joy exits.

In Control-Mastery Theory, traumatic experiences almost always result in a reduced capacity to experience pleasure and joy—and that tells you that traumatic experiences almost always involve, at some point, the experience of *shame*.[50] Even at the cellular level, the experience of shame inhibits certain neurological processes involved in the encoding of new information.

More research has been done in the last few decades on the relationship of shame to the development of psychopathology.[52] This offers a crucial lesson for parents. If we think we should make our children first feel *ashamed* for what they did wrong before we try to teach them the right way to do things, we're barking up the wrong tree. The experience of shame makes learning new things harder, not easier.

Some common pathogenic beliefs of teenagers are listed below. You'll notice that many, if not all of these beliefs are strongly related to guilt and shame.

If I am happy, comfortable, and successful it will make a best friend or other family member(s) feel inadequate and inferior—so my happiness causes others unhappiness.

If others don't respond well to me, it is my own fault and I am therefore bad, destructive, stupid, crazy, or "beyond fixing."

If others around me are often burdened, tired. or overwhelmed, it must be because I am too forceful, overpowering, or my needs/entire personality are just "too much."

If I do not meet expectations or complete tasks really well or perfectly, I do not deserve to be given the chance to do so in the future; my poor performance is fate and not correctable.

If my parents or caregivers drink, use drugs, get (or got) divorced, are depressed, anxious, or have a mental illness, or are violent with me, themselves, or each other, then it is my fault and/or my responsibility to fix them (this is a frequent, common pathogenic belief called the belief in "omnipotent responsibility" for suffering).

If I get punished or neglected, it is appropriate and deserved.

If I am lonely or isolated from my family, it is because I deserve to be, since it is a result of an inherent flaw, defect, or basic condition of "badness."

If I show my flaws and imperfections, I will be abandoned and left alone, since flaws keep people from being interested in and helping me (this pathogenic belief is also very common, especially in so-called "successful" or high-functioning teens: "If I look like I need help, nobody will help me").

If I erase, ignore, forget, suppress, diminish my own needs or put other's needs first and listen and comply with others' requests, I can finally get people to respond to my needs.

Using Knowledge About Pathogenic Beliefs to Help Yourself and Your Family

If I could give you a medal just for getting to this section, I'd give you one—you deserve it. But now we can put this all together in terms of *what you can do* to help yourself and your teenager.

Control-Mastery Theory operates on the tested assumption that people want to disconfirm their pathogenic beliefs and are often working to do so—although this work can be nonconscious. People have a drive to master their problems and conflicts and pursue their normal developmental goals. Unlike in Freudian theory, this theory believes we strive toward health and work relentlessly, consciously, and nonconsciously for health and connection with others. But we regulate that work, the timing and intensity of it, in proportion to how *safe* we judge the situation to be at any given time. Thus, *a sense of safety is what allows people to pursue their normal developmental goals—and as parents, you have a crucial role in fostering that safety.* We'll soon discuss how to do that, because as it turns out, teens especially are going to give you opportunities, at multiple times throughout every day, to help them feel safe. Another irony, right? We are continually able to make things hard for them and we are continually able to repair that (or at least to try). Some might call that the ultimate irony. I call it *parenting.*

So, you're telling me I have pathogenic beliefs, in relation to my experience in my own childhood? If I'm in pain or struggling, my kids are going to pick up on this and think they're at fault? And they're watching me like a hawk, so even if I think I'm hiding things, they can tell? So I can't avoid helping my children develop pathogenic beliefs? This is going to happen, no matter how much money I have or where we live or whether I make it all perfect for them?

Yes. Because, in fact, you can't make it *perfect* for your children. The life of humans and humans in families is such that you don't actually *know* what is *perfect* for your child, and even if you're a caring, loving person, you can't really know what your child will need, at each moment, *in advance.* In parenting, one size cannot fit all. One size can't even fit *one.* Perfect or right—or my preference, *a good approximation—is something that we realize after the fact.*

Part of the contribution of Weiss's early work was to confirm a classical psychoanalytic maxim about the work of psychotherapy. Weiss and his colleagues demonstrated early in their research that successful treatment in therapy always included the (re)emergence of warded-off mental contents (cognitions/thoughts, affects, feelings, emotions, and impulses).[53] In showing not only the criteria by which mental contents were warded off through defensive activity, but also the conditions under which these contents were brought to greater awareness, Weiss and his colleagues demonstrated empirically what Freud took as a given about pathogenesis, namely that there is an intimate link between the *themes* (like *worry* about hurting someone close to you or *guilt* over outdoing a parent or sibling) that are warded off and subsequent *symptom formation* (like depression or hypersexualization or drug-seeking behavior), but not necessarily between the affective correlates (anxiety, withdrawal and shut-down, hyper-activity, etc.) of a warded-off content and related behaviors. In other words, and in simple terms, you can more easily understand and productively work with what your children are struggling with by looking at: 1) what normal developmental mental health goals are being inhibited (the themes); and 2) how their symptoms function to keep inhibiting them from working on those goals.

Feminist theorists and clinicians at the Stone Center in Wellesley, Massachusetts have proposed the construction *relationship-differentiation* as a revision of the separation-individuation model. I refer to this process as the process of *developing related autonomy.*

Developing *related autonomy* is a primary mental health component for your teenager (See Chapter 9). Your children are not going to grow up and "separate" from you. That doesn't mean they won't mature and develop a strong sense of individual agency. But thinking in terms of related autonomy emphasizes the *relational* context in which all self-development takes place. This way of thinking puts connectedness to others and a more *fluid* capacity for identification at the core of human developmental "progress." Thus, disruptions in the capacity to empathize—disruptions in the capacity to engage with others and one's own relational world—can be understood, by definition, to be at the very heart of pathogenesis, because it defines pathology as being related to the inability to connect with others. If we cannot, especially as children, "connect" with others—regardless of the source of that disconnection (primarily medical, psychological, spiritual, or otherwise)—we lose the primary way that we immediately gather information about and come to know the world. Disruptions in the capacity to sense, tolerate, interpret, and respond to feelings and emotions are, by definition, *traumatic disruptions* since they threaten our capacity to engage with others and with our own relational world.

This long road brings us to a discussion of how parents can love, work, and play with their growing children, based upon the insights of Control-Mastery Theory. But first we have a stop to make, to consider how children/teens work in *therapy,* before we translate that to your home.

HOW DO CHILDREN AND PARENTS WORK IN THERAPY?

First and foremost, children come in to therapy to tell us their stories. According to Control-Mastery Theory, the dominant theme of most children's stories is that they feel responsible for their parents' problems, feel empathy for their parents, and want to fix them. They (mostly unconsciously) see the parents or caregivers as somehow damaged and want to respond to them. This perception of the parents as *flawed,* however, is usually kept from conscious awareness, for several reasons:

1. It is exquisitely painful for a child to recognize a parent's momentary or ongoing *liabilities*. It leaves the child feeling helpless, hopeless, and utterly abandoned as they negotiate the developmental dramas of childhood.

2. On the other hand, the child wants to distance from the parents' problems, to grow up and away from them. According to Control-Mastery Theory, the child most often feels *unconsciously* guilty and sad for the parents.

3. On the third hand (and the fact that there is seldom a "third hand" in a relational paradox is the reason for the development of a pathological compromise), the child inescapably needs the parents and whatever protection, attention, and love they can offer.

You can leave a partner—and sometimes that is hard enough—but you can't really leave your parents. I hope you don't really leave your kids, either.

There are several maladaptive ways of resolving the dilemma of negotiating children's own needs in the context of an altruistically based motivational system. These "solutions" take on a unique character depending upon the reasons for the parental unavailability to really see and be attuned to the child's physical and emotional development. But, in the main, the child can, as we've already seen:

1. 1) Try not to have many needs of their own;

2. 2) Try to *exaggerate* their needs and the strength of their demand that the environment respond to them;

3. 3) Try to determine which of their affects and needs are unacceptable and selectively regulate the experience of those affects and needs, while trying to control the situations during which those affects and needs might be triggered; and/or

4. 4) Try to banish from conscious awareness those most painful aspects of the caregiving environment.

These are only some of the *main* methods that children utilize, and there are plenty of others. As we know from Freud's work, human beings have a remarkable capacity for regulating painful experience, in the form of erecting defenses against both the painful affect and the situation/cause of that pain. For example, temporary relief might be obtained through use of *repression* (forgetting, and then forgetting I forgot); *projection* (seeing others as having the feelings I cannot tolerate); *reversal into the opposite* ("I don't hate my brother, he hates *me*"); *fantasy* (thinking and feeling in ways not very connected to reality); *dissociation/conversion* (*dissociation* is feeling detached and separated from reality—on a continuum from mild to severe; *conversion* is when one has a bodily effect with no neurological cause, like when a soldier becomes blind because of witnessing horrible violence, not because of a physical injury to the eyes; see Chapter 9); *rationalization/rumination* (endless thinking about or justifying something that really you don't believe, deep down); *omnipotence* (taking on full responsibility for the pain, thereby becoming its *possible* source of amelioration); *denial* (of affects, needs, impulses, wishes, thoughts…you name it); *procrastination* (a good strategy to not "outdo" the parent); *acting-out*; and many other defenses. We all do these things. Don't be worried if you recognize your behaviors. It's good to know that you are doing them to try to protect yourself and to stay safe. And if you do these things a lot or you do one all the time, it might indicate there is a trauma underneath there somewhere.

For therapists, the types, amounts, and successes of the defenses employed tell us a lot about the kind of relational traumas the child is coming to therapy with; they also sometimes point back to *unresolved* parental conflicts for which the child has become a bearer.[54]

As I mentioned earlier, children condemn in themselves whatever threatens their ties to their primary caregivers. They will condemn all motives, traits, affects, and behaviors that seem to upset, worry, sadden, hinder, drain, humiliate, betray, or otherwise hurt the parent. Children may condemn in themselves motives that are normally thought of as acceptable goals, if they infer that by pursuing that goal, the parent will be threatened or otherwise harmed. This former point bears repeating because it will, in large measure, determine the kinds of behaviors and emotions I am likely to see (and not see) in my therapy sessions.

What the child tries not to feel or think about in therapy is what they have either learned is unacceptable to their caregiver or they are on the *verge of* learning is unacceptable. This is a central point.

I want to emphasize the idea of "being on the verge" because children (and teens) will *test* us to see what behaviors and emotions they *may* need to get rid of in the future.

Take that example of a child experiencing a parent as very burdened by his needs. In order to figure out whether his needs overall (or just certain needs) are a problem, he *has* to present you with his needs and feelings surrounding the needs, to see how you'll react. He might sense you have a problem tolerating certain feelings or behaviors about him, so he has to bring them to you to see what you'll do. He's going to have needs his whole life. He wants to figure out which needs are okay and which needs drive people away. He loves you and thinks you're safe, so he's going to take a chance by demonstrating a need and hoping you don't get too overwhelmed by it. If you got overwhelmed that one time (or every few months), and you explain that it really wasn't about him—Daddy just has a stomachache, or a problem with work—then all may be relatively okay. You son can relax, start ignoring you and your needs again (because he's a kid), and go back to attending to his primary task: self-development. But if over and over again, he presents you with his normal needs and he feels you are overwhelmed and depleted, he's going to have to come up with a theory about *why*. And I can tell you that the *why* is going to include a theory about *him* being wrong or bad in some way.

On the way to developing a firm pathogenic belief, your children will test to see if they need to get rid of certain thoughts, affects, feelings, etc. They don't want to have to do it. And *on the way back* from working on something based upon a particular pathogenic belief, they will test you to see if it is safe enough to change their belief, and the behavior attached to it. *If it isn't safe enough, they won't change the pathogenic adaptation.* The therapist's job is to help create the conditions of safety necessary for pathogenic adaptations to be modified enough to allow the pursuit of normal developmental goals. The therapist does this job, in close relationship with the client, in part by behaving, feeling, and thinking in ways that disconfirm the child's pathogenic beliefs and/or ways that allow the child to know that they do not need to make a pathogenic adaptation with everyone, all the time, in every situation. This is enormously relieving for a child. *When a child is no longer focused on making pathogenic adaptations to their environment, they have an enormous amount of energy available to work on their normal development.* Bingo.

All this might seem intuitively wrong to you, but it isn't. Parents of teens usually call a therapist because they have a child that they are frustrated with (or in some cases at their wits end with), because of behaviors that are making them feel *upset, worried, sad, hindered, drained, humiliated, betrayed, and hurt.* So, how does it make sense that I told you that children want to make their parents happy, more than anything?

This is exactly the point. Your child will continue to *test* you (and their environment) by evoking these feeling states in the parents *precisely* because they need help in understanding how to modulate the affect themselves (and, of course, because they sense that you are having trouble doing this). Your child loves you and needs to develop. He is trying to fix the two of you *simultaneously*; that is what *testing behavior* is all about.

HOW DO CHILDREN AND PARENTS WORK AT HOME?: THE CONCEPT OF *TESTING*

I'm a parent. I get nervous at the idea that what I do at any moment—especially when I don't mean to—could possibly mess up my child. I know that what happens is always about genetic and environmental factors, but somehow I keep wondering if I'm doing something wrong. Look: Pathogenic beliefs develop. It just happens. It is so very hard to stop them from forming, because of the immature state of our children's psyche. But if we know that this happens, we can address the situation. We can *choose* to address the situation. In my view, this means that parenting could be a *holy* activity (See Chapter 10).

That's a very strong word to use—and I know it has religious connotations. But that's the way I think of the fact that with the very little beings we love, we are bound to create problems. And the very little beings that love us are bound to create problems for us, too. Being a parent means that our children, at each stage in their development, will retraumatize or restimulate us in relation to our own earlier traumas.[55] Each crisis for the child is also a potential crisis for the parent, and at the same time an opportunity for the parent's further growth, not only with their own child in the specific conflict at hand, but with their parents, their partner, their family, and close others. In more simple terms, how we respond to the fact that we are bound to hurt each other is an *ethical* question—and the potential for who we can become, based on what we choose, makes parenting, potentially, a kind of holy ground.

Control-Mastery Theory tells us that one reason for parents being underinvolved in the therapeutic process or so upset, attacking, and overinvolved with what therapists "*do* to their children" is because they themselves are hoping that the therapist will help them figure out something that simultaneously helps *both* parent and child.

In short, parents who bring their children into therapy often keep their distance because they are fearful I cannot help *them*. Or the parents stay away because they worry I will be overwhelmed by *their* difficulties, just as they are overwhelmed by their child's difficulties. Sometimes parents want to be heavily involved in the treatment, almost wanting to direct it, because they feel entirely overwhelmed by the magnitude of their difficulties and the "unquiet peace" they have in relation to their own pain.

Both teenagers and their parents *test* by shuttling back and forth between behaviors they fear are troubling. Or they shuttle back and forth between demonstrating problematic feeling states and hiding them. Why does the behavior often seem so contradictory? Children and parents shuttle between the poles because they are *testing* and trying to master their problems. They need to draw on and demonstrate/

withhold both sides of a problematic behavior or feeling, precisely because they never learned the right proportion of showing their feelings and behaviors and hiding them. They never learned well enough how to be attuned to their own needs (and thus often cannot attune to the real developmental needs of others). The child or parent's "resistances" or symptoms or "things that drive us nuts" are examples of *compromises* that were reached when earlier attempts at developmental mastery were met with a lack of attunement. By testing both poles, we learn to move toward a resolution of the tasks that were interrupted, and at the same are working to change *beliefs,* related *physiological patterns of response,* and concrete behaviors. *Children and teenagers must test their parents* because testing behavior represents the most elegant and efficient way of figuring out how much and just what parts of their identities are acceptable in the world. And they test parents because you are a big, important part of their world.

Control-Mastery Theory, basically, does not believe in the concept of *resistance,* at least not in the way we discussed that Freud talked about it. A strict Freudian therapist (or sometimes an angry, anxious parent) will say, "Why is he doing this to us? Doesn't he want to be happy/better/adjusted/normal?" Control-Mastery Theory looks at the concept of resistance and doesn't see ambivalence toward progress; it posits a *lack of safety in the internal or external environments.* I don't see resistance; I see a *form of work* or an *adaptation gone awry. And I assume that teenager wants a better way of doing it for themselves and their parents.* A Control-Mastery therapist (and now, increasingly, hopefully you) might ask questions like, and begin to approximate theories about:

> "How is his behavior an adaptation, an attempt to be *healthy* and pursue the goals listed in Chapter 9?"

> "What can I do to understand the pathogenic beliefs that might be influencing his behavior?"

> "How is my child *testing* me and what is she trying to figure out is safe to do or feel?"

> "What is the *theme* behind her behavior?"

Well, you might not include the phrase "Chapter 9" in your statement, but you get the picture.

THE IMPORTANCE OF *SAFETY* IN THE TESTING BEHAVIOR OF TEENAGERS

There are various and complicated (and simple and elegant) ways that teenagers (and all children) test their parents (and their therapists). Children test verbally, by telling you things; they test with their behavior, by doing things with you and away from you; they test by feeling things in your direction, and seeing what you do (or feel) or think in response to that. Not everything is a test—that would make the idea of testing ridiculous or at least very hard to work with.

How do you know if you're undergoing a test from your teenager? Well, think of it. If a theory isn't working for them, they'll be in pain and need to figure it out. If an emotional way of responding, or certain kinds of thoughts, or certain behaviors or actions are problematic for them, they'll be hurting in some way—something will stop working. And they'll find a way to give you the same experience. So, if the way you've been doing something (you know, feeling, thinking, behaving) with them gives them pain, they'll give you pain and something will stop working. It will be time to question your theory about what you're doing or who you think your child is or what they need. You'll know when you're being tested because it will often feel like picking up a hammer without a head, and trying to hit a nail with it. Something no longer works: That's what the philosopher Martin Heidegger called an *aporia*. If you Google this term, in Wikipedia you'll (hopefully) see:

> **Aporia** (<u>Ancient Greek</u>: ἀπορεία: *impasse; lack of resources; puzzlement; doubt; confusion*) denotes, in <u>philosophy</u>, a philosophical puzzle or state of puzzlement, and, in <u>rhetoric</u>, a rhetorically useful expression of doubt."[56]

Just because you aren't feeling the *aporia* doesn't mean everything is great. I'm just saying that you *don't have to wonder/worry all the time* if everything is a test or not. If things seem okay, then just go with the flow. Love your child, have fun, work hard, play well, take good care of yourself and your loved ones; no problem.

Remember that the goal of your child's testing behavior is to disconfirm a pathogenic belief (or a potential pathogenic belief), and to pursue their normal developmental goals? Which goals? The ones in Chapter 9 that describe a "mentally healthy" teen. Here are three major ways that teenagers will test you. I'll alternate the use of pronouns here, to indicate that boys and girls can use *either* kind of testing behavior.

1. Rejection Tests

Their behavior: Your teenager will act in ways that make you want to *reject* them.

The questions being asked by their behavior: Am I evil? Am I bad? Am I a cruel, inferior, or undeserving person? Do I have a right to exist, even? What am I entitled to, love- and care-wise, if parts of me aren't very good or great? Am I bad if I show initiative? Will you attack me? If I do something wrong, do I deserve retaliation, or can mistakes include correction and redemption?

Some ways to pass their tests: This could turn into a long section, so I'm going to pick one major point: *Make sure to make the distinction between your teen's behavior and her "being."* I think criticism—as *kind,* accurate feedback—is important. In couples therapy, we talk about a different denotation of criticism, in making a distinction between a *criticism* and a *complaint.* In this context, a criticism is about someone's *being:* "You're always so *lazy,* you never help me around the house." "You're so irritating and disorganized—why do you have to have your belongings in a mess like that?" Those are examples of criticisms. You are basically saying, *You are a certain way.* It's basically a way of telling someone: You are bad and you cannot change, because it's a personality or biologically based characteristic. When you offer a *complaint,* though, that indicates something temporary, more impersonal, and something that can be changed.[57] Here is a *complaint:* "You know me, Jack, I get irritated and really find it hard to get my own work done if you've left a mess in the kitchen and I have to deal with it. I need your help and I trust you can do better at cleaning up than you have been lately." This way of responding to difficult or disrespectful behaviors helps to avoid the message that your teenager is rejectable or bad in some unchangeable way. By the way, eye-rolling, sighing, and dirty looks—the tried and true triple play of parental disapproval—*does not* help disconfirm a teen's pathogenic belief that he or she is somehow rejectable, at the core.

2. Omnipotence Tests

Their behavior: Your teenager will act in ways that basically make you feel like you are being destroyed, like you have the weight of the world on your shoulders, especially around the experiences of *worry* and *anger.* Your child will do things to make you feel completely overwhelmed and unable to care for them and want to see if you'll basically give up your own life to deal with them.

Some questions being asked by their behavior: Am I too powerful or more powerful than anyone else (in the family)? Am I responsible for everything that happens in this family? Am I responsible for your troubles and pain? Am I selfish and bad if I just focus on my own self and development?

Some ways to pass their tests: One of the best ways of passing an omnipotence test is for you to model *not* taking on too much responsibility for either the good or the bad things that happen in your life. It also helps for your teen to see you (often) taking good care of your physical, emotional, mental, and spiritual health and *not* putting others first all the time. You might think you're modeling a lack of selfishness and a belief in "community" and helping others, but you may also be showing them that the weight of the world does, in fact, belong on your shoulders. If I am working with a psychotherapy client that I know is struggling with a sense of omnipotent responsibility for others, I might encounter a situation where I am going on vacation or have to miss a session. I am careful, in these situations, not to act shy about my vacation and not to apologize for missing a session. That doesn't mean I act like a jerk. It just means that I don't get quiet or sad about the fact that I'm doing something good for myself, knowing that my absence may not be "good" for this person. It's amazing—you might think that this could lead to the person feeling bad about me or abandoned, but many more times than not it leads to the person giving herself permission to enjoy her own moments of pleasure or "good times," even if people she cares about and loves aren't doing the same. The same is true for parenting. You might be presented with a teen that shows up in some state of turmoil, asking you to do something or imploring you to help her figure something out. You might think she can do it on her own, but then you begin to feel like a jerk or wonder, "What kind of mom (or dad) would I be if I say that I can't do this *now*?" You don't want her to be angry or disappointed in you, and she might tell you directly: "I will be angry or disappointed if you don't do this!" That might be just the moment to pull your blankie up tight around you, take a sip of tea and a bite of a cookie, and tell her, "I'm sorry, but I trust you to figure this out—and I'm way too comfy to get out of bed and go do this now...it's not that I mind that you asked, but right now isn't good."

3. Protection Tests

Their behavior: Your teenager will put themselves in harm's way and generally try to elicit your protection behavior. Your teenage might present you with "questionable" situations in which they need some kind of help, support, or protection and act is if there's nothing important at stake.

Some questions being asked by their behavior: Do I deserve to be protected from harm? Are my needs as important as others' needs? Am I weak or bad if I want or need help and protection? Am I hurting you or putting you out too much if I need your attention, care, and solicitude? Is it wrong or hurtful to others if I protect myself from them?

Some general ways to pass their tests: Try to respect their defenses and tests while they're doing them. They're now in a vulnerable position, so you can help by not making them feel ashamed or more vulnerable when they show feelings or behaviors that they are worried about. If you notice that they are testing you in this way, try to be consistent and unwavering, like a guardrail on the side of the freeway.

Passing a protection test might involve you showing *very strong* feelings about your child's right and need to be protected. But that strong feeling cannot be rage or any feeling condemning to your child. This type of test merits an example, because it is the kind of testing that teenagers often do.

Your daughter might come home from a dance or a party in a bad mood, being short with you and treating you disrespectfully. After a while at home (and maybe a few minutes of television-watching together), you might say, "Um, I don't think this is really about me, but you're not exactly treating me like someone you care about." She might groan and then tell you about how someone she really liked just sent her a text saying "It's over." She might say, "Whatever, it doesn't matter—I didn't like him all that much." You might feel very protective of her and so get angry about her being treated this way, not because someone decided not to get more involved, but because someone she had some connection with thought it was just fine to end that connection with a *text*. I think that is rude and disrespectful, and especially because that kind of behavior is on the increase—even among adults—I personally believe it should be fought against, as we establish new norms for digital communication. That's just my opinion. But let's say you agree with that, and think your daughter deserves more—that's it's a respect (and self-respect) issue. If you get angry at your daughter (or angry at the other person), you're kind of "taking over" the situation, and your daughter might just end the conversation and get angry with you, instead. There are lots of ways to pass that protection test. In fact, you probably already did. That was quick, right? Look at the sentence early in this paragraph that suggests a response. Your daughter presented you with a bad mood, and treating you disrespectfully without much consideration—just as had happened to her. That is called a *passive into active* test. She helped you feel the way *she* was feeling, in hopes you'd show her a way out of the bad feelings and get back on the path of standing up for herself and being treated with respect. Your response—to stay calm and just say directly that she is treating you without respect and that isn't going to fly with you—gives her two messages: I deserve to be protected when someone violates my sense of integrity *and* there is a calm, compassionate way of responding to boundary violations. Just do that a few hundred times and your daughter will, in many but not all cases, get some great messages about self-respect.

HOW YOUR TEENAGER WILL TEST YOU

Testing is also usually done by two methods: the "passive into active" method and the "transference" method.

In the *passive into active* method, you usually feel the strain, and your teenager appears very powerful to you. You're usually feeling "one down." Using this method, your daughter will be behaving with you as someone else behaved with her.

In passive into active testing, your teen is trying to get you to feel what he or she is feeling—and needs help sorting out. Her behavior will be a way of saying, "Someone did it to me, now I'm going to do it to you; please respond in a way that helps me figure out how to *better* respond when I encounter this situation."

This way of testing is safer for the teen, because they're in a position of power. It's a hard way to be tested, as a parent, because you think they're getting all the advantages and all the power and goodies and you're not in control. But it's hard to give up a belief, for example, that you are afraid of being a burden to someone, if you're busy being incredibly needy of him or her. It's "better" (or safer) from a child's point of view, to be the one doing the burdening, than the one being the burden. In a passive into active test, then, your teen will burden you and want to see if you *can give some, but not too much.* They want to figure out the right balance between self and self-in-relation. That's exactly what they are trying to figure out; this is Item 13 on the list of Core Components of Mental Health.

If you daughter is doing something that you think is a passive into active type of testing, then she is likely doing something that she: 1) experienced earlier as traumatic or problematic; or 2) anticipated as traumatic or problematic, by inference. In these kinds of tests, the teen is usually identifying with the parent in order to get help figuring out how to respond to the problematic behavior.

In the *transference* testing method, you usually feel pretty okay and safe, but your child may appear very worried, anxious, and fearful. In transference testing, your son behaves toward you in the very ways that are worrisome for him—they just are more exaggerated versions of the behavior, feelings, thoughts, or affects they are trying to figure out a "balance" about. Your son, though, might seem *stuck* in that behavior, and you might be puzzled as to why he isn't "moving on" or "getting it." He might be stuck and therefore repeating or offering up for you certain behaviors, feelings, thoughts, or affects that: 1) provoked a traumatic or problematic reaction from you (or your partner or any close other); or 2) are *anticipated,* by inference, to produce a traumatic or problematic reaction from you (or any caregiver or close other).

Using this method, your son is going to try to avoid remembering or otherwise experiencing *his own* responses to your behavior, in order to keep you happy or to maintain a connection. For example, your son might be worried that you'll be disappointed or left out or sad if he wants to spend less time with you in the family. He actually *wants* to have more independence but he fears or worries (based on inference, perhaps) that he'll really hurt your feelings if he initiates that behavior. So, rather than just walking up to you and saying, "Hey, Dad, you know I love you, but I hope you don't mind me not playing basketball with you every evening anymore," he might just ask you to do it more and more or start doing things that give you the opportunity not to have his company. He might watch to see if you take care of your own needs with your partner or always give in to what they want, for fear of making them feel left out or left behind. He might test you by presenting himself over and over to you in ways that are *dependent,* when what he's hoping is that you'll support his *independence.* He's going to watch whether you readily accept his dependence or whether you actually encourage his autonomy and aren't at all upset by it.

It's necessary to also know that if you pass their initial tests of a pathogenic belief (or family of related beliefs) and the beliefs they're trying to disconfirm are really intense and important, they won't just get better or consider the matter "closed," overnight; they will actually test you *more* and *more vigorously. They are developing, after all, and new levels of development and capacity require new levels and types and topics of testing.* Aren't you lucky?! Yes, I think so. Hang in there and increase your own supports and self-care. If you need a friend or a therapist, call one or both. It doesn't mean you've failed if you want and need help—remember, that's what you're trying to teach your child, so it's good modeling. Also, if you *pass* your teen's initial test, he will often bring up some new thought or feeling he hadn't shared before. In the example above, the mother's quick response that calmly demonstrated her need to be respected resulted in her daughter *telling her* about the very incident that was triggering the testing. That's one way to know you passed a test: You'll get *more* information, not less.

TESTING ISN'T EASY FOR YOUR TEENS, EITHER

A period of vigorous testing of you as a parent is often followed by your teen feeling guilty about what he she been doing, often accompanied by the remembrance and re-experiencing of difficult thoughts, feelings, and affects. The thoughts, feelings, and affects will be the very things your teenager had been hiding away and "storing," so to speak, in the behaviors that were making you (as a parent) worried, anxious, or angry. So, some guilt and then some progress forward can follow vigorous testing. Often, transference testing follows testing in a passive into active way. In other words, safer testing first (being in the one-up position of doing to you what they're trying to figure out) followed by riskier testing second (being in the one down position, and hoping you won't punish them or withdraw...and will somehow figure out how to pass their tests).

For example, your daughter has been really pushing your buttons about curfew, because she seems to ignore the limits you've set on her staying out. Perhaps she got into some trouble with partner violence and that's why you want her to follow the limits you've set. But the incident with her partner may have reinforced a pathogenic belief that she doesn't deserve to be protected. She might test her pathogenic belief that she doesn't deserve protection from harm by putting herself in harm's way again and seeing how you respond. If you're calm but firm about the limits, and insist on her intrinsic value and her *right* to be protected, you might pass her test. But when you pass her test, everything won't magically get better. She might talk about the time her boyfriend hit her after he was drinking at a party—that's a good sign. And she'll do so because you helped her feel safe to talk about a hard subject. But when she talks about it, she'll now have to experience the feelings, thoughts, and affects again—the ones she was managing by acting out with you...by testing you. These painful feelings and thoughts "hide away" inside behaviors that irritate or worry parents (like staying out too late or getting into unsafe situations) and seem to have nothing to do with the actual events connected to the pain (the partner violence). When you pass the tests of your teenager, you help bring them closer to their *actual* feelings about *actual* events. This is a beautiful thing, and it is also painful, at first, and sometimes for a while.

Different behaviors can test the same pathogenic beliefs, so you won't get the same behaviors from teen to teen or within the same teen. Testing will keep you on your toes—and it does, if it's been done the right way. You won't be able to figure out a "system" to pass the tests.

Unfortunately (or fortunately, because you get lots of chances), testing is often a long process, conducted sequentially. There is almost never a "single" test that you will get or have to pass. It's not like that. Testing is multilayered, multileveled, and it unfolds over time. That makes sense. If testing were quick and easy, there wouldn't be a need for it! Testing is about *safety* and about seeing whether or not certain affects, feelings, thoughts, or behaviors are problematic for you (and your teens). It's safer to do it slowly and repetitively. Plus, if you're looking to confirm a long-held or somewhat intransigent belief, are you going to believe someone who tells you once that they don't feel or think the way you fear? Once isn't enough; for most humans, once is not enough for learning and once is absolutely not enough for unlearning—especially unlearning a pathogenic belief.

Another crucial characteristic of the testing process is that passing tests is *always case-specific*. There really is no way to exactly pre-figure how to pass tests, because there is one thing required to pass *any* test: Your children require your real, authentic investment in the relationship. Sorry, one size won't fit all. You can't just make a list of things to do that will pass any test. Tests are too varied, too complex, and slightly different each time. In other words, you have to think practice-driven, not protocol-driven. Protocol-driven will not work for passing tests. If when your kids do "A"," you always do "B," it reads to them as canned, inauthentic, and dismissive. It works that way in therapy, too. And it makes parenting an *ethical* endeavor. More on that in the last chapter. But let's look at an example of how testing and responding to testing is always specific to the person, at that moment, by going back to the issue of parenting *style* for a moment.

Just be an authoritative parent, right? That would generally mean you would function democratically—to some degree—largely sharing decision-making, as your child gets older and more capable. You would ask your child what they're up to, what they're thinking about various issues, and really listen to them. You won't always agree or go along with them, but you'll be pretty interactive with them, inviting their input and soliciting their responses. Well, for a child who, by temperament, by genetics, by experience is anxious or "slow to warm up," this style of parenting can be *more* anxiety-provoking. It can send them into a deep worry that they're disappointing you by not being as outgoing, engaged, and verbally articulate as you want them to be or as their other sibling probably is. In this case, a cookie-cutter authoritative parenting move can actually help to create and confirm the pathogenic belief that by being different than you, your son or daughter is disappointing you and cannot make you happy. Think I'm kidding? Nope.

Sometimes children who have a hard time focusing need an authoritarian style with some interventions (but *minus* the anger). Children, in particular, with inattentive subtype of AD/HD often require structure, even though they get bored with it and rail against it. As they get older, they do eventually come to appreciate it and need it…as long as periods of structure can alternate with periods of freedom, with limits. Kids in this boat seem to need a lot of energy to innervate them to action. This "innervation" usually ends up being *yelling, arguing, or some transmission of anger.* Parents end up repeating and yelling and begging and cajoling and getting angry because it often *works*. It will, in many cases, get your son or daughter to do something they've been putting off forever. But all that yelling is exhausting for everybody and it starts taking a toll on the relationship. You can end up with a child who eventually does things, but that you don't particularly like very much. So, how do you get the energy of anger that seems to wake your child up? *Enthusiasm*. It's a way of keeping the same high *level* of energy while changing the *form*. Enthusiasm usually beats anger because it's positive; it might annoy your AD/HD child that you're so damn enthusiastic about things, but it won't piss him or her off the way *anger* will. I could give you 1,000 examples of this same idea. Sorry, but you can't phone it in, in advance, not even the "best" parenting style. And that is the problem with a *style*; it's a guideline, but it's not "the answer."

Crazy, huh? Nope, it's an elegant, sophisticated, complicated, and ingenious way to stay *safe*, and still work on overcoming things that hold you back. But in order to pass these tests, you have to have a firm grasp on what it is they are trying to do and what they really want. That's what Control-Mastery Theory calls the "unconscious plan." Okay, now I'm really nuts, right? I'm expecting you, after all of this, to just guess what is going on in their unconscious. You want me to read my son or daughter's mind? More theory-making!! Is this chapter ever going to end?

Yes, it's coming to an end. You don't have to guess or mind-read (well, you do, but not about what your teenager *really* needs and wants). I bet you know where to find a list of those things—it's in the next chapter.

P.S. You might think that this whole "healthy human being" stuff is only what *you* want for them. They really want an iPhone and an X-Box 360 and a trip to Aspen and a new Escalade and sex or love or to be left alone right now, and, and…. Your son or daughter might want some or all of these things. But what I believe they *really* want, what their bodies and souls want, is what's in Chapter 9. I think you'll agree, and now it's time to remember that you're the parent and you actually do know better about some things, so you're going to help your teen with working on the upcoming list, thank you very much.

Practical Help Tips

1) First and most important: It's all case-specific. Discovering the "right" intervention to support your teen and meet your needs, too, means knowing your teenager well. Solutions to problems in the family require your engagement and real commitment and that means solutions usually get found *after* a period of messiness, not before. So much suffering for parents (and teens) comes from trying to *avoid* messiness.

2) We are teaching our teens by the emotional state we are in as we parent. We are teaching our teens by our attitudes and underlying "theories" about who we are, what the world is like and what others are like. So, we are always teaching—*especially and most intently* when we're not teaching directly. It pays to know how this kind of "teaching" is happening, because it's what our kids *get* the most.

3) Parenting styles are important, but not all-important, when it comes to figuring out how to be with your teenager. Authoritative parenting is generally the most helpful parenting style but it won't work for *every* child. As with everything else in parenting, one size doesn't fit everyone.

4) Anything that happens in the family is going to happen in at least two directions. Try not to get stuck in the thought that your child is "doing something to you." Conversely, it's not productive to be thinking, "I'm going to do something that will make him [fill in blank with name of 'good' behavior]." Our behaviors with one another in the family are mutually influencing and mutually reinforcing. Yes, it's often hard to figure out just *how* your behavior is influencing a particular behavior from your teenager. But you can trust that *something* you are doing supports or does not support this behavior. And what gets our children *very* frustrated, angry, and confused is when you're doing something that both supports *and* undermines their behavior at the same time. The more we can approximate our own contribution to their troublesome (and positive) behaviors, the better for everyone in the family.

5) Try to really learn the approximation process involved in being The Approximate Parent. We're always doing this in the "background." We start from wherever we are, and we're making conscious and nonconscious decisions (involving feeling, thinking, believing, wishing, imagining, planning, and organizing). We're always making theories in the background about how the world, ourselves, and others work. Sometimes—for various reasons—our theories are wrong or inaccurate or cause problems. When this happens, you might get angry or frustrated or sad. Have a nice cry or talk to a good friend about your anger. But if you really want to *change* the situation, it's going to involve thinking deeply about what theory you've been using for that particular situation. You might need to change a particular theory about yourself, another, or the world. You might not know exactly how to change the theory; so you might have to get help or come up with a hypothesis for the time being and try it out, collect data, and reassess. That's called "approximating" and it is, in my opinion, an excellent way to parent a teenager. It's practical and is *practice-driven*.

6) *Your teenager's behaviors are questions.* Sometimes her behavior is a question about her identity—who should I be? Sometimes her behavior is a question about how to solve an interpersonal problem. Sometimes his behavior is a question about how you are doing. Sometimes the behavior is a question about what is safe to feel or think. If you're having trouble understanding your teenager's behavior, remember: It's likely a question about something, an attempt to come up with a theory for how things work. Try to think: What could this behavior be a question about?

7) *Review the useful and practical contributions from Control-Mastery Theory.* Remember what Kurt Lewin said about good theory being really useful? Theory isn't only for psychologists and scientists. It's for parents. Know what these terms/ideas mean (from a Control-Mastery perspective), because they will change—in positive ways—how you think and feel about being a parent: pathogenic belief, trauma, guilt, shame, survivor guilt, importance of *safety,* testing, and related concepts (passive into active, transference, rejection tests, protection tests, omnipotence tests, passing tests). This is as close as I can come to making a promise to you. If you really understand and apply this theory, being the parent of a teen will be easier and, most likely, way more interesting and less annoying.

8) *Try to understand and remember some of the most common pathogenic beliefs of teenagers.* You can consider these "beliefs" when you're trying to figure out why your teen isn't doing well or is really struggling; it may help you guess what's eating at them.

a) If I am happy, comfortable, and successful it will make a best friend or other family member(s) feel inadequate and inferior—so my happiness causes others unhappiness.

b) If others don't respond well to me, it is my own fault and am therefore bad, destructive, stupid, crazy, or "beyond fixing."

c) If others around me are often burdened, tired, or overwhelmed, it must be because I am too forceful, overpowering, or my needs/entire personality are just "too much."

d) If I do not meet expectations or complete tasks really well or perfectly, I do not deserve to be given the chance to do so in the future; my poor performance is fate and not correctable.

e) If my parents or caregivers drink, use drugs, get (or got) divorced, are depressed, anxious or have a mental illness, or are violent with me, themselves, or each other, then it is my fault and/or my responsibility to fix them (this is a frequent, common pathogenic belief called the belief in "omnipotent responsibility" for suffering).

9) *You're not your child's therapist.* Love your child, do your work, and try to have fun with him or her, but when things go wrong or you just don't understand your child's behavior, try to think like a Control-Mastery therapist, by asking these questions:

a) "How is his behavior an adaptation, an attempt to be *healthy* and pursue the goals listed in Chapter 9?"

b) "What can I do to understand the pathogenic beliefs that might be influencing his behavior?"

c) "How is my child *testing* me and what is she trying to figure out is safe to do or feel?"

d) "What is the *theme* behind her behavior?"

Suggested Reading: *Family: How Parents Teach When They* Aren't *Teaching*

The lists in the "Suggested Reading" sections are by no means comprehensive. I'm including what I consider to be the most informative, practical, relevant, or comprehensive readings on the topic(s) of the chapter. In other words, if you have limited time, these are the works I believe you might want to explore first. It doesn't mean all of these books are "easy reads." Sometimes a listed book will be very difficult, but worth the time.

Baumrind, D. et al. *Parenting for Character: Five Experts, Five Practices.* **Oregon: CSEE, 2008.**

Chess, S., & Thomas, A. *Know Your Child: An Authoritative Guide for Today's Parents.* **New York: Basic Books, 1989.**

Coleman, J. *When Parents Hurt: Compassionate Strategies When You and Your Grown Child Don't Get Along.* **New York: William Morrow Paperbacks, 2008.**

Coontz, S. *The Way We Never Were: American Families and The Nostalgia Trap.* **New York: Basic Books, 1993.**

Dreikurs, R., & Grey, L. *The New Approach to Discipline: Logical Consequences.* **New York: Plume, 1993.**

Foreman, S. A. *Breaking the Spell: Understanding Why Kids Do the Very Thing That Drives You Crazy.* **Charleston: BookSurge Publishing, 2009.**

Glennon, W. *Fathering: Strengthening Connection With Your Children No Matter Where You Are.* **San Francisco & Newburyport: Conari Press, 1995.**

Nelsen, J. N, & Erwin, C. *Parents Who Love Too Much: How Good Parents Can Learn to Love More Wisely and Develop Children of Character.* **New York: Three Rivers Press, 2000.**

Pugh, A. J. *Longing and Belonging: Parents, Children, and Consumer Culture.* **Berkeley: University of California Press, 2009.**

9

Does My Teen Have Good Mental Health?

You can pick up any one of a thousand books and find information about mental illness and disorders, but not necessarily find much about mental *health*. Mental health and the absence of disorders are not the same. Self-help books that promise happiness or success are not necessarily about mental health, either; in fact, they oftentimes work against health by deepening and amplifying the same sociocultural contradictions that actually increase risk for mental illness among youth. So, I want to approach this section from the point of view of a question that has never been asked of me in the close to two decades of doing my work: *How can I tell if my teenager has good mental health?*

As a parent you might think, "My teen doesn't smoke or drink; I know she doesn't lie very much if at all; and she's getting very good grades and is popular. I know she's mentally healthy!" You may or may not be surprised to learn that these signs are not necessarily indicators of good mental health, and depending upon the context, may actually be *risk* signals for mental health difficulties.

I'm not really sure where the conversation has gone about what constitutes mental health. (Caution, "old fogey" moment coming.) I remember that when I first started studying psychology as an undergraduate 30-some years ago, we all mostly talked about "community psychology" and how studying psychology and being in clinical practice were "political activities that served a vital function in a democracy." I admit that I still believe that, but I now rarely have the kinds of conversations that got me started in the profession. I think that some of the conversation about what constitutes mental health—and why supporting the mental health of our young people is so crucial—has morphed into some of the literature and research on "the science of happiness." I think this is really unfortunate. Not that I'm particularly against happiness *per se,* but happiness and mental health are not the same thing. In the shift that took root in the 1980s toward "happiness," "self-improvement,"

353

and, following the lead of insurance companies, "behavioral health,"[1] marriage and family therapists, social workers, psychologists, and psychiatrists have increasingly been called on to be (and thought of less as) *healing* forces in the community and more like technicians. We are in the business of relieving symptoms, very much in the tradition of the American "quick fix."

Before Freud and the "talking cure," and before the so-called European Enlightenment, if you were suffering it was a religious issue—a matter for the clergy. Just as psychology relieved religion of the "burden" of dealing with our mental health, now psychology is being relieved of the burden of dealing with human suffering and sadness. That's *your* job, now. It's up to you to heal yourself—we have the technology; if you don't use it, it's your problem.

One person who is still thinking a lot about these questions is Nancy McWilliams, professor of psychology at Rutgers University, author of numerous books and articles on clinical practice and diagnosis, and psychotherapist/psychoanalyst in private practice in New Jersey. Dr. McWilliams is "one of those people," for me, in the way that Mike Riera was "one of those people." You'll notice a theme throughout this work—the importance of mentoring and the transformative power of writing, to connect people and generations to one another, in the service of community.[2]

So Dr. McWilliams's work is going to help guide us through the question of what describes a mentally healthy teenager.[3] This work follows several of Nancy's presentations over the years, and is implied throughout much of her thinking about diagnosis and treatment. Though she primarily speaks about adults in her talks, the following 15 "mental health components" are fairly easily applied to a consideration of adolescents. You'll probably notice that all of these components are related and fit together. While that high degree of overlap suggests that the organization of components into a list of 15 is somewhat arbitrary, this list has the narrative power of illustrating how these components cannot be really separated; they point to and form a kind of "integrity" of the teenager and his or her mental health. That very sense of integrity—of being a whole (however incomplete)—is the idea you can aim for in assessing whether your particular teenager is mentally healthy. Another way of thinking of this is that as a healthy teenager makes progress in one of these areas, they will inevitably make progress in others.

The 15 Core Components of Mental Health

1. *They are able to love*

No, we're not talking about loving Call of Duty, Minecraft, your iPhone, or Facebook. Does your child have loving relationships with family members or peers? Can and do they make some sacrifices for that person, despite having other priorities?

Love, like work, is active and has its component parts. It is magical, but not simply magic. We cannot really love someone without being *toward* them in some way, and this directionality, this leaning toward another involves activities and behaviors, through which we perceive and otherwise experience the love of another or toward another. One way that children understand "being loved" (let's put it in quotes for now) has to do with a host of small micro-level behaviors we do with our faces when we turn in their direction. The *face* is not the only communicator/performer of those behaviors, because if that were true, then children blind from birth would not feel at all loved. So we have other sensory inputs, like touch, smell (yes, smell communicates all kinds of valuable information), and auditory stimuli. The sound of Dad's voice, Mom's smell, the sound and rhythm of the heartbeat, the degree of pupil dilation of the caregiver's eye, the temperature of the skin all convey *significant* data to the child (in some cases, prenatally), which allows the child the "building blocks" of the experience of being loved. And this interaction is by no means one-way.[4] The good and bad news is that these largely non-conscious processes (of perception and micro- and macro-level behaviors) continue throughout a lifetime. Your teenager is still (unless something is wrong) receiving these many messages. I argue throughout this book that these many non-verbal, non-conscious messages are louder and more clear than the verbal messages and they are being exchanged constantly—in work with your teen, in play and relaxation, and when you are just plain "loving" them. So, when I talk about the "capacity" or ability to love, I am talking not just about an overall articulated feeling ("I love Grandma") but about a host of other small and large behaviors, thoughts, and feelings, all with neurological correlates, conscious and nonconscious.

2. They are able to work

It might be nice if your child brought home some money from a job, but this isn't the only kind of work we're talking about. Can your teen work hard on a project, with some sustained effort, even if it's not as long as you'd like them to? Think about the parts of a "piece of work." You might think about the making of a meal, in all its aspects. Can your child identify some of the resources necessary to take the creation or maintenance of a meal from beginning to end? If they wanted fresh carrots, grown from soil, would they know how to get a seed? Would they know how to plant the seed and what kind of nutrients it needed to grow? Or know how to care for it while it grows or when to harvest it? Would they know how to access the information to learn how to turn a harvested carrot into a nutritious meal, with other ingredients? How to cook it? Can they gather the resources—people, information, tools, items from nature, manufactured products—to put it all together and figure out how to utilize them in a coherent fashion? Can they do these steps with a piece of music? A piece of art? A babysitting "business"? If so, they are able to work, which is, of course, more than "going to work." When you're thinking about "work" as a capacity, try to think first about whether they exhibit these skills and only then about whether you like what they're doing with the skills.

3. They are able to play and enjoy

The first two components come from the oral tradition of Freud's work—as Erik Erikson related that Freud was to have said that the goal of psychotherapy was to enable the patient "to love and to work."[5] It seems obvious now—at least to me—that being able to love and to work are inexorably intertwined. Our abilities to be industrious, to create, to sustain attention and cognitive energy are developed (or not) in relation to caregivers that model and provide these very components as we mature. Think of it this way: Work—by its very definition—requires mental and physical energy. The more our attention and energy are oriented toward scanning the environment to make sure we are not in danger, the more our energies are devoted to mere survival, the less attention and energy available for concentration on other tasks. Neurocognitive abilities related to survival develop first in the human being, for obvious reasons. If you're not alive, not much else matters. In order for attention and energy to be devoted to more complex tasks of development, we need to know we're safe and will survive. This fact alone weds the early childhood experiences of caretaking and love from the Other with the developmental "work" tasks necessary for brain and other cognitive and physical developmental progress. This could be thought of as an "attachment theory" perspective on the links between love and ability to work, and it has been well studied.[6]

But love and work and play are also forever linked (or should be, for purposes of study and living) because, as we know, the way that children primarily learn, love, and work is *through* play behaviors and the development of a psychological self at play, with others.[7] While the forms and types of play change and are changed by development, *play* has similar functions whether done by a 2-year-old or a 14-year-old, and those functions are legion: Play creates and extends new physical capacity; play brings new understandings of social relationships and social relating in general; plays produces pleasure and linkages in memory between experience and desire; play allows for the experience of "context" in learning of all kinds; play changes neurological patterns through the introduction of novelty, repetition, and consolidation of experience—and on and on in a list so long it could (and has) filled many books. *Playing* is a way of being toward and in the world and it is bound up in the other ways of being toward and in the world—loving and working. If your teenager can love and work, but cannot play, you don't have a fully healthy teenager in your house. I believe the same could be said for any other combination of these three factors, if one is missing.

4. *They are able to create and maintain attachments to others*

The processes of becoming and being attached with others[8] are complicated ones. Most psychologists look to work on attachment done by John Bowlby, Mary Ainsworth, and later, Mary Main for understanding how children form (or fail to form) and maintain attachments. Later work by Philip Shaver and Cindy Hazan extended these concepts of attachment to understand how adult romantic relationships form,[9] and psychologists like Peter Fonagy and Mary Target brought together insights from attachment and psychoanalytic theory to explain human beings' ability to attribute mental states such as beliefs, intentions, desires, pretending, knowledge, and the like, to oneself and others. This process—referred to as *mentalization* or having a theory of mind—includes the understanding that others have beliefs, desires, and intentions that are different from one's own. As you might imagine, this is crucial for the development of empathy and capacity for cooperation. Having a healthy and developed theory of mind really requires the fully functioning executive capacities of the prefrontal cortex. Until the brain is fully developed, teens and young adults can have difficulty guessing accurately what others are thinking, feeling, and intending, and often misinterpret cues like facial expression and tone of voice, especially with adults. It should make sense, then, that a highly functioning capacity for mentalization helps with the creation and maintenance of attachment. Less misunderstanding, greater ability to "read" others' mental states and needs, and more general ability to understand that we live in a world of others, with different and changing needs—these are all capacities that describe a healthy young adult, and make connection and cooperation much easier.

The quality, type, and length of attachments with others tell us a lot about a person's mental (and physical!) health. These ways of being with others are on a spectrum of "closeness" (from detached to clinging), "security" (from very unstable to highly stable), and "level of organization" (highly disorganized to highly organized or even rigid). Attachment theorists talk about secure, avoidant, ambivalent/resistant, and disorganized patterns of attachment, and in the last two decades began to study the interrelationship between temperament and attachment.[10] It can be particularly difficult for a child or a teen, for that matter, to feel intense fear with and intense need for the same person. Now, every child both fears and loves their parent. It goes with the territory. But I am talking about a situation in which the person who is providing physical punishment is continually threatening a child's physical safety. In this case, a child's attachment will most likely not be secure—the goal for healthiest "quality" of attachment. Securely attached infants, toddlers, and school-age children are much more likely to have more social success in forming relationships with others. And having a "secure base" to work from makes the process of acquiring motor and social skills more smooth. In teens, secure attachment is a factor that increases resilience—a kind of protection against the inevitable stresses and losses that come with adolescence.

If a child is attached with a "disorganized" pattern (such as those who are mal-treated, neglected, and abused might be), he or she is much more likely to have later dif-ficulties in relationships, often characterized by increased anxiety; in short, the world feels dangerous and the nervous system is continually in stress responding, looking to "fight, flight, or freeze." Children with disorganized patterns of attachment continually see relationships as a challenge to survival, not a place of relaxation, pleasure, or a "break" from difficulty—all things we hope to feel with close others.

Children with ambivalent attachments have elevated risk levels for those dis-orders characterized by self-attack, like depression, and those who are avoidantly attached more often act out and have trouble with others.[11]

In short, if relationships and safe interdependence on others is avoided, experi-enced as dangerous and chaotic or ambivalent and confusing, there is a significant narrowing down of what constitutes an acceptable "relationship." The ability to attach to and feel close to and understood by others, while still being able to have a strong, consistent sense that you won't be deeply hurt, abandoned, or neglected "on purpose," is therefore, one of the hallmarks of adolescent mental health.

5. They have a strong sense of self-efficacy[12] and authorship

While Dr. McWilliams speaks of agency,[13] I like to break that down and consider what it constitutes for teens, the feeling and sense that "I am choosing to act, and there is power in me to affect things." This connects very strongly to the idea that adolescence is defined as a search for identity—a cohesive sense of a self in the world, engaged and inspired, without having to know in advance that successful commerce with the world is guaranteed. A teen with a strong identity has the basic strength to persevere and feel able to act and choose, in an imperfect world, with an imperfect self. He or she is still the author of their life and that life *matters*. Erikson wrote of identity:

> As a quality of unself-conscious living, this can be gloriously obvious in a young person who has found himself as he has found his communality. In him we see emerge a unique unification of what is irreversibly given—that is, body type and temperament, giftedness and vulnerability, infantile models and acquired ideals—with the open choices provided in available roles, oc-cupational possibilities, values offered, mentors met, friendships made, and first sexual encounters.[14]

Teen life is filled with uncertainty and a foreshortened sense of time. This can create a tendency of thinking to be unnecessarily pessimistic, as a defense against the little and big disappointments of living. Adults (hopefully) have something that comes with time, experience, and a fully developed prefrontal cortex: *perspective*. A healthy adult realizes more easily that one lost chance or failed attempt doesn't mean "the end." They know that time changes things and reveals that sometimes things we think we wanted we're better off without. You know—all the platitudes (and truths) you try to tell your teen when they're let down or disappointed. But one reason why "being a teen" and "having depression" look so similar from the outside is the presence of what psychologist Martin Seligman called "a negative explanatory style" for both positive and negative events. That is to say, when things go well, a teen with a negative explanatory style will think she had nothing to do with the good thing (no sense of authorship), will think the good stuff won't last and is just a small part of her life. If something negative happens, that same teen will think it's all her fault (strong sense of authorship), is going to last forever, and will negatively affect all sorts of things in her life.[15]

You'll notice that when a pessimistic explanatory style predominates, the sense of efficacy is always diminished, but the sense of authorship changes depending upon whether the event was "good" or "bad." Got an "A" on a test? That's not about me. Got an "F" on a test? That's about me. If you're the author of events only when they go *badly* (a pessimistic explanatory style), then at least you can do something about the bad things. I can certainly understand this way of thinking.

It can be fairly effective—as a way of fending off the disappointments of daily life—to keep telling yourself that things won't work out and you don't have much power. I've seen numerous highly successful teens in my practice that use this "strategy." They often tell me it's better to predict disappointment and powerlessness and then be happily and pleasantly surprised. I think many of us can remember doing this when we were younger. The problem can be that it's hard to stop doing and our "magical thinking" can tell us—if things mostly do work out—that our worrying and not feeling efficacious or connected to our efforts actually help "cause" things to go right. While this attitude might help soften the blows, it also falsely diminishes a teenager's sense of power to decide and to do. A strong sense of "writing the story" of one's own life, and being able to accurately see one's role in things going well and badly allow for the ability to reflect on what happened, analyze the situation, and make adjustments. That whole process is about *engagement* in the world, which is one of the strongest protective factors for teenagers' mental health.

6. They are able to form fully developed, realistic ideas of themselves and others, which includes good parts and bad parts in the same person (and in oneself)

One of the signs of a person under psychological stress is the presence of what's called "all-or-nothing" thinking. If experiences (of oneself, of another, of the world in general) are felt as "all good" or "all bad," it generally makes it difficult if not impossible to have a sense of a solid, integrated identity. Why? Because if something (or someone) is all good or all bad, we usually want to possess them completely or reject them entirely. Both forms of relating to oneself, others, and the world cause a lot of pain. It means one must be constantly avoiding the bad and coveting the good and there's no in-between. If you feel something bad, you must remove that feeling completely, and will attack yourself if you can't get rid of the bad feelings. If you feel something good, you have to always feel that good feeling and will feel devastated if that good feeling doesn't last (and probably also attack and condemn yourself for failing to maintain the good feeling). This way of experiencing oneself in the world is not only painful, it also distorts perspective and time, since it's all about how you feel now, not how you felt in the past or might feel in the future. There is therefore no time for things to change and develop, and no sense of a self that lasts through time. It's all about *now* and whether things are good or bad, right now. That might sound kind of familiar if it sounds like being an infant—that's right. It's normal for infants, though, not for teenagers or adults.

Care of the self requires a view of the self over time, and a desire to be kind with one's body. This is difficult to do if you see yourself as bad at your core or cannot see that you're made up of both positive and negative qualities and worthy of care. If you don't believe you can change or know that living always includes both pain and pleasure, life will feel intensely frustrating.

On the other hand, teens with a sense of a self that persists over time (what's known in psychology as a strong sense of self and object constancy) know that they are responsible for taking care of themselves and others. They know (or come to know) that past hurts might be reparable, that pain today doesn't mean the end of pleasure tomorrow. They know that being or feeling alone today can be transformed by reaching out to someone. If a teen can hold in consciousness the image or idea or feeling of a kind or loving presence, they are safer and have real protection against the inevitable losses and disappointments of living. Suffering is so often mitigated by the imagination of a friend's smile or voice or a parent's face or a pet's sweet sounds or behaviors. But it is also assuaged by the remembrance of oneself, of a better time in the past or the imagination of more tender future. Both of those strategies require what's called "self and object constancy"[16] or the knowledge that we go on existing for others, and they for us, when we're not together. We don't disappear for others, or ourselves, when experiences are difficult or traumatic. This contributes in a powerful way to the sense of *identity,* and the related sense that I am a whole person, in a world of others. This is a bulwark against one of the most pervasive feelings of adolescence—loneliness.

I mentioned earlier that when a teen has a sense of "authorship" and efficacy, it follows that if things don't go well, there is something you can do about it. If you're "all bad," then what's the point? If you're capable of change, then you know that you, others, and the world always contain really excellent and really lousy things. When things are lousy, it helps to accurately assess what's up, what can be changed and what can't be changed. While you might not be able to change everything, you can change some things. So, an *accurate* view of "the good and the bad" increases a feeling of efficacy, and vice versa. It keeps us engaging with others and ourselves.

You might remember the story about the girl who would put her cell phone in a Ziploc bag and take it into the shower with her, so that she didn't miss a text. I'm not saying that this girl is not mentally healthy. But I am suggesting that if this feeling persists for the young girl—that she cannot really exist and her friends do not exist for her unless digital media can tether them to one another—it could be signaling a challenge to healthy self and object constancy.

Again, we're back to the link between engagement and mental health. Babies develop a sense of object permanence—the knowledge that things exist when they aren't visible to us—by making theories about what's going on and why it's happening. Theory-making is highly complex, a central way of understanding and responding to the world (and our own experience), and this book argues that we're born to do it. The psychologist Kurt Lewin once wrote, "There is nothing so practical as a good theory."[17] Researchers, philosophers, babies, children, teens, and adults all agree. If we're not able to analyze, evaluate, theorize, and try new behaviors or have different feelings as a result of that process, we're not healthy.

7. They are able to respond well to stress—both positive and negative stress—and be resilient and perseverant

Everyone experiences stress. "Stress" is one of those words that everyone uses but few really understand. "I'm so stressed!" has become one of those stereotypical teen phrases.

Dr. Mardi Horowitz is one person who understands stress very well. He's spent a good part of his long career researching and writing about what he calls "stress response syndromes." We might as well say, as long as life is happening, stress is always happening to our organism. Positive and negative events are both stressful—they impinge upon our being and call for a response. Most of those responses will be nonconscious, but some will be conscious, and those are the ones we usually care the most about. The question, though, is whether stress is perceived and responded to as problematic or dangerous. According to Horowitz, we need to process information about the event, as it unfolds, in order to make the determination of danger, risk, or trauma. As adults (or teens) it would be both inefficient and problematic just to shut down (dissociate) every time something happens. This is what newborns often do—they fall asleep in part to help limit the amount of stimulation being received and information processing to do. But we need to stay awake and able to respond, and that means processing what's happening, trying to make sense of it, usually by relating those new, strong experiences to things we already know. Each person responds to experience in a different way. This should be obvious for adults.

Imagine you're a camera operator, filming two people going to see one of those old-fashioned B-horror movies. One person watches the film with a look of intense engagement, excitement, and pleasure as they engage in the experience. The other person looks terrorized, worried, and scared and eventually has to leave. "Wasn't that a blast?" asks the first friend. The other answers, "Are you kidding me, that was that most *awful* thing I've ever seen! I never want to do that again!"

From the point of view of the observer, the two people saw the same movie, and had the same "experience." Both people experienced some elements of stress—physiological changes precipitated by release of catecholamine hormones (adrenaline or noradrenaline), causing increased heart rate, rapid pulse, pupil dilation, flushing, etc. But the person who experienced it as "a blast" interpreted their stress as relatively positive and related it to other experiences (like riding a roller-coaster, for example) associated with fun. This person's affect[18]—their bodily response to the stimulation, before they processed the experience in thought—was probably similar to the other person's. But the experience of emotions is a mixture of the physical response to the stress, perceived and interpreted by the individual. I think of it this way: Affect is *biology* and emotion is biology *plus* biography. In other words, if person two associates and remembers similar bodily experiences as when they viewed the horror film as being *dangerous,* it is not likely that they will find it a "blast!" They might not experience positive stress (*eustress*) but might instead experience a kind of traumatic stress (*distress*) and move into what Walter Bradford Cannon described as "fight or flight" mode.[19] Once we're busy processing that information as traumatic and dangerous, it's a very different process, with very different effects on our bodies and in our thinking.

So, what happens to your teen when he's "stressed"? Does he find it a challenge and kind of exciting or does he feel undone by it? Does your son (who plays the clarinet) feel kind of nauseous but also a little excited right before a performance at school, or does it occasion several days of withdrawal, school refusal, stomachaches, and tearful bedtimes? Does your daughter (who has a big speech coming up tomorrow in English class) say, "I've practiced a lot, I'm just going to do the best I can tomorrow and listen to some music and not think about this right now"? Or does she obsessively pore over the speech to the point of having a headache, refusing dinner, and trying to find ways to get out of showing up in class?

Everyone needs a way to deal with stress—a defense against stress when it feels like "too much," and a way to process the information contained in the challenge to our bodies/feelings. When we're relatively healthy, we have quite a few ways to deal with stress. We forget some stuff that's too hard. We make jokes about it. We might ask for help. We might sleep more during a stressful time…or exercise more. We might give ourselves little "treats" when we successfully get through a stressful event. All of these are pretty healthy ways of dealing with stress. And these are all pretty minor stresses. It would be great if all of America's young people had only to worry about clarinet recitals or speeches. But teenagers in America are dealing with considerably more than that, and some of those stresses are normal and expectable and some are not. Here's a glimpse of what teens face, in whole or part:

Dealing with rapid physical changes	Drug and alcohol use choices
Sexual orientation	Sexual activity
Gender issues	Driving and getting a license (if that's even possible)
Meeting parental expectations	Meeting peer expectations
Meeting teacher expectations	Status and worry over status
College/college choices (or not having any choices about this)	Jobs/job market/recession
Violence at home	Violence at school/bullying
Abuse	Neglect
Poverty	Racism and other prejudices
Homophobia	Sexism
Making and keeping friends	Dealing with arguments with friends and changing loyalties
Worry about friends	Romantic relationships
Depression	Anxiety
Other mental health challenges	Learning disabilities and other cognitive barriers to learning
Balancing their parents' needs with their own wishes and desires	Dealing with conflicting messages about sex
Dealing with conflicting messages about drugs	Worrying about physical appearance and fitting in
Divorce and family conflict	Sports, drama, clubs, Internet use, social networking, extracurricular activities (or the lack of those forms of connecting with others, or trying to balance all these with pretty much no time to do it all)

Whether your teenager is able to deal productively with these stressors says a lot about their level of mental health. Teens who are flexible in their responses to stress reach out for help from others, have a *variety* of strategies and defenses, and don't need to only shut down or act out in order to pull resources toward them. Teens who are responding to stress in a healthy way learn to ask and act on the following questions:

1. WHAT is most stressful for me?

2. HOW does the stress affect me specifically?

3. WHEN am I most vulnerable to stress?

4. WHEN is stress good for me?

5. WHAT can I think, feel, or do right now to reverse the stress process?

We're beginning to put some things together now about mental health. Healthy stress responding requires object constancy, since it involves the feeling of care for oneself and the expectation that others can help. It requires a strong sense of agency—the knowledge that action can ameliorate stress and that positive action can be successful. Stress is a part of life, and life is so much about love and work and play—all ripe opportunities for practice and learning. Moderate amounts of stress even improve our learning and performance, while too much stress can impair us in significant ways. Too little stress, and our motivation for action decreases. So, what's the right amount of stress? It's different for each person, and if your teen is healthy, they're engaged in the process of figuring this out. By the way, they'll need your help with this.

8. They have an assessment of themselves ("self-esteem") that is both realistic and reliable

Over 100 years ago the still-much-underrated American philosopher and psychologist William James defined self-esteem as a ratio:

> Our self-feeling in this world depends entirely on what we back ourselves to be and do. It is determined by the ratio of our actualities to our supposed potentialities; a fraction of which our pretensions are the denominator and the numerator our success:

> thus, Self-esteem = Success / Pretensions

> Such a fraction may be increased as well by diminishing the denominator as by increasing the numerator. To give up pretensions is as blessed a

relief as to get them gratified; and where disappointment is incessant and the struggle unending, this is what men [sic] will always do.[20]

We can feel good about our whole self—as a mixture of various selves, of varying strengths and weaknesses—in one of two ways: by increasing our "successful commerces" in the world, or by decreasing our pretensions (or our expectations for ourselves). This first point is extremely important because, in my opinion, it really accounts for why multiple attempts by government and private industry over the last 50 years to "increase self-esteem" have failed. When James talked about more success in commerce, he was speaking of the industrious in the world—real success at achievement, with others, and not just "feeling good" about yourself, no matter your lack of achievement. I agree with Martin Seligman and others who have criticized the so-called "self-esteem" movement.[21] This is the huge misunderstanding of self-esteem: that we can help children (or ourselves) feel better by simply "thinking good thoughts" about ourselves. It gets to a related point, too, deeply researched by Carol Dweck and her colleagues, about the problems with global, non-specific praise—praise that doesn't actually relate to real accomplishment in the world.

When my son was about 4, he brought a picture over to me for inspection. It was, as you might suspect, a bit of a mess: various overlapping crayon scribbles that, because they were done with such alacrity, tore through the drawing paper. He shoved the paper toward my eyes and said, "Look!" "Oh, that's beautiful, honey, thank you!" You know, a typical busy parent's response that says, "Yeah, that's fine but I'm busy now and maybe if I tell you how fantastic this is, you'll feel great and leave me alone." Well, what did you expect? I told you in the beginning of this book that I blew it all the time. So I gave him my boilerplate answer and I looked down at his sweet little face, on which shone a growing frown. "What's wrong?" I asked him. "It's NOT beautiful. It's a mess. Why are you saying it's beautiful?" Yikes. After that, we made a deal. "How about this?" I asked. "If it's kind of a mess, I'll say it's kind of a mess." He smiled and bounced down the stairs.

Even at 4, my son knew the emptiness of global praise and he knew his drawing sort of sucked. What he wanted was encouragement to continue his work, not undue praise for an activity that he knew was unsuccessful. When we tell our kids, "You can succeed at anything you want to do!" they know it just isn't true if their actual experience in the world does not match that overblown statement. That's one strong reason why consideration of self-esteem requires knowledge about how your child is actually performing on task understanding and completion, because that kind of industriousness and "successful commerce" is one big part of what allows a child to feel successful in the world. If a child's "great feeling" about herself doesn't match the reality of her performance, her self-esteem will not rise or it will be extremely fragile.

But the other part of the equation is equally important. We can decrease our suffering and feel better about who we are by realistically lowering our expectations, too. James wrote, in 1895:

> Many Bostonians, *crede experto* (and inhabitants of other cities, too, I fear), would be happier women and men to-day, if they could once for all abandon the notion of keeping up a Musical Self, and without shame let people hear them call a symphony a nuisance. How pleasant is the day when we give up striving to be young, - or slender! Thank God! we say, *those* illusions are gone. Everything added to the Self is a burden as well as a pride.[22]

Giving up "pretensions" of success at everything is one of the most difficult aspects of modern American teenage life—at least for those with privilege and some wealth. Part of the complex effects of racism includes daily attacks on genuine self-esteem that are not easy to throw off. I would venture to say that many African-American youth (and many children of color) do not have the same expectations for success in American culture as do their white counterparts, and so the issue of status and anxiety over status surfaces in complex ways among citizens of color.[23] And as we discussed in the chapter on Status and Identity, feeling bad about oneself has been made so much easier in America now owing to the explosion in what constitutes the reference group for deciding upon what success means and what successful people are entitled to.

I purposely am drawing attention to this issue because I believe that this particular component of mental health—realistic and reliable self-esteem—is under attack for all American teenagers. It's one of my primary reasons for writing this book and points to the importance of being able to think about who you are and what you do in the world in a way that is accurate and results in an overall positive feeling about "me" and "my place in the world." Recent articles and books that castigate the self-esteem "movement," and *only* draw attention to the more narcissistic, anxiety-fueled parental concerns over a misunderstood but valid concept (self-esteem) may help move product, but they are often unfair, unscientific, and lacking in nuance. A 2011 *Atlantic* piece is a good case in point. The author—herself a psychotherapist and parent—cites Jean Twenge and Dan Kindlon's work, too, but gives examples such as: If you rush in too quickly to comfort your toddler when she trips on a rock, then "these toddlers become the college kids who text their parents with an SOS if the slightest thing goes wrong, instead of attempting to figure out how to deal with it themselves."[24] It might be true that constantly rushing in too quickly to help your child with everything might make your particular child overly dependent, but the author's implication of general causality is facile and inflammatory. It may needlessly cause parents to feel guilty about whether their son or daughter is sending too many texts. It might help a few parents reflect on whether they are overinvolved in their child's life at college, but I think the way articles like this are written isn't worth the minor potential benefits for some parents.

9. They have a developing ethical "muscle"

Another axiom of this book is that human beings need (and often desire) a way of orienting themselves to the world that takes into account the inevitable conflict between needs. This conflict can be between human and "non-human animal," between human and "environment," or between human and human. In 1929 Freud wrote—after plagiarizing it from another, as Freud seemed fond of doing)[25]—*homo homini lupus:* Man is a wolf to his fellow-man. This fact forms one of the "discontents" of living in the world. Seneca the Younger disagreed when he wrote some 1,865 years earlier that "Man is something sacred for man." Which one was correct? Are they both accurate? What does it matter? What, if anything, would either of these views obligate us to? If we're all "just animals" then it's "kill or be killed" and get what you can for yourself while you're on the planet. If we're all holy, then the Sanskrit phrase *Tat Tvam Asi* would apply,[26] meaning that we are identical to the Divine, it is of and in us all, or, in Christian terms, we are all "made in the likeness of God." If this is true, what would this obligate us to do in terms of how we organize our lives and how we treat one another (and everything else of the world)?

Well, as of the writing of this book, those questions have not been definitively answered, although millions have thought and felt about, and hundreds of thousands have written about these questions. What seems to me less in question is that the *way* you answer the question—whether we are wolves or holy beings—has an enormous impact on what you do in the world and how you decide what to do. Will you consider others and their needs? Will you only consider the needs of others if they match your own?

I realize that I am being very subjective—and it is a subjective issue to consider the development of ethics as primary. That is exactly the point: I take it as an axiom that *being toward these questions* is *a,* if not *the* fundamental aspect of human mental health and it defines our very subjectivity. And this is a subjectivity that is oriented toward others and what is beyond others, to the holy, the sacred and the profane, simultaneously. This reminds me of what philosopher Emmanuel Levinas was addressing when he wrote, "Ethics is an optics."[27] My ethical stance toward the Other, and my responses to the Other, are the first and last perspectives for all other questions.

The ability to orient oneself toward another is a basic human capacity available from before birth, in various forms biological and psychological (at the very least).[28] Empathy is one piece of the ethical landscape. It is variously described (and increasingly scientifically studied) as theory of mind or "the ability to attribute mental states—beliefs, intentions, desires, pretending, knowledge, etc.—to oneself and others, and to understand that others have beliefs, desires, and intentions that are different from one's own."[29]

A robust capacity for empathy is comprised of many developmental milestones and is not just a given. It is being understood—as are so many things about human development—as a socially mediated neurological function, which can be amplified or diminished but which is part of our genetic heritage.[30] You'll recognize some of these developmental pieces related to brain development in several researcher/theorists' definitions. For example, Heinz Kohut called empathy the "capacity to think and feel oneself into the inner life of another person."[31] And more to our point, Simon Baron-Cohen[32] defined it this way:

> Empathy is about spontaneously and naturally tuning into the other person's thoughts and feelings, whatever these might be... There are two major elements to empathy. The first is the cognitive component: Understanding the other's feelings and the ability to take their perspective... [T]he second element to empathy is the affective component. This is an observer's appropriate emotional response to another person's emotional state.[33]

I like that definition because it emphasizes, like Kohut did, both the *feeling* and *thinking* aspects of being oriented toward others, and they toward us. Both definitions suggest that as empathy develops, so does the sense of obligation to the other—not in the sense of some awful burden I owe to someone, but in the sense of *consideration*. Real consideration means taking into account the fact that I and the other person feel and think differently, but we both feel and think. It can call forth an examination of what my needs and the other's needs might be, in *that moment* of consideration. It means that the development of ethics is an *active* and *always incomplete* process, in parallel to the ways that neurobiological capacities involved in the tasks that make up ethical relationships are always developing and plastic. If your son or daughter *does not have to think or feel,* in deciding how to approach, treat, care for, or refuse another, they are not exercising the ethical *muscle,* so to speak. In this view, mental health implies the *ongoing* activity of ethical development, including assessment, data gathering, theorizing, and behavior change. It implies failure and recalibration. Even if your teenager is mentally healthy, that does not mean that he or she will always think about you or their friends and "do the right thing." It doesn't mean that they'll refrain from asking you for a ride to a friend's house at 11 P.M., while you are in bed with the flu. But it does mean that if, over time and with your help, they aren't slowly "getting" that other people have lives, too, that their excitement might be someone else's fear, or that not everyone lives like they do (or wants to), there is something wrong with the ethical muscle and there is an impact on their mental health.[34]

10. They can recognize, understand, articulate, and manage their feelings and thoughts (and have the awareness of their bodies necessary to carry out these capacities) and have flexible means of doing so

I've referred to the importance of feeling (and affect) tolerance in many different contexts, calling it the most important (set of) tasks for teenagers to learn.

Teens are given multiple opportunities throughout the day to feel bad (and strongly so) about themselves and others. And as we saw in the chapter on Alcohol, Drugs, and Parties, teens certainly know of quick ways of changing their feeling states into something more tolerable. Their immature amygdalae and other parts of the brain increase the opportunity for misunderstanding their own and others' emotions. As we saw in our discussion of stress, everybody responds differently to different affective responses. You'll recall that a person's emotional response to a situation is about the person's biology *plus* their biography. One person's increased heart rate signals "excitement," while it quickly signals "danger" to another. The areas of the brain—like the periaqueductal gray (PAG) and the ventromedial prefrontal cortex—that are heavily involved in decision-making about fear, risk, and danger develop differently with each person, based upon experience, even though those areas have the same general *purpose* of function from person to person.

With the adolescent propensity toward misinterpretation—plus a lack of knowledge about how the *same* affect can produce different feelings and emotions in others—you can see that accurate empathy is a learned skill. It requires engagement and practice. But it's not just a matter of whether your teenager can understand and tolerate other people's feelings. We can and will have really difficult, painful feelings throughout our lives. Some of you will say, yeah, that's my definition of my own adolescence: difficult and painful feelings. Mental health for your teenager then must include a growing capacity to tolerate their own negative affect and thoughts and come to see them as parts of being alive. Why? I put a fine point on this before: If an adolescent cannot tolerate their own thoughts or feelings, they either move toward ending their life or they try to limit their negative thoughts and feelings with some behavior that quickly gets the reward center of the brain firing or "tunes down" the part of the brain that signals danger. You know the stuff: alcohol, drugs, sex, gambling, video games (and now, for some, tweeting, posting on Facebook, or checking email), or any addictive-risk behaviors.

I know it seems simplistic, but it's been my experience that sometimes explaining to a teen client that the nervous, sick feeling they get before they "put themselves out there" for evaluation of some kind, is a result of increased cortisol and adrenaline and isn't something to be too worried about. I explain the function of those two stress hormones—that they need some of the effects of the hormones to actually do a good job—and we talk about the difference between normal and abnormal stress. For some, this is kind of interesting and enough to get them to reinterpret those "sick" feelings as precursors to something exciting or potentially positive. The emotional relationship to public speaking or playing soccer or confronting a parent *changes* and may not have to be *avoided* or *denied* completely.

Another way that we all deal with difficult emotions and affect is to *project them* on to other people. We've all probably, at points in our lives, gotten really upset or angry with someone, only to later realize that we'd accused them of doing something that we were actually doing or feeling ourselves. We can use *projection* as a defense—and it's a pretty common defense—when we encounter something difficult to feel, like the sense of shame or humiliation…or feeling like a failure. Just think of how many times you've had this argument with a partner:

"Why aren't you more supportive? I didn't blow it, you did!"

"I *am* supportive of you. Who told you that you're really good at that and you should go for it? I don't know what you're talking about."

"No, you're not; you're always ready to tell me I can't do something or shouldn't try!"

"Um…honey…that sounds like you. You always tell me that you feel like you shouldn't even try or you put yourself down for something you're actually good at."

"Oh. Um. Yeah, that does sound like me."

So, we can use the defense of projection when we've made the (usually nonconscious) decision that it's better to get rid of a difficult emotion (like feeling shame/failure for something that didn't work out), than to *feel* it. Our good mental health and the good mental health of our children is in part dependent upon our ability to *tolerate* feelings and thoughts about ourselves and others and not to have to (always) project them onto others or the world in general. It means not having to condemn (and then "get rid of") difficult thoughts and feelings, so that we can work with them, learn from them, and transform them into positive action. Here's a thought I've had: *I wonder what it would be like if I just took that brownie in the display.* Here's another thought: *I wonder what it would be like to just take that money. Or to kiss that woman.* I could keep going. When someone has pretty good mental health, they know there's a difference between having a thought and acting on a thought. They don't have to either distort or deny or avoid the thought or feeling—all activities that take up an enormous amount of time and energy, time and energy that could be used for normal developmental tasks.

There are many different kinds of defenses against difficult thoughts and feelings and some are more adaptive, social, or dangerous than others.[35] Using *humor* is considered a defense against difficult feelings and thoughts, and the (somewhat) careful use of humor can connect us with others and help us feel less isolated in our own difficult thoughts and feelings. The use of displacement—taking your feelings about yourself or a situation out on someone else, a.k.a. the "kicking the dog" syndrome—is very common. You're mad at the guy who cut you off on the highway so when you get home you yell at your partner or daughter. We've all done it. But if you are *constantly* and *solely* doing that—taking your hard feelings out on others—it will likely be problematic for you in a variety of different ways. If you are constantly seeing others and the world as "all good" or "all bad"—the defenses of primitive idealization and devaluation—you will be suffering greatly and your mental health will be compromised.

While everyone suffers, *how* a person suffers has a lot to do with the defenses they use to understand, manage, and deal (or not deal) with the difficulties of life. It's good—mental health–wise— to have a *range* of conscious behavioral choices when responding to negative thoughts and feelings, as well as a range of nonconscious, more automatic responses to the same.

11. They have awareness of where they're at now and who they might want to be, and have some measure of the distance between the two

This particular component of good mental health is really an amalgamation of many or all of the other components. It is called different things, but following Dr. McWilliams, let's call this the *capacity for insight.* Most people understand the word insight from a "self-help" or therapeutic kind of context. When we have an "insight" in counseling or therapy we (usually suddenly) understand how things fit together in our life and we (usually suddenly) feel better. I don't actually think that therapy works this way, but it's a common understanding that the goal of therapy is "insight." One problem with this understanding is that it suggests that "feeling better" or "being healthy" is a process of thinking, primarily. You have to be *smart* to have insights or the therapist has to "give" you insights into your situation so that you can change or feel better. Being able to see "inside" yourself—to experience your own thoughts and feelings—is very important, but it's not really what Dr. McWilliams means, nor is it "enough" to feel better or differently about yourself, others, or the world. In McWilliams's view, insight describes something about the "space between where the person was and the ability to act on new abilities and qualities of a changed self."[36]

I remember having a conversation with a 16-year-old boy once who told me that he realized at some point he wasn't feeling as scared about the prospect of meeting new people when he entered a new situation. I asked him, "Do you remember when we first started meeting and you told me that you'd never be able to make friends—it just wasn't in your nature?" He laughed and said he remembered that. I asked him, "How did you get from *that* to *this*?" That is a question about *insight*, because it is a reflection on the space between his previous felt lack of capacity and the current quality of his changed self. Peter Fonagy and Mary Target wrote about the *reflective function* and its crucial role in the development of the ability to attach successfully with others:

> Reflective function is the developmental acquisition that permits the child to respond not only to other people's behavior, but to his *conception* of their beliefs, feelings, hopes, pretense, plans, and so on. Reflective function or mentalization enables children to *"read" people's minds....* By attributing mental states to others, children make people's behavior *meaningful* and predictable. As children learn to understand people's behavior, they can flexibly activate, from multiple sets of self-other representations organized on the basis of prior experience, the one(s) best suited to respond adaptively to particular interpersonal transactions.[37]

Having insight requires a consideration of self and others, so it is a process related to reflective functioning, mentalization, having theory of mind—all ways of saying *an awareness, memory, and ability to reflect on self and other, and organize that experience into ways of responding.* You can see the obvious link with the development of what I am calling the "ethical muscle," and why that is a neuro-psychological, developmental acquisition, as part of good mental health—and not a statement about the "goodness" or "badness" of a child. This also points to a bridge between the way children are treated and the possibilities for ethical development. As with most other disruptions and retardation of normal development, maltreatment plays an enormous role in limitations around ethical thinking, feeling, and behaving. The complexity of those limitations grows over time, and an adolescent who is maltreated is not only behind in the development of reflective capability but they are also in a much more powerful position to hurt others with their choices. Parents play a central, but not singular role, in helping their children understand complex relationships and work through ruptures in those relationships in ways that head toward repair, rather than disintegration.

12. *They have a developing theory of mind*

This is a component that is covered in all of the other components as well, and is one of the most critical parts of mental health and being a self in relation to others. Let's go over some examples here that point to difficulties in developing a *theory of mind,* or what Fonagy and others call *mentalization*. An immature mentalization capacity might sound like this conversation with a middle-school child:

> *Dad:* Hey bud. How was school today?
> *Franklin:* Bad.
> *Dad:* What happened? Why was it bad?
> *Franklin:* I hate Justin. That kid knows just how to push my buttons.
> *Dad:* What do you mean?
> *Franklin:* He makes me so mad. He just does exactly the thing that will make me angry. Like today he was ignoring me completely.
> *Dad:* I'm sorry. I know you have trouble with Justin. But are you sure that Justin is ignoring you on purpose?
> *Franklin:* What do you mean? He pisses me off when he won't talk to me. I hate when he does that to me.

This is an example of what Fonagy or McWilliams would call an "unmentalized" way for Franklin to understand the situation. Franklin thinks that because he feels angry—or any way for that matter—his friend Justin meant to make him feel that way. Franklin isn't thinking of Justin as a separate person with separate motives and feelings. It isn't too unusual for a middle-schooler to think that others mean to hurt them, but as teens get older, one wants to see increasing capacity and much more subtlety in understanding the mentality of other people as complicated and varied. It should be obvious that a growing capacity for mentalization goes along with a growing capacity for understanding and tolerating negative affect (or for enjoying good feelings, for that matter). As teens get older, they generally share less information with us as parents. This can leave them to primarily deal with their peers, as a way of processing difficult experiences. If they are good at thinking of multiple motives for behavior and separating their own feelings from the intentions of others, they will be more mentally healthy. An example of that would be shown in Franklin responding to his dad's questions with something like: "Justin was pushing my buttons again today. I get angry when he ignores me but I think things are rough for him since his mom got sick." This suggests some real nuance in understanding the motivations of others and recognizes another person as having a different and separate subjectivity than our own.

13. They have a reasonable balance between taking care of things on their own—and feeling good about that—and relying on the capacities and presence of others

Bear with me—this section is on the long side, but for good reason. The balance of depending upon close others and being self-reliant has enormous bearing on adolescence and thinking about the overall health of our teenagers. This is no more true than in the period of preparation for leaving home—arguably one of the most difficult developmental milestones for parents and teenagers alike.

We need others. We want to *feel* that we can do things "on our own," even as the mastery we seek involves help along the way. I work with many teenage girls, for example, who have relationships and feel they couldn't possibly survive without their partner. Yes, teens can feel particularly intensely attached in love relationships. But I have an equal number of adults who struggle *constantly* with discovering a balance between feelings of need and dependence on close others versus some admixture of good old American self-reliance and—for women who choose men as partners—some of the wisdom from feminist theory and struggle to "not need a man to be complete." One male client of mine recently pleaded with me, in quite some pain, "But isn't that what love is *all about*—the feeling that you can't live without your wife? I mean, why else would I get married; that's what love is."

This balance between what Yale Professor of Psychology and Psychiatry Sidney Blatt called "relatedness" (attachment) and "self-definition" (separation) is a key component in the development of mental health.[38] This is a lifelong process, and one that significantly influences not only our mental but also our physical health, which are, in any case, always intertwined. Blatt believed that leaning too heavily on one or the other pole constituted risk for the development of mental health problems like depression and severe anxiety.

For many decades, parents were told by folks in my profession—and it became part of the common lore—that when kids reach adolescence, they begin to *separate* from their parents, psychologically, in preparation for physical separation. In Western, highly industrialized cultures, this was seen as a normal developmental achievement, as it still is today. This evolutionary-oriented behavior, which Professor Linda Spear refers to as the "expansion of interests to more distant and unfamiliar regions," is a feature of emerging adolescence (across species) and represents a sexual strategy to avoid inbreeding.[39] Adolescents seem to leave home; this is normal. But for human adolescents, physical and psychological "separation" has come to be conflated. We don't really separate, in the sense of being torn asunder. I have come to prefer the term *related autonomy*,[40] because, albeit clumsy and jargonish, it more closely describes what happens with us—*par excellence*—in adolescence. Adolescence is about defining who you are, what your self is made of and what it will do, in relation to and over against others (especially *close Others*).[41]

Since we are, in my view, always in relation to parents, caregivers, or close others regardless of physical proximity, we are always engaged in this dance between self-definition and self-in-relationship. We want to feel and be autonomous actors, the authors of our choices and the trajectories (and stories) about our lives, but as humans we live in a *social* world. We can't go off and not be social group animals for a while and then become human again. This is one of the greatest difficulties of adolescence—discovering a balance between self needs and the needs of close others—and it's captured so well in my favorite definition of maturity as "doing what you want, even if your parents want you to do it."

In Chapter 3, we imagined the inner dialogue of a child, over a period of years, sounding something like this:

> I am a teenager. I am almost an adult. My job is to be and become my Self. My very own Self. I want to do it myself. I *should* do it myself. But I need my parents. I need my friends a lot, but that's not really a problem to me. I guess I need teachers; I don't know, it depends upon the teacher. I love some (or all) of my extended family and care what they think, too, but not like with my parents. *I hate disappointing them.* I'd rather they punish me and get it over with than "be disappointed." I just want what I want, and want it *now* and I wish they'd understand. What I want is increasingly different than my parents. I say I don't care, but I do. *It makes me feel guilty.* But instead, I usually get angry, then they get angry back and sort of punish me and strangely I feel better...kind of a distraction from the guilt, and I feel more okay to want what I want. I'm selfish. No, I'm not; they're selfish. It will be so great to leave—*I think.* I really want them to be happy. And happy with me. I want to be happy, too. *How do I have both of those?* Thank God it's the weekend.

This inner dialogue, so to speak, is the result of an ongoing (normal) series of conflicts and questions that describe the formation of a healthy sense of *related autonomy*—or balance of self and self-in-relation. Figuring out this balance and having related autonomy has a strong bearing on whether intense guilt and psychopathology emerge, or a feeling of strength, self-direction, and authorship ("efficacy") and a good feeling about needing others.[42]

Adolescence is traumatic, for reasons we discussed in the chapter on Family. I am defining trauma as falling upon a continuum of "threats to engagement with (especially close) others." One can imagine, for example, developmentally appropriate separation as (relatively) traumatic, as calling for responses from the care-giving environ, and as (potentially) creating both developmental crises and opportunities. An example is found in a child going off to preschool for the first time. This is a (relatively) traumatic event usually for parent and child, and not because your child was crying for an hour and didn't want you to leave or because you hid in the bushes and looked into the childcare room. It's because it's a *threat to ongoing engagement with close others*. Your child doesn't yet know you'll be returning and doesn't know what will happen until that time. You don't know your child will be okay; you hope she will, but you can't be sure. Those are minor threats to safe engagement that most all of us survive. But these "threats" occur for the rest of our lives, and so we constantly have relatively small or large crisis or "traumas" to contend with. It's one reason why I think that *living is grieving*.

Humans can and do continually regulate their nonconscious mental life in order to seek ongoing safe engagement with others. More and more science is showing how we are born to do this by paying exquisite attention to the faces of close others—including eye movement and gaze/contact, movement of the brow and small musculature of the face, slight openings of the mouth, and a host of other bidirectional clues that set numerous neurological, gross physical and emotional processes in motion in a cycle of responding and counter-responding.

So, threats to the physical and neuropsychological processes involved in seeking safe engagement are what I'm calling *trauma*. Trauma can—but doesn't always—help produce mental illness. Risk and resilience factors always come into play to help determine whether one person's relative trauma (threat to ongoing engagement with particular, close others) is another person's trigger for psychopathology, like depression or post-traumatic stress.

But in the realm of mental health, it's important for you to know (as a parent) that there is a particular way that we all respond to traumas (big and small). If a particular thought or belief or physical state (affect) or emotion or other mental content is assessed to be too dangerous—and remember that this assessment is always taking place nonconsciously—if it is judged to be a threat to maintaining a tie to a significant relationship, whoever the "offending party" is gets uninvited to the dance. In other words, until a person judges it is safe to think, wish, feel, believe, or otherwise be aware of something, those things will be banned from awareness. This "banning" (which includes one of our normal defensive processes we discussed earlier) is preferred to the severing of a tie to a close other.[43] That's often not a bad thing. If something is too painful to know or feel about our parents or our partner, maybe it's okay not to think or feel it. But if you are constantly being forced to deny your own experiences or your differing needs or your wishes for yourself, in order to preserve a relationship, then your own development becomes strained and can sometimes stall and delay, in the service of expending more conscious and nonconscious energy and time toward making sure others near you are not being hurt by you being who you are. Disruption in the ability to exercise or practice attuning to what one feels and thinks necessarily results in (degrees of) disruptions in engagement. In short, it hurts and it's dangerous. Remember, "feeling, understanding, articulating, and managing" affect (and emotions) is the most important task of adolescence, because if teens don't do it in healthy ways, they'll do it in unhealthy ways.

Sometimes the "hurt" can take the form of holding back the pursuit of an otherwise normal developmental goal—like, say, leaving home. Sometimes that "hurt" can take the form of a physical hurt, like chronic headaches or stomachaches/gastrointestinal upset. Sometimes that "hurt" can be a constant, pervasive condemnation of your own needs and feelings, as in certain kinds of debilitating depression. Sometimes it doesn't feel like "hurt," it feels more like "worry" and it takes the form of an actual anxiety disorder. Sometimes the balance shifts so far to the side of doing what will please the other, your teen can be physically and emotionally hurt by that other person—that's called abuse or domestic violence. It's rather shocking that a year 2000 study indicated that at least 25 percent of teens aged 12–19 reported experiencing violence in a relationship.[44] All of these challenges to mental health, therefore, have a relationship to how well your teenager can find *related autonomy,* or a balance between self and other.

Michael Friedman's work outlines a view of guilt, altruism, and psychopathology (all alluded to in my imagined inner dialogue of your teenager), to argue that both Freud and sociologist W. Trotter were correct: We are aggressive animals concerned with our own survival, and "herd" animals concerned with the perceived needs of others, not because we choose to be, but because *we must be.*[45]

The conceptualization of trauma in this book draws upon features of the above theories but pays special attention to the interpersonal aspects of how trauma begins and points to a *continuum* of severity. It is thus possible to speak of a *relatively* severe traumatic event, grounded in altruistic concern, occasioned by loss, engendering feelings of helplessness and loss of control in relation to the witnessed or imagined suffering of another in which thoughts, wishes, feelings—and new neural connections— are created, maintained, or strengthened. Adolescence is a relatively traumatic developmental period, then, with leaving home/senior year a particularly intense version of this trauma.

Your child wants to leave home, and probably part of them doesn't. They want to be dependent and a large part of them does not. They want to do it on their own and they want help (as long as it's not too directly from you and you don't take too much credit for it). They feel guilty for leaving you behind. They really do. They wonder if you'll be okay—that's the altruistic concern, which, I believe, we carry from birth: We want more than anything for our parents to be happy. This also is has an evolutionary function; it's not just a feeling of altruism for close kin (although it is that, too).[46] If you're happy, you're more likely to care—and care well—for a dependent being in your charge. This feeling of guilt for leaving another behind is sometimes called "separation guilt" or *survivor guilt*. It is based on the (false) idea that there are only so much of the good things in life to go around and that if one person has good things, another must suffer. It sees happiness and access to all the good things in life—including the pursuit of normal developmental goals—as being a zero sum game. If I leave, you lose. If I'm happy, you're unhappy (or less happy). If you get your way, I won't get mine. It's a kind of all-or-nothing distortion in our thinking and it's characteristic of thinking under stress. It's also a characteristic pattern of thinking for animals (such as humans) that live in groups and live their lives in close proximity to others.[47]

It's probably pretty clear now how the balance between self-definition and self-in-relationship is related to good mental health and how complex this balancing act can be. The balancing act is always about *adaptation* to a world of others. And you know from reading about adolescent brain development how "massively plastic" your teen's brain is in adaptation to reality, and how much "reality"—culture, environment, experiences with close others—changes things at the cellular level on up. It seems to be what we are designed to do, rapidly and intensely during adolescence. Dr. Harold Sampson, one of the kindest and smartest folks I've had the pleasure to work with and learn from, puts it succinctly:

> Adaptation to reality is a central psychic concern, and a central organizer of mental life, from birth.... As part of this effort, [one] seeks to acquire reliable knowledge (i.e., beliefs) about [one's] *interpersonal* [italics mine] world. These beliefs are central to a person's conscious and unconscious mental life. They organize personality and psychopathology.[48]

14. They feel for themselves—and others feel, too—a sense of passion and "aliveness" to their life

Another colleague and mentor of mine, Dr. Harvey Peskin, has written for years about the ongoing effects of intense, prolonged interpersonal trauma. He speaks in particular of victims of the Holocaust who, many decades "after" the event, are like the "walking dead." For some, intense and unspeakable trauma may leave the body present but without vitality, without a sense of excitement for a future. For those who survived the Holocaust, this seems understandable. But this loss of passion and vitality seems less comprehensible in a young person who has barely had a chance to cultivate links in the world between desire, pleasure, curiosity, industriousness, and action.

Christopher Bollas, a psychoanalyst and a wonderfully passionate writer, wrote in *The Evocative Object World*:

> You are riding in a train, absorbed by the sights flying by. It passes an airport, crosses a canal, traverses a meadow, climbs a long, low hill graced by rows of vineyards, descends into a valley choked with industrial parks... Each location evokes sets of associations. The airport reminds you of the coming summer and your holiday abroad. It recalls the plane that brought you to this part of the world in the first place; the never-ending expansions of airports... Crossing the canal you think of a longed-for trip on a canal boat, yet to be accomplished, signifying the potential remainders of a life... You think of your mother and father-in-law's former house which was alongside a small canal. You might also think of the dentist and a root canal. And so it goes.[49]

The description of everyday kinds of associations might seem banal, but for me they make me long to travel. Alain de Botton is particularly good at describing the longing for travel, as well as thoughts and impulses to the contrary.[50] But what Bollas and de Botton are also pointing to is a kind of parallel evocativeness between the world of objects and our inner worlds of thought and feeling—and the creative impulses that join the two. One could say that there is a vitality in the description, but it could also be said it is a *description of vitality*—a vigorousness about and in response to living, both to the fact of living and to what is encountered on the journey.

When you look at a healthy young child of 4, for example, you see this vitality, with a remarkable integrity. "He is so...himself!" you might say, watching your own 4-year-old bound toward you, arms flung open wide, all eyes and cheeks and limbs flying in excitement to relate his worlds—inner and outer, which really don't have fine distinction—to you, for you...because he *has to*. That kind of wholeness, integrity, and vitality, if it's present and not captured by physical or mental illness or the cruelty of all types of violence or war, is unmistakable. If you've felt it in yourself, you can say, "I know the feeling—of being alive!"

Many parents of adolescents are either grieving the loss of the expression (to them) of this vitality or they are wondering if it is there. If it never seems to have been there, you might already know something is wrong—probably one of the mental health issues listed above.

But it's not unusual for a teenager to *hide* signs of vitality from a parent or caregiver. After all, showing you what she loves *potentially* exposes your daughter to your disagreement, disapproval, faint praise, or condemnation. It also exposes her to the vulnerability and risk of your *approval*. I often think of one of my prototypical "parenting teens" stories in relation to this kind of "hiding" and the maturity definition of "doing what you want, even your parents want you to do it."

When my son was about 15½ he came home proud and excited from one of the local thrift stores, wanting to show me his most excellent purchase of some hiking boots—which he'd obtained at a most excellent price. I was happy for him, truly happy; I know how exciting a good thrift store find can be. But I told him to hang on—I had something to show him, too. I ran into the bedroom and grabbed a pair of identical hiking boots that I'd bought a few months earlier. I thought it was so cool that we had similar taste in shoes. Needless to say, I never saw him wear *his* shoes again.

Trite, but it makes the point. Sometimes as a teen you have to hide even your little enthusiasms, for fear your parent will co-opt *your* successes and *make them their own.* The point, you remember, is for your teen to develop his or her *own* sense of identity, not to mirror your identity or take their cues from you, at least not directly. It's very hard for teens.

Think of it like this: They have a job to do. You hired them, and it's an incredibly important job and they know it. They have to succeed at the job. But your teen cannot ask you directly how to do the job. There isn't really a job description, either. It's a huge organization—your teen arrives at the job and everybody is busy and they pretty much look like they know what they're doing and they must get to work, too. So, they can't ask you for help but they have to please you (and their co-workers) or at least figure out the priorities in relation to who gets pleased and what the consequences of different levels of success might be. How are they going to learn the job and be successful, without asking the boss directly for instructions?

That's kind of the task for American adolescents. Their job is to develop a sense of their own identity, as over against yours. For reasons we've discussed in this book, they have to do it without asking you directly: Who am I supposed to be and how do I do it, with all these pressures and varying expectations and conflicts of needs? Nonetheless, they have to figure out all the challenges, and adjust to their changing bodies and feelings and thoughts, in whatever social setting they happen to be, which is either overflowing with, adequate, or sorely lacking the necessary resources for the job.

Well, that's adolescence. What would you do? (What did you do?) Where are they going to get the information to do the job? I'll tell you where—the Internet. Why? We already figured out why. It's on and available 24/7, 365. Don't know what to do? Google it. Are you in one of the 12.4 percent of American households that don't at present have Internet access or a smart phone or tablet?[51] Then what would you do? Same thing teens do to get answers to other questions—they ask their friends for information. And I know if I wanted accurate, up-to-date, scientifically studied information, say, on birth control or responding to your partner's eating disorder or self-harm behavior, I know what I'd do—okay, wait for the punch line: *I'd ask a 15-year-old, right?*

Okay, great, so I'm a teen, trying to figure out "My Job" and I've basically got the Internet and my peers. (Let's not even get into how much the Internet is absolutely jam-packed with biased, inaccurate information.) What about teachers? Yes, your teens will ask teachers questions about themselves—if they trust them. Sometimes your son or daughter will trust a teacher or coach too much, though, and ask that teacher or coach things they should be asking of a parent. And sometimes teachers and coaches are not yet fully aware of all the issues surrounding good boundaries, and then you have can have young, highly relatable adults in positions of great power and influence with your teen, who is rapidly developing his or her sexual and social self. That is a recipe for some problems. It's not that teachers shouldn't be in advisory roles to youth. In fact, it's one of the most important roles they can play with teenagers. But in my view, they cannot and should not be *friends* with teenagers. That is a very unequal relationship of power and authority with a teenager, and when things go wrong, it's the adult that must bear the brunt of that responsibility. Teens look adult-like, but they are not the same as adults. *In so very many ways, they are not the same as adults,* even as their capacities can outstrip an adult's.

So, let's get back to this issue of hiding vitality. Teens do it to a degree with their parents. They might let it shine with a sports, music, drama, or dance coach (if they trust the coach). They might let it shine (at times, in certain muted ways) with a teacher, as long as they're not *too* worried about being evaluated negatively for their choices and enthusiasms. They're mostly going to let it shine *with their close peers or alone,* depending upon their temperament, the setting, their cultural background, etc. So, if you don't see your son's vitality and aliveness like you used to, ask your son's friend's *parent* if he or she sees it. Don't pry too much, but ask them if your son seems happy and engaged. Ask a favorite teacher, coach, or aunt or uncle about how your son seems with them and try not to express your jealousy to your child (that everyone else gets the good stuff, while you get the complaining and arguing). I'm not saying you should just suffer alone this very real grief around how teenagers can go underground with their enthusiasm.[52] I'm just saying that you might want to get other people to talk to about this, so that your teen doesn't feel (more) guilty for being happy with people other than you. This is another one of those examples of "separation" guilt or a kind of "survivor guilt" and when our kids have to put away their happiness because it makes you jealous and upset, it's really lousy for their development.

As I'm sure you know, and I mentioned earlier, many things can occasion the absence of aliveness, but there are common factors on the list of neuropsychological reasons for the lack of aliveness, and those have to do with defenses against traumatic experience. If your teen experiences threats to ongoing engagement with people important to him or her, there can be *trauma.* There are many ways to defend against trauma and its effects, and *dissociation* is one very powerful, primitive defense.

Dissociation is part of the overall stress response syndrome linked with the "freezing" part of "fight, flight, or freeze." You can enter a state of weak or strong dissociation. When you sit and "space out" and look out the window, you're in a weak version of that state. Things seem to just happen and you're not terribly connected to them. It can be kind of (or very) pleasant. Babies do it when they're overstimulated and so do children and adults. But when dissociation gets really serious is when your brain thinks that a tiger has your neck in its jaw and the tiger is about to bite down. In other words, if you're at that point, it's all over. There is absolutely nothing left to do but wait to die. The perception of time slows down. Our perception of space changes. Our hearing changes. If you see a tiger and you are a few hundred yards away, you will likely get a huge shot of adrenaline and cortisol in your nervous system and your large muscle groups will be activated. Glucose will flow away from parts of your brain associated with nuanced thinking (why bother, after all?) and blood will flow to the periphery of the body, to prepare for flight (or fight). Personally, if I had a few hundred yards' head start and a jeep, I'd flee, but that's just me. If you can't escape (or think you can't escape) and your brain has decided it's all over, then the changes associated with "freeze" will set in, activating a much more ancient[53] part of the vagal nerve response.

In our normal state of experiencing things—where say, you go into a store—you remember the experience as a *whole*. You connect visiting the store with the time of day, the sounds and sights and smells of the store, and you can probably recall the events that happened there, in some roughly linear order. You had the experience and now you have *declarative* (or explicit) memories (facts about what happened), sense memories (smell, sights, tastes, etc.), and a coherent narrative for the trip to the store. But in a state of dissociation, things are experience as disassociated. You might have heard something, but don't connect it with what was actually happening at the moment. You might smell something but have no memory later of how you felt smelling this smell. Your thoughts and memories and feelings and story about what happened are not all together, available to you, so that you are "there" having a full experience.

When teenagers (or adults) are lacking vitality, it could be that the defensive capacity to dissociate is at work. *Dissociation* is not the only defensive procedure that can rob a person of their connection, engagement, or feeling of vitality and aliveness, but it is a particularly powerful process and it usually happens when we're significantly overwhelmed and/or traumatized, and we're (consciously and nonconsciously) hoping to avoid that kind of experience ever again.

But what about teenagers for whom there seems to be little or no apparent trauma in their lives? Psychologist Donald Winnicott's work suggests the idea that a person can be normal without figuratively being alive or vital.[54] It seems he had in mind the teenagers that psychologist Madeline Levine profiled in her 2006 book *The Price of Privilege*. The subtitle of that book is the point, though: *How Parental Pressure and Material Advantage are Creating a Generation of Disconnected and Unhappy Kids*. I've seen my fair share of children in this state of "unaliveness" about which Dr. Levine wrote. Now, Dr. Levine doesn't need me defending her, but when I presented at a conference with her—to the very group of highly successful, affluent parents that she was writing about—and I listened to her research and approach, it was clear that she did not write that book to bash or blame parents or destroy the notions of "hard work" or "rewards" and "success." She was, however, pointing to a strong correlation between being given everything you could want—or given it too soon or in the form of global praise, or being rescued from failure—and a significantly increased risk for the kinds of feeling states that look like "deadness" in adolescents. My clinical experience supports the notion that psychiatrist and educator Rudolf Dreikurs pointed to with his rule of thumb "Never do anything for a child what he can do for himself."[55] In my view, Dreikurs was one smart cookie and one of the original parent educators who translated psychologist Alfred Adler's work into practical thinking about parenting that is still fresh and salient 50 years later. But I don't know about the "never" part, because sometimes it benefits parent and child to actually do some things that both parties know the child can do. It's sort of a nice, kind, and cozy thing to do. But when it's a steady diet of doing for the child what they can do, it's called *overindulgence*, and it has nasty consequences, including robbing your child of initiative, will, perseverance, knowing their feelings, dealing with failure and correcting, understanding emotion, and developing a strong, solid identity that contains the experience of *aliveness*.

15. They have the ability to perceive and deal with failure, loss, and things larger than themselves

Speaking of overindulgence, here's our last constituent part of adolescent mental health to consider. And it's a big one. I mentioned earlier that I felt that *living is grieving*. The Buddhists say, "All life is suffering." In *Civilization and Its Discontents*, Freud wrote that:

> We are threatened with suffering from three directions: from our own body, which is doomed to decay and dissolution and which cannot even do without pain and anxiety as warning signals; from the external world, which may rage against us with overwhelming and merciless forces of destruction; and finally from our relations to other men [sic]. The suffering which comes to us from this last source is perhaps more painful to us than any other.[56]

Freud goes on to say that we've failed miserably in preventing this suffering and that perhaps it's because of our own selves—a "piece of unconquerable nature…our own psychical constitution."[57]

Seems like between Freud and the Buddhists we've covered just about all the forms of suffering. Let's see, it's all of life and it come from the natural world itself, others, and ourselves. Check. We should just say what someone's grandma once told me: "Life's got a paddle fit just right to everyone's behind."

I know, life is filled with pleasure, too, and beauty, and the glory and majesty and grace of God—I'm not saying this ain't so. I'm just saying, you pretty much have to agree to the suffering part, even if you're not suffering (right now). That's why I think living is grieving. There is always some loss, something to let go of or to surrender to.

Alain de Botton, tour guide for inner and outer worlds, once again takes us to just the right place:

> …the behaviour of others and our own flaws are prone to leave us feeling small. Humiliation is a perpetual risk in the world of men. It is not unusual for our will to be defied and our wishes frustrated. Sublime landscapes do not therefore introduce us to our inadequacy; rather, to touch on the crux of their appeal, they allow us to conceive of a familiar inadequacy in a new and more helpful way. Sublime places repeat in grand terms a lesson that ordinary life typically introduces viciously: that the universe is mightier than we are, that we are frail and temporary and have no alternative but to accept limitations on our will; that we must bow to necessities greater than ourselves.[58]

What de Botton describes here as the *sublime* is an answer to the depressing thought or feeling that "surrender" to something larger than ourselves is a weakness or solely a *loss*. When something is so much larger than yourself and has the power to begin and end you literally or figuratively—the ocean, the desert, love[59]— it's not a *problem*, it's something you respond to. So we add—aided with the wise vision of Dr. McWilliams—that the ongoing adaptation to a world and forces bigger than us is our last component of assessing mental health. This adaptation is largely unconscious but it is so necessary, it takes up much of our conscious attention as well—we just tend to fight that.

This is highly "philosophical," and *very* practical. I understand that I didn't just give you a list of signs and symptoms of mental illness, so that you could see if your child has AD/HD or bipolar disorder, for example. These lists are easy to find in some of the books recommended at the chapter's end.

We've seen described throughout the book a theory of practice moving toward (approximating) correction and conscious adaptation to the situation. It's how we function, when we're healthy. It's what we want, even if we don't sit down and say, "Yeah, I want a better capacity for mentalization in 2013" or "I think I'll deal with grieving and acceptance in relation to the sublime during my trip this year." But I believe it's what we want, and I believe it's what your teenagers want. And so much of your *helping* your teenagers develop these capacities rests upon just knowing that *that is what they're really aiming for.* You son might talk about wanting the newest Nike Air Jordans or your daughter might talk about just *having* to go to meet a particular friend or she'll die, or you may argue with them about cell phone use or drug use or curfew or 1,000 other things. It might not stop your child from working your last nerve, but it can make a difference in you staying close and connected if you know that all these "little" things are actually signs of their development—either progressing or moving in a problematic direction. The more reliably you are able to catalog the behavior and what it might mean in terms of their development, the less you'll take it personally and feel offended or disrespected by it. It doesn't mean you should tolerate mistreatment and disrespect. It just means that understanding their affect and what it's about and what they're working on can get you *interested* and a bit calmer and more engaged…and that's just better for everyone.

You can help your son or daughter (and yourself) by trying to slow it all down and take some time to think about which of these 15 components of mental health your child is working on, when they're doing what they're doing, because they are working on it all the time, 24/7, 365 days a year.

It's important to say that these are not the only components of adolescent mental health, but they arguably cover the *major* developmental capacities that describe a healthy teen. Many of the so-called disorders that are characteristic of the adolescent period, as well as many, if not all of the "Big Problems" that confront parents, have to do with one or more of the components of adolescent mental health listed above.[60] Clear thinking and conceptualization—thanks to Dr. McWilliams—about what makes a teen psychologically healthy also provides something of a roadmap for clinicians, teachers, parents, and other caring adults to intervene positively in the lives of those teens. That's why thinking about teens and mental health only in terms of "problems" or diagnoses doesn't work. It gets us too focused on just relieving symptoms and doesn't shed enough light on where we're headed (in helping our teens). I've never met anyone who is perfectly mentally healthy. It's about having goals and something to aim for. Otherwise, as Yogi Berra is quoted as having said, "You've got to be very careful if you don't know where you're going, because you might not get there."

Practical Help Tips

1) Thinking about what mental health means for a teenager is just as important as thinking about the "problems" of adolescence. Good mental health is not just about the absence of problems—it's about the development of positive capacities in an imperfect environment. It's about *fidelity.*

2) A shorthand "mental health" test includes an assessment of how your teen can love, work, and play alone and with others. Can your child *combine* these three important human activities? Does doing one activity crowd out all others?

3) Teens and adults think and feel in different ways, from a neurobiological point of view. No, that doesn't mean your teen is "crazy." It does mean that applying to your teen your standards or methods for thinking, feeling, and figuring out what to do is not really fair or accurate. Your teen doesn't actually function in the same way you do—through no fault of her own.

4) What looks like a big personality problem may be a stress problem. One of the signs of a person under psychological stress is the presence of what's called "all-or-nothing" thinking. If experiences (of oneself, of another, in the world in general) are felt as "all good" or "all bad," it generally makes it difficult, if not impossible to have a sense of a solid, integrated identity. This condition can make you think, "What the [bleep] is wrong with this kid?" The answer might actually be: "I'm stressed, and my capacity for thoughtfulness, balance, and perspective is not home at the moment. Please leave a message." Try to help your child lower their stress level. Do the same for yourself. Then, and only then, make an assessment about their overall state and capacity. In this instance, time and patience are your friends.

5) When you're really getting irritated and frustrated with your teen, look at that long list of what teens face. I know many parents think teens have it easy. Everything is done for them and they have everything they need and often everything they want. And yes, some teens are overindulged and overprotected. But if you think your teen has no reason to be stressed, just take a look again at that list. Almost every teenager in America is dealing with many of the items on that list, on an hourly basis.

6) Teens (and parents) who are dealing adequately with the stressors in their lives learn to ask and act on the following questions:

a) WHAT is most stressful for me?

b) HOW does the stress affect me specifically?

c) WHEN am I most vulnerable to stress?

d) WHEN is stress good for me?

e) WHAT do I need to or can I think, feel, or do right now to reverse the stress process?

7) I've referred often to the importance of tolerating and working with affects and feelings, calling it the most important (set of) tasks for teenagers to learn. Teenagers need your help in understanding their physical responses to situations (understanding their affect), their experience of those responses in the context of their lives (understanding their emotions), and managing those situations. Teenagers need help articulating their emotions and knowing where in their bodies those emotions take root. They need help dealing with strong emotions, especially strong negative emotions, in ways that are safe. Their good mental health and the process of identity formation depends upon this.

8) In the realm of mental health, everyone uses defenses against painful experience. Defenses are normal. It doesn't help to tell yourself to stop being defensive. It doesn't help to tell your teen, "Stop being so defensive." It does help to wonder: What am I defending against and how can I feel safer? It does help to get your teen to wonder: What is he feeling he needs to defend against and how might he feel safer to experience it—without having to defend so much? It helps to wonder: *Why* do I feel I have to defend against that feeling or thought, rather than just having it and moving on?

9) Try to focus on helping your teen deal with loss, not avoid it. Big and small losses and "failures" happen all the time, every day. If we are busy avoiding this fact then we are busy teaching our teen to get *anxious* about losses—rather than to stay calm and accept and deal intelligently with what comes, without getting undone.

10) Teens need practice, to develop well and healthfully. Try not to do for them what they can do for themselves or others. That doesn't mean you should neglect them. That's too far on one end of the spectrum. But doing *everything* for them and protecting them from failure or messiness is at the other far end of the spectrum of balanced support. I think it's better with some teens to error on the side of asking too much of them, and then helping them sort out how to deal with "too much."

11) Finally, in terms of mental health, look for signs of "aliveness" in your teen. Look for signs of engagement with others, with projects, with ideas. Your teen may "hide" these from you, so if you're not sure how vital they are, ask other people in your teen's life. If your teen is engaged in their own inner life, a life with others, a life of curiosity and care and excitement and loss and failure, take a huge breath of relief. You're doing a good job with them, and they're doing a good job with you.

Suggested Reading: *Does My Teen Have Good Mental Health?*

The lists in the "Suggested Reading" sections are by no means comprehensive. I'm including what I consider to be the most informative, practical, relevant, or comprehensive readings on the topic(s) of the chapter. In other words, if you have limited time, these are the works I believe you might want to explore first. It doesn't mean all of these books are "easy reads." Sometimes a listed book will be very difficult, but worth the time.

Atwood, T. *The Complete Guide to Asperger's Syndrome.* Jessica Kingsley Publishers, 2008.

Bolick, T. *Asperger Syndrome and Adolescence: Helping Preteens and Teens Get Ready for the Real World.* Beverly: Fair Winds Press, 2004.

Bourne, E. J. *The Anxiety and Phobia Workbook.* Oakland: New Harbinger Publications, 2011.

Bowlby, J. *A Secure Base: Parent-Child Attachment and Healthy Human Development.* New York: Basic Books, 1988.

Cooperman, S. A., & Gilbert, S. D. *Living with Eating Disorders (Teen's Guides).* New York: Checkmark Books, 2009.

Costin, C. *The Eating Disorder Sourcebook: A Comprehensive Guide to the Causes, Treatments, and Prevention of Eating Disorders.* New York: McGraw-Hill, 1999.

Dellasega, C. *The Starving Family: Caregiving Mothers and Fathers Share Their Eating Disorder Wisdom.* Wisconsin: Champion Press, 2005.

Fonagy, P., Gergely, G., Jurist, E., & Target, M. *Affect Regulation, Mentalization, and the Development of Self.* New York: Other Press, 2005.

Fox, A. F., & Kirschner, R. *Too Stressed to Think?: A Teen Guide to Staying Sane When Life Makes You Crazy.* Minneapolis: Free Spirit Publishing, 2005.

Hallowell, E. M., & Ratey, J. J. *Driven To Distraction: Recognizing and Coping with Attention Deficit Disorder from Childhood Through Adulthood.* New York: Touchstone, 1995.

Herman, J. L. *Trauma and Recovery: The Aftermath of Violence—From Domestic Abuse to Political Terror.* New York: Basic Books, 1993.

Horowitz, M. *Stress Response Syndromes: Personality Styles and Interventions.* New York: Jason Aronson, Inc., 2001.

Lieberman, A. F. *Emotional Life of the Toddler.* New York: Free Press, 1995.

Neumark-Sztainer, D. *"I'm, Like, SO Fat": Helping Your Teen Make Healthy Choices about Eating and Exercise in a Weight-Obsessed World.* New York: The Guilford Press, 2005.

Porges, S. W. *The Polyvagal Theory: Neurophysiological Foundations of Emotions, Attachment, Communication, and Self-regulation.* New York: W. W. Norton & Company, 2011.

Price, J., & Fisher, J. E. *Take Control of Asperger's Syndrome: The Official Strategy Guide for Teens With Asperger's Syndrome and Nonverbal Learning Disorders.* Waco: Prufrock Press, 2010.

Riera, M. *Staying Connected to Your Teenager: How to Keep Them Talking to You and How to Hear What They're Really Saying.* Cambridge: Da Capo Press, 2003.

Robison, J. E. *Be Different: Adventures of a Free-Range Aspergian with Practical Advice for Aspergians, Misfits, Families & Teachers.* New York: Crown Archetype, 2011.

Saperstein, J. A. *Atypical: Life with Asperger's in 20⅓ Chapters.* New York: Perigee Trade, 2010.

Seligman, M. E. *The Optimistic Child: Proven Program to Safeguard Children from Depression & Build Lifelong Resilience.* New York: Harper Paperbacks, 2005.

Tompkins, M. A., & Martinez, K. A. *My Anxious Mind: A Teen's Guide to Managing Anxiety and Panic.* Washington, D.C.: Magination Press, 2009.

Wallerstein, J. S. *What About the Kids? Raising Your Children Before, During, and After Divorce.* New York: Hyperion, 2003.

10
The Ethical Dimension of Parenting Teenagers

This last chapter of the book—signaling the end—is also a beginning. I want to begin the end with some final assumptions and premises. I want to make more explicit some of the "theories" and principles that float in the background of my mind as I live my life, engage in my clinical practice, and offer support to parents of teenagers.

Some of these theories and ideas, like the five that open this final chapter, are more abstract and obtuse and don't seem to have any practical application, at least not in the moment. In that case, does it mean there is some *hidden* principle at work, masquerading as a mere theory? Maybe. The harder a theory is to critique, respond to, and negotiate around, the more it can seem like it points to an ineluctable truth. Those theories feel more like *principles,* and it's hard to think about and change what feels inevitable. But I've lived a while now, and no matter how hard I try to keep some aspect of my thinking tentative and open to change, I still find some things are appearing to be principles or, at the very least, ideas that seem very true to me and that I value highly. Here are five of those things:

Sometimes there is truth in a lie.

Sometimes we have to remember the future to heal the past.

Sometimes we have to do the wrong thing.

Sometimes suffering is necessary, but only the right *kind of suffering.*

Sometimes both principles and people fail us, and we fail them too—that can be the best thing.

Let's look at two *common* definitions for the word *principle*. Webster's Dictionary defines the word as a "truth admitted either without proof, or considered as having been before proved; a settled law or rule of action in human beings." And Guido Alpha's definition of principle, as cited in Wikipedia, reads:

> A principle is a law or rule that has to be, or usually is to be followed, or can be desirably followed, or is an inevitable consequence of something, such as the laws observed in nature or the way that a system is constructed. The principles of such a system are understood by its users as the essential characteristics of the system, or reflecting [the] system's designed purpose, and the effective operation or use of which would be impossible if any one of the principles was to be ignored.[1]

We often try to be principled parents or to parent according to certain principles. On its face that sounds like a good idea. We're just trying to teach our fundamental values to our children. But considering the definition above, parenting *by principle*—no matter what the principle—can get you (and your child) into some pretty difficult situations. It raises questions (especially from curious, thinking teenagers) like: "How did you get sole access the system's 'designed purpose' such that you always know how things should go?" "Is it *really* true that if I don't follow your suggestions, rules, or 'laws' my life will actually become *impossible* to operate in?" "Is it actually the case that I don't know how this system ("me") is constructed and you're the only one with access to knowledge about the inevitable, fundamental groundwork to how the system works?" "On what basis can I decide (or can I ever decide) whether what you say or do or tell me to do is *wrong*?" "Can one argue against principles or are they always 'considered to have been proved'?" "What about *my* principles—the things I think, feel, and believe are inviolate?"

> It's 4:30 P.M. I walk up the stairs of our apartment, knowing that I will find him in front of the television, half-opened soda bottle—all the carbonation now gone—and pizza box strewn on the floor next to him as if we live in some college dorm, homework undone and probably unconsidered. We've played this scenario over and over again, hundreds of times. But this time, there's been a suicide that day at a colleague's school and I'm feeling pretty raw and tender toward my son. I want to just bolt up the stairs and tell him I love him. I think of this the whole way home: Just walk up the stairs and tell him you love him; just tell him straight away; walk up the stairs and say, "I love you." I put the key in the door and I can feel my heart beating fast. I am literally saying to myself, like Homer Simpson, over and over again the words, "Say I love you, say I love you." I round the turn at the top of the stairs, and there he is, just as predicted, just as I've seen him a

hundred times before. But this time I open my mouth, survey the situation, feel my heart beating harder, and say, "Is your homework done?!" *What is wrong with me?*

I'm not sure where I got the following theory from and if turns out someone else (or many people) also thought of it, please let me know. I've found this particular theory to be very powerful. Over the last 26 years as a parent, I've noted something happening, over and over again. I started checking it out with other parents and with my clients and kept getting confirmation. The idea is this: *Whatever developmental stage your child is going through at any particular time, the fact of that happening is going to stimulate in you conscious (but mostly nonconscious) thoughts, feelings, moods, hopes, fantasies, and beliefs (all of these together I just call "cognitions") that are echoes of whatever* you *were going through at that particular developmental stage.*

Here is one illustration of the theory. When your child is around 2, he or she will begin to go through the developmental stage that includes the psychosocial conflict Erik Erikson referred to as "autonomy versus shame and doubt." The major question your child is trying to figure out has to do with whether or not she can do things on her own (without it upsetting you too much) or whether she always needs to be dependent on the help of others. If your child successfully negotiates this stage, with your help, she will gain the basic virtue of *will*. Kids at this stage, which lasts a couple of years, are trying to establish a sense of their own authorship and self-efficacy (in some ways, just like in adolescence). They want to feel and *be* somewhat independent (without being punished) and are gaining a sense of personal control over their bodies. Success at new tasks leads to feeling autonomous, failure (or blame for their independent strivings) leads to feelings of shame. It's interesting to note how one psychologist, Sylvan Tomkins, talks about shame, not as an emotion per se, but as an *attenuator* of emotion. In other words, shame is the thing that *limits other things.*[2] Shame stops us from doing whatever we were going to do or feeling whatever we might have felt. It is an attempt to keep us from doing or feeling or thinking something that has already been experienced as unsafe—and you're still worried will be too unsafe to pursue. It's one reason why the experience of shame is such a powerful experience. It's worth keeping this in mind because it's an experience *par excellence* of adolescence and functions to *stop* teens from doing some things and *induces* them to do others.

In any case, your toddler is going to be working on issues involving independence, autonomy, embarrassment, shame, and trying to do what they want without disappointing close others too much. The theory that I'm suggesting means that these same issues will be "on your plate," too, in a particularly intense way, when your child hits this developmental stage. I think that this partly happens because, of course, similar behavioral cues spark memories and remind your conscious mind and your body of similar experiences in your life. But this phenomenon of having your child's developmental struggles echoed in your life also occurs because your child's behavior—for example, touching the light socket when you don't want him to or running away from you at the store or screaming when he doesn't get his way— is a powerful reminder that your child has *different* needs than your own (now) and those needs have to be negotiated.

By the time your first child reaches the age of 2, you're probably realizing more and more that you're in this for the long haul, and the haul is definitely going to feel *long*. You might start to have feelings of being trapped, even if you deeply love your child. This might bring up some of the same feelings in relation to your partner, who may or may not be helping out with your child's newfound and challenging behaviors. If you keep along with this thread of thinking, it's easy to see how your child's developmental stage can easily induce in you a lot of feelings around *independence, autonomy, embarrassment, shame,* and trying to do what *you* want without disappointing close others too much.

Now, if you consider that this is going to happen again and again, around each developmental stage in your child's life, you'll know that parenting is going to stimulate in you affect, feelings, moods, and cognitions *about the way you were parented.* And this will always be going on *while* you're being a parent. The intensity of those echoes will rise and fall, as your child enters or leaves a particular developmental phase. Amazing, huh? This theory—which I haven't yet named—exemplifies something about why I believe that *parenting is a* holy *activity*, something out of (and into) the realm of the ethical.

If, as Emmanuel Levinas wrote, *ethics* is indeed an optics, then parenting your children (and your teens, especially) is a study of refining the processes by which we see more clearly into the nature of something that, by definition, is bright and ever-changing.

I am particularly fond of a brief description I found on the American Mathematical Society (AMS) website. The Society produces a CD that contains some of the "Mathematics Awareness" materials published by AMS. "Mathematical Moments" is a compilation of short articles on *applied mathematics*—the practice-based realm of mathematics that is intimately connected to research, but ultimately about using math to figure out real-world problems. Here is the text from Mathematical Moment 38:

> Twinkling stars are fun for songs but frustrating for astronomers. Current technology uses *adaptive optics* to adjust for turbulence in the atmosphere and deliver an accurate image of stars, planets, and satellites. Correcting for atmospheric distortion involves linear algebra, geometry, and

statistics to determine the extent of the distortion and continually adjust deformable mirrors which refocus light waves back along their true paths.[3]

Okay, it's a stretch—but only a small stretch because it offers a *poetic* way of thinking about parenting teens. Parenting propels us simultaneously back into our own past and toward our parents (which no doubts connects our parents, if they're still alive, back to *their* parents, and so on). It connects us in the moment, by complex equation, to our own children. It connects us forward to thinking about what we want our children to become. *Parenting is a nexus of past, present, and future, in which all three can be changed, depending upon what we choose.* It is the opportunity for healing some of our own past hurts through the opportunity of reflecting on and grieving our own past and figuring out and deciding to make it better for our own future, our child's future, and their children's futures. And the opportunities will present themselves pretty much every day—we can take them up or leave them alone, but they are always there, waiting.

Becoming a parent or raising your teenagers is neither *inherently* a spiritual practice nor grounds for ethical development. In other words, the ethical dimension of parenting teenagers is neither something that is a *given,* nor something that *has to be followed,* like it or not. It is a choice. *The ethical dimension of parenting is something you* can *choose, but* do not have to *choose.* If you were forced into it, as "the way things are," it would not be in the realm of the ethical; it would be about acting in accordance with the nature of something that could not be otherwise. It would be like congratulating a pencil for obeying Newton's First Law of Motion[4] and staying on the table. The pencil isn't *deciding* to stay put until a strong wind (or a teenager) comes along and knocks it on the floor; it has no choice.

But you can *choose the good*—just like you're trying to teach your teens, that they can choose the right things for themselves and their lives with others. You'll recall that I said that if it was all so easy—just a matter of following principles, like an object follows the laws of motion—you'd just pick the "best" parenting style and follow it. But I also noted that you can't do that, because choices around parenting are always *case-specific.* One size doesn't fit all. *One size* can't *fit all. That's why parenting is so hard. That's why parenting can engender so much sadness and loss, as well as joy. That's the ethical dimension in parenting—that you have the choice to face the difficulty.*

Am I being too glum here? I don't think so. I've said many times in the book that living is grieving. If you're alive, you're coming up against limitations and losses and you have to adjust and adapt. You can't make life *perfect* for your children. The life of humans and humans in families is such that you don't actually *know* what is *perfect* for your child; even if you're a caring, loving person, you can't really know *in advance* what your child will need, at any given moment. In parenting, *a good approximation is something we can see only after the fact.*

So parenting teenagers can hurt and can engender some suffering. Being a teenager does the same. How do you know if you're doing the "right" thing? Parents ask themselves this question all the time. Teens ask themselves this question all the time.

In 16 years of seeing clients in psychotherapy, I've rarely come across a teenager who, having done something "wrong," upon reflection could not describe *a singular moment* in the sequence of events leading up to the "wrongdoing" at which they heard a voice or had a feeling (or often, both), telling them: *Don't do this.*

I remember a particularly difficult time between my son and me, during his junior year in high school. We were arguing a lot, but not talking very much. He could feel my disappointment in his schoolwork and I worried often about his disengagement with anything school-related. Getting him to do anything that resembled a "chore" was almost pointless, or so I thought. I felt "used" and taken for granted a lot and was getting weary of working hard and getting what felt like no help from him. I remember being close to tears one evening—you know, that feeling in your eyes and your chest where at any minute you *could* cry. I don't know if he remembers this, but that night he wrote me a letter and left it for me outside my door. In the letter he wrote:

> I know sometimes I do the wrong thing. I know I should get up and clean off the table, like you've asked me to a hundred times, but I just sit there. I know that when you come home from work you're tired and you're trying to help people and you need help, too, and I'm laying on the sofa and I know you're going to ask me if I did my homework or if I did the dishes. But I just sit there and I tell myself "okay, in a minute—before Dad gets back—go do the dishes," and I just sit there and then you come home and you're angry with me. I'm sorry. But I want to you know, though that even though I don't do the right thing, I want to do the right thing.

When I first read the letter, I felt that my heart softened a little bit—then I burst into the tears I'd been choking back for three days. I knew that he didn't write this to me so that I would forgive him when he fails to do his tasks. I knew that he didn't even write it so that I would cut him some slack when he does things late. He wrote it so that I would not give up on him and I would not forget him. He wanted me not to forget the man *he is becoming* that is alive inside him, even in the absence of action that demonstrates his maturity—or doing what he wants, even if I want him to do it. Even at 16, he knew there was a present self *in motion* (or at rest on the couch in front of the television), and a self he wished to become. He wanted me to remember his *future.*

Teenagers often do know the right thing to do and more often than not they do the right thing; they *want* to do the right thing. But when they tell me (or you) that they *knew* what they should have done—*How do they know?* How can they come to this knowledge, and why don't they act on this knowledge more often, *if they "know" already?* Sometimes being able to act on what you know is a matter of practice. Sometimes it's a matter of time. Sometimes it's a matter of education—of something being *led out of them,* gently—by someone close, someone who loves them.

I believe that ethical development—as a part of human development—has something to do with feeling, and it has to do with a kind of human echolocation in and using the *body.* Human echolocation, like that of other animals, is an ability or strategy used to detect objects in the environment by sensing echoes from those objects. In the moment your teenager *feels* and locates a feeling in the body, he or she is beginning to engage in the exercise of those muscles of apperception, hearing and responding to the call from *oneself*—this is ethical development. It is a kind of approximation about ourselves, others, and the world, by echolocation, using *feelings.* If you're doing this practice, this kind of approximation, at the same time your teen is doing it, it will help them more than you'll ever know.

Because parents, too, come in to my office to get support for helping their teens, even though many times they spend a fair amount of time sitting on the sofa describing exactly what they know they need (and want) to do—just like in the example of my own behavior that opens this chapter. You *know,* but you *don't* always do it or *can't* always do it. That is a kind of *suffering* that is not unique to parenting, but it is a type of feeling you will have if you are choosing to enter the ethical dimension of parenting teens.

The ethical dimension of parenting suggests that this is a kind of necessary suffering and if it isn't fought against or denied or pushed away too much, it gives us what we need: a *certain kind* of sadness, and a *certain kind* of joy.

In Eric G. Wilson's book *Against Happiness: In Praise of Melancholy*, he writes eloquently about the importance of these "certain kinds" of sadness and joy.[5] It's not that Wilson is opposed to people being happy, but rather he is pointing to the emptiness (and in some ways, impossibility) of working toward a life of joy *without* sadness. So much of our lives and the lives of our teens are filled with incompleteness and not knowing. His counsel, though, is to recognize these incomplete states and "*seek* the sorrowful joy [italics mine]." For me, and I believe for parents of teens, the key wisdom is that we have a unique opportunity when we *seek,* rather than just *endure* the sorrowful joys of parenting our adolescents.

Sometimes being an approximate parent to your teens requires *lying.* Can you believe I'm saying that, in a chapter about the ethical dimension of parenting? It is a certain kind of lying, and it's best illustrated by Anthony Bloom.

Anthony Bloom was born in Switzerland but returned to Russia prior to the First World War. He spent the second part of his childhood in present-day Iran. After the

Russian Revolution ended, his family crossed north over mountainous Kurdistan on horseback in horse-driven carts, then traveling down the rivers Tigris and Euphrates in a barge. The family found an English boat bound for India, and from there headed toward Southampton. Weather delayed them, and then the lack of seaworthy transportation delayed them. Finally the family made it to Gibraltar, but the luggage kept going all the way to Southampton. It took 14 years for them to get the luggage back. In the 14 years they tried (and waited) to get the luggage back, they traveled through Spain, France, Austria, and Yugoslavia, staying in Austria for a while and then finally settling in France in 1923, where Anthony would live for 27 years.

Anthony Bloom taught mathematics and Latin. After secondary school he studied science and medicine in France; in 1939 he became a doctor, and soon after that he was called into the second World War, performing surgery and working in the French resistance. Bloom was strongly anti-religious, but his father was not. One day after not seeing his son for an extended period, his father said to him: "I was worried about you." Bloom asked, "Did you think I'd had an accident?" His father replied, "That would have meant nothing, even if you had been killed. I thought you had lost your integrity."

In 1948 Anthony Bloom was ordained, secretly taking his vows to be a monk—since he could not openly profess his faith and serve as a physician at that time. There is so much more to the story of this man that I will not tell here. Born June 1914, Andrei Borishovich Bloom ("Anthony" Bloom) died in August 2003, Metropolitan Anthony of Sourozh, Archbishop of the Russian Orthodox Church. In those 89 years, he traveled great physical, psychological, and spiritual distances and died a very beloved figure.

In 1970, Anthony of Sourozh wrote:

> When you live in your family, and you work out of doors, and are doing a heavy kind of work, you may come back physically worn out. If at that moment your mother, your sister, your father or whoever else, said 'Do you love me?' you would say 'I do.' If the other person goes on investigating, 'Do you really love me at this moment?' what you could honestly have said is 'No, I feel nothing but my aching back and worn out body.' But you are perfectly right in saying 'I love you' because you know that underneath all the exhaustion, there is a live current of love.[6]

⁓

The father of a 16½-year-old came to see me to talk about his son, who was smoking pot and not doing his homework.[7] His son, he thought, was probably angry about his parents' divorce a few years back, and he was a loving, very open man, who encouraged his son to talk about any feelings he might have. Still, his boy remained pretty silent about it. But lately, school was becoming something for which he had no real feeling, let alone passion…and he couldn't really see the point of getting good grades and doing homework—or even caring about these things. "I don't know what I'm going to do, or want to do in the future, so why should I really care about these things like doing Latin or finishing my math homework?" The father wondered whether his son was depressed, but he knew that deep down, it probably wasn't depression…it was something more, something bigger. He knew his son was wrestling with something about life, about his own life, and he wanted to know how to help him.

His father, like most parents, tried to understand, but usually ended up telling him that he wanted him to keep doing his homework and get good grades. The father was no idiot; he shared his concerns about the pot-smoking and, more important, told his son he was worried about him. That was good.

So, the father went to talk with an old family friend about his son's predicament, and the friend remembered a time when the family (including the friend) were together at the lake and the boy's mom wanted him to swim from the dock out to the raft, about 100 meters offshore. This was a real rite of passage in this family. The boy was about 8 or 9 at the time and had never before swum in a lake. His mom tried just about every psychological trick in the book (she was a psychologist) to help get the boy into the water and to bridge the distance between the dock and the raft. (You'll see in a minute how psychologists can be absolutely useless at crucial times.) She tried to cajole him, promise him good things if he reached the raft, tried using encouragement and cheerleading—"Come on, you can do it, I know you can do it, I believe in you!"—and all kinds of other tricks like saying, "It's fine, I'll wait, I know you probably can't do it" (reverse psychology, gag me). This went on for 15 minutes and the boy stood frozen on the dock and then eventually dissolved into a puddle of tears.

The friend had remembered this story and reminded the father of it, and then said, "See, that's what he's had as a model most of his life—trying to be cajoled and pushed and tricked to get past the point where his desire met his fear. He just gets terrified, and there is a point past which he can't go…so he gives up."

The father was heartened by hearing his friend's reminiscence because he told me, "You know, my friend really had it right, because yesterday I told my son I wanted to have a talk with him and as we walked my son opened up and told me":

> You know, Dad, I *do* actually care about things other than smoking
> weed and not doing my work. It's just that I always get to this point with
> everything where I sort of glide for a while and do okay with things I'm

interested in, but then I reach a point where I know I'm going to have to actually work really hard to get past a certain point, and I just give up. I do that with everything, especially with things I'm interested in myself...not just stupid things like homework. In some way, I even actually *want* to do the homework. I don't know, I can't explain it.

His dad felt really grateful that his son had opened up to him, but there was still this nagging worry of what to do about it. I told him even though his ex-wife (the boy's mom) had had a good impulse—to help her son past the point of fear—she was going about it, in my opinion, in a way that interfered with her son's development, especially, perhaps, his *ethical* development. I thought the problem was that she was making it all about her and her own reactions and desires. So I suggested to the father another scenario to imagine, based upon the story his friend had related to him about their time at the lake and this rite of passage:

Imagine you're on the dock with your son. You know he's scared. *Assume* that he wants to get to the raft. Just quietly tell him, "Look, every single human being reaches a point with everything they try to do where their desire and interest reaches a wall...when they know that going farther means doing something that makes their stomach hurt and their chest tighten and makes them want to throw up or run away. You won't even be sure you want this thing you're struggling with. And even if you did want it, you feel certain you'll fail or you're pretty damned sure you will. You just know in your heart that at the very least you'll make a fool of yourself. You just know that there is a right way to do this thing, and that most people other than you could do it, but you can't. But there is another, exquisitely quiet voice, that is calm, for no good reason, and it is curious about what is on the other side of doing the thing you're certain you'll fail about. You don't know what it is, but you know there's something there you want, that's for you. When the curiosity and wish to know what's on the other side is just a hair's weight heavier than your fear and worry, you'll jump in...or you'll find that you already jumped in."

I decided to tell this story, once, to a group of 300 graduating seniors. I'm not sure what, if anything, they got from it. But I realized that I wanted to tell them, because I was talking about their entire adolescence, up to that point...to the point of being on the eve of leaving home. So, at the end of the speech, I added these words:

Some of you have jumped. Some of you are on the dock. All of you don't really know what next year will really be like, on the other side. Once you get there, there will be another side, and another raft on the horizon.

Listen. It's all meaningful, and so are your lives. You all matter. The raft doesn't matter much, but your choices do, and so does the pain, and the not-knowing and your fear and your curiosity.

For your teens to develop their ethical being,[8] as part of their identity, they want and need you nearby, whispering (not shouting) in their ear: "You *matter,* what you choose matters, others matter, it's all meaningful, despite the mess and the fear and unknown and the 'successes' you get or think you need or want. Keep going, keep trying, keep learning." Remember *fidelity?*

Practical Help Tips

This tip is in the form of an exercise. I think you'll find this valuable. I often used this exercise in a parenting workshop I used to lead called "Teaching Values and Responsibility." You can do this at home—you'll need a pen or pencil, a large sheet of paper (if possible, 11x14), and some crayons or colored pens/pencils.

Step 1: You're going to make a grid on a piece of paper. This grid will be a calendar of your week. Across the top, in the columns, write the days of the week. Down the left side, in the rows you've drawn, write the hours of the day, in two-hour increments, e.g., 8–10 A.M.; 10–12 P.M.; 12–2 P.M., etc.

Step 2: Fill in the squares of the calendar with a basic description of your activities. It should look something like this:

	MONDAY	TUESDAY
8–10 A.M.	Commute, work at store	
10–12 P.M.	Work	
12–2 P.M.	Lunch, work	
2–4 P.M.	Work	
4–6 P.M.	Commute, make dinner	
6–8 P.M.	Make/eat dinner; dishes	
8–10 P.M.	Help T.J. w/ homework	
10–12 A.M.	Review work, read, TV	
12–2 A.M.	Sleep	
2–4 A.M.	Sleep	
4–6 A.M.	Sleep	

Step 3: Go through the list of values, below, and pick your top three values—the values that are closest to your heart, the ones that matter the most and that you feel you organize your life around. Give each "value" a color, e.g., "Religious Faith/Spirituality" is blue, "Family" is green, "Creative Expression" is yellow.

Step 4: Go through the list of activities on your calendar. Color-code each activity that is an expression of your values.

For example, if every Sunday morning you go to church, or every morning at sunrise you get up and pray, or every Saturday afternoon you carve out time to draw and paint or do art projects with the kids, then make the squares the "value color" represented by that activity. You might code the first two activities blue for "religious faith" and the last one yellow "creative expression." Or you might see it as "family" and color it green. You get the idea.

Step 5: Once you've done this for all the activities in your typical week, look at the paper. Ask yourself:

1. How much color, overall, is on the chart?

2. If the chart seems somewhat lacking in color, then ask yourself: Am I happy? Are my kids and my partner happy? How can I manage to weave my highest values into where I actually put my body each hour of each day? How are the others in my family doing with their own charts? Can I help them? How can I continue living my values?

3. If there is a lot of color on the chart, then ask yourself: Am I happy? Are my kids and my partner happy? How did I manage to weave my highest values into where I actually put my body each hour of each day? How are the others in my family doing with their own charts? Can I help them? How can I continue living my values?

A List of Values

1) Accomplishment: Making a contribution, reaching goals, producing results

2) Altruism: Action on behalf of the other; service

3) Belonging: Acceptance as a member of worth in a group

4) Compassion: The mixture of altruism and knowledge of human frailty

5) Creative Expression: Expressing ideas/values in novel, unique ways, with art, music, dance, song, math—you name it

6) Diversity: Appreciation of difference in people, ideas, and situations

7) Excitement: Maintaining a stimulating, active life

8) Fairness: Distributing benefits and burdens according to compassion

9) Family: The creation, recognition and maintenance of compassionate relationship with those you love

10) Friendship: The creation, recognition, and maintenance of intimate relationships and mutual caring

11) Happiness: Feeling joy, well-being, and deep pleasure with others

12) Health: Soundness of mind, body, and spirit

13) Independence: Ability to set course of action *in light of* but not controlled by others

14) Integrity: Having a high degree of match between your words, deeds, and beliefs

15) Knowledge: Engagement in the pursuit of truth, understanding, and scholarship

16) Loyalty: Duty, allegiance, and commitment to others in conscious obligation

17) Pleasure: Seeking an enjoyable, leisurely life

18) Power: Pursuit of control, authority, and influence (could be over or alongside others)

19) Religious Faith/Spirituality: Creating, discovering, and maintaining a relationship to God/Allah/Brahma/The Natural World...choose your own words

20) Respect: Preservation of the inherent worth and value of each person...re-spect, to look again, with compassion

21) Security: Freedom from fear, danger, and uncompassionate thoughts and beliefs about others and ourselves

22) Social Good: Working for the common good, the good of society

23) Stewardship: Holding oneself accountable for human, financial, and ecological resources

24) Wealth: Accumulation of material possessions

25) Wisdom: Active pursuit of understanding what is true, right, and lasting

What are your own values that aren't listed here? If you have other values, just define them and give them a color, per the instructions above.

Suggested Reading: *The Ethical Dimension of Parenting Teens*

The lists in the "Suggested Reading" sections are by no means comprehensive. I'm including what I consider to be the most informative, practical, relevant, or comprehensive readings on the topic(s) of the chapter. In other words, if you have limited time, these are the works I believe you might want to explore first. It doesn't mean all of these books are "easy reads." Sometimes a listed book will be very difficult, but worth the time.

Bellah, R. N. *Habits of the Heart: Individualism and Commitment in American Life.* San Francisco: HarperCollins, 1986.

de Zengotita, T. *Mediated: How the Media Shapes Our World and the Way We Live in It.* New York: Bloomsbury USA, 2006.

Jenkins, H. *Confronting the Challenges of Participatory Culture: Media Education for the 21st Century.* In John D. and Catherine T. MacArthur Foundation Series on Digital Media and Learning. Cambridge: The MIT Press, 2009.

Needleman, J. *Why Can't We Be Good?* New York: Tarcher, 2007.

Riera, M. and Di Prisco, J. *Right From Wrong: Instilling a Sense of Integrity in Your Child.* New York: Perseus Books, 2002.

Endnotes

INTRODUCTION

1. I alternate the use of pronouns throughout the book between "he" and "she" to indicate that the concepts apply to either of those genders. Sometimes writers call this stage "Identity versus Role *Diffusion*," rather than Role *Confusion*. They are related in Erikson's writing. I believe the gist of the idea is that during the period of adolescence, the child really must have a crisis about their identity and struggle to find who they are and want to be. Those teens that have made a strong commitment to an identity tend to be better adjusted and more happy than those who have not. But if a teen doesn't struggle toward the experience and expression of identity or commit to an identity, they're in a state that Erikson called "identity diffusion." They feel out of sync and as if they do not have a place in the world—there is no strong feeling of belonging.

2. Mike Riera has since published amplifications and extensions on that original work that are equally valuable, such as *Field Guide to the American Teenager* (with Joe DiPrisco), *Surviving High School*, and *Staying Connected to Your Teenager*.

3. This is discussed in detail in Chapter 3, "Identity Development, Relationships, and Status."

4. See, for example, *The Encyclopedia of Adolescence*, ed. R. M. Lerner, A.C. Petersen, and J. Brooks-Gunn (New York: Garland, 1991), 492. See also, *Gale Encyclopedia of Childhood and Adolescence*, ed. by S. Gale and J. Kagan Gale Group (New York: Gale Publishing, 1997).

5. If we leave aside "parenting" books that are represented as parenting books—of which there are some great ones—the honor for "best" might just go to Thomas de Zengotita's *Mediated: How the Media Shapes Your World and the Way You Live in It*. Apart from Erik Erikson's work, I haven't read another book that so captures the processes of identity formation in America at the turn of this century. Part smartarse philosophical and intellectual masterpiece and part travelogue through the minds of adolescents (and adults) on "media"—you know those ads, "This is your brain on drugs." Zengotita strikes me as the De Tocqueville of the 21st century. In terms of understanding the effects of digital media, either de Zengotita is not a fish or he is an exception to Culkin's dictum that "whomever discovered water...was certainly not a fish."

6. You'll find this concept alluded to throughout the current work. Habermas did not originate the concept of *Lebenswelt* or *Life-World*, but his understanding and furthering of the concept was first

introduced to the public in 1936 by philosopher Edmund Husserl.

7. See Luckmann, T.L. & Berger, P.L. *The Social Construction of Reality: A Treatise in the Sociology of Knowledge* (New York: Doubleday & Company, 1967). And thanks to Stephen Colbert for the neologism.

8. I'm not sure what kind of therapist I've become. I do my work. I believe that it's up to each one of my clients to decide for themselves whether I'm "good" at it or not. My intention to be of service is important, but not ultimately what counts. What did they actually get from our relationship?; that's the thing. Since I think that way about my work, you'll probably notice I think that way about parenting teens, too.

9. I want to comment here on why I keep referring *only* to American teens. Some of what I've written could apply to teens with similar socioeconomic conditions, i.e., advanced capitalist, democratic, highly industrialized societies. Some of what I've written will apply to more and more teens as more and more of the adolescent lifeworld in that particular country is dominated by forces of state and market. But for now, I'm sticking with what I know and that's why this book pertains to American teens—there will be enough variations by geography and economic status to provide plenty of argument about the generalizability of approaches represented in this book, in any case.

10. Investigations into what children think and do are now much more common. Many provocative and influential insights came from the work of Jean Piaget, Albert Bandura, Lev Vygotsky, John Watson, Margaret Mahler, John Bowlby, Anna Freud, and Peter Blos, for example. But others like Rudolf Steiner, Maria Montessori, Rudolf Dreikurs, and John Dewey, and more recently, outstanding thinkers like Daniel Stern, Richard Lerner, Alison Gopnik, and others—who work across many disciplines—are making enormous contributions to our understanding of child and adolescent development.

11. As an aside, teens do have "youth," which in itself is a high status quality, and can substitute for not having a job, in some cases.

CHAPTER 1: DO I HAVE A TEEN IN MY HOUSE?

1. *The Adolescent Brain: Learning, Reasoning, and Decision Making*, Ed. V.F. Reyna, S.B. Chapman, M.R. Dougherty, and J. Confrey (Washington, D.C.: American Psychological Association, 2012.

2. Winters, K.C. "Alcohol and the Adolescent Brain: Tastes Great, Less Functioning." Paper presented at the 3rd Las Vegas Conference on Adolescents, Las Vegas, 2005.

3. Two of those books are *The Adolescent Brain* and Linda Spear's *The Behavioral Neuroscience of Adolescence*. Those are two good examples, but you'll find a list of other good references at the end of the chapter, if you want to learn about the growing sciences of adolescent development.

4. I happen to believe that most of these influences—the way others influence and change us and the ways we influence and change those very same others, as well as the way we change "things," "processes," and other parts of the natural world—are *primarily* nonconscious. I *would* think that, though: I'm a psychotherapist. So, for me, maturation in the lifeworld *is* development. For folks like philosophers, cognitive scientists, psychologists, those are fighting words, or rather, what Raymond Williams called "keywords." See Williams, R. *Keywords: A Vocabulary of Culture and Society* (Oxford: Oxford University Press), 1976.

5. See Joseph Weiss, "Unconscious Mental Functioning," *Scientific American* (1990): 103-109. See also P. Lewicki, M. Czyzewska and T. Hill, "Nonconscious Information Processing and Personality," in *How Implicit Is Implicit Learning?*, ed. D. Berry (New York and Oxford: Oxford University Press, 1997), 48-72 and P. Lewicki, T. Hill and M. Czyzewska, "Nonconscious Acquisition of Information," *American Psychologist* 47 (1992): 796-801.

6. See, for example, Joshua Coleman, *When Parents Hurt: Compassionate Strategies When You and Your Grown Child Don't Get Along* (New York: William Morrow Paperbacks), 2008.

7. This saying is often attributed to Chicago writer Peter De Vries, but the exact source of the quotation is uncertain.

8. Data for the 2010 United States Census are not fully compiled, although they do provide intercensus estimates, available at http://www.census.gov/popest/data/intercensal/national/nat2010.html. Cf. National Adolescent Health Information Center. Fact Sheet on Demographics: Adolescents. San Francisco, CA: University of California, San Francisco, 2003.

9. See Linda Spear, *The Behavioral Neuroscience of Adolescence* (New York: W. W. Norton & Company, 2009).

10. U.S. Census Bureau. (2003b). *American FactFinder, Census 2000 summary file 1* [Tabulated Data]. Washington, D.C.: Author. [Available at (12/03): http://factfinder.census.gov/servlet/BasicFactsServlet]

11. U.S. Census Bureau. (2003b). *American FactFinder, Census 2000 summary file 1* [Tabulated Data]. Washington, D.C.: Author. [Available at (12/03): http://factfinder.census.gov/servlet/BasicFactsServlet]

12. See J. Fields, "Children's Living Arrangements and Characteristics: March 2002" (Current Population Reports, P20-547) [Detailed Tables]. *Washington, D.C.: U.S. Census Bureau* (2003), http://www.census.gov/population/www/socdemo/hh-fam.html, accessed March 14, 2012.

13. If your daughter has, before the age of 8, developed armpit or pubic hair, more mature outer genitals, breasts, and had her first period, there is evidence for what's called "precocious puberty" and you should seek medical advice. While these changes can and do happen as early as 6 or 7, they're still cause for checking things out with her doctor. If your son has, before the age of 9, developed armpit or public hair, testicle growth, facial hair, voice deepening, and significant increase in musculature, you should also check with your doctor. See D.M. Styne and M.M. Grumbach, "Puberty: Ontogeny, Neuroendocrinology, Physiology and Disorders," in *Williams Textbook of Endocrinology*, ed. by H.M. Kronenberg et al. (Philadelphia: Saunders Elsevier, 2008), Chapter 24.

14. Puberty typically unfolds over a period of about 3½ years. If all of the signs of puberty are present for your son or daughter within a year or 18 months, you should have them checked by a doctor for potential issues around their endocrine system functioning—the system responsible for the production and release of hormones in the body. Disorders of the endocrine system can be serious, because these hormones impact just about every aspect of human maturation from physical growth and metabolism of nutrition to mood and ability to regulate mood. See, for example, Catharine M. Gordon and M.R. Laufer, "Physiology of Puberty," in *Pediatric and Adolescent Gynecology*, ed. by D.P. Goldstein, S.J.H. Emans and M.R. Laufer (Philadelphia: Lippincott, Williams & Wilkins), 120-55.

15. Puberty that occurs too late is called "delayed puberty" and is characterized for girls by lack of breast development by 13 or not having a period by 16. For boys, signs would be no testicular enlargement by 14 or lack of other signs of puberty within 4-5 years after enlargement of penis and

testicles. See C. Traggiai & R. Stanhope, "Disorders of Pubertal Development," in *Best Practice & Research Clinical Obstetrics & Gynaecology* 17, no. 1 (2003): 41–56.

16. See Parent et al., "The Timing of Normal Puberty and the Age Limits of Sexual Precocity: Variations Around the World, Secular Trends, and Changes After Migration," in *Endocrine Reviews* 24, no. 5 (2003): 668-693.

17. There is a big difference between a *principle* and a *theory*. This difference is, in effect, what this book is all about. More on this in the final chapter on The Ethical Dimension of Parenting Teenagers.

18. See D. Riva and C. Giorgi, "The Cerebellum Contributes to Higher Functions During Development: Evidence From a Series of Children Surgically Treated for Posterior Fossa Tumours," in *Brain* 123 (2000): 1051-1061.

19. See Joseph LeDoux, *Synaptic Self: How Our Brains Become Who We Are* (New York: Penguin, 2003).

20. For a detailed discussion of neuroanatomy of the brain, see Jay N. Giedd et al., "Anatomic Magnetic Resonance Imaging of the Developing Child and Adolescent Brain," in *The Adolescent Brain Learning, Reasoning, and Decision Making*, ed. by V.F. Reyna et al. (New York: American Psychological Association, 2012), 15-35.

21. See P.M. Thompson et al., "Growth Patterns in the Developing Brain Detected by Using Continuum Mechanical Tensor Maps," in *Nature* 404, no. 9 (2000): 190-193.

22. See V.F. Reyna and S.E. Rivers, "Current Theories of Risk and Rational Decision Making." *Developmental Review* 28 (2008): 1-11.

23. See J. G. Giedd, "Structural Magnetic Resonance Imaging of the Adolescent Brain," in *Annals of the New York Academy of Sciences* 102 (2004): 77-85.

24. See V.F. Reyna and M.R. Dougherty, "Paradoxes of the Adolescent Brain in Cognition, Emotion, and Rationality," in *The Adolescent Brain Learning, Reasoning, and Decision Making*, ed. by V.F. Reyna et al. (New York: American Psychological Association, 2012), 431.

25. See V.F. Reyna and F. Farley, "Risk and Rationality in Adolescent Decision-Making: Implications for Theory, Practice, and Public Policy," in *Psychological Science in the Public Interest* 7 (2006): 1–44.

26. See G. Kaati et al., in "Cardiovascular and Diabetes Mortality Determined by Nutrition During Parents' and Grandparents' Slow Growth Period," in *European Journal of Human Genetics* 10 (2002): 682–688.

27. See D. Grafodatskaya, B. Chung, P. Szatmari P. and R. Weksberg, "Autism Spectrum Disorders and Epigenetics," in *Journal of the American Academy of Child and Adolescent Psychiatry* 49, no. 8 (2010): 794-809.

28. See A. R. Isles and L.S. Wilkinson, "Epigenetics; What Is It and Why Is It Important to Mental Disease?" in *British Medical Bulletin* 85, no. 1 (2008): 35-45.

29. See W. Reik, "Stability and Flexibility of Epigenetic Gene Regulation in Mammalian Development," in *Nature* 447 (2007): 425–432.

30. See, for example, the Introduction to Sebastian Seung's *Connectome: How the Brain's Wiring Makes Us Who We Are* (New York: Houghton Mifflin Harcourt Publishing, 2012).

31. See E. Clifford, "Neural Plasticity: Merzenich, Taub and Greenough," in *Harvard Brain*, 16 (1999): 16-20.

32. In my relatively non-scientific brain, I have a hard time understanding experience-independent events. It seems to me that if something happens in the world, it is dependent upon something other than itself. In any case, I think of those as "experience-we-haven't-yet-discovered-related events." I think the scientists might mean "experiences internal to the body."

33. Hebb, D.O. *The Organization of Behavior: A Neuropsychological Theory* (New York: Wiley-Interscience, 1949).

34. Some, like Steven Pinker and Clay Shirkey, seem to argue—when looking at the "effects" of the Internet and digital media on the human brain—that plasticity is really no big deal. The brain changes, so what; it doesn't fundamentally change and rewire its basic functioning. Technology and the introduction of new technology always "change" the human brain and thinking—that's a description of human development, not a cause for alarm. I just have to say that I strongly disagree, especially in relation to adolescents. See Chapter 4 of this volume for more on this topic.

35. See A. Pascual-Leone et al, "Modulation of Muscle Responses Evoked by Transcranial Magnetic Stimulation during the Acquisition of New Fine Motor Skills," in *Journal of Neurophysiology* 74, no. 3 (1995): 1037–45.

36. See A. Thomas and S. Chess, *Temperament and Development* (New York: Brunner/Mazel, 1977).

37. Hebb, *Organisation*, 62.

38. See T.P. Pons et al., "Massive Cortical Re-Organization After Sensory Deafferentation in Adult Macaques," in *Science* 252, no. 5014 (1991): 1857-1860.

39. See T.A. Comery, C.X. Stamoudis, S.A. Irwin, and W.T. Greenough, "Increased Density of Multiple-Head Dendritic Spines on Medium-Sized Neurons of the Striatum in Rats Reared in a Complex Environment," in *Neurobiology of Learning and Memory* 66, no. 2 (1996): 93-96.

40. See R.D. Fields, "White Matter in Learning, Cognition and Psychiatric Disorders," in *Trends in Neurosciences* 31 (2008): 361-370.

41. See R. Westerhausen et al., "Effects Of Handedness and Gender on Macro- and Microstructure of the Corpus Callosum and its Subregions: A Combined High-Resolution and Diffusion-Tensor MRI Study," in *Cognitive Brain Research* 21, no. 3 (2004): 418–26.

42. See J. Stamatakis " Why Did the Absence of the Corpus Callosum in Kim Peek's Brain Increase His Memory Capacity?" *Scientific American Mind* (2011), accessed April 2, 2012, http://www.scientificamerican.com/article.cfm?id=why-did-the-absence-of-the-corpus.

43. Fields, "White Matter," 2008.

44. Giedd et al., "Anatomic Magnetic Resonance," 2012.

45. *Ibid.*, 28.

46. See R.K. Lenroot et al., "Sexual Dimorphism of Brain Developmental Trajectories During Childhood and Adolescence." *NeuroImage* 36 (2007):1065-1073.

47. See A. Koskey, "Sonoma County Teen Survives Plunge From Golden Gate Bridge." *San Francisco Examiner*, accessed March 5, 2012, http://www.sfexaminer.com/local/2011/03/sonoma-county-teen-survives-plunge-golden-gate-bridge.

48. See R.C. Kessler et al., "Lifetime Co-occurrence of DSM-III-R Alcohol Abuse and Dependence With Other Psychiatric Disorders in The National Comorbidity Survey," in *Archives of General Psychiatry* 54 (1997): 313-321. See also T. Paus, M. Keshavan, and J.N. Giedd, "Why Do Many Psychiatric Disorders Emerge During Adolescence?" in *Nature Reviews Neuroscience* 9, no. 12 (2008): 947-957.

49. See B.J. Casey et al., "The Storm and Stress of Adolescence: Insights From Human Imaging and Mouse Genetics," in *Developmental Psychobiology* 52, no. 3 (2010): 225–235.

50. See K. Blair et al., "Response to Emotional Expressions in Generalized Social Phobia and Generalized Anxiety Disorder: Evidence For Separate Disorders" in *American Journal of Psychiatry* 165 (2005): 1193–1202.

51. See A. Rae Simpson, "Raising Teens: A Synthesis of Research and a Foundation for Action." Project on the Parenting of Adolescents, Center for Health Communication, Harvard School of Public Health, copyright 2001 by A. Rae Simpson and the President and Fellows of Harvard College. The report is available online at http://hrweb.mit.edu/worklife/teens-youngadults-overview/.

52. Simpson, "Raising Teens," 32.

CHAPTER 2: THE BIG PROBLEMS

1. I hope you'll think of the concept of *status* here. The less status one is afforded, the harder it is to retain our equanimity in the face of this lack of regard, compassion, and care. This is one of the reasons we seek and desire high(er) status. It's not that we're just narcissistic; status makes a difference in how you are treated, in your physical and psychological health, and in your access to resources that ease the difficulties of living.

2. See G. Stanley Hall's *Adolescence: Its Psychology and Its Relation to Physiology, Anthropology, Sociology, Sex, Crime, Religion, and Education (2 Vols).* (New York: Appleton Press, 1904). Cf. J. J. Arnett, "Adolescent Storm and Stress, Reconsidered," in *American Psychologist* 54, no. 5 (1999): 317-26.

3. Some of the grownups we see in the film at 49, for example, are so very clearly deeply connected in terms of personality, lifestyle choices, and social class to the person they were at 7. However, many of the children in the film made remarkable changes, fueled by parents, teachers, and social institutions. Maturation and development were powerfully at work with each child. A particularly poignant example is the case of Neil, who while suffering for many years with crippling anxiety and depression (with its strong biological propensities), nonetheless ends up heavily and productively involved in local community-building and politics, with the help of others.

4. See R. D. Enright et al., "Do Economic Conditions Influence How Theorists View Adolescents?" in *Journal of Youth and Adolescence* 16, no. 6 (1997): 541-559.

5. I think that the East/West dichotomy, too, is a false one, but that is for a different kind of book.

6. There are so many ways, too, of describing "the postmodern," as if there is such a *thing*. That very activity of defining the postmodern made many a career in the 1970s, '80s, and '90s. We've all got to make a living. See, for example, S. Connor, *Postmodernist Culture: An Introduction to Theories of the Contemporary* (Oxford: Blackwell Publishers, 1989) and also J.F. Lyotard, *The Postmodern Explained: Correpsondence, 1982-85* (Minneapolis: University of Minnesota Press, 1992).

7. See, for example, Stephanie Coontz's fine volume *The Way We Never Were: American Families and the Nostalgia Trap* (New York: Basic Books, 1993).

8. The U.C. Berkeley Parents Network began as a small online support community primarily for people who worked at Cal Berkeley. The online bulletin board allowed people in the university community to exchange parenting information of all kinds. It has blossomed over the years to include

people from all around the Bay Area, asking the broadest range of questions about their infants, children, teens, and young adults. In the online forum, parents generally answer other parents and get to hear a wide sweep of (almost entirely uncensored) opinions and thoughts. You can visit them online at http://parents.berkeley.edu.

9. Quote from Michael Josephson, president of the Josephson Institute Center for Youth Ethics. This was Josephson's response to the 2002 "Ethics Report Card." Available online at: http://character-counts.org/programs/reportcard/2002/index.html.

10. See, for example, Michael Lewis, *The Big Short: Inside the Doomsday Machine* (New York: W. W. Norton & Company, 2011). See also G. Morgenson and J. Rosner, *Reckless Endangerment: How Outsized Ambition, Greed, and Corruption Led to Economic Armageddon* (New York: Times Books, 2011).

11. See P. Cumsille, N. Darling, and M.L. Martinez, "Shading the Truth: The Patterning of Adolescents' Decisions to Avoid Issues, Disclose, or Lie to Parents," in *Journal of Adolescence* 2 (2010): 285-96. As quoted in Bronson, P., & Merryman, A. *NurtureShock*: *New Thinking About Children* (New York: Twelve, 2009). See also N. Darling, "Discipline," in *Adolescence in America: An Encyclopedia*, eds. R. Lerner and J. Lerner (Denver: ABC-Clio), 223-226.

12. And while they might not say they agree, they will often repeat what you said to a friend or group of friends, as if it's coming from them. But most teens would be horrified if you overheard this and chimed in, "I taught her that!"

13. See N. Darling, "Parenting Style and Its Correlates," accessed April 3, 2012, http://www.eric.ed.gov/PDFS/ED427896.pdf. See also N. Darling, P. Cumsille, L. Pena-Alampay and J.D. Coatsworth, "Individual and Issue-specific Differences In Parental Knowledge and Adolescent Disclosure in Chile, the Philippines, and the United States," in *Journal of Research on Adolescence*, 19 (2009): 715-740. See also N. Darling, "Putting Conflict in Context," in *Monographs in Child Development*, 73 (2008): 169-175. And finally, see N. Darling, P. Cumsille, and M.L. Martínez, M., "Individual Differences in Adolescents' Beliefs About the Legitimacy of Parental Authority and Their Own Obligation to Obey: A Longitudinal Investigation," in *Child Development* 79 (2008): 1103-1118.

14. See L.E. O'Connor, J.W. Berry, J.W. Weiss, J. and D. Schweitzer, "Survivor Guilt, Submissive Behavior and Evolutionary Theory: The Down Side of Winning in Social Competition," San Francisco, 1996. Unpublished paper. See R.F. Baumeister and M.R. Leary, "The Need to Belong: Desire for Interpersonal Attachments As a Fundamental Human Motivation," in *Psychological Bulletin* 117, no. 3 (1995): 497-529. See also R.F. Baumeister, A.M. Stillwell and T.F. Heatherton, "Guilt: An Interpersonal Approach." *Psychological Bulletin* 115 (1994): 243-267.

15. See Carl R. Rogers, "The Development of Insight in a Counseling Relationship," in *Journal of Consulting Psychology* 8, no. 6 (1944): 331-341.

16. See S. Chess and A. Thomas, *Know Your Child: An Authoritative Guide for Today's Parents* (New York: Basic Books, 1989).

17. There is a strong correlation between the kind of negative views of the self associated with stress responses, depression, and social disengagement. See, for example, M.S. Caldwell, K.D. Rudolph, W. Troop-Gordon, and D.Y. Kim, "Reciprocal Influences Among Relational Self-Views, Social Disengagement, and Peer Stress During Early Adolescence," in *Child Development*, 75, no. 4 (2004): 1140-1154.

18. See D. Norman and T. Shallice, "Attention to Action: Willed and Automatic Control of Behaviour," in *Cognitive Neuroscience: A Reader*, ed. M.S. Gazzaniga (Oxford: Blackwell, 2000).

19. See J. Lehrer, "Accept Defeat: The Neuroscience of Screwing Up," in *Wired* (Jan. 2010).

20. See M. Krakovskky, "How Do We Decide? Inside the 'Frinky' Science of the Mind," accessed March 5, 2012, http://www.gsb.stanford.edu/news/bmag/sbsm0802/feature-babashiv.html.

21. See A.D. Baddeley and G.J.L. Hitch, "Working Memory," in *The Psychology of Learning and Motivation: Advances in Research and Theory (Vol. 8)*, ed. G.A. Bower (New York: Academic Press, 1974), 47-89.

22. That's Alan Baddeley's phone number at the University of York, in case you need to reach him and talk with him about his theory.

23. See George A. Miller's classic piece, "The Magic Number Seven Plus or Minus Two: Some Limits on Our Capacity to Process Information," in *Psychological Review* 63, no. 2 (1956): 81-97.

24. I wonder whether or not the "automatic" impulse to grab the cake is based on the body's need for glucose—quick energy—under stress. Perhaps the choice of cake is actually "smarter" from a brain perspective, but not so good from a health or weight management perspective. There are roughly double the amount of calories in a piece of chocolate cake than a bowl of fruit, and the cake "reads" as much more sugar-loaded. Animal studies have shown that high-cognitive-load activity can deplete extracellular glucose in parts of the brain associated with memory, and that glucose coming from outside the system reverses this depletion and enhances task performance. See E.C. McNay, T.M. Fried and P.E. Gold, "Decreases in Rat Extracellular Hippocampal Glucose Concentration Associated with Cognitive Demand During a Spatial Task," in *Proceedings of the National Academy of Sciences of the United States of America* 97, no. 6 (2000): 2881–2885.

25. Bronson and Merryman, *NurtureShock*, 2009.

26. See, for example, J.G. Smetana, "The Role of Trust in Adolescent-Parent Relationships: To Trust You Is to Tell You," in *Trust and Trustworthiness During Childhood and Adolescence*, ed. K. Rotenberg (New York: Cambridge University Press, 2010), 223-46. See also M. Tasopoulos-Chan, J.G. Smetana, J.Y. Yau, "How Much Do I Tell Thee? Strategic Management of Information With Parents Among American Adolescents from Mexican, Chinese, and European Backgrounds," in *Journal of Family Psychology* 23 (2009): 364-374.

27. Two people who've done a lot of writing on communication are Niklas Luhmann and Jurgen Habermas. Luhmann, in particular, paints a very different picture of "communication":

> Just like life and consciousness, communication is an *emergent* [italics mine] reality, a state of affairs ***sui generis***. It arises through a synthesis of three different selections, namely, selection of ***information***, selection of the ***utterance*** of this information, and a selective ***understanding or misunderstanding*** of this utterance and its information. None of these components can be present by itself. Only together can they create communication. Only together— and that means only when their selectivity can be made congruent. Therefore communication occurs only when a difference of utterance and information **is** understood.

In Luhmann's view, which is both widely praised and condemned, communication is not something people do, it's something that happens as a byproduct of the ways complex structures interact in life. I introduce his work in order to make the point that what communication "is" is highly debated, often highly abstract, and one of those keywords, the definition of which has broad sociopolitical and philosophical implications. Quote from N. Luhmann, "What Is Communication?" in *Communication Theory* 2, no. 3 (1992): 251–259.

28. See I.J. Roseman and C.A. Smith, "Appraisal Theory: Overview, Assumptions, Varieties, Controversies." *Appraisal Processes In Emotion: Theory, Methods, Research. Series in affective science*, eds. K.R. Scherer, A. Schorr and T. Johnston, (Oxford: Oxford University Press, 2001), xiv. 3-19.

29. See A.T. Beck, *The Cognitive Theory of Depression* (New York: Guilford Press, 1979).

30. Cf. E. Aronson, E., T.D. Wilson, and R.M. Akert, *Social Psychology*. 7 ed. (Upper Saddle River: Pearson Education Inc., 2005.)

31. See S. Schachter, S, and J.E. Singer, "Cognitive, Social and Physiological Determinants of Emotional State." *Psychological Review* 69 (1962): 379-99.

32. See S.L. Schneider and C.M. Caffray, "Affective Motivators and Experience in Adolescents' Development of Health-Related Behavior Patterns," in *The Adolescent Brain Learning, Reasoning, and Decision Making*, eds. V.F. Reyna, S.B. Chapman, M.R. Dougherty, and J. Confrey (New York: American Psychological Association, 2012), 291-334.

33. This crucial finding has been supported in the explosion of imaging studies and empirical researches on nonconscious mental functioning done by people like Joseph LeDoux, Antonio Damasio, Pawel Lewicki, and hundreds of others. Since Joe, Hal, and members of the Mt. Zion Psychotherapy Research Group (now SFPRG) formulated their theory positing high degrees of efficient, fast, and accurate nonconscious processing, it is almost an axiom now in cognitive neuroscience that our brains do much more and much more efficient nonconscious assessment and organization than we do consciously.

34. See Joseph Weiss, *How Psychotherapy Works: Process and Technique* (New York: Guilford Press), 20.

35. See, for example, M. Hilbert, "Toward a Synthesis of Cognitive Biases: How Noisy Information Processing Can Bias Human Decision Making," in *Psychological Bulletin* 138 no. 2 (2012):211-237.

36. See P. Ekman and E.L. Roenberg, *What the Face Reveals: Basic and Applied Studies of Spontaneous Expression Using the Facial Action Coding System (FACS)* (New York & London: Oxford University Press, 2005). See, A.A. Baird et al., "Functional Magnetic Resonance Imaging of Facial Affect Recognition in Children and Adolescents," in *Child Adolescent Psychiatry* 38, no. 2 (1999): 195-99. See also D. Yurgelun-Todd, "Emotional and Cognitive Changes During Adolescence," in *Current Opinion in Neurobiology* 17, no. 2 (2007): 251-257.

37. It is not about how to deal with bullying or fighting—at least not directly. You'll realize more as you read on that most of this book is not about *what to do* in certain situations. It's about how to *think about* what's going on and get some distance on specific behaviors.

38. See Lynn Ponton's excellent volume, *The Romance of Risk: Why Teenagers Do the Things They Do* (New York: Basic Books, 1998), 6.

39. See D.V. Ary et al., "Adolescent Problem Behavior: The Influence of Parents and Peers." *Journal of Behavior Research & Therapy*. 37 (1999): 217-230. See also D.V. Ary et al., "Development of Adolescent Problem Behavior," in *Abnormal Child Psychology* 27 (1999): 141-150.

40. See B.J. Casey, S. Getz, and A. Galvan, "The Adolescent Brain," in *Developmental Review* 28, no. 1 (2008): 62-77.

41. For a discussion of various models of risk-taking behavior in adolescents, see for example V.F. Reyna and S.E. Rivers, "Current Theories of Risk and Rational Decision Making," in *Developmental Review* 28 (2008): 1-11.

42. See G.S. Berns, S. Moore, and C.M. Capra, "Adolescent Engagement in Dangerous Behaviors Is Associated With Increased White Matter Maturity of Frontal Cortex" (2009), accessed March 1, 2012, http://www.plosone.org/article/info:doi%252F10.1371%252Fjournal.pone.0006773.

43. See A.A. Baird, J.A. Fugelsang, and C.M. Bennett, "What Were You Thinking? A Neural Signature Associated With Reasoning in Adolescence." Accessed March 1, 2012, http://faculty.vassar.edu/abbaird//research/presentations/pdfs/CNS_05_ab.pdf

44. See Abigail Baird, "In Teen Music Choices, Anxiety Rules," in *Scientific American*, March 2010, accessed March 15, 2012, http://www.scientificamerican.com/article.cfm?id=in-teen-music-choices-fear-rules.

45. This quote opens dana boyd's wonderful piece on social networking. See danah boyd's "Why Youth (Heart) Social Network Sites: The Role of Networked Publics in Teenage Social Life," ed. David Buckingham (Cambridge: MIT Press, 2007), accessed March 4, 2012. Please go to http://headrush.typepad.com/creating_passionate_users/2006/03/ultrafast_relea.html to see quote from this girl's mother, Kathy Sierra.

46. Many others, including eminent researcher Laurence Steinberg at Temple University, have made the point. See for instance, Laurence Steinberg, "Social Neuroscience Perspective on Adolescent Risk-Taking," in *Developmental Review* 28, no. 1 (2008): 78-106.

47. Spear, *Behavioral Neuroscience*, 49.

48. See for example J.D. Payne and L. Nadel, "Sleep, Dreams, and Memory Consolidation: The Role of the Stress Hormone Cortisol," in *Learning & Memory* 11 (2004): 671-678.

49. See for example L. Steinberg, "Hormone Contributions to Adolescent Behavior," paper presented at the Biennial meetings of the Society for Research on Adolescence, Alexandria, 1988. See also L. Steinberg and A. Morris, "Adolescent Development," in *Annual Review of Psychology*, 52, (2001): 83-110.

50. Many thanks to Dr. Shirtcliff for use of her paper. See E.A. Shirtcliff, "Neuroendocrine and Neural Contributions to Pubertal Development, Normative Adolescent Development and Affect-Related Behavior Problems." Background Paper for the Workshop on the Science of Adolescence Health and Development, National Academy of Science, 2005, accessed March 2, 2012, http://www.bocyf.org/090805.html.

51. See Bessel van der Kolk, "Psychobiology of Posttraumatic Stress Disorder," in *Textbook of Biological Psychiatry*, ed. J. Panksepp (New York: Wiley-Liss, 1996), 319-38.

52. See J.B. Persons, J. Davidson, and M.A. Tompkins, *Essential Components of Cognitive-Behavior Therapy for Depression* (Washington, D.C.: American Psychological Association, 2001).

53. It should be noted that this list would change considerably depending upon how safe your child is at any given moment. If your child is dealing with drugs, gangs, violence, poverty, and racism, their list of problems will quickly get narrowed down to "staying alive and safe." But these other problems on the list will not vanish or they will reappear, as safety is more possible.

CHAPTER 3: IDENTITY DEVELOPMENT, RELATIONSHIPS, AND STATUS

1. You may still be able to see some of these videos by visiting YouTube and searching for "Am

I Pretty" or "Am I Ugly." See also Youth Radio's always excellent reporting on the phenomenon, searchable online at http://www.youthradio.org/news/.

2. See R. Coles, *Erik H. Erikson: The Growth of His Work* (New York: Little, Brown & Company, 1970).

3. See L. Steinberg and A. Morris, "Adolescent Development," in *Annual Review of Psychology*, 52, (2001): 83-110.

4. See Erik Erikson's *Childhood and Society* (New York: W.W. Norton & Company, 1963), 260.

5. Erikson alternately referred to this stage as "Ego Identity vs. Role Diffusion" in different articles and editions of his work covering the same or elaborations on the material presented in "Eight Ages of Man."

6. Steinberg and Morris, "Adolescent Development," 2001.

7. See, for example, S.J. Schwartz, J.E. Cote, and J.J. Arnett, "Identity and Agency in Emerging Adulthood: Two Developmental Routes in the Individualization Process," in *Youth & Society* 37, no. 2 (2005):201-229.

8. Erikson, *Childhood and Society*, 263.

9. See Madeline Levine's *The Price of Privilege: How Parental Pressure and Material Advantage Are Creating a Generation of Disconnected and Unhappy Kids* (New York, HarperCollins, 2006), as well as Denise Clark Pope's *Doing School: How We Are Creating a Generation of Stressed-Out, Materialistic, and Miseducated Students* (New Haven: Yale University Press, 2003).

10. I don't want to unnecessarily hammer on this point about the uniqueness of American popular culture in these effects. Substance abuse, significant increases in binge drinking, depression, and Internet/digital media addictions are becoming more and more common in countries where consumerism has taken over cultural and national psyches. The phenomenon of globalization, fueled by the connectivity afforded by the Internet, export American culture throughout the world, and as democracy and consumer culture trace the globe hand-in-hand, the problems associated with teens and status anxiety begin to surface around the world. It's not a happy thing to report that Japan and South Korea are, in fact, far ahead of the United States in recognizing and treating gaming and general Internet addiction, with numerous programs set up to help kids' withdrawal from constant use of digital media. See, for example, http://www.nytimes.com/2010/05/29/world/asia/29game.html on South Korea's attempts to address Internet addiction.

11. From Walter Lippmann, *Public Opinion* (New York: Free Press, 1965 [1922]), 158.

12. Martin Lindstrom's two recent works are excellent examples. Lindstrom helped develop many of the techniques and practices currently in use in targeted marketing. See *Buyology: Truth and Lies About Why We Buy* (New York: Crown Business, 2010) and his most recent work, *Brandwashed: Tricks Companies Use to Manipulate Our Minds and Persuade Us to Buy* (New York: Crown Business, 2011).

13. The entire Intersperience website is worth a view. See P. Hudson, "Digital Ties That Bind. Future Thinkers Update," accessed March 9, 2012, http://www.intersperience.com/article_more. asp?art_id=42.

14. See, for example, S. Baron-Cohen, "Precursors to a Theory of Mind: Understanding Attention in Others." In *Natural Theories of Mind: Evolution, Development and Simulation of Everyday Mindreading*, ed. A. Whiten, (Oxford: Basil Blackwell, 1991), 233-51.

15. To read more about the incredibly important phenomenon associated with shame, see Don Na-

thanson's important volume, *Shame and Pride: Affect, Sex, and the Birth of the Self* (New York: W. W. Norton & Company, 1992).

16. The "Facebook Depression" study, as its now called (all over the Internet), originally appeared in the journal *Pediatrics,* and it is a lousy study; it actually isn't a study, it's a clinical report and when the media pick up and run with something like this, it's hard to get that horse back in the barn. It also makes it difficult for future work that is actually well done and may show a causal relationship between individuals prone to depression already and their time spent on Facebook or similar social networking site. This is a good example of how quickly (and poorly) the media can pick up and run with a "science" or "research" study and repeat it without any real assessment of the study. See, for example, John Grohol's 2010 online piece, "Pediatrics Journal Gets It Wrong About 'Facebook Depression,'" accessed March 12, 2012, http://www.cchrint.org/2011/03/29/pediatrics-journal-gets-it-wrong-about-facebook-depression/.

17. See Alain de Botton's outstanding work *Status Anxiety* (New York: Pantheon, 2004), vii.

18. de Botton, *Status Anxiety*, 26.

19. de Botton, *Status Anxiety*, 7.

20. As an aside, teens do have "youth," which in itself is a high status quality, and can substitute for not having a job, in some cases.

21. *Ibid.*, 117.

22. See J. Dickler "The Coming Millionaire Boom." CNN Money Online, accessed March 1, 2012, http://money.cnn.com/2011/05/05/pf/millionaire_rise/index.htm.

23. See R. Frank, "U.S. Has Record Number of Millionaires." The Wealth Report (online Blog of *Wall Street Journal*), accessed March 14, 2012, http://blogs.wsj.com/wealth/2011/06/22/u-s-has-record-number-of-millionaires/.

24. de Botton, *Status Anxiety*, 26.

25. *Ibid.*, 8–9.

26. See Erik Erikson, *Insight and Responsibility* (New York: W. W. Norton & Company, 1964).

125. For the 1978 edition, Erikson added the words "and confusion" to this definition of fidelity.

27. See J.E. Cote and C.G. Levine, *Identity Formation, Agency, and Culture: A Social Psychological Synthesis* (Philadelphia: Psychology Press, 2002), 202-03.

CHAPTER 4: PARENTING IN THE DIGITAL AGE

1. *Haptics* is the science of applying touch (tactile) sensation and control to interaction with computer applications.

2. See J. Valentino-DeVries, "Learning to Play 'Angry Birds' Before You Can Tie Your Shoes," accessed January 21, 2012, http://blogs.wsj.com/digits/2011/01/19/learning-to-play-angry-birds-before-you-can-tie-your-shoes/.

3. See M. Prensky, "Digital Native, Digital Immigrants," in *On the Horizon*. MCB University Press, 9, no. 5 (2001): 1-6.

4. I'm not sure this means much on its own, but if you put it together with a 2012 study by market researchers Intersperience that says that iPad use in U.K. households is dominated by 2-year-olds, maybe it means something more.

5. See M. McLuhan, *Understanding Media: The Extensions of Man*, ed. W. Terrence Gordon (Corte

Madera: Gingko Press, 2003 [1964]), 31.

6. See, for example, J. Brockman, *Is the Internet Changing the Way You Think? The Net's Impact on Our Minds and Future* (New York: Harper Perennial, 2011).

7. It's important to note that these observations are supported by published, peer-reviewed research; it's a prejudice I have for the scientific method and its (albeit tentative) results. Chapter 2 is more closely marked for citation of source around adolescent development.

8. See, for example, Po Bronson and Ashley Merryman's "The Science of Teen Rebellion," in *Nurtureshock* (New York: Twelve, 2010), 133-54.

9. See, for example, S. Baron-Cohen, "Precursors to a Theory of Mind: Understanding Attention in Others," in *Natural Theories of Mind: Evolution, Development and Simulation of Everyday Mindreading*, ed. A. Whiten (Oxford: Basil Blackwell, 1991) 233-51.

10. It seems that it is a bit of a "myth" about the brain containing 100 billion nerve cells. It doesn't mean there aren't close to this amount, but the origin of the phrase "100 billion nerve cells" is now in question. See, for example, Suzana Herculano-Houzel's research ("Neuro myth-busting") on the number of neurons in the brain online at http://www.nature.com/neurosci/neuropod/index.html. Scientists like Marsel Mesulam, director of cognitive neurology at Northwestern, and Van Weeden at Harvard think it's more like 40 billion nerve cells, arranged in a relatively organized grid-like pattern, following the contours of brain tissue.

11. This is now known as Hebb's Rule. See D.O. Hebb's *The Organization of Behavior: A Neuropsychological Theory* (New York: Wiley-Interscience, 1949), 62.

12. See, for example, Jay N. Giedd et al., "Anatomic Magnetic Resonance Imaging of the Developing Child and Adolescent Brain," in *The Adolescent Brain Learning, Reasoning, and Decision Making*, ed. by V.F. Reyna, S.B. Chapman, M.R. Dougherty, and J. Confrey (New York: American Psychological Association, 2012), 15-35.

13. Recent works like Madeline Levine's *The Price of Privilege* challenge this notion that poverty is tantamount to high risk for drug and alcohol use. Numerous studies have found that children in relatively affluent households, especially in the independent school world, are in fact at higher risk for substance use disorders.

14. See P. Ekman and E.L. Roenberg, *What the Face Reveals: Basic and Applied Studies of Spontaneous Expression Using the Facial Action Coding System (FACS)* (New York & London: Oxford University Press, 2005). See also A.A. Baird et al. "Functional Magnetic Resonance Imaging of Facial Affect Recognition in Children and Adolescents," in *Child Adolescent Psychiatry* 38, no. 2 (1999): 195-99.

15. The work being done at Vassar and UCLA has been headed up largely by Abigail A. Baird and Adriana Galvan, respectively. See Chapter 2 on "The Big Problems," for a fuller explication of Galvan's and Baird's studies.

16. This comes from a piece written by a 17-year-old girl to an online parenting forum, in response to a discussion of parties and drugs. Her letter was printed online in the UC Berkeley Parents Network Online Newsletter, Nov 19, 1999. See Chapter 5, "Alcohol, Drugs, and Parties" for the full letter.

17. Nicholas Carr, *The Shallows: What the Internet Is Doing to Our Brains* (New York: W. W. Norton & Company, 2011), 6.

18. See C. Thompson, "Your Outboard Brain Knows All," in *Wired*, accessed February 22, 2012,

http://www.wired.com/techbiz/people/magazine/15-10/st_thompson.

19. See V.J. Rideout, U.G. Foehr, and D.F. Roberts, *Generation M2: Media in the Lives of 8 to 18-year-olds* (Menlo Park: The Henry J. Kaiser Family Foundation, 2010).

20. Nielsen Company and NM Incite. *State of the Media: U.S. Digital Consumer Report Q3-Q4 2011* (New York: Nielsen Company, 2012).

21. This is a quote from an interview with media critic Robert McChesney. The entire interview and more material on teens and digital marketing is available online at http://www.pbs.org/wgbh/pages/frontline/shoes/cool/interviews/mcchesney.html.

22. Martin Lindstrom's *Buyology: Truth and Lies About Why We Buy* (New York: Crown Business, 2010) and his most recent work, *Brandwashed: Tricks Companies Use to Manipulate Our Minds and Persuade Us to Buy* (New York: Crown Business, 2011).

23. See Carr, *The Shallows*, 4.

24. This is not a typo. As long as I've been following Dr. boyd's work, since the late 1990s, she's gone by danah boyd, with a lower-case *d* and *b*.

25. See boyd, d. *The Social Lives of Networked Teens* (New Haven: Yale University Press, 2008).

26. See Pamela Paul's *New York Times* 2012 online piece, "Cracking Teenagers' Online Codes," accessed February 28, 2012, http://www.nytimes.com/2012/01/22/fashion/danah-boyd-cracking-teenagers-online-codes.html?_r=2&pagewanted=all.

27. The *New York Times* article referred to in the previous note is very telling. danah talks about being saved by the online world and what it offered in terms of connectivity with others, and she certainly had experiences as a youth that made the online world attractive and salvific. But I can't help but wonder what strong bias this gives her research to show us that "it's all going to be okay," because it all turned out pretty great for her.

28. Data on digital media use in this section comes from the U.S. Digital Consumer Report: Q3-4 2011, published by The Nielsen Company, 2012.

29. Data for the 2010 United States Census are not fully compiled, although they do provide inter-census estimates, available at http://www.census.gov/popest/data/intercensal/national/nat2010.html.

30. See, for example, a 2012 Harvard study that shows tablet use can cause significant shoulder and neck pain. J.G. Younga et al., "Touch-Screen Tablet User Configurations and Case-Supported Tilt Affect Head and Neck Flexion Angles," in *Work 41* (2012):81-91, doi 10.3233/WOR-2012-1337.

31. Descriptions of the "real" (and the problems with identifying what exactly might be real in the media) is from Thomas de Zengotita's excellent volume, *Mediated: How the Media Shapes Our World and the Way We Live in It* (New York: Bloomsbury USA, 2006), 19-21.

32. de Zengotita, *Mediated*, 8.

33. See A. Lenhart et al., "Teens, Kindness and Cruelty on Social Network Sites: How Teens Navigate the New World of 'Digital Citizenship,'" A Report of the Pew Internet & American Life Project, accessed March 17, 2012, http://www.pewinternet.org/Reports/2011/Teens-and-social-media.aspx.

34. See "Digital Overload," recorded talk at the San Francisco Jewish Community Center, December 22, 2011, http://tunein.com/radio/Binah-p143382/.

35. See J. Melkle's 2012 piece in *The Guardian*, "Twitter Is Harder to Resist Than Cigarettes and Alcohol, Study Finds," accessed April 1, 2012, http://www.guardian.co.uk/technology/2012/feb/03/twitter-resist-cigarettes-alcohol-study.

36. This is arguably the *essence* of Nicholas Carr's book—not that digital technology is evil, but

simply and powerfully that it changes us, our neurology, and that means certain capacities will be lost while others are found. I read his work as a plea for attention to and conversation around this fact, not a wholesale condemnation of this fact. It's noteworthy how polarizing this topic can be; many "critics" of Carr freely admit they haven't even *read* his work—they somehow just disagree with it *on principle*.

37. Carr, 210.

38. *Ibid.*, 116.

39. Postman, N. "The Educationalist As Painkiller. "Accessed April 20, 2012, http://neilpostman. org/articles/Postman-TheEducationistAsPainkiller.pdf.

40. See S.K. Morris, "A Comparison of Learning Outcomes in a Traditional Lecture-Based Versus Blended Course Module Using a Business Simulation With High Cognitive Load," Doctoral Dissertation, University of San Francisco, 2011.

41. See Brockman, "*Internet Changing…*", 2011.

42. See M. Goh, "Chinese Teen Sells Kidney For iPad and iPhone," in *The Two Way* (NPR's News Blog), April 12, 2012, accessed April 14, 2012, http://www.npr.org/blogs/thetwo-way/2012/04/07/150195037/chinese-teen-sells-kidney-for-ipad-and-iphone.

43. Carr, 47.

44. See d. boyd, *Why Youth (Heart) Social Network Sites: The Role of Networked Publics in Teenage Social Life*, ed. David Buckingham (Cambridge: MIT Press, 2007).

45. See, for example, G. Duncan, "Tweet Lightly: How Social Media Could Someday Affect Your Credit Score, Insurance, And More." *Digital Trends*, accessed March 2, 2012, http://www.digitaltrends.com/social-media/tweet-lightly-how-social-media-could-someday-affect-your-credit-score-insurance-and-more/. Duncan's "someday" is already here.

46. See TARGUSinfo Inc., "Taking Online Targeting to the Next Level," accessed March 2, 2012, http://www.targusinfo.com/files/PDF/white_papers/TakingOnlineTargetingtotheNextLevelWhitepaper.pdf.

47. See, for example, S. Lyall's 2011 *New York Times* piece, "Scandal Shifts Britain's Media and Political Landscape," accessed March 24, 2012, http://www.nytimes.com/2011/07/08/world/europe/08britain.html?pagewanted=all.

48. See L. Maggid, "Many Ways to Activate Webcams Sans Spy Software" (2010), accessed March 2, 2012, http://news.cnet.com/8301-19518_3-10457737-238.html.

49. Much of this section follows Joseph Turow's excellent work. There are several other fine works on the subject noted in the Suggested Readings for this chapter. See J. Turow, *The Daily You: How the New Advertising Industry is Defining Your Identity and Your Worth* (New Haven: Yale University Press, 2012).

50. The PBS series *Frontline* produced an in-depth program on the relationship between media, marketing, and teenagers in the program *The Merchants of Cool*. Interview materials, references, excerpts, and reactions from teen viewers of the program are all available online at http://www.pbs.org/wgbh/pages/frontline/shows/cool/. The show is well worth watching for teens and parents alike—a great activity to do together.

51. For example, *Between States and Markets: The Voluntary Sector in Comparative Perspective*, ed. Robert Wuthnow (Princeton: Princeton University Press, 1991).

52. See R. Purushotma, M. Weigel, K. Clinton, and A.J. Robison, *Confronting the Challenges of Participatory Culture: Media Education for the 21st Century* (Cambridge, The MIT Press, 2006), 3.

53. National Association for Media Literacy Education. 2007. Core Principles of Media Literacy Education in the United States. http://namle.net/wp-content/uploads/2009/09/ NAMLE-CPMLE-w-questions2.pdf (accessed March 15, 2012).

54. See John Culkin, "Why Study the Media? Thoughts from John Culkin," in *Film Study in the High School: An Analysis and Rationale* (1964), from the introduction to John Culkin's doctoral dissertation; Harvard Graduate School of Education. Copyright 2012, reproduced with permission of Center for Media Literacy in the format Tradebook via Copyright Clearance Center.

55. Carr, N. The Shallows: What the Internet Is Doing to Our Brains, 45.

56. *Ibid.*

57. See T. Lewis, *Empire of the Air: The Men Who Made Radio* (New York: HarperCollins, 1991).

58. This discussion of the advent of the printing press—from *The Shallows*—provided a paradigm for the ways in which new technology changes our behavior and politics, just as we create, influence, and modify that technology. Carr also uses the example of the printing press as a way of explaining how new technology always vigorously supplants older technology.

59. Carr, N. The Shallows: What the Internet Is Doing to Our Brains, 45.

60. See, for example, Clay Shirky's 2011 Foreign Affairs piece, "The Political Power of Social Media: Technology, the Public Sphere, and Political Change," accessed March 24, 2012, http://www.foreignaffairs.com/articles/67038/clay-shirky/the-political-power-of-social-media.

61. Statistics on firearm death from the National Center for Injury Prevention and Control, a program of the Centers for Disease Control (CDC) in Washington, D.C. See the WISQARS Injury Mortality Reports, 1999-2007, accessed March 2, 1012, http://webappa.cdc.gov/sasweb/ncipc/mortrate10_sy.html.

62. See B. Stelter, "In Slain Teenager's Case, A Long Route to National Attention," in *New York Times* (online), accessed March 25, 2012, http://www.nytimes.com/2012/03/26/business/media/for-martins-case-a-long-route-to-national-attention.html?pagewanted=all.

63. See "Late Night: Jon Stewart Accuses Spike Lee of 'Cyberbullying,'" in *Los Angeles Times* (Entertainment), accessed March 30, 2012, http://latimesblogs.latimes.com/showtracker/2012/03/late-night-jon-stewart-accuses-spike-lee-of-cyberbullying.html.

64. See D. Stableford, "Trayvon Martin Case Exposes Worst in Media," in *Yahoo!News,* accessed April 1, 2012, http://news.yahoo.com/blogs/cutline/trayvon-martin-case-exposes-worst-media-210020839.html.

65. See R. Mackey, "Bloggers Cherry-Pick from Social Media to Cast Trayvon Martin as a Menace," in *New York Times* (The Lede, Blogging the News with Robert Mackey), accessed April 2, 2012, http://thelede.blogs.nytimes.com/2012/03/29/bloggers-cherry-pick-from-social-media-to-cast-trayvon-martin-as-a-menace/.

66. Cf. M. Pujazon-Zazik, M. and M.H. Park, "To Tweet, or Not to Tweet: Gender Differences and Potential Positive and Negative Health Outcomes of Adolescents' Social Internet Use," in *American Journal of Men's Health* 4, no. 77 (2010). doi: 10.1177/1557988309360819. The Abstract of that study is worth quoting:

> Adolescents and young adults are avid Internet users. Online social media, such as social networking sites (e.g., Facebook, MySpace), blogs, status

updating sites (e.g., Twitter) and chat rooms, have become integral parts of adolescents' and young adults' lives. Adolescents are even beginning to enter the world of online dating with several websites dedicated to "teenage online dating." This paper reviews recent peer-reviewed literature and national data on 1) adolescents' use of online social media, 2) gender differences in online social media and 3) potential positive and negative health outcomes from adolescents' online social media use. We also examine parental monitoring of adolescents' online activities. Given that parental supervision is a key protective factor against adolescent risk-taking behavior, it is reasonable to hypothesize that unmonitored Internet use may place adolescents at significant risk, such as cyber bullying, unwanted exposure to pornography, and potentially revealing personal information to sexual predators.

CHAPTER 5: ALCOHOL, DRUGS, AND PARTIES

1. For instance, the *Diagnostic and Statistical Manual* lists four criteria for substance abuse and defines abuse as "a maladaptive pattern of substance use leading to clinically significant impairment or distress as manifested by one (or more)" of the listed criteria within the period of one year, including: 1) repeatedly using a substance and not being able to meet major role obligations because of that use; 2) repeatedly using the substance in dangerous situations (like while driving); 3) repeatedly using a substance despite having had legal problems; or 4) using and continuing to use a substance despite the fact you've had ongoing social, interpersonal, work, family, or school problems caused by or made worse by the effects of the substance. If one or more of those conditions are met, it is considered substance abuse. However, if your teen used a substance (like heroin) once and it resulted in a car accident or major injury, or if your teen used a substance in a way in which it was not intended (like huffing the nitrous oxide from a Reddi-Whip canister—called doing "whippets"), that might also be called abuse because of the serious risk involved and the use of a substance in a way in which it was not intended. See the *Diagnostic and Statistical Manual of Mental Disorders: DSM-IV.* Washington D.C.: American Psychiatric Association, 1994, 181-183.

2. The Chicago Recovery Alliance has done significant work to promote the motto of harm reduction: Any Positive Change. The message behind the motto is that there is always something you can do to reduce the harm associated with drug and alcohol use and abuse.

3. This is one reason why I don't particularly like the title of Michael Bradley's book or his approach in *Yes Your Teenager Is Crazy! Loving Your Kid Without Losing Your Mind.* In the book he uses the categories of "normal" and "insane," and talks about teen rages, suggesting parents act as "dispassionate cops" with their kids. There was a lot of money behind the marketing for this book and the hyperbole certainly helped get consumer attention. Bradley reviews much of the same brain science I'm looking at, so I don't disagree with his sources. But why perpetuate a stereotype about "crazy teens" and support (however weakly) the view that teen behavior is beyond their own control (the rather accepted definition of what it means to be "crazy")? A basic premise of *The Approximate Parent* is that teens and parents have enormous potential and actual capabilities to manage and control their experiences, for the better, even in the face of biological, social, and psychological in-

fluences that push toward risk-taking and "bad" decisions—and they do not need their parents (or anyone) acting as a "cop" to support better decision-making.

4. See, for example, R. Davenport-Hines, *The Pursuit of Oblivion: A Global History of Narcotics* (New York: W.W. Norton & Company, 2002). See also, S.M. Fitzpatrick et al., "Evidence for Inter-Island Transport of Heirlooms: Luminescence Dating and Petrographic Analysis of Ceramic Inhaling Bowls from Carriacou, West Indies," in *Journal of Archaeological Science*, accessed February 23, 2012, doi:10.1016/j.jas.2008.08.007.

5. You'll recall from Chapter 2 that adolescent brains prefer low-effort, high-reward activities.

6. This cogent definition comes from a presentation at Kaiser Permanente, Northern California, "A History of the Harm Reduction Movement," by Don McVinney, MSSW, M.Phil., ACSW, C-CATODSW, CASAC, National Director of Education and Training, Harm Reduction Coalition, New York.

7. See Patt Denning, Jeannie Little, and Adina Glickman's *Over the Influence: The Harm Reduction Guide for Managing Drugs and Alcohol* (New York: The Guilford Press, 2003). I think this is one of the best basic books out there on drug use.

8. Denning , Little, and Glickman, *Over the Influence*, 9.

9. See, for example, D. Kamerow, "The Papal Position on Condoms and HIV," accessed March 2, 2012, doi.10.1136/bmj.b1217 PMID19321547 and Roehr, B. "Pope Claims That Condoms Exacerbate HIV and AIDS Problem," accessed March 2, 2012, doi:10.1146/bmj.b1206 PMID 19321545.

10. See S. Tobias, "Anxiety and Cognitive Processing of Instruction," in *Self-Related Cognition in Anxiety and Motivation*, ed. R. Schwarzer (New York: Erlbaum, 1986), 35-54. See also Nathanson, *"Shame and Pride,"* 1992. This points to one reason why confrontational approaches to drug treatment fail and why it's not a good idea to make your teenager feel lousy about him or herself and *then* to try to have a teaching moment. Their brains are doing avoidance, withdrawal, attack self, or other...not listening to and storing away your good advice.

11. From Mike Riera's *Staying Connected to Your Teenager: How to Keep Them Talking to You and How to Hear What They're Really Saying* (Cambridge: Da Capo Press, 2003), 6.

12. This is going to be a lousy example in the future, as kids seem to be able to play "Angry Birds" before they learn to tie their shoelaces. See J. Valentino-DeVries January 2011 *Wall Street Journal* (online) piece, "Learning to Play "Angry Birds" Before You Can Tie Your Shoes," accessed March 23, 2012, http://blogs.wsj.com/digits/2011/01/19/learning-to-play-angry-birds-before-you-can-tie-your-shoes/.

13. The peripheral nervous system (PNS) is sort of roughly divided into three main functional entities: autonomic, somatic, and sensory systems. Sensory/somatic neurons (*afferent* neurons) relay impulses toward the central nervous system, coordinating body movements and taking in information from the environment; motor neurons (*efferent* neurons) of the autonomic nervous system relay impulses away from the central nervous system and take care of the nonconscious functions like responding to danger, changing our heartbeat and blood pressure, temperature, digestion, and all the physical sensations we associate with fight, flight, or freeze, e.g., the release of adrenaline.

14. See S.W. Porges, *The Polyvagal Theory: Neurophysiological Foundations of Emotions, Attachment, Communication, and Self-regulation* (New York: W. W. Norton & Company). Problems associated with vagal nerve regulation and function are some of the most interesting and promising areas of research happening right now, with broad implications for education, psychotherapy and

healing from trauma. The number one mental health issue with adolescents is related to anxiety and mood and this is intimately wrapped up in the functioning of the vagus nerve.

15. You'll have to keep in mind that this really is a terrible simplification of the workings of the synapses, which, like the spaces between musical notes, could be argued to be as important as the nerve cell itself. Some of the chemicals in the synapse further the transfer of electrical signals between neurons while others retard or stop the signals by working on yet more chemicals in the synapse. Some of these chemicals modify glutamate modulators, such as serotonin, dopamine, testosterone, and estrogen—vital chemicals that affect almost all aspects of human feeling and functioning. See, for example, Joseph LeDoux's excellent work, *The Emotional Brain: The Mysterious Underpinnings of Emotional Life* (New York: Simon and Schuster, 2003).

16. See A. Mühlberger et al, "Stop Looking Angry and Smile, Please: Start and Stop of the Very Same Facial Expression Differentially Activate Threat- and Reward-Related Brain Networks," in *Social Cognitive and Affective Neuroscience* 6, no. 3 (2011): 321-329. See also, D. Sabatinelli et al., "Pleasure Rather Than Salience Activates Human Nucleus Accumbens and Medial Prefrontal Cortex," in *Journal of Neurophysiology* 98, no. 9 (2007): 1374–1379.

17. This idea of a set structure called the "limbic system" is considered pretty well outmoded by one of the world's leading researchers on emotions and "emotional processing," fear, learning, and memory. See, for example, the *Edge* interview with Joseph Ledoux, "Parallel Memories: Putting Emotions Back Into The Brain. A Talk With Joseph LeDoux," accessed March 15, 2012, http://edge.org/3rd_culture/ledoux/ledoux_p2.html.

18. See A. Galvan, "Risky Behavior in Adolescents: The Role of the Developing Brain," in *The Adolescent Brain Learning, Reasoning, and Decision Making*, eds. V.F. Reyna et al. (Washington, D.C.: The American Psychological Association, 2012), 267-289.

19. So, let's stop talking about *whether* drugs and alcohol affect adolescent development and maturation. Of course they do, they are *drugs; that's what drugs do.* Let's talk about *how* they affect it. When I say this to teens, it makes sense to them and the science backs it up. I won't say to teens that drugs and alcohol are evil and will ruin and rot your brain. But I will say that drugs affect your brain and body and that is a fact and why wouldn't they want to know *how* that is? I haven't met a teen yet that didn't say, "Sure, I want to know how."

20. See S. Ramsden et al, "Verbal and Nonverbal Intelligence Changes in the Teenage Brain," in *Nature* (2011, epub ahead of print).

21. I am indebted to Dr. Ken Winters, Ph.D., whose cogent presentation on teens and addiction informs this section. I first heard Professor Winters present this material in 2005 in Las Vegas, Nevada at his workshop entitled, "Alcohol and the Adolescent Brain: Tastes Great, Less Functioning." Dr. Winters is a professor in the Department of Psychiatry at the University of Minnesota and also serves as senior scientist at the Treatment Research Institute in Philadelphia, Pennsylvania. Material included by permission of Dr. Winters, 2012.

22. This is admittedly a high-level overview and doesn't begin to cover all the changes that happen in the brain in the presence of drugs or alcohol, but I think it's a good, basic way to understand the power of the process in its relation to the reward pathway.

23. See A.J. Silva et al, "CREB and Memory," in *Annual Review of Neuroscience* 21 (1998): 127-148.

24. There are certainly studies, though, that compare previous-year rates of alcohol dependence, for

example, that show that rates of alcohol use disorders are highest among teens 17-20, higher than for adults over 20. See, for example, D. Falk, H-y Yi and S. Hiller-Sturmhöfel, "An Epidemiologic Analysis of Co-Occurring Alcohol and Drug Use and Disorders: Findings From the National Epidemiologic Survey of Alcohol and Related Conditions (NESARC)." *Alcohol Research & Health* 31, no. 2 (2008):100–110.

25. The definitions of both of these kinds of substance use disorders is now being revised and is out for public comment and review by the American Psychological Association. In late 2012 or early 2013 the APA is supposed to release the 5th revision of the Diagnostic and Statistical Manual (DSM-V). The new DSM proposes folding in the two categories into one category of *Substance Use Disorder.*

26. See R.E. Tarter et al., "Predictors of Marijuana Use in Adolescents Before and After Licit Drug Use: Examination of the Gateway Hypothesis," in *American Journal of Psychiatry* 163, no. 12 (2006): 2134–40.

27. See F.J. Rose and J. Kaprio, "Genes, Environments, and Adolescent Substance Use: Retrospect and Prospect from the *FinnTwin* Studies," in *Acta Psychologica Sinica* 40, no. 10 (2008): 1062-1072.

28. See, for example, L.M. Scheier and G.J. Botvin, G.J., "Effects of Early Adolescent Drug Use on Cognitive Efficacy in Early-Late Adolescence: A Developmental Structural Model," in *Journal of Substance Abuse* 7, no. 4 (1995): 379-404.

29. The Monitoring the Future study (MTF) is funded by the National Institute on Drug Abuse (part of the National Institutes of Health) and is conducted at the Survey Research Center at the University of Michigan. You can view historical results of the surveys online at www.monitoringthefuture.org.

30. The MTF study did not include the use of "synthetic" marijuana in its survey results, but will do so in the future. Also, while the MFT study suggests that the drop in "perceived risk" for using weed might be related to a much more high-profile national discussion of medical marijuana and legalization, it seems to me we would also need to consider other events that occurred around 2007. Can anyone think of something that started in 2007 that might have affected tens, if not hundreds of millions of Americans?

31. Ketamine is now being touted as a treatment for the rapid relief of depression among adolescents.

32. See L.D. Johnston, P.M. O'Malley, J.G. Bachman, and J.E. Schulenberg, *Monitoring the Future National Results on Adolescent Drug Use: Overview of Key Findings, 2011* (Ann Arbor: Institute for Social Research, The University of Michigan, 2011), 11.

33. I'm going to be *very* unscientific here and suggest that the decrease in street drug usage and increase in prescription drug usage among teens that began in the mid-1990s has something to do with the Internet, which began in its modern form around 1994. I will be glad to retract or amplify this sentiment if someone wants to send me some good research on the topic.

34. Overall trend data between the two studies has itself been studied and appears very similar. Data from the Youth Risk Behavior Surveillance System (YRBSS) also comes out yearly as part of the *Youth Risk Behavior Survey*. It is available online at http://apps.nccd.cdc.gov/youthonline.

35. See W.B. Hansen and J.W. Graham, "Preventing Alcohol, Marijuana, and Cigarette Use Among Adolescents: Peer Pressure Resistance Training Versus Establishing Conservative Norms," in *Preventive Medicine* 20, no. 3 (1991): 414-430.

36. See M.P. Martens et al., "Differences Between Actual and Perceived Student Norms: An Examination of Alcohol Use, Drug Use, and Sexual Behavior," in *Journal of American College Health* 54, no. 5 (2006): 295-300.

37. This piece was written by a 17-year-old girl to an online parenting forum, in response to a discussion of parties and drugs. Her letter was printed online in the UC Berkeley Parents Network Online Newsletter, Nov 19, 1999.

38. See D. Inaba, D and W.E. Cohen, *Uppers, Downers, All Arounders: Physical and Mental Effects of Psychoactive Drugs* (Medford: CNS Productions, 2007).

39. See, for example, T. Foroud, H.J. Edenberg, and J.C. Crabbe, "Who Is at Risk for Alcoholism," in *Alcohol Research and Health* (a publication of the National Institute on Alcohol Abuse and Alcoholism (NIAAA)) 33, nos. 1 and 2 (2010): 64-75.

40. See R.C. Kessler et al., "Lifetime Co-occurrence of DSM-III-R Alcohol Abuse and Dependence With Other Psychiatric Disorders in the National Comorbidity Survey," in *Archives of General Psychiatry* 54 (1997): 313-321.

41. For example, see J. Biederman et al., "Does Attention-Deficit Hyperactivity Disorder Impact the Developmental Course of Drug and Alcohol Abuse and Dependence?," in *Biological Psychiatry* 44 (1998): 269-273.

42. See A. Verdejo-Garcia, A. Bechara, E.C. Recknor, and M. Perez-Garcia, "Negative Emotion-Driven Impulsivity Predicts Substance Dependence Problems," in *Drug Alcohol Depend.* 91 (2007): 213-219.

43. See T.H. Kelly et al., "Individual Differences in Drug Abuse Vulnerability: D-Amphetamine and Sensation-Seeking Status," in *Psychopharmacology* (Berl) 189 (2006): 17-25.

44. See J. Sareen, M. Chartier, M.P. Paulus, and M.B. Stein, "Illicit Drug Use and Anxiety Disorders: Findings from Two Community Surveys," in *Psychiatry Research* 142 (2006): 11-17.

45. Galvan, A. "Risky Behavior in Adolescents: The Role of the Developing Brain." In *The Adolescent Brain Learning, Reasoning, and Decision Making*, edited by V.F. Reyna, S.B. Chapman, M.R. Dougherty, & J. Confrey, 267-89. New York: American Psychological Association, 2012.

46. Co-authored with Joe Di Prisco.

47. This definition of "Party" is from *The Urban Dictionary* (Online), retrieved 3/15/12 at http://www.urbandictionary.com/define.php?term=party.

48. As a reminder, here's that "ideal" parenting state we can hope for and reach toward, even if we don't get to it: "calm, firm, matter-of-fact, loving, but meaning business."

49. See Mike Riera and Joe DiPrisco's *Field Guide to the American Teenager: A Parent's Companion* (Cambridge: Da Capo Press, 2001), 153-54.

50. See S.W. Porges, *The Polyvagal Theory: Neurophysiological Foundations of Emotions, Attachment, Communication, and Self-regulation* (New York: W. W. Norton & Company).

51. Control-Mastery Theory refers to these problematic "lessons" as *pathogenic beliefs*, because they warn off the person who holds them from pursuing certain normal, developmental goals. For example, if you learn that you can't possibly confront or argue with someone you care about, you are going to avoid confrontation. Since one human being always has different needs at different times than another human being, not being able to argue or negotiate or confront someone when your needs differ is bound to create some problems. There are many ways to solve that problem: You could ignore your own needs or not know what they are; you could comply with someone else's

desires all the time; or you could try to sneak or hide your own needs, in an attempt to get them met indirectly. And these strategies are exactly the strategies that children employ, in order to not confront or disappoint or argue with their parent(s).

52. A few references are worth noting here. See M.L. Skinner et al., "Observed Parenting Behavior with Teens: Measurement Invariance and Predictive Validity Across Race," in *Cultural Diversity and Ethnic Minority Psychology* 17, no. 3 (2011): 252. See M.H. Licea, "Risk Factors Associated with Adolescent Alcohol and Cigarette Use," Cal. State University Long Beach. See also K.W. Griffin et al., "Parenting Practices As Predictors of Substance Use, Delinquency, and Aggression Among Urban Minority Youth: Moderating Effects of Family Structure and Gender," in *Psychology of Addictive Behaviors* 14, no. 2 (2000):174. Finally, see S.D. Lamborn, N.S. Mounts, L. Steinberg, and S.M. Dornbusch, "Patterns of Competence and Adjustment Among Adolescents from Authoritative, Authoritarian, Indulgent, and Neglectful Families," in *Child Development* 62, no. 5 (1991): 1049-1065.

53. See, for example, M.D. Resnick et al., "Protecting Adolescents from Harm: Findings from the National Longitudinal Study on Adolescent Health," in *Journal of the American Medical Association* 278, no. 10 (1997): 823-832.

54. That is a kind of "overconfidence" and I think it often leads to withdrawal or overinvolvement.

55. See Mike Riera and Joe DiPrisco's *Field Guide to the American Teenager: A Parent's Companion* (Cambridge: Da Capo Press, 2001), 153-54.

CHAPTER 6: THE SEXUAL CULTURE OF AMERICAN TEENS

1. See, for example, P.J. Magistretti, L. Pellerin, and J.L. Martin, "Brain Energy Metabolism: An Integrated Cellular Perspective," in *Psychopharmacology: The Fourth Generation of Progress*, eds Floyd Bloom and David Kupfer (Philadelphia: Lippincott Williams & Wilkins, 1995) and P.J. Magistretti and L. Pellerin, "Brain Energy Metabolism: Relevance to Functional Imaging," in *Philosophical Transactions of the Royal Society of London B* 354 (1999): 1155-1163.

2. See Roland Barthes, *The Empire of Signs*, Trans. Richard Howard (New York: Hill & Wang, 1970).

3. See A. Holman and A. Sillars, "Talk About 'Hooking Up': The Influence of College Student Social Networks on Nonrelationship Sex," in *Health Communication*, 1–12 (2011): 1-12.

4. See H. Jenkins, *Confronting the Challenges of Participatory Culture: Media Education for the 21st Century (John D.. and Catherine T. MacArthur Foundation Reports on Digital Media and Learning)* (Cambridge: The MIT Press, 2009).

5. By the way, I'm not trying to upset or be disrespectful of anyone who reads this and thinks it's *horrible* that I would suggest that sexual activity and intercourse was a "way to get to know someone" if you believe it's for marriage only, and only done with your spouse, after marriage. I'm just talking about the range of adolescent behavior in the past and present.

6. As of mid-2012, Facebook currently lists the following relationship status "choices" for a Facebook profile: single, married, in a relationship, it's complicated, in an open relationship, separated, divorced, widowed, in a civil union, and in a domestic partnership.

7. I don't say this from a political perspective on the right or left; it's just what happened. See J.S. Hacker and P. Pierson's well-researched *Winner-Take-All Politics: How Washington Made the Rich*

Richer—and Turned Its Back on the Middle Class (New York: Simon & Schuster, 2011).

8. See *Youth, Pornography and the Internet*, eds. D. Thornburgh and H.S. Lin (Washington, D.C.: National Academies Press, 2002).

9. See K. Hall, "Billy Gray, Bud from *Father Knows Best*, Collects Racing Motorcycles," in *Southern Antiquing and Collecting Magazine*, accessed March 15, 2012, http://www.go-star.com/antiquing/billy_gray.htm.

10. See Hacker and Pierson, *Winner-Take-All Politics*.

11. From Nicholas Carr, *The Shallows: What the Internet Is Doing to Our Brain* (New York: W.W. Norton & Company, 2010), 116.

12. See, for example, M. Griffiths, "Sex on the Internet: Observations and Implications for Internet Sex Addiction," *Journal of Sex Research* 38, no. 4 (2001): 333-342.

13. See *Youth, Pornography and the Internet*, eds. D. Thornburgh and H.S. Lin (Washington, D.C.: National Academies Press, 2002).

14. From Ariel Levy's *Female Chauvinist Pigs: Women and the Rise of Raunch Culture* (New York: Free Press, 2005), 5. All quotations in this chapter are with the permission of the author. I want to thank Ariel for her generous support and care about women and girls—and *all* adolescents.

15. Levy, *Female Chauvinist Pigs*, 30.

16. *Ibid.*, 29.

17. See, for example, Stephen Hinshaw and Rachel Kranz's excellent volume *The Triple Bind: Saving Our Teenage Girls from Today's Pressures* (New York: Ballantine Books, 2009). Levy also addresses this point in *Female Chauvinist Pigs*.

18. Levy, *Female Chauvinist Pigs*, 128.

19. *Ibid.*, 156.

20. See American Psychological Association Task Force on the Sexualization of Girls. 2010. "Report of the APA Task Force on the Sexualization of Girls," accessed April 1, 2012, http://www.apa.org/pi/women/programs/girls/report-full.pdf.

21. See D. Satcher, "The Surgeon General's Call to Action to Promote Sexual Health and Responsible Sexual Behavior." Washington, D.C.: U.S. Department of Health and Human Services, Office of the Surgeon General (2001), accessed April 1, 2012, http: www.surgeongeneral.gov/library/sexualhealth/call.pdf.

22. See American Psychological Association, Task Force on the Sexualization, 2010.

23. See Kaiser Family Foundation, "SexSmarts Survey: Teens and Sexual Health Communication," accessed April 1, 2012, http://www.kff.org/youthhivstds/3240-index.cfm. See also J. Zalow's 2009 online article, "Girls and Dieting, Then and Now," in *Wall Street Journal* (online), accessed April 1, 2012, http://online.wsj.com/article/ SB10001424052970204731804574386822245731710.html.

24. See C. Timberg and D. Halperin, *Tinderbox: How the West Sparked the AIDS Epidemic and How the World Can Finally Overcome It* (New York: Penguin Press, 2012).

25. See Raymond Williams, *Keywords: A Vocabulary of Culture and Society* (New York: Oxford University Press USA, [1976] 1985).

26. See M.H. Bornstein, W. Kessen, and S. Weiskopf, "Color Vision and Hue Categorization in Young Human Infants," in *Journal of Experimental Psychology: Human Perception and Performance* 2, no. 1 (1976): 115. See also A.M. Brown, "Development of Visual Sensitivity to Light and Color Vision in Human Infants: A Critical Review," in *Vision Research* 30, no 8 (1990): 1159-88.

27. See D.J. Kelly et al., "The Other-Race Effect Develops During Infancy," in *Psychological Science* 18 (2007): 1084–1089. See also L.D. Scott and L. Monesson, "The Origin of Biases in Face Perception," in *Psychological Science*, 20, no. 6 (2000): 676-680.

28. See "Why White Parents Don't Talk About Race," in Po Bronson and Ashley Merryman's *NurtureShock: New Thinking About Children* (New York: Twelve, 2009), 45-69.

29. See D.G. Smith et al., *Diversity Works: The Emerging Picture of How Students Benefit* (Washington, D.C.: Association of American Colleges and Universities, 1997).

30. See, for example, B.D. Tatum, *Why Are All the Black Kids Sitting Together in the Cafeteria? (And Other Conversations About Race)* (New York: Basic Books, 1997) or M. Wright, *I'm Chocolate, You're Vanilla: Raising Healthy Black and Biracial Children in a Race-Conscious World* (San Francisco: Jossey-Bass, 2000).

31. There are hundreds of such studies demonstrating parent-child communication as a protective and risk-lowering factor regarding adolescent drug and alcohol use. See, for example, J. White, "The Contribution of Parent–Child Interactions to Smoking Experimentation in Adolescence: Implications for Prevention," in *Health Education Research* 27, no. 1 (2011): 46-56. See also M.A. Miller-Day, "Parent-Adolescent Communication about Alcohol, Tobacco, and Other Drug Use," in *Journal of Adolescent Research* 17, no. 6 (2002): 604-616.

32. See Deborah Tolman's fine work, *Dilemmas of Desire: Teenage Girls Talk about Sexuality* (Cambridge: Harvard University Press, 2005).

33. See, for example, E.A. Borawski, C.E. Levers-Landis, L.D. Lovegreen, and E.S. Traol, "Parental Monitoring, Negotiated Unsupervised Time, and Parental Trust: The Role of Perceived Parenting Practices in Adolescent Health Risk Behaviors," in *Journal of Adolescent Health*, 33, no. 2 (2003): 60-70. See also, R.L. Repetti, S.E. Taylor, and T.E. Seeman, "Risky Families: Family Social Environments and the Mental and Physical Health of Offspring," in *Psychological Bulletin*, 128, no. 2 ((2002): 330-366.

34. See M.H. Zimmer-Gembeck and M. Helfand, "Ten Years of Longitudinal Research on U.S. Adolescent Sexual Behavior: The Evidence for Multiple Pathways to Sexual Intercourse, and the Importance of Age, Gender and Ethnic Background," in *Developmental Review* 28 (2008): 153-224.

CHAPTER 7: PROTECTING THE WISH TO LEARN

1. From Erik Erikson's *Childhood and Society* (New York: W.W. Norton & Company, 1963), 260.

2. From John Dewey's "My Pedagogic Creed," in *School Journal* 54 (January, 1897): 77-80.

3. See S. Yanow, "Ella Fitzgerald," accessed March 16, 2012, http://www.allmusic.com/artist/p6503.

4. See M. Ruggieri, "Music Notes," in *Richmond Times-Dispatch*, 2000, D. 13.

5. See G. Kaufman, "Yes, Britney Really Is Naked in the 'Toxic' Video: VMA Lens Recap," *MTV News* (08/25/04), accessed March 17, 2012, http://www.mtv.com/news/articles/1490554/vma-lens-recap-britneys-toxic-video.jhtml?headlines=true.

6. See the "Room Noise" music blog, accessed March 17, 2012, http://room-noise.com/2011/01/11/is-britney-spears-a-musical-genius/.

7. See Alain de Botton's *Status Anxiety* (New York: Pantheon, 2004), vii.

8. Sometimes it takes a while, and a lot of money (or the latest Adobe Photoshop suite) to get to

"very good looking." A recent *Daily Mail* story alleges that Jennifer Anniston spends about $8,000 a month on her beauty regimen. Accessed March 17, 2012, http://www.dailymail.co.uk/femail/article-2114414/Jennifer-Anistons-monthly-beauty-broken-down.html. You might want to take a look at websites like "Chill Out Point" or "Celebrities Without Makeup" to see the rather extensive digital makeovers that most celebrities go through on their ways to appearing "beautiful" in public all the time (http://www.chilloutpoint.com/misc/celebrities-before-and-after-photoshop.html or http://seehere.blogspot.com/2006/08/celebrities-without-makeup.html).

9. See Andrew Matson's 2009 article on Andy Hildebrand, "Inventor of Auto-Tune: 'I'm Innocent!'" *The Seattle Times* (Online), accessed March 17, 2012, http://seattletimes.nwsource.com/html/matsononmusic/2009389530_post.html.

10. See Nicholas Carr, *The Shallows: What the Internet Is Doing to Our Brains* (New York: W. W. Norton & Company, 2011), 3-4.

11. This is a quote from Branford Marsalis, one of the stars of the film *Before the Music Dies*. Shapter, A. (Director, Writer) & Rasmussen, J (Producer, Writer). (2006). *Before the Music Dies*. Roadwings Entertainment. More information available online at http://www.roadwingsentertainment.com/before-the-music-dies/.

12. See Council for American Private Education (CAPE), "Facts and Studies," accessed March 18, 2012, http://www.capenet.org/facts.html.

13. According to the National Center for Education Statistics (NCES), basic achievement "denotes partial mastery of the knowledge and skills fundamental for proficient work at a given grade," proficient achievement "represents solid academic performance, and competency over challenging subject matter," and advanced achievement "signifies superior performance at a given grade." The level proficient represents the standard all students are expected reach. For further information, see http://nces.ed.gov/nationsreportcard/science/achieveall.asp.

14. *Ibid.*, accessed March 19, http://www.capenet.org/pdf/Outlook355.pdf.

15. See W.H. Jeynes, "The Relationship Between Parental Involvement and Urban Secondary School Student Academic Achievement," in *Urban Education* 42, no. 1 (2007): 82-110. See also W.H. Jeynes, "Religion, Intact Families and the Achievement Gap," in *Interdisciplinary Journal of Research on Religion* 3, no. 3 (2007): 1-24.

16. See Child Trends DataBank, "High School Dropout Rates," accessed March 19, 2012, http://www.childtrendsdatabank.org/?q=node/300.

17. See, for example, Stephen Holden's (9/23/10) *New York Times* film review of *Waiting for Superman*—a profile of Geoffrey Canda's work with the Harlem Children's Zone in New York, accessed March 19, 2012, http://www.nytimes.com/2010/09/24/movies/24waiting.html.

18. See V.E. Frankl, *Viktor Frankl – Recollections: An Autobiography*, trans. J. and J. Fabry (New York: Plenum Publishing, 1996; originally published in 1995 as Was nicht in meinen Büchern steht).

19. See B. Moreno, *The Statue of Liberty Encyclopedia* (New York: Simon and Schuster, 2000), 172.

20. See M. Weber, *The Protestant Ethic and the Spirit of Capitalism* (New York: Charles Scribner's Sons, 1959).

21. See J. Koebler, "High School Notes: National High School Graduation Rates Improve," in *U.S. News and World Report* (online), accessed March 19, 2012, http://www.usnews.com/education/blogs/high-school-notes/2011/06/13/national-high-school-graduation-rates-improve. The article reports that "One fifth of the country's dropouts attended school in one of the 25 districts, mainly

found in large cities, that the report dubbed the 'epicenters of the graduation crisis.' In New York City and Los Angeles alone, more than 35,000 students dropped out of school in 2008."

22. See YouTube video of a interview with Dr. Frankl, http://www.youtube/watch?v=9ElxGric_6g, accessed April 18, 2012. The full video and more interviews with Dr. Frankl are available at the Official Website of the Viktor Frankl Institute Vienna (http://logotherapy.univie.ac.at/).

23. If you're inclined to watch the Louis C.K.'s show *Louie* based on this description let me just issue a warning that the show is not your average family television sitcom. It's of a very adult nature; the scene described in this book is completely tame compared with the rest of the episode.

24. See P. Gonzales et al., "Highlights from TIMSS 2007: Mathematics and Science Achievement of U.S. Fourth- and Eighth-Grade Students in an International Context," accessed March 21, 2012, http://nces.ed.gov/pubsearch/pubsinfo.asp?pubid=2009001.

25. See, for example, H. Remschmidt and M. Belfer, "Mental Health Care for Children and Adolescents Worldwide: A Review," in *World Psychiatry* 4, no. 3 (2005): 147-153.

26. For U.S. statistics, see, for example, J.A. Martin et al., "Births: Final data for 2007." *National Vital Statistics Reports* 58, no. 24 (2010). For other countries, see *United Nations Statistical Division. Demographic Yearbook 2007* (New York: United Nations, 2008).

27. See T. Sato, "Internet Addiction Among Students: Prevalence and Psychological Problems in Japan," in *JMAJ* 49, nos. 7-8 (2006): 279-283.

28. See M. Krasny's "Schools Under Stress," *Forum* (KQED Radio Broadcast), May 8, 2012. Accessed May 8, 2012, http://www.kqed.org/a/forum/R201205080900.

29. Quote from John Dewey as cited in Denise Clark Pope's *Doing School: How We Are Creating a Generation of Stressed Out, Materialistic, and Miseducated Students* (New Haven: Yale University Press, 2003), xiii.

30. See S. Leckart, "The Stanford Education Experiment Could Change Higher Learning Forever," in *Wired Science* (March 20, 2012), accessed March 27, 2012, http://www.wired.com/wired-science/2012/03/ff_aiclass/all/1.

31. See J. Keane, "What Is Google X?" in *The Washington Post* (Business section online), accessed April 12, 2012, http://www.washingtonpost.com/business/technology/what-is-google-x/2011/11/14/gIQAfR06KN_story.html.

32. See C. Atiyeh, "MIT Puts the Brakes on Autonomous Driving," accessed May 15, 2012, http://editorial.autos.msn.com/blogs/autosblogpost.aspx?post=5d72a73e-3345-4a94-98a3-0a2d993eff3d?icid=autos_2804.

33. See J. Stern, "Google Glasses: Will You Want Google Tracking Your Eyes?" in *ABC News Blogs* (Technology Review), accessed April 12, 2012, http://abcnews.go.com/blogs/technology/2012/04/google-glasses-will-you-want-google-tracking-your-eyes/.

34. See M. McLuhan, *Understanding Media: The Extensions of Man*, ed. W. Terrence Gordon (Corte Madera: Gingko Press, 2003 [1964]), 31.

CHAPTER 8: FAMILY: HOW PARENTS TEACH WHEN THEY *AREN'T* TEACHING

1. See, for example, S.M. Lee, M.H. Daniels, and D.B. Kissinger, "Parental Influences on Adolescent Adjustment: Parenting Styles Versus Parenting Practices," in *The Family Journal: Counseling and Therapy for Couples and Families 14*, no. 3, (2006): 253-259. See also the work of V. Brenner &

R.A. Fox, "An Empirically Derived Classification of Parenting Practices," in *Journal of Genetic Psychology: Research and Theory on Human Development* 160, no. 3 (1999): 1-14.

2. See K.E. Williams, J. Ciarrochi, and P.C.L. Heaven, "Inflexible Parents, Inflexible Kids: A 6-Year Longitudinal Study of Parenting Style and the Development of Psychological Flexibility in Adolescents," in *Journal of Youth and Adolescence*, 2012 (Epub ahead of print).

3. See, for example, N.M. Astone and S.S. McLanahan, "Family Structure, Parental Practices and High School Completion." *American Sociological Review*, 56, no. 3 (1991): 309-320.

4. These styles follow Diana Baumrind's descriptions. See D. Baumrind, "The Influence of Parenting Style on Adolescent Competence and Substance Use," in *Journal of Early Adolescence* 11, no. 1 (1991): 56-95.

5. See E.E. Maccoby, "The Role of Parents in the Socialization of Children: An Historical Overview." *Developmental Psychology*, 28 (1992): 1006-1017.

6. See E.E. Maccoby and R.N. Mnookin, *Dividing the Child: Social and Legal Dilemmas of Custody* (Cambridge, Harvard University Press, 1992).

7. By "arguing" I really mean to imply all the normal activities of scientists—debating, studying, conversing, publishing, revising, etc.

8. See C.V. Luskin, "Eleanor Maccoby: How Much Do Parents Matter? Reading and Misreading Behavior Genetics," in *Bing Times Online* 2001, accessed March 27, 2012, http://www.stanford.edu/dept/bingschool/cgi-bin/bt/aug2001/eleanor-maccoby-how-much-do-parents-matter-reading-and-misreading-behavior-genetics/. See also W. Collins et al., "Contemporary Research on Parenting: The Case for Nature and Nurture," in *American Psychologist* 55, no. 2 (2000): 218-232.

9. See R.J. Comer, *Abnormal Psychology* 7th edition (New York: Worth Publishers, 2009).

10. See, for example, the discussion of historical antecedents for psychopathology and treatment in Comer, 2009.

11. See Stephanie Coontz, *The Way We Never Were: American Families and the Nostalgia Trap* (New York: Basic Books, 1992).

12. I prefer Alan Rappoport's modification of the term to "pathogenic adaptations," for a number of reasons. See A. Rappoport, "Freeing Oneself from Pathogenic Adaptations: A Contribution to Control-Mastery Theory," *Psychotherapy Bulletin* 31, no. 4 (1996): 27-33. In this piece (5) he wrote: I have advanced the idea that pathogenic beliefs are more accurately and productively seen as pathogenic *adaptations*, that such a view would be more consistent with the fundamental tenets of Control-Mastery Theory, that "disconfirming" pathogenic beliefs means gathering evidence that the adaptations which were required of us in early life can be safely relinquished, and that passive-into-active testing is engaged in, as is transference testing, for the purpose of gathering this evidence [italics mine].

13. I think it is somewhat unfortunate that Joe Weiss chose the term "belief" because it seems to make his theory a purely cognitive one. Since publication of the 1986 volume, Weiss has clarified his use of term "belief" and suggested that pathogenic beliefs are more structurally complex since they always include affects (and thus, predictable physiological correlates) and emotions (or in the language of Donald Nathanson, "memory plus affect," and schemas of likely behavioral responses, as well as beliefs about these responses and the entire relational environment—people, places and things). Joe made clear to me in conversations over the years that by "pathogenic belief" he implies something closer to what Bowlby discussed in terms of internal "working models" and dominant

and sub-systems of internal working models or what Nathanson—in expanding on Sylvan Tom-kins's "script theory"—discusses in terms of the development of "affect scripts," that is, *means of organizing and managing affective experience*. In this book, I'm going to use the terms "pathogenic beliefs" and "pathogenic adaptations" interchangeably. See Donald Nathanson's *Shame and Pride: Affect, Sex, and the Birth of the Self* (New York: W. W. Norton & Company, 1992), 245. See also John Bowlby's excellent volume Vol. 2, *Attachment and Loss. Separation: Anxiety and Anger* (New York: Basic Books, 1973), 203, for a definition of "working models."

14. When Joe Weiss writes about a *pathogenic belief*, or we consider a family of pathogenic beliefs, we are discussing something akin to Bowlby's idea of the working model, which has become "un-serviceable":

Much psychopathology is regarded as being due to models that are in greater or less degree inadequate or inaccurate. Such inadequacy can be of many kinds: a model may be unserviceable, for example, because it is totally out-of-date, or because it is only half revised and therefore remains half out-of-date, or else because it is full of inconsistencies and confusions. Some of the pathological sequelae of separation and bereavement can be understood in these terms (Bowlby, 1969, 82).

15. Thus the theory is highly relational and treatment is case-specific, sharing many of the same insights as Self Psychology, Intersubjectivity Theory, Cognitive-Behavioral Theory, and the range of relational theorists and clinicians from Margaret Mahler and John Bowlby to Donald Winnicott and Harry Stack Sullivan.

16. From Joseph Weiss, *How Psychotherapy Works* (New York: Guilford Press, 1993), 194.

17. Later, Freud would write about *Eros* and *Thanatos*, or two forces/principles that helped to de-termine and shape the various conflicts and possibilities of mental (and cultural) life. See S. Freud, *Civilization and its Discontents*, trans. Joan Riviere (New York: W. W. Norton & Company, 1961 [1930]), 97.

18. The issues of "identifications" and "compliances" are complex throughout the psychoana-lytic and psychological literature. The ideas are extremely important for parenting practices, however. When Weiss and his colleagues speak of *identification* and *compliance* they are talking about processes by which a person adapts to their interpersonal reality. Thus, these processes are rooted in real experience and are about survival and adaptation to, rather than defenses *against* reality (as Freud saw them). To identify with someone is to take on their most defining characteristics and to adopt them as if they were one's own. This process is largely noncon-scious (although it can certainly be conscious) and can include the adoption of physical, physi-ological, and psychological characteristics of the other. The conscious aspect of identification is seen in our colloquial use of the term, for example, when we say, "Yes, I really liked her speech and how she came up working hard. I can really identify with her perseverance." Often the process is nonconscious, though, and a child can adapt to his or her interpersonal world by identifying with a parental belief or attitude—about the world, others, or himself. This pro-vides one way for the child to "get along" and be in agreement—a position he or she imagines will be safer, in most ways, especially if the adoption of a particular belief or quality seems to please the parent. A *compliance* is like the *motivational* component of an identification. A child can comply with parental beliefs or wishes by having certain feelings, thoughts, attitudes, or behaviors that represent an *identification* with the parent of some kind. If a child believes that the parent sees him as lazy, he might act in compliance with this belief, to please the parent and

install them as an "accurate judge of character." In this way, the child "wins" (somewhat), by acting as the parental attitude/belief would predict—so the parent is "right," and he remains safe—but he "loses," because he has to continue to act lazy to maintain that tie to the parent, thus making it harder to pursue any normal developmental goal that calls for initiative and a lack of "laziness." He also loses in the sense that he will often bear the brunt of criticism from the parent and self-condemnation. This provides a partial description of how many pathogenic beliefs are adopted—through identifications and "implemented" originally by the child as a strategy of adaptation to reality, but backfiring because this pathogenic adaptation requires the reduction in all kinds of capacities toward greater competence, in order to maintain ties to caregivers. See also H. Sampson, "Repeating Pathological Relationships to Disconfirm Pathogenic Beliefs: Commentary on Steven Stern's 'Needed Relationships,'" in *Psychoanalytic Dialogues* 4, no. 3 (1994): 357-61.

19. In helping to determine *how* we do what we do, the processes of identifying with and complying with our parents' views of the world cannot be governed only by shadowy impulses impervious to reality, based upon getting immediate gratification. The process of figuring out how and why we do what we do is referred to in the psychological literature as the "development of motivational tendencies" and Control-Mastery Theory understands this as the normal human process of *adapting* to reality, not a flight from reality. The problem, however, is that these adaptations may not end up serving us as adults.

20. See S. Freud, "The Ego and the Id," in *The Standard Edition of the Complete Psychological Works of Sigmund Freud*, trans., ed. James Strachey, Vol. 19 (London: Hogarth Press, 1923), 1-66.

21. Weiss, 1993, 3.

22. *Ibid.*, 35.

23. These are, of course, the components that Seligman outlined in *The Optimistic Child* as pertaining to a negative explanatory style. This style of cognition is associated with proneness to depression, and I think it points to a good explanation for why parents of children with undiagnosed AD/HD (who are already more prone to depression) often get depressed, themselves. It's true that if your child has AD/HD you are more likely to have it, too (since it is an inheritable disorder), and since depression and AD/HD are highly co-occurring anyway, that might be one explanation. But Seligman's theory of explanatory styles speaks to an environmental factor for depression in the parents of kids with AD/HD and other learning disabilities.

24. See R. Shilkret, R. (1995). "The Origins of Pathogenic Beliefs: Comments on the Developmental Aspects of Control-Mastery Theory." Unpublished paper, 1995.

25. See, for example, S. Prior, *Object Relations in Severe Trauma* (Northvale, N.J.: Jason Aronson, Inc., 1996). In this work Prior utilizes Freud's (1920, 1923, 1926) conception of trauma to note that trauma points to an overwhelming of the psyche, object loss, and the fear of annihilation. But he is keen to point out that Freud's conception of trauma is neither fully developed nor sufficiently *relational*. Prior cautions about the difficulty of delineating a univocal concept of trauma:

> What happens to the psyche when it is overwhelmed is what theories of
> trauma need to explain. Each theory characterizes the traumatic event, the dam-
> age to the psyche, the defensive mobilization, and the long-term consequences

in different terms. Because all the theories contain the term trauma, one might think they are all talking about the same thing. Surely, one might say, they are all about trauma. But each theory of trauma gives new or different significance to the concept. ...In the theory I devise, trauma is understood as *damaging the capacity to relate to others, producing specific relational dynamics*, and evoking annihilation anxiety. Because the theory defines the concept, we must allow the initial definition to be imprecise [italics mine]. (Prior, 1996, 14.)

26. This note is for the psychoanalytic-minded folks. Prior's caution is wise, because it points to the difficulty (but not impossibility) in operationalizing such an intersubjective experience. For Judith Herman, psychological trauma "is an affliction of the powerless...[where] the victim is rendered helpless by overwhelming forces...[and where] the common denominator of psychological trauma is a feeling of 'intense fear, helplessness, loss of control, and threat of annihilation.'" See J.L. Herman, *Trauma and Recovery* (New York: Basic Books, 1992), 33.

In Greenacre's usage of the term *trauma*, he spoke of any condition "definitely unfavorable, noxious, or drastically injurious to the development of the young individual." See P. Greenacre, "The Influence of Infantile Trauma on Genetic Patterns," in *Emotional Growth* (Vol. 1), 260-299 (Madison: International Universities Press, 1971 [1967]), 277. Greenacre's definition reminds us that theories of trauma are often discussed in terms of injuries to self and as occurrences of childhood. However, when Niederland introduced the phenomenon of survivor guilt into the psychoanalytic literature, it represented a reconceptualization of the concepts of both guilt and trauma. Niederland's studies of Holocaust survivors led him to conclude that his patients were not suffering because of unconscious, ambivalent, hostile wishes toward their friends and family members, but because of these patients' unconscious beliefs that their *having survived represented a betrayal of their loved ones*. See W.G. Neiderland, "The Problem of the Survivor," in *Journal of Hillside Hospital* 10 (1961): 233-247. Drawing on his traditional psychoanalytic background, Erich Lindemann, one of the pioneers in the study of crisis and trauma, defined traumatic experience in relation to the arrested development of the sexual and aggressive drives, and trauma was revealed as arising "on the occasion of a crisis or at a time when the legitimate expression of these drives is expected":

> If the sex drive is the one that has been repressed, varying degrees of impairment of the capacity for sexual enjoyment may ensue. Such arrested development of drives toward sex or aggression often results from overstimulation—excessive provocation of the drives at a time when the person is too young, too inexperienced to understand or handle them—in which case we speak of a traumatic experience. [See E. Lindemann, *Beyond Grief: Studies in Crisis Intervention* (New York: Jason Aronson, 1979), 174.]

27. See, for example, S. Freud, "Further Remarks on the Neuro-psychoses of Defense," in *The Standard Edition of the Complete Psychological Works of Sigmund Freud,* trans. and ed. James Strachey, Vol. 3, (London: Hogarth Press, 1896), 159-185; Neiderland, 1961 and W.G. Neiderland, "The Survivor Syndrome: Further Observations and Dimensions," in *Journal of the American Psy-*

choanalytic Association 29, no. 2 (1981): 413-425; A. Modell, "On Having the Right to a Life: An Aspect of the Superego's Development, in *International Journal of Psycho-Analysis* 46 (1965): 323-331; and A. Modell, "The Origin of Certain Forms of Pre-Oedipal Guilt and the Implications for a Psychoanalytic Theory Of Affects," in *International Journal of Psycho-analysis* 52 (1971): 337-346.

28. See M. Bush, "The Role of Unconscious Guilt in Psychopathology and Psychotherapy." *Bulletin of the Menninger Clinic* 53, no. 2 (1989): 102.

29. The approach is much more akin to the altruistic-adaptive hypothesis of human motivation proposed by sociologist W. Trotter (1919) that Freud considered and rejected in *Group Psychology and the Analysis of the Ego* (1921). See W. Trotter, *Instincts of the Herd in Peace and War* (New York: The MacMillan Company, 1919) and S. Freud "Group Psychology and the Analysis of the Ego," in *The Standard Edition of the Complete Psychological Works of Sigmund Freud,* trans. and ed. James Strachey, Vol. 18 (London: Hogarth Press, 1921), 65-143.

30. See J. Bowlby, "Attachment and Loss: Retrospect and Prospect," in *American Journal of Ortho-psychiatry* 52, no. 4 (1982): 664-678.

31. See M. Hoffman, "Is Altruism a Part of Human Nature?" in *Journal of Personality and Social Psychology* 40 (1981): 121-137.

32. See M. Nergaard and G. Silberschatz, "The Effects of Shame, Guilt, and the Negative Reaction in Brief Dynamic Psychotherapy," in *Psychotherapy* 26 (1989): 330-337; and N. Nichols, "Crisis Intervention Through Early Interpretation of Unconscious Guilt," in *Bulletin of the Menninger Clinic* 53, no. 2 (1989): 115-122.

33. See P. Fretter, "A Control-Mastery Case Formulation of a Successful Treatment for Major Depression," in *In Session: Psychotherapy in Practice* 1, no. 2 (1985): 3-17; L.E. O'Connor, "Survivor Guilt and Depression." Paper presented at the Annual Meeting of Division 39 of the American Psychological Association, San Francisco, California, 1995; and L.E. O'Connor, J.W. Berry, and J. Weiss, "Interpersonal Guilt, Shame and Psychological Problems," in *Journal of Social and Clinical Psychology* 18, no. 2 (1996): 181-203.

34. See S. Weatherford (Gassner), "Reply to 'Commentary on a New View of Unconscious Guilt,'" in *Bulletin of the Menninger Clinic* 53, no. 2 (1989): 143-148.

35. See M. Friedman, "Survivor Guilt in the Pathogenesis of Anorexia Nervosa," in *Psychiatry* 48 (1985): 25-39.

36. See J. Weiss, "Unconscious Guilt," in *The Psychoanalytic Process: Theory, Clinical Observations, and Empirical Research,* eds. J. Weiss, H. Sampson, & the Mt. Zion Psychotherapy Research Group (New York: Guilford Press, 1986), 43-67.

37. See Weiss, et al. 1986, Bush, 1989 and S. Weatherford Gassner, 1989.

38. See Modell, 1965 and 1971. See also H. Loewald, H., "The Waning of the Oedipus Complex," in *Journal of the American Psychoanalytic Association* 27 (1979): 751-775.

39. See Weiss, et al. 1986, Bush, 1989 and S. Weatherford Gassner, 1989.

40. See L.E. O'Connor, "Role Guilt and the Development of Pathogenic Beliefs." San Francisco, 1997.

41. See L.E. O'Connor et al., "Interpersonal Guilt: The Development of a New Measure," in *Journal of Clinical Psychology* 53, no. 1 (1997): 73-89.

42. See Freud, 1923, 1926, and 1930. See also M. Klein, "On the Theory of Anxiety and Guilt," in *Envy and Gratitude and Other Words, 1946–1963* (New York: Delacorte Press, 1975 [1948]). See

also Modell, 1965, 1971.

43. Shame has been understood, to a lesser extent, as a contributor to psychopathology. But since the work of Helen Block Lewis and Heinz Kohut, researchers and theoreticians began to focus on shame as the more problematic of the human emotions. See, for example, *The Role of Shame in Symptom Formation*, ed. H.B. Lewis (New York: Lawrence Erlbaum Associates, 1987); and H.B. Lewis, "Shame and Guilt in Human Nature," in *Object and Self: A Developmental Approach*, eds. S. Tuttman, C. Kaye, and M. Zimmerman (Madison: International Universities Press, 1981), 235-265; and M. Lewis, *Shame: The Exposed Self* (New York: Free Press, 1992); and H. Kohut, *The Analysis of the Self: A Systematic Approach to the Psychoanalytic Treatment of Narcissistic Personality Disorders* (Madison: International Universities Press, 1971). Shame and guilt (which often arise together) powerfully organize our social lives and when linked to pathogenic beliefs can lead to severe inhibitions and potential pathology. Lewis argued that both shame and guilt were *socially* derived emotions, oriented toward restoring lost or threatened attachments. Freud, Darwin, and other 19th-century thinkers held a predominantly self-oriented view of social phenomena in which the "self" was deemed the most salient focus of investigation. O'Connor points to a certain lack of understanding of how evolutionary processes may have developed, which supports not only "purely" competitive but fundamentally cooperative, mutual ties to others, beginning with family members, close kin, friends, and significant others in the environment:

If one believes that the "self" is the main unit...of the social group, then emotions focused on the self—or threats to the self—become primary. However, if one considers that *groups* may be an equally significant unit of organization and of selection, then an emotion related to the group, such as guilt, may be primary. Weiss's theory...incorporates an understanding of man as a group-based social animal, with empathy and the need to belong as primary motivations. (See O'Connor, Berry & Weiss, 1996, p. 2.)

44. See, for example, M. Slavin and D. Kriegman, D. (1992), *The Adaptive Design of the Human Psyche* (New York: Guilford Press, 1992), or R.L. Trivers, "The Evolution of Reciprocal Altruism," in *Quarterly Review of Biology* 46 (1971): 35-37.

45. See, for example, R.F. Baumeister and M.R. Leary, "The Need to Belong: Desire for Interpersonal Attachments As a Fundamental Human Motivation," in *Psychological Bulletin*, 117, no. 3 (1995): 497-529; and R.F. Baumeister and D.M. Tice, "Anxiety and Social Exclusion," in *Journal of Social and Clinical Psychology* 9, no. 2 (1990): 165-195.

46. June Price Tangney's work is of particular importance in this area. See J.P. Tangney and K.W. Fisher, *Self-conscious Emotions: The Psychology of Shame, Guilt, Embarrassment and Pride* (New York: Guilford Press, 1995), 343-367; J.P. Tangney, "Assessing Individual Differences in Proneness to Shame and Guilt: Development of the Self-Conscious Affect and Attribution Inventory," in *Journal of Personality and Social Psychology* 59 (1990): 102-111; J.P. Tangney, "Moral Affect: The Good, the Bad and the Ugly," in *Journal of Personality and Social Psychology,* 61 (1991): 598-607; also J.P. Tangney, P. Wagner, and R. Gramzow, "Proneness to Shame, Proneness to Guilt, and Psychopathology," in *Journal of Abnormal Psychology* 101, no. 3 (1992): 469-478.

47. See K.E. Kugler and W.H. Jones, "On Conceptualizing and Assessing Guilt," in *Journal of Personality and Social Psychology* 62 (1992): 318-327.

48. It was just this question that Control Mastery–oriented researchers Lynn O'Connor, Jack Berry, Joseph Weiss, and their colleagues sought to answer in the early 1990s, through a program of

studies on emotion and pathogenesis. They began their series of studies using a measure developed by June Price Tangney, which defined guilt in a widely accepted formulation as "a self-conscious emotion related to the sense that one has done some specific wrong for which one can make reparation" (O'Connor, 1995). Tangney had defined shame as the feeling that something was globally wrong with them. In other words, in guilt, I *did* something wrong, whereas in shame, *I am wrong*. The results of their studies were published in 1997 and suggested that when controlling for shame, survivor guilt continued to be significantly correlated with the development of symptoms. In each study, O'Connor and her colleagues found that interpersonal guilt was significantly correlated with psychological problems (and that survivor guilt and shame were highly correlated). The studies also suggested that some types of unconscious guilt are more highly correlated with pathology than shame, and that some types of guilt are more maladaptive than others. In particular, omnipotent responsibility guilt can be held in place by extreme feelings of shame and a pervasive self-attribution system in which guilt over specific negative incidents is multiplied and linked, the replay of these scenes creates global moods, depressive affect, and tendencies to interpret upcoming and past life events as fatefully negative (this relates to the pervasiveness of pessimistic explanatory styles). In the case of pathological guilt, one indeed functions with the belief described by Modell (1971) that "one does not have the right to a life." High proneness to shame may be an indication of unconscious survivor guilt (O'Connor, 1995).

49. See S. Tomkins (1962, 1963). The affect/modulator "shame" exists only in terms of other affects. Shame is an *impediment* to positive affects; it is an *amplifier*, not really an affect on its own. Shame reduces our level of interest in a situation, as well as modulates enjoyment/joy. Shame is painful in direct proportion to the degree of positive affect it limits. If we seek pleasure, we will experience shame, since shame "occurs whenever desire outruns fulfillment." Shame reduces our level of interest or proximity to a situation when every other stimulus operates to continue the process of amplifying our interest.

50. In some cases, the "failure" or holding oneself back evident in survivor guilt would be syntonic with self- views, and not necessarily show up in all measures of depression. However, as noted above, these feelings, beliefs, attitudes, and self-attributions do seem to be picked up by measures of interpersonal guilt, which are correlated with the presence of symptoms.

51. See, for example, S. Tobias, 1986, and Nathan, 1992.

52. The work of June Price Tangney is particularly important in this regard.

53. See L.M. Horowitz et al., "On the Identification of Warded-off Mental Contents," in *Journal of Abnormal Psychology* 84 (1975): 545-558.

54. See S.M. Johnson, *Character Styles* (New York: W.W. Norton & Company, 1994). Stephen Johnson's lucid and important work is very much in line with a Control-Mastery view of traumogenesis. If we take even a quick view of Johnson's character-developmental approach, we can see how nicely his view of developmental interruptions or malattunement relates to the idea of pathogenic belief formation.

55. The idea of *retraumatization* is found in Robert Stolorow's work. See R. Stolorow, *Trauma and Human Existence: Autobiographical, Psychoanalytic, and Philosophical Reflections* (Psychoanalytic Inquiry Book Series) (New York: Routledge, 2007).

56. This definition of "aporia," retrieved from http://en.wikipedia.org/wiki/Aporia. I wanted the most common/generic definition of this term since it has so many philosophical implications if borrowed from someone like Paul Ricoeur or Martin Heidegger.

57. This should sound like the insights from cognitive behavioral theory or the work of Martin Seligman and others who emphasize that people with negative explanatory styles see negative events in the world as being personal, pervasive, and permanent. When you *criticize* your teen in this way, you deliver the message that they are at fault, not for a specific reason, but because of who they are, which they cannot change. In other words, a criticism is personal, pervasive, and permanent and usually makes the person who receives it feel *shame*.

CHAPTER 9: DOES MY TEEN HAVE GOOD MENTAL HEALTH?

1. There are advantages and disadvantages to a third-party payer system. But insurance companies have enormous power, and have utilized that power to change the way we think about "healing" and the function of psychotherapy. Insurance companies now offer some parity between paying for medical and mental healthcare (as if they were completely different), but still only reimburse practitioners on the basis of whether the documented intervention will reduce the kinds of behaviors that cost money. In other words, it's about reducing hospitalization, lowering number of missed workdays, reducing proneness to accident and medical illness, and overall minimizing the fiscal impact of the behaviors in question. I'm not arguing that that's bad. I'm saying it fundamentally changes the relationship between patient—who is now called a *client*, in part, to better fit the consumer model—and practitioner. It puts a primary emphasis on client behavior, symptom reduction, and doing what saves money, not necessarily on healing the client via a *relationship*.

2. Though we've only met professionally a few times, Dr. McWilliams's work is one of the most powerful reasons I'm still a psychotherapist to this day. I'm deeply indebted to her. She has been an intellectual mentor for me and a powerful beacon for staying focused on what really matters in clinical practice—the healing relationship, in general, and specifically, how closely tracking the client's subjective experience, really knowing the client, is fundamental in treatment. In short, one size does not fit all, and while there is much to be learned from lists, books, and manuals, real help doesn't become a possibility unless you take "set" and "setting" (so to speak) into deep account.

3. While this material is implied in her earlier work and covered in some detail in the *Psychodynamic Diagnostic Manual* (PDM), of which Dr. McWilliams is an associate editor, much of this discussion follows several of her presentations from 2010-11 on "Mental Health: A Vanishing But Critical Concept." See also *Psychodynamic Diagnostic Manual*, ed. PDM Task Force (Silver Spring, MD: Alliance of Psychoanalytic Organizations, 2006).

4. See Daniel Stern's wonderful *The Interpersonal World of the Infant: A View from Psychoanalysis and Developmental Psychology* (New York: Basic Books, 2000) and Allison Gopnik's *The Philosophical Baby: What Children's Minds Tell Us About Truth, Love, and the Meaning of Life* (London: Picador, 2010). See also S.W. Porges's fascinating *The Polyvagal Theory: Neurophysiological Foundations of Emotions, Attachment, Communication, and Self-regulation* (New York: W. W. Norton & Company, 2011).

5. See E. Erikson, *Childhood and Society* (New York: W.W. Norton & Company, 1963).

6. For example, see C. Hazan and P.R. Shaver, "Love and Work: An Attachment-Theoretical Perspective," in *Journal of Personality and Social Psychology* 59, no. 2 (1990): 270-280.

7. See K.W. Fischer, "A Theory of Cognitive Development: The Control and Construction of Hierarchies of Skills," in *Psychological Review* 87, no. 6 (1980): 477.

8. See, for example, J. Cassidy and P.R. Shaver, *Handbook of Attachment: Theory, Research, and Clinical Applications* (New York: The Guilford Press, 1999).

9. Hazan and Shaver identified four patterns of attachment between adults that roughly correspond to the patterns of childhood attachment. Those adult patterns included: secure, anxious-preoccupied, dismissive-avoidant, and fearful-avoidant patterns.

10. The kind and quality of attachment is mediated by temperament/biological factors, which are largely determined at birth, but we know how plastic humans are…biology and biography are always in dialogue.

11. For more information on the relationship between attachment pattern and development of psychopathology, see J. Bowlby, *Attachment*. Vol. 1, *Attachment and Loss* (New York: Basic Books, 1969) and J. Weiss et al., *The Psychoanalytic Process: Theory, Clinical Observations, and Empirical Research* (New York: Guilford Press, 1986) for an extension of Bowlby's concept of the internalized working model in the idea of the "pathogenic belief. " Children who develop pathogenic beliefs about themselves and the world will warn themselves against pursuing normal developmental goals. In Weiss's theory of psychopathology, difficulties and failures of attachment play *a* if not *the* key role in the disruption and delay of healthy development in adolescence and adulthood.

12. Definition of "Self-Efficacy" from *Wikipedia* (online dictionary), retrieved April 1, 2012 from http://en.wikipedia.org/wiki/Self-efficacy.

13. The term "agency" has very strong philosophical resonances here that I wish to avoid. See, for example, J. Martin et al., *Psychology and the Question of Agency* (Albany: State University of New York Press, 2003).

14. See E.H. Erikson, "Reflections on the Dissent of Contemporary Youth," in *International Journal of Psychoanalysis* 51 (1970): 11-22.

15. Martin Seligman writes that people with negative explanatory styles view negative events as personal, pervasive, and permanent, whereas they view positive events as impersonal, specific, and temporary. He has argued that there is a strong link between proneness to depression and cognitive explanatory style. See, for example, M. Seligman, *The Optimistic Child* (New York: Harper, 1996).

16. Jean Piaget delineated six stages of what he called "object permanence," and the concept refers, in its most basic sense, to the idea that objects go on existing when they cannot be seen, heard, or touched. If a child does not attain these stages of object permanence, he or she does not develop a "separate" sense of self. See J. Piaget, *The Construction of Reality in the Child* (New York: Basic Books, 1954) [*La construction du réel chez l'enfant* (1950), also translated as *The Child's Construction of Reality* (London: Routledge and Kegan Paul, 1955)].

17. See K. Lewin, *Field Theory in Social Science: Selected Theoretical Papers*, ed. D. Cartwright (New York: Harper & Row, 1951), 159.

18. See R. B. Zajonc, "Feelings and Thinking: Preferences Need No Inferences," in *American Psychologist*, 35, no. 2 (1980): 151-175.

19. See Walter Bradford Cannon's *Bodily Changes in Pain, Hunger, Fear and Rage* (New York: Appleton-Century-Crofts, 1929).

20. See W. James, *The Principles of Psychology* (Orig. 1895) (Mineola: Dover Publications, [1895] 1950), 311. Reprinted by permission of Dover Publications.

21. Seligman sets out his critique strongly in *The Optimistic Child*, but this view is shared and supported by others who write about youth culture and proneness to depression, and how the emphasis on

"feeling good" over actually helping children become critical reflectors of their own and other's interactions—successes and failures—can actually lead to feeling worse and clinical levels of depression. See, for example, *The Optimistic Child* or San Diego State University's Jean Twenge's research on adolescent development, entitlement, and problems with the conceptualization of self-esteem in *Generation Me: Why Today's Young Americans Are More Confident, Assertive, Entitled—and More Miserable Than Ever Before* (New York: Free Press, 2007).

22. See W. James, *The Principles of Psychology* (Orig. 1895). (Mineola: Dover Publications, [1895] 1950), 311. Reprinted by permission of Dover Publications.

23. Even when children of color come from economically privileged backgrounds, status is felt and understood in ways different than for their white peers and has different effects. This is not an adequately researched area of inquiry. It's also worth noting that increased levels of risk-taking and problematic behavior are seen both among high and low SES adolescents. See, for example, J. Humensky, "Are Adolescents with High Socioeconomic Status More Likely to Engage in Alcohol and Illicit Drug Use in Early Adulthood?" in *Substance Abuse Treatment, Prevention, and Policy 5*, no. 19 (2010): 1-10, accessed April 9, 2012, doi:10.1186/1747-597X-5-19.

24. See, for example, L. Gottlieb, "How to Land Your Kid in Therapy: Why the Obsession With Our Kids' Happiness May Be Dooming Them to Unhappy Adulthoods. A Therapist And Mother Reports," in *The Atlantic* (July/August 2011), 64-78.

25. This dictum was a centerpiece of Freud's work in *Civilization and Its Discontents*. The phrase "homo homini lupus" appears in Plautus's *Asinaria* (495, "lupus est homo homini") and in the work of Thomas Hobbes (and probably many others), prior to Freud's use of the phrase in 1929. Seneca wrote "man is something sacred for man" ["Homo, sacra res homini (...)"] in Lucius Annaeus Seneca, *Epistulae morales ad Lucilium*, XCV, 33, 65 A.D.

26. This phrase is found throughout the Vedic literature, but it is repeated throughout Chapter 6 of the *Chāndogya Upaniṣad*, part of the Sama Veda, as the great sage Aruni is instructing his son about the nature of divinity and humanity.

27. This phrase comes from the preface to Emmanuel Levinas's *Totality and Infinity: An Essay on Exteriority*, trans. Alphonso Lingis (Pittsburgh, Duquesne University Press, 1969).

28. Daniel Stern's work is particularly good at describing this. See, for example, *The Interpersonal World of the Child* and *The Birth of a Mother*.

29. See, S. Baron-Cohen, "Precursors to a Theory of Mind: Understanding Attention in Others," in *Natural Theories of Mind: Evolution, Development and Simulation of Everyday Mindreading*, ed. A. Whiten (Oxford: Basil Blackwell, 1991), 233.

30. Some fascinating work is being done that builds on discoveries in the 1990s by Italian researchers (in Parma) on the "mirror neuron" in monkeys. It is a subject for debate as to whether humans have similar neurons and whether they are "responsible" for the capacity to imagine the inner world of the other, but these neurons may have some implication for the study of how "theory of mind" develops. See G. Rizzolatti and L. Craighero, L., "The Mirror-neuron System," in *Annual Review of Neuroscience* 27 (2004): 169-192.

31. See H. Kohut, A. Goldberg, and P.E. Stepansky, *How Does Analysis Cure?* (Chicago: University of Chicago Press, 1984).

32. See *The Lost Self: Pathologies of the Brain and Identity*, eds. T.E. Feinberg and J.P. Keenan (Oxford: Oxford University Press, 2005).

33. See S. Baron-Cohen, *The Essential Difference: The Truth about the Male and Female Brain* (New York: Basic Books, 2003).

34. If you have a child who has AD/HD or Asperger's Disorder or another learning disability, you'll argue that this lack of consideration is all too familiar and you just know your child is healthy and loving. I agree. But I'm not saying that problems with empathic capacity or difficulty exercising the "ethical muscle" will ruin a person's entire mental health. I am saying, though, that it will present *challenges*—as will anything that interferes with relating with others. And this is important to consider, because if you find that your child doesn't seem to have this "ethical muscle" developing, it would be good to ask yourself or a professional whether one of the above conditions are present, before you just assume that they're a "bad" kid or have no ethical sense. That's why I make such a strong link between the ethical sense and challenges to mental health. It's easier to think our kids are lazy, bad, or good-for-nothing than to think they might have something going on with their mental health involving disruptions or problems with executive functioning implicated in mature empathic responding.

35. See, for example, N. McWilliams, *Psychoanalytic Diagnosis: Understanding Personality Structure in the Clinical Process* (New York: Guilford Press, 1994).

36. Quote from Nancy McWilliams from the Conference Proceedings of "Mental Health: A Vanishing But Critical Concept," January 29, 2011, San Rafael, California.

37. See P. Fonagy and M. Target, "Attachment and Reflective Function: Their Role in Self-Organization," in *Development and Psychopathology* 9 (1997): 679–700.

38. Dr. Blatt's most recent work is a testimony to his career-long contributions to the understanding of human personality development. See S. Blatt, *Polarities of Experience: Relatedness and Self-Definition in Personality Development, Psychopathology, and the Therapeutic Process* (Washington, D.C.: American Psychological Association, 2008).

39. See L. Spear, *The Behavioral Neuroscience of Adolescence* (New York: W.W. Norton & Company, Inc.,2010), 16.

40. *Autonomy* in general is a much-discussed topic in philosophy, psychology, and psychoanalysis. My use of this phrase comes from my years with the San Francisco Psychotherapy Research group, and conversations with Drs. Joseph Weiss, Harold Sampson, and Lynn O'Connor, in particular.

41. Forgive me for being so personal here, but I found out just how powerful "related autonomy" was in the most visceral ways when my own father died. It was as if a "layer of protection" had someone vanished between the raw world and myself. I realized in losing him that just about everything I had been thinking and feeling (conscious and nonconscious) had been with reference and in relation to him. We didn't always agree and we had different ways of seeing the world, but my views and feelings were often derived from his or against his. But what seemed true after he died was that most things were thought or felt or referenced, somehow, *with him in mind.*

42. The Control-Mastery approach to trauma, guilt, and psychopathology reflected here is thus more akin to the *altruistic-adaptive* hypothesis of human motivation proposed by sociologist W. Trotter (1919), which Freud considered and rejected in *Group Psychology and the Analysis of the Ego* (1921). It takes account of the interpersonal nature of trauma and psychopathology as the result of the conflict between one's own needs and the perceived needs of others. This hypothesis assumes an altruistic motive system and set of biologically based prosocial instincts, like those proposed by John Bowlby.

43. See, for example, H. Sampson et al., "Defense Analysis and the Emergence of Warded-Off Mental Contents: An Empirical Study," in *Archives of General Psychiatry* 26 (1972): 524-532. See also J.E. LeDoux, "Emotion, Memory and the Brain," in *Scientific American* (June 1994): 50-57; and J. Weiss, *How Psychotherapy Works* (New York: Guilford Press, 1993).

44. See Kaiser Family Foundation, "SexSmarts Survey: Teens and Sexual Health Communication," accessed April 1, 2012, http://www.kff.org/youthhivstds/3240-index.cfm.

45. See M. Friedman, "Toward a Reconceptualization of Guilt," in *Contemporary Psychoanalysis* 21, no. 4 (1985): 501-547.

46. See C.D. Batson, *The Altruism Question: Toward a Social-psychological Answer* (New York: Lawrence Erlbaum, 1991); M. Hoffman, "Is Altruism a Part of Human Nature?" in *Journal of Personality and Social Psychology* 40 (1981): 121-137; R.L. Trivers, "The Evolution of Reciprocal Altruism," in *Quarterly Review of Biology* 46 (1971): 35-37. See also R.F. Baumeister and M.R. Leary, "The Need to Belong: Desire for Interpersonal Attachments as a Fundamental Human Motivation," in *Psychological Bulletin* 117, no. 3 (1995): 497-529.

47. See L.E. O'Connor, J.W. Berry, J.W. Weiss, J. and D. Schweitzer, "Survivor Guilt, Submissive Behavior and Evolutionary Theory: The Down Side of Winning in Social Competition," San Francisco, 1996. Unpublished paper.

48. See H. Sampson, "The Problem of Adaptation to Reality in Psychoanalytic Theory," in *Contemporary Psychoanalysis* 26 (1990): 690.

49. See C. Bollas, *The Evocative Object World* (New York: Routledge, 2008), 4.

50. See, for example, Alain de Botton's *The Art of Travel* (New York: Pantheon, 2002).

51. See Nielsen and NM Incite. (2012). *State of the Media: U.S. Digital Consumer Report Q3-Q4 2011*. Nielsen Company.

52. By the way, they can often do this during the first years in college, if they go to college, which can lead you to think they hate it there, when they don't.

53. See, for example, S.W. Porges's description in Chapter 1 of *The Polyvagal Theory* on the function of various pathways of vagal nerve response.

54. See, for example, D.W. Winnicott, Maturational Processes and the Facilitating Environment: Studies in the Theory of Emotional Development (London: Hogarth Press, 1965).

55. See R. Dreikurs, "The ABC's of Guiding the Child," accessed April 19, 2012 online at http://www.carterandevans.com/portal/images/pdf/article70.pdf.

56. See S. Freud, *Civilization and its Discontents*, trans. Joan Riviere (New York: W. W. Norton & Company, 1961 [1930]), 77.

57. *Ibid.*, 33.

58. See A. De Botton, *The Art of Travel* (Kindle Locations 1611-1616). New York: Vintage. Kindle Edition, 2008-11-19.

59. And to this list I would add *music,* for my own personal reasons.

60. I realize that this is not a typical chapter on "mental health," because there is no discussion of the "disorders" and what to do about them. There are a wealth of these kinds of materials on mental health disorders arranged in just that way, e.g., How to spot AD/HD, or the 10 Signs of Depression In Teens. One good website to consult first if you're trying to find information on a disorder is the National Institute of Mental Health website at http://www.nimh.nih.gov/health/publications/index.shtml (to search for publications by topic). You can get consistently good material there on just about every disorder, and

it beats searching randomly online—there is a lot of misinformation about mental health on the Internet, as you've probably seen for yourself. It can be hard to sort it all out; the NIMH site is a good place to start. See also the list of Internet Resources for Parents.

CHAPTER 10: THE ETHICAL DIMENSION IN PARENTING TEENS

1. See G. Alpa, "General Principles of Law," in *Annual Survey of International & Comparative Law* 1, Article 2 (1994).

2. Sylvan Tomkins and later Donald Nathanson understood the shame response not as a primary affect, but as ancillary, as the impediment to the primary affect pair "excitement-joy." This matches well with the understanding from Control-Mastery Theory that the development of pathogenic beliefs in response to traumatic experience results in the inhibition of certain otherwise desirable life goals and/or the capacity to experience joy. See S. Tomkins's two volumes on affect, *Affect, Imagery, Consciousness. Vol. 1, The Positive Affects* (New York: Springer, 1962) and *Affect, Imagery, Consciousness. Vol. 2, The Negative Affects* (New York: Springer, 1963). See also D. L. Nathanson, *Shame and Pride: Affect, Sex, and the Birth of the Self* (New York: W. W. Norton & Company, 1992).

3. Available online at http://msc2010.org/MSC2010-CD/Mathematical%20Moments/mm-index.html.

4. Newton's First Law states: Every body perseveres in its state of rest, or of uniform motion in a right line, unless it is compelled to change that state by forces impressed thereon. From Isaac Newton's *Principia* (1687), trans. Andrew Motte (1729).

5. Erik G. Wilson's *Against Happiness: In Praise of Melancholy* (New York: Farrar, Straus and Giroux, 2008).

6. In Anthony Bloom's *Beginning To Pray* (New York: Paulist Press, 1970), 57-58.

7. A very special thanks to B. for this story. His relationship with his children and, more important, his relationship to life—to what his soul brings into this life—has transformed me in just about every way. He's one of the best humans I've been graced enough to know. I just don't know how I got that lucky.

8. Some of you might call this the "soul" or "spirituality" or a life in G-d. I certainly have no problem with that. I just think of it in terms of *ethics*, because that focuses my attention on what we do with one another, face to face, every day, what we mean or long to be and how we measure the distances or closeness between those things.

References

The Adolescent Brain Learning, Reasoning, and Decision Making. Edited by V.F. Reyna, Chapman, S.B. Dougherty, M.R. & Confrey, J. Washington, D.C.: American Psychological Association, 2012.

Alliance of Psychoanalytic Organizations. *Psychodynamic Diagnostic Manual.* Edited by PDM Task Force. Psychodynamic Diagnostic Manual Publishing, 2006.

Alpa, G. "General Principles of Law." *Annual Survey of International & Comparative Law 1,* no. 1 (1994).

American Psychological Association Task Force on the Sexualization of Girls. 2010. Report of the APA Task Force on the Sexualization of Girls. www.apa.org/pi/women/programs/girls/report-full. pdf (accessed April 1, 2012).

Arnett, J.J. "Adolescent Storm and Stress, Reconsidered." *American Psychologist 54,* no. 5 (1999): 317-26.

Aronson, E., Wilson, T.D., & Akert, R.M. *Social Psychology.* 7 ed. Upper Saddle River: Pearson Education Inc., 2005.

Ary, D.V., Duncan, T.E., Duncan, S.C. & Hops, H. (1999). "Adolescent Problem Behavior: The Influence of Parents and Peers." *Journal of Behavior Research & Therapy,* 37 (1999): 217-230.

Ary, D.V. et al. "Development of Adolescent Problem Behavior." *Abnormal Child Psychology* 27 (1999): 141-150.

Astone, N.M., & McLanahan, S.S. "Family Structure, Parental Practices and High School Completion." *American Sociological Review* (1991): 309-320.

Atwood, T. *The Complete Guide to Asperger's Syndrome.* Jessica Kingsley Publishers, 2008.

Baddeley, A.D. & Hitch, G.J.L. "Working Memory," in *The Psychology of Learning and Motivation: Advances in Research and Theory (Vol. 8),* edited by G.A. Bower, 47-89. New York: Academic Press, 1974.

Baird, A.A. 2010. "In Teen Music Choices, Anxiety Rules." www.scientificamerican.comarticle. cfm?id=in-teen-music-choices-fear-rules (accessed March 15, 2012).

Baird, A.A. et al. "Functional Magnetic Resonance Imaging of Facial Affect Recognition in Children and Adolescents." *Child Adolescent Psychiatry* 38, no. 2 (1999): 195-99.

Baird, A.A., Fugelsang, J.A., Bennett, C.M. "What Were You Thinking? A Neural Signature Associated With Reasoning in Adolescence." http://faculty.vassar.edu/abbaird//research/presentations/pdfs/ CNS_05_ab.pdf (accessed March 1, 2012).

Baron-Cohen, S. "Precursors to a Theory of Mind: Understanding Attention in Others." In *Natural Theories of Mind: Evolution, Development and Simulation of Everyday Mindreading*, edited by A. Whiten, 233-51. Oxford: Basil Blackwell, 1991.

————. *The Essential Difference: The Truth about the Male and Female Brain*. New York: Basic Books, 2003.

Barthes, R. *The Empire of Signs*. Translated by Richard Howard. New York: Hill & Wang, 1970.

Batson, C.D. *The Altruism Question: Toward a Social-psychological Answer*. Lawrence Erlbaum, 1991.

Baumeister, R.F. & Leary, M.R. "The Need to Belong: Desire for Interpersonal Attachments As a Fundamental Human Motivation." *Psychological Bulletin* 117, no. 3 (1995): 497-529.

Baumeister, R.F. & Tice, D.M. "Anxiety and Social Exclusion." *Journal of Social and Clinical Psychology*, 9, no. 2 (1990): 165-195.

Baumeister, R.F., Stillwell, A.M. & Heatherton, T.F. "Guilt: An Interpersonal Approach. *Psychological Bulletin* 115 (1994): 243-267.

Baumrind, D. "The Influence of Parenting Style on Adolescent Competence and Substance Use." *Journal of Early Adolescence* 11, no. 1 (1991): 56-95.

Baumrind, D. et al. *Parenting for Character: Five Experts, Five Practices*. Oregon: CSEE, 2008.

Beck, A.T. *The Cognitive Theory of Depression*. New York: Guilford Press, 1979.

Bellah, R. N. *Habits of the Heart: Individualism and Commitment in American Life*. New York: HarperCollins, 1986.

Berns, G.S., Moore, S. Capra, C.M. 2009. "Adolescent Engagement in Dangerous Behaviors Is Associated with Increased White Matter Maturity of Frontal Cortex." www.plosone.org/article/info:doi%252F10.1371%252Fjournal.pone.0006773 (accessed March 1, 2012).

Between States and Markets: The Voluntary Sector in Comparative Perspective. Edited by R. Wuthnow, Princeton: Princeton University Press, 1991.

Biederman J. et al. "Does Attention-Deficit Hyperactivity Disorder Impact the Developmental Course of Drug and Alcohol Abuse and Dependence?" *Biological Psychiatry* 44 (1998): 269-273.

Blair K. et al. "Response to Emotional Expressions in Generalized Social Phobia and Generalized Anxiety Disorder: Evidence for Separate Disorders." *American Journal of Psychiatry* 165 (2005): 1193-1202.

Blatt, S. *Polarities of Experience: Relatedness and Self-Definition in Personality Development, Psychopathology, and the Therapeutic Process*. Washington, D.C.: American Psychological Association, 2008.

Bloom, A. *Beginning to Pray*. Mahwah: Paulist Press, 1970.

Bolick, T. *Asperger Syndrome and Adolescence: Helping Preteens and Teens Get Ready for the Real World*. Beverly: Fair Winds Press, 2004.

Bollas, C. *The Evocative Object World*. New York: Routledge, 2008.

Borawski, E.A. et al. "Parental Monitoring, Negotiated Unsupervised Time, and Parental Trust: The Role of Perceived Parenting Practices in Adolescent Health Risk Behaviors." *Journal of Adolescent Health* 33, no. 2 (2003): 60-70.

Bornstein, M.H., Kessen, W. & Weiskopf, S. (1976). "Color Vision and Hue Categorization in Young Human Infants." *Journal of Experimental Psychology: Human Perception and Performance* 2, no. 1 (1976): 115.

Bourne, E. J. *The Anxiety and Phobia Workbook*. Oakland: New Harbinger Publications, 2011.

Bowlby, J. *Attachment*. Vol. 1, *Attachment and Loss*. New York: Basic Books, 1969.

_____. Vol. 2, *Attachment and Loss. Separation: Anxiety and Anger*. New York: Basic Books, 1973.

_____. "Attachment and Loss: Retrospect and Prospect." *American Journal of Orthopsychiatry* 52, no. 4 (1982): 664-678.

_____. *A Secure Base: Parent-Child Attachment and Healthy Human Development*. New York: Basic Books, 1988.

boyd, d. *Why Youth (Heart) Social Network Sites: The Role of Networked Publics in Teenage Social Life*, edited by David Buckingham. Macarthur Foundation Series on Digital Learning–Youth, Identity, and Digital Media. Cambridge: MIT Press, 2007.

_____. *The Social Lives of Networked Teens*. New Haven: Yale University Press, 2008.

Brenner, V., & Fox, R.A. "An Empirically Derived Classification of Parenting Practices." *Journal of Genetic Psychology: Research and Theory on Human Development* 160, no. 3 (1999): 343-357.

Brockman, J. *Is the Internet Changing the Way You Think? The Net's Impact on Our Minds and Future*. New York: Harper Perennial, 2011.

_____. 1997. "Parallel Memories: Putting Emotions Back Into the Brain. Edge: A Talk With Joseph LeDoux." http://edge.org/3rd_culture/ledoux/ledoux_p1.html (accessed March 5, 2012).

Bronson, P., & Merryman, A. *NurtureShock: New Thinking About Children*. New York: Twelve, 2009.

Brown, A.M. "Development of Visual Sensitivity to Light and Color Vision in Human Infants: A Critical Review." *Vision Res.* 30, no. 8 (1990): 1159-88.

Brown, M. L., & Rounsley, C. A. *True Selves: Understanding Transsexualism—For Families, Friends, Coworkers, and Helping Professionals*. San Francisco: Jossey-Bass, 2003.

Bruner, J.S. *Relevance of Education*. New York: W.W. Norton & Company, 1971.

Bush, M. "The Role of Unconscious Guilt in Psychopathology and Psychotherapy." *Bulletin of the Menninger Clinic* 53, no. 2 (1989): 97-107.

Caldwell, M.S., Rudolph, K.D., Troop-Gordon, W., & Kim, D.Y. (2004). "Reciprocal Influences Among Relational Self-Views, Social Disengagement, and Peer Stress During Early Adolescence." *Child Development*, 75, no. 4 (2004): 1140-1154.

Cannon, W.B. *Bodily Changes in Pain, Hunger, Fear, and Rage*. Appleton-Century-Crofts, 1929.

Carr, N. *The Shallows: What the Internet Is Doing to Our Brains*. New York: W. W. Norton & Company, 2011.

Casey, B.J. et al. "The Storm and Stress of Adolescence: Insights from Human Imaging and Mouse Genetics." *Dev Psychobiol.* 52, no. 3 (2010): 225–235.

Casey, B. J., Getz, S., & Galvan, A. "The Adolescent Brain." *Developmental Review* 28, no. 1 (2008): 62-77.

Cassidy, J. & Shaver, P.R. *Handbook of Attachment: Theory, Research, and Clinical Applications*. New York: Guilford Press, 1999.

Chess, S., & Thomas, A. *Know Your Child: An Authoritative Guide for Today's Parents*. New York: Basic Books, 1989.

Chin, E. *Purchasing Power: Black Kids and American Consumer Culture*. Minneapolis: University Of Minnesota Press, 2001.

Clifford, E. "Neural Plasticity: Merzenich, Taub and Greenough." *Harvard Brain*, 16 (1999): 16-20.

Coleman, J. *When Parents Hurt: Compassionate Strategies When You and Your Grown Child Don't Get Along*. New York: William Morrow Paperbacks, 2008.

Coles, R. *Erik H. Erikson: The Growth of His Work*. New York: Little, Brown & Company, 1970.

Collins, W. et al. "Contemporary Research on Parenting: The Case for Nature and Nurture." *American Psychologist 55*, no. 2 (2000): 218-232.

Comer, R.J. *Abnormal Psychology*. New York: Worth Publishers, 2009.

Comery, T.A., Stamoudis, C.X., Irwin, S.A., & Greenough, W.T. "Increased Density of Multiple-Head Dendritic Spines on Medium-Sized Neurons of the Striatum in Rats Reared in a Complex Environment." *Neurobiology of Learning and Memory 66*, no. 2 (1996): 93-96.

Committee on Integrating the Science of Early Childhood Development & Youth, and Families Board on Children, and National Research Council. *From Neurons to Neighborhoods: The Science of Early Childhood Development*. Madison: National Academies Press, 2000.

Connor, S. *Postmodernist Culture: An Introduction to Theories of the Contemporary*. Oxford: Blackwell Publishers, 1989.

Coontz, S. *The Way We Never Were: American Families and the Nostalgia Trap*. New York: Basic Books, 1993.

Cooperman, S. A., & Gilbert, S. D. *Living with Eating Disorders (Teen's Guides)*. New York: Checkmark Books, 2009.

Costin, C. *The Eating Disorder Sourcebook: A Comprehensive Guide to the Causes, Treatments, and Prevention of Eating Disorders*. New York: McGraw-Hill, 1999.

Cote, J.E. & Levine, C.G. *Identity Formation, Agency, and Culture: A Social Psychological Synthesis*. Philadelphia: Psychology Press, 2002.

Culkin, J. "Why Study the Media? Thoughts from John Culkin." In *Film Study in the High School: An Analysis and Rationale*. From the introduction to John Culkin's doctoral dissertation; Harvard Graduate School of Education, 1964. Copyright 2012; Reproduced with permission of Center for Media Literacy in the format Tradebook via Copyright Clearance Center.

Cultural Politics in Contemporary America. Edited by Angus, I. & Jhally, S. Routledge, 1988.

Cumsille, P., Darling, N. & Martinez, M.L. "Shading the Truth: The Patterning of Adolescents' Decisions to Avoid Issues, Disclose, or Lie to Parents." *J Adolescence* no. 2 (2010): 285-96.

Darling, N. "Parenting Style and Its Correlates" (accessed April 3, 2012), www.eric.ed.gov/PDFS/ED427896.pdf.

_____. "Discipline." In Lerner, R. & Lerner, J. (Eds). Adolescence in America: An Encyclopedia (pp. 223-226). Denver, CO: ABC-Clio, 2001.

_____. "Putting Conflict in Context." *Monographs in Child Development* 73 (2008): 169-175.

Darling, N. Cumsille, P., & Martínez, M.L. "Individual Differences in Adolescents' Beliefs About the Legitimacy of Parental Authority and Their Own Obligation to Obey: A Longitudinal Investigation." *Child Development* 79 (2008): 1103-1118.

Darling, N., Cumsille, P., & Pena-Alampay, L., Coatsworth, J.D. "Individual and Issue-Specific Differences in Parental Knowledge and Adolescent Disclosure in Chile, the Philippines, and the United States." *Journal of Research on Adolescence* 19 (2009): 715-740.

Darling-Hammond, L. *The Flat World and Education: How America's Commitment to Equity Will Determine Our Future*. New York: Teachers College Press, 2010.

Data on digital media use comes from the U.S. Digital Consumer Report: Q3-4 2011 published by The Nielsen Company, 2012.

Davenport-Hines. R. *The Pursuit of Oblivion: A Global History of Narcotics*. New York: W.W. Norton & Company, 2002.

de Botton, A. *The Art of Travel*. New York: Pantheon, 2002.

_____. *Status Anxiety*. New York: Pantheon, 2004.

"Definition of 'party,'" retrieved March 15, 2012 at the *Urban Dictionary* (Online), www.urbandictionary.comdefine.php?term=party.

Dellasega, C. *The Starving Family: Caregiving Mothers and Fathers Share Their Eating Disorder Wisdom*. Wisconsin: Champion Press, 2005.

Denning, P., Little, J., & Glickman, A. *Over the Influence: The Harm Reduction Guide for Managing Drugs and Alcohol*. New York: The Guilford Press, 2003.

De Tocqueville, Alexis. *Democracy in America*, edited by E.D. Heffer. New York: The New American Library, 1956

Dewey, J. *Democracy and Education*. New York: Simon & Brown, 2011.

_____. *Experience and Education*. New York: Free Press, 1997.

_____. "My Pedagogic Creed." *School Journal* 54 (1897): 77-80.

de Zengotita, T. *Mediated: How the Media Shapes Our World and the Way We Live in It*. New York: Bloomsbury USA, 2006.

Dickler, J. 2011. "The Coming Millionaire Boom." CNN Money Online. http://money.cnn.com2011/05/05/pf/millionaire_rise/index.htm (accessed March 1, 2012).

DiClemente, C.C. *Addiction and Change: How Addictions Develop and Addicted People Recover*. New York: The Guilford Press, 2003.

Dreikurs, R., & Grey, L. *The New Approach to Discipline: Logical Consequences*. New York: Plume, 1993.

Dreikurs, R., & Soltz, V. *Children: The Challenge. The Classic Work on Improving Parent-Child Relations—Intelligent, Humane & Eminently Practical*. New York: Plume, 1991.

Duncan, G. 2012. "Tweet Lightly: How Social Media Could Someday Affect Your Credit Score, Insurance, and More." *Digital Trends*. www.digitaltrends.comsocial-media/tweet-lightly-how-social-media-could-someday-affect-your-credit-score-insurance-and-more/ (accessed March 2, 2012).

Ehrenreich, B. *Bait and Switch: The Futile Pursuit of the Corporate Dream*. London: Granta Books, 2006.

Ekman, P. & Roenberg, E.L. *What the Face Reveals: Basic and Applied Studies of Spontaneous Expression Using the Facial Action Coding System (FACS)*. New York & London: Oxford University Press, 2005.

The Encyclopedia of Adolescence. Edited by Lerner, R. M., Petersen, A. C., & Brooks-Gunn, J. New York: Garland, 1991.

Enright, R.D., Levy, V.M., Harris, D. & Lapsley, D.K. "Do Economic Conditions Influence How Theorists View Adolescents?" *Journal of Youth and Adolescence* 16, no. 6 (1997): 541-559.

Erikson, E. H. *Insight and Responsibility*. New York: W. W. Norton & Company, 1964.

_____. *Childhood and Society*. New York: W.W. Norton & Company, Inc., 1963.

_____. Reflections on the Dissent of Contemporary Youth. *International Journal of Psychoanalysis*, 51 (1970): 11-22.

_____. *Identity: Youth and Crisis*. W. W. Norton & Company, 1994.

"Facts and Studies" (On U.S. private schools), retrieved 4/1/12 at www.capenet.org/facts.html.

Falk, D., Yi, H.-Y. & Hiller-Sturmhöfel, S. "An Epidemiologic Analysis of Co-Occurring Alcohol and Drug Use and Disorders: Findings From the National Epidemiologic Survey of Alcohol and Related Conditions (NESARC)." *Alcohol Research & Health* 31, no. 2 (2008):100–110.

Fields, J. 2003. Children's Living Arrangements and Characteristics: March 2002 (Current Population Reports, P20-547) [Detailed Tables]. Washington, DC: U.S. Census Bureau. www.census.gov/population/www/socdemo/hh-fam.html (accessed March 14, 2012).

Fields, R.D. "White Matter in Learning, Cognition and Psychiatric Disorders." *Trends in Neurosciences* 31 (2008): 361-370.

Fischer, K.W. "A Theory of Cognitive Development: The Control and Construction of Hierarchies of Skills." *Psychological Review* 87, no. 6 (1980): 477.

Fitzpatrick, S.M. et al. Evidence for Inter-Island Transport of Heirlooms: Luminescence Dating and Petrographic Analysis of Ceramic Inhaling Bowls from Carriacou, West Indies. *Journal of Archaeological Science* 3, no. 3 (2008): 596-606.

Foley, S. F., Kope, S. A. K., & Sugrue, D. P. *Sex Matters for Women: A Complete Guide to Taking Care of Your Sexual Self*. New York: The Guilford Press, 2011.

Fonagy, P., Gergely, G., Jurist, E., & Target, M. *Affect Regulation, Mentalization, and the Development of Self*. New York: Other Press, 2005.

Fonagy, P. & Target, M. "Attachment and Reflective Function: Their Role in Self-Organization." *Development and Psychopathology*, 9 (1997).

Foreman, S. A. *Breaking the Spell: Understanding Why Kids Do the Very Thing That Drives You Crazy*. Charleston: BookSurge Publishing, 2009.

Foroud, T., Edenberg, H.J. & Crabbe, J.C. "Who Is at Risk for Alcoholism." *Alcohol Research and Health* (publication of the National Institute on Alcohol Abuse and Alcoholism) 33, nos. 1 and 2 (2010): 64-75.

Fox, A. F., & Kirschner, R. *Too Stressed to Think?: A Teen Guide to Staying Sane When Life Makes You Crazy*. Minneapolis: Free Spirit Publishing, 2005.

Frank, R. 2011. "U.S. Has Record Number of Millionaires." The Wealth Report (Online Blog of *Wall Street Journal*). http://blogs.wsj.comwealth/2011/06/22/u-s-has-record-number-of-millionaires/ (accessed March 14, 2012).

Frankl, V. E. *Viktor Frankl—Recollections: An Autobiography*. Translated by J. and J. Fabray. New York: Plenum Publishing, 1996. (Originally published in 1995 as *Was nicht in meinen Büchern steht*.)

Fretter, P. "A Control-Mastery Case Formulation of a Successful Treatment for Major Depression." *In Session: Psychotherapy in Practice* 1, no. 2 (1995): 3-17.

Freud, S. "Further Remarks on the Neuro-psychoses of Defense." In *The Standard Edition of the Complete Psychological Works of Sigmund Freud*, translated and edited by James Strachey, Vol. 3, 159-185, London: Hogarth Press, 1896.

_____. "Group Psychology and the Analysis of the Ego." In *The Standard Edition of the Complete Psychological Works of Sigmund Freud,* translated and edited by James Strachey, Vol. 18, 65-143, London: Hogarth Press, 1921.

_____. "The Ego and the Id." *Standard Edition,* In *The Standard Edition of the Complete Psychological Works of Sigmund Freud,* translated and edited by James Strachey, Vol. 19, 1-66, London: Hogarth Press, 1923.

_____. "Inhibitions, Symptoms and Anxiety." In *The Standard Edition of the Complete Psychological Works of Sigmund Freud,* translated and edited by James Strachey, Vol. 18, 65-143, London: Hogarth Press, 1921.

_____. "Civilization and its Discontents." In *The Standard Edition of the Complete Psychological Works of Sigmund Freud,* translated and edited by James Strachey, Vol. 21, 59-148, London: Hogarth Press, 1930 [1929].

Friedman, M. "Survivor Guilt in the Pathogenesis of Anorexia Nervosa." *Psychiatry* 48 (1985): 25-39.

Frontline program, "The Merchants of Cool." Interview materials, references, excerpts, and reactions from teen viewers of the program. Retrieved 2/10/12 at www.pbs.org/wgbh/pages/frontline/shows/cool/.

Gale Group, Gale, S. & Kagan, J. *Gale Encyclopedia of Childhood and Adolescence.* Farmington Hills: Gale Publishing, 1997.

Galvan, A. "Risky Behavior in Adolescents: The Role of the Developing Brain." In *The Adolescent Brain Learning, Reasoning, and Decision Making*, edited by V.F. Reyna, S.B. Chapman, M.R. Dougherty, & J. Confrey, 267-89. New York: American Psychological Association, 2012.

Giedd, J. "Structural Magnetic Resonance Imaging of the Adolescent Brain." *Annals of the New York Academy of Sciences* 102 (2004): 77-85.

Giedd, J. et al. "Anatomic Magnetic Resonance Imaging of the Developing Child and Adolescent Brain." In *The Adolescent Brain Learning, Reasoning, and Decision Making*, edited by V.F. Reyna, S.B. Chapman, M.R. Dougherty, & J. Confrey, 15-35. New York: American Psychological Association, 2012.

Glennon, W. *Fathering: Strengthening Connection With Your Children No Matter Where You Are.* San Francisco & Newburyport: Conari Press, 1995.

Gopnik, A. *The Philosophical Baby: What Children's Minds Tell Us About Truth, Love, and the Meaning of Life.* London: Picador, 2010.

Gordon, Catharine M., Laufer, MR. "Physiology of Puberty." In *Pediatric and Adolescent Gynecology*, edited by D.P. Goldstein, S.J.H. Emans & M.R. Laufer, 120-55. Philadelphia: Lippincott, Williams & Wilkins.

Gottlieb, L. "How to Land Your Kid in Therapy. Why the Obsession With Our Kids' Happiness May be Dooming Them to Unhappy Adulthoods. A Therapist and Mother Reports." *The Atlantic*, 2011, 64-78.

Grafodatskaya, D., Chung, B., Szatmari P. & Weksberg, R. "Autism Spectrum Disorders and Epigenetics." *Journal of the American Academy of Child and Adolescent Psychiatry* 49, no. 8 (2010): 794-809

Greenacre, P. "The Influence of Infantile Trauma on Genetic Patterns." *Emotional growth* (Vol. 1), International Universities Press (1971 [1967]): 260-299, p. 277

Griffin, K.W. et al. "Parenting Practices as Predictors of Substance Use, Delinquency, and Aggression Among Urban Minority Youth: Moderating Effects of Family Structure and Gender." *Psychology of Addictive Behaviors* 14, no. 2 (2000): 174-184.

Griffiths, M. "Sex on the Internet: Observations and Implications for Internet Sex Addiction." *Journal of Sex Research* 38, no. 4 (2001): 333-342.

Grohol, J.M. 2010. Pediatrics Journal Gets It Wrong About "Facebook Depression." www.cchrint. org/2011/03/29/pediatrics-journal-gets-it-wrong-about-facebook-depression/ (accessed March 12, 2012).

Hacker, J. S., & Pierson, P. *Winner-Take-All Politics: How Washington Made the Rich Richer—and Turned Its Back on the Middle Class.* New York: Simon & Schuster, 2011.

Hall, G.S. *Adolescence: Its Psychology and Its Relation to Physiology, Anthropology, Sociology, Sex, Crime, Religion, and Education (2 Vols).* New York: Appleton Press, 1904

Hall, K. "Billy Gray, Bud from *Father Knows Best,* Collects Racing Motorcycles." In *Southern Antiquing and Collecting Magazine.* Acworth, Georgia: McElreath Printing & Publishing, Inc. www. go-star.comantiquing/billy_gray.htm (accessed March 15, 2012).

Hallowell, E. M. *CrazyBusy: Overstretched, Overbooked, and About to Snap! Strategies for Handling Your Fast-Paced Life.* New York: Ballantine Books, 2007.

Hallowell, E. M., & Ratey, J. J. *Driven to Distraction: Recognizing and Coping with Attention Deficit Disorder from Childhood Through Adulthood.* New York: Touchstone, 1995.

Hansen, W.B., & J.W. Graham. "Preventing Alcohol, Marijuana, and Cigarette Use Among Adolescents: Peer Pressure Resistance Training Versus Establishing Conservative Norms." *Preventive Medicine* 20, no. 3 (1991): 414-430.

Harm Reduction: Pragmatic Strategies for Managing High-Risk Behaviors. Edited by Marlatt, G.A., Larimer, M.E. & Witkiewitz, K. New York: Guilford Press, 2011.

Hazan, C. & Shaver, P.R. "Love and Work: An Attachment-Theoretical Perspective." *Journal of Personality and Social Psychology* 59, no. 2 (1990): 270-280.

Hebb, D.O. *The Organization of Behavior: A Neurological Theory.* New York: Wiley-Interscience, 1949.

Herman, J. L. *Trauma and Recovery: The Aftermath of Violence—From Domestic Abuse to Political Terror.* New York: Basic Books, 1993.

"High Levels of Satisfaction Among Private School Students," retrieved April 1, 2012 at www.capenet. org/pdf/Outlook355.pdf

"High School Dropout Rates," retrieved April 1, 2012 at www.childtrendsdatabank.org/?q=node/300

Hilbert, M. "Toward a Synthesis of Cognitive Biases: How Noisy Information Processing Can Bias Human Decision Making." *Psychological Bulletin* 138 no. 2 (2012):211-237.

Hinshaw, S., & Kranz, R. *The Triple Bind: Saving Our Teenage Girls from Today's Pressures.* New York: Ballantine Books, 2009.

Hochschild, A. R. *The Managed Heart: Commercialization of Human Feeling.* Berkeley: University of California Press, 1983.

Hoffman, M. "Is Altruism a Part of Human Nature?" *Journal of Personality and Social Psychology* 40 (1981): 121-137.

Holden, S. "Waiting for Superman," *New York Times Online* (movie review), accessed March 19, 2012, http://www.nytimes.com/2010/09/24/movies/24waiting.html

Holman, A. & Sillars, A. "Talk About 'Hooking Up': The Influence of College Student Social Networks on Nonrelationship Sex." Health Communication (2011): 1–12.

Horowitz, L.M. et al. "On the Identification of Warded-Off Mental Contents." Journal of Abnormal Psychology 84 (1975): 545-558.

Horowitz, M. Stress Response Syndromes: Personality Styles and Interventions. New York: Jason Aronson, Inc., 2001.

Hudson, P. 2012. "Digital Ties That Bind. Future Thinkers Update." www.intersperience.comarticle_more.asp?art_id=42 (accessed March 2, 2012).

Humensky, J. "Are Adolescents with High Socioeconomic Status More Likely to Engage in Alcohol and Illicit Drug Use in Early Adulthood?" Substance Abuse Treatment, Prevention, and Policy 5, no. 19 (2010):1-10, accessed April 9, 2012, doi:10.1186/1747-597X-5-19.

Inaba, D., & Cohen, W. E. Uppers, Downers, All Arounders: Physical and Mental Effects of Psychoactive Drugs. Medford: CNS Productions, 2007.

Isles, A.R. & Wilkinson, L.S. "Epigenetics; What Is It and Why Is It Important to Mental Disease?" British Medical Bulletin 85, no. 1 (2008): 35-45.

Ito, M., et al. Hanging Out, Messing Around, and Geeking Out: Kids Living and Learning with New Media. In John D. and Catherine T. MacArthur Foundation Series on Digital Media and Learning. Cambridge: The MIT Press, 2009.

Jackson, M. Distracted: The Erosion of Attention and the Coming Dark Age. Amherst: Prometheus Books, 2008.

James, C. Young People, Ethics, and the New Digital Media: A Synthesis from the GoodPlay Project. Cambridge: The MIT Press, 2009.

James, W. The Principles of Psychology. Mineola: Dover Publications. (1950 [1895]): 311.

Jenkins, H. Convergence Culture: Where New and Old Media Collide. New York: NYU Press, 2006.

_____. Confronting the Challenges of Participatory Culture: Media Education for the 21st Century. In John D. and Catherine T. MacArthur Foundation Series on Digital Media and Learning. Cambridge: The MIT Press, 2009.

Johnson, S.M. Character Styles. New York: W.W. Norton & Company, 1994.

Johnston, L. D., O'Malley, P. M., Bachman, J. G., & Schulenberg, J. E. Monitoring the Future National Results on Adolescent Drug Use: Overview of Key Findings 2011. Ann Arbor: Institute for Social Research, The University of Michigan, 2012.

Josephson Institute Center for Youth Ethics. "2002 Ethics Report Card," a biannual project of the Josephson Institute, available at http://charactercounts.org/programs/reportcard/2002/index.html (accessed on March 5, 2012).

Kaati, G., et al. "Cardiovascular and Diabetes Mortality Determined by Nutrition During Parents' and Grandparents' Slow Growth Period." European Journal of Human Genetics 10 (2002): 682–688.

Kaiser Family Foundation. 2002. "SexSmarts Survey: Teens and Sexual Health Communication." www.kff.org/youthhivstds/3240-index.cfm. (accessed March 3, 2012).

Kamerow, D. 2009. The Papal Position on Condoms and HIV. Doi.10.1136/bmj.b1217 PMID19321547 (accessed March 2, 2012).

Kaufman, G. 2004. "Yes, Britney Really Is Naked in the 'Toxic' Video: VMA Lens Recap." www.mtv.comnews/articles/1490554/vma-lens-recap-britneys-toxic-video.jhtml?headlines=true (accessed April 1, 2012).

Kelly, D.J. et al. "The Other-Race Effect Develops During Infancy." *Psychological Science* 18 (2007): 1084–1089.

Kelly, T.H. et al. "Individual Differences in Drug Abuse Vulnerability: D-Amphetamine and Sensation-Seeking Status." *Psychopharmacology* 189 (2006): 17-25.

Kessler, R.C. et al. "Lifetime Co-occurrence of DSM-III-R Alcohol Abuse and Dependence With Other Psychiatric Disorders in the National Comorbidity Survey." *Archives of General Psychiatry* 54 (1997): 313-321.

Kessler, R.C. et al. "Lifetime Prevalence and Age-of-Onset Distributions of DSM-IV Disorders in the National Comorbidity Survey Replication." *Archives of General Psychiatry* 62 (2005): 593–602.

Kilbourne, J. *Can't Buy My Love: How Advertising Changes the Way We Think and Feel*. New York: Free Press, 2000.

Kindlon, D. & Thompson, M. *Raising Cain: Protecting the Emotional Life of Boys*. New York: Ballantine, 2000.

Klein, M. *"Envy and Gratitude" and Other Works, 1946-1963: On the Theory of Anxiety and Guilt*. New York: Delacorte Press, 1975 [1948].

Koebler, J. 2011. "High School Notes: National High School Graduation Rates Improve." www.usnews.comeducation/blogs/high-school-notes/2011/06/13/national-high-school-graduation-rates-improve (accessed April 1, 2012).

Kohn, A. *What Does it Mean to be Well Educated? And More Essays on Standards, Grading and Other Follies*. Boston: Beacon Press, 2004.

Kohut, H. *The Analysis of the Self: A Systematic Approach to the Psychoanalytic Treatment of Narcissistic Personality Disorders*. International Universities Press, 1971.

Kohut, H., Goldberg, A. & Stepansky, P.E. *How Does Analysis Cure?* Chicago: University of Chicago Press, 1984.

Koskey, A. 2011. "Sonoma County Teen Survives Plunge From Golden Gate Bridge." www.sfexaminer.comlocal/2011/03/sonoma-county-teen-survives-plunge-golden-gate-bridge (accessed March 5, 2012).

Krakovskky, M. 2012. "How Do We Decide? Inside the 'Frinky' Science of the Mind." www.gsb.stanford.edu/news/bmag/sbsm0802/feature-babashiv.html (accessed March 5, 2012).

Kugler, K.E. & Jones, W.H. "On Conceptualizing and Assessing Guilt." *Journal of Personality and Social Psychology* 62 (1992): 318-327.

Kuhn, C., Swartzwelder, S., & Wilson, W. *Buzzed: The Straight Facts About the Most Used and Abused Drugs from Alcohol to Ecstasy*. New York: W. W. Norton & Company, 2008.

Kurcinka, M. S. *Kids, Parents, and Power Struggles: Winning for a Lifetime*. New York: Harper Paperbacks, 2001.

Lakoff, G., & Johnson, M. *Metaphors We Live By*. Chicago: University Of Chicago Press, 1980.

Lamborn, S.D., Mounts, N.S., Steinberg, L. & Dornbusch, S.M. "Patterns of Competence and Adjustment Among Adolescents From Authoritative, Authoritarian, Indulgent, and Neglectful Families." *Child Development* 62, no. 5 (1991): 1049-1065.

Lanier, J. *You Are Not a Gadget: A Manifesto*. New York & London: Vintage, 2011.

Lareau, A. *Unequal Childhoods: Class, Race, and Family Life*. Berkeley: University of California Press, 2003.

Leckart, S. "The Stanford Education Experiment Could Change Higher Learning Forever," in *Wired Science*, accessed March 27, 2012, www.wired.comwiredscience/2012/03/ff_aiclass/all/1.

LeDoux, J.E. "Emotion, Memory and the Brain." *Scientific American* (1994): 50-57.

_____. *The Emotional Brain: The Mysterious Underpinnings of Emotional Life*. New York: Simon & Schuster, 1998.

_____. *Synaptic Self: How Our Brains Become Who We Are*. New York: Penguin, 2003.

Lee, S.M., Daniels, M.H. & Kissinger, D.B. "Parental Influences on Adolescent Adjustment: Parenting Styles Versus Parenting Practices." *The Family Journal: Counseling and Therapy for Couples and Families*. 14, no. 3 (2006): 253-259.

Lehrer, J. "Accept Defeat: The Neuroscience of Screwing Up." *Wired*, 2010.

Lenhart, A. et al. 2011. "Teens, Kindness and Cruelty on Social Network Sites: How Teens Navigate the New World of "Digital Citizenship." www.pewinternet.org/Reports/2011/Teens-and-social-media.aspx (accessed March 17, 2012).

Lenroot et al. "Sexual Dimorphism of Brain Developmental Trajectories During Childhood and Adolescence." *NeuroImage* 36 (2007):1065-1073.

Lessig, L. *The Future of Ideas: The Fate of the Commons in a Connected World*. New York: Random House, 2001.

Levin, D. E., & Kilbourne, J. *So Sexy So Soon: The New Sexualized Childhood and What Parents Can Do to Protect Their Kids*. New York: Ballantine Books, 2008.

Levinas, E. *Totality and Infinity: An Essay on Exteriority*. Translated by Alphonso Lingis. Pittsburgh: Duquesne University Press, 1969.

Levine, M. *The Price of Privilege: How Parental Pressure and Material Advantage Are Creating a Generation of Disconnected and Unhappy Kids*. New York: HarperCollins, 2006.

Levy, A. *Female Chauvinist Pigs: Women and the Rise of Raunch Culture*. New York: Free Press, 2005.

Lewicki, P., Czyzewska, M. & Hill, T. "Nonconscious Information Processing and Personality." In *How Implicit Is Implicit Learning?*, edited by D. Berry, 48-72. New York and Oxford: Oxford University Press, 1997.

Lewicki,P., Hill, T., & Czyzewska, M. "Nonconscious Acquisition of Information." *American Psychologist* 47 (1992): 796-801.

Lewin, K. *Field Theory in Social Science: Selected Theoretical Papers*. Edited by D. Cartwright. New York: Harper & Row, 1951.

Lewis, H.B. "Shame and Guilt in Human Nature." In *Object and Self: a Developmental Approach*, edited by C. Kaye and M. Zimmerman S. Tuttman, 235-65. Madison: International Universities Press, 1981.

Lewis, M. *The Big Short: Inside the Doomsday Machine*. New York: W. W. Norton & Company, 2011.

Lewis, M. *Shame: The Exposed Self*. New York: Free Press, 1992.

Lewis, T. *Empire of the Air: The Men Who Made Radio*. New York: HarperCollins, 1991.

Licea, M.H. "Risk Factors Associated With Adolescent Alcohol and Cigarette Use." Masters, California State University, Long Beach, 2011.

Lieberman, A. F. *Emotional Life of the Toddler*. New York: Free Press, 1995.

Lindemann, E. *Beyond Grief: Studies in Crisis Intervention*. New York: Jason Aronson,1979, 174.

Lindstrom, M. *Buyology: Truth and Lies About Why We Buy*. New York: Crown Business, 2010.

_____. *Brandwashed: Tricks Companies Use to Manipulate Our Minds and Persuade Us to Buy*. New York: Crown Business, 2011.

Lippmann, W. *Public Opinion*. New York: Free Press, 1965 [1922].

Loewald, H. "The Waning of the Oedipus Complex." *Journal of the American Psychoanalytic Association* 27 (1979): 751-775.

The Lost Self: Pathologies of the Brain and Identity. Edited by Feinberg, T.E. & Keenan, J.P. New York & London: Oxford University Press, 2005.

Luckmann, T.L. & Berger, P.L. *The Social Construction of Reality: A Treatise in the Sociology of Knowledge*. New York: Doubleday & Company, 1967.

Luhmann, N. "What Is Communication?" *Communication Theory* 2, no. 3 (1992): 251–259.

Luskin, C.V. 2001. "Eleanor Maccoby: How Much Do Parents Matter? Reading and Misreading Behavior Genetics." www.stanford.edu/dept/bingschool/cgi-bin/bt/aug2001/eleanor-maccoby-how-much-do-parents-matter-reading-and-misreading-behavior-genetics/ (accessed 4/2/12).

Lyall, S. 2011. "Scandal Shifts Britain's Media and Political Landscape." www.nytimes.com2011/07/08/world/europe/08britain.html?pagewanted=all (accessed 3/24/12).

Lyotard, J.F. *The Postmodern Explained: Correspondence, 1982-85*. Minneapolis: University of Minnesota Press, 1992.

Maccoby, E.E. "The Role of Parents in the Socialization of Children: An Historical Overview." *Developmental Psychology* 28 (1992): 1006-1017.

Maccoby, E.E. & Mnookin, R.N. *Dividing the Child: Social and Legal Dilemmas of Custody*. Cambridge: Harvard University Press, 1992.

MacKenzie, R. J. *Setting Limits with Your Strong-Willed Child: Eliminating Conflict by Establishing Clear, Firm, and Respectful Boundaries*. New York: Three Rivers Press, 2001.

Maggid, L. 2010. "Many Ways to Activate Webcams Sans Spy Software." http://news.cnet.com8301-19518_3-10457737-238.html (accessed March 1, 2012).

Magistretti, P.J., Pellerin, L. & Martin, Jean-Luc. "Brain Energy Metabolism: An Integrated Cellular Perspective." In *Psychopharmacology: The Fourth Generation of Progress*, edited by Floyd Bloom & David Kupfer. Philadelphia: Lippincott Williams & Wilkins, 1995.

Martens, M.P. et al. "Differences Between Actual and Perceived Student Norms: An Examination of Alcohol Use, Drug Use, and Sexual Behavior." *Journal of American College Health* 54, no. 5 (2006): 295-300.

Martin, J. et al. *Psychology and the Question of Agency*, Albany: State University of New York Press, 2003.

Matson, A. "Inventor of Auto-Tune: 'I'm Innocent!'" in *The Seattle Times* Online (Matson on Music), accessed April 20, 2012, http://seattletimes.nwsource.com/html/matsononmusic/2009389530_post.html

McChesney, R. *Rich Media, Poor Democracy: Communication Politics in Dubious Times*. Urbana: University of Illinois Press, 1999.

McLuhan, M. *Understanding Media: The Extensions of Man*. Edited by W. Terrence Gordon. Corte Madera: Gingko Press, 2003 [1964].

McNay, E.C., Fried, T.M. & Gold, P.E. "Decreases in Rat Extracellular Hippocampal Glucose Concentration Associated with Cognitive Demand During a Spatial Task." *Proceedings of the National Academy of Sciences of the United States of America* 97, no. 6 (2000): 2881–2885.

McWilliams, N. Conference proceedings of "Mental Health: A Vanishing But Critical Concept," January 29, 2011, San Rafael, California.

_____. *Psychoanalytic Diagnosis: Understanding Personality Structure in the Clinical Process*. New York: Guilford Press, 1994.

Melkle, J. 2012. "Twitter Is Harder to Resist Than Cigarettes and Alcohol, Study Finds." www.guardian.co.uk/technology/2012/feb/03/twitter-resist-cigarettes-alcohol-study (accessed April 1, 2012).

Miller, G.A. "The Magic Number Seven Plus or Minus Two: Some Limits on Our Capacity to Process Information." *Psychological Review* 63, no. 2 (1956): 81-97.

Miller-Day, M.A. "Parent-Adolescent Communication About Alcohol, Tobacco, and Other Drug Use." Journal of Adolescent Research 17 (2002): 604-16.

Modell, A. "On Having the Right to a Life: An Aspect of the Superego's Development." *International Journal of Psycho-Analysis*, 46 (1965): 323-331.

_____. "The Origin of Certain Forms of Pre-Oedipal Guilt and the Implications for A Psychoanalytic Theory of Affects." *International Journal of Psycho-analysis* 52 (1971): 337-346.

Moreno, B. *The Statue of Liberty Encyclopedia*. New York: Simon and Schuster, 2000.

Morgenson, G. & Rosner, J. *Reckless Endangerment: How Outsized Ambition, Greed, and Corruption Led to Economic Armageddon*. New York: Times Books, 2011.

Morozov, E. *The Net Delusion: The Dark Side of Internet Freedom*. New York: PublicAffairs, 2011.

Morris, S.K. "A Comparison of Learning Outcomes in a Traditional Lecture-Based Versus Blended Course Module Using a Business Simulation With High Cognitive Load." Doctoral, University of San Francisco, 2011.

Mühlberger, A., et al. "Stop Looking Angry and Smile, Please: Start and Stop of the Very Same Facial Expression Differentially Activate Threat- and Reward-Related Brain Networks." *Social Cognitive and Affective Neuroscience* 6, no. 3. (2011): 321-329.

Mysko, C. *Girls Inc. Presents: You're Amazing! A No-Pressure Guide to Being Your Best Self*. Avon: Adams Media, 2008.

Nathanson, D.L. *Shame and Pride: Affect, Sex, and the Birth of the Self*. New York: W. W. Norton & Company, 1992.

National Adolescent Health Information Center. "Fact Sheet on Demographics: Adolescents." San Francisco, CA: University of California, San Francisco, 2003.

National Association for Media Literacy Education. 2007. "Core Principles of Media Literacy Education in the United States." http://namle.net/wp-content/uploads/2009/09/ NAMLE-CPMLE-w-questions2.pdf (accessed March 15, 2012).

Needleman, J. *Why Can't We Be Good?* New York: Tarcher, 2007.

Negt, O., Kluge, A., & Labanyi, P. *Public Sphere and Experience: Toward an Analysis of the Bourgeois and Proletarian Public Sphere (Theory and History of Literature)*. Minneapolis: University of Minnesota Press, 1993.

Neiderland, W.G. "The Problem of the Survivor." *Journal of Hillside Hospital* 10 (1961): 233-247.

_____. "The Survivor Syndrome: Further Observations and Dimensions." *Journal of the American Psychoanalytic Association* 29, no. 2 (1981): 413-425.

Nelsen, J.N, & Erwin, C. *Parents Who Love Too Much: How Good Parents Can Learn to Love More Wisely and Develop Children of Character.* New York: Three Rivers Press, 2000.

Nelsen, J.N., & Glenn, H.S. *Raising Self-Reliant Children in a Self-Indulgent World: Seven Building Blocks for Developing Capable Young People.* New York: Prima Lifestyles, 1988.

Nelsen, J.N., Lott, L., & Glenn, H.S. *Positive Discipline A-Z, Revised and Expanded 2nd Edition: From Toddlers to Teens, 1001 Solutions to Everyday Parenting Problems.* New York: Three Rivers Press, 1999.

Nergaard, M., & Silberschatz, G. "The Effects of Shame, Guilt, and the Negative Reaction in Brief Dynamic Psychotherapy." *Psychotherapy* 26 (1989): 330-337.

Neumark-Sztainer, D. *"I'm, Like, SO Fat": Helping Your Teen Make Healthy Choices about Eating and Exercise in a Weight-Obsessed World.* New York: The Guilford Press, 2005.

Newton, I. *Principia.* Translated by Andrew Motte, 1729 [1687].

Nichols, N. Crisis Intervention Through Early Interpretation of Unconscious Guilt. *Bulletin of the Menninger Clinic* 53, no. 2 (1989): 115-122.

Nielsen Company and NM Incite. *State of the Media: U.S. Digital Consumer Report Q3-Q4 2011.* New York: Nielsen Company, 2012.

Norman, D.A., & Shallice T. "Attention to Action: Willed and Automatic Control of Behaviour." In *Cognitive Neuroscience: A Reader*, edited by M.S. Gazzaniga. Oxford: Blackwell, 2000.

O'Connor, L.E. "Survivor Guilt and Depression." Paper presented at the Annual Meeting of Division 39 of the American Psychological Association, San Francisco, 1995.

_____. "Role Guilt and the Development Of Pathogenic Beliefs." San Francisco, 1997.

O'Connor, L.E., et al. "Interpersonal Guilt: The Development of a New Measure." *Journal of Clinical Psychology* 53, no. 1 (1997): 73-89.

O'Connor, L.E., Berry, J.W. & Weiss, J. "Interpersonal Guilt, Shame and Psychological Problems." *Journal of Social and Clinical Psychology* 18, no. 2 (1996): 181-203.

O'Connor, L.E., Berry, J.W. & Weiss, J. & Schweitzer, D. "Survivor Guilt, Submissive Behavior and Evolutionary Theory: The Down Side Of Winning in Social Competition." San Francisco, 1996.

Panksepp, J. *The Archaeology of Mind, Neural Origins of Human Emotion.* New York: W.W. Norton & Company, 2010.

Parent et al. "The Timing of Normal Puberty and the Age Limits of Sexual Precocity: Variations Around the World, Secular Trends, and Changes After Migration." *Endocrine Reviews* 24, no. 5 (2003): 668-693.

Pascual-Leone, A., et al. "Modulation of Muscle Responses Evoked by Transcranial Magnetic Stimulation during the Acquisition of New Fine Motor Skills." *Journal of Neurophysiology* 74, no. 3 (1995): 1037–45.

Patton, C. *Inventing AIDS.* New York: Routledge, 1990.

Paul, P. 2012. "Cracking Teenagers' Online Codes." www.nytimes.com2012/01/22/fashion/danah-boyd-cracking-teenagers-online-codes.html?pagewanted=all (accessed February 28, 2012).

Paus, T., Keshavan, M. & Giedd, J.N. "Why Do Many Psychiatric Disorders Emerge During Adolescence?" *Nature Reviews Neuroscience* 9, no. 12 (2008): 947-957.

Payne, J.D. & Nadel, L. "Sleep, Dreams, and Memory Consolidation: The Role of the Stress Hormone Cortisol." *Learning & Memory* 11 (2004): 671-678.

Pearce, J. C. *From Magical Child to Magical Teen: A Guide to Adolescent Development.* South Paris: Park Street Press, 2003.

Persons, J. B., Davidson, J., & Tompkins, M. A. *Essential Components of Cognitive-Behavior Therapy for Depression.* Washington, DC: American Psychological Association, 2001.

Piaget, J. *The Construction of Reality in the Child* (Basic Books, 1954) *[La construction du réel chez l'enfant* (1950), also translated as *The Child's Construction of Realit.]* London: Routledge and Kegan Paul, 1955.

Pons, T.P. et al. "Massive Cortical Re-Organization After Sensory Deafferention in Adult Macaques." *Science* 252, no. 5014 (1991): 1857-1860.

Ponton, L. *The Romance of Risk: Why Teenagers Do the Things They Do.* New York: Basic Books, 1998.

Pope, D. Clark. *Doing School: How We Are Creating a Generation of Stressed Out, Materialistic, and Miseducated Students.* New Haven: Yale University Press, 2001.

Porges, S.W. *The Polyvagal Theory: Neurophysiological Foundations of Emotions, Attachment, Communication, and Self-regulation.* New York: W. W. Norton & Company, 2011.

Postman, N. *Technopoly: The Surrender of Culture to Technology.* New York & London: Vintage, 1993.

————. *The Disappearance of Childhood.* New York: Vintage/Random House, 1994.

Prensky, M. "Digital Native, Digital Immigrants." *On the Horizon.* MCB University Press, 9, no. 5 (2001): 1-6.

Price, J., & Fisher, J. E. *Take Control of Asperger's Syndrome: The Official Strategy Guide for Teens With Asperger's Syndrome and Nonverbal Learning Disorders.* Waco: Prufrock Press, 2010.

Prior, S. *Object Relations in Severe Trauma.* Northvale, N.J.: Jason Aronson, Inc., 1996.

The Psychoanalytic Process: Theory, Clinical Observations, and Empirical Research. Edited by J. Weiss, H. Sampson & the Mt. Zion Psychotherapy Research Group. New York: Guilford Press, 1986.

Pugh, A. J. *Longing and Belonging: Parents, Children, and Consumer Culture.* Berkeley: University of California Press, 2009.

Pujazon-Zazik, M. & Park, M.J. "To Tweet, or Not to Tweet: Gender Differences and Potential Positive and Negative Health Outcomes of Adolescents' Social Internet Use." *American Journal of Men's Health* 4, no. 77 (2010).

Purushotma, R., Weigel, M., Clinton, K. & Robison, A.J. *Confronting the Challenges of Participatory Culture: Media Education for the 21st Century.* Cambridge: The MIT Press, 2006.

Ramsden, S., et al. "Verbal and Nonverbal Intelligence Changes in the Teenage Brain." *Nature* (epub ahead of print), 2011.

Rappoport, A. "Freeing Oneself From Pathogenic Adaptations: A Contribution to Control-Mastery Theory." *Psychotherapy Bulletin* 31, no. 4 (1996): 27-33.

Ravitch, D. *The Death and Life of the Great American School System: How Testing and Choice Are Undermining Education.* New York: Basic Books, 2011.

Reik, W. "Stability and Flexibility of Epigenetic Gene Regulation in Mammalian Development." *Nature* 447 (2007): 425–432.

Repetti, R.L. et al. "Risky Families: Family Social Environments and the Mental and Physical Health of Offspring. *Psychological Bulletin,* 128, no. 2 (2002): 330-366.

Resnick, M.D., et al. "Protecting Adolescents from Harm: Findings from the National Longitudinal Study on Adolescent Health." *Journal of the American Medical Association* 278, no. 10 (1997): 823-832.

Reyna, V.F. & Dougherty, M.R.. "Paradoxes of the Adolescent Brain in Cognition, Emotion, and Rationality." In *The Adolescent Brain Learning, Reasoning, and Decision Making,* edited by V.F. Reyna, S.B. Chapman, M.R. Dougherty, & J. Confrey, 431-436. New York: American Psychological Association, 2012.

Reyna, V.F., & Farley, F. "Risk and Rationality in Adolescent Decision-Making: Implications for Theory, Practice, and Public Policy." *Psychological Science in the Public Interest* 7 (2006): 1–44.

Reyna, V.F. & Rivers, S.E. "Current Theories of Risk and Rational Decision Making." *Developmental Review* 28 (2008): 1-11.

Rideout, V.J., Foehr, U.G, & Roberts, D.F. *Generation M2: Media in the Lives of 8 to 18-year-olds.* Menlo Park: The Henry J. Kaiser Family Foundation, 2010.

Riera, M. *Uncommon Sense for Parents of Teenagers.* Berkeley: Celestial Arts, 1995.

————. *Surviving High School: Making the Most of the High School Years.* Berkeley: Celestial Arts, 1997.

————. *Staying Connected to Your Teenager: How to Keep Them Talking to You and How to Hear What They're Really Saying.* Cambridge: Da Capo Press, 2003.

Riera, M. & Di Prisco, J. *Field Guide to the American Teenager: A Parent's Companion.* Cambridge: Da Capo Press, 2001.

————. *Right From Wrong: Instilling a Sense of Integrity in Your Child.* New York: Perseus Books, 2002.

Ritchart, R., Church, M. and Morrison, K. *Making Thinking Visible: How to Promote Engagement, Understanding, and Independence for All Learners.* San Francisco: Jossey-Bass, 2011.

Riva, D., & Giorgi, C. "The Cerebellum Contributes to Higher Functions During Development: Evidence From a Series of Children Surgically Treated for Posterior Fossa Tumours." *Brain* 123 (2000): 1051-1061.

Rizzolatti, G., & Craighero, L. "The Mirror-Neuron System." *Annual Review of Neuroscience* 27 (2004): 169-192.

Robison, J. E. *Be Different: Adventures of a Free-Range Aspergian with Practical Advice for Aspergians, Misfits, Families & Teachers.* New York: Crown Archetype, 2011.

Roehr, B. 2009. "Pope Claims That Condoms Exacerbate HIV and AIDS Problem." doi:10.1146/bmj.b1206 PMID 19321545 (accessed March 2, 2012).

Roffman, D. M. *Sex and Sensibility.* New York: Perseus Books Group, 2002.

Rogers, C.R. "The Development of Insight in a Counseling Relationship." *Journal of Consulting Psychology* 8, no. 6 (1944): 331-341.

The Role of Shame in Symptom Formation. Edited by H.B. Lewis. Mahwah: Lawrence Erlbaum Associates, 1987.

Room Noise Music Blog. "Is Britney Spears a Musical Genius?" http://room-noise.com2011/01/11/is-britney-spears-a-musical-genius/ (accessed April 1, 2012).

Rose, F.J. & Kaprio, J. "Genes, Environments, and Adolescent Substance Use: Retrospect and Prospect from the *FinnTwin* Studies." *Acta Psychologica Sinica* 40, no. 10 (2008): 1062-1072.

Roseman, I.J., Smith, C.A. "Appraisal Theory: Overview, Assumptions, Varieties, Controversies." *Appraisal Processes in Emotion: Theory, Methods, Research. Series in Affective Science.* Edited by K.R. Scherer, A. Schorr and T. Johnson, 3-19. Oxford: Oxford University Press, 2001.

Ruggieri, M.. "Music Notes." *Richmond Times-Dispatch.* (2000): D. 13.

Sabatinelli, D, et al. "Pleasure Rather Than Salience Activates Human Nucleus Accumbens and Medial Prefrontal Cortex." *Journal of Neurophysiology* 98, no. 9 (2007): 1374–1379.

Sahlberg, P. *Finnish Lessons: What Can the World Learn from Educational Change in Finland?* (Series on School Reform). New York: Teachers College Press, 2011.

Sampson, H. "The Problem of Adaptation to Reality in Psychoanalytic Theory." *Contemporary Psychoanalysis.* 26 (1990): 677-691.

———. "Repeating Pathological Relationships to Disconfirm Pathogenic Beliefs: Commentary on Steven Stern's 'Needed Relationships.'" *Psychoanalytic Dialogues* 4, no. 3 (1994): 357-61.

Sampson, H., Weiss, J., Mlodnosky, L., & Hause, E. "Defense Analysis and the Emergence of Warded-Off Mental Contents: An Empirical Study." *Archives of General Psychiatry* 26 (1972): 524-532.

Sang-Hun, C. 2010. "South Korea Expands Aid for Internet Addiction." www.nytimes.com2010/05/29/world/asia/29game.html (accessed March 23, 2012).

Saperstein, J. A. *Atypical: Life with Asperger's in 20⅓ Chapters.* New York: Perigee Trade, 2010.

Sareen J., Chartier, M., Paulus, M.P. & Stein, M.B. (2006). "Illicit Drug Use and Anxiety Disorders: Findings from Two Community Surveys." *Psychiatry Res.* 142: 11-17.

Satcher, D. 2001. "The Surgeon General's Call to Action to Promote Sexual Health and Responsible Sexual Behavior." Washington, DC: U.S. Department of Health and Human Services, Office of the Surgeon General. www.surgeongeneral.gov/library/sexualhealth/call.pdf (accessed April 1, 2012).

Schachter, S & Singer, J.E. "Cognitive, Social and Physiological Determinants of Emotional State." *Psychological Review* 69 (1962): 379-99.

Scheier, L.M. & Botvin, G.J. "Effects Of Early Adolescent Drug Use on Cognitive Efficacy in Early-Late Adolescence: A Developmental Structural Model." *Journal of Substance Abuse* 7, no. 4 (1995): 379-404.

Schneider, S.L. & Caffray, C.M. "Affective Motivators and Experience in Adolescents' Development of Health-Related Behavior Patterns." In *The Adolescent Brain Learning, Reasoning, and Decision Making,* edited by V.F. Reyna, S.B. Chapman, M.R. Dougherty, & J. Confrey, 291-334. New York: American Psychological Association, 2012.

Schore, A. N. *Affect Regulation and the Origin of the Self: The Neurobiology of Emotional Development.* Philadelphia: Psychology Press, 1999.

Schulz, K. *Being Wrong: Adventures in the Margin of Error.* New York: Ecco, 2011.

Schwartz, S.J., Cote, J.E. & Arnett, J.J. "Identity and Agency in Emerging Adulthood: Two Developmental Routes in the Individualization Process." In *Youth & Society* 37, no. 2 (2005):201-229.

Scott, L.S. & Monesson, L. "The Origin of Biases in Face Perception." *Psychological Science* 20, no. 6 (2000): 676-680.

"Seeing More Clearly," an online article published by the American Mathematical Society, retrieved at http://msc2010.org/MSC2010-CD/Mathematical%20Moments/mm35s-adaptiveoptics.pdf

Self-Conscious Emotions: The Psychology of Shame, Guilt, Embarrassment and Pride. Edited by J.P. Tangney & K.W. Fischer. New York: Guilford Press, 1995.

Seligman, M. E. *The Optimistic Child: Proven Program to Safeguard Children from Depression & Build Lifelong Resilience.* New York: Harper Paperbacks, 2005.

Seneca, L.A. *Espistulae morales ad Lucilium.* XCV, 33, 65 A.C.E.

Seung, S. *Connectome: How the Brain's Wiring Makes Us Who We Are.* New York: Houghton Mifflin Harcourt, 2012.

Sheff, D. *Beautiful Boy: A Father's Journey Through His Son's Crystal Meth Addiction.* New York: Simon & Schuster Ltd., 2008.

Sheff, N. *Tweak: Growing Up on Methamphetamines.* New York: Atheneum, 2009.

Shilkret, R. "The Origins of Pathogenic Beliefs: Comments on the Developmental Aspects of Control-Mastery Theory." Mt. Holyoke: 1995.

Shirky, C. 2011. "The Political Power of Social Media: Technology, the Public Sphere, and Political Change." www.foreignaffairs.comarticles/67038/clay-shirky/the-political-power-of-social-media (accessed March 24, 2012).

Shirtcliff, E. A. 2005. "Neuroendocrine and Neural Contributions to Pubertal Development, Normative Adolescent Development and Affect-Related Behavior Problems." Background Paper for the Workshop on the Science of Adolescence Health and Development, National Academy of Science, www.bocyf.org/090805.html (accessed March 2, 2012).

Silva, A.J. et al. "CREB and Memory." *Annual Review of Neuroscience* 21 (1998): 127-148.

Simmons, R. *Odd Girl Out: The Hidden Culture of Aggression in Girls.* New York: Mariner Books, 2003.

Simpson, A. R. "Raising Teens: A Synthesis of Research and a Foundation for Action." Project on the Parenting of Adolescents, Center for Health Communication, Harvard School of Public Health, 2001.

Skinner, M.L. et al. "Observed Parenting Behavior With Teens: Measurement Invariance and Predictive Validity Across Race." *Cultural Diversity and Ethnic Minority Psychology* 17, no. 3 (2011): 252.

Slavin, M. & Kriegman, D. *The Adaptive Design of the Human Psyche.* New York: Guilford Press, 1992.

Smetana, J. G. "The Role of Trust in Adolescent-Parent Relationships: To Trust You Is to Tell You." In *Trust and Trustworthiness During Childhood and Adolescence*, edited by K. Rotenberg, 223-46. New York: Cambridge University Press, 2010.

Smith, D. G. et al. *Diversity Works: The Emerging Picture of How Students Benefit.* Washington, D.C.: Association of American Colleges and Universities, 1997.

Spear, L. *The Behavioral Neuroscience of Adolescence.* New York: W. W. Norton & Company, 2009.

Stamatakis, J. 2011. "Why Did the Absence of the Corpus Callosum in Kim Peek's Brain Increase His Memory Capacity?" www.scientificamerican.comarticle.cfm?id=why-did-the-absence-of-the-corpus (accessed April 2, 2012).

Steinberg, L. "Hormone Contributions to Adolescent Behavior." Paper presented at the Biennial meetings of the Society for Research on Adolescence, Alexandria, 1988.

_____. "A Social Neuroscience Perspective on Adolescent Risk-Taking." *Developmental Review* 28, no. 1 (2008): 78-106.

Steinberg, L., & Morris, A. "Adolescent Development." *Annual Review of Psychology*, 52, (2001): 83-110.

Stern, D.N. *The Interpersonal World of the Infant: A View from Psychoanalysis and Developmental Psychology*. New York: Basic Books, 2000.

Stolorow, R. *Trauma and Human Existence: Autobiographical, Psychoanalytic, and Philosophical Reflections. Psychoanalytic Inquiry Book Series*. New York: Routledge, 2007.

Styne, D.M. & Grumbach, M.M. "Puberty: Ontogeny, Neuroendocrinology, Physiology and Disorders." In *Williams Textbook of Endocrinology*, edited by H.M. Kronenberg, S. Melmed, K.S. Polonsky, & P.R. Larsen, Chapter 24. Philadelphia: Saunders Elsevier, 2008.

Tancer, B. *Click: What Millions of People Are Doing Online and Why it Matters*. New York: Hyperion, 2008.

Tangney, J.P. "Assessing Individual Differences in Proneness to Shame and Guilt: Development of the Self-Conscious Affect and Attribution Inventory." *Journal of Personality and Social Psychology, 59* (1990): 102-111.

_____. "Moral Affect: The Good, the Bad and the Ugly." *Journal of Personality and Social Psychology* 61 (1991): 598-607.

_____. "Shame-Proneness, Guilt-Proneness, and Psychological Symptoms." In *Self-Conscious Emotions: The Psychology of Shame, Guilt, Embarrassment and Pride*, edited by J.P. Tangney & K.W. Fischer, 343-67. New York: Guilford Press, 1995.

Tangney, J.P. & Fisher, K.W. (1995). *Self-Conscious Emotions: The Psychology of Shame, Guilt, Embarrassment and Pride*. Guilford Press.

Tangney, J.P., Wagner, P. & Gramzow, R. "Proneness to Shame, Proneness to Guilt, and Psychopathology." *Journal of Abnormal Psychology* 101, no. 3 (1992): 469-478.

TARGUSinfo Inc. 2009. "Taking Online Targeting to the Next Level." www.targusinfo.comfiles/PDF/white_papers/TakingOnlineTargetingtotheNextLevelWhitepaper.pdf (accessed March 2, 2012).

Tarter, R. E. et al. "Predictors of Marijuana Use in Adolescents Before and After Licit Drug Use: Examination of the Gateway Hypothesis." *American Journal of Psychiatry* 163 (12) (2006): 2134–40.

Tasopoulos-Chan, M., Smetana, J. G., & Yau, J. Y. (2009). "How Much Do I Tell Thee? Strategic Management of Information With Parents Among American Adolescents from Mexican, Chinese, and European Backgrounds." *Journal of Family Psychology* 23 (2009): 364-374.

Tatum, B.D. *Why Are All the Black Kids Sitting Together in the Cafeteria? (And Other Conversations About Race)*. New York: Basic Books, 1997.

Thomas, D. and Brown, J.S. *A New Culture of Learning: Cultivating the Imagination for a World of Constant Change*. New York: CreateSpace, 2011.

Thomas, A., & Chess, S. *Temperament and Development*. New York: Brunner/Mazel, 1977.

Thompson, C. 2007. "Your Outboard Brain Knows All." www.wired.comtechbiz/people/magazine/15-10/st_thompson (accessed February 22, 2012).

Thompson, M., & Barker, T. *Speaking of Boys: Answers to the Most-Asked Questions About Raising Sons*. New York: Ballantine Books, 2000.

Thompson, P.M. et al. "Growth Patterns in the Developing Brain Detecting by Using Continuum Mechanical Tensor Maps." *Nature* 404, no. 9 (2000):190-193.

Timberg, C., & Halperin, D. *Tinderbox: How the West Sparked the AIDS Epidemic and How the World Can Finally Overcome It.* New York: Penguin Press, 2012.

Tobias, S. "Anxiety and Cognitive Processing of Instruction." In *Self-Related Cognition in Anxiety and Motivation,* edited by R. Schwarzer, 35-54. New York: Erlbaum, 1986.

Tolman, D.L. *Dilemmas of Desire: Teenage Girls Talk about Sexuality.* Cambridge: Harvard University Press, 2005.

Tomkins, S. *Affect, Imagery, Consciousness. Vol. 1, The Positive Affects.* New York: Springer, 1962.

_____. *Affect, Imagery, Consciousness. Vol. 2, The Negative Affects.* New York: Springer, 1963.

Tompkins, M.A., & Martinez, K.A. *My Anxious Mind: A Teen's Guide to Managing Anxiety and Panic.* Washington, D.C.: Magination Press, 2009.

Traggiai, C, Stanhope, R. "Disorders of Pubertal Development." *Best Practice & Research Clinical Obstetrics & Gynaecology* 17, no. 1 (2003): 41–56.

Trivers, R.L. "The Evolution Of Reciprocal Altruism." *Quarterly Review of Biology* 46 (1971): 35-37.

Trotter, W. *Instincts of the Herd in Peace and War.* New York: MacMillan Company, 1919.

Turkle, S. *Alone Together: Why We Expect More from Technology and Less from Each Other.* New York: Basic Books, 2011.

Turow, J. *The Daily You: How the New Advertising Industry Is Defining Your Identity and Your Worth.* New Haven: Yale University Press, 2012.

Twenge, J. M. *Generation Me: Why Today's Young Americans Are More Confident, Assertive, Entitled—and More Miserable Than Ever Before.* New York: Free Press, 2007.

Twenge, J. M., & Campbell, W. K. *The Narcissism Epidemic: Living in the Age of Entitlement.* New York: Free Press, 2009.

"United States Census, 2010 Intercensus Estimates," retrieved at www.census.gov/popest/data/intercensal/national/nat2010.html.

U.S. Census Bureau. (2003b). American FactFinder, Census 2000 summary file 1 [Tabulated Data]. Washington, DC: Author. (Available at (12/03): http://factfinder.census.gov/servlet/BasicFactsServlet)

Valentino-DeVries, J. 2011. "Learning to Play 'Angry Birds' Before You Can Tie Your Shoes." http://blogs.wsj.comdigits/2011/01/19/learning-to-play-angry-birds-before-you-can-tie-your-shoes/ (accessed January 21, 2012).

van der Kolk, B.A. "Psychobiology of Posttraumatic Stress Disorder." In *Textbook of Biological Psychiatry,* edited by J. Panksepp, 319-38. New York: Wiley-Liss, 1996.

Verdejo-Garcia A., Bechara, A., Recknor, E.C. & Perez-Garcia, M. "Negative Emotion-Driven Impulsivity Predicts Substance Dependence Problems." *Drug Alcohol Dependence* 91 (2007): 213-219.

Verklin, D., & Kanner, B. *Watch This, Listen Up, Click Here: Inside the 300 Billion Dollar Business Behind the Media You Constantly Consume.* New York: Wiley, 2007.

Wallerstein, J. S. *What About the Kids? Raising Your Children Before, During, and After Divorce.* New York: Hyperion, 2003.

Watkins, S. C. *The Young and the Digital: What the Migration to Social Network Sites, Games, and Anytime, Anywhere Media Means for Our Future.* Boston: Beacon Press, 2009.

Weatherford, S. (Gassner). Reply to "Commentary on a New View of Unconscious Guilt." *Bulletin of the Menninger Clinic* 53, no. 2 (1989): 143-148.

Weber, M. *The Protestant Ethic and the Spirit of Capitalism*. New York: Charles Scribner's Sons, 1959.

Weiss, J. "Unconscious Guilt." In *The Psychoanalytic Process: Theory, Clinical Observations, and Empirical Research*, edited by J. Weiss, H. Sampson & the Mt. Zion Psychotherapy Research Group, 43-67. New York: Guilford Press, 1986.

_____. "Unconscious Mental Functioning." *Scientific American* (1990): 103-109.

_____. *How Psychotherapy Works: Process and Technique*. New York: Guilford Press, 1993.

Wellman, V. "$2,000 on the Face and $6,000 on the Body: Jennifer Aniston's Monthly Beauty Bill Broken Down," *Mail Online* at http://www.dailymail.co.uk/femail/article-2114414/Jennifer-Anistons-monthly-beauty-broken-down.html (accessed March 24, 2012).

Westerhausen R. et al. "Effects of Handedness and Gender on Macro- and Microstructure of the Corpus Callosum and its Subregions: A Combined High-Resolution and Diffusion-Tensor MRI Study." *Cognitive Brain Research* 21, no. 3 (2004): 418–26.

Westheimer, R. K. *Sex for Dummies*. New York: Hungry Minds, Inc., 1995.

White, J. "The Contribution of Parent–Child Interactions to Smoking Experimentation in Adolescence: Implications for Prevention." *Health Education Research* 27, no. 1 (2011): 46-56.

Williams, K.E., Ciarrochi, J. & Heaven, P.C.L. "Inflexible Parents, Inflexible Kids: A 6-Year Longitudinal Study of Parenting Style and the Development of Psychological Flexibility in Adolescents." *Journal of Youth and Adolescence*, 2012 (epub ahead of print).

Williams, R. *Keywords: A Vocabulary of Culture and Society*. Oxford: Oxford University Press, 1976.

Winters, K.C. "Alcohol and the Adolescent Brain: Tastes Great, Less Functioning." Paper presented at the 3rd Las Vegas Conference on Adolescents, Las Vegas, 2005.

Wright, M. *I'm Chocolate, You're Vanilla: Raising Healthy Black and Biracial Children in a Race-Conscious World*. San Francisco: Jossey-Bass, 2000.

Yarrow, K. & O'Donnell, J. *Gen BuY: How Tweens, Teens and Twenty-Somethings Are Revolutionizing Retail*. San Francisco: Jossey-Bass, 2009.

Youth, Pornography and the Internet. Committee to Study Tools and Strategies for Protecting Kids From Pornography and Their Applicability to Other Internet Content. Edited by National Research Council, D. Thornburgh & H.S. Lin, Washington, D.C.: National Academies Press, 2002.

Yurgelun-Todd, D. "Emotional and Cognitive Changes During Adolescence." *Current Opinion in Neurobiology* 17, no. 2 (2007): 251-257.

Zajonc, R. B. "Feelings and Thinking: Preferences Need No Inferences." *American Psychologist*, 35, no. 2 (1980): 151-175.

Zalow, J. 2009. "Girls and Dieting, Then and Now." *Wall Street Journal* (online). http://online.wsj.comarticle/SB10001424052970204731804574386822245731710.html (accessed April 1, 2012).

Zilbergeld, B. *The New Male Sexuality*. New York: Bantam Books, 1999.

Zimmer-Gembeck, M.H. & Helfand, M. "Ten Years of Longitudinal Research on U.S. Adolescent Sexual Behavior: The Evidence for Multiple Pathways to Sexual Intercourse, and the Importance of Age, Gender and Ethnic Background." *Developmental Review* 28 (2008): 153-224.

Zittrain, J. *The Future of the Internet—and How to Stop It*. New Haven: Yale University Press, 2008.

Internet Resources for Parents

LOCAL BAY AREA ONLINE PARENT RESOURCES

http://nahic.ucsf.edu/about/about-nahic

National Adolescent Health Information Center at UCSF. The goals of the NAHIC are to serve as a national resource for adolescent health information and research; and to assure the integration, synthesis, coordination, and dissemination of adolescent health–related information. This is a good source for up-to-date, relevant research on teens.

www.alamedasocialservices.org/public/services/children_and_family/child_abuse.cfm

Child and Family Services Department. Information for Alameda County provides specific information on child abuse information and reporting for families and health professionals.

http://parents.berkeley.edu

UC Berkeley Parents Network is simply an amazing online community with information about everything you'd ever want to know about parenting in the Bay Area...by parents, for parents.

www.pamf.org/teen/hotlines.html

Palo Alto Medical Foundation provides a listing of Bay Area and national crisis lines and hotlines, from suicide and self-injury to grief support and sexuality information.

www.parentsplaceonline.org

Parents Place provides comprehensive, results-oriented mental health services for children, teens, and their families, emphasizing prevention and early intervention. Through individual counseling, play therapy, socialization groups, family therapy, and consultations to parents, Parents Place gives families access to the tools they need whenever they need them. Parents Place also provides consultation, staff training, prevention, and early intervention services to licensed early childhood programs that serve low-income children and families.

www.kidsturn.org

Kids' Turn helps children understand and cope with the loss, anger, and fear that often accompany separation or divorce. They provide education, training, and groups for kids and parents separately and together.

www.ldaca.org

Learning Disabilities Association of California (LDA-CA) is a 501(c)(3) nonprofit volunteer organization of parents, professionals, and adults with learning disabilities. Its purpose is to promote and support the education and general welfare of children and adults of potentially normal intelligence who manifest learning, perceptual, and/or behavioral handicaps.

www.namicalifornia.org

NAMI California educates families, professionals, and the public about the recent explosion of scientific evidence that shows serious mental illnesses are neurobiological brain disorders. NAMI California works to provide a strong, coherent system that offers a continuum of care for the persistent, long-term needs of people with mental illness. NAMI California strives to eradicate stigma and advocates for increased research to uncover causes and new, effective treatments.

www.fvlc.org

Family Violence Law Center (FVLC) provides family law attorney service in English and Spanish for domestic violence victims in Alameda County and can provide legal referrals for other areas of the country. Services are available in any language through their confidential interpreter program. They provide help with things like restraining orders, legal representation in divorce, and assistance with child custody and visitation arrangements.

www.jfcs.org/services

Jewish Family and Children's Services is a nonsectarian, nonprofit organization that provides services to individuals and families of all ages and backgrounds. This link provides referrals and up-to-date resources, including services related to domestic violence.

DO-IT-YOURSELF RESEARCH SITES FOR PARENTS

www.eric.ed.gov

The Education Resources Information Center (ERIC), sponsored by the Institute of Education Sciences (IES) of the U.S. Department of Education, produces the world's premier database of journal and non-journal education literature. The ERIC online system provides the public with a centralized website for searching the ERIC bibliographic database of more than 1.1 million citations going back to 1966. More than 107,000 full-text non-journal documents (issued 1993-2004), previously available through fee-based services only, are now available for free.

http://thomas.loc.gov/Thomas

THOMAS was launched in January of 1995, at the inception of the 104th Congress. It is a service of the Library of Congress, and the key link to legislative information on the Internet.

www.nolopress.com

Nolo Press has long been a fixture in the "doing it yourself" world. Nolo Press publishes hundreds of legal books, forms, and software, many related to issues involving the family.

www.nimh.nih.govhealth/index.shtml

National Institute of Mental Health provides a comprehensive website to help parents, educators, clinicians, and researchers on a wide range of mental health topics. The site is not a substitute for professional help, but it represents a trusted place to start if you have questions about mental health.

www.webmd.com

WebMD provides up-to-date information on medical concerns of all sorts. Aside from the detailed info on everything from allergies to weight control, WebMD offers an assortment of quizzes, calculators, and other resources on topics such as diet and nutrition, infertility, men's and women's health issues, and sexuality. The site is helpful, but should not be used as a substitute for getting professional help.

A FEW GOOD SITES FOR YOUR TEENS

www.goaskalice.columbia.edu
Go Ask Alice! is the health question and answer Internet service produced by Alice!, Columbia University's Health Education Program—a division of Health Services at Columbia. This site has several great features: Question & Answers of the week, with the most recently published inquiries and responses—updated every week; Search GAA! lets you find health information by subject via a search of the ever-growing *Go Ask Alice!* archives containing nearly 3,000 previously posted questions and answers and gives you the chance to ask and submit a question to *Alice!*

www.youthradio.org
Youth Radio promotes young people's intellectual, creative, and professional growth through education and access to media. What can I say about this organization? I love radio and I love what Youth Radio does. They teach media education, broadcast journalism, technical training, and production activities, providing unique opportunities in social, professional, and leadership development for youth ages 14–24. They help connect youth with their communities through media literacy and professional development. Nobody is perfect, but I think the overall mission and work of this organization exemplifies the way learning for adolescents should take place.

www.pamf.org/teen/hotlines.html
Palo Alto Medical Foundation provides a listing of Bay Area and national crisis lines and hotlines, from suicide and self-injury to grief support and sexuality information.

www.howstuffworks.com
How Stuff Works is for geeks and non-geeks alike. This is just a cool site. Want to know how something works? This is where you'll probably find out about it. This can be used to impress your physics teacher, if you're in the mood.

www.dmv.ca.govdl/dl.htm
Department of Motor Vehicles for the State of California. The site links to information about how to get your driver's license and permit.

www.jfcs.org/services/youth
Jewish Family and Children's Services is a nonsectarian, nonprofit organization that provides services to individuals and families of all ages and backgrounds. This link provides referrals and up-to-date resources, including a range services for kids and families.

EDUCATION AND SCHOOLS—GENERAL RESOURCES AND RESEARCH

www.edsource.org/about_who_we_are.html
EdSource reports and researches California school performance and keeps tabs on finances affecting California schools, while also broadening the education policy and school reform topics it researches. They have also widened their audiences to include policymakers, researchers, K–12 and college educators, education media, and parent and community leaders. This is a fantastic source for information on what's going on with California public education.

www.ed-data.k12.ca.us/Pages/Home.aspx

Ed-Data is a partnership of the California Department of Education, EdSource, and the Fiscal Crisis & Management Assistance Team (FCMAT), designed to offer educators, policymakers, the legislature, parents, and the public quick access to timely and comprehensive data about K-12 education in California. Want to know how your child's school compares to other schools? Want to know what percentage of the dollars on your school district has are spent on instruction? This is the place to find out.

www.wested.org/cs/we/print/docs/we/home.htm

WestEd was formed in 1966 and is now a nationally renowned nonprofit research, development, and service agency, striving to enhance and increase education and human development within schools, families, and communities. You can check here for information about WestEd's projects: www. wested.org/cs/we/print/docs/we/prog_proj.htm.

www.greatschools.net

GreatSchools.net is a comprehensive source of information on elementary, middle, and high schools around the country. A nonprofit organization, GreatSchools.net provides information about public, private, and charter schools in all 50 states and detailed school profiles for California, Arizona, Texas, Florida, Colorado, New York, and Washington.

www.nais.org

The National Association of Independent Schools (NAIS) provides this searchable database of member schools across the United States and around the world. Each record contains basic contact information about the school and financial aid possibilities, including a link to the school's website when available. In addition to individual school records, families may also get information about regional or state independent school associations by using the association search feature.

LEARNING DISABILITIES AND DIFFERENCES

www.ldaamerica.org

LDA (Learning Disabilities Association of America) offers support to people with learning disabilities, their parents, teachers, and other professionals. At the national, state, and local levels, LDA provides cutting-edge information on learning disabilities, practical solutions, and a comprehensive network of resources. You can use this link to go directly to the Parents' section of LDA America: www.ldaamerica.org/aboutld/parents/index.asp.

www2.ed.gov/ocr

The Office of Civil Rights of the Department of Education works to promote student achievement and preparation for global competitiveness by fostering educational excellence and ensuring equal access. You can find good information here about the transition to college for students with learning disabilities.

www.wrightslaw.com/info/sec504.index.htm

WrightsLaw provides news, information and guidance on the Individuals with Disabilities Education Improvement Act of 2004 (IDEA), the nation's law that works to improved results for infants, toddlers, children and youth with disabilities, as well as other information on the ADA (Americans With Disabilities Act) and other laws affecting students with disabilities.

www.iser.com

Internet Special Education Resources (ISER) is a nationwide directory of professionals who serve the learning disabilities and special education communities. They help parents and caregivers find local special education professionals to help with learning disabilities and attention deficit disorder assessment, therapy, advocacy, and other special needs.

www.ets.org/disabilities

Educational Testing Services' Disabilities section was developed in conjunction with the Office of Disability Policy, and provides information on standardized testing accommodations to qualified individuals. This website will help you or your student understand and apply for accommodations for SAT, SATII, ACT, AP, and other standardized tests.

www.chadd.org

Children and Adults with Attention-Deficit/Hyperactivity Disorder (CHADD) is a real gem. CHADD is a national non-profit organization founded in 1987 in response to the frustration and sense of isolation experienced by parents and their children with AD/HD. Many individuals and families dealing with AD/HD turn to CHADD, the national organization representing individuals with AD/HD, for education, advocacy, and support. The organization is composed of dedicated volunteers from around the country who play an integral part in the association's success by providing resources and encouragement to parents, educators, and professionals on a grassroots level through CHADD chapters.

www.kidsource.comkidsource/content3/college.planning.LD.html

The *KidSource* website focuses on helping students with learning disabilities plan for college—choosing a school, making the transition to college, and a host of other topics are included.

www.ldonline.org

Learning Disabilities Online (LD Online) is a very comprehensive, thorough resource to support families, students, and educators around understanding and working with all kinds of learning disabilities. Go to www.ldaonline.start to get right to the resources you need. The website primarily serves parents whose kids (kindergarten through high school) have learning difficulties, including: learning disabilities, attention problems (including AD/HD), and information for kids who struggle with similar problems but who don't qualify for special education.

PARENTING AND PARENT EDUCATION

http://contemporaryfamilies.org

The Council on Contemporary Families was founded in 1996 and is based at the University of Miami. CCF is a nonprofit, non-partisan organization dedicated to providing the press and public with the latest research and best-practice findings about American families. CCF is made up of demographers, economists, family therapists, historians, political scientists, psychologists, social workers, sociologists, as well as other family social scientists and practitioners.

www.cfw.tufts.edu

The Child & Family WebGuide provides approved links to websites and videos on topics of interest to parents. It is also used by students and professionals in the fields of child development, education, and psychology. The WebGuide primarily provides links to organizations and videos that have a legitimate research basis for the material they provide. At the request of parents, the Resources/Recreation section contains sites with information about specific programs and things to do, and this material is not research-based. Users of the WebGuide can search particular age groups (topics by age).

www.parentsplaceonline.org

Parents Place provides comprehensive, results-oriented mental health services for children, teens, and their families, emphasizing prevention and early intervention. Through individual counseling, play therapy, socialization groups, family therapy, and consultations to parents, Parents Place gives families access to the tools they need whenever they need them. Parents Place also provides consultation, staff training, prevention, and early intervention services to licensed, early childhood programs that serve low-income children and families.

www.hsph.harvard.edu/chc/parenting

The Harvard Project on the Parenting of Adolescents provides one of the most comprehensive and cogent pieces of research on teens and what their developmental needs are in relation to privacy. A. Rae Simpson's full report is an excellent source of general information on parenting teens. You can follow Dr. Simpson's more recent work at: http://hrweb.mit.edu/worklife/raising-teens/.

www.parentseducationnetwork.org

Parents Education Network is a coalition of parents collaborating with educators, students, and the community to empower and bring academic success to students with learning and attention difficulties.

ADOLESCENTS, ETHICS, AND CHARACTER DEVELOPMENT

www.scu.edu/ethics

The Markkula Center for Applied Ethics at Santa Clara University is one of the preeminent centers for research and dialogue on ethical issues in critical areas of American life. The center works with faculty, staff, students, community leaders, and the public to address ethical issues more effectively in teaching, research, and action. The center's focus areas are business, health care, biotechnology, character education, government, global leadership, technology, and emerging issues in ethics.

http://charactercounts.org/programs/reportcard/index.html

Josephson Institute Center for Ethics is a public-benefit, nonpartisan, nonprofit membership organization founded by Michael Josephson in honor of his parents. Since 1987, the Institute has conducted programs and workshops for over 100,000 influential leaders including legislators and mayors, high-ranking public executives, congressional staff, editors and reporters, senior corporate and nonprofit executives, judges and lawyers, and military and police officers. This site makes for intriguing reading on the latest large-scale survey on youth and ethical behavior.

CONNECTING AS A CITIZEN: WEBSITES FOR CONGRESS AND SENATE

www.senate.gov

Senate.gov provides links to the U.S. Senate, including staff listings, legislation, and Senate records.

www.house.gov

House.gov provides links to the U.S. House of Representatives, including staff listings, legislation, and House of Representatives records.

CONNECTING TO OTHERS: WAYS TO GIVE

www.charitywatch.org/aboutip.html

CharityWatch (formerly American Institute of Philanthropy) is a nonprofit charity watchdog and information service, aiming to maximize the effectiveness of every dollar contributed to charity by providing donors with the information they need to make more informed giving decisions. This is a great site to find out where to give and how your dollars and time might be best utilized.

PHYSICAL, SOCIAL, MENTAL, AND EMOTIONAL DEVELOPMENT AND HEALTH

http://intramural.nimh.nih.govchp/index.html

The Child Psychiatry Branch of the National Institute of Mental Health conducts research on the diagnosis, treatment, and neurobiology of childhood psychiatric disorders. Brain imaging, genetic, and drug treatment studies are ongoing and described on this site. This is where Judith Rapoport and Jay Giedd work—and for a research geek interested in adolescent brain development, this is *the* place. It's certainly not the only place where great brain research is happening, but it's a good one.

www.humanconnectomeproject.org/about

The Human Connectome Project is another one of those places where great brain research is happening. The Human Connectome Project is a joint endeavor of the Laboratory of Neuro Imaging at UCLA (LONI, www.loni.ucla.edu/) and the Martinos Center for Biomedical Imaging (www.nmr.mgh.harvard.edu/martinos/flashHome.php) at Massachusetts General Hospital. The project is funded by National Institute of Health.

www.pbs.org/wgbh/pages/frontline/shows/teenbrain

"Inside the Teenage Brain" is a *Frontline* special that chronicled how scientists were exploring the recesses of the brain and finding some new explanations for why adolescents behave the way they do. These discoveries could change the way we parent, teach, or perhaps even understand our teenagers, but must be understood in the context of this brain science being in its early stages.

www.nami.org

NAMI is a nonprofit, grassroots, self-help, support, and advocacy organization of consumers, families, and friends of people with severe mental illnesses, such as schizophrenia, schizoaffective disorder, bipolar disorder, major depressive disorder, obsessive-compulsive disorder, panic and other severe anxiety disorders, autism and pervasive developmental disorders, attention deficit/hyperactivity disorder, and other severe and persistent mental illnesses that affect the brain.

www.nationaleatingdisorders.org

The National Eating Disorders Association (NEDA) is the largest not-for-profit organization in the United States working to prevent eating disorders and provide treatment referrals to those suffering from anorexia, bulimia, and binge eating disorder and those concerned with body image and weight issues.

www.nimh.nih.gov/health/topics/child-and-adolescent-mental-health/index.shtml

National Institute of Mental Health provides a menu of services regarding adolescent mental health disorders and treatment, news and information, and publications and research materials.

www.nimh.nih.govpublicat/eatingdisorders.cfm#intro

National Institute of Mental Health provides extensive information on eating disorder symptoms, causes, treatments, and references for further exploration.

www.nimh.nih.govpublicat/depression.cfm

National Institute of Mental Health provides extensive information on depression, including information on symptoms, causes, treatments, and references for further exploration.

www.nimh.nih.govpublicat/bipolar.cfm

National Institute of Mental Health provides extensive information on bipolar disorder, including information on symptoms, causes, treatments, and references for further exploration.

www.sfbacct.com

The San Francisco Bay Area Center for Cognitive Therapy (SFBACCT) is a treatment group but also provides a lot of good information about Cognitive Behavioral Therapy (CBT). CBT has been shown to be the most effective treatment for anxiety and related disorders. SFBACCT provides individual therapy, training, referrals, and education.

www.olweus.org/public/index.page

Olweus Bullying Prevention Program, developed by Dan Olweus—arguably one of the world's experts on bullying and aggression among children. This downloadable program description provides an outline for this SAMHSA model program to reduce bullying in elementary, middle, and high schools.

www.harmreductiontherapy.org

The Harm Reduction Therapy Center offers outpatient therapy and treatment services to people interested in an alternative approach to addiction. Part of the larger public health harm reduction movement that includes needle exchange programs, safer sex education, and other interventions to prevent the spread of HIV and other diseases, the Harm Reduction Therapy Center (HRTC) has as its goal to reduce the damage to individuals, families, and communities caused by drug and alcohol use, by changing, reducing, or eliminating drug and alcohol use.

http://www.niaaa.nih.gov/alcohol-health

National Institutes on Alcohol Abuse and Alcoholism website includes information from the latest research studies, a searchable database of resources along with treatment referral information.

www.nida.nih.gov

National Institutes of Drug Abuse website contains excellent basic information about just about all drugs of abuse, including material on assessment, treatment, and general education resources. See www.nida.nih.govparent-teacher.html for the parent/teacher section.

www.samhsa.gov

The Substance Abuse and Mental Health Services Administration (SAMHSA) provides this online resource for locating drug and alcohol abuse treatment programs. The Substance Abuse Treatment Facility Locator lists: private and public facilities that are licensed, certified, or otherwise approved for inclusion by their state substance abuse agency; and treatment facilities administered by the Department of Veterans Affairs, the Indian Health Service, and the Department of Defense. SAMHSA endeavors to keep the Locator current. Their "model programs" list features treatment approaches that have been been tested in communities, schools, social service organizations, and workplaces across America, and have provided solid proof that they have prevented or reduced substance abuse and other related high-risk behaviors.

http://dancesafe.org

DanceSafe is a nonprofit harm reduction organization promoting health and safety within the rave and nightclub community. This is a controversial organization but you should know about it, because most teenagers know about it and they've helped save a lot of lives. They train volunteers to be health educators and drug abuse prevention counselors within their own communities, utilizing the principles and methods of harm reduction and popular education.

www.thecapcenter.org

The Child Abuse Prevention Center provides national and international training, education, research, and a resource center dedicated to protecting children and building healthy families.

www.rainn.org

The Rape, Abuse & Incest National Network (RAINN) is the nation's largest anti–sexual assault organization. RAINN operates the National Sexual Assault Hotline at 1.800.656.HOPE and carries out programs to prevent sexual assault, help victims, and ensure that rapists are brought to justice. Inside, you'll find statistics, counseling resources, prevention tips, news, and more.

www.childtrends.org/index.cfm

Child Trends is a 26-year-old nonprofit, nonpartisan research organization dedicated to improving the lives of children by conducting research and providing science-based information to improve the decisions, programs, and policies that affect children and their families. Once you get to the site, click on the link for reports and information on adolescent sexual behavior.

www.themediaproject.comhome.htm

The Media Project provides services to the entertainment industry regarding sex information and education. Since many television and film projects use the Media Project to gather current information about sex and sexuality, this is a good source for parents who want up-to-date information about teens and sex and want to know what sorts of information is being supplied to the media. Their services include a HELPline, tailored meetings, and industry-wide informational briefings.

www.siecus.com

SIECUS (the Sexuality Information and Education Council of the United States) has served as the national voice for sexuality education, sexual health, and sexual rights for over 40 years. SIECUS affirms that sexuality is a fundamental part of being human, one that is worthy of dignity and respect. They advocate for the right of all people to accurate information, comprehensive education about sexuality, and sexual health services.

www.kff.org/entpartnerships/seventeen/index.cfm

The Kaiser Family Foundation partnership with *Seventeen* magazine provides candid information based on teen research regarding sex and dating.

www.abanet.org/publiced/teendating.shtml

The American Bar Association Division for Public Education sponsors a National Teen Dating Violence Prevention Initiative in an attempt to inform teens, parents, educators, and the general public about the facts surrounding teen violence in dating. You can click here for their downloadable fact sheet or teachers can click on the following link to download the Teen Dating Violence Prevention Classroom Guide for some really excellent tips on bringing up the topic during advisories or class discussions.

http://www.nsvrc.org/organizations/87

The National Youth Violence Prevention Resource Center is a "one-stop shop" for information on youth violence prevention, sponsored by the Centers for Disease Control and Prevention and other dederal agencies. This link provides information on teen dating violence and abuse.

http://hrweb.mit.edu/worklife/raising-teens/index.html

The Raising Teens Project is spearheaded by A. Rae Simpson, Ph.D. and is the culmination of a groundbreaking initiative to pull together current research on the parenting of adolescents and to distill from it key messages for the media, policymakers, practitioners, and parents. This initiative was launched in collaboration with the Harvard Center for Health Communication and was funded by the John D. and Catherine T. MacArthur Foundation.

INTERNET AND DIGITAL MEDIA

www.mediaandwomen.org

The Girls, Women + Media Project is a 21st-century, nonprofit initiative and network working to increase awareness of how pop culture and media represent, affect, employ, and serve girls and women—and to advocate for improvement in those areas. The Project also seeks to educate and empower all consumers and citizens about consumer rights and responsibilities regarding the media, and to promote universal media literacy.

www.parentfurther.comtechnology-media

The Search Institute assists families and educators to maximize the benefits and minimize the harm of mass media on children through research, education, and advocacy. This is a good site to help you make wise media choices.

www.digitalcenter.org/pages/site_content.asp?intGlobalId=22

USC Annenberg Center for the Digital Future conducts long-term longitudinal studies on the impact of computers, the Internet, and related technologies on families and society. The results from the first year of the project were released to nationwide acclaim in October 2000 and the project continues, using a combination of well-accepted scientific survey methods and techniques for social science data analysis.

www.pewinternet.org/topics/Teens.aspx

The Pew Internet & American Life Project is one of seven projects that make up the Pew Research Center, a nonpartisan, nonprofit "fact tank" that provides information on the issues, attitudes, and trends shaping America and the world. The Project produces reports exploring the impact of the internet on families, communities, work and home, daily life, education, health care, and civic and political life. The quality of their work is outstanding—this is the place to look for great research on teens and digital media.

http://cyber.law.harvard.edu

The Berkman Center for Internet & Society was formed at Harvard University to explore and understand cyberspace; to study its development, dynamics, norms, and standards; and to assess the need or lack thereof for laws and sanctions. This is one of the best nonprofit research sites on the Internet.

www.benton.org

The Benton Foundation aims to articulate a public interest vision for the digital age and to demonstrate the value of communications for solving social problems. There is good information here about policy discussions on digital media.

www.kff.org/entmedia/internet.cfm

The Henry J. Kaiser Family Foundation is a nonprofit, private operating foundation focusing on the major health care issues facing the nation. The Foundation is an independent voice and source of facts and analysis for policymakers, the media, the health care community, and the general public. The link above goes directly to the Foundation's study on children and Internet use. The Foundation is not associated with Kaiser Permanente or Kaiser Industries; they also offer research on child and television use at http//www.kff.org/entmedia/tv.cfm.

www.wiredkids.org

Wired Kids, Inc. is a U.S. charity dedicated to protecting all Internet users, especially children, from cybercrime and abuse. It operates several programs and websites designed to help everyone learn how to protect their privacy and security online and to teach responsible Internet use.

www.kff.org/entmedia/1535-index.cfm

See *Henry J. Kaiser Family Foundation description above.* This link is for "Kids & Media at the New Millennium," one of the most comprehensive national public studies ever conducted of young people's media use. The study, based on a nationally representative sample of more than 3,000 children ages 2–18, shows how much time kids spend watching TV and movies, using computers, playing video games, listening to music, and reading.

www.commonsensemedia.org

Common Sense Media is dedicated to helping children and families understand the impact of media and digital activities. They are a non-partisan, not-for-profit organization, and provide reliable information and tools to assist families in having good choices around the media they consume.

www.screenit.com

ScreenIt.com provides information to parents about movie content prior to their kids viewing the material. While I don't usually provide links to paid sites, this might be of interest to parents who want to get detailed information before you allow certain movies to be viewed. A yearly subscription is about $50, as of 2012.

www.parentfurther.comtechnology-media

The Search Institute assists families and educators to maximize the benefits and minimize the harm of mass media on children through research, education, and advocacy. This is a good site to help you make wise media choices.

Index

Permissions

Use of the "Vini, Vedi, Vici" model of addiction in Chapter 5 by permission of Dr. Ken Winters, Professor, Department of Psychiatry, University of Minnesota.

Selections on media literacy in Chapter 4 (Practical Help Tips) by permission of the National Association of Media Literacy Education.

Description of "Harm Reduction" from *Over the Influence:the Harm Reduction Guide For Managing Drugs and Alcohol* by Patt Denning, Jeannie Little and Adina Glickman © 2003 by Patt Denning, Jeannie Little and Adina Glickman. Used by permission of Guilford Press.

"The Ten Tasks of Adolescence" is from *Raising Teens: A Synthesis of Research and a Foundation for Action*, copyright 2001 by A. Rae Simpson and the President and Fellows of Harvard College. Used by permission of Dr. A. Rae Simpson. For the most current information on the Raising Teens project online, see: http://hrweb.mit.edu/worklife/teens-youngadults-overview/.

Selection from THE PRINCIPLES OF PSYCHOLOGY by William James © [1895] 1950. Used by permission of Dover Publications.

Selection from THE EVOCATIVE OBJECT WORLD by Christopher Bollas © 2008 by Christopher Bollas (orig. Routledge). Used by permission of Taylor & Francis (originally a Routledge book).

Selections from MEDIATED: How the Media Shapes Our World and the Way We Live in It by Thomas de Zengotita. Copyright © 2006 by Thomas de Zengotita. Used by permission of Bloomsbury USA.

About the Author

Michael Y. Simon, LMFT is a Licensed Marriage and Family Therapist in private practice in Oakland, California. Michael is a sought-after local and national speaker on the subjects of teens and families and has worked with thousands of children, youth and families since 1990. He served for many years as a high school counselor, ran or developed programs that directly served children from birth to 18 and taught psychology, philosophy and religious studies at several American universities. He is the founder of Practical Help for Parents—a support organization for parents, educators and mental health professionals who work daily in support of adolescents. Most importantly, he's the proud parent of a sweet, kind, 26 year-old man who, as a teenager, couldn't be bribed to write a paragraph, and as an adult, would like nothing more than to write for a living. How's that for neural plasticity?